HISTORY OF NORTH AFRICA

History of
NORTH AFRICA

TUNISIA · ALGERIA · MOROCCO

From the Arab Conquest to 1830
Edited and revised by R. Le Tourneau

by
CHARLES-ANDRÉ JULIEN

Translated by
JOHN PETRIE

Edited by
C. C. STEWART

PRAEGER PUBLISHERS
New York · Washington

BOOKS THAT MATTER

Originally published as *Histoire de L'Afrique du Nord*
by Payot, Paris, in 1952

Published in the United States of America in 1970
by Praeger Publishers, Inc., 111 Fourth Avenue,
New York, N.Y. 10003

English translation © 1970 by Routledge & Kegan Paul, Ltd.
London, England

All rights reserved

Library of Congress Catalog Card Number: 79-104771

Printed in Great Britain

Contents

List of Illustrations	page vi
List of Maps	vii
Author's Preface to the Second French Edition	viii
Author's Note on the English Edition	x
English Editor's Preface to the English Edition	xii
Introduction: North Africa at the Time of the Arab Conquest	xv
1 THE ARAB CONQUEST AND THE KHARIJITE KINGDOMS	1
2 THE ARAB AND BERBER DYNASTIES (NINTH–ELEVENTH CENTURIES)	37
3 THE BERBER EMPIRES: THE ALMORAVIDS AND THE ALMOHADS	76
4 THE RETURN TO BERBER KINGDOMS	138
5 THE SHARIFIAN EMPIRE: 1553–1830	220
6 TURKISH RULE IN ALGERIA AND TUNISIA: 1516–1830	273
7 GENERAL SURVEY	336
Glossary	345
Bibliography	353
Index	423

List of Illustrations

❈

1. Block diagram of Fez   page 39
   (after E. F. Gautier, *Les Siècles obscurs du Maghreb*, Paris, 1927)

2. The site of Achir of Ziri   65
   (after E. F. Gautier, *op. cit.*)

3. Relation of Qalʿa of the Beni Hammad to Bougie   71
   (after E. F. Gautier, *op. cit.*)

4. Plan of the Mosque of the Kutubiya at Marrakesh   131
   (after H. Terrasse, *L'art hispano-mauresque des origines du XIIIe siècle*, Paris, 1932)

5. Kairouan during the Hafsid period   153
   (after R. Brunschvig, *La Berbérie orientale sous les Hafsides des origines à la fin du XVe siècle*, Paris, 1940 and 1947)

6. Tunis under the Hafsids   157
   (after R. Brunschvig, *op. cit.*)

7. The city of Fez during the Merinid period   180
   (after R. Le Tourneau, *Fès avant le Protectorat*, Casablanca, 1949)

8. Plan of the Bou ʿInaniya Madarsa at Fez   202
   (after E. Pauty, 'Le plan de l'Université Qarawiyin à Fès', in *Hespéris*, III, 1923)

9. Algiers under the Turks   289
   (after J. Lespès, *Alger*, Paris, 1930)

List of Maps

❋

1	Conquests in the Maghrib and Europe in the 7th and 8th Centuries (after R. Roolvink, *Historical Atlas of the Muslim Peoples*, Amsterdam, 1957)	page 9
2	The Mediterranean in the 9th Century (after R. Roolvink, *op. cit.*)	25
3	Stages of the Fatimid Conquests, 902–921 (after H. W. Hazard, *Atlas of Islamic history*, Princeton, 1951)	54
4	The Maghrib and Spain on the eve of the rise of the Almoravids (after R. Roolvink, *op. cit.*)	69
5	The Almoravid Empire and Western Mediterranean in 1100 (after R. Roolvink and H. W. Hazard, *op. cit.*)	78
6	The Almohad Empire in the early 13th Century (after R. Roolvink, *op. cit.*)	95
7	The Maghrib and Spain at the end of the 13th Century (after Ch.-A. Julien, *Histoire de l'Afrique du Nord*, Paris, 1952)	181
8	The Portuguese and Spanish in Morocco (early 16th Century) (after Ch.-A. Julien, *op. cit.*)	214
9	Morocco in the 16th and 17th Centuries (after Ch.-A. Julien, *op. cit.*)	231
10	Morocco in the 18th Century (after Ch.-A. Julien, *op. cit.*)	268
11	Algeria and Tunisia under the Turks (after Ch.-A. Julien, *op. cit.*)	283

Preface to the Second French Edition

North Africa was incorporated in the Orient in consequence of its conversion to Islam. Before this was complete the country had put up a strong defence of its individual personality, expressed not only in revolts but also in apostasies every time the invader was brought to a halt and in heresies and schisms markedly national in character. The process of Islamisation began as early as the end of the seventh century, but did not reach finality until after the triumph of the Almohads in the twelfth century; and Islam became militant and popular in Morocco only by way of reaction against the Christian invasions. Thereafter the Maghrib and Islam were inseparable. They are so still, and no problem—social, political or national—can be understood unless account is taken of its Muslim aspects. Herein lies the interest of that long period of North African history during which the country, left to itself and cut off from European influences, witnessed the rise and fall of dynasties without ever itself achieving a lasting unity. In the last twenty years our previous knowledge has been modified, sometimes radically, by the work of Messieurs Brunschvig, Cateau, Ceillié, Emerit, Lévi-Provençal, Le Tourneau, Marçais, Penz, Ricard and Terrasse, to mention only the leading names. The study of the Kharijites and the Fatimids has undergone mere alterations of detail, and the chapters devoted to the Almoravids, Almohads, Saadians, Alawites and Turks have required no more than partial revision. On the other hand everything relating to the Idrisid, Hafsid and Merinid dynasties has had to be largely or entirely recast. Finally, the concluding chapter is new in every respect.

For such a task to be brought to a successful conclusion, there was need for an historian who had acquired a grasp of the past not

Preface to the Second French Edition

only as a matter of intellectual culture but also as the fruit of personal research. Monsieur Le Tourneau, Professor in the Faculty of Letters, historian and Arabist, has been good enough to devote his talents to the difficult and unrewarding task of revision, for which I am profoundly grateful to him. His thesis on Fez before the Protectorate,[1] which gives expression to a deep and close acquaintance with Muslim society, covers the entire history of Muslim Morocco. His recent book on contemporary Islam,[2] shows the wide extent of his knowledge and the interest he brings to the present no less than to the past. (Thanks to the copious bibliography at the end of the book, the reader will be in a position either to pursue questions further or to follow up personal research.) At a time when the rise of Muslim nationalisms points to the need for a knowledge of the past of the Maghrib, *The History of North Africa from the Arab Conquest to 1830*, so fittingly revised by Monsieur Le Tourneau, will make it possible to be fully conversant with the latest state of historical knowledge.

CHARLES-ANDRÉ JULIEN
[1952]

Notes

1. R. Le Tourneau, *Fès avant le Protectorat* (Casablanca, 1949).
2. *L'Islam contemporain* (Paris, 1952).

Author's Note on the English Edition

❋

The first edition of *Histoire de l'Afrique du Nord* appeared in 1931 when the lanterns for the celebration of the Centenary of the Fall of Algiers were being extinguished, when the official and Roman Catholic demonstrations at Tunis extolled a half-century of French Protectorate and when the conquest of Morocco was concluded. Falling within this euphoric period of triumphant colonisation, the effort to revise the imperialist inspiration of conventional history received a cool if not hostile reception from the *colons*. Some French and English historians were offended by my iconoclastic zeal which, in fact, took into consideration only the bare truth, sparing no one. For the first time a history of the Maghrib did not concentrate upon the European conquest and colonisation but was open to economic, social, religious and artistic subjects. The Maghribians were clearly aware, to which their gratitude has testified, of the impact of a work which revived a past of which they had been left unaware. In 1970 some Tunisian scholars translated into Arabic the first volume which is concerned with ancient times. The readers today are no longer surprised at the points of view which were 'disgraceful' forty years ago. The part which I have been able to play in dissipating stubborn preconceptions remains one of my greatest satisfactions.

The English translation, done from the text which was revised in 1952 by my colleague R. Le Tourneau, an Islamic scholar, brings me new satisfaction. I have been pleased to take up my work again through the translation of John Petrie, who has faithfully preserved the easy style that I had endeavoured to give to the French text. The original work contained 357 illustrations which, for lack of time, could not be reproduced, but otherwise with the typography and presentation that Routledge and Kegan

Author's Note on the English Edition

Paul are accustomed to give to their publications, the English language readers will benefit from advantages that were not available to those who read the book in French. All this is to the credit of C. C. Stewart who has placed at the service of the readers the most praiseworthy skill and erudition. The new maps, the notes at the end of chapters and especially the rich and critical bibliography which are his work, stress the extent to which his contributions have been effective. Translator and editor have worked with skilful hands. I am deeply grateful to them.

Paris, 1970   CH. ANDRÉ JULIEN
Professeur honoraire d'histoire de la colonisation à la Sorbonne
Doyen honoraire de la Faculté des Lettres de Rabat

Preface to the English Edition

❂

The French edition of this second volume of M. Ch.-André Julien's *Histoire de l'Afrique du Nord* has long been accepted as a convenient reference by students and general readers of Middle Eastern, West African and North African history. In the 1952 edition, updated by M. Le Tourneau, the student of Islamic history has a useful synthesis of earlier research and a valuable bibliographic guide. With its appearance now in English, it is hoped that this volume may help to fill a gap which exists for the English reader, for whom few historical surveys encompassing the whole of the Maghrib are now available.

The reader being introduced to M. Julien's volume for the first time shall find it in many ways a unique contribution to Maghribi historiography. Although the author does not ignore recent research into linguistics, sociology, economics, art and archaeology —indeed, he weaves this material carefully into the fabric of his presentation—the core of his narrative in the first four chapters comes directly from the Arab writers themselves. Here is the strength of the work for the student of Islamic history, as well as one of the more important qualifications on its use for the reader unfamiliar with North African history and Arabic. The narrative in the early chapters, dependent as it must be upon Arab authors, tends likewise to be subject to the frame of reference held by those authors. The reader will find this leads to rather sharp value judgments being made against the non-Arab or non-orthodox principals, and he may well be reminded that he is receiving the account of a conquering people by those people. M. Julien has well captured the spirit of the Arab authors in this, but it is well to bear in mind that this was done through the French translations of the Arab historians, geographers, travellers, etc. Therefore, the narrative which has been taken from the translations of de Slane,

Preface to the English Edition

Fagnan, Motylinski, Masquery, Lévi-Provençal, etc., is subject to the accuracy of the individual translator, the manuscripts available to him at the time he did the work, and the supplementary material at his disposal—archaeological excavations, geographical surveys, ethnographical information, etc.—much of which is the result of only recent research. As a result, several instances might be cited in which portions of the translations from the Arabic accounts quoted in this volume fall short of what they might be. Rather than retranslate those portions quoted here, however, I have attempted to mention Arabic editions of the works quoted, as well as more recent French and English translations. Where the translations of specific Arabic words or phrases may be called into question, these have been rendered into an Anglicised transliteration, with long vowel markings, but the author's translation has been faithfully preserved. This should not seriously handicap the general reader and the Arabist will, most likely, already know the relative accuracies of the translations referred to here, or, for individual words and phrases, he will be able to consult an Arabic dictionary for more precise translations.

A few alterations to the French second edition have been made here, largely for the convenience of the reader concerned with a general survey of North African history, but also for the student of the Maghrib interested in locating the material which M. Julien drew upon for this volume. I have attempted to cite all the important references which were quoted or mentioned in the French edition, but this has not always been possible where a particular author has written widely on the subject under discussion or the original reference was vaguely stated. Therefore, where precise references have not been cited I have referred the reader to an extract from the author in which he deals with the issues under discussion, though not in the precise words quoted by M. Julien. In instances where quotations are short or of limited relevance to the development of a particular point, I have not always noted their source in the belief that the general reader might find the pedantic citation of all works employed by M. Julien somewhat cumbersome. For the same reason the many *Encyclopedia of Islam* articles concerning persons, places, dynasties and terminology which are cited in M. Julien's bibliography have not been mentioned again in the text. Where alternate works or editions have presented themselves,

History of North Africa

I have used the one which might be most conveniently located, either by its recent imprint or its availability in English.

Several additional maps have been included and slight revisions have been made to those maps in the French edition which have been reprinted. Place and institutional names have been retained as in the French edition since the greater part of supplementary and detailed maps available to the reader will be of French origin, and these spellings are used today in the independent Maghribi states. Personal names, except insofar as they are otherwise transliterated by the individuals concerned, and book titles in Arabic have been rendered into a simple English transliteration, without diacritical marks. The Arabist will recognise the correct spelling and the general reader should have little difficulty in sounding out the correct pronunciations. Berber terms and Berberised terms and names have been retained in the French transliteration which is their accepted form in the Maghrib today. Dates are all given in Christian years, though where I have felt the Hijira date illustrates more clearly the period of an event or man in relation to the advent of Islam, it too has been given. A brief glossary has been appended to the book in order to clarify terms and their usages in Maghribi Islam.

A note introducing the bibliography further elaborates the minor changes made there. *Encyclopedia of Islam* references have been condensed, as most readers will be aware of its value as a standard work of reference, items have been rearranged to make them more easily read, and an effort has been made to bring the bibliography up to date and to include more English language material.

Finally, I should like to thank M. Regragri at the Bibliothèque Générale et Archives du Maroc, Rabat, and M. Monteil, of I.F.A.N., Dakar, and their staffs who have kindly permitted my use of their respective libraries and assisted me in the location of a number of references in the preparation of this edition. I am also indebted to Mrs. Eva Watkin and my wife for their assistance in preparing the translated manuscript, and to Mr. P. Sluglett for his aid in the final stages of preparation of the manuscript.

Dakar, 1968   C. C. S.

Introduction: North Africa at the Time of the Arab Conquest[1]

When the Byzantines reconquered the former Roman provinces in the autumn of 533 and drove out the Vandals, it seemed that they were merely resuming that imperial tradition the continuity of which had been broken for a century or so by Genseric and his successors. In point of fact Byzantine Africa bore little or no resemblance to the Africa of the Romans, which perhaps explains why the Byzantines played so limited a role when the Muslim conquerors appeared on the scene.

The territory occupied by the Byzantines was much smaller. Mauretania Tingitana was reduced to Septem (Ceuta), Caesariana to Cherchel (Caesarea); Sitifiana had lost its western part and Tripolitania its northern; only Numidia, Proconsular and Byzacena remained as they had been. The territories thus left to themselves slowly freed themselves of Roman civilisation and turned gradually back to the ancient Berber practices. In the countryside, where Roman penetration had been slight, the transition was short and easy. In the towns and townships it was with some reluctance that the Romanised Berbers moved gradually away from a manner of life they had come to appreciate. In any case the Berbers, whether countrymen or townsfolk, had regained the custom of political independence, which they valued highly. Even within the zone subjected to Byzantium, the need for political emancipation was making itself felt; great Berber confederations were beginning to appear, reasonably independent to all appearances, of the governor of Carthage.

Moreover, the Byzantines themselves did not bring to Africa the same solid contribution as the Romans had done. They had arrived complete with their religious disputes, as vehement as they were subtle, and these the Arab invasion of Egypt served only to aggravate. Indeed, the refugees who had sought asylum in Africa included some monophysites. They had proselytised, had stirred up feeling and sown the seeds of discord in every Christian community of the country.

Finally, the Byzantine officials did not always show themselves loyal and devoted servants of central authority. They examined their orders carefully before carrying them out—when they did carry them out. The death of Heraclius and the ascension to power in 641 of Constant II, an emperor who was little more than a boy, served only to accentuate this centrifugal tendency. In 646 the patrician Gregory, Byzantine governor of Africa, embarked on rebellion against the government of Byzantium and had himself proclaimed emperor.

Such was the Africa that was about to undergo attack by the Muslims—a country lacking cohesion, in the process of withdrawing from a dying civilisation, gradually abandoning Roman institutions in favour of a return to ancestral traditions, and by no means fully subject to its Byzantine leaders, who were themselves cutting loose from their mother-city.

Notes

1. Cf. Ch.-A. Julien and C. Courtois, *Histoire de l'Afrique du Nord: des origines à la conquête arabe* (Paris, 1951).

CHAPTER 1
The Arab Conquest and the Kharijite Kingdoms

❈

1. The Arab Conquest

A HISTORY OF LEGEND

Islam and North Africa are so closely superimposed that it is easy to forget what struggles it cost the Muslim East to overlay the Berber West.

Clearly it is the visible—and enormous—consequences of the Arab conquest and conversion of the natives that strike us. There occurred, as Gautier affirms, 'a huge revolution. The country passed through the bulkhead, watertight everywhere else, separating Occident from Orient. Compared with such a leap into the unknown, our own French and Russian revolutions appear as trifling affairs.'[1]

This leap into the unknown was not taken willingly by the Maghrib. We know indeed that its resistance was long and savage, but it would be unwise to hope to know more than this. There are no written records, no accounts by foreign travellers, no European chronicles. To fill the gaps left by the poverty of inscriptions, the insufficiency of coinage and the want of reliable documents, we have to fall back on Arab chroniclers writing very much later than the events they relate.

'In our present stage of knowledge', writes William Marçais, the man best equipped to assess the value of the documents, 'the best view, in my opinion, is that our scanty information regarding this heroic and legendary age derives from four traditions—an oriental tradition represented by Waqadi,[2] who lived at Medina and Baghdad at the end of the eighth century; a Spanish tradition represented by a descendant of the conqueror Musa b. Nusair, who lived in Andalusia at the end of the thirteenth century; an African tradition represented by the descendant of another conqueror, Abu al-Muhajir, who lived at Kairouan at the same period; and finally an Egyptian tradition represented by Ibn 'Abd al-Hakam,[3] who died at Cario in 871. This is the only one that has been transmitted to us directly and in full.'[4]

Ibn 'Abd al-Hakam wrote towards the end of the ninth century and related traditions gathered in Egypt in the eighth century. The word 'traditions' is not lightly employed in this context. The sources are cited in the same way as the traditionalists recounted the 'sayings' of the Prophet Muhammad. The author gives the chain of testimonies he has been able to reconstruct until he reaches the final link, that is, an individual who was, or *could have been*, an eyewitness of the facts in question. Apart from this, concern for enlightenment and for the establishment of points of law is only too clear. History is far less interesting in itself than for the sake of the arguments to be drawn from it by the juridical school to which 'Abd al-Hakam belonged. We have to be conscious of the inevitable distortion due to this way of looking at things if we are to realise what precautions are necessary in using this author's work. It is a source of valuable information, but it is not, strictly speaking, a work of history, or even simply a chronicle.

Later annalists—we have several from the eleventh to the fifteenth centuries—afford far more details, but without citing many other sources beyond those indicated above. They give the impression of having embroidered a rather empty canvas, and they must be used with at least as much caution as Ibn 'Abd al-Hakam himself. Ibn Khaldun, alone, displays not only a great freedom of judgment and critical spirit, but also the need to understand and to explain. Unfortunately his account of the conquests is seven centuries later than the events, and it is impossible to recover his sources.[5] The most disturbing feature of both his work and that of the historians of the eleventh to the fifteenth centuries (al-Maliki,[6] Ibn al-Athir,[7] Ibn 'Idhari,[8] Nuwairi[9]) is the wealth of detail in contrast with the dearth prevailing in the chroniclers of the eighth and ninth centuries (Ibn 'Abd al-Hakam, al-Baladhuri,[10] and the Pseudo-Ibn Qutaiba[11]). 'The leading figures in the tragedy', observes W. Marçais, in drawing attention to this contrast, 'are endowed by the later authors with clearer features, better defined

The Arab Conquest and the Kharijite Kingdoms

roles, and a more lively and dramatic bearing. It will naturally be right to attribute these improvements to progress in literary skill rather than to the availability of recent documentation.'[12] In short, in studying the Arab occupation, we are reduced to employing biographies which are as fictional as they are edifying.

Must we then on that account give up all hope of accuracy? Or should we, following Gautier's example, resolutely bring some order into the chaos of wars, insurrections and collapse of kingdoms, by trying to 'interpret and interpolate' the Arab chronicles? This method, which is, if not the best, at least the only one to offer any satisfaction, carries with it an element of the subjective, the risk of which cannot be concealed by the brilliant success of Gautier's *Siècles obscurs du Maghreb*. If, when stitching cobwebs, even with threads of shot silk, we fail to produce solid fabric, the fault does not lie with the workman.

We can also, as G. Marçais has recently done, by patient study of the documents, recover from them what they can be made to yield—a by no means negligible portion of certainties, and a host of question marks. In doing this, we must not forget to restore the whole to its setting in the historical context, in the general history, that is, of the Mediterranean basin. Isolated though it may have been at this period of slow and uncertain communications, the Maghrib is and was a Mediterranean country, sharing more or less in the life of this geographical unity running from the Straits of Gibraltar to the Near East. To this North Africa had already been linked in Carthaginian times, and was to be still more closely united by the Muslim conquest, by the Arab invasions, by the adventurous careers of a few such men as Idris, Ibn Rustum, Ibn Tumart, and finally by the Turkish thrust in the sixteenth century.

THE TREACHEROUS MAGHRIB

When the Arabs came to Byzantine Africa, they had not, since crossing the Suez isthmus in 640, met with any serious obstacle. Fewer than 4,000 men and one battle had sufficed to settle the fate of Egypt, where the invaders received an enthusiastic welcome from the persecuted Copts. By autumn 642 Barqa, chief city of Pentapolis, had fallen into their hands, to be followed by the whole of Cyrenaica. From there they launched raids, southwards as far as the Fezzan (Zwila) and westwards as far as Tripoli, which they took by storm in 643.

So far they had encountered only Berber tribes, and the apathy of the exarch encouraged them to go on with their invasion. Nevertheless they limited permanent occupation to Cyrenaica and refrained from crossing the Djebel Nefousa. It is said that their general 'Amr, encouraged by his successes, would have liked to attempt an expedition into Ifriqiya, that is Tunisia, but the caliph 'Umar was against it. The forceful letter attributed to the caliph by the historian Ibn 'Abd al-Hakam may not be authentic but at the very least it reflects the repugnance which, at a later date, Arabs of the ninth century felt for the ambush-ridden African campaigns. 'No,' was 'Umar's reply to 'Amr's proposal to march on Ifriqiya, 'it is by no means Ifriqiya, but rather the treacherous country (*al-mufarriqa*) that misleads and betrays and which no one shall attack so long as I live.'[13] Ibn 'Abd al-Hakam, that conscientious compiler of traditions, goes so far as to furnish a variant—'so long as the water of my pupils shall bathe my eyes[14] [Ifriqiya shall not be invaded]'. The two readings leave no doubt of the feelings attributed to the caliph.

IBN SA'D'S EXPEDITION

'Uthman, who succeeded him in 644, broke with these methods and authorised his foster-brother 'Abd Allah ibn Sa'd, governor of Egypt, to carry out a raid. Ibn Sa'd made a first push forward in 645 or 646, but it was in 647 that he successfully concluded that great expedition which Arab historiography embellishes with marvellous or romantic incidents.

In order to parry the invasion, the patrician Gregory became reconciled with the Berber tribes and adopted the fortified point of Sufetula (Sbeitla) as his strategic base, without however making it his capital. Ibn Sa'd, who had first secured the spot where Kairouan was later to be built, fell back towards the south-west. After several days of watching and waiting, he attacked the Byzantine army in the plain of Sbeitla, and there destroyed it. Gregory perished in the battle, perhaps at the hand of 'Abd Allah ibn al-Zubair, whom legend credits with too many virtues to be above suspicion.

Hardly more weight can be given to the romantic exploits of the

The Arab Conquest and the Kharijite Kingdoms

patrician's daughter Yamina. It is with great satisfaction that Arab historians have described this beautiful Amazon, riding beneath a parasol of peacock feathers or appearing unveiled at the top of a tower. But she who had been destined for the conqueror of Ibn Sa'd became the prize of a man of the Ansars, and escaped slavery only by throwing herself from the back of her camel so as to break her neck. This tragic tale, though doubtless of pure invention, nevertheless gives graphic expression, as Gautier has observed, to the abhorrence that must have been felt by aristocratic Grecian ladies when they fell into the coarse hands of the nomads.[15]

The Arab raid had been prompted by the desire for booty, and the pillaging of Sufetula and the forays into southern Byzacena were extremely profitable. However, Ibn Sa'd had reason to fear a counter-attack based on the strongpoints in the north, to which he was incapable of laying siege. When the Byzantines proposed a large war indemnity on the condition of his leaving Byzacena, he accepted readily and returned to Egypt with all his treasures. The expedition had lasted hardly more than a year (647-648).

Short as it was, it had struck a heavy blow at Byzantine rule. In southern Byzacena, pillaged and depopulated, the Berber tribes broke loose from control by Carthage. The patrician's death added to the disorder and to the chronic rivalries. But of greater importance, the experiment had shown to the Arabs the feebleness of Greek resistance and the vast profits to be made from raiding expeditions. Clearly the invaders would soon be back.

THE CALIPHATE CRISIS

However, the disorder that followed 'Uthman's assassination brought seventeen years of respite to Africa. The spread of the Arab empire had created problems that only a series of crises could resolve. The second caliph, 'Umar, had hoped to maintain law and order by so organising the state's finances as to furnish the conquerors with allowances tenable at his discretion. But this arrangement, depending as it did on the caliph's pleasure and the systematic exploitation of the conquered, could not work without jealousies and revolts. 'Uthman, who kept this system despite its imperfections, fell victim to it just as 'Umar had done. The new caliph, 'Ali, although he was Muhammad's son-in-law, met with even greater difficulties. While dealing with a mutinous governor of Syria, he was skilfully involved in an arbitration concerning 'Uthman's murder, was declared to have forfeited his office and soon afterwards was assassinated in 661. Mu'awiya had not even waited until after his death to have himself proclaimed caliph in July 660. With him began the 'Umaiyad dynasty, which was to attempt to organise a centralised national monarchy, with its capital at Damascus.

Egypt, which served as the base for campaigns against North Africa, had been directly involved in these disturbances. Egypt had risen against 'Uthman's governors, had forced Ibn Sa'd to quit the country and had dispatched the caliph's assassins to Medina. The country had then fallen under the authority of 'Ali until 658, when one of Mu'awiya's lieutenants had taken possession of it. Political and religious quarrels had naturally thrust plans for attacking the Maghrib into the background. The new dynasty, having entrusted the government of Egypt to the aged amir, who had by no means abandoned his designs on Ifriqiya, resumed plans for expansion towards the west.

MU'AWIYA'S EXPEDITION

Africa had not taken advantage of its respite to re-establish its former positions of power, any more than Constantinople had used the occasion of Gregory's death to re-establish its authority. On the contrary, the emperor Constant II had published a new edict, the *Type*, which, without referring either to monothelism or to bitheism, proclaimed harsh sanctions against all who should not adhere strictly to the ancient symbols. In doing so he had stirred to revolt the orthodox Christians of Africa, who were as submissive to the pope's authority as they were hostile to the imperial will. It is possible that a usurper named Gennadius may have taken advantage of this situation to maintain an independent principality for some years and then, finding himself threatened by a rival who enjoyed the emperor's backing, may have entered into negotiations to secure Muslim support. When the emperor regained control, his possessions amounted to no more than the remnants of an exarchate, and he had to abandon the first-line fortresses and limit himself to guarding the approaches to central Tunisia.

Everything written by Arab historians regarding the attacks on

The Arab Conquest and the Kharijite Kingdoms

the Berber tribes between 660 and 663 should be taken with caution. In 665 the former leader of the Egyptian ʿUmaiyad party, Muʿawiya Ibn Hudaij, made his way into Byzacena under orders from the caliph, defeated a Byzantine army which had landed at Hadrumetum, carried and sacked the fortress of Jaloula, and then returned to Egypt laden with booty.

PERMANENT OCCUPATION: ʿUQBA IBN NAFIʿ

Shortly afterwards ʿUqba ibn Nafiʿ, who had already carried out a brilliant raid into the Fezzan, organised a third expedition. This differed from its two predecessors in that it resulted in a permanent settlement. It was in fact in 670 that he founded Kairouan, in the very heart of Byzacena, on a vast semi-desert plain, having first rid the place of its population of reptiles and wild beasts by pronouncing a ritual formula on three consecutive days. 'I am inclined,' he said, according to the historian al-Nuwairi, 'to build a city that can serve as an armed stronghold (*qairawān*) for Islam to the end of time.'[16]

Kairouan was indeed an armed stronghold against the Byzantines, who were able to make use of the coastal towns for an offensive, but it was chiefly against the Berbers, who thereafter constituted the only really dangerous adversaries. Thus Kairouan not only guarded the road to Egypt, which had to be kept clear for supplies and as a possible line of retreat but it also faced the Aurès which was becoming the hard core of resistance.

Although thus taken over Ifriqiya became not an autonomous province, but a dependency of Egypt. Indeed, ʿUqba was unceremoniously relieved of his command, to be replaced by Abu al-Muhajir, one of the new governor's entourage. Possibly the founder of Kairouan was reproached for his exclusively military views, his imperious attitude towards the Berber chiefs, his systematic massacres and his forays as full of risk as they were devoid of advantage. It seems that, in contrast with his predecessor, Abu al-Muhajir entered into negotiations with the Berber chiefs with a view to securing their support against the Byzantines.

It is said also that he advanced as far as 'the springs of Tlemcen' and took prisoner the powerful and clever Kosaila, prince of the Awraba. In all, Abu al-Muhajir's policy, though less striking than that of ʿUqba, seems to have been more successful.

'UQBA'S WESTWARD MARCH

The disgrace of 'Uqba was not final. In 681 he was given supreme command in Africa and at once undertook a foray in the grand style into the Maghrib, though it would be unwise to guarantee that this incident actually occurred.

By way of sating his vengeful spirit, he dragged after him Abu al-Muhajir and Kosaila in chains. It is said that he spared the Berber chief none of the affronts that the latter had visited upon him. He made no attempt to besiege the fortified places in the north of the Aurès, and after an encounter with native troops reinforced with Greek elements—Rums—near Baghai and Lambaesis, and then at Tiaret, he pushed on as far as Tangier.

According to the account given by the Arab historians, the patrician Julian (Ilyān or Yulīan) rather than fighting him, received him with rich gifts.[17] 'Uqba sought his advice about the Visigoths of Spain, the Rums and the Berbers of the Maghrib. On the strength of the information thus secured, he penetrated into the Sous and there carried out a great massacre of the inhabitants and a most profitable round-up of lovely girls, taking God to witness that the Atlantic alone hindered him from hastening still further to the slaughter of infidels.

All of this is very curious, and Gautier has used it as a basis on which to construct a theory. In his view, the ease with which Tingitana was occupied is comparable with the similar cases of Ifriqiya and, a little later, Spain: all the North African countries that had felt the influence of Carthage sided readily with the Muslims.[18] But most of the details are found only in historians of a later date. In Ibn 'Abd al-Hakam, and then not even in all the traditions he reports, we find no more than a reference to the Sous—a vague enough term with later Arab geographers, the exact meaning of which in the eighth century would need to be established[19]—and 'Uqba's celebrated saying as he halted at the seashore (but which sea?) and called God to witness that he could go no further. There is no mention of Tangier, and not a single detail of this extraordinary ride into unknown country. There is none the less matter for reflection and doubt; it is certain that 'Uqba did his utmost to extend the Muslim empire westwards and that to that end he waged war in the Aurès. It would be incautious to assert more than

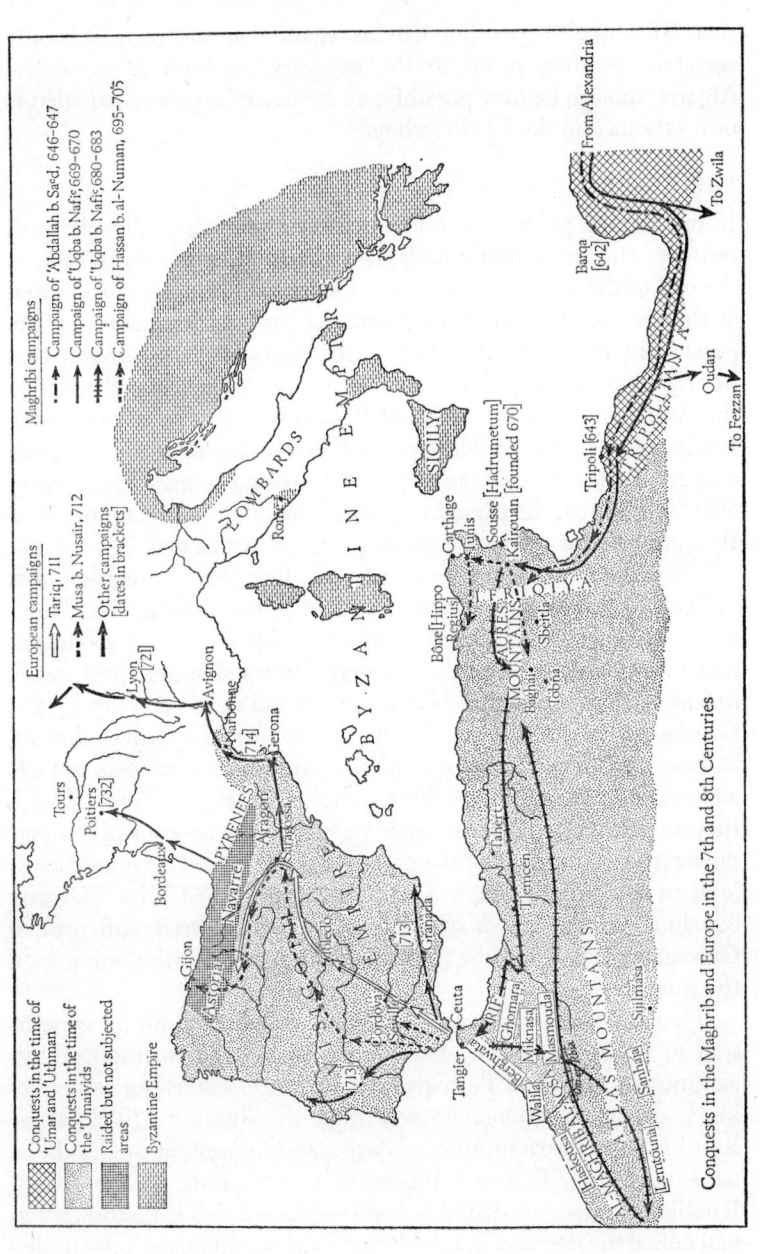

Conquests in the Maghrib and Europe in the 7th and 8th Centuries

that. 'If 'Uqba's expedition can be regarded as authentic, it is only sensible, pending proof to the contrary, to limit it to central Algeria, though he may possibly, at the most, have reached what is now Orania and the Chélif valley.'[20]

THE BERBER RESISTANCE: KOSAILA

If on certain points we follow writers later than the eleventh century, and more particularly Ibn Khaldun, who was writing at the end of the fourteenth century, we are led to the conclusion that at this period the history of North Africa was dominated by the personality of Kosaila. Gautier indeed goes so far as to assume that he was king of the Jedar or at the very least that he commanded the Awraba. These were settled Branès, thoroughly imbued with Latin and Christian civilisation and disposed to make common cause with the Greeks against the Muslim Arabs. 'The victory over Sidi 'Uqba,' he concludes, 'was probably to a greater degree a Byzantine victory than any subsequent Berber victory.'[21]

Given the scarcity of documents and their lack of precision, it is difficult to make an exact assessment of Kosaila's influence. However, the ancient traditions handed on by Ibn 'Abd al-Hakam make it possible to state that he played a considerable part in the defeat of 'Uqba and that he was supported in his activity by the Greeks of North Africa. They, no longer themselves having sufficient military force to oppose the Muslim attacks, seem to have succeeded in raising the Berbers, concerned though they were with their own interests, against the invaders. In the absence of military power the Byzantines still possessed some political influence, at least in the eastern Maghrib. Were Kosaila and his men already Muslims, as the late historians assert, or did they still profess Christianity? It would be imprudent to give a definite opinion on the question.

What is certain is that in 683, on his way back from his expedition to the west, 'Uqba was trapped by a large coalition of Byzantines and Berbers. Perhaps he was not completely in control of his booty-laden troops. At any rate, at Thubunae (Tobna) he split his army into a number of corps, and himself, at the head of a weak squadron, followed the route to the south of the Aurès. Kosaila, who had evaded him at some place which is unknown and had rallied the Berber tribes and the Greek contingents, surrounded

The Arab Conquest and the Kharijite Kingdoms

him at the edge of the desert near Thabudeos (Tahoudha at the mouth of the Oued el-Abiod) and killed him together with his 300 horsemen. It is known that ʿUqba's body lies in the mosque of the oasis bearing his name (Sidi ʿUqba) some three miles south of Tahoudha, under a modest *qubba* (dome), to which come as pilgrims the descendants of those who joined forces to put him to death.

The victory appeared decisive; ʿUqba's policy was terminating in disaster. In the face of the combined efforts of Berbers and Greeks, the Arabs were abandoning all their conquests beyond Barqa. Kosaila, after making an entry into Kairouan, became for three years the veritable leader of Ifriqiya and the eastern Maghrib. The Berber converts to Islam were quick to apostatize as, according to a celebrated passage in Ibn Khaldun,[22] they did so often—as many as twelve times in 70 years. Africa seemed determined to preserve its independence under a Berber leader, taking as its centre the Aurès which constituted the heart of the resistance.

But the Arabs were incapable of remaining inactive after such a defeat. The caliph ʿAbd al-Malik had to delay his revenge in order to contend with the powerful pretender ʿAbd Allah al-Zubair, the former conqueror of the patrician Gregory. He, on the strength of his kinship with Aisha, the prophet's widow, had rallied a great part of the Muslim empire to his cause. ʿAbd al-Malik took advantage of a period of tranquillity to give Zuhair ibn Qais command of an army which met that of Kosaila at Mems near Kairouan. In 686 the Berber and Byzantine troops were defeated after a fierce battle and Kosaila was killed. This was only a relative defeat; Zuhair withdrew, leaving only a garrison at Kairouan, and was surprised and killed at Barqa by a Byzantine landing party.

THE KAHINA

If we follow Ibn Khaldun,[23] and Gautier's attractive exegesis,[24] we are led to the conclusion that the death of Kosaila involved serious consequences. In the defensive war, the Byzantines, with their command of the great ports from Hadrumetum (Sousse) to Hippo Regius (Bône) and of numerous inland citadels, had acted only as auxiliaries of the Berbers. They took advantage of the Arab departure and of rivalries between tribal chiefs to consolidate their authority in Byzacena. The Awrāba lost control of operations, which passed to a tribe of the eastern Aurès, the Jerāwa.

These Jerāwa, according to Gautier, were not a sedentary people, any more than their culture and religion resembled those of the Greeks, but were Zenata, 'almost pure-blooded, great camel-riding nomads, newcomers and recent intruders into the Maghrib,'[25] with no roots in the country's past, and no common interest with the old Africa. If this productive hypothesis could be confirmed, it would throw light on the new direction given to the struggle by the Queen of the Aurès, the Kahina.

The change occurred at a particularly dangerous time. 'Abd al-Malik, who had at last put down Ibn al-Zubair in 692, and after him religious revolts in the Persian provinces, aimed at vigorous action in Ifriqiya. In fact the governor, Hassan ibn al-Nu'man al-Ghassani, introduced new methods; as a first step he liquidated the Byzantine danger by carrying Carthage by assault in 695. The emotion felt at Constantinople was as great as at the time of the success of Genseric, and the emperor Leontios felt obliged to fit out a fleet, which fortunately succeeded in retaking the city.

Meanwhile Hassan had turned his attention to the Berbers of the Aurès. He had learned, so it is said, that they were ruled over by a powerful queen surnamed the Kahina, that is, the prophetess. We are assured by Ibn Khaldun that this woman, whose very name is unknown (perhaps Damya or Dichya?) practised Judaism, as did the folk of her tribe.[26] There have even been attempts to find proof of this in her surname, which is, however, purely Arab. Few African heroes have given rise to so many legends as this heroine to whom G. Marçais gives the picturesque appellation of the 'Berber Deborah'. Let us, moreover, take note that in Barbary, women have frequently played principal roles, at least during the Almohad period. We have only to recall the importance of Yusuf ibn Tashfin's wife, Zainab—who also had a knowledge of magic— of several Almoravid princesses and of Ibn Tumart's own sister, who stood by him in his last moments along with the most beloved of his disciples. None, however, attained such heights as did the Kahina. In fact, we know little more about her than her name, her renown and her savage resistance to the invader—a resistance nurtured, as it seems, by Berber patriotism and Jewish faith.

One fact seems certain—that the Kahina reconstituted the Berber bloc, crushed the Arab army on the banks of the Meskiana (between Aïn-Beïda an Tébessa) and threw it back into Tripolitania.

The Arab Conquest and the Kharijite Kingdoms

HASSAN'S VICTORY

But not long afterwards, in 698, Hassan once more invaded Byzacena and recaptured Carthage. All he found in the city was a handful of Rums, in too wretched a state to care about the change of masters. The other inhabitants had reached the islands of the Mediterranean. In place of the fallen capital Hassan immediately laid the foundations of a new city—Tunis—at the head of the gulf, its principal role being that of a marine arsenal unlikely to be successfully attacked from the open sea. However, the caliph's ships had scattered the Byzantine fleet, the last that was able to cruise along the coasts of Africa, and the command of the sea was passing to the Arabs. Soon the Greeks retained no more than the strongpoint of Septem, with some fragments of Mauretania Secunda, Tingitana, Majorca, Minorca and a very few towns in Spain. These, it seems, represented the full extent of an exarchate which lasted another ten years.

There remained the Berbers to conquer. This time their disunity made victory easy. The Kahina seems to have governed the Maghrib for a term of five years, in accordance with nomadic principles. The results were not slow to show themselves.

All the Arab historians confirm that the invaders found valuable auxiliaries among the Rums and the sedentary Berbers. If it is true that the queen aimed at warding off the return of the Arabs by sacking the countryside and leaving neither trees nor walls standing, it is easy to understand her having aroused townsfolk and farmers against her, whether Greeks or natives. Hassan was too clever not to profit from such a situation. Moreover, 'Abd al-Malik, who had just victoriously put down the last pretender's revolt in 702, sent Hassan a large army enabling him to take the offensive.

On the eve of the final battle, the Kahina ordered her sons to go over to the enemy. In a useful comparison, Gautier has shown how natural such an action is to a Berber leader for whom his family's supremacy over the tribe takes precedence of all else.[27] The aged queen fought a desperate battle, possibly near Tabarka, and was then, in company with her faithful adherents, pushed as far as the Aurès. She was killed near a well, known thereafter as Bīr el-Kāhina, and her head was sent to the caliph as a trophy. With her death, the era of illustrious defence came to an end.

BRANÈS + BUTR = SEDENTARY PEOPLES + NOMADS

Thus in the course of the Arab conquest it would seem that the eternal conflict between sedentary peoples and nomads was a feature of primary importance. This antithesis would go far to clarify the history of Barbary if we could superimpose it on the classification adopted by Ibn Khaldun,[28] and discover the geographic and economic reality underlying the genealogical fiction. This is what Gautier has attempted in one of his bold hypotheses that makes one take a fresh look at history as it has been traditionally narrated.[29] According to this view, the camel-riders, whom the initiative of the Severi had enabled to form huge tribes, as elusive as they were mobile, were those Berbers whom the Arab historian calls *Butr*, descendants of a legendary namesake Maghdis al-Abtar, whereas the sedentary folk traced their origins to the Branès (*Barānis*), whose ancestor was Bornos. Each group included, not kinsmen, but populations of a like way of life.

This would explain the obstacles encountered by the Arab conquest and the disunity that allowed it to triumph. The subjection of the old townsfolk of Ifriqiya required little effort. Organised and regular government, essential for their life and business, mattered far more to them than liberty. But in Numidia a social drama had been unfolding ever since the Vandal period. Dating from the days of Roman rule the cultivators had gradually been forced out by small mobile herdsmen and above all by the great camel-mounted nomads. In turn these two population groups, the Branès and the Butr, embodied Berber resistance, the sedentary Awrāba under Kosaila and the nomadic Jerāwa under the Kahina. The revolt of the sedentary folk against nomadic practices was decisive for the victory of the invaders and enabled them to push their conquests and their conversions towards the west. 'In the Maghrib', Gautier concludes, 'sedentary folk and nomads were never able to attempt co-existence without mutual revulsion. Herein lay the triumph of the Arab invasion, the decisive turning-point was there. It was Hassan who went beyond it.'[30]

This hypothesis, then, is capable of application to the specific case of the Arab invasion. The two views have been discussed with the serious attention they merit by W. Marçais. To him it seems

The Arab Conquest and the Kharijite Kingdoms

impossible to identify the Butr with the nomads and the Branès with the sedentary people.

A large proportion of the Zenata, outstanding representatives of the Butr branch, were undoubtedly riders of camels. But it is difficult to attribute the character of great nomads to many others of the Butr—to the village-dwelling Koumīya, for example, to the Metaghra 'living in fixed abodes in cabins,' to the Nefousa farmers of the Tripolitanian hills or to the Jerāwa of the Aurès. And on the other hand it remains the fact that among the Brānis we find the greatest of all the nomads—the Sanhāja of the Sahara. According to the testimony of Ibn Khaldun there were, among the Brānis-Haouwāra, both nomadic and sedentary folk at the same time; and also that an entire branch of the Brānis-Ketāma—the Sedouīkech—lived in tents and raised camels. The Ketāma are generally regarded as Kabyles: in that case the Sedouīkech would afford us the curious variety of the Kabyle who was a shepherd and a tent-dweller.[31]

If the Arab historians failed to note a contrast in ways of life that was perfectly familiar to them, the reason is that such did not correspond with the realities of the Maghrib. W. Marçais, with all the weight of his authority as a linguist, puts forward in his turn, but with due caution, a personal explanation of the division. 'Perhaps', he says, 'it was originally based on differences in costume observed by the Arabs among the first Berber tribes they got to know—hooded Berbers (*Brānis*, plural of *burnus*, garment with a hood) and Berbers with short garments or without hoods (*butr*, plural of *abtar*, shortened garment). It must be said that all this is pure hypothesis. In due course, the primitive meaning of this distinction would have been lost... in proportion as it came to embrace all the aborigines with whom the conqueror entered gradually into contact.'[32]

It is probable that as they pursued their westward advance the invaders encountered tribes bearing identical names, sometimes at points far removed from one another. These names would be drawn from conditions of life (the Ifren may have been cave-dwellers) if not from totems. 'And since similarity of name was for them the most cogent indication of kinship, they saw in tribes bearing the same names (some living in the east and some in the west of the Maghrib; some living the lives of great or petty nomads and some as settled farmers; some on the confines of the Sudan and some in the mountains of the Tell) descendants of a single ancestor who had been scattered by the vicissitudes of destiny.'[33] Thus an Arab historian applying the same criterion today to the mountaineers 'would group in the one family the Moroccan Djebāla who live in houses, the Constantine Djebāla who live in huts, the Tunisian Djebālīya who breed camels and spend part of the year in tents',[34] and would give them all a common and eponymous ancestor, Djebal. Such was no doubt the process which made it possible to trace the Sanhaja back to Sanhaj and the Matmata to Matmat.

Gautier's hypothesis, so attractive otherwise, must therefore be rejected in so far as it is too systematic. But it does lay stress on the impact in social matters of the Arab conquest and on that account it deserves consideration. It is a fact, observed on many occasions, that in times of political crisis the nomads leave their isolation and appear in the settled lands in order to profit from the turmoil. Later it was to be the Almoravids bursting into the disrupted Morocco of the eleventh century, the Merinids appearing in the region of the lower Moulouya as the Almohad empire gave its first signs of weakness, and quite close to our own times al-Hiba and his blue men ascending the Rio de Oro when the Alawite dynasty was near its downfall. After the considerable disturbances created by the Muslim invasions, at least in the eastern parts of North Africa, the nomads' arrival on the scene was not surprising.

On the other hand, Gautier's hypothesis underlines the importance of ways of life closely involved in the bonds of blood, which the Arab chroniclers, with their incorrigible concern for genealogy, too easily tend to underestimate. There are numerous examples of tribes supposedly descended from a single ancestor but in reality made up of unrelated elements united by a single way of life. Only the fiction of adoption has served to give them the characteristic of ethnic unity to which the entire Maghrib is so deeply attached.

As for the respective roles of Kosaila and the Kahina, it seems unwise to attempt a precise evaluation on the basis of the available documents, unreliable and contradictory as they are. That lively personage Kosaila—'first champion of Berber independence'—has gained greatly in prominence from elaboration over the centuries.

The Arab Conquest and the Kharijite Kingdoms

Baladhuri does not so much as know him. Al-Bakri makes him flee from Tobna pursued by Musa ibn Nusair. The Pseudo-Ibn Qutaiba makes him die in 702 while disputing the passage of the Moulouya with the same Musa. Ibn ʿAbd al-Hakam is not too sure whether Kosaila or 'the son of the Kahina' should have the credit for the death of ʿUqba Ibn Nafiʿ; perhaps indeed he regards them as one and the same person. None of these ancient chroniclers attributes to 'Kacīla the title of chief of the Aoureba', and there is moreover nothing to justify situating their principal habitat in the Aurès at the time of the Arab conquest. The whole traditional narrative, so well suited to minds accustomed to epics, does not stand up to confrontation with the documents, and it would perhaps be imprudent to credit the figure of Kosaila with more historical accuracy than that of the Roland of the *chansons de gestes*.

There remains the theory of the two Aurès, borrowed by Gautier from Masqueray.[35] It is supposed to rest on a distinction, based on a multitude of errors and today rejected by all Berber scholars, between the dialect of the west Aurésian Chaouia, descendants of Kosaila's subjects, and that of the east Aurésian Chaouia, descendants of the Kahina's subjects. 'Masqueray's thesis regarding the duality of the Chaouia country seems therefore very thin. Until more is known it would be better not to attach too much weight to it.'[36]

Thus the circumstances of the Berber resistance confound our investigation. What more can one do, in the present state of affairs, than recall on the one hand the common version of the conquest, as it is customarily taken from the Arab historians by a selection that does not always conform to the exigent demands of criticism, while on the other hand setting out the hypotheses and debate inspired by the traditional narrative in two minds of singular range and penetration?

Does this mean that Gautier's attempt is useless? Far from it. Indeed—quite apart from the author's delightful style—there remains the fact that more than any of his predecessors he has laid emphasis on the distinction between the 'folk in dwellings of hair' and the 'folk in dwellings of clay' and has demonstrated all the inferences that can be drawn from this by an historian who is also a geographer. The fact is that, with rare exceptions, of which that of W. Marçais is the most brilliant, the criticisms of Gautier's theory have been conspicuously inadequate. It is only too clear, as his principal opponent has readily acknowledged, that 'the historians of the Maghrib will be unable to evade a single one of the questions he poses'.[37]

MUSA IBN NUSAIR

Hassan, who on his return to Kairouan had undertaken the organisation of an orderly financial system, fell under the caliph's suspicion and was recalled. Musa ibn Nusair was then given the governorship of Ifriqiya, thereafter independent of Egypt, and had only to enlarge the successes of his predecessor. It is very difficult to fix the time of this appointment within ten years, so much do the dates given differ; 705 is the one most generally adopted.[38]

Musa first subdued the far Maghrib to the Atlantic, and pushed on as far as Sijilmasa in the Tafilalet. He failed to capture Septem, but finally and permanently occupied Tangier. The country was at that time inhabited by Berber tribes of the Sanhaja group—the Ghomara on the Mediterranean coastline, the Berghwata, along the Atlantic between the Straits of Gibraltar and the mouth of the Oum er-Rbia, the Miknasa in the centre, the Masmouda on the western slope of the Great Atlas and along the coast from the Oum-er-Rbia to the Sous, the Haskousa between the Sous and the Draʿ, and the Lemta and the Lemtouna on the left bank of the Draʿ. On these tribes—some Christian, some Jewish, but mostly devoted to nature cults—as on the apostate populations of the rest of Barbary, he imposed Islam by means of an energetic policy of conversion. Spain, where in 711 an army of Berbers commanded by one of their number, Tariq, put an end to the Visigoth empire in one battle, afforded an outlet to the newly converted. It was they who conquered the peninsula and in 732 penetrated into Gaul as far as Poitiers. Their withdrawal after the victory of Charles Martel was due not so much to the enthusiasm of the Franks as to the revolts provoked in the far Maghrib by the allotment of Spanish lands to the benefit exclusively of the Arabs and by the exactions and violence of the governors of Tangier.

The invaders had been able to rally to their cause the town-dwelling middle classes of Ifriqiya and Tingitana, and for the moment to divert the Berbers' ardour in the direction of conquest and loot. But the subjection of the Berber masses, despised and

The Arab Conquest and the Kharijite Kingdoms

exploited by the Arabs, was no more than an illusion. 'The conquest of Africa', as Hassan had already observed, 'is an impossible thing.' His successors realised to their cost that permanent occupation was far more difficult than warlike expeditions on horseback.

II. The Berber Resistance

KHARIJISM

Every insurrection must have an ideological basis. The Egyptian fellahin who rose in 2000 B.C. in order to wrest from the aristocracy the secrets opening the way to immortality, the Donatists who combated Catholic time-serving and the coalition of Roman governors, bishops and landed proprietors—these did no more than give expression in religious terms to their hatred for those in possession of and for established authority. It was equally natural that the Berbers whom the Arabs had converted should come to base their opposition on Islamic grounds, thus being able to put forward their social demands under the guise of a religious ideal.

Kharijism became, in one respect, an episode in the class-struggle and a manifestation of xenophobia, just as Donatism had been. If the Maghrib was the chosen territory of these two heresies—or rather of these two schisms of a revolutionary nature—the reason was that nowhere else did the feeling for asceticism and egalitarianism, both indissolubly linked with a hatred of the masters, reach such a degree of intensity.

The primary cause of the Kharijite schism was probably the arbitration to which the caliph 'Ali had to agree under pressure from his troops. A group of auxiliaries preferred to withdraw at once rather than sanction by their presence a decision that committed God's word to the judgment of men. After 'Ali's condemnation many of his supporters secretly left Koufa (on the western arm of the Euphrates) where the army was quartered, and went to join the original dissidents. It was on account of this exodus that the schismatics were given the name of Kharijites (those who go out).

If we disregard the rapidly multiplying rival sects, we note that the Kharijites were unanimous in proclaiming with regard to the caliphate what Wellhausen has very aptly called their 'nonconformity'.[39] For them any imam who deserted the right path must be denounced and removed from office. This moral and religious criterion led them to accept Abu Bakr and venerate 'Umar but reject 'Uthman after the sixth year of his reign, as also 'Ali after his adherence to the arbitration. Accordingly any one of the faithful, if worthy, could be designated caliph by the community without regard to any privilege arising from race, 'were he even a black slave'. In practice their moral requirements were exigent in the extreme. Faith was not sufficient justification without works, and anyone committing a capital sin was to be regarded as an apostate and—according to some—shut out for ever from the company of the faithful and doomed to death along with his family.

The Kharijites organised punitive expeditions against the supporters of the 'Umaiyads, in the course of which they stained the eastern empire with the blood of religious murders, but they were not brought under control until the time of the Abassid caliphs, who allowed them to exist only as a sect. It was under the last of the 'Umaiyads that their emissaries in the Maghrib began to spread their egalitarian puritanism, which received an enthusiastic welcome. Three principal tendencies gave rise to strife among the adherents of the movement. Azrakism represented extremism to the left, Ibadism the right and Sufrism the left. Of these, the two last-named played a considerable part in African history. Kharijism was naturally modified by the Berbers to suit their revolutionary temperament. Sufrism, which was opposed to terroristic methods as a matter of principle, was converted into a doctrine of direct action, as was Azrakism in the east.

The Kharijites' opposition to Sunni orthodoxy, the tangible representatives of which were Arab despotism and Arab bureaucracy, swiftly assumed the form of an insurrection. Gautier has sought to show that it had an essentially Zenata character.[40] W. Marçais, on the other hand, distinguishes two eighth-century foci of insurrection, both capable of striking a mortal blow at the Arab occupation[41]—one in Morocco, threatening Spain with isolation or contamination; the other in the eastern extremity of Barbary in the south of the Constantine area, in Tunisia and Tripolitania. The triumph of this latter could have jeopardised the future of the new capital and communications with bases in the east. Without

The Arab Conquest and the Kharijite Kingdoms

question, the Zenata played a role in the east, but in Morocco the movement caught the interest chiefly of the Branès and did not at the outset spread to central Zenatia, that is, to eastern Morocco, Orania and the plain of the Chélif.

ARAB OPPRESSION AND BERBER REACTION

The Maghrib and Spain were at that time under governors installed at Kairouan. These, according to the vicissitudes of politics, belonged either to the Qaisite clan or to that of the Yemenites, the triumph of Islam having done nothing to diminish ancestral rivalries.

In addition to this instability, Africa suffered the irresistible fiscal demands of the caliphs. To prevent the spread of Islam from exhausting the treasury, the 'Umaiyads had conceived the ingenious idea of requiring the newly converted to pay land tax (*kharāj*) and poll tax (*jizīya*) which were properly due only from infidels. The Arabs had no consideration for these recently-converted Muslims, least of all for the wild Berbers. Was not the governor Yazid observed to boast of introducing into the Maghrib the methods practised by al-Hajjaj in Iraq?[42] A worthy model indeed was this al-Hajjaj, at least for the clarity with which he had affirmed his principles of government to the inhabitants of Kufa. 'I observe', he announced in his speech delivered after taking up office, 'heads which have come to ripeness and must now be harvested. Already I see the blood running over your turbans and down your beards. By Allah, I will bind you hand and foot as we bind thorn bushes the more easily to cut them. I will thrash you like camels that have left the herd.' If that was the sort of rule imposed on the Berbers, it can be understood why they revolted and killed Yazid.

A few years later the caliph Hisham, anxious to stiffen the tax system organised by 'Umar, found in the governors of Tangier and Sous agents so zealous that they provoked a rising on the part of the tax-payers in 739–740. It was the Kharijites who took the lead. At the head of the revolting Ghomara, Miknasa and Berghwata marched a water-carrier, Maisara, who was, naturally, a Sufrite. He was designated Caliph, but that did not prevent his being deposed and executed as soon as he fell under suspicion for lack of zeal. Under his leadership the Kharijites soon became masters of Tangier, despite intervention by the governor of Spain. In 740 their new leader, Khalid ibn Hamid, defeated the hostile army in the 'battle of the nobles', in which the Arab general perished together with 'all the heroes' surrounding him. According to Ibn Khaldun this was on the Chélif.[43] If it was indeed so, it would have to be assumed that the eastern focus of Kharijism had got a hold in central Zenatia, which would confirm Gautier's thesis.[44] But the other Arab historians, with greater probability, situate the battle in northern Morocco. The discrepancy might be due to a copyist's error in the text of Ibn Khaldun, which, W. Marçais suggests, might have 'read Sebou instead of Chélif. Apart from the length of a loop, and disregarding diacritical marks which scribes habitually omit or restore erroneously, the two names are written in virtually the same fashion.'[45] Thus the uncertainty of the available documents once more calls for great circumspection.

Hisham then thought it necessary to take counter-action and dispatched his best troops from Syria under the amir Kulthum. They met the same fate at Baqdoura on the Sebou in 742. The authority of Damascus might have been thought to be permanently impaired, had not, in the same year the new governor of Egypt, Handhala ibn Safwan, arrived in time to win the twin victories of al-Qarn and al-Asnam in April and May 742. Thus he halted the two Kharijite armies which had invaded Ifriqiya and were threatening Kairouan.

THE DISTURBANCES IN IFRIQIYA

The defeat of the Kharijites, and the difficulties encountered by the 'Umaiyads at the same period in maintaining their hold on the caliphate, made it possible for an Arab reaction, seditious in character, to succeed in Ifriqiya. In 744, the very year in which the revolts broke out in the east that resulted six years later in the inauguration of the Abbasid dynasty, a great lord, 'Abd al-Rahman ibn Habib, great-grandson of 'Uqba, proclaimed his independence of Tunis. It is said that, moved by religious scruples and shrinking from civil war between Arabs, Handhala preferred to return to Syria without fighting, but when he did so in February–March 745, he cursed Ifriqiya as a land of sedition and revolt. The last 'Umaiyad and the first Abbasid rulers were too occupied to dispute the usurper's rights. When finally the caliph al-Mansur

The Arab Conquest and the Kharijite Kingdoms

showed his intention of exacting obedience, 'Abd al-Rahman resumed the role of rebel and offered asylum to the fugitive 'Umaiyads. One of these managed to reach Cordova where he founded an amirate, later transformed into an independent caliphate, in 756. But the end of 'Abd al-Rahman's reign was disturbed by palace quarrels, and in 755 he was stabbed to death by his brothers.

The conflicts following his death enabled a southern Tunisian Sufrite tribe, the Ourfejjouma, to take Kairouan and there to abandon itself to the worst acts of savagery. It was necessary to resort to other Kharijites, the Ibadites of the Djebel Nefousa, who, under the leadership of their first imam, Abu al-Khattab, had recently expelled the Abbasid governor of Tripoli.

It is said that Abu al-Khattab, indignant at the atrocities committed by the rival Kharijite sect, threw his forces on Kairouan where, notwithstanding his principles of moderation, he was responsible for the horrible massacre of the Ourfejjouma. At that time his authority extended from Tripolitania, where he resided, to Ifriqiya, where in June 758 he installed as governor at Kairouan 'Abd al-Rahman ibn Rustum, a noble of Persian extraction who had been brought up in the city.

Thus, as in the time of Kosaila, the Berbers were regaining control of the eastern part of North Africa, while the west, except during the period from the conquests of Musa ibn Nusair to the revolt of Maisara, had retained its independence. But the invaders left in the country a religious ferment which was to continue there. Islam might adopt heterodox forms in Barbary, it might leave outside its grasp many tribes in the mountains and even in the plains. But it was there, firmly planted in men's souls and already victorious over the beliefs that had preceded it.

The new governor of Egypt, Ibn al-Ash'ath, sent two armies against Abu al-Khattab; they were defeated. Finally he took command in person of a third and, in August 761, after a dearly won victory at Taworgha (south-east of Zliten in Tripolitania) he was able to recover possession of Kairouan.

THE KHARIJITES OF THE CENTRAL MAGHRIB

Though he was master of Ifriqiya, where he endeavoured to eradicate schism, Ibn al-Ash'ath had no hold on the rest of the

Maghrib. His victory was indeed an indirect cause of the creation of an Ibadite kingdom where Kharijism could blossom freely. Immediately after the capture of Kairouan, Ibn Rustum succeeded in evading the victor and went to the slopes of the Djebel Jozzoul, where he found the city of Tahert or Tihert (now Tagdemt) not far from a former Roman station (now Tiaret) where his faithful following elevated him to the imamate a few years later (776 or 778).

About the same period Abu Qurra, who commanded the powerful tribe of the Ifren, established a Sufrite kingdom in the neighbourhood of Tlemcen. We know nothing of its internal history, but its military role was considerable.

The Kharijites of these two kingdoms, together with those of the Djebel Nefousa and several other Berber groups, were a cause of much trouble to the governor of Kairouan, 'Umar ibn Hafs 'Hazarmard'.

Under the leadership of Abu Qurra, thirteen army corps surrounded him at Tobna in the Zab. The Arabs owed their safety solely to the greed of the Safrite prince who, in return for 40,000 dirhems, removed his most numerous and formidable contingents. 'Umar managed with some difficulty to extricate himself from Tobna and to get back to Kairouan, where the Berbers besieged him. Thus in 771 the Kharijites held not only the central Maghrib, but Ifriqiya as well.

However, the caliph dispatched from the east a powerful army commanded by Yazid ibn Hatim, who was under orders to replace 'Umar. It is said that after learning this 'Umar was killed in a sortie. The Berbers marched ahead of the Abbasid troops, under the leadership of a former Kharijite governor of Tripoli, Abu Hatim, who had played an important part at Tobna, and had directed the siege of Kairouan. The Ibadites invested him with the title of 'imam of defence' but in 772 he suffered a severe disaster in Tripolitania west of Jenbi. It was, say the Arab historians, the last of the 375 battles in which the Berbers had engaged the army from the time of their revolt against 'Umar ibn Hafs.[46]

Yazid employed strong measures against the Kharijites of Ifriqiya during the fifteen years of his governorship (772–787). At his hands the Ourfejjouma tribe, already drained of their resources by Abu al-Khattab, disappeared almost entirely. The Nefzawa

The Mediterranean in the 9th Century

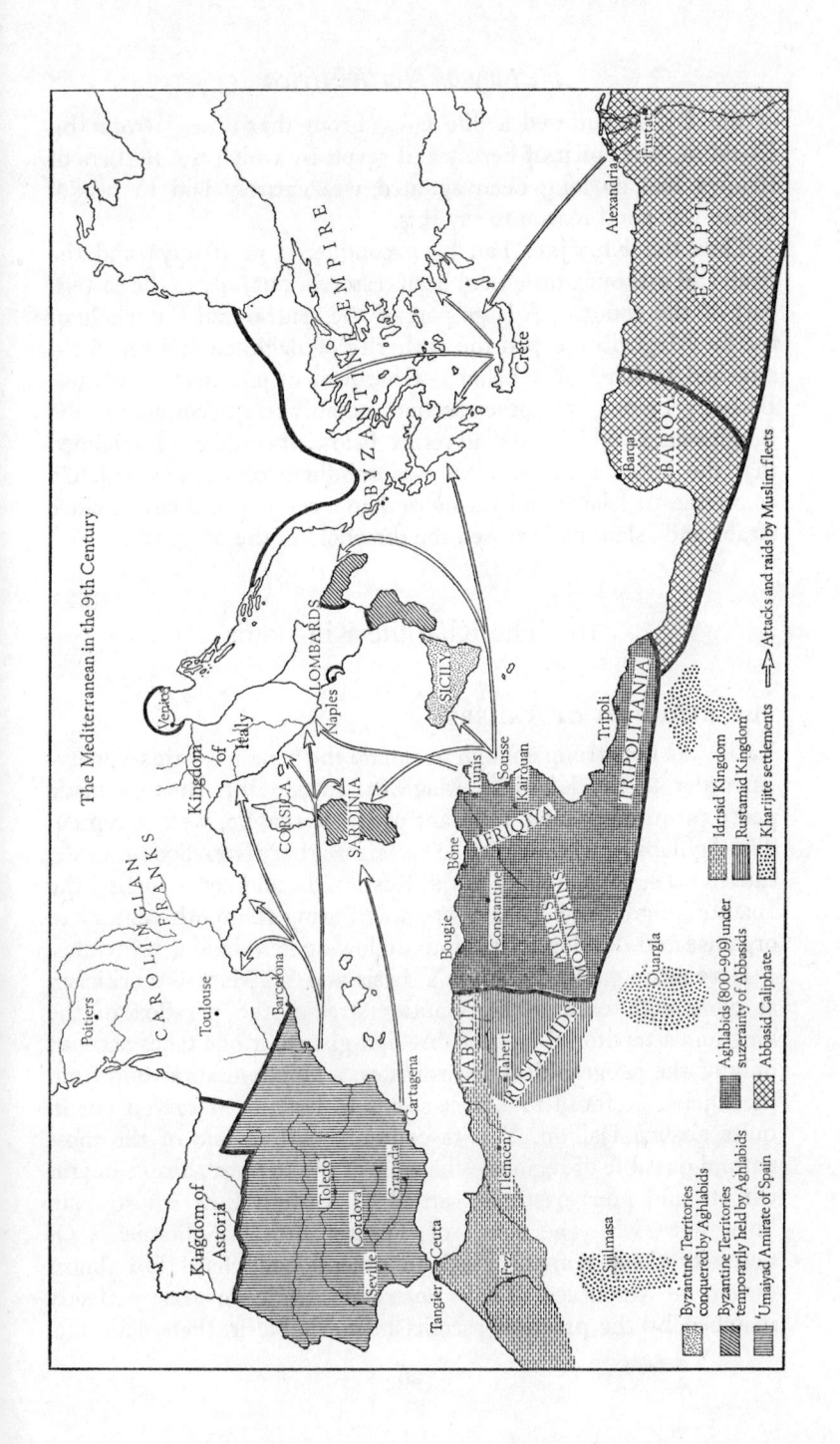

Byzantine Territories conquered by Aghlabids
Byzantine Territories temporarily held by Aghlabids
'Umaiyad Amirate of Spain
Aghlabids (800-909) under suzerainty of Abbasids
Abbasid Caliphate
Idrisid Kingdom
Rustamid Kingdom
Kharijite settlements
⟶ Attacks and raids by Muslim fleets

of the Djérid suffered a like fate. 'From this time,' wrote Ibn Khaldun, 'the spirit of heresy and revolt by which the Berbers of Ifriqiya had so long been agitated was entirely laid to rest.'[47] There was good reason to say this.

Thus the Kharijites had been conquered in Ifriqiya and the Arab and orthodox order had been restored, but only in the eastern part of the country. A large part of the central and the whole of the far Maghrib escaped the authority of Baghdad and remained attached to heterodox beliefs—Kharijism in one place, and new Berber religions in another section, notably in the country of the Berghwata, to which we shall return below. It could not be claimed that the land of the Berbers was subdued, or even completely converted to Islam; and yet more than a century had lapsed since Arabs and Islam had crossed the threshold of the Maghrib.

III. The Kharijite Kingdoms

THE KINGDOM OF TAHERT

Yazid was not strong enough to extend the benefits of this Varsuvian order to the Kharijite Maghrib. In 787 Ibn Rustum made peace proposals which, for want of an alternative, were accepted. The Aghlabids, who reigned in eastern Barbary from 800 onwards, caused no serious anxiety to the Rustumids, and consequently the Ibadite kingdom of Tahert was able during the tenth century to organise and develop in freedom, following its religious principles.

Here again we find Gautier's thesis and W. Marçais's criticism at odds with each other. Gautier stresses the paradox of the kingdom's territorial lay-out. 'At first glance, if one takes account only of the geographical co-ordinates, a kingdom sprawling from the Djebel Nefousa to Tiaret seems to have been carved out in quite absurd fashion. Yet its contours outline one of the most natural possible of regions—the zone of the steppes', a zone of arid climate and poor pastures, settled by 'eastern Butr whose main links were with the south of Tunisia and Tripolitania'.[48] Of necessity these nomads lived an exceptionally hard life almost devoid of resources. Their doctrinal asceticism was perfectly matched by the practical asceticism inevitable in their daily life.

The Arab Conquest and the Kharijite Kingdoms

And their mysticism, too, found in the desert the most fitting of settings.

It is unfortunate that Gautier did not take account of a document of our own times which fits his thesis so well. Ernest Psichari recalls the 'great facilities for meditation' afforded to men by that 'land of the spirit', the Sahara; and he sought instinctively—the word is his—'the contemplators, the dreamers of the steppes, men whose flesh had been consumed and their hearts pared down by fasting'. This youthful officer, tormented by the summons of the faith, felt himself drawn, almost against his will and under the pressure of the desert, to the Berber, nomad and mystic. What Psichari has to say could be applied to the Ibadites without altering a single word.

But, replies W. Marçais, the constructive elements of Rustumid Kharijism were not these Zenata nomads of the central Maghrib, who were 'only too much given to faction and rebellion, had little devotion for the Kharijite cause',[49] and made it difficult for the princes of Tahert to exercise their authority. 'Fortunately for them, they could also reckon among their subjects the people of the Aurès, small mobile herdsmen and farmers, and the mountain villagers of Tripolitania. These people furnished them with loyal soldiers and ardent propagandists, and filled the public granaries with the products of their tithes. . . .'[50]

Our attention, however, is claimed less by the disposition of tribes within the Rustumid kingdom than by the way of life of the Kharijites as their own masters, above all in their capital, where the leaven worked virtually in a sealed chamber. Two chronicles give us some information on the subject. One is the work of a Muslim not a member of the sect, Ibn Saghir,[51] who lived at Tiaret under the last of the imams. The other was written by a Kharijite scholar of Ouargla, Abu Zakariya',[52] towards the end of the eleventh century. The first was edited and translated by Motylinski. The other was translated by Masqueray from a Mzabite original wrongly thought to have been lost. The Polish Professor Zmogorzewski, who devoted himself to the study of Kharijism and discovered numerous unpublished documents in the Mzab country, was to have seen to its publication, but he died without having done so.

The Ibadites had established their capital at Tahert on a slope rising some 3,000 feet above the pastoral steppe. There the nomads came to summer their flocks and to exchange the produce of stock-raising for the cereals of the Tell. On arrival the chiefs went to make contact with the city notables, and then returned to camp until their departure. The fame of the Rustumid capital drew the brethren of the sect, who came hastening from Iraq to bring the contributions of the faithful and to drink in the atmosphere of triumphant Kharijism, but they also came to realise less disinterested speculations. Many did not return. 'There was not a foreigner', writes Ibn Saghir, 'who stopped in the city but settled among them and built in their midst, attracted by the plenty there, the equitable conduct of the imam, his just behaviour towards those under his charge and the security enjoyed by all in person and property. Soon one could not see a house in the town without hearing it said, "This belongs to such an one from Kufa; that house to such an one from Basra; that other to such an one from Qairouān; behold, here is the mosque of the men of Qairouān and their market; there is the mosque and the market of the Basrians, and there is that of the folk from Kufa."'[53]

For a long time those wishing to judge the architectural culture of the Rustumids have merely looked at the ruins of Sedrata (near Ouargla) where the inhabitants of Tahert took refuge after their capital had been captured by the Fatimids in 911. These ruins disclose an architecture having connections with that of Ifriqiya, decoration similar to that of the Coptic monasteries, and elements inspired by contemporary Egyptian public buildings and possibly by the palaces of Mesopotamia. The richly decorated dwellings erected at Sedrata must have been reminiscent of the houses of the men from the east at Tahert which Ibn Saghir greatly admired.

In 1941 G. Marçais and A. Dessus-Lamare explored the site of Tahert and undertook several digs.[54] Their task was made more difficult by the fact that from 1835 to 1841 the amir 'Abd al-Qadir had in his turn established himself on the location of the former Rustumite capital and left traces of his settlement there.

However, they were able to definitely identify part of the Rustumite walls, considerable water reservoirs, fragments of pottery and the kasbah where the Rustumid amirs had their seat. From their researches they concluded that Tahert was principally a well-guarded fortress equipped to withstand sieges, and that the extremely simple architecture of the kasbah showed similarities to

The Arab Conquest and the Kharijite Kingdoms

Syrian castles of the seventh century. On the other hand the pottery fragments they found enabled them to assert that the art of the Tahert ceramists was crude and rudimentary.

Accordingly, these architectural data, though still fragmentary, do permit us to give a certain credence to Ibn Saghir's account, which describes the imam constructing his own ceiling with mortar handed to him by a slave. It is true that things were different later on, and the delegates from Kufa, coming to Tahert for the second time, 'beheld castles built and gardens planted'.[55] These splendours, if splendours there were, must still have been modest enough, to judge from the ruins of Sedrata; in any case, current investigations have yielded no trace of them.

A THEOCRATIC GOVERNMENT

At the head of the Ibadite kingdom was an imam designated by the community of the faithful. He governed, in accordance with the Koran and the Tradition, subjects who owed him absolute obedience. Before bowing to the wishes of the notables, Ibn Rustum made them give a solemn undertaking in God's name to submit to all his orders that accorded with justice. If the imam transgressed the divine will which ought to be his inspiration, his decisions were *ipso facto* precluded. 'A conflict between the imam and the clergy', G. Marçais observes, 'naturally assumed the form and scale of a schism. The internal history of Tahert was to a great extent to be the history of the schisms that held authority in check.'[56]

The imam had to live an ascetic life. Ibn Rustum, busy filling in the cracks in his terrace with mortar, finished his task before coming down from his ladder to receive Ibadite messengers arrived from Iraq. He offered them buttered cakes and melted butter. 'The room was bare, save for the cushion he slept on, his sabre and his lance; and in another part of the house there was a tethered horse.' He held money in contempt to the point of sending back a second embassy, on the ground that the community was no longer so poor as to accept gifts. The imam Ya'qub 'touched neither dinar nor dirhem with his hands. . . . If he had need of a coin he fetched them out (from under a pack-saddle where they were put by the majordomo) with a rod.' He would swallow a full glass of milk—so Ibn Saghir tells us—'and went on thus for three days, taking neither food nor drink, nor going to stool'.[57] When travelling he would never accept a dish from his host.

It was the imam's duty to direct the state, to interpret the laws, to render justice, to preside over the prayers and to receive the tithe for alms-giving. He was spied on, and often sharply censured, by notables and clergy. Appointments to responsible posts were a trial of his impartiality. For example, secret meetings between the nomads and the principal Ibadites resulted in demands for the dismissal of the qadi, the treasurer and the chief of police. The designation of the qadi, with his responsibility for the administration of justice, was a matter of great consequence. He was a personage capable of opposing the imam and punishing the powerful. One qadi was seen to humiliate his friend and protector who had given the appearance of exercising pressure on his independence; another to throw his seal and registers into the hands of the amir, whose son had abducted a young girl. Also, the community took all possible precautions and sometimes had the holder of the office sent for from the depths of the Djebel Nefousa.

At harvest time Ibn Rustum's alms-collectors levied tithes not only on cereals but also on sheep and camels. When the collection was complete, the grain was distributed to the poor and then the sale of the sheep and camels took place. When the imam had sent to the governors the amounts representing their administrative budgets, the balance was used for the purchase of woollens and oil and these were distributed proportionately to each family, preference being given to the poor of the Ibadite sect. The expenses of government were charged to the product of the poll tax, of the *kharāj*, of lands and other revenues. Any surplus was devoted to public works of benefit to the Muslims.

By virtue of his position the imam was an expert theologian, for life at Tahert was conducted in a permanent state of religious fever. Cultivated minds, attracted by Kharijite radicalism, were not afraid of controversy. They even showed tolerance towards unbelievers. Did not certain men in the east go so far as to limit as strictly as possible the differences separating them from Jews and Christians? According to Ibn Saghir there were in the Rustumid capital Christians among the notables surrounding the imam Abu Hatim. One of these, a noted horseman, was counted among the city's defenders. When the amir Abu Bakr was in danger, the

The Arab Conquest and the Kharijite Kingdoms

Christians at once joined the Rustumids. The Kharijites were very ready to promote discussions with their opponents in the hope of converting them. Ibadites and Mu'tazilites arranged meetings for public debate in the valley of the Mina. Eastern jurists, one of whom enjoyed great reputation with the people, did not conceal even their intention 'to halt the progress of the Ibadites and to stamp out their doctrine.'[58] These controversies evolved over points—often very subtle—of dogma, law or grammar. Nothing could be more scholastic than the dialogue between a Kharijite and Ibn Saghir concerning the marriage of girls who have not attained the age of puberty.[59] The influence of the scholars was considerable. One of them, 'learned in the sciences of law, theology, records, grammar and language', used to receive a tithe from his admirers at Sijilmasa. Polemical works were written in increasing numbers and manuscripts were collected, but with all their training in theological argument, the Ibadites devoted themselves with equal ardour to secular studies.

Puritanism subjected this Geneva of the Maghrib to a censorship of public morals. But, if restraining influences failed in time of civil war, moral corruption worked havoc. 'The inhabitants made public and scandalous use of intoxicating liquors, and of young men for the satisfaction of their vices.' But when order was established once more, morality was restored 'by means of blows, imprisonment and throwing into irons'. The wine jars were broken and the sodomites had to flee 'to the tops of the mountains or the depths of the valleys'.[60]

Every Ibadite, resolved to shrink from no measure for the greater glory of God, was potentially a rebel. Often the imam kept his place only by means of adroit political manipulation. If a conflict broke out, coalitions promptly formed and took up arms. When the amir Abu Bakr, disturbed by his favourite's ostentation and popularity, had him assassinated, a war followed which lasted for seven years. The merchants took advantage of it to finance the rebels, and the turbulent tribesmen threw themselves into the fray. 'The parties', writes Ibn Saghir, 'were fired by warlike passion resembling that of the pre-Islamic period and fought on either side for glory and renown.'[61] Clashes sometimes arose from hatred between tribesmen and town-dwellers, more often from popular discontent at the abandonment of customary practices. On the death of the imam Aflah there were found those ready to challenge the procedure adopted for designating his son. 'God requires of you an account of your conduct, O Nefousa,' cried one of them. 'When an imam dies you put another in his place without submitting the matter to the Muslims and without, by consultation, enabling them to choose him who is most pious and who accords with them the best.'[62] There was no shortage of men who maintained 'a haughty attitude' towards the new amir Abu Bakr. When Abu Hatim's entourage wanted to screen him 'from the vulgar gaze and to surround him with royal pomp . . . the people refused and insisted on their right to approach him freely at any moment as they had been accustomed to do before he became imam'.[63] Between the lines of Ibn Saghir's narrative one can discern a steady effort on the part of nobles and clergy to form an aristocracy which could impose its guidance on the amir. The imam Aflah b. al-Wahhab cautioned the principal Ibadites against the appointment of a qadi from the mountains who 'takes no account of rank or of the noble birth of any man whatever . . . (and) will apply the laws in their full rigour without troubling to mitigate them in order to ingratiate himself with you.'[64] The *qaids* and those close to 'Abd al-Wahhab induced him to break an undertaking given to the nomads by laying before him the danger of yielding to their pressure and the advantages of an authoritarian policy. The result was an Arab insurrection. The imam suppressed it, but it left 'a ferment of hatreds working among the groups which had suffered losses by death'.[65]

Notwithstanding these endless clashes, the society of Tahert seems not to have been warlike by temperament. Battles were not particularly bloody, fugitives were often not pursued, the wounded were not killed, and opposing sides would consent to mediation. Therein no doubt lay the cause of the fall of the Rustumid kingdom. The imams were unable to organise a firm and reliable army, and the result was that in 911, at the very first assault, Shiite troops took their capital without difficulty.

The destruction of Tahert, though it condemned the Ibadites to relinquish the 'way of defence' for the 'way of secrecy', extinguished neither the Kharijite faith nor the theological literature of its adepts. Scattered through the Algerian and Tunisian Sahara, they continue to exist today in the Djebel Nefousa, on the island of

The Arab Conquest and the Kharijite Kingdoms

Djerba, at Ouargla and in the Mzab. At the cost of great effort and considerable expenditure the Mzabites maintain oases on an unproductive soil and in their towns with their cold, bare mosques—Ghardaia, Melika and the sacred Beni Isguen—they preserve a religious intransigence which is sometimes in contrast with the life their merchants and clever business men lead in the Tell.

THE KINGDOM OF SIJILMASA AND THE BERGHWATA

We have unfortunately very little information about another Kharijite kingdom which, according to the geographer al-Bakri, was founded at Sijilmasa in 757 by Berbers of the Sufrite sect, the Miknasa, who were in revolt against the governor of Kairouan.[66] This was the kingdom of the palm-grove oases of the desert. What Ibn Khaldun tells us indicates that the faithful freely made use of their right to depose their imams. Discontented with the behaviour of the first amir, 'his people bound him hand and foot and left him exposed on a mountain top until he died'.[67] There were some theologians of repute among them, and one of these had gained great renown for his studies at Medina. The chief ruler of the Benu Midrar dynasty seems to have been Abu Mansur al-Yasa', who in the course of a reign of 34 years (790-823) completed the building of Sijilmasa and the conquest of the oases. He took the logical step of seeking reconciliation with the kingdom of Tahert by marrying his son to Ibn Rustum's daughter.

A particularly remarkable heresy was the one that grew up in the far Maghrib in Chaouia country among the tribes forming the Berghwata group. About 744 these tribes, who had joined in the Kharijite schism and had taken part in the expeditions of the water-carrier Maisara, followed their chief Salih in his plan to organise a new religion.

Salih, proclaiming himself the prophet of the Berbers, composed a Koran in his own language and established a kind of religious code which laid down prohibitions, no doubt of local origin, and some modifications of ritual. This heresy, whether it is rightly attributed to Salih or was renewed or even instituted by his grandson Yunus, represents one of the most original attempts to Berberise a religion imported into the Maghrib by an invader.

These schismatic or heretical kingdoms, which are of such great interest to us, failed to secure the attention of Arab historians. It

History of North Africa

was with zeal of a very different order that they studied the two orthodox dynasties which were founded at the two extremes of the Maghrib at the beginning of the ninth century—that of the Idrisids of Fez and that of the Aghlabids of Ifriqiya.

Notes

1. E. F. Gautier, *L'Islamisation de l'Afrique du Nord. Les siècles obscurs du Maghreb* (Paris, 1927), pp. 233–4 (2nd edition, Paris, 1937; notes here are taken from the 1st edition).
2. Abu 'Abd Allah Muhammad b. 'Umar al-Waqidi (A.H. 130–207/A.D. 747–822); see J. Horvitz, 'al-Wakidi', *Encyclopedia of Islam*, IV.
3. Ibn 'Abd al-Hakam ('Abd al-Rahman b. 'Abd Allah b. 'Abd al-Hakam b. A'yan), *Futuh Ifriqiyya wa al-Andalus*: see A. Gateau, tr. and ed., *Conquête de l'Afrique du Nord et de l'Espagne* (2nd ed. 1948), II; and *Histoire des Berbères* (tr. M. de Slane, Alger, 1852–6), 4 vols. (reprinted, Paris, 1925–56), I, appendix I.
4. W. Marçais, 'Un siècle de Recherche sur le Passé de Algérie musulman', in J. Alazard and C. Albertini, *Histoire et Historiens de l'Algérie* (Paris, 1931), p. 150.
5. Ibn Khaldun, *Kitab al-'Ibar*; for parts about North Africa see *Histoire des Berbères* (ed. M. de Slane, Alger, 1847), 2 vols.; also *Histoire des Berbères* (tr. M. de Slane, Alger, 1852–6), 4 vols. (reprinted, Paris, 1925–56).
6. al-Maliki: I have been unable to identify this historian (ed.).
7. Ibn al-Athir (A.H. 555–630/A.D. 1160–1234), *al-Kamil fi al-Ta'rikh*; see E. Fagnan, tr. and ann., *Annales du Maghreb et de l'Espagne* (Alger, 1901).
8. Ibn 'Idhari (Abu 'Abdallah Muhammad al-Marrakushi), flourished at the end of 7th century A.H./13th century A.D., *al-Bayan al-mughrib fi akhbar al-Maghrib*; see R. Dozy, ed., *Histoire de l'Afrique et de l'Espagne* (Leiden, 1848–51), 2 vols.; see also E. Fagnan, tr., *Bayan al-maghrib*, 2 vols. (Alger, 1901–14).
9. al-Nuwairi (Shibab al-Din Ahmad b. 'Abd al-Wahhab al-Bakri al-Kindi al-Shafi'i), (A.H. 677–732/A.D. 1279–1332), *Nihayat al-arab fi funun al-adab*, tr. in part by M. de Slane, 'Conquête de l'Afrique septentrionale', in *Histoire des Berbères* (Alger, 1852), (reprinted Paris, 1925–56), I, appendix II, 314–397.
10. Ahmad b. Yahya b. Jabir al-Baladhuri (d. A.H. 279/A.D. 892), his two extant works are: *Futuh al-Buldan* and *Ansab al-Ashraf*; see C. H. Becker, 'al-Baladhuri', *Encyclopedia of Islam*, I.
11. C. Brockelmann, 'Ibn Qutaiba', *Encyclopedia of Islam*, II, the reference here is to *Kitab al-Imama wa al-siyasa* (Cairo, 1322, 1327),

The Arab Conquest and the Kharijite Kingdoms

ascribed to Ibn Qutaiba, but probably of Maghribi or Egyptian origin in his lifetime (A.H. 213–276/A.D. 828–889).
12. W. Marçais, 'Les siècles obscurs du Maghreb', *Revue critique d'historie et de littérature* (1929), pp. 255–70; reprinted in W. Marçais, *Articles et Conférences*, Publications de l'Institut d'Etudes Orientales, Faculté des Lettres d'Alger (Paris, 1961), p. 77.
13. Ibn 'Abd al-Hakam (tr. de Slane), *op. cit.*, I, 304.
14. *Ibid.*, I, 304.
15. E. F. Gautier, *op. cit.*, p. 226.
16. al-Nuwairi (tr. de Slane), *op. cit.*, I, 327.
17. *Ibid.*, I, 332–3; Ibn Khaldun (tr. de Slane), *op. cit.*, I, 287.
18. E. F. Gautier, *op. cit.*, p. 221.
19. See J. Ruska, 'al-Sus al-Aqsa', *Encyclopedia of Islam*, IV.
20. R. Brunschvig, 'Ibn 'Abdalh'akam et la conquête de l'Afrique du Nord par les Arabes', *Annales de l'Institut d'Etudes Orientales*, Faculté des Lettres d'Alger, VI (1942–7), p. 138.
21. E. F. Gautier, *op. cit.*, p. 243.
22. Ibn Khaldun (tr. de Slane), *op. cit.*, I, 289.
23. *Ibid.*, III, 193.
24. E. F. Gautier, *op. cit.*, p. 245 *et seq.*
25. *Ibid.*, p. 245.
26. Ibn Khaldun (tr. de Slane), *op. cit.*, I, 208.
27. E. F. Gautier, *op. cit.*, pp. 252–3.
28. Ibn Khaldun (tr. de Slane), *op. cit.*, I, 168 *et seq.*
29. E. F. Gautier, *op. cit.*, 'Butr', pp. 204–11; 'Branès', pp. 211–14.
30. *Ibid.*, p. 254.
31. W. Marçais (1961), *op. cit.*, pp. 73–4.
32. *Ibid.*, p. 74.
33. *Ibid.*, p. 75.
34. *Ibid.*, p. 75.
35. E. Masqueray, 'Le Djebel Chechar', *Revue Africaine*, XXII (1878), pp. 44–5; and E. F. Gautier, *op. cit.*, pp. 192, 242.
36. W. Marçais (1961), *op. cit.*, p. 78.
37. *Ibid.*, p. 82.
38. al-Nuwairi (tr. de Slane), *op. cit.*, I, 338–9 and note 1, p. 339.
39. For an English translation of one of Wellhausen's more general surveys, see M. G. Weir, *The Arab Kingdom and its Fall* (Calcutta, 1927); references to the Kharijites, pp. 63–8.
40. E. F. Gautier, *op. cit.*, pp. 264–9.
41. W. Marçais (1961), *op. cit.*, p. 78.
42. al-Nuwairi (tr. de Slane), *op. cit.*, I, 356.
43. Ibn Khaldun (tr. de Slane), *op. cit.*, I, 217.
44. E. F. Gautier, *op. cit.*, p. 269.
45. W. Marçais (1961), *op. cit.*, p. 79.
46. al-Nuwairi (tr. de Slane), *op. cit.*, I, 384; Ibn Khaldun (tr. de Slane), *Ibid.*, I, 223.
47. *Ibid.*, I, 224.

48. E. F. Gautier, *op. cit.*, pp. 300–1.
49. W. Marçais (1961), *op. cit.*, p. 79.
50. *Ibid.*, p. 79.
51. A. de Motylinski, ed. and tr., 'Chronique d'Ibn Saghir sur les imams rostémides de Tahert', *Actes du XIV Congrès des Orientalistes*, 3rd part (Paris, 1908).
52. Abu Zakariya' Yahya b. Abi Bakr; the work referred to here is *Kitab al-sira wa akhbar al-a'imma*, in E. Masqueray, tr., *Chronique d'Abou Zakaria, Livre des Benî Mzab* (Alger, 1878).
53. Ibn Saghir (tr. Motylinski), *op. cit.*, p. 68.
54. G. Marçais and A. Dessus-Lamare, 'Recherches d'Archeologie musulmane: Tihert-Tagdemt', *Revue Africaine* (1946), pp. 24–57.
55. Ibn Saghir (tr. Motylinski), *op. cit.*, p. 69.
56. G. Marçais, *La Berbérie Musulmane et l'Orient au Moyen Age* (Paris, 1946), see p. 107.
57. Ibn Saghir (tr. Motylinski), *op. cit.*, pp. 64–72 for a biographical account of Ibn Rustum.
58. *Ibid.*, p. 116.
59. *Ibid.*, pp. 124–6.
60. *Ibid.*, p. 123.
61. *Ibid.*, p. 102.
62. *Ibid.*, p. 91.
63. *Ibid.*, p. 116.
64. *Ibid.*, p. 82.
65. *Ibid.*, p. 77.
66. al-Bakri, *Kitab al-Masalik*; see M. de Slane, ed. and tr., *Description de l'Afrique septentrionale* (Alger, 1857–8); (2nd, corrected ed., Alger, 1911–13); (notes taken here from the 3rd ed., Paris, 1965), p. 282.
67. Ibn Khaldun (tr. de Slane), *op. cit.*, p. 261.

CHAPTER 2

The Arab and Berber Dynasties
(Ninth–Eleventh Centuries)

❦

In the history of the Maghrib the period that runs from the middle of the ninth to the middle of the eleventh century is one of confusion, with two waves of nomads breaking over the country—one, the Almoravids, coming from the western Sahara, the other, the Hilalians, coming from the deserts of the east.

It was a period of transition, during which the Berbers were discarding the links that had bound them for a time to the east, but did not yet feel sure enough of themselves to dispense with the very east whose political sway they were repudiating. Except in Ifriqiya they rejected the authority of the Abbasid caliphs, but were nevertheless very ready to welcome exiles from the east and to take them as leaders. They drank at the springs of Muslim law and oriental art and, in their towns, though these still lacked much of what makes a city, they did their best to live in the manner of the age-old civilisations of Damascus or Baghdad.

Thus, by a strange paradox, the point of time at which politically the Berbers were seeking to emancipate themselves was also that at which they were becoming deeply imbued with Semitic civilisation and were endeavouring—for the first time apparently since the beginning of time—to become easterners.

Our documents for this period are more numerous and more reliable than for the one which precedes it. It is true that we still have only too often to be content with writers of much later date, and the genius of an Ibn Khaldun cannot blind us to the fact that he is as far removed in time from the Idrisids and Aghlabids as we are [in 1952] from the Hundred Years War. But we do have older sources, some of which, like the works of the geographers al-Ya'qubi[1] and Ibn Hawqal,[2] were written by eyewitnesses. Without finding ourselves in full daylight—Gautier's term 'dark ages' remains fully valid—we can step forward a little less hesitantly and allow ourselves a few firm assertions.

1. The Idrisid Dynasty

IDRIS SETTLES IN THE FAR MAGHRIB

In 788 there arrived at Tangier a fugitive from the east, Idris ibn 'Abd Allah, a descendant of 'Ali and Fatima. Having compromised himself in a rebellion of the Alids against the Abbasids, he had escaped by chance from the massacre that followed the victory of the Abbasids over the rebels at Fakhkh, near Mecca, in 786. Accompanied only by a single freedman, the faithful Rashid, he had made his way as far as Tangier. It had proved impossible for him to settle either in Ifriqiya, which continued loyal to the caliphate, or in the central Maghrib, which was in the hands of the Kharijites. Tangier was too remote, and he did not stay there, but became the guest, and later the leader or rather the imam (a term of the Shi'a vocabulary) of the Awraba tribe settled around the former Roman city of Volubilis, now known as Walila. Is there any need to believe, as Gautier does, that Idris was able to assume the command of this tribe because it consisted of still Romanised Berbers?[3] We may rather think, with Terrasse, that these Berbers, whether Romanised or not, made Idris welcome because he was a sharif and an opponent of the detested caliph, and probably also because of his outstanding personal qualities.[4]

Moreover, the Awraba were soon joined by a number of Arabs hostile to the Abbasids. Perhaps Idris had the plan, as did the Fatimids at a later date, of using the Maghrib as a base from which to launch a campaign to reconquer the heritage of his fathers. Be that as it may, considering Walila too small, he founded a new city, Madinat Fas (on the site of the present Andalusian quarter of Fez), and began to carve out a kingdom for himself with the assistance of several Northern Moroccan Berber tribes. In turn he attacked Tamesna (in the Salé region), Fazaz (in the region of Azrou-Aïn Leuh) and Tlemcen of which he took possession. But hardly had

The Arab and Berber Dynasties (Ninth–Eleventh Centuries)

his successes become known than the caliph Harun al-Rashid had him poisoned by one of his emissaries in 791–792.

IDRIS II AND THE FOUNDATION OF FEZ

Idris left no son to succeed him, but one of his Berber concubines, Kenza, was pregnant, and two months after Idris's death she gave birth to a boy who in his turn was given the name of Idris. He grew up in the safe-keeping of his mother and Rashid, amid the veneration of the Awraba Berbers, who saw in him the inheritor of the *baraka*,[5] that beneficent power transmitted from father to son by the descendants of the Prophet.

The child must have come up to the simple hopes placed in him, for when he was only eleven years old he was solemnly acknowledged as heir to his father's political power. But other influences were at work on him besides those of the Awraba. Arabs from Ifriqiya and Andalusia came to join his entourage at Walila, and probably awakened inherited affinities in him, for it was from among them that he chose his chief collaborators. Indeed in 808 he went to the length of having the Awraba leader, Abu Laila Ishaq, put to death. This was doubtless at the instigation of his new companions, but we know nothing of the circumstances. The year following this murder, Idris and his Arabs, who no longer felt safe at Walila, decided upon the town of Fez, which had been founded some twenty years earlier as the abortive capital which Idris I had had no time to bother about, and which was still no more than a Berber market town.

The young prince chose to leave the town as it was, preferring to settle opposite it across the river on the left bank. He built a

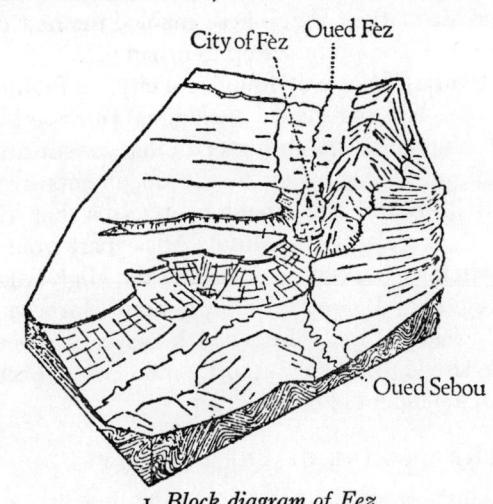

1 *Block diagram of Fez*

mosque, a market and a palace that was certainly far from grandiose, in which he lodged his Arabs. Such was the birth of the future city of the men of Kairouan, its original name being al-ʿAliya (the high town). This at least is the account put forward by Lévi-Provençal in an important study devoted to the foundation of Fez.[6] All of the arguments which he sets forth carry conviction, at least so far as we are concerned. No one after reading it could fail to realise that there are two traditions for the foundation of Fez, or that this one mentioned above, though poorer in details, is both as ancient and as well supported as that of the *Rawd al-Qirtas*.[7] Futhermore it explains the hitherto mysterious juxtaposition of the two original towns of Fez.

Gautier has rightly laid stress on the abundance of water flowing or trickling through the site of Fez.[8] Water certainly was an important factor with both Idrises in making their choice. Moreover, there are plentiful building materials in the neighbourhood. Finally, it is situated on the most convenient road between the Atlantic plains and the central Maghrib, crossed at this point by a north-south road running from Tangier to the Tafilalet.

Soon both of the twin cities received a sudden influx of new inhabitants—several hundred familes from Cordova and Kairouan who, in 818 and 825, had been forced into exile by the vicissitudes of politics and who brought advanced techniques to the newly created city of Fez. These enabled the new city to dispense with a period of apprenticeship to urban life.

Idris II not only founded a city, he founded the first Moroccan state. Not that he succeeded, as Terrasse has observed,[9] in combining under his authority all that constitutes the Sharifian empire of today. According to the documents available to us (notably al-Bakri and Ibn Khaldun) it seems that 'the greater part of the Atlantic plains, the Middle Atlas apart from its northern edge, the whole of the central Atlas and the High Atlas, almost all the oasis region and a good deal of eastern Morocco remained outside the Idrisid empire.'[10] Idris had, however, succeeded in grouping under a single Muslim authority numerous Berber tribes until then independent of one another.

THE DECLINE OF THE DYNASTY

The new kingdom was imposing, but brittle. It did not withstand

The Arab and Berber Dynasties (Ninth–Eleventh Centuries)

the death of its founder, who disappeared prematurely (whether by accident or assassination is not clear) in 828. The ancient Berber spirit of political fragmentation and local autonomies had not vanished. On the advice of their Berber grandmother Kenza, the two sons of Idris II parcelled out his kingdom between them, thereby destroying his political achievement but not his civilising mission, due to the spreading influence of Fez, the only 'city' which might be so called in the Morocco of those days.

The Idrisite principalities continued in existence in spite of difficulties until the advent of the Fatimids in 921. Thereafter the last Idrisids clung to the mountains near Tangier until the generals of Cordova put an end to the dynasty in 974.

II. The Aghlabid Dynasty

AN INDEPENDENT DYNASTY

At the other end of Barbary, in Ifriqiya, an Arab governor of the Zab, Ibrahim ibn al-Aghlab, founded a dynasty which, without breaking with the Abbasid caliphs, remained entirely independent.

The ruler from whom the dynasty took its name, al-Aghlab ibn Salim (765–767) had so far enjoyed the caliph's confidence as to be raised to the amirship, but had experienced only the difficulties of power and had died under the arrows of the soldiery. His son Ibrahim was far from Kairouan during the years when the strong-willed Yazid ibn Hatim was restoring order. He was then appointed governor of the Zab and subsequently he made skilful use of the insurrections in Ifriqiya to set himself up as mediator and in turn to secure the title of Amir in 800.

Until the beginning of the tenth century his descendants succeeded one another without difficulty and there was never any serious dispute between Kairouan and Baghdad. Though towards the end of the dynasty the caliphs intervened in the quarrels between the amir and the people of Tunis, in general they were satisfied with an honorific suzerainty and refrained even from confirming the nomination of new amirs. As for the Aghlabids themselves, the devolution of power by the caliphs served to increase their prestige with the Arab soldiery. The loyalty of the army enabled them to have recourse to Abbasid subventions, so that they never showed any sign of breaking the links that were, in fact, of very little inconvenience.

SPREAD OF AGHLABID POWER

These princes ruled over Ifriqiya, the land of the settled folk, the exact limits of which—if such indeed there were—are unknown to us. To the south-east they held Tripoli, but the immediately surrounding country was in the hands of the Ibadites of Djebel Nefousa, who were very much in control of the narrow coastal road leading to the town until the day in 896 when an unexpected conflict enabled the amir to crush his formidable adversaries. In the south, the Djérid, utterly drained of resources, represented a partly Kharijite, but totally pacified, territory. In the south-west, in the Zab and the Hodna, a minority of active and loyal Arabs kept these distant provinces in subjection to Kairouan until 865. Garrisons, almost independent, dotted the roads leading to the Zab and guaranteed freedom of passage. The Aurès naturally constituted a hostile bloc in which Kharijism flourished in its most extreme form of Nakkarism, opening the way for Mu'tazilite rationalism. From its upheaval the amir prudently stood aside, content in those parts with only theoretical authority. Finally in the west, Bône came under the Aghlabids, as also did the country of the fierce Kotama, whose respectful submission was maintained by the fortress of Belezma. In fact, however, lesser Kabylia eluded them, no less than the Aurès.

In Ifriqiya proper the amir had little difficulty in maintaining his control over the coastal region from Gabès to Sousse; the Qamouda, to the south-west, between Kairouan, Gafsa and Tébessa; and the region between Kairouan and Tunis—all of them urbanised territories, sufficiently Arabised and orthodox. However, he had also to reckon with the Berber tribes of the north-west, neighbours of the Kotama, and the mixed populations, civilised but independent, of the north-east. The inhabitants of Kairouan and Tunis were no more inclined to discipline than were these Berber tribes.

Islamised Berbers naturally constituted the majority, but the descendants of the Arab invaders were numerous—perhaps 100,000. The Christians—Berbers converted long ago or

The Arab and Berber Dynasties (Ninth–Eleventh Centuries)

descendants of the Romans, and all included under the name of Africans (*Afāriq*)—had not disappeared and held an important position, due to their traditional culture and despite their internecine quarrels. There were also to be found, according to al-Ya'qubi, a number of Rums, that is, the broken remnants of Byzantine garrisons of former times, now in the process of being assimilated.[11] In the towns, Jews particularly as physicians, constituted an intellectual élite. Christians and Jews do not appear to have been greatly troubled by contact with Muslims. The Arabs, on the other hand, even of most humble origins, loathed the Muslim Berbers. Kharijism had caused the conquerors sufficient trouble to explain their growing 'Berberophobia', and it is not difficult to understand why the ascetic Bohloul should have given a banquet on the day he received proof that he was indeed one hundred per cent Arab.

A SOCIETY OF DEVOTEES

We can form a sufficient idea of the Muslim society of Ifriqiya, not so much from the dull accounts of the chroniclers as from the books called *Tabaqāt*, the object of which was to determine the conditions under which the traditional documents (*hadith*), constituting sacred custom (*sunna*), were handed down. One of the oldest of these, the *Classes of the Scholars of Ifriqiya*, affords a number of intimate little sketches which make it possible to form a vivid idea of life at Kairouan.[12]

The atmosphere of Ifriqiya in the ninth century, like that of all Islam, was surcharged with devotion. But among the mass of the Berber people, with their strong dislike of half-measures, this devotion took on a peremptory character and those who practised it occupied an outstanding place in society. Whatever the environment they sprang from, men of religion commanded respect, even admiration, from these people who by the end of the eighth century were passing through a crisis of asceticism. The holy man Bohloul, who despised man's vile body to the point of never undressing and of converting latrines into oratories, made such a mark by his austerity and his Sunni intransigence that his fame spread as far as Samarkand.[13]

The movement intensified under the early Aghlabids. Many were the Muslims who felt the need to withdraw from the world, sometimes permanently, or, more often, to go into retreat in the frontier fortresses, the *ribats*, which were places of intense prayer as well as military strongpoints.

But Ifriqiya was not only a land of spontaneous faith, it was also an extremely active theological centre. 'What are the inhabitants of Kairouan talking of today?' was the question asked by a traveller on his return from Iraq. 'Of the names and attributes of God,', was the answer a young man gave him.[14]

Under the influence of Iraq, simple asceticism appears from 830 onwards to have given way to controversy. The East and Andalusia sent their scholars to Ifriqiya, where the number of disciples increased. Arabs, chiefly from Kairouan, went to Iraq or to Medina in order to sit at the feet of masters of repute and returned, ecstatic with their newly acquired knowledge, to proselytise in their own country. Thus there came into being a class of scholars, theologians and jurists whose arguments the public followed avidly.

They were not all professionals. Many worked at their trade as potters or brickmakers, as merchants of furs or cotton goods, as exact and exacting tradesmen inclined to give short weight when serving the customer with provisions, or as land owners. And the populace held them in esteem, feeling them to be close to itself and involved in its daily life. Naturally enough they became the spokesmen of the people and the amir had to reckon with them, the more so that their independence and, as a general rule, their contempt for honours deprived the government of any means of applying effective pressure.

THE PROBLEM OF THE CREATION OF THE KORAN. MU'TAZILISM

The questions which were being discussed were those in which the whole of the Islamic world was then interested. Foremost, there was the emotionally charged question of the creation of the Koran. Orthodox theologians, whose minds had been opened by discussion with Christians to the concept of the eternal and uncreated character of the word of God, asserted that the Koran, as a revelation spoken by Allah, was uncreate even as He was. Each copy of the Arabic Koran, like the Koran in heaven, existed from all eternity and was identified with the word of God, which was 'to be found between the pages within the binding'.

The Arab and Berber Dynasties (Ninth–Eleventh Centuries)

These assertions were vigorously contested by the Mu'tazilites, who found them destructive of the divine unity and maintained that the Koran was created. On other essential points they also broke with orthodoxy. They were advocates of free will and set up a symbolic exegesis of the Koran in opposition to prevailing anthropomorphic conceptions. In the name of the unchangeable and indestructible unity they rejected such divine attributions as could not be distinguished from the divine essence, and whose indefinite repetition amounted merely to the single statement: *God is*. Finally, they regarded reason (*'aql*) as a basic source of religious knowledge.

The conflict was to continue until it was brought to an end by al-Ash'ari, who died in 935. He, after breaking with Mu'tazilism, became the founder of orthodox scholastic theology (*kalām*). Employing all the resources of his dialectic methods, he demonstrated that the Koran is in essence and reality identical with the uncreate and eternal word of God, and thus ensured the triumph of orthodoxy.

By the end of the eighth century the Mu'tazilites constituted an independent and courageous minority in Ifriqiya, yielding neither to the uncompromising Berber masses, in whose eyes doctrines of this kind amounted to denials of divinity, nor to the traditionalists. But they were caught between the two lines of thought as in the jaws of a vice. The crystallisation of Muslim dogma at the end of the ninth century brought the condemnation of their endeavours, and the triumph of the Shiites was to strike them a mortal blow.

MALIKISM. SAHNUN

Closely intermingled with theological arguments were those relating to Muslim law (*fiqh*) which regulated not only the religious life of the faithful, but their civil and economic life as well. Of the four orthodox schools of law in Islam to which it is 'lawful' to belong, two played an important part in Ifriqiya. One of them was Hanifism, the least strict in Islam, Persian in inspiration and fathered by the imam Abu-Hanifa, who died about 767. The other was Malikism, more strict in interpretation and hostile to rational interpretations; this was the product of the celebrated imam of Medina, Malik ibn Anas, who died in 795.

Malikism, which was perfectly suited to the Berber mentality, triumphed, as might be expected, in Ifriqiya and subsequently throughout North Africa, where it is still predominant. But its success was not immediate. The great Anas ibn al-Furat, who was to lead the Aghlabid armies invading Sicily, had introduced Malikism into Ifriqiya, but was not himself free from compromising associations with the rival school. It was one of his disciples, Sahnun, an able and militant theologian and celebrated author of the *Mudawwana*, as austere as he was independent, who broke with his master's erring ways to preach a strict Malikism, the triumph of which he ensured.

The small Hanifite élite bravely kept up the struggle, with the energetic support of certain amirs, but it was compromised at the end of the ninth century by its contacts with the Mu'tazilites and submerged under the hostile and violent mass of Malikite Berbers. There then prevailed throughout Ifriqiya a particularly uncompromising brand of Malikism. 'We are told', said a man from Baghdad one day to a man of Kairouan, 'that the Prophet used to say . . .' 'According to what we are told', interrupted the other, 'Malik is of a different opinion,' 'May your faces be blackened on the day of the Last Judgment, O people of the Maghrib', exclaimed the Baghdadi, 'you set up Malik's word against the word of the Prophet!'[15]

THE AMIRS

Not all the amirs were thoroughly orthodox. Some showed signs of Hanifite leanings and one was a Mu'tazilite, but they could not ignore public opinion, so much so that, beginning with Sahnun, they selected the qadis of Kairouan, whose influence was considerable, from among the Maliki disciples.

Rather than theological argument, they preferred their refined palace life in accordance with the taste of Baghdad, surrounded by female musicians, concubines and minions, eunuchs raised by their favour to the highest rank, the many princes of royal blood and the Arab lords who had joined their cause, white freedmen and the faithful black guard. They would listen to songs and poems and the jests of buffoons, wander through gardens or glide by boat across stretches of water, play at games or watch horse races. They were often cultivated, artistic and broad-minded; sometimes they were cruel; nearly always they were drunkards.[16]

The Arab and Berber Dynasties (*Ninth–Eleventh Centuries*)

The founder of the dynasty, Ibrahim I (800–812) was an outstanding personality, erudite, able and daring. ʿAbd Allah I (812–817) was a tyrant whose one concern was to exploit his subjects. In Ziyadat Allah I (817–838) who checked the revolt of the army and began the conquest of Sicily, poetic taste existed side by side with ferocious drunkenness. Abu ʿIqal (838–841) displayed admirable qualities during his short reign. Muhammad (841–856) delighted in ignorance and debauch; Ahmad (856–863) in virtue and building; Muhammad II—after the brief interim of Ziyadat Allah II (864–875)—in wine and hunting. The most famous amir of the dynasty was Ibrahim II (875–902), a genuine statesman but unbalanced enough to satiate himself with the slaughter of his kinsmen: he ended his days piously, fighting against the Christians in Sicily, having abdicated his authority. The eminent ʿAbd Allah II, a learned theologian and popular although a Muʿtazilite, perished at the hands of his son after one year's rule. This son, Ziyadat Allah III (903–909), was a wild degenerate who was unable to withstand the attacks of the Shiites and fled to the east, where he lived out his days wretchedly.

Their taste for magnificence illustrated itself in numerous buildings, for the construction of which they employed the former Christian slaves who had now become their dependents (*muwāla*). Some three miles from Kairouan, Ibrahim I built the palace of Qasr al-Qadim, which became the nucleus of a great fortified city. Similarly Ibrahim II built Raqqada just over five miles from the capital. This was the seat of government, and also a place of moral corruption abhorred by the pious folk of Kairouan. He divided his time between it and Tunis.

MILITARY AND RELIGIOUS ARCHITECTURE

For the protection of the country the amirs adapted Byzantine fortresses, notably at Belezma and Baghai (the former Bagai), and they drew chiefly on them as models for the construction all along the coast of *ribats*, as at Sousse and Monastir, or of strong walls, as at Sfax.

But it was naturally on religious buildings that most care was lavished, above all on the Great Mosque at Kairouan, the original construction of which was attributed to ʿUqba ibn Nafiʿ, its first mihrab being, so it is thought, still preserved.[17] Ziyadat Allah rebuilt it in 836 and it was twice enlarged in the course of the ninth century. Its construction follows the oriental plan, little modified since the days of the Prophet, and its basic element consists of a rectangular pillared hall having before it a courtyard flanked on three sides with porticoes. With the vast open space of its courtyard, its Syrian minaret with three superimposed towers, its cupola, its mihrab in marble, and above all its prayer hall crowded with innumerable columns and dimly lit by the light filtered through the doors, it is impressive in its mysterious majesty.

The great Mosque of the Olive Tree at Tunis, with its important subsidiary buildings; the mosque, of smaller dimensions, at Sousse; the Mosque of the Three Doors at Kairouan, its façade so tastefully decorated by horse-shoe arcading; and finally the mosque at Sfax, which was later remodelled—these too are evidence of the building activity of the Aghlabids.

In the construction of public buildings use was made of every kind of material—puddled clay, unfired brick, baked brick and ashlar—and Roman ruins were drawn on freely. Decoration was modelled on the technique of the Christian period, the motifs of which, such as branches and rosettes, were reproduced. The ancient symbol of the vine, common to pagan and Christian alike, predominated. With the leaves either open or entwined, it was to be found everywhere in the floral decoration of Muslim buildings in Ifriqiya.

GOVERNMENT

The Aghlabids were not entirely given over to pleasure and building. Far from playing the role of idle rulers, they made a point of organising a regular government on the lines of that of Baghdad. Having little confidence in the Arab aristocracy, they chose their assistants from among the princes of the blood, whose loyalty could be relied on, or from among those under their control—dependents, personal servants, eunuchs, even Christians.

Like the Abbasids, they had a vizier, albeit without real power; a chamberlain, who was both law officer and military leader; a postmaster, who combined with his duties those of chief of police; and a number of secretaries. They selected their generals for valour, not by rank, and they entrusted the various administrative tasks—correspondence, levying of taxes, care of the official seal—to humble clerical officials. In the matter of justice on the other

The Arab and Berber Dynasties (Ninth–Eleventh Centuries)

hand the post of qadi of Kairouan, with the additional administrative functions it carried, was given only to outstanding personalities notable for their conscientiousness even more than for their knowledge. Provincial governors wielded great authority under the amir's supervision.

It has to be admitted that functions of the officials were not well defined and their spheres of authority dangerously overlapped. But the men who made up the service, all Arabs and all selected at the amir's pleasure, were indebted to him for everything and remained loyal to him.

The Aghlabids had an economic policy, or at any rate a water policy, as is witnessed by the many reservoirs and aqueducts they constructed. It appears that in the ninth century Ifriqiya experienced a revival of prosperity. But the amirs' fiscal policy was deplorable. They imposed the land tax on all their subjects, even Muslims, collected tithes in money and not in kind and established taxes not warranted by the Koran, in particular on markets and the movement of provisions. This situation, made worse by the exactions of officials, played some part in contributing to the fall of the dynasty.

THE JUND AND THE CAMPAIGN IN SICILY

The amirs would willingly have brought about the fusion of Arabs and Berbers, but they did not succeed. Though the Berbers caused them few difficulties, the Arab military forces sometimes brought the dynasty very near to disaster. The *jund*—whether the word is taken to mean former soldiers discharged without pay and half-starving, or the standing force in the amir's service—was rent by tribal quarrels, garrison rivalries and conflicting ambitions, and constituted a large number of men who were in a state of anarchy and permanent readiness to revolt. In order to be in control of it, the Aghlabids had to exert all their strength and to create a prætorian guard of negroes, whose fidelity was beyond question. But when they had broken the *jund* and annihilated the frontier garrisons, notably the one at Belezma, they were left without an army capable of withstanding the Shi'a offensive.

To the warlike activity of the rebellious army, Ziyadat Allah I offered the unexpected outlet of a war against the Christians of Sicily. In Africa the amirs were living peaceably with their neighbours, especially since the *jundis* had clearly demonstrated their unwillingness to become involved in conflict with Berbers, and for a long time the great island, on which the Arabs had conducted numerous raiding expeditions, had looked like an easy prey. Byzantium was not concerned about so distant a matter as Sicily and relied for its defence on the small Italian republics. Meanwhile, the amirs were creating a fleet and turning Ifriqiya into a maritime state.

In 827 Ziyadat Allah, in answer to a call from a rebellious Greek leader, landed an army of *jundis* and Berbers in Sicily under the command of the qadi Asad, who had made himself the apostle of the war. Four years later the Arabs took Palermo, which they made their capital and in 843, after a number of reverses partly due to rivalries between African and Spanish contingents and to epidemics, took Messina. Then in 859, after more than thirty years of effort, they took the 'belvedere of Sicily', Enna (Castrogiovanni).

Neither the intermittent efforts of Byzantium, nor interventions by Venice, the small republics and even the Carolingian emperor Louis II, could halt the progress of the Aghlabid troops in Sicily and after that in Southern Italy. Syracuse fell in 878, and Taormina in 902. Thereafter the Arabs held all Sicily save for a few posts of no importance. The emperor Leo VI, renouncing his Italian possessions, was obliged by the Aghlabid victories to devote himself to a purely eastern policy during the second half of his reign.

Ziyadat Allah III was able, at the beginning of the tenth century, to observe that Sicily was free from all serious danger. Thus the amirs' external policy reaped an incontestable success, but, while they were weakening themselves with a distant war, they were no longer to find in Ifriqiya, where they had destroyed the *jund* and the frontier garrisons, forces capable of standing up to the Kotama contingents which the Shi'a missionary Abu 'Abd Allah sent against the last and most cowardly of the line.

III. Fatimid Rule over the Maghrib

THE SHI'A MOVEMENT

The Fatimid dynasty had its origin in a legitimist schism, that of the Shi'a, and its founder was a refugee from the east, 'Ubaid Allah. Its support came from a Berber tribe of Kabylia, the Kotama.

The Shi'a schism, as did the Kharijite, arose from the question

The Arab and Berber Dynasties (Ninth–Eleventh Centuries)

of the succession of the caliphs. To this it stood in opposition by virtue of its strict adherence to the descendants of 'Ali, whose hereditary legitimacy ruled out any possibility of election.

Since 'Ali ought to have been acknowledged as caliph on the death of the Prophet, whose cousin and son-in-law 'Ali was, the first three caliphs were all usurpers. As for the 'Umaiyads—who were assured their power by the slaughter in 680 of 'Ali's second son, Husain, and his kinsmen on the battlefield at Kerbela—and their successors the Abbasids, the Shiites never admitted that their *de facto* rule could extinguish the indefeasible rights of the descendants of 'Ali and his wife Fatima.

The actions of the Shiites met with harsh repression at the hands of the caliphs. Vanquished, imprisoned, scattered in small clandestine and powerless groups, they delegated certain of their number for propaganda (*dā'i*) and these undertook individual conversions and the initiation of the faithful. The sect as a whole was reduced to constructing the comforting doctrine of the hidden imam. This faultless imam, last descendant of 'Ali, awaits, unseen by men, the propitious hour when he will appear as imam Mahdi, saviour of the world. This world he will govern in person by divine right, ensuring the triumph of peace and dispensing unparalleled prosperity to all Muslims.

The Shiites split into numerous sub-sects according to the particular descendant of 'Ali to whom they ascribed their expectation of parousia. The Ismailis, who regarded the seventh imam, Isma'il, as the last of the visible imams, received the adherence of the Fatimids. The descendants of Isma'il lived as hidden imams, sending out *dā'i* from their retreats. These spread among the masses an allegorical doctrine which owed its attraction to the mysterious character of the initiatory rites and to the hierarchy of degrees of knowledge offered to the aspirations of the faithful. This hidden but intense propaganda resulted in a vast increase of Shi'a adherents, on the strength of which the expected Mahdi made his appearance at the beginning of the tenth century, in the person of 'Ubaid Allah.

THE MAHDI 'UBAID ALLAH

The Mahdi had his headquarters at Salamiya, a small town in Syria situated not far from Hama to the east of the Orontes. In about 864 it had become the centre of Ismaili propaganda. There is a great uncertainity about the origins of the Mahdi; he may have been a descendant of that famous Persian sectary, the oculist Maimun, one of the outstanding personalities of the Shi'a movement. However that may be, he declared himself a Fatimid, was accepted as such (it was only later that his opponents cast doubt on his ancestry), became an Ismaili grand master, and sent his *dā'ī* throughout Mesopotamia, Persia and the Yemen.[18]

But it was on the soil of the Maghrib that the Shi'a seed yielded an unexpected harvest, which the Kotama tribes served to fertilise.

THE KOTAMA

The Kotama occupied Lesser Kabylia to the east of the Babors, between Djidjelli, Sétif and Constantine, and at the eastern extremity of Roman Mauretania. This was an intermediate zone between the wildness of the mountain-dwellers and the traditional civilisation of Numidia, ideal for the restoration of an empire.

The amirs were officially masters of Kabylia but rarely risked asserting their rights there. 'The Kotama', writes Ibn Khaldun, 'never had to suffer the least act of oppression at the hands of the Aghlabids.'[19] Which means that Kairouan acknowledged itself incapable of exercising its authority over them.

Situated as they were on the edge of Ifriqiya, the Kotama nourished an instinctive hostility for the Arab conquerors, which they displayed by welcoming the rebellious *jundis*. From the time when they succeeded in expressing that hostility under the traditional guise of religious opposition organised by a leader, it assumed the character of a violent conflict, in which the Aghlabid dynasty met its downfall.

It is not thought that their country was Kharijite in the eighth century, albeit cases are cited of Kotama who aided the Ibadite imam Ibn Rustum, or inclined to Nakkarism. It was two Ismaili *dā'ī* commissioned with propaganda in the Maghrib who began to spread Shi'a doctrines among them as early as the first years of the reign of Ibrahim II, but it was Abu 'Abd Allah who did the real work [of propagation].

THE DĀ'Ī ABU 'ABD ALLAH

Abu 'Abd Allah, originally a missionary of inferior grade and later

The Arab and Berber Dynasties (Ninth–Eleventh Centuries)

confidential agent for the Mahdi—whom it is said, he did not know personally—must have possessed exceptional qualities as organiser, psychologist and diplomat. He had spoken at Mecca with Kotama pilgrims who, possibly in 893, brought him home with them. There he settled at Ikjan (not far from the present site of Chevreul), an impregnable fortress in Lesser Kabylia safe from Aghlabid attacks.

We do not know exactly through what stages the preaching of his mission went. It seems to have run into opposition from certain chiefs, whom nothing short of force could put down. He succeeded, however, in combining the Kotama into an army deeply inspired by a single religious ideal, and this army he launched against Ifriqiya. The capture of Mila in 902 proved that the time was ripe. 'Abd Allah II, who had just received the amirate from his father Ibrahim II, hastened to meet the $dā'ī$ and defeated him, but failed utterly in his march through the snow-clad mountains towards Ikjan. The amir's assassination by Ziyadat Allah III was soon followed by a fresh offensive on the part of Abu 'Abd Allah. He took possession of Sétif in 904, recovered Mila, crushed the Arab army near Belezma, carried the fortresses of Tobna and Belezma in 905 and occupied all the important strategic points on the routes leading to Ifriqiya during 907–908. On 27 March 909, having put the last Aghlabid army to flight, probably near Laribus, he entered Raqqada, where the amir had fled in a most wretched state.

Everywhere he spared the people, promising them that he would abolish taxes contrary to the Koran, and above all put down jurists and men of religion whose influence could be dangerous, however, he did have all negroes executed. He restored law and order by putting down brigandage, and he minted coinage. When he deemed his authority to be firmly enough established, he appointed a Shi'a qadi, caused the faithful to be invited to adopt the beliefs of the conquerors, and then set off to meet his master the Mahdi, in whose name he had been acting.

THE MAHDI'S TRIUMPH

'Ubaid Allah, whose propaganda was causing anxiety to the caliph, had left Salamiya in 902 in order to join his $dā'ī$, who had kept him informed of his progress. While passing through Egypt in the garb of a merchant, he had barely escaped prison. On his journey he probably benefited from the help of the governor of Tripoli, by no means a disinterested party, who neglected to arrest him, and that of the officials at Qastiliya (Djérid) who received the orders too late. Giving up the idea of joining Abu ʿAbd Allah, he had finally taken refuge, we do not know exactly where, with the Midrarid ruler of Sijilmasa, who may have had him interned. It was there that on 26 August 909 the Kotama army arrived to set him free, having in passing made a complete sweep of the Rustumid kingdom of Tahert.

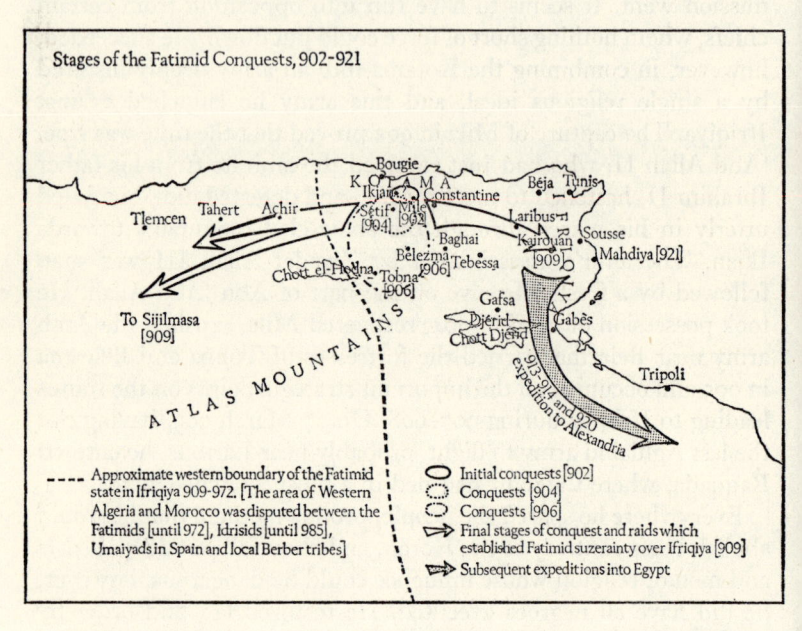

Stages of the Fatimid Conquests, 902-921

---- Approximate western boundary of the Fatimid state in Ifriqiya 909-972. [The area of Western Algeria and Morocco was disputed between the Fatimids [until 972], Idrisids [until 985], Umaiyads in Spain and local Berber tribes].
◯ Initial conquests [902]
◯ Conquests [904]
◯ Conquests [906]
⇨ Final stages of conquest and raids which established Fatimid suzerainty over Ifriqiya [909]
⇨ Subsequent expeditions into Egypt

It was a triumphal return. On 15 January 910 ʿUbaid Allah made a ceremonial entry into Raqqada, where he officially assumed the appellation of *al-Mahdi* and the title of Commander of the Faithful (*Amīr al-Muminīn*). The installation of the Mahdi in the Aghlabid capital marked the triumph of the Shiʿa movement and even more that of the tribe of the Kotama. It was the tribe of Kotama who had constituted the army of the *dāʿi*, as they were to furnish the contingents which conquered the Maghrib and Egypt under the command of Fatimid leaders. It was a highly symbolic success of immense implications, as Gautier has made clear in forceful terms,[20] for, in the total revenge of the Maghrib against the foreign ruler, it brought the Arab conquest definitely to an end. They were not

The Arab and Berber Dynasties (Ninth–Eleventh Centuries)

nomads, but sedentary peasants of Kabylia, who formed the framework of the state created by the Arab caliph 'Ubaid Allah. Their tribe, drained by the battles in the Maghrib, in Egypt or in Sicily, and worn out by the enjoyment of power, however, paid for its prodigious adventure and disappeared from the Maghrib.

EARLY DAYS OF THE MAHDI

The Aghlabid princes had formed administrative staffs which the Mahdi had only to use in order to govern Ifriqiya. 'Government offices', writes Ibn Khaldun, 'were organised, taxes began to come in regularly and governors and other officials were established in every town.'[21] Opponents, naturally few in number, were put to the sword.

'Ubaid Allah had scarcely acceded to power when he showed himself to be an energetic and authoritarian leader, with little taste for accepting the tutelage of his propagandist Abu 'Abd Allah. The latter had at his side an evil genius in the person of his brother Abu al-'Abbas who kept urging him to revolt. 'It is you who have founded an empire,' he would repeatedly remind him. Abu 'Abd Allah tried in vain to persuade the Mahdi to share power with him, then went so far as to criticise governmental decisions and even to express doubts whether 'Ubaid Allah was genuinely the Mahdi. All this was reported to the ruler, whose first action was to have one of the Kotama chiefs put to death; the others took fright and formed a conspiracy. 'Ubaid Allah did not react at once, being restrained no doubt by a remnant of affection and gratitude for the man who had brought him to power. Finally he decided to act, and on 31 July 911 had Abu 'Abd Allah and his brother executed.

The Kotama, whose attachment had been to the missionary far more than to the Mahdi, and who were, moreover, disappointed that they were not at liberty to pillage and hold to ransom the rich territory of Ifriqiya as they wished, at once rebelled. The Mahdi's energetic stand quieted them for a time, but in the spring of 912 they grouped around a pseudo-Mahdi and took up arms again, drawing with them the tribes of the Zab (southern Constantine region). 'Ubaid Allah had great difficulty in mastering them. To do it, he had to entrust an army to his young son Abu al-Qasim, who was scarcely twenty years old, and who on this occasion displayed the measure of his valour.

The Kotama revolt was not the only one; earlier in the autumn of 911 the inhabitants of Tahert had risen against Shi'a authority with the support of the Zenata tribe of the Maghrawa. At the end of 912 it was the turn of the population of Tripoli, their patience exhausted by the abuses perpetrated by the Kotama garrisoned there. Finally a part of Sicily rallied round an Aghlabid prince, acknowledged the authority of the caliph of Baghdad and harassed the Shi'a troops until 915, so far at least as the confused chronology of the period allows events to be dated without a great degree of error.

THE EGYPTIAN EXPEDITIONS

No sooner had 'Ubaid Allah terminated these serious risings than he turned his arms against Egypt. Indeed, so far as he was concerned, the Maghrib was not an end in itself, but merely a point of departure. By virtue of his descent he considered himself as legitimate heir of the entire Muslim empire. That was why, as soon as Ifriqiya was pacified, he tried to gain possession of Egypt, which in his mind could be no more than a new stage towards the conquest of the entire caliphate.

As early as winter 913–914 he organised an expedition which, under the command first of a Shi'a leader and then of the heir to the throne in person, Abu al-Qasim, had no great difficulty in occupying Alexandria and al-Faiyum and threatening Fustat. But the caliph of Baghdad, al-Muqtadir, sent one of his best generals, the eunuch Munis the Brave, against the invaders. After several bloody encounters, Abu al-Qasim, too far from his base, had to hastily retreat and returned to Raqqada on 26 May 915.

A second attempt was made four years later, still under the command of Abu al-Qasim. Alexandria was once more occupied without a fight, and Fustat once more threatened. The Shi'a troops got as far as Gizeh, and once more Munis took the field. A supporting fleet dispatched by 'Ubaid Allah was totally destroyed by Abbasid ships before the port of Rosetta on 11 May 920. Abu al-Qasim held on with desperate obstinacy, but finally had to withdraw under the combined attacks of Munis, famine and plague; he was back in Mahdiya in November 921.

FOUNDATION OF MAHDIYA

During this period, 'Ubaid Allah had changed capitals. At this

The Arab and Berber Dynasties (Ninth–Eleventh Centuries)

time it was almost a Muslim tradition that a new dynasty did not establish itself in the city in which its predecessor had exercised its authority. Apart from this, Raqqada, the city of the Aghlabids, situated as it was in the middle of a vast plain, had insufficient natural protection against possible enemies, of whom, as events at the outset of the reign had shown, there was no lack. Finally, 'Ubaid Allah, as has been seen, had his thoughts fixed more on Egypt and the eastern Mediterranean than on the Maghrib. Accordingly he was anxious to establish himself on the coast, where he could fit out maritime expeditions.

After searching for a good site in the direction of Carthage and Tunis, he chose a small peninsula lying between Sousse and Sfax which had once sheltered a Roman, indeed even a Phoenician, port. Here again the chronology is uncertain. Ibn 'Idhari puts the foundation of the new capital in 912,[22] immediately after the revolt at the beginning of the reign. Ibn al-Athir gives the date as 915.[23] Whatever the precise date may be, 'Ubaid Allah settled there in 921 and gave it the name it still bears—el-Mahdiya, the town of the Mahdi.

The archaeological data studied by G. Marçais enables it to be stated that Mahdiya was principally a very stoutly defended fortress and a combined military port and arsenal.[24] There were a mosque and palaces, of course, but no luxury; the new capital of the Fatimids had the air far more of a garrison town than of a princely seat.

THE EXPEDITIONS INTO THE MAGHRIB

As has been seen, 'Ubaid Allah's main concern was with Egypt and the East. However, he probably had to realise that his failures in the East were partly attributable to the instability of his authority in Africa. His first expedition towards the western Maghrib certainly took place after his first defeat in Egypt and, furthermore, he committed himself more deeply [to the Maghrib] after the second defeat, as though drawing a lesson from his lack of success in the east.

Abu 'Abd Allah's lightning campaign to rescue his master at Sijilmasa had opened the Maghrib of the high plains, inhabited by the Kharijite Zenata, to the Shiites. But there, even more than elsewhere, their rule was challenged, since between occupiers and occupied there ran such differences of doctrine, race and way of life

—Kharijites against Shiites, Zenata against Sanhaja, nomad or mobile pastoralists against sedentary farmers. Placing these factors in perspective, we may well share the opinion of Terrasse[25] that the key question in the events that were to unfold up to the end of the tenth century throughout the western half of the Maghrib was not so much the triumph of the Shiite or the Kharijite movement as the supremacy of Zenata or Sanhaja, all of which was to be overlaid by the rivalry between the Fatimid empire and the Umaiyad empire of Cordova.

Nevertheless, in 917, at the very outset of hostilities, ʿUbaid Allah attacked the principality of Nakour (Alhucemas) which maintained excellent relations with the amirate of Cordova. The aged amir of Nakour was killed, but several members of his family were able to escape to Spain. A few months later they returned and with the overt help of Cordova recovered the heritage of their forefathers by force of arms.

This was a mere skirmish; the conquest of the far Maghrib began in earnest in 922, when ʿUbaid Allah had for a time dropped his plans for eastern conquest. Under the command of the chief of the Miknasa, Masala ibn Habbus, the Shiʿa troops marched westwards and had little difficulty in reducing the Idrisid Yahya IV to the state of a vassal, and then of acquiring Sijilmasa. Shortly afterwards Yahya, having not proved sufficiently obedient in the eyes of his new masters, was expelled and replaced by a Miknasa amir, Musa ibn Abi al-ʿAfiya. A part of Morocco, the districts of Fez and Sijilmasa, came under the protectorate of the Fatimids through the medium of the Miknasa.

The sovereign of Cordova, though still occupied in putting down the seditions his grandfather had bequeathed to him, nevertheless could not remain indifferent to what was happening in the far Maghrib. He did not participate directly, but encouraged rivals to the Miknasa, their kinsmen the Maghrawa Zenata.

For approximately twenty years the Miknasa and Maghrawa fought each other for the possession of northern Morocco, while from time to time the Idrisids tried to stir up trouble. Abd al-Rahman III, who had proclaimed himself caliph at Cordova in 929, placed garrisons in the towns of Melilla, in 927, and more particularly Ceuta, in 931, in order to provide against any contingency, and shortly afterwards persuaded Musa ibn Abi al-ʿAfiya to join

The Arab and Berber Dynasties (Ninth–Eleventh Centuries)

his cause. Two large-scale operations launched by the Fatimids in 933 and 935 led to no clear result. While it can be said that on the eve of Abu Yazid's insurrection the Fatimids had a foothold in Morocco, their position was far from assured.

FATIMID OPRESSION

'Ubaid Allah's methods of government were to bring Fatimid authority into very serious danger. The Mahdi's administration seems to have been quite pitiless. Notwithstanding the promises of the *dā'ī*, the necessity of securing the revenues without which the state could not manage led to the establishment of a system of finance and taxation as irregular and as excessive as that of the Aghlabids. Ibn 'Idhari mentions in 919 'the most hateful exactions of the Shi'a, for whom any and every pretext was good enough for despoiling the people',[26] already sorely tried by plague and the increasing cost of living. If one adds to this that the Berbers, as convinced and impenitent Malikis, found no attraction in the heresy of a master who altered the liturgy at his pleasure, it can be understood that even during the reign of its first sovereign the new dynasty inspired a hostility probably stronger even than that to which the Aghlabids fell victims.

We can indeed speak of an actual resistance movement springing up into Ifriqiya by way of reaction against the Shi'a doctrine—a resistance involving clandestine operations, the organisation of armed bands, torture and martyrdom, and the approving, but cautious, smiles of the bourgeois of Kairouan. The opposition was undertaken and directed by two categories of pious men—the Maliki doctors of Kairouan and the mystics and ascetics (*al-suliha*) who frequented the *ribat* and were fairly numerous. The common man had such regard for both, and their prestige was such, that the Shi'a proceeded with great circumspection before attacking them.

In a Maghrib in complete upheaval as a result of conquest, subject to armed conflicts and crushed by taxation, the rising against Fatimid exploitation broke out once more under the religious and social guise of extremist Kharijism.

ABU AL-QASIM

Legend has it that the Mahdi foresaw that the Kharijite storm would strike the whole of the Maghrib but would finally be broken before the walls of Mahdiya. After some preliminary disturbances, the tempest broke in the reign of his son Abu al-Qasim al-Qaim in 934–946. The new caliph participated directly in his father's imperialist policies, had taken Constantine and Tripoli, and had commanded the two expeditions against Egypt. As soon as power was in his hands he made a third attempt, which began with the capture of Alexandria but ended in yet another reverse. He launched his corsairs against the coast of Provençe and was able for a time to occupy Genoa. In the Maghrib, having without difficulty rid himself of a pretended son of the Mahdi, he defeated Musa ibn Abi al-'Afiya, who had gone over to the 'Umaiyads, and whose territories, as also those of Tahert which had rebelled, he entrusted to the Idrisids.

Abu al-Qasim seems to have been a rough and courageous prince, always in search of battle. He was a fanatical Shi'a, and also a man of authority. In his father's lifetime, it was in his name, says Ibn Hammad, that dispatches and diplomas of appointment were issued and to him that petitions were addressed and delegates were referred. In order to impress the common people, following a custom which had not hitherto reached Barbary, he had a horseman to carry over his head a sunshade 'resembling a buckler mounted on the end of a lance ... entirely made up of jewels and stones so precious that everyone was struck with admiration and the eyes of all beholders were delighted'.[27]

It is probable that at this time Fatimid administration maintained, and perhaps heightened the ruthless character it had borne during the period when Abu al-Qasim was taking an active part in public business in his capacity as heir apparent. The awakening of the oppressed was indeed violent.

THE REVOLT OF ABU YAZID, THE MAN ON THE DONKEY

The spirit and leader of the revolt was a Zenata of the Djérid, Abu Yazid, nicknamed 'the man on the donkey'. He was born about 885, probably in the Sudan, where his father was a merchant. He was a most unusual character, this shabby, limping agitator, whose fiery propaganda succeeded in raising the Maghrib and brought the Fatimid dynasty to the brink of ruin. He was far from uneducated. 'As soon as he reached puberty', writes Ibn Hammad, 'he

The Arab and Berber Dynasties (Ninth–Eleventh Centuries)

studied the Ibadite dogma so thoroughly that he became one of the sect's ablest doctors in law and dialetic.'[28] As might be expected, he joined the Nakkarites, the most austere and uncompromising of the Kharijites of the Maghrib.

The apostolate ran in his veins. When teaching the Koran at Tozeur, he used his influence over the children to preach the overthrow of the Mahdi. His propaganda in the Djérid was so effective that he became a source of anxiety to the Shi'a authorities and had to emigrate to the very seat of Kharijism, Tahert, where he continued to maintain a school.

It was after the Mahdi's death that his activity developed. Mounted on a grey donkey, surrounded by his four sons and his wife—she was one of his proselytes—clad, like the common people, in a simple jallaba and offering an example of the most rigorous asceticism, he went through the central Maghrib exhorting the Berbers to drive out the Fatimids and replace them with a council of shaikhs, that is, of clergy, in accordance probably with the usage adopted in Kharijite states.

This revolutionary propaganda offered to a poverty-stricken proletariat the shining prospect of a just and worthy government sprung from its own ranks, which the faithful were invited to install by force of arms, and it met with overwhelming success, particularly in the Aurès. Abu Yazid's intransigence was, however, matched by a precise judgment of political necessity. He negotiated, though without success, for the support of the Umaiyad ruler of Cordova, and made use of the covert Malikism of the inhabitants of Kairouan to secure their temporary association with his cause. Religious opposition was at last finding its opportunity to break into the light.

The man on the donkey swiftly conquered Ifriqiya. There he and his bands showed no pity. Abu Zakariya', among others, recites the horrors perpetrated by 'the foe of Allah',[29] with a wealth of detail that must be viewed with some suspicion, coming as it does from an Ibadite moderate roused to opposition by the extremists.

Far from being regarded as shocking, this violence attracted the crowds. They rushed to join the movement and thought they were going to force the Fatimids to renounce their authority. The flood of humanity thus gathered took the the route formerly followed by Abu 'Abd Allah and his Kotama. By way of the valley of the Oued

Mellègue it flowed out into northern Tunisia, where al-Qaim's troops attempted in vain to contain it. Abu Yazid defeated them near Béja, secured Tunis with the connivance of the Sunni inhabitants, crossed the Tunisian Dorsal and entered Kairouan— where the Maliki doctors persuaded him to halt the pillaging of his horde. There he triumphed over an army sent from Mahdiya under one of the best Shi'a generals and finally, in November 944, laid siege to Mahdiya, the sole fragment of the Fatimid empire to remain in the caliph's hands. The siege was marked by furious assaults, in the course of which Abu Yazid, who personally took part in the fighting and several times narrowly escaped being killed, almost succeeded in carrying the town. When the besieged had nothing left, they received supplies brought by a column which forced the blockade; it was commanded by the chief of the Sanhaja of Achir (Boghari region), Ziri Ibn Manad, who by this action probably saved the Shi'a dynasty.

Such a resistance was too much for the multitude assembled by Abu Yazid; its enthusiasm ebbed as quickly as it had mounted. There being nothing left to loot, many went home; others accused the aged cripple of playing the ostentatious sovereign. He had to abandon the siege of Mahdiya in September 945, after which he tried to regroup his forces around Kairouan. Soon he found himself faced with a new adversary. Al-Qaim had died on 16 May 946, and his son Abu al-'Abbas Isma'il al-Mansur had succeeded him and was exerting all his energies to drive out the rebel. A few days after assuming power, he entered Kairouan and there he remained despite the staggering blows delivered by Abu Yazid. Finally, on 15 August 946, a bloody battle fought under the walls of the town settled the fate of the rebellion.

There followed an extraordinary man-hunt lasting another year. Cut off from the Sahara by a skilful manœuvre of al-Mansur, Abu Yazid took refuge in the Hodna mountains and gave a final proof of his indomitable energy by fighting to the very end surrounded by the last of his faithful adherents.

Al-Mansur was deprived of the pleasure of being able to put his adversary to death. Despite every care, he died of his wounds in August 947. 'His corpse', writes Ibn Khaldun, 'was flayed and the skin stuffed with straw and put in a cage as a plaything for two apes which had been trained to this task.'[30]

The Arab and Berber Dynasties (Ninth–Eleventh Centuries)

The caliph, who had thanked God on seeing the rebel's broken body at his feet, paid homage to his own merits by taking the title of al-Mansur the Victorious. His victory outstripped the usual bounds of military success, in that it finally liquidated Kharijism, that great revolutionary force of the Muslim Maghrib. It left the way clear for the sedentary Kabyles, who, having carved their triumph in the flesh of the nomads, were to attempt the task of piecing the torn and scattered fragments of Barbary into a unified state.

THE LAST FATIMIDS OF THE MAGHRIB

The great task of al-Mansur's reign (946–953) had been the repression of the Kharijite revolt. Security was so entirely assured that he was able to quit the refuge of Mahdiya and in 947 to build a new town, Çabra or Mançouriya, in the immediate neighbourhood. This he made an active centre of commerce to the detriment of its neighbour. In the west a single expedition was enough to restore order. This was noteworthy for the freeing of Tahert, under siege by a former officer of the Fatimids who had become governor of the Maghrib on behalf of the caliphs of Cordova.

Nevertheless, the Spaniards had taken advantage of Abu Yazid's rebellion to eliminate the political influence of the Fatimids from the entire far Maghrib; their own influence extended the full length of the coast as far as Algiers, where Friday prayers were said in the name of the caliph of Cordova.

In Sicily too the Fatimids' situation was difficult. A revolt broke out there in the spring of 947 while al-Mansur was pursuing Abu Yazid in the Hodna. After a brief period of peace, revolt broke out worse than before, after the Christians of the island appealed to the Byzantines for troops, which were sent. The Fatimid governor finally succeeded in mastering the situation and, after inflicting a decisive defeat on his opponents, was able to have a great mosque built at Reggio di Calabra: 'a single stone removed from the building would have been the signal for the destruction of every church in Sicily and in Ifriqiya.'[31]

The reign of the caliph al-Mu'izz (953–975) marks both the zenith and the end of Fatimid rule over Barbary. At Mançouriya the caliph built palaces, the Persian names of which may indicate the first impress of Mesopotamian civilisation. His general Jawhar, a former slave of al-Mansur, with the aid of the Sanhaja contingents of Ziri, defeated a Midrarid ruler of Sijilmasa, who had returned to orthodoxy, had assumed the title of Prince of the Faithful and had coinage minted in his name. He followed this in 958 by taking possession of Fez and bringing the whole country into subjection as far as Tangier and Ceuta. A second campaign conducted nine years later with equal success served to counteract the 'Umaiyad influence and to establish peace within the country such as the Maghrib had not known for a long time.

Al-Mu'izz was then able to realise Fatimid ambitions regarding Egypt, the political decay of which he was well aware. Jawhar, at the head of an army of—it is said—100,000 men, entered the capital with ease in 969, and at once laid the foundations of a new quarter, from which emerged what is now the city of Cairo. When he had been victorious over several armies sent in relief, he summoned the caliph, who joined him in June 973, four years after he had established himself in Old Cairo. Thereafter, Egypt was ruled by the Fatimids for two centuries.

On leaving Ifriqiya, where the descendants of the Prophet had never felt at home or at ease, the caliph took with him not only 'the treasures' of the empire and the palace furnishings',[32] thus making clear his intention of effecting a definitive removal, but also the governmental staff and the coffins of his forefathers. Naturally he retained in Egypt the Kotama contingent which Jawhar had led there. It was the Sanhaja who succeeded to the privileged position which their victory had secured for the Kotama. Indeed it was to their chief, Bologguin, son of Ziri, that al-Mu'izz entrusted the task of governing the Maghrib in his name.

IV. The Sanhaja Dynasties and the Hilalian Invasion

ZIRI'S ACHIR

The namesake of the Berber dynasty who inherited rule over Ifriqiya had been the loyal and active lieutenant of the Fatimids. In their conflicts with the troops of Abu Yazid and the Zenata nomads who ruled to the west of Tiaret, his interventions had played a decisive part. Moreover, the caliph al-Qaim had

The Arab and Berber Dynasties (Ninth–Eleventh Centuries)

authorised him to assert his newly-founded power by the building of a capital to serve him as strongpoint and magazine at Achir (east of Boghari on the slopes of the Djebel Lakhdar).

G. Marçais, who has investigated the remains of the Zirid constructions on the site, has indicated that they display the progress made by the founder of the dynasty.[33] Ziri must have been satisfied at the outset with a narrow space on the summit of a rock surrounded by precipices. Then he moved to a more extensive village, which he emptied of its inhabitants and wealth when he finally raised his capital on a vast site occupying probably almost 90 acres.

The third Achir grew rapidly in importance. Situated in a position ideal for a capital, on the natural frontier separating the plains

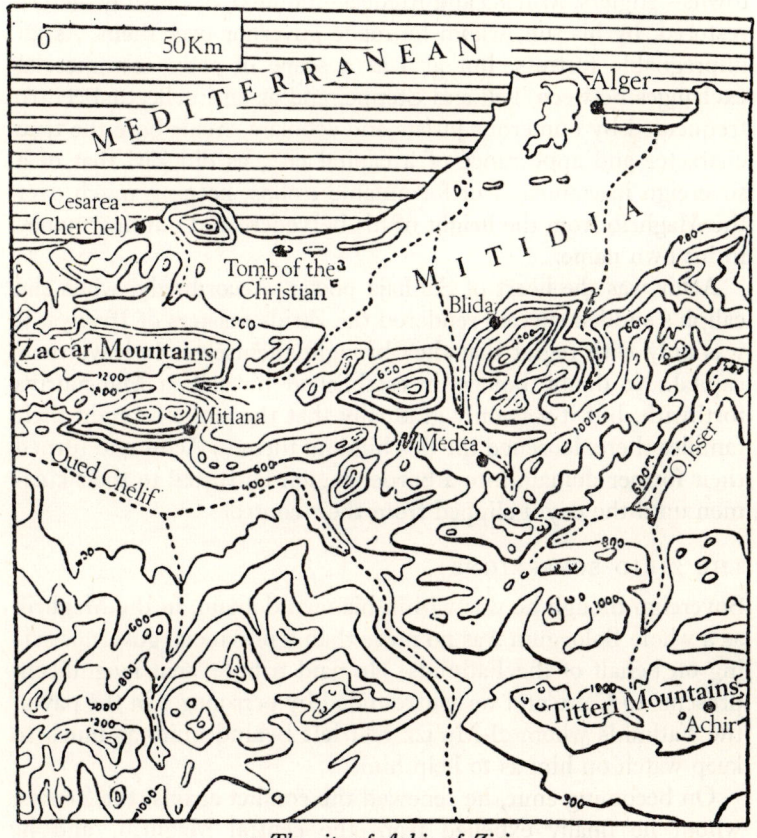

2 *The site of Achir of Ziri*

of the western Tell from the Kabyle mountains of the east, it commanded the road that follows the hilltops on its climb from the coast and kept watch over the nomads of the plain.

Its rise was encouraged by the caliph, who went so far as to assist its building by the dispatch of craftsmen and materials. Ziri transferred the inhabitants of other towns to it, and possibly also undesirables who did not feel safe elsewhere, and then surrounded it with thick walls. Early in the eleventh century al-Bakri reports that 'we are assured that throughout the region there is no stronger place, none more difficult to take or more apt to discourage the enemy', for ten men suffice for its defence.

To ensure his command over communications, Ziri had three towns—Algiers, Miliana and Médéa—founded, or possibly merely restored, by his son, whom he made governor over them. As an impregnable fortress, but also as a scene of active commercial exchanges between Tell and Steppe, and as an intellectual centre frequented by numerous jurists and scholars, Achir bore the true character and appearance of a capital city, as did Ziri that of a sovereign in command of formidable troops, keeping watch over the Maghrib from the height of his belvedere and minting money in his own name.

Achir was the heart of Sanhaja power. Accordingly, when the caliph's sudden success rendered the Zirids masters of Ifriqiya, it was only with regret that they brought themselves to leave their capital. No doubt Bologguin established himself at Mançouriya forthwith, but it was only gradually that the amirs brought their families there, loosened the ties binding them to Achir and turned their former domain into a border region entrusted to their kinsmen until the day it slipped from their control.

THE ZIRID SOVEREIGNS

Sovereign though he was within his own domain, in the Maghrib as a whole Bologguin was no more than a provincial governor acting on behalf of the Fatimids. He paid tribute, sent magnificent presents to Cairo and was surrounded by personages in the pay of the Fatimids whom al-Mu'izz had left behind quite as much to keep watch on him as to help him.

On becoming amir, he renewed the conflict against the Zenata, whom he finally expelled from the central Maghrib, and he

The Arab and Berber Dynasties (Ninth–Eleventh Centuries)

destroyed Tiaret and took Tlemcen, the population of which he transported to Achir. In 978 the new Fatimid caliph al-'Aziz agreed to entrust him with the command of Tripolitania which until then had come under the authority of a separate governor.

In 979 Bologguin resumed once more the conflict against the Zenata and their 'Umaiyad protectors, and in 980 he secured possession not only of Fez but of the whole of Morocco. He fell back, however, from an assault on Ceuta, where the 'Umaiyad vizier had fortified his position. His last successes were fleeting, for as soon as his troops had departed, the Zenata resumed prayers in the name of the caliph of Cordova from the Moulouya to Tangier.

It was his son and successor al-Mansur (984–996) who was the first to attempt to shake off the Fatimid yoke. As soon as he assumed power he declared to the notables of Kairouan who had come to congratulate him, 'I am not one of those who are appointed by a stroke of the pen and are dismissed in the same fashion, for I have inherited this kingdom from my father and my ancestors'.[34] The Fatimid reaction was not slow in coming. An official propagandist (*dā'ī*) was sent from Cairo to the Kotama country, who in 986 raised those rugged warriors against al-Mansur. The rebellion lasted two years, but was crushed by the Zirids with the utmost cruelty; a second revolt in 989 met with no better fate. It was the end of the Kotama; the Sanhaja of Achir had established their hegemony over the entire eastern half of the Maghrib.

The rest of the Maghrib, however, they abandoned to the Zenata. Indeed, after a vain attempt in 985 to restore his influence over Fez and Sijilmasa, al-Mansur left the entire west to his ancient enemies and to the Spanish dictator al-Mansur ibn Abi 'Amir, and entered into formal relations with them. Thus after the departure of the Fatimids, who had turned their ambitions elsewhere, a state of comparative equilibrium was established between the Zenata and the Sanhaja, who had been rivals for three-quarters of a century and who were mutually to rest and enjoy the fruits of their conquests.

Badis (996–1016) returned to something comparable to submission to the caliph of Cairo, but it did him little good. When his uncle Hammad was seceding in 1014, he received no help from Egypt, although the rebel acknowledged the suzerainty of the Abbasids. His son and successor al-Mu'izz (1016–1062), who was invested with authority at the age of eight, did not follow the same course.

Whether this was due to his early training under the aegis of a Sunni master, or to a desire to satisfy public opinion which, at Kairouan as in Ifriqiya as a whole, was intensely hostile to the Shi'a movement, the fact is that gradually al-Mu'izz loosened his ties with Cairo, and finally, in 1048, proclaimed the suzerainty of Baghdad.

THE ZIRID STATE

Ifriqiya was thus reaching the same political state as the rest of Barbary. After a period of subjection to the caliphate and of obedience to eastern princes having no connection with Baghdad, it was attaining independence under a Berber prince. We should not be misled by the rendering of homage to the Abbasids; it was a mark much more of the break with Cairo than of any new attachment to Baghdad.

Ifriqiya, however, gradually became distinct from the rest of Barbary, even from the marshland of Achir where the Zirid dynasty had arisen, simply because eastern influence had penetrated more deeply in Ifriqiya than elsewhere. The amirs were not slow to accommodate themselves to their role of the caliph's delegates, which they even maintained with oriental splendour. One of them put all the prodigality of a noble of ancient lineage into the distribution of thousands of dinars. They prized knowledge, works of art, poetry and, above all, luxury. They found pleasures in entertainments in which they made great display of sumptuous materials, valuable horses and exotic animals. The dowry of the daughter of al-Mu'izz, it is said, amounted to ten mule-loads and was worth a million dinars. The procession as it passed by, and the fantastic feats of the horsemen, inspired 'in the provinces descriptions worthy of fairy-tales'. On his mother's death, the amir had the logwood coffin fitted with gold nails and strings of huge pearls. At Mançouriya the Zirid al-Mansur raised a sumptuous dwelling, and al-Mu'izz had several palaces built.

The amirs' munificence was rooted in the wealth of Ifriqiya. It seems that during the period of their rule the country enjoyed real prosperity. Cultivation covered areas now barren, villages crowded where nothing is left today but solitude. At Béja a thousand camels a day were needed to remove the grain. On this favoured soil there swarmed not only merchants and craftsmen, drawn by commercial and industrial activity, but also men of letters and jurists from

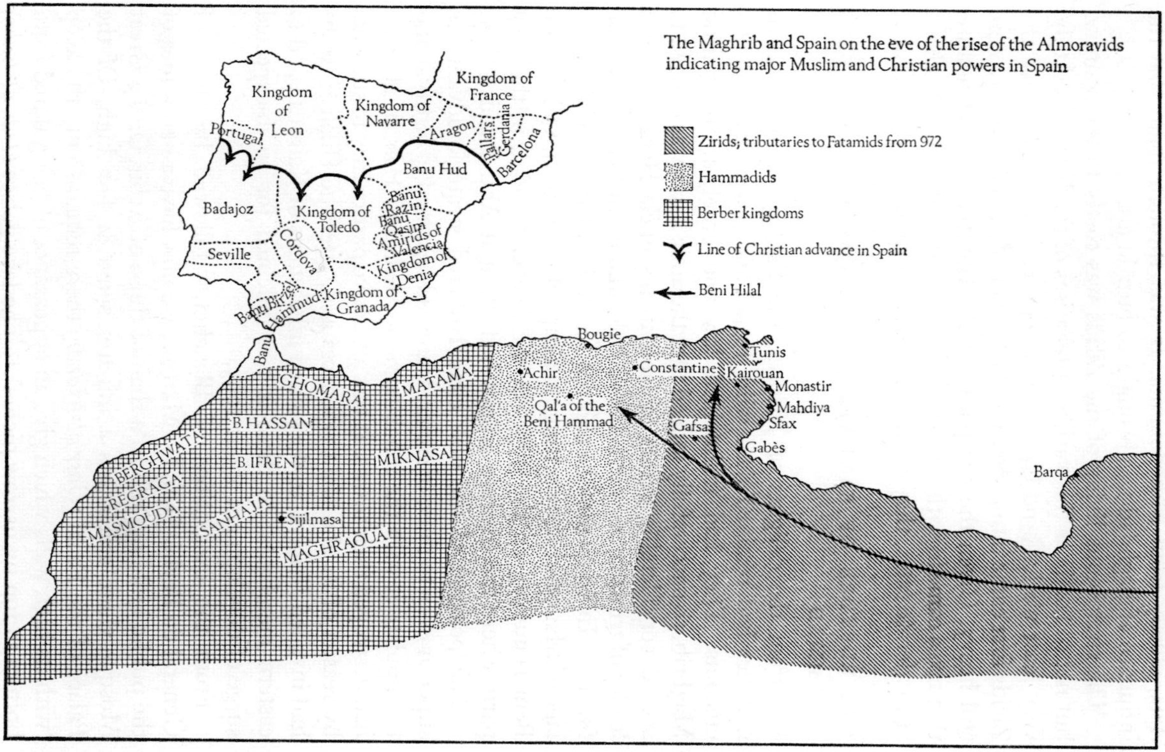

The Maghrib and Spain on the eve of the rise of the Almoravids indicating major Muslim and Christian powers in Spain

Asia, chiefly from Mesopotamia. It was through them that the influence of Baghdad was brought to bear in art.

The sumptuous living of the Zirids was costly to the country, but not so costly as the warlike enterprises of the Fatimids. At the very least we have no hint of fiscal oppression, except when the Zirids first came into power and the financial demands of Cairo were still heavy. Given the prosperity of the country, we may assume that taxes came in without too much difficulty and that, though set at moderate rates, they sufficed to meet the dynasty's expenditure.

THE RUPTURE OF SANHAJA UNITY. QAL'A OF THE BENI HAMMAD

Far from the delights of Ifriqiya, the Sanhaja of the western marches had retained their wild, brutal and proud manners and customs. They had maintained law and order in the central Maghrib, so successfully indeed that the amir Badis was obliged to accord considerable grants of land to his uncle Hammad. This leader of tribal bands was becoming too important to remain docile for long. In 1007–1008 he showed his desire to shake off the tutelage of Mançouriya by setting up a capital in his turn, Qal'a of the Beni Hammad, on the slopes of the Djebel Maadid, in the very parts where the Sanhaja armies had brought Abu Yazid to bay.

The position of the new citadel offered strategic advantages superior even to those of Achir. Hammad hastened to fortify it and to populate it with the inhabitants of Msila and Hamza, after he had destroyed their towns. It was attractive particularly to students by reason of its abundant resources and, after the Hilalian Arabs had invaded Ifriqiya, to the ruined inhabitants of Kairouan and to eastern merchants; to these it was indebted for an unexpected surge of development about 1065.

From the excavations of Blanchet,[35] followed by those of General de Beylié[36] and G. Marçais, we now have a better idea of the public buildings of Qal'a than of those of Achir. Of the Great Mosque there still exists a minaret some 81 feet high. Of the Palace of the Fanal (*Qasr al-Manār*) there remains only the keep 'with its high walls which give an appearance of being fluted from bottom to top by narrow niches'.[37] The lake palace (*Dār al-Bahr*) was destroyed to ground level, but its plan can be reconstructed from the foundations. It consisted of an agglomeration of buildings

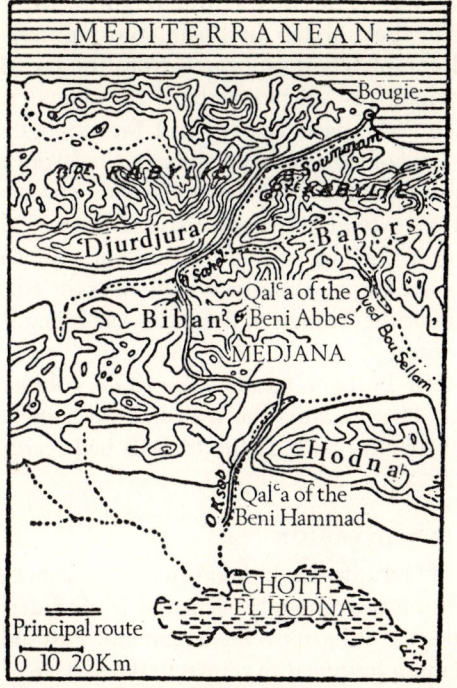

The Arab and Berber Dynasties (Ninth–Eleventh Centuries)

3 Relation of Qal'a of the Beni Hammad to Bougie

and gardens, comprised reception rooms, private apartments and baths for the masters, and owed its name to a vast basin in which aquatic tournaments were held. No other Muslim palace of the eleventh century can be so precisely reconstructed.

At Qal'a, as at Mançouriya, the artistic principles of Cairo, and more particularly of Baghdad, were supreme—porcelain mosaics, sculptured plaster, stalactites of enamelled terra cotta, stylised vegetable decoration and geometric ornamentation, but more heavily executed and often retaining a provincial look.

The Zirids naturally tried to take action against the independence of the Hammadids. Badis besieged Hammad at Qal'a but died without achieving success. Al-Mu'izz had no more success, and in 1017 he had to reconcile himself to a *fait accompli*. There were thereafter two Sanhaja dynasties independent of each other and always ready to begin hostilities.

While the Sanhaja were triumphant in the east, the Zenata had no important rivals in the west of the Maghrib. After the collapse of the 'Amirite dictatorship in Spain, the political influence of Cordova had completely disappeared from the far Maghrib. The Zenata, for a long time dependants of the 'Umaiyads, had very naturally taken their place, but without forming a coherent state. Like the Muslims of the Iberian peninsula, they were divided into a number of principalities often at odds with one another. Their influence did not extend over the whole of Morocco; they had been obliged to halt in the face of powerful Berber confederations—the Masmouda of the High Atlas, the Ghomara of the Rif and the Jbel, the Berghwata of the Tamesna, these two last being heterodox and highly deviationist.

While eastern Barbary retained a certain cohesion under the Zirids and the Hammadids, the west had reverted to the state of political disunity out of which the Idrisids had scarcely succeeded in dragging it.

THE HILALIAN INVASION

The princes of Qal'a, to mark their separation from the Zirids, had thrown off Fatimid sovereignty. When al-Mu'izz decided, in turn, to break with the Shi'a movement and the Fatimids, the Hammadids thereupon hastened to return to the service of Cairo and to set themselves up as its official delegates. Thus they were at first the sole beneficiaries of the invasion which the Fatimids unloosed on the Maghrib.

The caliph had received with ill temper the news of the break proclaimed by al-Mu'izz. He took his revenge by turning loose on Ifriqiya the ravaging Beni Hilal Arabs, whom for their misdeeds he had had to intern in Upper Egypt. In so doing he solved two problems in a single move, by ridding himself of extremely embarrassing guests and by punishing a rebel.

The Beni Hilal, soon followed by the Sulaim, who were no better, hastened to make full use of the opportunity afforded them. Between 1050 and 1052 they hurled themselves on Ifriqiya, defeated the amir, who had hoped to find in them auxiliaries against the Hammadids, sacked Kairouan and ravaged the country. 'Like an army of grasshoppers', wrote Ibn Khaldun employing a Koranic simile, 'they destroyed everything in their path'.[38] In 1057 the Zirids had to take refuge in Mahdiya, where they tried in vain

The Arab and Berber Dynasties (Ninth–Eleventh Centuries)

to reconquer their lost cities. Ifriqiya was turned over to anarchy; towns, principalities, little Arab states sprang up spontaneously.

Waves of nomads broke over the country without ceasing, trailing women and children after them and thrusting back those who had gone before them. The Hammadids made allies of the nomads. With their aid, al-Nasir was able to make incursions into Ifriqiya, but he quickly became their puppet rather than their master. By dint of laying Hammadid territory waste, they finally secured from the sultan al-Mansur, successor to al-Nasir, half of his harvest. Soon he had to abandon Qal'a, which was under direct threat, and in 1090 to settle in another capital, Bougie, founded eighteen years earlier at the point where the main road, of which Qal'a was the southern extremity, reached the sea. There the dynasty still maintained itself respectably until the Almohad conquest.

The Hilalian invasion is undoubtedly the most important event of the entire mediaeval period in the Maghrib. It was that invasion, far more than the Muslim conquest, that transformed the Maghrib for centuries. Before the Hilalians, the country—Islam apart—had remained profoundly Berber in language and custom. It had resumed its Berber character politically in so far as it had shaken off the authority of the east. We have seen how it had even achieved a state of equilibrium, somewhat precarious perhaps, between the great ethnic families established there from time immemorial.

The Bedouins brought with them their language, readily distinguished from the urban dialects bequeathed by the first Muslim conquerors. This Bedouin Arabic is the source of most of the rural Arab dialects spoken in North Africa today.

They also brought their pastoral habits. It appears that before their advent sedentary and nomadic Berbers had succeeded after a fashion in dividing up the lands they needed. The arrival of the Hilalians threw this harmony between the two ways of life demanded by the climate and configuration of the Maghrib into a melting pot. With them nomadism became an invading torrent. Lands made for the cultivation of cereals or fruit-growing were wrested from their proper use, villages and secondary towns were choked into ruin and agriculture was permitted to exist only in a narrow strip along the coast, around the remaining towns and in the interior of mountain masses which the Arab flood swept round without penetrating. Examples abound—Ifriqiyian agriculture retreated towards the Sahel, Cap Bon and the Bizerta region, while the olive lands of the centre were given over to flocks; the Hammadid kingdom was forced to retire to Bougie; Kairouan was reduced to the rank of a small town after having been a capital for centuries; Kabylia walled itself up in its mountains and remained shut against newcomers.

Politically the consequences of the Hilalian invasion were no less important. Gradually the Arabs pushed back westwards the Zenata nomads who had formerly constituted the kingdom of Tahert. In Ifriqiya they at once caused the break-up of the Zirid kingdom, from which sprang several small principalities, each upheld by an Arab tribe settled in the neighbourhood. Finally the Hammadid kingdom, the leaders of which had thought they could make use of the Arabs, shrank to the vicinity of Bougie, and was very lucky not to perish altogether. We then observe the paradoxical phenomenon noted by G. Marçais[39]—the Sanhaja, Berber mountaineers though they were, turned to the sea, and at Mahdiya and Bougie created maritime principalities. But it was too late; the Normans were already established in southern Italy and Sicily, and were to constitute an obstacle to the seagoing ambitions of the Hammadids and Zirids.

All these changes, be it noted, on the whole were slow and gradual. We should speak not so much of a rushing torrent, as of the inexorable flood of the rising tide—hardly a single memorable battle, no spectacular action, just a sustained pressure, almost gentle, but irresistible.

Notes

1. al-Ya'qubi, *Kitab al-buldan*; see G. Weit, tr., *Textes et traductions d'auteurs orientales* (Cairo, 1937).
2. Ibn Hawqal, *Kitab al-masalik wa al-mamalik* (written *c.* 977); see M. de Slane, tr., 'Description de l'Afrique', *Journal Asiatique* (1842).
3. E. F. Gautier, *op. cit.*, pp. 281–2.
4. H. Terrasse, *Histoire du Maroc, des origines à l'établissement du Protectorat français*, 2 vols. (Casablanca, 1949–50), I, 112–33.
5. For an elaboration on the significance of *baraka* in the far Maghrib, see E. Westermark, *Ritual and Belief in Morocco* (London, 1926), I, 35–261.

The Arab and Berber Dynasties (Ninth–Eleventh Centuries)

6. E. Lévi-Provençal, 'La fondation de Fès', *Annales de l'Institut d'Études Orientale* (1938), IV, 23–53.
7. Ibn Abi Zar', *Rawd al-Qirtas*; for a poor French translation, see A. Beaumier, *Raud al-Qirtas* (Paris, 1860), p. 44 *et seq.*
8. E. F. Gautier, *op. cit.*, p. 285.
9. H. Terrasse, *op. cit.*, I, 123.
10. *Ibid.*, p. 123.
11. al-Ya'qubi (tr. Weit), *op. cit.*, p. 213.
12. Abu al-'Arab, *Tabaqat 'ulama' Ifriqiyya*; see Muhammad Ben Cheneb, ed. and tr., *Classes des savants de l'Ifriqiya*, Publications de la Faculté des lettres d'Alger (Alger, 1914–20), LI–LII.
13. *Ibid.*, p. 117.
14. *Ibid.*, see p. 269 *et seq.*
15. *Ibid.*, p. 308.
16. See al-Nuwairi (tr. de Slane), *op. cit.*, I, 398–447 for brief accounts of each of the amirs' reigns.
17. For detail concerning the Great Mosque of Kairouan see G. Marçais, *Manuel d'art Musulman*, 2 vols. (Paris, 1926–7), I, 15.
18. Concerning the disputed ancestry of 'Ubaid Allah, see Ibn Khaldun (tr. de Slane), *op. cit.*, II, 506–8.
19. *Ibid.*, I, 292.
20. E. F. Gautier, *op. cit.*, pp. 317–18.
21. Ibn Khaldun (tr. de Slane), *op. cit.*, II, 512.
22. Ibn 'Idhari (tr. Fagnan), *op. cit.*, I, 236–7.
23. Ibn al-Athir (tr. Fagnan), *op. cit.*, p. 314.
24. G. Marçais (1926), *op. cit.*, I, 130–5.
25. H. Terrasse (1949), *op. cit.*, I, 176.
26. Ibn 'Idhari (tr. Fagnan), *op. cit.*, I, 257.
27. Ibn Hammad; see M. Vonderheyden, ed. and tr., *Histoire des rois 'Obaidides (Les Califes fatimides)*, (Alger, 1927), p. 27.
28. *Ibid.*, p. 34.
29. Abu Zakariya (tr. Masqueray), *op. cit.*, p. 236 *et seq.*
30. Ibn Khaldun (tr. de Slane), *op. cit.*, II, 539.
31. Ibn al-Athir (tr. Fagnan), *op. cit.*, p. 354.
32. *Ibid.*, p. 370; Ibn Khaldun (tr. de Slane), *op. cit.*, II, 550.
33. G. Marçais (1926), *op. cit.*, I, 101–3.
34. Ibn 'Idhari (tr. Fagnan), *op. cit.*, I, 352.
35. P. Blanchet, 'Description des monuments de la Kalaa des Beni Hammad', *Nouvelles archives des Missions*, XVII, 1908–9, p. 3 *et seq.*
36. General de Beylié, *La Kalaa des Beni Hammad. Une capitale berbère de l'Afrique de Nord au XIe siècle* (Paris, 1909), p. 77 *et seq.*
37. G. Marçais (1926), *op. cit.*, I, 114–15, 120–1.
38. Ibn Khaldun (tr. de Slane), *op. cit.*, I, 34.
39. G. Marçais (1946), *op. cit.*, pp. 215–88.

CHAPTER 3

The Berber Empires: The Almoravids and the Almohads

❊

At the very moment when the Arab tribes from the south-east were setting foot on the soil of the Maghrib, another nomadic group, this time Berber, was forming in the western Sahara and making ready in its turn to break over North Africa in waves from the south-west. These were the veiled Sanhaja known to history as the Almoravids. In the space of a bare half-century they were to constitute an enormous Berber empire in the western half of the country and in Spain.

Three-quarters of a century later, around a nucleus of sedentary Berbers of the High Atlas, the Masmouda, a second Berber empire was to be formed still vaster in extent, since it included the whole Muslim west from Tripoli to Cuenca and Agadir; this was the Almohad empire. Thus over nearly two centuries the people of the Maghrib succeeded by their own unaided exertions in erecting huge political structures such as these original inhabitants of the land had never before, it appears, managed to create.

Until about 1920 virtually the only information available regarding this important epoch in the history of the Maghrib dated from between one and two centuries later than the events themselves. Only the geographers al-Bakri[1] and al-Idrisi,[2] and the chroniclers al-Marrakushi[3] and Ibn al-Athir,[4] a man of the east, were contemporary with the latest of the facts they recorded. Since then Arabists and archaeologists, particularly in Morocco, the cradle of both empires, have found documents and buildings which afford better knowledge and understanding of men and events. Many points are indeed still obscure, and there are doubtless many discoveries yet to be made. Nonetheless we can follow quite

The Berber Empires: The Almoravids and the Almohads

closely the evolutionary curve of the Almoravid and Almohad empires and assign some reasons for their final downfall.

1. The Almoravids

The original cell of the Almoravid empire was a powerful Sanhaja tribe of the Sahara, the Lemtouna, whose place of origin was in the Adrar in Mauritania. Their custom was to traverse chiefly the desert regions stretching from the oases of southern Morocco to the country of the blacks. Perhaps as a protection against the evil eye, they wore a veil covering the lower part of their faces, the *litham*. Accordingly they were called the wearers of the litham (*al-mulathamun*). They were never without it and were highly contemptuous of the 'fly-catchers' with uncovered faces.

The geographer al-Bakri assures us that they knew neither how to till the ground nor how to sow, and that their only wealth lay in their flocks from which they received their nutriment. 'Many of them would live their whole life through without having eaten bread, if merchants from the Muslim countries or the lands of the blacks did not give them some to taste, or make them a present of flour.'[5]

For their subsistence they relied on stock-raising, and also on caravan traffic, which had developed considerably in the western Sahara since the end of the ninth century. 'As suzerains of the negro kings of the Sudan and masters of the Atlantic Sahara, the veiled Sanhaja were undoubtedly the chief beneficiaries of this caravan traffic, whether by acting as carriers themselves or by levying dues of passage and protection on the caravans of others.'[6]

These tough nomads were converted to Islam in the ninth century, and expended the ardour of still very ignorant neophytes in holy wars against the negro infidels. After fighting under a single leader, they finally split up for more than a century, until the day when an energetic amir, Abu 'Abd Allah Muhammad ibn Tifawat, assumed control of them.

IBN YASIN

About the middle of the eleventh century the Lemtouna and their neighbours the Godala had as chief the successor to Abu 'Abd

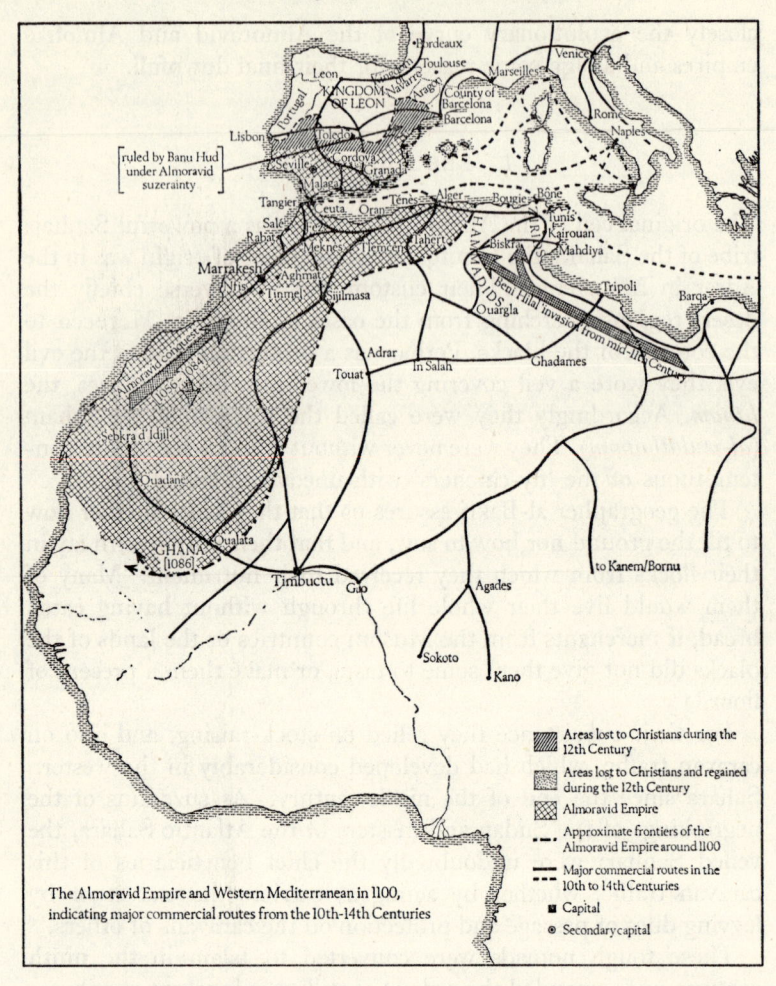

The Almoravid Empire and Western Mediterranean in 1100, indicating major commercial routes from the 10th-14th Centuries

- Areas lost to Christians during the 12th Century
- Areas lost to Christians and regained during the 12th Century
- Almoravid Empire
- Approximate frontiers of the Almoravid Empire around 1100
- Major commercial routes in the 10th to 14th Centuries
- Capital
- Secondary capital

Allah, Yahya ibn Ibrahim al-Gadali, who, together with a group of notables, undertook the pilgrimage to Mecca. On his way back he met at Kairouan a renowned Maliki professor of law, a native of Morocco, Abu 'Imran al-Fasi. Realising his own ignorance, Ibn Yasin asked him for one of his disciples to teach the Koran to the Sanhaja tribes of the desert. But none of the townsmen surrounding the master wanted to preach to such rough company. Abu 'Imran then gave Yahya the name of a Moroccan scholar of the far

78

The Berber Empires: the Almoravids and the Almohads

Sous who would be able to find a capable and devout preacher among his students. One of these, ʿAbd Allah ibn Yasin, did agree to follow the chief of the Lemtouna into the desert.

From what can be learned about him from the text of al-Bakri, who was practically his contemporary, ʿAbd Allah ibn Yasin appears as an odd sort of personage. He appeared to be learned in the eyes of the ignorant Saharans, but he had the knowledge only of a petty scholar of the Sous, which is to say a slender stock of learning.[7] He was a great lover of women, incontestably able for all that, and was endowed with a personal prestige that enabled him to maintain among the Sanhaja nomads a vigorous discipline founded on strokes of the lash. He was a man of action, a leader of men rather than a man of doctrine. In point of fact it would be wrong to speak of an Almoravid doctrine. At the outset his preaching did not attract the free nomads, who were more concerned to satisfy their passions than to burden themselves with rules of ethics. Ibn Yasin then prevailed on two Lemtouna chiefs and seven Godala notables to establish under his direction a military monastery (*ribat*) on an island in a river (the Niger or Sénégal?) or more probably in the Tidra islands off the Mauritanian coast between the Baie du Lévrier and Cap Timiris. There the inmates—the men of the ribat or Almoravids (*murābitun*) would be able to lead a life in strict conformity with unadulterated Malikism.

The members of the community lived on fruit, what they could hunt or fish, and meat which, after being dried, had been pounded and covered with melted fat or butter. They drank practically nothing but milk. Under the rigorous direction of their spiritual leader, they worked on an equal footing for the triumph of Islam. On entry into the sect, it was necessary, according to al-Bakri, to undergo harsh ordeals in order to be cleansed of one's pollutions. The drinker or the liar received eighty strokes of the lash, the fornicator one hundred. Sometimes indeed Ibn Yasin increased the punishment. Failures in religious duty entailed punishments according to a scale—five blows for being late for public prayer, twenty for omitting one of the ritual prostrations, and as many as the judge deemed fit if the culprit raised his voice in the mosque. To make up for prayers left unsaid in the past, the novice was required to repeat the midday prayer four times before it was celebrated publicly.[8]

THE FIRST CONQUESTS

The fame of the Almoravids' sanctity and the high quality of their discipline soon attracted a thousand men trained to the military life and resolved by force of arms to impose strict observance on unbelievers and on unzealous Muslims. These armed monks quickly subdued the Sanhaja tribes. Their success soon brought together 30,000 men—an incredibly large force in that desert land—firmly determined to satisfy simultaneously their keen appetite for proselytism and for pillage. Ibn Yasin, who remained the religious leader of the Almoravids, but was too adroit to aspire to personal power, put the troops under the command of a Lemtouna chief, an initiate [in the movement] from the beginning, Yahya ibn 'Umar. He made fruitful expeditions, northwards in the valley of the Oued Dra' and southward in the Sudan. Soon he was summoned to intervene at Sijilmasa.

The dynasty of the Benu Midrar had been finally driven out of the Tafilalet in 976-977 by a Zenata chief and vassal of the 'Umaiyad sovereign of Cordova, by the name of Khazrun ibn Falfal al-Maghrawi, and his descendants proclaimed their independence. Certain learned men, suffering under the impieties and persecutions of the ruler of Sijilmasa, asked for the aid of the Almoravids. They intervened the more readily for being able thus to satisfy their religious zeal, to appease their family quarrels with the Zenata and to give free rein to their desires to pillage. Ibn Yasin took the city in 1055-1056, and had all its places of pleasure and musical instruments destroyed. He acquired enormous booty after massacring all the Maghrawa he could find. Thereafter Sijilmasa was no longer self-governing, but its subjection to the rulers of the Maghrib never went very far, and the tribes of the Tafilalet, the inhabitants of the city and the local governors continually stirred up sedition. Just before the capture of Sijilmasa, in 1054, the Almoravids penetrated as far as the negro kingdom of Ghana, where they took the important city of Aoudaghost, south of present-day Tagant [Mauritania].

On Yahya's death in 1056, his brother Abu Bakr ibn 'Umar was given command of the troops by Ibn Yasin, and he enlarged the field of conquest northwards. His first objective was the Sous, where he gained possession of the capital Taroudant in 1056, and

The Berber Empires: the Almoravids and the Almohads

caused the disappearance of a small Shi'a principality which the Fatimids had established there but in which Almoravid rule was not able to be firmly implanted. Next he made his way into the Atlas massif as far as Aghmat, meeting, by all accounts, with no difficulty. There he married the king's widow, the lovely and willing Zainab, nicknamed 'the wise woman', who later played an important political role.

The heretical Berghwata, whom the Almoravids next attacked, did not permit themselves to be easily led into the paths of orthodoxy. Indeed, Ibn Yasin's army was routed and he himself was killed. A harsh offensive by Abu Bakr was required to maintain control of the situation. A new danger was appearing in the east. A ruler of Qal'a of the Beni Hammad, Bologguin ibn Muhammad ibn Hammad, marched with a large army as far as Fez, which he captured. On the way back he was assassinated, says Ibn Khaldun, with the support of the Sanhaja, who had become disgruntled at so many expeditions into hostile and distant lands'.[9] The Zirids could not without mortal danger afford the useless and costly luxury of western conquests.

It is not known whether the Almoravids clashed with the Zirids. Other projects may have claimed their attention at this time. The desert Sanhaja were fighting among themselves, and in 1061 Abu Bakr had to go to the desert to bring their dissensions to an end. He left command of the troops in the Maghrib to his cousin Yusuf ibn Tashfin, and in addition he left him his wife, Zainib, who rapidly acquired a great influence over her new husband.

We have now reached the critical moment of the Almoravid dynasty. Threatened as they were by the Beni Hammad, threatened in the rear by probably serious internal struggles, settled in a country still incompletely subdued, the Saharans might have been swept away at any time. Certainly that is al-Bakri's opinion. 'Today', he wrote in the year 460 (1067–1068), 'the Almoravids have as their amir Abu Bakr ibn 'Umar, but their empire is fragmented and their power divided. They maintain themselves now in the desert.'[10] This was taking no account of the advantages they still held. The Beni Hammad had other concerns and the tribes of Morocco were not yet capable of uniting against the invader. Furthermore, the Almoravids had their religious prestige, which was considerable in a Morocco still only superficially converted to

Islam. They had a local woman, Zainib, who, through the narratives of the chronicles, must have been an exceptionally remarkable person. They had an experienced army reinforced by Christian and black mercenaries, and finally, the Almoravids had a man hitherto unknown (al-Bakri does not even mention him) who was to reveal himself as a great conqueror, and well able to take advantage of any opportunity.

IBN TASHFIN

Ibn Tashfin, at this time some fifty years old, was a typical man of the Sahara. Such he appears in the portrait sketched of him in the *Qirtas*—'Complexion brown, stature middling, lean, little beard, voice soft, eyes black, nose aquiline, Muhammad's lock falling over the tip of the ear, eyebrows running into each other, and hair crinkly. He was courageous, resolute, dignified, active, generous, charitable; he disdained worldly pleasure, and was austere, just, and holy. He was modest even in his clothing, never wearing anything but wool, to the exclusion of any other material; he lived on barley, meat and camel's milk and held strictly to this diet until his death.'[11] Under his leadership the Almoravid empire made rapid progress, no less because of his qualities as a general than because of his strict religious observance. This religiosity brought him valuable contacts and understandings among the pious Muslims who were subjects of the Maghrawa of Fez. When Abu Bakr learned of his lieutenant's conquests in the far and central Maghrib, he came to claim his command, but though, on Zainib's advice, he was given rich presents, his intervention was unsuccessful and he had to return to the desert. When Abu Bakr died, in 1087–1088, Ibn Tashfin was able to assume power unchallenged.

Meanwhile, Ibn Tashfin asserted his authority at once by the building of a camp in the northern foothills of the Atlas on the upper waters of the Oued Tensift. He could not then—in 1060? —have imagined that out of this would emerge the great capital of Marrakesh. The Arab historians have not stinted detail, more or less apocryphal, regarding the creation of a city for which such a fair future lay in store. The site, which belonged to an old Masmouda woman, was reputed to be a brigands' lair. Ibn Tashfin purchased it out of his private fortune, set up the Almoravid tents there and personally took a hand in the work of building the

The Berber Empires: The Almoravids and the Almohads

mosque. 'He girded himself', says the *Qirtas*, 'with a belt, and worked in the clay and at the building work along with the labourers, out of humility towards God.'[12] This last description illustrates clearly the character of the holy man; the historic spot north-west of the Koutoubiya is still pointed out. From its first foundation, Marrakesh has given the appearance of a Saharan city, with its palm-groves planted in a climate by no means encouraging to the palm-tree, but for a desert people it is the only tree of any importance.

From this operational base, with the valour of his troops taking the place of ramparts, Ibn Tashfin launched expeditions into the western and central Maghrib. He took Fez in 1069, thus terminating the Zenata hold on northern Morocco, penetrated into the Rif, marched along the valley of the Moulouya, and brought the Beni Snassen and Oujda into submission. Having acquired the mastery of all Morocco, he marched eastwards, took possession of Tlemcen, Oran, Ténès and Ouarsenis, and in 1082 laid siege to Algiers, but he did not attack eastern Barbary or even the Kabyle bloc. After organising his conquests and entrusting their management to Almoravid officers, he returned to Marrakesh as though he regarded himself as having achieved his task, but shortly afterwards, grave events led him to intervene in Spain.

THE KINGS OF THE TAIFAS

Despite his prestige, the 'Umaiyad caliph of Cordova had been unable to withstand the rivalries of the Muslims of the peninsula. Arabs from the east, Berbers from the Maghrib, Andalusian renegades and liberated Christian slaves took advantage of the slightest weakness on the part of authority to settle their quarrels by armed force. To contain them had required nothing less than the strong action of the all-powerful vizier Ibn Abi 'Amir al-Mansur (the Almanzor of the Spaniards) whose dictatorship rested on the support of his Berber troops. After the death of his son al-Muzaffar in 1008, no authority was powerful enough to arrest the disintegration of the caliphate. During the quarter century preceding the expulsion of the last 'Umaiyad (1009–1031) more than ten pretenders appeared and disappeared.

It was owing to this state of anarchy that the provincial governors or notables gradually formed twenty-three independent principalities covering a vast expanse of territory, from Aragon in the north and Valencia in the east as far as Andalusia and Murcia in the south and the former Lusitania in the west. They were called the kings of the 'parties' (*muluk al-tawā'if*; in Spanish *reyes de Taïfas*). At Badajoz a Berber officer of the Miknasa tribe, who said he was of Arab extraction, founded the dynasty of the Aftasids (1027-1094). In the south, smaller Berber kingdoms—Hamudids of Malaga (1016-1057) and Zirids of Granada (1012-1090)—did the same. In the south-east liberated slaves ruled over what were known as the slave kingdoms of Valencia and Almeria. In Aragon ('the upper frontier') after the flourishing dynasty of the Toujibids (1019-1039) had come to an end, their vassals of Lerida, the Hudids, also of Arab origin, established themselves as masters of Saragossa from 1039 to 1110. The most important of these kingdoms was that of Seville (1023-1091) controlled by the 'Abbadids, descended from Syrians, who extended their territories in the direction of what is now Portugal, of Malaga, Cadiz and Badajoz and over the south-western part of the former caliphate, and who finally secured possession of Cordova. Seville then became the chief political, intellectual and artistic centre of the peninsula.

The Christians took advantage of the crumbling of Muslim strength and the chronic rivalries between the Muslim princes to work for the liberation of the territory (*reconquista*). As early as 1054 King Ferdinand I, after annexing Leon and Galicia to Castile, had demonstrated his intention of concentrating his efforts against the unbelievers by refusing to annex Navarre. His successful offensives had reduced the kings of Seville, Badajoz, Toledo and Saragossa to tributary rank and had enlarged his frontiers in every direction. In 1063 Pope Alexander II declared a grant of special indulgence to any who would go to fight the Muslims of Spain, and knights of France came in numbers to join their peers across the mountains. At the same period the new kingdom of Aragon began the struggle against the kings of Saragossa and Huesca. A combined operation by the two champions of Christendom might have been decisive, but the disturbances over the succession that ensued on Ferdinand's death in 1065 paralysed the reconquest.

King Alphonso VI had once more to reunite all the territories of central and western Spain north of the Tagus before he could

The Berber Empires: the Almoravids and the Almohads

resume his father's policy in 1072. It was during the conflicts which set Christian against Moor and Taïfa against Taïfa that the mercenary leader Rodrigo Diaz de Vivar played a predominant political role. Nicknamed the 'champion' (*Campeador*) by the Spaniards and 'my master' (*sayīdī, sīdī*; in Spanish *mio Cid*) by the Muslim soldiers, he placed his sword sometimes at the service of the king of Castile, more often at that of the Hudid dynasty of Saragossa, and above all at the service of his personal ambition. It is probable that but for the bitter rivalries between Alphonso and the Cid the reconquest might have been extremely rapid, to such a condition were the Taïfas reduced.

The ruler of Castile imposed a double tribute on the king of Seville, al-Muʿtamid, who had sided against him in the quarrels over the succession, and reduced the king of Toledo to the rank of vassal. In 1083 he led a large and victorious expedition across the entire Muslim territory as far as Tarifa. Then, in 1085, he took advantage of a revolt by the Toledans to take possession of their city, which he made into a formidable base of operations. Furthermore he succeeded in extending his conquest from the Tagus to the Turia, in keeping Murcia under threat and in forcing all the Taïfas of east and south to pay tribute. In the north the king of Saragossa had difficulty in resisting the attacks of the king of Aragon and the counts of Barcelona.

The kings of the Taïfas had to choose between submission to Alphonso VI and emigration. Al-Muʿtamid is said to have forcefully declared that he preferred being a cameleer in Africa to being a swineherd in Spain. There was a third possible way of emerging from the dilemma—to oppose the Christians with Muslim reinforcements from overseas. The great mystical and popular movement then affecting Islam was making itself felt in Spain. The cordial relations between Christians and Moors were giving way to a hostility not so much political as religious. The kings could not ignore the deep emotional inclinations of their people. For the defence of the true faith they had recourse to those same Berber warriors against whom they had directed the revolution that had brought about the fall of the caliphate. They decided that to sue for the intervention of the Almoravids would be less fraught with risk than that of the Hilalians whom they had first considered asking.

ALMORAVID INTERVENTION

From 1074 at least, Yusuf ibn Tashfin had been receiving requests from various quarters to intervene in Spain, either to come to the aid of the Muslims under pressure from the Christian threat or to side with one Muslim prince against another.[13] Not being inclined temperamentally to rush into mad enterprises, he waited till he had secured command of the Straits of Gibraltar before committing himself. Having acquired Ceuta in 1083, he yielded to al-Mu'tamid's urgent solicitations only on the condition of gaining control over Algeciras. At that time, however, he seems to have entertained no ambitions with regard to Spain, a country of which he knew nothing. His sole object was that the holy war which was being urged upon him should be waged in the most favourable conditions possible.

He landed with a powerful army at Algeciras, which he transformed into a fortified base, made contact with al-Mu'tamid at Seville, and then, with reinforcements from Seville, Granada, Malaga, Almeria and Badajoz, marched on Toledo. The hostile troops met in the fields of Azagal (Zallaqa or Sacralias, near Badajoz) on 23 October 1086. Ibn Tashfin demanded the conversion of Alphonso to Islam; Alphonso replied that he would resort to the arbitration of war. A turning movement by the Almoravids was the determining factor in a victory so complete that the king of Castile was nearly captured and was forced to withdraw from the region and to lift the siege of Saragossa. The repercussions of this victory throughout the Muslim world were as considerable as those of the capture of Toledo by Alphonso VI. Ibn Tashfin was from that time regarded as one of the principal champions of a threatened Islam.

The progress of the Muslim armies was interrupted by the departure of Ibn Tashfin for Morocco, to which he was recalled by the death of his son. He left al-Mu'tamid no more than 3,000 Berbers. The Christians then resumed the offensive in the direction of Murcia and Almeria, and in 1088 or 1090 al-Mu'tamid decided to present himself in person before Ibn Tashfin to beg the Almoravids to intervene once more. In answer, Ibn Tashfin put out of action the powerful military base of Aledo, south-west of Murcia, which the Taïfas had previously attacked without success, and so he restored the situation.

The Berber Empires: the Almoravids and the Almohads

Everything presaged a large offensive by the combined forces of Almoravids and Moors. But the Muslim kingdoms of Spain were too weak to furnish Ibn Tashfin with effective support, and too divided not to tempt the Berber leader to augment his power at their expense. Soon he was acting no longer as an ally but as a master. The kings of the Taïfas, scholarly and corrupt, may have despised the unpolished and austere man of the Maghrib. Not so the common folk, victims of Christian reprisals, nor the jurisconsults (*fuqahā*, singular *faqīh*), both of whom contrasted the scepticism of the Andalusian amirs with the strict Malikism of these Berbers, whom they regarded as the emissaries of God. Strong in this two-fold support, Ibn Tashfin was able to establish himself as an arbiter of quarrels, to exile kings and to confiscate their territories. The *fuqahā* legitimated each one of his encroachments with a *fatwa*. He thus succeeded in re-establishing by 1094 the unity of Islam in Spain. However, he respected the kingdom of Saragossa, which he regarded as a buffer state between Christians and Almoravids. Valencia, held first by the Cid and then by his widow Chimeneas, did not fall into the hands of the Almoravids until 1102. When Yusuf died in 1106–1107—at the age of nearly one hundred, it is said—he bequeathed to 'Ali, his 23-year-old son by a Christian slave, a vast empire comprising Muslim Spain as far as Fraga (south-west of Lerida) in the north and the islands of Majorca, Minorca and Ibiza.

'ALI AND THE DEFENCE OF MALIKISM

Despite his youth, the new Almoravid ruler acceded to power without difficulty—one among many proofs of Yusuf's extraordinary prestige. He was even more pious than his father, with a piety bordering on bigotry and rendering him the docile instrument of the *fuqahā*. Moreover, far from having received the rough education of the desert, he had spent the greater part of his youth in Spain and had been brought up as an urban dweller, far from the characteristic conditions of tribal life. Finally, he was debilitated and lacking in vigour. 'His way of setting about things was good and his sentiments were lofty. He esteemed continence and hated injustice, and was worthy of ranking among ascetics and hermits rather than among princes and conquerors. . . . He was content to exercise a nominal sway and to draw the proceeds of taxation, and had no thought save to pass the night in prayer and the day in fasting ... but of the interests of his subjects his neglect was utter and entire.'[14] It is not therefore surprising that during his reign, as the same Marrakushi indicates, the sole thought of the grandees of the empire, women included, was to follow their own inclinations, with no concern for the common interest.[15]

In these circumstances Almoravid power was of short duration. The cause of their fall, as of their triumph, lay in religion. 'Ali was as much of an uncompromising Maliki as his father had been. In Spain, just as in the Maghrib, Malikism stifled intellectual effort and religious feeling. It ruled out any allegorical interpretation of the Koran and any personal inquiry into the meaning of the law by reference to sources. Thus, by furthering a coarse anthropomorphism and legalistic theology, it was considered heresy even to question the meaning of one of Muhammad's words, and the study of the Koran and the *hadiths* was abandoned. It professed to devote itself to juridical science (*fiqh*) in accordance with second-hand orthodox manuals on the doctrine of specific cases, or applied *fiqh*, that is, on the systematic working out of positive law under its various individual heads (*furū'*). This desiccated casuistry, emptied of any religious content, only encouraged interminable canonical and juridical arguments. Most anyone could consider himself qualified to give *fatwas* on most any point. This dropping of the Koran and the Tradition in favour of dry casuistry called forth a vigorous protest by the greatest and most original theologian of Islam, al-Ghazali (1058–1112). He showed in his *Revival of Religious Learning* (*Ihyā 'ulūm al-dīn*)[16] that the *fiqh*, as understood by the Malikis of the strict observance, was no more than a purely temporal pursuit having no link with religion. He denounced the way in which the *fuqahā'* took a far from disinterested hand in politics, their feeling for self-advertisement and their foolishness in claiming to assure the salvation of the soul by means of an empty legalistic exercise, whereas religion is above all a matter touching the heart. We can understand how his works scandalised the Malikis not so much in dogmatic matters as in the severity of the judgments he passed on *fuqahā'*. Accordingly these latter persuaded 'Ali, the foe of theology, to have al-Ghazali's works burnt and to threaten anyone possessing fragments of them with confiscation of goods and death. This sin against the spirit was to prove

The Berber Empires: the Almoravids and the Almohads

fatal to the Almoravids, as is illustrated by the success of the Almohad movement.

ALMORAVID BUILDINGS IN THE MAGHRIB

For all their piety, the Almoravids did not govern Spain with the aid only of orthodox Berbers. They found themselves transported into an environment where tradition went too deep and culture was too refined to permit a complete obliteration of the past. As leaders not only of the Saharans, but also of all the Muslims of the west—as their title of *amir al-muslimin* proclaims—they turned for assistance to the most distinguished personages in the country. They rejected neither scholars nor artists, and even, in the words of an Arab historian, surrounded themselves 'with such a multitude of the most outstanding secretaries and men of letters the like of which was never seen in any age.' Ibn Bajja (Avenpace, d. 1138), who was not only a philosopher but also a musician of repute, was for twenty years vizier to the governor of Granada and Saragossa, the Almoravid 'Ali's brother-in-law. Gradually the uncouth men of the veil absorbed the Spanish environment, which softened their austerity and opened their eyes to joys other than those of battle. Through them the Maghrib experienced the spread of that Andalusian civilisation which had already found its way into Ceuta and Fez. While Spain received from Africa the soldiers of the faith, it gave back to it in turn architects, craftsmen and a culture that reached at least certain urban centres.

After the break between the 'Umaiyads and the Abbasid caliphate, Muslim art in the peninsula had developed freely. The Almoravids, with no earlier models before their eyes and with no direct relations with the east, came under the influence of the architecture of Cordova and Granada. In the public buildings they erected in western Barbary they made use of massive pillars in place of columns, of the semicircular arch *outrepassé* (or Norse arch) which Spain had borrowed from Ifriqiya, where it had been in use for the past two centuries, and of the arch cut out in foils in place of the broken arch, not *outrepassé*, of Kairouan.

Unfortunately nothing remains of the mosque at Marrakesh or of the oratories at Fez which Ibn Tashfin had ordered to be constructed. We can, however, still find in all its essentials—despite alterations carried out in the fourteenth century and under the

Turks—the Great Mosque of Algiers with its prayer hall having eleven five-bayed naves, reminiscent of Tlemcen. It was 'Ali who enlarged the Mosque of al-Qarawiyin at Fez, which had been founded in the ninth century and had become too small to hold the crowd of the faithful. It was 'Ali also who founded the most important Almoravid edifice, the Great Mosque at Tlemcen.[17]

This is a building measuring some 150 by 180 feet, approached by a square court each side of which is some 60 feet in length, and which, following a practice characteristic of Almoravid art, is lined on the east and the west with naves which are extensions of those of the prayer hall. This hall comprises thirteen six-bayed naves bordered, as at Algiers and Fez, with stone-built pillars supporting broken or foiled Norse arches. A ribbed cupola rises in the middle. Another, placed in front of the mihrab, exhibits fretted sections which make of it 'an admirable aerial lace hung above the drum'. The arrangement of the corbelling of the lantern, with its multiple rising masses one above another, enables us to recognise 'the first dated example in the west of a cupola with stalactites'.[18] In the decoration the floral motif predominates, in its final form of single or double palm, finely ribbed and copiously intermingled with acanthus. The mihrab is notable for elegant ornamentation offering great similarity to that of the mihrab at Cordova.

The palaces built at Marrakesh and Tagrart have been destroyed. It was 'Ali who in 1120 constructed the first ramparts of Marrakesh. There still exist ruins of the two fortresses of the Ouergha country and the Marrakesh foothills, the Amergo and the Tasghimout, which kept watch over the Rif people and the Masmouda. It seems unlikely that the Almoravids added to works of public utility. 'Ali is, however, credited with a canal which made it possible to irrigate the gardens of Fez, and with a bridge over the Tensift built by Spanish technicians. 'The Almoravids, as liaison officers, so to speak, between Spain and Africa, turned for the construction of their works both to Saharan water-engineers and to Andalusian architects.'[19]

DECADENCE AND DOWNFALL OF THE ALMORAVIDS

The reign of Ibn Tashfin represented the zenith of Almoravid power in Spain. His son 'Ali continued the conflict with the Christians of Castile but, despite the victory of Uclés (near

The Berber Empires: the Almoravids and the Almohads

Taraneón in the Cuenca region) failed to penetrate enemy territory. His forces were so weakened that when the death of Alphonso VI in 1109 was followed by disturbances in Castile and Leon, the only advantage he could derive from them was to occupy Saragossa for a few years, from 1110 to 1118.

Without the help of Castile, which was temporarily reduced to anarchy, Aragon and Barcelona went forward with the reconquest. The king of Aragon, Alphonso the Battler, recaptured Saragossa in 1118, and pushed his frontiers across the Ebro, invaded the regions of Valencia, Murcia and eastern Andalusia, and in 1126 for the first time reached the sea at Salobreña (south of Granada) facing Barbary. After a great success at Arnisol (near Lucena, some 40 miles south-east of Cordova) he settled 14,000 Andalusian Arabic-speaking Christians (*Muzarabs*) in the districts taken from the Muslims north of the Ebro. He then turned his energies northwards, but met with failure before Fraga and Lerida. However, the count of Barcelona enlarged his territories at the expense of Lerida and Tortosa and imposed tribute on the governor of the Balearics. From 1144 to 1147 King Alphonso VII, who had settled his dynastic difficulties, made an increasing number of large-scale raids (*algarades*) in Andalusia, ravaging the country as far as Almeria.

When 'Ali died in 1143, the Christians were pushing back the amirs of Cordova and Seville everywhere, while the Almohads were occupying the greater part of Morocco. It was then that the Muslims of Spain began to revolt against the authority of 'Ali's son Tashfin. They may have been aggrieved at the way their leaders had been corrupted by the atmosphere of Andalusia and at the protection extended to the Christian army at Fez commanded by Reverter; they were beyond doubt aggrieved at the brutal exercise of authority by the Almoravid princes. However, they took advantage of conflicts waged by Tashfin ibn 'Ali against the Almohads of the Maghrib to revolt in the Algarve under the leadership of a disciple of al-Ghazali, and after that in Valencia, Murcia, Cordova and Almeria. Muslim Spain was once more the scene of a regime similar to that of the Taïfas after the fall of the caliphate. It was in the course of the struggles between Almoravids and Andalusian Muslims that one of the rebellious chiefs called upon the Almohads to intervene, and it was this that led to the downfall, in Spain as in Barbary, of Almoravid power.

CONCLUSION

The first impression one draws from this story is of a brilliant fire of straw, its ashes quickly scattering and leaving no trace.

In political terms, failure was total. The Almoravid empire was dismembered as quickly as it had been formed, a process regarded with entire indifference by peoples who seem to have offered no serious opposition to the Almohads. In Spain the situation in 1145 was the same as when Yusuf ibn Tashfin first intervened, and the country lay rent and powerless before the Christian offensive. Finally, it cannot be established that either the Almoravid sovereigns or their advisers succeeded in establishing any real governmental machine. It seems likely that the original Saharan institutions and Andalusian traditions constituted a very odd mixture, lacking any sort of solidity or durability. However, the tribes of Morocco did learn from their Saharan masters the habit of obedience to a single political power, and for that the task of their successors was rendered so much easier.

In matters of religion failure, despite appearances, was less absolute. Though Almoravid thought may be quite lacking in richness or originality, though the doctors of law may have been masters only of casuistry, it remains true that the Almoravids caused to disappear numerous heresies which had flourished in the far Maghrib since the eighth century. They gave the country a religious unity which it has consistently maintained ever since.

Taking everything into consideration, it is in the sphere of culture and civilisation that the Almoravid movement left its most lasting traces. This is an odd paradox if we reflect on the Saharan origins of the men of the veil and their small stock of creative imagination. In fact the Almoravids did not create an original culture, but made themselves agents for diffusing Andalusian culture throughout the western Maghrib. The city of Fez, whose name is associated with the memory of the Merinids, probably owes more to Yusuf ibn Tashfin and his son than to the rulers of the thirteenth and fourteenth centuries. The same could be said of Tlemcen and Algiers, not to mention Marrakesh. It is generally agreed that this nascent urban civilisation was deeply indebted to neighbouring Spain. That is not to say that there had been no previous contact between Muslim Spaniards and Moroccans, but

The Berber Empires: the Almoravids and the Almohads

they had never lived in such close and continuous contact as in the time of the Almoravids. Here, it must be added, we lack documents. If we know about the life of Seville at the beginning of the twelfth century,[20] we have no details at all of daily life in Fez or Marrakesh. We are accordingly obliged to note the influence of Andalusia without being able to study the way in which it was brought to bear.

Altogether, brilliant though the Almoravid period was, it was no more than a prelude. It was the Almohads who were to profit from the efforts of their predecessors, which, though far from negligible, were without lasting effect.

11. Ibn Tumart, Mahdi of the Almohads

IBN TUMART

Just at the point of time when 'Ali's repression seemed to be ensuring the triumph of pure and unadulterated Malikism, a movement of reaction against Muslim scholasticism was being organised by the Almohad community which was to destroy the power of the Almoravids. Its triumph was not only that of one sect over another, but also that of Kabyle mountaineers over great Saharan nomads, a belated riposte to the victory of the Sanhaja over the Zenata of the central Maghrib.

It was in fact in the mountainous region of southern Morocco, very probably the Anti-Atlas, that at the end of the eleventh century the Mahdi of the Almohads, Ibn Tumart was born. Igliz or Igilliz, the little village of which his father may have become headman, had been built on the lands of the Hargha tribe, which occupied the southern slopes of the mountain in the direction of the Oued Sous. His family, which belonged to the village aristocracy, was extremely pious. Later it was linked with the Prophet by means of ingenious genealogies through the Idrisids.

Even in childhood Ibn Tumart's religious zeal attracted attention. He was assiduous in attendance at the mosque and displayed a precocious learning which may have earned for him the nickname of 'torch' (*asafū*). There is no doubt that he swiftly acquired authority over his fellow-tribesmen. The young scholar's departure for the east some time between 1105 and 1110, with the aim of completing his studies there, must have been a great occasion for the village and even for the tribe. Marrakesh seems not to have detained him for long, and it is not known whether he made a sojourn in Spain during which he would have been introduced to the writings of the Cordovan theologian Ibn Hazm (died 1064). The points of agreement between the ideas of the Zahiri scholar and the Mahdi are very probably not fortuitous. In particular, both display the same aversion to private opinion arising out of the free exercise of reason (*ra'y*), and rely solely on the sacred book (*kitāb*), tradition (*sunna*) and general consensus (*ijmāʿ*).

Then, without being able to reconstruct the stages of his journey from the documents, we find Ibn Tumart in the East. We do not know why he failed to make the pilgrimage to Mecca, but we do know that he completed his education at Baghdad, and possibly Damascus. There he was initiated into the study of juridical sources (*usūl al-fiqh*) so much despised by the Malikis of the Maghrib, who devoted themselves solely to applied *fiqh* (*furūʿ al-fiqh*).

Though he was acquainted with the doctrines of al-Ghazali, there is no certainty that, as legend later firmly asserted, he met with the master. But he applied himself chiefly to studying the theology of al-Ashʿari (873–935) the founder of orthodox scholasticism (*kalām*). By means of the method of figurative interpretation (*ta'wīl*) he learnt how to resolve the painful discrepancy between belief in the spiritual and immaterial character of divinity and the anthropomorphic language of the Koran. Thus he became a full supporter of Ashʿarite dogmatism, which he rendered supreme in the Maghrib.

Ten years or so after leaving Igliz, Ibn Tumart set off home for Morocco, breaking his journey at Alexandria, which was at that time an active centre of Ashʿarite studies. He may have reached Tunisia by sea, landing at Mahdiya, because later legend pictures him smashing the jars of wine on board, delivering sermons to the crew and converting the most recalcitrant, after having calmed a fearful tempest with his voice. It is probable that the ideas of Ibn Tumart did not at this point constitute a coherent system and that he did not yet conceive of himself as the sinless imam, but rather as a reformer of evil morals. Doubtless he was too confident of his own

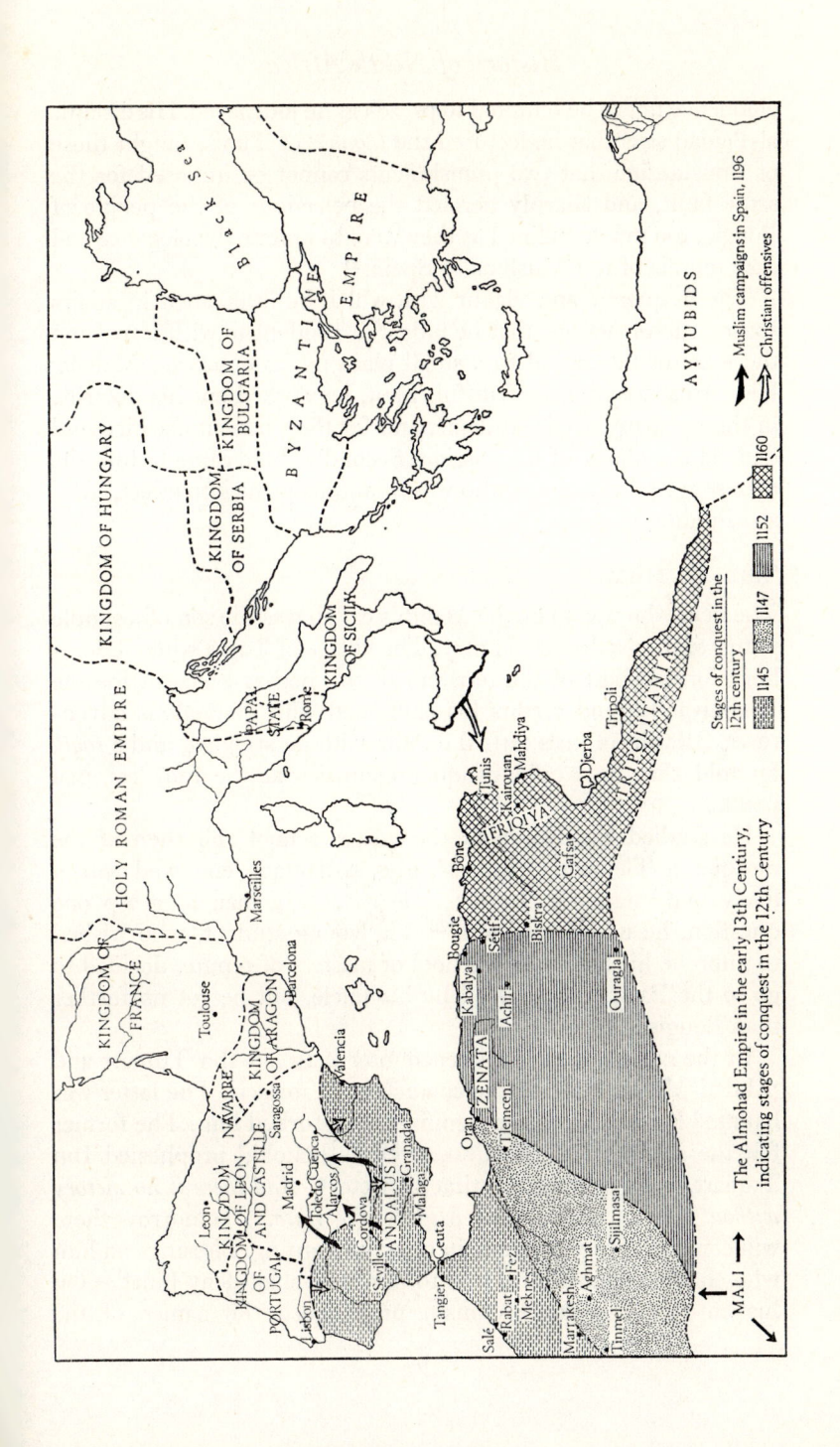

The Almohad Empire in the early 13th Century, indicating stages of conquest in the 12th Century

eloquence not to be tempted to preach as he journeyed. His disciple al-Baidaq says that he lectured the *fuqahā* of Tunis, taught those of Constantine that two punishments cannot be imposed for the same fault, and sharply berated the behaviour of the people of Bougie, too much inclined as they were to imitate the elegance and easy morals of the Muslims of Spain.[21]

The frequency and vigour with which he intervened in affairs roused such reactions that he judged it prudent to withdraw from the Hammadid capital to a small place on its outskirts, Mallala. His retreat was doubly fruitful. First, he worked out his doctrine in the company of his students, and for their benefit clarified and defined the object of his mission. Secondly there came to him the man sent by Providence who was to put his plans into effect, 'Abd al-Mumin.

'ABD AL-MUMIN

The man who was to be the Mahdi's caliph was the son of a simple potter of the Nédroma country. The village of Tagra where he was born formed part of the territory of the Berber Zenata tribe the Koumiya. Legend credits his childhood with marvellous adventures. Swarms of bees settled on him without stinging, and a *faqīh* foretold that he would conquer countries at the four cardinal points.

He studied the Koran at the village school and then at the mosque at Tlemcen. 'He was', says al-Baidaq, 'endowed with a lively understanding. In the time it takes a man to grasp one question, he understood ten.'[22] The young student, who wished to improve his talents in a school of masters of repute, decided to go to the East, accompanied by his uncle, but he got no further than Bougie.

In the course of time the encounter between Ibn Tumart and 'Abd al-Mumin took on the character of a miracle. The latter was haunted by dreams whose significance disturbed him. The former felt the approach of the Chosen One. 'Behold,' prophesied Ibn Tumart, 'now is come the time of victory. *And there is no victory without the aid of Allah the Mighty, the Wise.*[23] Tomorrow there will come near to you a man in quest of learning. Blessings on him who shall recognize him, woe to him who shall deny him!'[24] On his entering, the sinless imam pronounced the names of the

The Berber Empires: the Almoravids and the Almohads

newcomer's father and village and invited him not to seek in the East the learning he could find where he stood.

The account of his conversion, given by the Mahdi's companion, is moving in its simple grandeur.

> When evening fell, the Imam took 'Abd al-Mumin by the hand and they departed. In the middle of the night the Sinless One called to me, "Abu Bakr [al-Baidaq], give me the book in the red box.' I handed it to him and he added, 'Light the lamp for us.' He began to read the book to him who was to be Caliph after him, and as I held the lamp I heard him say, 'The mission on which the life of religion depends will triumph only through 'Abd al-Mumin ibn 'Ali, the torch of the Almohads!' The Caliph-to-be, on hearing these words, began to weep and said, 'O *faqih*, I was in no way qualified to play this part. I am but a man in search of that which can cleanse him of his sins.' 'That which will cleanse you of your sins,' replied the Sinless One, 'is the role you will play in the reform of this world below.' And he gave him the book, saying, 'Happy be the peoples whom you will lead, and woe to them who set themselves against you, from the first to the last.'[25]

THE MAHDI'S DOCTRINE

This account probably brings together a number of discussions which the great influence of Ibn Tumart must have kept to a minimum. However, 'Abd al-Mumin gave up the idea of continuing his journey, and for several months studied day and night under the Mahdi's direction. The Mahdi must by now have formulated his doctrine. In it there can be distinguished from this time a moral science and a theology; to these were to be later added a political doctrine.

The morality with which Ibn Tumart began his reforming activity was characterised by extreme rigour and by a predominant concern to use only the original sources, that is the Koran, and the Prophetic Tradition of Medina. Thus it was that he recommended the segregation of the sexes, abstinence from all fermented liquor and from all blameworthy amusement (music was one such), modest attire for women, *et cetera*. None of this is novel from the doctrinal point of view, but, if we are to believe the account given by al-Baidaq and later chroniclers, the practice of the Maghrib at that time, from Tunis to Marrakesh, was very different. Thus it was a profound moral reform that Ibn Tumart preached, and its results can still be observed in North African society today.

The essential basis of his theology is the affirmation of the oneness of God (*tawhīd*). Hence the name of the doctrine's adepts—*al-muwahhidun* or *Almohads* (those who proclaim the oneness of God). On the other hand God is spirit, and the Koranic texts which involve the Creator's sight or hearing have to be explained by means of a figurative interpretation (*ta'wīl*). These principles necessarily entail condemnation of the anthropomorphists (*mutajassimun*) who interpret literally the Koranic texts just mentioned, as also of the polytheists (*mushrikun*) who attach such importance to God's attributes (His goodness, His generosity, His clemency and so on) that the one Divinity appears to be broken up, as it were, into a number of autonomous powers. Finally the oneness of God carries by the way of corollary His omnipotence, and this in turn entails absolute predestination—'All things created emanate from His predestination and His foreknowledge. . . . Every man awaits that which has been allotted to him.'[26]

There is no great originality in any of this. In any case, Ibn Tumart shunned originality and personal interpretation (*ra'y*). Only the traditional Sources (Koran, Tradition, consensus of the doctors) found favour with him. Here we meet an echo of the tendencies of thought of oriental Islam, particularly of the doctrine of al-Ash'ari who presented traditional ideas under a renovated guise. Indeed, in the *Book of Ibn Tumart*[27] we can read a series of logical and abstract demonstrations which are set forth in the manner of al-Ash'ari.

Ibn Tumart parted company with the original theologians and took on the appearance of an innovator when it came to the diffusion of the doctrine. The oriental theologians, even al-Ghazali, were intellectuals living in their ivory tower with no idea what the people might benefit from their meditations. Ibn Tumart, on the contrary, aimed at propagating his doctrine very widely. To that end he most often used the Berber language, Arabic being far from widespread in the Morocco of those days. Then again he wrote—always in Berber—small pamphlets or treatises of which we have a few samples (see footnote 27). Finally he perfected mnemonic

The Berber Empires: the Almoravids and the Almohads

methods which may appear simple-minded to us, but which certainly took into consideration the human material he had to mould. Thus each man in a group was given by way of name one word of a phrase that had to be learnt. Every day at roll-call each man gave his name in unvarying order, the order of the phrase in question. At the end of a few days, the phrase had been learnt.

The political doctrine, centred on the Shi'a idea of the Mahdi and the sinless Imam, was not to emerge until later, when Ibn Tumart returned to Morocco and there encountered Almoravid authority. It seems that he tried at first to lead the Almoravids back to the right path, but then, seeing them persist in error, he not only denounced that error but also affirmed the condemnation which—according to certain traditions, though these are extremely obscure—the Prophet had pronounced against them. It was only at this point that the idea of the Mahdi was put in the forefront.

Such are the main points of Ibn Tumart's thought so far as it can be reconstructed from the documents currently available. Soon concern for the state was set by Ibn Tumart on the same, if not higher, level as morals and theology. He became the champion of a cause quite as much political as religious. Under his successor 'Abd al-Mumin politics were unequivocally to take precedence.

FOUNDATION OF THE ALMOHAD COMMUNITY

The sojourn at Mallala could not be indefinitely prolonged. Ibn Tumart must, like all mountaineers, have felt the need to return to his natural habitat. There happened to pass by two pilgrims from the Atlas on their way to the East, and he questioned them in their own tongue, for they knew no Arabic. Doubtless their answers revealed to him the muffled discontent the Berbers of the Atlas held against the Almoravids on the plain. 'When evening was come', recounts al-Baidaq, 'the Master said to us, "Make ready to leave for the Maghrib, if it be pleasing to Allah."'[28] And such were the beginnings of Almohad power.

The meagre caravan, some ten souls, marched westward by way of the Ouarsenis, Tlemcen, Oujda, Guercif and Fez. Everywhere Ibn Tumart held himself out as a censor of morals, not as Mahdi. Often he inspired awe and succeeded in making his precepts respected. Sometimes, however, he encountered open resistance, as in a village in the Taza region where he was threatened with a beating if he did not leave immediately. In such cases Ibn Tumart did not persist and went on his way. In urban circles, where the religious were more enlightened, he found support among influential people attracted by his learning and his eloquence. It was probably the protection of a notable at Fez that enabled him to escape retribution after he had sacked the music merchants' shops. Thereafter the Sinless One soon reached Marrakesh by way of Meknès and Salé.

The date A.H. 514 (A.D. 1120–1121) is the one given by the majority of chroniclers for his arrival at Marrakesh. Up to this point the chronology of Ibn Tumart's life is quite uncertain. There are five or six dates of birth, ranging from 1075 to 1097, no reliable information about the date of his departure for the East, the length of his stay there, the date of his return, or the duration of his march across the Maghrib from Mahdiya to Marrakesh. Even the faithful al-Baidaq, valuable though he is in so many respects, seems to take special care to avoid chronological exactitude. It is clear how difficult it is to discriminate between pious legend and history.

At Marrakesh Ibn Tumart gave a stirring display of his character as a reformer of morals. He is said to have insulted the amir's own sister, who used to go out without a veil, and to have censured the amir for wearing one. All the historians assure us that he entered into a controversy with the Maliki doctors which nearly resulted in his being imprisoned.

It appears to be well established that he met the Almoravid ruler 'Ali ibn Yusuf and caused that pious man the gravest embarrassment. In one respect 'Ali saw Ibn Tumart only too clearly as one who could disturb the peace, who could prove dangerous, and who had been able to contrive secret understandings even within the Almoravid court. Yet in another respect he could not refrain from being struck by his theological learning and his austere virtue. Moreover, he felt himself under the domination of the powerful, almost magnetic, personality of this strange wanderer. Thus all the influence of his counsellors was needed to make him decide on severe action. But Ibn Tumart was warned in time.

Once more, the unending peregrination had to be resumed. The caravan took to the mountains, always pursued by the hostility of the amir's servants. Thus the Mahdi had to leave Aghmat after a short stay, but finally he was able to halt at the village of his birth

The Berber Empires: the Almoravids and the Almohads

and, perhaps in 1121 or 1122, undertake his work of propagation among the tribes.

For three years he prayed and preached. But the political leader in him made no concession to the theologian. Shortly afterwards the representatives of several tribes acknowledged him as imam and swore not to desert him in holy war against the Almoravids. When he had received their oath, he proclaimed himself the Mahdi, the Imam known and infallible, sent by God to destroy error and bring about the triumph of the true faith. To his immediate disciples he gave the name of *tulba* because under him they studied the true learning. The faithful, whose spiritual leader he was, received the title of *Almohads* or unitarians.

In 1125, to more effectively exert his influence over the mountaineers and to prepare for his offensive against the Almoravids, he established himself in a place situated at the entry to a small plain, as fertile as an oasis, in the upper valley of the Oued Nfis. This place, Tinmel, had the double advantage of being in the heart of the Masmouda tribes and of affording an excellent strategic position.

ORGANISATION OF THE COMMUNITY

It was at Tinmel that Ibn Tumart brought into being and organised his community, following the pattern of Muhammad and the group of his first companions at Medina. Like the Prophet, he acted as spiritual director, judge and commander-in-chief; but he also acted as a Berber chief well acquainted with his people, their state of mind and their social and political habits.

Indeed, unlike Yusuf ibn Tashfin, who was able to find support in the ready-made confederation of the Almoravid tribes, Ibn Tumart had to manage as best he could with a patchwork of tribes, all extremely jealous of their independence and easily offended, whose social structure and political tendencies must have very closely resembled those described by Montagne in his book *Les Berbères et le Makhzen dans le sud du Maroc*.[29] How was he to bring these disparate elements to lead a common political life and to shape them into a force coherent enough to shake the power of the Almoravids?

To solve this problem, Ibn Tumart devised a social organisation about which our information is poor and which, probably for that reason, appears extremely complicated. We can distinguish the following components:

1 The Mahdi's 'household' (*ahl al-dār*), a score of men including the three brothers of Ibn Tumart, who constituted his general staff and were responsible to him exclusively.

2 Two 'councils', that of the Ten and that of the Fifty, obviously suggested by the assemblies of notables which play so large a part in the 'Berber republics'. The former was composed of Ibn Tumart's ten companions who were the first to recognise him as Mahdi. The various lists that have come down to us reveal some discrepancies. Nevertheless, certain names are always to be found in them—'Abd al-Mumin, Abu Hafs, 'Umar al-Hintati (one of the first notables from the mountains who joined after the flight from Marrakesh), and 'Abd Allah ibn al-Bashir al-Wansharisi, one of the first disciples, who was recruited in the central Maghrib. These ten personages formed a kind of privy council consulted by the Mahdi on all matters of importance.

The council of the Fifty comprised representatives in varying numbers of the principal mountain tribes and took part in affairs much less often than did the Ten. It was a kind of consultative assembly.

3 At least for purposes of military reviews, and probably also of battle-order, the tribes were ranged in an order of precedence worked out in great detail. The Hargha tribe, which was the Mahdi's own, took the lead. Certain important persons, like 'Abd al-Mumin, were attached to the Hargha probably by a tie of adoption. The people of Tinmel came next, followed by the other mountain tribes. The *'abīd*, probably black slaves, brought up the rear.

4 Within each of these groupings there existed another hierarchy, based not on ethnic connections, but on the functions exercised by each individual. In the first place was the *muhtasib*, whose exact role is unknown, but who certainly acted as group-leader. Next came the *mizwar*, one for the original Almohads and one for those who had joined later. Then the 'minters' (*sakākīn*), who were responsible for minting coinage and perhaps also for collecting taxes. After them the regular army (*jund*), the muezzins, the combatants (probably reserve troops), the *hafidh* and the men of the

The Berber Empires: the Almoravids and the Almohads

hizb (in charge of worship) and finally the archers, freedmen or slaves.

All this hierarchic society was subject to strict rules and kept firmly in hand by the Mahdi. Regular attendance at spiritual exercises was compulsory. Neglect of religion might entail flogging, even death. However, the aim of the sermons of the Sinless One was to force into the minds of the Berbers a Muslim system of law which often ran contrary to their own tradition (*qānūn*), and in this propagandising the statesmen played as large a part as did the theologian. Anyone not entirely devoted to the cause deserved the fate of the infidels. Thus it was that on the 'day of sorting' he engaged in a radical purge of suspect elements by having them all executed, and did away in the same fashion with a whole tribe on which he could not rely. By these forceful actions he assured his authority over the mountaineers.

We may suppose that he also resorted to other methods for bringing his supporters into subjection. The *Rawd al-Qirtas* and Ibn al-Athir, both unfavourable to the Almohads, give us a picture of Ibn Tumart and 'Abd al-Mumin playing on the credulity of the people by crude wizardry.[30] The facts are probably twisted and exaggerated in the interest of their case, but they are not necessarily false. We know from other sources that Ibn Tumart, like many other southern Berbers, was versed in the sciences of divination, and magical practices certainly had a prominent place in the daily life of the Chleuhs, as they still do today.

However, Ibn Tumart succeeded in organising a regular state in the Atlas, with revenues drawn from taxation and fanatical troops ready for ruthless war against the Almoravids. The first attempt of the Saharans against the Almohads, in 1122, had ended in a serious defeat. Out of fear for an incursion by the mountaineers, the Almoravids were reduced to fortifying Marrakesh and Aghmat. It was as well they did, for in 1128 after an expedition against Tinmel, they were thrown back into their capital and besieged for forty days, but the affair finished fortunately for them, and they crushed the Almohad army in a sortie. On hearing the news, the Mahdi showed great coolness. When he learnt that 'Abd al-Mumin was alive, he ordered al-Baidaq, 'Go back to him and tell him, "Nothing is lost! Do not be disturbed!"'[31]

Four months later Ibn Tumart, feeling very unwell, let it be known that he desired to make a long retreat as a reason for withdrawing into his house. In another four months he was dead (1127–1128 or December 1129). In order to prevent the Almohads so soon after a defeat from rejecting 'Abd al-Mumin, who was after all still a foreigner, the Mahdi's death was long concealed—for more than two years, Ibn Khaldun assures us.[32] Ibn Tumart's entourage scrupulously respected his orders. Even Abu Hafs 'Umar, leader of one of the most powerful groups of the Masmouda, whose joining the cause at the outset had contributed largely to its success, did not rise up against the designated successor. In 1129–1130, after the adherence of the Ten, followed by that of the Fifty, he even conducted an active campaign of propaganda among the Almohads, who consented to swear the oath between his hands [i.e. at his feet].

III. The Almohad Empire

THE CONQUEST OF MOROCCO

'Abd al-Mumin took the title of Caliph of Ibn Tumart, in imitation of Abu Bakr, who had been the Caliph of Muhammad. As soon, apparently, as he acceded to power he assumed, or allowed his followers to give him, the title of Prince of the Faithful (*Amir al-Muminin*). He continued the organisation instituted by the Mahdi and took counsel with the assemblies. However, he never enjoyed the same prestige with the Masmouda as the Sinless One had held. He even had to put down plots and later to surround himself with a guard recruited from among members of his own tribe.

At first he acted on the unchanging mountaineer tactics prescribed by the Mahdi to his lieutenants, 'Do not go down into the plain, but let the enemy climb up to you.'[33] Then he tried swift raids which disclosed the enemy's weak points. Finally he determined to venture on an expedition.

First he occupied the southern provinces of Morocco, and made his way slowly northward without ever leaving the mountainous regions—for the Almoravid army was still formidable—as far as the Ouergha valley and the Rif, which surrendered to him. He

The Berber Empires: the Almoravids and the Almohads

abandoned the idea of taking Ceuta and then, aided by tribal quarrels, continued his march to the north-east. The new Almoravid ruler, Tashfin ibn 'Ali, tried to oppose him with his contingents, Reverter's Christian militia, a few Zenata allies and reinforcements sent by the Hammadids. But Reverter perished in an encounter in 1144–1145, and the Almohads, it is said, had the pleasure of crucifying his corpse. With his death the Almoravid troops lacked too greatly in cohesion and leadership to resist the disciplined ardour of the unitarian troops of 'Abd al-Mumin and his own clear will. After a defeat near Tlemcen on 22 February 1145 (?) Tashfin was pushed back into the Oran plain; he failed to escape by sea and in the course of a night march he fell with his horse from the top of a cliff. The Almohads cut off the head of the corpse, embalmed it and sent it to Tinmel. With the last true Almoravid sovereign, the brief hegemony of the Saharans came to an end, struck down by the Kabyles of the Atlas. Once again the relentless warfare between nomads and settled folk had caused one empire to crumble and was clearing the way for the establishment of a new one.

The death of Tashfin did not mean the end of the war, even in western Barbary. His son, only a youth, had been installed in power at Marrakesh. The caliph left the task of investing Tlemcen to one of his lieutenants. He himself attacked Fez, which he took after a siege of nine months, and then Marrakesh, which was taken and the population left to be massacred in 1146.

After the Almohad victory the young Almoravid ruler sought 'Abd al-Mumin to spare him. 'Abd al-Mumin was about to do this when one of his companions cried, 'Hither, come hither, O Almohads. See how 'Abd al-Mumin sets himself against us! He desires to raise up lions' whelps to oppose us!' Meanwhile one of the Almoravid amirs spat in the young prince's face and reproached him with the words, 'Are you entreating your father or someone able to have pity on you? Be brave, like a man!'[34] And after that sharp awakening of pride the Almoravid line was extinguished.

The capture of Marrakesh did not, however, spell triumph for 'Abd al-Mumin. Serious revolts at once broke out, first in the Sous and then on the Atlantic coast where the remnants of the Berghwata took up arms and sowed revolt among the neighbouring Dokkala. Fortunately for the Almohads these risings were neither concerted nor even simultaneous. By the end of the year 1148 Morocco had been wholly brought under the new authority.

THE ALMOHADS IN SPAIN

Even before the capture of Marrakesh the Almohads had been summoned to Spain by those who had risen against the Almoravids. Accordingly they had no great difficulty in establishing themselves in the western part of Andalusia, though not in accordance with any preconceived plan. Even if it is assumed as likely that 'Abd al-Mumin desired to supplant the Almoravids in Spain as in the Maghrib, he was too sensible to attempt both campaigns at the same time. He limited himself therefore to answering the summons addressed to him by dispatching troops under the orders of two brothers of Ibn Tumart. These behaved so high-handedly that the Almohads quickly roused everyone against them and had to evacuate part of their positions. Nothing short of the reckless offensive waged against Muslim territory by Alphonso VIII of Castile could have brought about a fresh appeal to the Almohads for help. Time was at a premium; the Christian king was already besieging Cordova. In 1150, following the Almohad intervention, 'Abd al-Mumin received a delegation of notables from western Andalusia who had come to acknowledge him as sovereign. But nothing more than a vague and limited protectorate was yet involved.

DESTRUCTION OF THE HAMMADID KINGDOM

The Almohads' first campaign beyond the Moulouya had carried them as far as Tlemcen and Oran. Seven years later, a fresh expedition resulted in the destruction of the Hammadid kingdom. Since the removal of Sultan al-Mansur in 1090 from Qal'a to Bougie—founded by his predecessor al-Nasir in 1062–1063—the new capital had become one of the principal cities of Barbary.

> Ships touch there, [wrote al-Idrisi at the time of the Almohad triumph] caravans come thither, and it is a repository of merchandise. The inhabitants are rich and more skilled in various arts and crafts than men generally are elsewhere, so that commerce is in a flourishing state. The merchants of this city do business with those of West Africa as well as with those of the

The Berber Empires: the Almoravids and the Almohads

Sahara and the East. Much merchandise of every kind is warehoused. Around the city are cultivated plains which yield wheat, barley and fruit in abundance. Great vessels are built there, ships and galleys, for the surrounding mountains are heavily wooded and produce resin and tar of excellent quality . . . The inhabitants engage in exploiting iron mines which yield very good ore. In a word, the city is a hive of industry.[35]

Bougie was also prominent as an intellectual capital. An historian who was a native of the city was able to draw up the biographies of 104 local celebrities in law, medicine, poetry and religion.[36]

The freedom of behaviour of the people of Bougie was what had shocked Ibn Tumart. They wore special tunics, dressed like women, loved music and drank wine. Men and women celebrated the end of Ramadan by mingling on the esplanade. Neither the Mahdi's powerful influence nor his cudgellings had availed to cure them of their immoral ways.

Despite the progress of the Hilalians, the Hammadid kingdom had still experienced great prosperity under al-Mansur. The sultan had reinforced his Sanhaja and Zenata troops with Arab mercenaries for the fight against the Almoravids, and had brought their eastward advance to a halt by taking Tlemcen in 1102–1103. He had also succeeded in recovering Bône and Constantine from the Zirids and in subduing Berber revolts.

After him Hammadid power continuously declined. However, al-ʿAziz (1104–1121) had succeeded in occupying Djerba and in pushing back the Arabs from the Hodna. But his son Yahya (1122–1152), who thought of nothing but hunting and women, was unable to prevent the Genoese from attacking Bougie, and he was even less capable of halting the Almohad invasion.

After provisionally settling the situation in Spain, ʿAbd al-Mumin, whose forces had increased, decided to strike a major blow in the central Maghrib. He made his way, by forced marches and in the utmost secrecy, to Bougie. In 1151, without striking a blow his advance-guard entered Algiers and Bougie, whence Yahya had fled, and subsequently his son captured and sacked Qalʿa.

RESISTANCE OF THE HILALIANS

The Arabs understood the danger. They found themselves faced with Kabyles powerfully organised and capable of contending with them for the advantages they had been able to wrest from the weakness of governments. The shaikhs of Ifriqiya, abandoning their rivalries for a time, decided to unite with the intention of using their own resources to push the enemy back to the far west. In 1152 they concentrated near Béja and made their way in great disorder towards Bougie. 'Abd al-Mumin, on his way back to Morocco, turned about in the Mitidja and led the enemy after him as far as Sétif. The Hilalians felt that they were risking everything. They had brought with them their wives and children, who were to act as the stakes of battle. In order not to be tempted to retire, they had even hobbled their camels. After four days of carnage, Almohad discipline gained the upper hand and the Arabs fled as far as Tébessa, harassed all the way. 'Abd al-Mumin made no reprisals. He divided the booty among his companions, but he restored their families to the vanquished, and he received their shaikhs with honour at Marrakesh.

FROM ALMOHADS TO MUMINIDS

As far as we can judge from a very uncertain chronology, it was at this point that 'Abd al-Mumin determined to make use of the Almohad movement to the benefit of his own family. Whether the initiative came from him, or from certain Almohad personalities, or again from Arab chiefs who had recently submitted, we do not know. What is certain is that 'Abd al-Mumin agreed without much resistance to designate as his successor his son Abu 'Abd Allah Muhammad in place of Shaikh Abu Hafs 'Umar who had originally been designated. A year later, in 1156, he distributed among his other sons the governorships of the principal provinces of the empire,[37] however, each of them had at his side an Almohad shaikh responsible for his training. The official distinction made between the *sayyid*—descendants of 'Abd al-Mumin—and the *shaikhs*—descendants of the other great Almohad families—dates from this period.

It is probable that the institutions devised by the Mahdi continued without noticeable change, but in practice they were from that time emptied of their content. The original formula set out by Ibn Tumart, that sort of federative and aristocratic republic which appeared to be acceptable to the Berbers, gave way to a family

The Berber Empires: the Almoravids and the Almohads

monarchy for which those same Berbers had a strong distaste. Our only clue to the alterations made by 'Abd al-Mumin in the Mahdi's system is to be found in the anonymous chronicle *al-Hulal al-mawshiyya*,[38] which relates to the class of *hafidh*. Under 'Abd al-Mumin these were no longer reciters of the Koran. The author describes them as learning riding, swimming and archery and as receiving a general education of a high standard. A military training school is what inevitably comes to mind.

His contemporaries fully understood the implications of the measures taken by 'Abd al-Mumin. If Abu Hafs 'Umar and the majority of the Almohad shaikhs resigned themselves more or less willingly, a few took part in open revolt, notably two of the Mahdi's brothers, 'Abd al-'Aziz and 'Isa. They fled from Fez, where they were residing under surveillance, and attempted to gain control of Marrakesh.[39] But 'Abd al-Mumin was a man of energy and he succeeded in imposing the new order.

THE STATE OF EASTERN AND CENTRAL BARBARY: CHRISTIANS AND HILALIANS

The Sétif disaster did not bring the Hilalian invasion to an end. The caliph contented himself with establishing a governor at Bougie and returned to Morocco. Though the Zenata bloc in the central Maghrib was still scarcely penetrated, Tripolitania and Ifriqiya had already suffered irreparable disasters. In Tripolitania the invaders had Arabised a section of the Berbers, but were suffering from raids by the elusive camel-riding tribes. Little was left of agriculture around the towns or, more important, of commerce. The ports were in danger and Barqa was partly abandoned. The only towns to survive were fortified ones like Lebda, or those allied by treaty with the nomads, such as Awjala (south of Barqa) which the Arabs kept in existence for their own trade. From Tripoli to the Djérid the country was ruined, but the ports of the eastern coast of Ifriqiya had put up a better defence. Gabès, which had fallen to the Hilalian Beni Jami' in 1099, had assimilated its new masters. These, until the Norman conquest, acted like settled rulers, concerned to ensure and improve the economic prosperity of their possessions. Date cultivation continued to flourish there and local trade was prosperous. The enclosed towns of the coast had saved themselves from the Arab danger only to fall into the hands of the Christians. Over the period 1118-1127 the Norman count of Sicily, Roger II, who was already in possession of Messina, had been engaged in unsuccessful attempts to gain a footing on the coast of Ifriqiya with the intention of securing control of Mediterranean trade. He had even tried to organise an African crusade with the assistance of the count of Barcelona and the city of Savona, but had been temporarily diverted from his objective by the conquest of the other Norman states of southern Italy and a papal quarrel. When he had secured the title of King from the pope in 1130, he once more took up the project he had in mind. In this he had the good fortune to be able to entrust command of the expeditions to the Grand Amir (Admiral) George of Antioch, who, like his brother, had left the service of the Zirid prince of Mahdiya to place at the disposal of Roger II his profound knowledge of Arabic and the African coast. Roger took advantage of the unsettled situation in Ifriqiya to impose his suzerainty on Mahdiya and to gain possession of Djerba in 1134. From there in 1143 his fleet struck at Djidjelli, and in 1146 the small ports between Cherchel and Ténès, the Kerkenna islands and Tripoli. With the capture of Tripoli he decided to organise his occupation on a permanent footing by installing a garrison in each port. In the two following years he took Gabès, Mahdiya, Sfax and Sousse and put an end to the power of the Zirids. His territory at this point extended from Tripoli to Tunis. Sfax continued to live by fishing and what was left of its olive groves, and Sousse by commerce and textiles. The king of the Two Sicilies did not try to conquer Ifriqiya and left the natives of the occupied regions to their own administration and customs, and he avoided entering into their religious quarrels.

While the coastal towns conserved a reflection of their former splendour, Kairouan was dying. The townsfolk burdened by the nomads' taxation, were deserting the city. Mançouriya and Raqqada were no more than ruins. The Arabs were laying waste the central plains and western Ifriqiya, and were in occupation of Carthage and the rich plain of Béja. Tunis, despite its internal dissensions and its changes of government, had been able to establish trade relations with the powerful neighbouring tribes and to increase its prosperity. The wheat supply of the Djérid was at the mercy of the nomads; they had imposed their patronage on

The Berber Empires: the Almoravids and the Almohads

Baghaï and taken possession of the lands of the Zab, from which they had expelled the Berber owners. It was impossible to move outside the towns without risk. But the invasion did not extend beyond the Hodna, the Babors and Cap Bougaroun.

The towns of Numidia were less imperilled than those of Ifriqiya. Constantine had even concluded a profitable agreement with the nomads, but the insecurity of the country had increased.

From Tripolitania to the Hodna there was no uniform political system. Relations between Berber and Arab varied with the respective strength of the adversaries. The nomads were complete masters of the Béja plain, where the former owners had been reduced to servitude. They had imposed on the inhabitants of Badis (at the foot of the Aurès) and of Baghaï a burdensome and precarious domination, which did, however, permit trade and agriculture to carry on, although with great difficulty. In the stronghold towns north of Qal'a, there were truces by which the families of murdered parties were guaranteed the price of the blood shed by the murderer's people, but these never took effect when Arabs were to blame. Towns needed to enjoy the strong position of a Tunis or a Constantine if they were to incorporate the nomads within the organisation of their trade and cultivation of their crops without serious risk.

OCCUPATION OF IFRIQIYA

The Hilalians had not remained indifferent to the Christian invasion, for which they were partly responsible. No doubt, their form of Islam might appear to be lacking in zeal in comparison with that of the Almoravids or Almohads, but contact with the infidel so far aroused it as to make them refuse the help of Roger II against the Almohad invasion of 1151. Later they endeavoured to support revolts which had been stirred up in Christian territory as a result of an order given by the officers to preach against the Almohads; but their zeal did not carry them to the point of resisting the Normans' subsidies. Whether it was that the Almohads' plans had their approval, or that they feared a fresh disaster like that of Sétif, they did not oppose the expedition which 'Abd al-Mumin attempted in Ifriqiya. Indeed, according to one Arab historian, 'their principal chiefs joined his retinue'.

If we are to believe Ibn al-Athir, the conquest of Ifriqiya had been planned long beforehand.[40] Indeed, the capture of Mahdiya by the Normans dates from 1156. The Muslim inhabitants of the former Zirid capital, having taken refuge in the neighbouring centre of Zawila, promptly sent a deputation to 'Abd al-Mumin begging him to help them return to their own city. He took their request into consideration, but he needed more than two years to complete preparations for the expedition, which he did not want to fail. In 1159 he left Marrakesh with a powerful army, while his fleet sailed eastward. He had had mounds of grain placed at intervals along his route to supply his army. The people were greatly impressed by the discipline of the Almohad forces. Their arrival in Ifriqiya quickly put an end to the prevailing anarchy. 'Abd al-Mumin subdued the petty dynasties that had sprung up after the destruction of the Zirid empire, entered Tunis and Sousse and then laid siege to Mahdiya. It took several months of close blockade, and the defeat of a relieving fleet from Sicily, to bring the city to agree, on 22 January 1160, to an honourable surrender. Its fall marked the end of Norman rule in Africa. The king of Sicily made no attempt at counter-action. At Palermo it was thought, and wisely, that it would be imprudent to become involved in a war against the Almohad power at a time when the kingdom needed to preserve all its forces, whole and entire, against the inevitable conflict with the emperor Barbarossa, who was to put the very existence of the kingdom in danger.

'Abd al-Mumin's conquest of Ifriqiya marks a most important date in the history of the Maghrib. It was the first occasion for a long time, perhaps indeed the very first, that this enormous country had known political unity under a leader sprung from its own soil. And this unification, which had already been outlined by the Fatimids and their Kotama, was the work of settled mountaineers. But at the very moment when he had just completed this great work, 'Abd al-Mumin made a decision that was to contribute to its downfall. Aware as he was of the power of the nomadic Arabs in Ifriqiya, he wished to break it while at the same time seeking contingents from them for the operations in Spain which he was considering. Perhaps too he did not regret having at his command men of his own who would enable him, in case of need, to consolidate his new dynasty. Accordingly, he forcibly moved several Arab tribes to the far Maghrib and settled them in the

The Berber Empires: the Almoravids and the Almohads

Atlantic plains which had been depopulated by the massacre of the Berghwata and Dokkala, who had revolted twelve years previously. Thus, at the very moment when he had ensured the triumph of the settled Berbers, he brought the whole western part of the Maghrib into the domain of Arab nomads who were to introduce into it their own way of life and their habits of anarchy.

DISTURBANCES IN SPAIN. IBN MARDANISH

The news from Spain brought the stay of the Almohad army in Ifriqiya to an end.

The Almohad protectorate over the western part of Andalusia had probably been consolidated, but all the rest of Andalusia and the Levant were beyond the control of 'Abd al-Mumin and formed an independent state, at the head of which there had been, for an uncertain period, a Spaniard of Christian origin, Ibn Mardanish (Martinez?). The only thing accurately known is that as early as 1153 'Abd al-Mumin had invited him to make his submission.[41] Far from complying, he had set himself up as the Almohads' enemy, had negotiated with neighbouring Christian rulers and had even taken advantage of the caliph's campaign in Ifriqiya to extend his possessions towards the west and to threaten Cordova. Such an attitude 'Abd al-Mumin, at the height of his power, could not tolerate. Accordingly, in 1161 he crossed the Straits in person for the first time and spent two months at Gibraltar in order to issue his orders on the spot.

The Almohads succeeded with some difficulty in pushing Ibn Mardanish back towards the east and in 1162 recovered Granada, which he had taken by surprise, but they failed to crush him. 'Abd al-Mumin had no wish to rest on this partial victory. With the assistance of his son Abu Ya'qub Yusuf, whom he had recently acknowledged as his heir in place of Muhammad, who had been deemed unworthy of the succession, he established himself early in 1163 in the fortress of Ribat al-Fath (Rabat), which he had had built as early as 1150. Here he assembled numerous troops and a considerable fleet,[42] which were certainly destined for Spain. But death interrupted his plans; he died at Ribat al-Fath in May 1163.

THE GOVERNMENT OF THE CALIPH

'Abd al-Mumin was not content to be a conqueror. He was anxious to organise his conquests. The *Qirtas* tells us that in 1159 he began an immense geographical survey from Cyrenaica to the Atlantic. 'From this area one-third was deducted for mountains, rivers, salt lakes, roads and deserts. The remaining two-thirds were made subject to the land tax (*kharāj*) and the amount to be paid by each tribe in grain and money was fixed. This was the first time this was done in Barbary.'[43]

This survey, an innovation introduced by a chief of state concerned to make certain of his fiscal resources, derived its legality from the caliph's religious ideas. In his eyes the Almohad community alone was orthodox. All non-Almohad Muslims, and even Almohads suspected of being unzealous, were classified as unbelievers. The community was entitled to seize their property, which became *hubus* on which the occupiers paid *kharāj*. The state collected a large part of the *kharāj* for its own benefit, and this, together with the Koranic taxes, sufficed to supply the treasury.

Not all the tribes, however, were liable to the *kharāj*. 'Abd al-Mumin was not content to enlist the nomads in the armies of Spain, but also used them for maintaining order in Barbary. Thus Hilalians occupied lands belonging to the community in Morocco. A part of the country between Mina and the Moulouya was allotted to the Zenata Beni 'Abd al-Wad. Another tribe camped in the Bougie region. These *makhzan* tribes were not merely exempt from the *kharāj* but enforced its payment on settled tribes. They owned slaves to work their lands and could pasture their flocks freely. In return they owed the caliph military service and formed the *jaish* [army] of the Almohads.

ABU YA'QUB YUSUF

However great his prestige, 'Abd al-Mumin had to reckon with the influence and susceptibilities of the shaikhs to assure the succession. He had already had to revoke for the benefit of Abu Ya'qub Yusuf the decision taken in favour of another of his sons.

The chroniclers have left us several contradictory versions of Abu Ya'qub's accession to power. Ibn Khaldun himself gives two different accounts of the event.[44] According to some the new sovereign was received without resistance.[45] According to others he found himself the object of more or less open opposition on the part of Abu Hafs 'Umar and several Almohad shaikhs and was not

The Berber Empires: the Almoravids and the Almohads

able to assume the title of Caliph until five years after his father's death, following his victory over the revolting Ghomara. The *Almohad Official Letters*[46] give much support to this second version.

'Abd al-Mumin had proven himself as a great ruler, an active conqueror, an administrator with new and resolute ideas and an artist with unfailing taste. He left to his son a vast empire comprising the whole of the Maghrib and the greater part of Muslim Spain. Abu Ya'qub (1163–1184) did not let power fall into the hands of women. Acting upon his father's advice, he turned for help to the untouched reserve constituted by the Arab tribes. It was with contingents from them that in 1170 he resumed the war with Ibn Mardanish, who, supported by the Christian kings of Aragon, Castile and Barcelona was beginning to renew his incursions into Almohad territory. In 1172 family treachery, to which Ibn Mardanish fell victim, and his death during the siege of Murcia, facilitated the triumph of Abu Ya'qub. The rebel's sons entered the caliph's service and all Muslim Spain acknowledged Almohad authority.

REBELLIONS IN THE MAGHRIB

Not only in Spain did Abu Ya'qub find immediate opportunity to demonstrate his energy, but in the Maghrib as well. Indeed, immediately after 'Abd al-Mumin's death the Ghomara in the north of Morocco revolted, drawing in their wake their neighbours the Sanhaja. Abu Hafs 'Umar did not succeed in putting down the rebellion, which on the contrary spread from the Mediterranean coast to the Ouergha. Finally Abu Ya'qub assumed control of operations and brought the mountaineers under control in 1167.[47]

Scarcely had he finished in that quarter when he had to turn his attention to the other extremity of the Maghrib. The inhabitants of Gafsa, oppressed by their Almohad masters, had just revolted and called in as their leader a descendant of the dynasty which had ruled in the town until the Almohad conquest. Here again the measures taken were too weak at the outset. Moreover the rebels were encouraged by an adventurer of Armenian origin, Qaraqush, who had been established in Tripolitania since 1172 and undoubtedly desired to gain possession of Ifriqiya. The revolt was put down only after Abu Ya'qub had laid siege to Gafsa and taken it, in 1180. The caliph transported a certain number of families from the insurgent Arab tribe, the Riyah, to Morocco, but his action was of no avail; he left eastern Barbary embittered by famine, disturbed by brigandage and ready to welcome leaders preaching rebellion.

THE HOLY WAR IN SPAIN

Shortly after the defeat of Ibn Mardanish, Abu Ya'qub had concluded a truce of seven-years with the Christians. It was observed more or less for a few years and was then broken by the Christians, whose champion was now Alphonso IX of Leon. Abu Ya'qub, committed in Ifriqiya, could not at first react. It was not until 1184 that he organised an expedition against the town of Santarem, and there he met his death in combat at the age of 46. His 24-year-old son Abu Yusuf Ya'qub, later surnamed al-Mansur, succeeded him without difficulty.

THE INSURRECTION OF THE BENI GHANIYA

In the eastern and central Maghrib, ruined by the Bedouin invasions and gradually slipping further away from the Almohad empire, a new leaven of dissolution was contributed by the amazing adventure of two mercenary leaders from Majorca. The Almoravid Beni Ghaniya had not been satisfied merely with carving out a principality in the Balearics with the object of holding Mediterranean commerce to ransom. They were well aware of the insurrections in Ifriqiya, the discontent of the inhabitants of the former Hammadid capital and the weakness of the Almohad garrisons. Without warning 'Ali ibn Ghaniya landed 4,000 wearers of the *litham* near Bougie and occupied the city on 13 November 1184 without striking a blow. He had no trouble in rallying to his cause the dispossessed Hammadid princes and above all the Hilalian tribes. Owing to Arab help he quickly captured Algiers, Miliana, and Qal'a of the Beni Hammad, and then laid siege to Constantine. The new caliph, after restoring the situation in Spain, was obliged to put forth a strenuous effort in order to recover his towns, relieve Constantine and throw 'Ali and his brother Yahya back towards the Djérid. The chance effect of defeat was to bring the Beni Ghaniya into the region most favourable to their plans. There they came on tribes hostile to Almohad rule and—owing to the support of the Beni Sulaim, a large nomadic tribe who had not yet penetrated into the Maghrib—they were able to bring

The Berber Empires: the Almoravids and the Almohads

about a junction with the Turcoman soldiers of Qaraqush, who were already masters of the Fezzan and Tripolitania.

'Ali and Qaraqush, invested by the Abbasid caliph with special powers, occupied Ifriqiya except for Tunis and Mahdiya. Al-Mansur succeeded, with a small well-disciplined army, in defeating them near Gabès and in taking Gafsa. He chastised the town harshly for its 'adultery' with the Almoravids, and then transported the families of three Arab tribes to Morocco *en masse*. It was a fleeting triumph. The remote location of Ifriqiya made it impossible for the masters of the far Maghrib to count on its loyalty. Yahya, who succeeded his brother 'Ali, reappeared in the Djérid, and with the help of the Sulaim rid himself of the Turcomans of Qaraqush, who, as allies, were excessive in their demands. He took Mahdiya, where an Almohad amir had made himself independent, and fortified Gabès, which he made his capital. He occupied Béja, Biskra, Kairouan and Bône, and finally took Tunis in 1203. Owing to an army in which Arab contingents, Hilalian or Sulaimid, predominated, he had succeeded in forming an Almoravid empire out of central Barbary extending from Bône to the Djebel Nefousa and running southward as far as Biskra.

ALARCOS

Al-Mansur had been content with a brief campaign in Ifriqiya; it was Morocco and above all Spain that held his attention. At the time of his accession he had found a difficult situation in Spain. The king of Castile, Alphonso VII, had succeeded with the help of the king of Aragon in taking Cuenca from the Almohads, while the king of Leon was penetrating into Estremadura. These successes led to a general offensive against the Muslims. The archbishop of Toledo, as much a general as a dignitary of the church, led the knights of Alcantara, whose order had just been founded, against the districts of Cordova and Jaen. The reign of Abu Ya'qub finished with the disaster of Santarem. The caliph al-Mansur limited himself to hurriedly restoring the situation, and then after his campaign in Ifriqiya made careful preparation for revenge. Alphonso tried to parry the danger by asking the Cortes for subsidies for the next campaign and by seeking the help of Leon and Navarre, but he did not receive the help he was counting on and was not even able to employ the full military resources of

Castile. However, he did not hesitate to launch his improvised army of ill-disciplined troops against the Almohad forces, which inflicted a severe defeat on him at Alarcos (west of the present site of Ciudad Real) on 18 July 1196. Al-Mansur was able to dispatch expeditions against Toledo, Madrid, Alcala and Cuenca.

THE ALMOHAD EMPIRE UNDER AL-MANSUR

The majority of Arab chroniclers depict the reign of Ya'qub al-Mansur as the most brilliant period of the Almohad empire. As recently as 1946 a Moroccan historian, Mohammed er-Rachid Mouline, devoted a study in Arabic to *The Epoch of al-Mansur the Almohad*[48]

Indeed, apart from the revolt of the Beni Ghaniya—and that was quickly contained, temporarily at least—the reign of al-Mansur was particularly untroubled. There was no tribal revolt, even when the Almoravids were trying to re-establish their power, there were hardly any family difficulties, and there was no reaction on the part of the Almohad shaikhs, who seemed to accept Muminid primacy as a *fait accompli*. Peace reigned. It was the time when a woman could 'go from Barqa to the Oued Noun without being molested or even spoken to'.

It was also the period when the growth of public buildings begun under 'Abd al-Mumin was at its height. Great mosques were built or finished. A new town of great proportions arose all around the fortress of Ribat al-Fath. Public works were executed at Marrakesh —a water supply, the building of a hospital, and roads. Finally, the prince, a man of great culture and attracted by intellectual life, had gathered round him a court of poets, scholars and philosophers, at which Averroes made his appearance before falling into disgrace for a time.

At the very moment of its flowering the Almohad empire was undergoing far-reaching changes which were to hasten its downfall. Our information on the point is no more than fragmentary and not always exact, and we are driven to conjecture rather than certainty. However, under Ya'qub al-Mansur the Almohad doctrine, which his father and grandfather had allowed to become 'official'—that is, to lose its life and strength—became once more a subject of major interest and recovered its vigour. Jews were ordered to wear a special garb, Malikis were harried and their

The Berber Empires: the Almoravids and the Almohads

books burned—al-Marrakushi gives us a list of Maliki works he saw burned at Fez—and philosophers were harassed.[49] In addition, the caliph advocated a return to the two chief sources of religion, the Koran and the Tradition, to the exclusion of all else, including the Mahdi himself, as al-Marrakushi emphasises. Later the Almohad Caliph al-Mamun, in a letter cited in the anonymous chronicle *al-Hulal-al-mawshiyya*, was even to assert that in his soul and conscience al-Mansur repudiated the doctrine of Ibn Tumart and, but for his sudden death, would undoubtedly have publicly avowed his opinions. Here we are on debatable ground where categorical assertions are not in order. We may, however, believe that a certain unease was in the air of Marrakesh during al-Mansur's last year of power and that doubt had again been cast more or less openly on the doctrinal foundations of the movement.

THE CALIPH AL-NASIR

The successor of al-Mansur was not the man to pacify so serious a malaise. Among the conventional portraits the Maghribi chroniclers painted of their rulers, that of Muhammad al-Nasir (1199–1214) by al-Marrakushi stands out by its revealing precision. This is how he describes the young monarch of eighteen: '... He often kept his eyes cast down and was much given to silence, this being due chiefly to a defect of speech by which he was affected. He was inscrutable, but gentle and courageous withal, little inclined to shed blood and with no great mind for carrying out anything to which he had not given much thought....'[50] To which we may add this from the *Qirtas*: 'He was unable to bring his business to a successful conclusion without much labour and managed his empire alone, relying solely on his own opinion.'[51] A timid and solitary young man it was who inherited an immense empire which was less solid and closely knit than it appeared at the time.

THE SUBMISSION OF IFRIQIYA AND THE GOVERNMENT OF ABU MUHAMMAD IBN HAFS

The victory of Alarcos temporarily weakened Christian resistance. The caliph al-Nasir took advantage of it to concentrate his efforts against the Almoravids of eastern Barbary, whose oppression lay heavily on the people there. His fleet recaptured Tunis and his army entered Gafsa and then Mahdiya. Yahya, after defeat in a desperate battle, took refuge in the desert.

Al-Nasir believed that Ifriqiya would withstand fresh Almoravid assaults only if it were strongly held. He did not turn to his family for a governor, whom he wished to make a veritable viceroy, but appointed the shaikh Abu Muhammad, whose double triumph over Alphonso of Castile and Yahya had left him in an unrivalled position. This appointment took on particular importance because Abu Muhammad was the son of the Abu Hafs whose loyalty had enabled 'Abd al-Mumin to accede to the caliphate. An Arab author assures us that in order to overcome the shaikh's resistance al-Nasir declared that he regarded him as his equal and would agree, should occasion arise, to yield to him his own position at Marrakesh, which we can take to mean that the Hafsids' influence over the community remained strong enough for the caliph to reserve a privileged place in the empire for them.[52]

The charge entrusted to Abu Muhammad was no sinecure. He had to ward off incessant risings stirred up by Yahya's prodigious activity in setting other Arabs of rival tribes against the Arabs of the Almoravid army. The victory he gained at Chebrou (near Tébessa) with the support of the Sulaim threw Yahya back into the central Maghrib. There the Arabs of his army in concert with the Zenata, freed from the Sanhaja grasp, laid waste to the country, which did not recover. 'The hearths there are dead,' observed Ibn Khaldun two centuries later, 'and the cockcrow is heard no more.' It was not in Barbary but in Tripolitania, where Abu Muhammad pursued him, that Yahya made his final attempt. Behind him were arrayed the shaikhs of the Arab tribes, who were in danger of being barred by the forceful government of Ifriqiya from access to grazing-ground and profitable booty. The battle of the Djebel Nefousa in 1209 was one of the most important 'days of the Arabs' in Barbary. The nomads of the Almoravid army had committed their families and their goods as the stake of battle. They lost everything and had to flee southward in disorder. However, Yahya's career was not ended. Driven out of Ifriqiya and Tripolitania, he succeeded in 1212 in taking Waddan (in the oasis of Djofra) and the neighbouring oases from his former ally Qaraqush, whom he had crucified. He remained in Waddan, awaiting the moment when he could once more appear in the Maghrib, access

The Berber Empires: the Almoravids and the Almohads

to which was for the moment closed to him by Abu Muhammad.

Thus Ifriqiya was thereafter protected from the Almoravid peril, but at the price of according quasi-independence to its governor. It became increasingly clear that this province was much too distant from Marrakesh, and called for much too specialised a form of management, for the caliph's authority to be effective. On the other hand, the appointment of a Hafsid to Tunis is proof that the prestige of the Almohad shaikhs was still very much alive and had indeed probably been strengthened in so far as the caliph's eccentric personality permitted.

LAS NAVAS DE TOLOSA

The caliph relied completely on the Hafsid shaikh to command the struggle against the Almoravids, particularly because affairs in Spain required his entire attention. Alphonso was preparing his revenge for Alarcos by calling for aid from all the rulers of Spain, the kings of Portugal and even the pope, who had a crusade preached against the Almohads. Knights and adventurers hastened from all quarters. Al-Nasir deemed the situation sufficiently serious to leave Marrakesh in February 1211 and to take command of the army. The campaign was protracted and ended in disaster. A powerful Christian army, in which all Spain except Leon was represented, crossed the Sierra Morena and inflicted a decisive defeat on the Almohads at al-'Uqab (Las Navas de Tolosa) on 16 July 1212. The plague alone halted the triumphal march of the Christians to the south. Counter-action, attempted with initial success by the general Abu Sa'id, resulted in a further defeat in 1213. When Alphonso died in the following year, the break-up of the Muslim states in Spain had already begun.

THE BREAK-UP OF THE EMPIRE

The caliph was not of the stature to restore so serious a situation. He returned from Morocco to abdicate in favour of his son Yusuf al-Mustansir, and in December 1213 or January 1214 died in circumstances which are still obscure, so widely do the chroniclers' accounts differ about it. Al-Mustansir (1214–1224), who was only sixteen years old and had no thought for anything but his pleasures, inherited a weighty responsibility. Though he was able to shift the task of protecting Ifriqiya on to Abu Muhammad, the central

History of North Africa

Maghrib, handed over to the Zenata, was slipping out of his control. Even in Morocco the Beni Merin, hitherto subject to Almohad authority, were sending bands of marauders as far as the Tell. Abu Muhammad's death in 1222 made the situation even worse. The council of government had designated his son as his successor, but the caliph, disturbed by the independence of the Hafsids, recalled him and replaced him by an incapable governor. Yahya took advantage of the occasion to reappear in the central Maghrib, where he carried on warfare for ten years, from 1226 to 1237, until he was reduced to carrying out surprise raids as a bandit chieftain.

The last years of the monarchy (1224–1269) were disturbed by rivalries between the shaikhs, who claimed to subject the new caliph to investiture by them (*baiʿa al-khāssa* 'proclamation by the élite'), and the descendants of ʿAbd al-Mumin. Stress should also be laid on the increasingly frequent intervention of the Arab tribes settled in Morocco. These, appealed to by the various pretenders, took a part they had not sought in the highly confused political game of the day. Thus these Arabs, who had been settled scarcely three-quarters of a century before, gradually came to constitute a political power whose role was sometimes decisive and was to continue so until the beginning of the twentieth century.

Abu Muhammad ʿAbd al-Wahid died by strangulation in 1224, and his successor al-ʿAdil died by drowning in a palace pool in 1227. Two pretenders then laid claim to the caliphate—al-Mamun, brother of al-ʿAdil, in Andalusia, and Yahya ibn al-Nasir, the candidate of the shaikhs, at Marrakesh. The civil war which ensued opened the way for the Christians to take a hand in the affairs of the Maghrib. In 1230 King Ferdinand III supplied al-Mamun with 12,000 horsemen for the capture of Marrakesh. Al-Mamun's triumph marked the beginning of a violent reaction against the Almohads. He massacred the shaikhs and their families, took political measures contrary to those of his predecessors, and from the elevation of the kasbah pulpit repudiated the doctrine of the Mahdi, whose very memory he declared accursed, in favour of the Sunni teaching.

In the case of the king of Castile, al-Mamun paid his debt by authorising the foundation of the church of Notre-Dame, where the Christians were able to hold public worship. This church was destroyed as early as 1232, but the bishopric of Marrakesh

The Berber Empires: the Almoravids and the Almohads

continued in existence until the fourteenth century, so long as there were Christian military forces retaining officers' privileges, at least on a private footing. Al-Mamun even undertook to prevent the Christians posted to his service from apostatizing, while he acquiesced in such conversions to Christianity as might take place in his territory. The state of Almohad decadence by 1228 is clear, for its ruler to accept such conditions.

Ferdinand III gained a further advantage from the crisis. Having become the joint sovereign of Castile and Leon, he no longer found himself faced with a united Almohad state, but with the petty Muslim kingdoms of Valencia, Murcia and Arjona (northwest of Jaen, near Andujar). The most important of the three kings, the king of Murcia, who commanded the whole south-eastern region (from Alicante to Alhama) declared himself a vassal of Ferdinand in 1241, and the king of Arjona, who had established his capital at Granada, sought alliance with him in 1246. With the capture of Seville two years later, Ferdinand secured all Muslim Spain except for the kingdom of Granada, where the Nasrids, while barely subsisting for two and a half centuries, enabled Andalusian civilisation to cast one final ray of glory. Ferdinand died in 1252 just when he was preparing for a landing in Morocco. With him the *reconquista* of Muslim territory in Spain ended its violent period.

In Barbary Almohad power suffered blows no less severe. Yahya took advantage of the caliph's absence at the siege of Ceuta, and of the opposition roused by his Almohad policy, to recapture Marrakesh. Al-Mamun died on his way back, in 1232. His young son, al-Rashid (1232-1242), continued the conflict with Yahya and became master of his own capital only after having his rival assassinated.

The unity of the empire, already breached by the defeats in Spain, could not withstand the palace revolutions. The amir of Tlemcen, Yaghmorasan ibn Ziyan, proclaimed his independence in 1235-1236 and created the Zenata kingdom of the Beni 'Abd al-Wad. In Ifriqiya the Hafsid governor Abu Zakariya broke with the caliph in 1228, and subsequently, in 1236-1237, took the title of Amir and made his capital at Tunis.

However, Seville acknowledged al-Rashid as caliph in 1238, and a few months later Ibn al-Ahmar, the Nasrid of Granada, was negotiating with the ruler of Marrakesh. These facts are the measure of the extreme uncertainty prevailing throughout what had been the Almohad empire. With al-Saʿid (1242–1248) the situation grew even worse. The Hafsids extended their conquests as far as Tlemcen, while the Merinids were infiltrating as far as Meknès and levying taxes wherever they established themselves. Al-Saʿid then made a great effort, the last one, to restore the Almohad empire in its entirety, at least in the Maghrib. Being determined to push as far as Tunis, he forced the Merinids to negotiate and even to supply him with a token contingent. He appeared to be about to destroy the Beni ʿAbd al-Wad when he fell into an ambush and was killed. The army at once surged back towards Morocco. The Merinids were awaiting it at the crossing over the Moulouya at Guercif; they annihilated it and immediately afterwards gained possession of Fez. Except as a shadow, Almohad power existed no longer.

In 1262 ʿUmar al-Murtada (1248–1266), whose territory was bounded to the north by the Oum er-Rbia, had to agree to pay tribute in order to save Marrakesh. In their hour of danger the Almohads weakened themselves still further by family hatreds. Al-Murtada's cousin Abu Dabbus went over to the enemy in 1266, overthrew the caliph and had himself proclaimed in his place. It was then that the Merinid, who regarded himself as having been betrayed by his ally, put an end to the Almohad dynasty by taking possession of Marrakesh in September 1269.

IV. Almohad Culture

THE CALIPHS

Culturally the outlook seemed bleak indeed at the advent of Almohad rule. The Mahdi tolerated no wavering in matters of faith, condemned luxurious dress and sought out musical instruments in order to destroy them. According to the *Qirtas*,[53] the first concern of ʿAbd al-Mumin, when he entered Fez, was the whitewashing of the sculptures and gildings of the Great Mosque. It is possible that the first Almohads condemned the adornment of public buildings, which scandalised them. It is nonetheless true

The Berber Empires: the Almoravids and the Almohads

that if such feelings existed, they quickly disappeared on contact with the exigencies of power, and above all with the Andalusian environment. 'Abd al-Mumin had several copiously decorated mosques built, including the two Kutubiyas (the first having been destroyed on his orders because of an error in orientation) and the mosque at Tinmel. It was on Spanish soil that 'Abd al-Mumin, at the end of his life, 'issued an invitation to poets whom previously he had never received save at their request'.

After the reign of Abu Ya'qub it is impossible to differentiate Spain from Maghrib—or rather the Maghrib from Spain, since residence in the latter came to be much more to the caliph's liking. He was happier at Seville, the pleasure capital, than at Cordova, the metropolis of intellect. He astonished Ibn Rushd (Averroes) at their first interview by his philosophical erudition and took such pleasure in Ibn Tufail's company that, according to one of the master's disciples, he would 'remain in the palace at his side for days and nights without appearing'. He had the Great Mosque at Seville built, laid the foundations of his minaret, the famous Giralda, and laid out the plan of the kasbah at Marrakesh, of which the enclosing wall and palace, neither of which remain, were built for him.

Al-Mansur, like his father, was imbued with Andalusian culture. He was not only a general but also a builder, creator of the Mosque of the Kasbah at Marrakesh, of the Giralda, of the agglomeration of walls and monumental gates at Rabat, and finally of the gigantic Mosque of Hasan at Rabat, which remained unfinished. Through the Almohad caliphs Hispano-Moorish art was diffused in Barbary, and the Berbers and Arabs who made up the occupation forces in the towns of Spain proved equally susceptible to Andalusian influences.

ECONOMIC ACTIVITY

Andalusian civilisation then took on a character which was all the more brilliant because it coincided with the restoration of order brought about by the Almohads in their exercise of power. The caliphs put an end to the financial disorder of the Taïfas and encouraged the agriculture of a 'land of blessing', as an Arab writer of the eleventh century called it. Industry continued to thrive. There was trade in silkworms at Jaen, Alicante had its shipyards, and at Almeria silk was woven on 800 looms, and instruments of copper and iron were manufactured. This industrial activity made its influence felt in the Maghrib. Ceuta was as much renowned as Jativa for its production of a paper called *sebti*, and at Fez there were mills for the same manufacture.

Commerce was very active. Alicante, Almeria and Cordova had famous markets. Spain's chief export to Morocco consisted of timber from its forests, but there were also grain, manufactured items, linen and products of the East. The Almohads reformed the monetary system instituted by the Almoravids. Instead of enclosing the inscription on their dinars in a circle, they bounded it in part with a square; and as the unit of their system they adopted the double denier, which corresponded more closely to the former dinar.

The Maghrib did not trade only with Spain. Tunis, Bougie, Constantine, Oran, Tlemcen and Ceuta—where there was a Marseillais *funduk*[54] in 1236—exchanged merchandise with Pisa, Genoa, Venice and Marseilles. Texts annotated by Sayous[55] have thrown light on the methods adopted by the merchants of Ifriqiya in their business dealings with the Christians.

In the Almohad period the Muslims, who had been the first to organise their commercial procedure to comply with the requirements of international trade, had brought their methods to a high pitch of efficiency, and the Christians took these as models. Despite the differences in religion, despite even the growth of privateering, over which the African rulers were losing control, relations and exchanges between Christians and Muslims continued to develop. In the twelfth and early thirteenth centuries Christians came to Tunis not only to do business, but also to settle. In the Maghrib they bought mainly sheep and goat skins and wax, and sold textiles, oriental products and even wine.

The Pisans displayed the greatest activity and in 1157 succeeded, by means of a rudimentary treaty, in securing guarantees for their persons and their merchandise. A *funduk* was set aside for the warehousing of their goods and they were treated with consideration. At the very beginning of the thirteenth century some merchants of Tunis sent letters in friendly and pressing terms to a Pisan who had left the city after it had been seized and offered him every assurance. 'Do not hesitate to come back,' a dragoman wrote

The Berber Empires: the Almoravids and the Almohads

with emphasis, 'you will meet with an excellent reception everywhere, and likewise those who come with you. Prices of merchandise are good and you will be able to make all the purchases you wish.'[56] And a Muslim leather merchant went further. 'Tranquillity and business are in a good state, better even than at the time of your departure. You will be received and treated here extremely well, as formerly.'[57] These letters disclose warm and personal relations between merchants of Pisa and Tunis. And indeed the trade conducted by the Pisans in Ifriqiya was considerable. Their principal exchanges were of grain for wool, leather, alum and wax. The Muslims trusted them so far as on occasions to allow them credit.

The Genoese and the Marseillais employed the methods in use on the markets of Europe—the ordinary loan, in theory interest-free, and the maritime loan, which allowed a high return since marine risks were borne by the lender. There were also the *commenda* contract, under which the lender took a share of the merchant's profits, and the *societas*, in which the profits were distributed between the work done and the capital sums contributed by the shareholders. The Genoese were the first to employ the contract of exchange with Tunis. The Marseillais invested much capital in commerce and carriage of goods. Twenty contracts signed by the merchant-capitalists Manduel between 1212 and 1246 show that through Jewish agents in Bougie, Ceuta, Oran and Tlemcen they sold Arabic coinage (*millares* or half-dirhems) which they used to have minted for export, particularly at Montpelier. As for the Venetians, it was only under the Hafsids that they held a role of any importance at Tunis.[58]

THE ARMY AND FLEET

To secure their authority in Barbary and above all in Spain, the Almohads had a well organised army. This was in the beginning recruited from Berber tribes and later from Arab nomads, and in it there even figured contingents of Turks, captured during the conflict with Qaraqush, and Christian troops. As the proportion of these foreigners increased and the numbers of Masmouda contingents diminished, the Almohad army lost its original spirit—we might say its national valour—and turned into a professional force. The caliph's guard was of great importance. It was the duty of the loyal soldiers surrounding his tent to let themselves be killed rather than allow it to be approached. In attack the troops charged in successive waves, with lances, swords, arrows and slings. Against fortifications they used towers, sometimes of six storeys.

Once the Almohads had occupied Cadiz they had at their disposal the powerful fleet of the Beni Maimoun. The Berber Yusuf, who had served in the vessels of Roger II, King of Sicily, and later had been appointed admiral by Abu Ya'qub, had made the caliph's squadron the foremost in the Mediterranean. Indeed in 1190 Saladin asked for its assistance with the intention of halting the Christian kings on their route to Syria, but he probably did not obtain it; his involvement with Qaraqush was not calculated to earn him the goodwill of Abu Ya'qub.

The power of the Almohad empire, its wealth and the reputation of its army and fleet conferred great prestige on the caliphs. An Arab writer goes so far as to declare that the Muslims of Cairo and Alexandria hoped that Abu Ya'qub would conquer Egypt. Saladin's request indicates at the very least that he regarded the ruler of the Maghrib as best fitted to defend the threatened Islamic East.

THE PHILOSOPHY OF IBN TUFAIL AND IBN RUSHD

Hispano-Moorish culture added still further to the prestige of the Almohads throughout the Muslim world. The two greatest Arab philosophers of the twelfth century were intimates of the caliphs. Ibn Tufail (1110–1185) was secretary to a son of 'Abd al-Mumin at Ceuta and Tangier, and later became the appointed physician to Abu Ya'qub who often called on him for advice. Ibn Rushd (Averroes, 1126–1198) took the place of Ibn Tufail with the caliph but fell into disgrace, though only briefly, under al-Mansur. Both wielded an influence on mediaeval philosophy that extended even to Christendom. Leibniz could still find matter for praise in Pocock's Latin adaptation of Ibn Tufail's philosophic novel *The Living One, Son of the Vigilant* (*Hayy ibn Yaqzān*). This describes how a child, alone on a desert island, ascends from sense knowledge, by means of which he succeeds in establishing a highly advanced practical industry, to the abstract forms of bodies. He then continues to the idea of general causes—the sky which he conceives of as spherical with the world as a huge living creature—

The Berber Empires: the Almoravids and the Almohads

finally attaining the concept of God, endowed with will, wise, skilled and merciful, whose qualities emerge from the study of natural beings. An attempt at preaching the philosophy of the *Hayy* in a neighbouring country comes to nothing and the Living One, together with a pious adherent by whom he has been joined, returns to his island to devote himself to pure contemplation, leaving images and symbols to ordinary folk. Thus Ibn Tufail defined with precision the respective positions of mysticism and religion.

It was on the advice of Ibn Tufail that Ibn Rushd undertook the writing of commentaries on the Greek philosophers, translations of whose writings the caliph found obscure. Not all his works are extant in Arabic; some are known only through translations into Hebrew or Latin, and some are lost. He was not so much an original philosopher as an analyst and commentator. His triple commentary on Aristotle, adapted to the three levels of education, exerted very great influence. In philosophy Ibn Rushd departed from Avicenna and Ibn Bajja only on secondary questions. On two points in particular he held his own interpretation—in his theory of the production of substantial forms, which was directed against Avicenna, and in his theory of the intellect, which refuted an interpretation of Alexander of Aphrodisias. He paid much attention to the relations between scientific reason and faith, which must harmonise. Both mark stages in thinking. The part of the multitude is to adhere to the literal meaning; interpretation is the responsibility of the philosopher, whose knowledge is the very worship he offers to God. It can be understood how this syncretic philosophy, which took it for granted that a single truth could present itself in diverse forms, caused disquiet to the professional theologians and brought its author under suspicion of heresy.

MUSIC

The Andalusian and Maghribi circles in which Ibn Tufail and Ibn Rushd lived were interested not only in philosophy but also in music and art. It was by way of the Maghrib that the theory of music, of intervals and modes, spread from the East, where it had been formulated, to Spain, where it remained virtually intact. It was chiefly at Seville that, in the words of Averroes, music was 'cultivated with passion'. The philosophers discussed the aesthetics of music, the effect of sounds on the human soul and their power of expression. Averroes spurned plaintive and frightening melodies and the slavish imitation of things irrational and unworthy of man, such as the cries of animals and the noises of nature, on account of their evil influence on the hearer. He also forbade all music produced by different instruments, including even all the musical modes. For him the essential aim of music was ethical in character —to inspire men to strength and temperance. Accordingly he despised Arab melodies, which had as great a success in the cities of the Maghrib as in those of Andalusia. Even today lovers of the 'music of Granada', which is regarded as the most elegant and expressive form, are to be found in numbers in Barbary. This music was an art of townsmen. The country Berbers retained their own song with its emphatic melodic lines and its crude and simple strains; in its instrumental form their music employed a primitive flute or a barrel musette with a flapping reed of wood (*ghaïta*).

ARCHITECTURE

This too was an urban art. Like that of the Almoravids, Almohad art had a dynastic character. Thus it was at its height by the time 'Abd al-Mumin's authority was firmly established in the far Maghrib. It was the finest period of Muslim art in the West.

'Abd al-Mumin praised God by building mosques at Taza and at Marrakesh, where it has been possible to reconstruct the plan of the first Kutubiya—it is now destroyed but its foundations have been excavated. He built another at Tinmel in memory of the Mahdi, in which Hispano-Moorish tradition, contributions from the East and local influences, are all combined. He also ordered the fortress of Ribat al-Fath built, which stood on the site of the present Kasbah of the Oudaya at Rabat. His son Abu Ya'qub built the Great Mosque at Seville and the kasbah at Marrakesh. According to tradition Ya'qub al-Mansur directed the preliminary work on the Mosque of Hasan at Rabat, the building of the Mosque of the Kasbah at Marrakesh, and the completion of the Giralda at Seville and of the minaret of the Kutubiya. The Mosque of Hasan was imposing in appearance. It extended over an immense space of more than some 200 by 151 yards, and had sixteen doors. The minaret in rose-pink stone, which stood in the middle of the façade, still exists.

The Berber Empires: the Almoravids and the Almohads

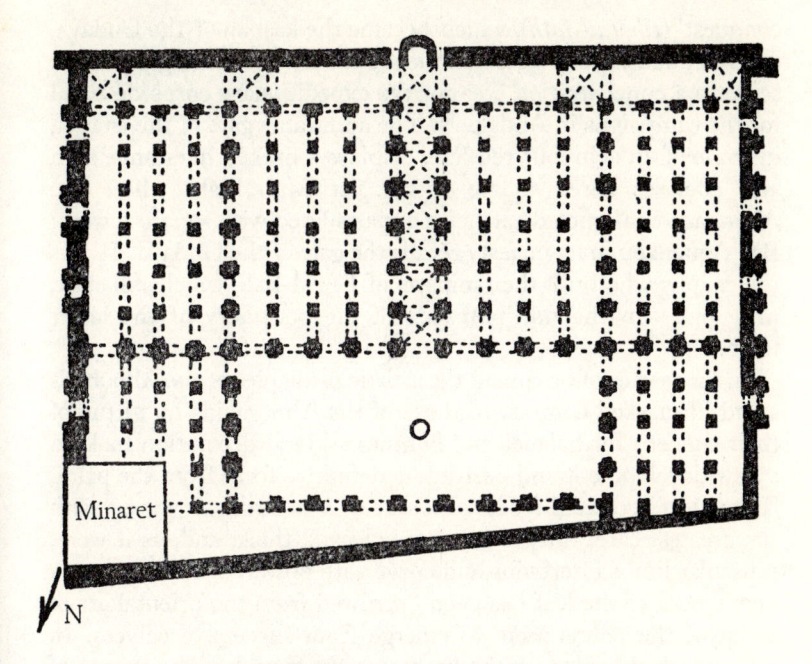

4 Plan of the Mosque of the Kutubiya at Marrakesh

Of Almohad minarets, square in plan and topped with a central lantern, only the one at Kutubiya still exists in its entirety. It comprises six floors of superimposed chambers, in which the architects freely diversified the system of vaulting. The lantern, a little tower in itself, is crowned with a ribbed cupola and completed by a minaret on which stand three spheres of gilded copper. The highest point of the building is more than 200 feet from the ground.

Nothing is left of the Almohad palaces, or of the great hospital at Marrakesh, built in unusually luxurious style by al-Mansur, the most renowned builder of the dynasty. This caliph raised numerous fortifications, but his principal construction was the citadel of the town of Rabat. The enormous earthen rampart ran to nearly 4 miles in length, and was pierced by gates, of which the most remarkable and best preserved is the one called Bab er-Rouah. The vast conglomeration of military buildings constituting the 'camp of conquest' (*ribāt al-fath*), which became the kasbah of the Oudaya, was intended to keep watch on the mouth of the Bou Regreg and to serve as a concentration area for the expeditionary corps destined for the campaigns in Andalusia. The admirable gate of the citadel, in stone of an ochreous red hue, displays a broken horseshoe arch and encloses three square rooms. At Marrakesh, where the Almohads constructed earthen ramparts lined with square towers; Bab Aguenaou in its majesty recalls the gate of the Oudaya. It was the caliphs who built the ramparts of Fez al-Bali, which still exist, principally on the northern side of the periphery of the lower town.

In the matter of ornament the artistic principles of the Almohads stand in marked contrast to those of the Almoravids by virtue of their concern for balance and lightness. Floral decoration took on a new development and derived its definitive form from the palm. 'Every leaf is treated for its own sake and its outline is drawn with the greatest care. Shapes become bold and thick, and, as it were, muscular limbs intertwine and curve with powerful movements. A new model of the leaf has been borrowed from the oriental art of Ifriqiya; the palms seem to emerge from successive calyces. In sculptured plaster work the limbs are cut from broad patterns of shade, and in lattice decoration the smooth palm makes its appearance, with no intervening detail to distract the eye from the sinewy scrollwork of the lobes.'[59] Geometric ornamentation was no less elegant and vigorous. 'The foiled arches, their extrados often formed by subtle interlaced designs with several branches, display in their powerful curves and long points a unique combination of elegance and strength. In borders the principle of interlacing is carried to its extreme logical consequences and architectural interlaced work covers the faces of minarets.'[60] The artists of the twelfth century were colourists who lavished the polychromy of porcelain mosaics (*zulaij*) on their minarets. The turquoise blue tiles of the Kutubiya crown the minaret with jewels sparkling in the sun.

Almohad art, the study of which in Morocco has been led by Terrasse and the late H. Basset, was the outcome of efforts extending over centuries. It mingled oriental ideas with Andalusian traditions. Out of all these elements it formed a personal aesthetic which was as majestic and powerful as the rulers themselves. This

The Berber Empires: the Almoravids and the Almohads

grandeur is to be found in its immense many-domed mosques boldly thrusting their minarets to heaven, in the robust materials, even in the dried earth of its ramparts, and in a decoration closely linked with its architecture and displaying a broad and stylised treatment with a concern for order and clarity. It has been rightly said by Gsell that this art constitutes 'a masterpiece of harmonious discipline'.

Almohad art reached its zenith under the first caliphs. By the thirteenth century decadence had set in, and the minaret of the mosque of Hasan was never finished. The great empire broke up, and the dynasties which shared in the spoils never attained the same political and artistic grandeur.

CONCLUSION

The work of the Almohads, at least as brilliant as that of the Almoravids, had more lasting effects.

From the political point of view, their failure is obvious. As in the ninth century, the Maghrib was broken into three parts which were not to be reunited again—Ifriqiya under the Hafsids, the central Maghrib under the Beni 'Abd al-Wad, and the far Maghrib under the Merinids. The Masmouda and the Muminids had not succeeded in establishing Berber unity in lasting fashion. This failure was due to a large number of causes which have been analysed with great insight by Terrasse in his *Histoire du Maroc*.[61]

In the first place the attempt at unification came too late. By the time the Almohads achieved power the worm had been too long in the fruit and its ravages had gone too deeply. By the middle of the twelfth century the Hilalian Arabs had the entire mastery of Ifriqiya and had penetrated deep into the central Maghrib. At the same time, the Ma'qil Arabs, the last to come, were infiltrating into the far Maghrib—along the Saharan edge. Both had already entered into alliance with the Zenata Berbers, thus constituting a very powerful nomadic mass capable of counteracting the attempts of the settled folk at hegemony. It is known that the Arabs, allies of the central power when it was strong but ready to defect at the first opportunity, played a centrifugal role in the empire, notably during the long adventure of the Beni Ghaniya and later at the time of the state's decline, dating from 1224. But the results of their activity were perhaps more decisive in the economic field.

These devoted herdsmen wrested many regions from agriculture and turned them into vast grazing grounds on which they practised extensive stock raising. Elsewhere they reduced the cultivators to the condition of ill-paid and hopeless serfs. Finally, as pillagers by ancestral instinct, they impeded commercial relations which had been so prosperous at the outset of the Almohad epoch.

The caliphs of Marrakesh saw this Arab problem clearly enough. They thought to resolve it by moving the nomads to Morocco, but in doing so they merely contaminated the far Maghrib, hitherto immune, while failing to establish peace in Ifriqiya.

Furthermore, these Berber mountaineers were unable to broaden their political ideas to match the scale of the empire they had carved out. The original Almohads, the Masmouda, were unwilling to take the other peoples of the empire into partnership in their activity, i.e. in their government. In Spain, in Ifriqiya and in the central Maghrib their proud behaviour was that of conquerors: hence the perpetual revolts and the final cracking of the structure as soon as the caliph was no longer a man capable of contending with them.

Even within the conquering clan the Muminids allotted themselves the greatest share at the expense of the other Almohad families. This policy of arrogating power antagonised the other families, who took advantage of the first opportunity to recover what they regarded as their right. It was a short-sighted policy which led only to chaos, except in Ifriqiya with the Hafsids.

When we consider religion, the accomplishments of the Almohads look very different. Their doctrine did not endure, but they did complete the work of unification begun by the Almoravids. They did so by encouraging the growth of the Muslim mystical movement which was latent in the Maghrib but had never been able to fully develop. 'It is very striking', writes Terrasse, 'that the great mystical leaders of the Maghrib—those who were to remain the most popular of its saints—nearly all lived under the Almohads and died at the end of the twelfth century—Sidi Harazam in 1173, Mulay Bushaib in 1174, Mulay Bu 'Azza in 1176, Sidi Bu Madian, Mulay 'Abd al-Slam ibn Mshish and Sidi Bal 'Abbas al-Sabti in 1188.'[62] Thereafter religious peace was to reign uninterrupted in the Maghrib under the aegis of Malikism. In contrast, Maghribi rigorism (segregation of men and women,

The Berber Empires: the Almoravids and the Almohads

strict observance of fasting, scrupulous abstinence from forbidden foods) had its origin in the moral code of Ibn Tumart.

Finally, it cannot be denied that the Almohads created a veritable culture of their own and did not, like their predecessors, rest content with making themselves mere agents for the diffusion of Andalusian culture. It was a forceful and austere culture, in which fortresses and mosques took precedence over palaces and gardens, and philosophy over poetry, but one whose grandeur and originality are incontestable.

We may then regard the half-century from 1160 to 1210 as the period in which the Berber Maghrib was at its height.

Notes

1. al-Bakri (tr. de Slane), *op. cit.*
2. al-Idrisi, *Kitab nuzhat al-mushtaq fi khtiraq al-afaq*, written c. 1154 for Roger II of Sicily; it constitutes a complete description of the world known to the Arabs in the middle of the 12th century. For an edition and partial translation see R. Dozy and J. M. de Goeje, *Description de l'Afrique et de l'Espagne* (Leiden, 1866).
3. al-Marrakushi, *al-Mu'jib fi talkhis akhbar al-Maghrib*, written c. 1224 in the East by a Moroccan who had been in contact with Almohad rulers and artists. An edition was published by R. Dozy, *The History of the Almohades* (Leiden, 1847–81); and a translation is available by E. Fagnan, 'Histoire des Almohades', *Revue Africaine* (1891–2), and *Histoire des Almohades* (Alger, 1893).
4. Ibn al-Athir (tr. Fagnan), *op. cit.*
5. al-Bakri (tr. de Slane), *op. cit.*, p. 310.
6. H. Terrasse (1949), *op. cit.*, I, 213.
7. al-Bakri (tr. de Slane), *op. cit.*, p. 318.
8. *Ibid.*, pp. 371–2.
9. Ibn Khaldun (tr. de Slane), *op. cit.*, II, p. 47.
10. al-Bakri (tr. de Slane), *op. cit.*, p. 373.
11. Ibn Abi Zar' (tr. Beaumier), *op. cit.*, pp. 190–1.
12. *Ibid.*, p. 194.
13. E. Lévi-Provençal, 'Les Mémoires de 'Abd Allah, dernier roi ziride de Grenade', *Al-Andalus*, III, IV (1935–6), IV, 72.
14. al-Marrakushi (tr. Fagnan, 1891–2), *op. cit.*, pp. 146–7.
15. *Ibid.*, p. 147.
16. For an English translation see N. A. Faris, *The Book of Knowledge* (Lahore, 1962); a thorough discussion of al-Ghazali is available in M. Watt, *Muslim Intellectual, A Study of al-Ghazali* (Edinburgh, 1963).

17. For a description of the Great Mosque of Tlemcen see G. Marçais (1926), *op. cit.*, I, 313–20.
18. *Ibid.*, I, 319.
19. *Ibid.*, I, 359.
20. See E. Lévi-Provençal, *Séville musulmane au XIIe siècle* (Paris, 1947).
21. al-Baidaq (Abu Bakr b. 'Ali al-Sanhaji), 'L'Histoire des Almohades', in E. Lévi-Provençal, tr., *Documents inédites d'histoire almohade, fragments inédites du 'Legajo' 1999 du fonds arabe de l'Escurial* (Paris, 1928), part 3, pp. 75–7.
22. *Ibid.*, p. 85.
23. *Koran*, sura iii, verse 122.
24. al-Baidaq (tr. Lévi-Provençal), *op. cit.*, p. 81.
25. *Ibid.*, pp. 86–7.
26. *Koran*, sura.
27. J. Luciani, ed., *Le livre d'Ibn Toumert (Mowat'tʻâ)* (Alger, 1903); translated in part by Massé, 'La profession de foi ('Agîda) et les guides spirituals (morchida) du Mahdi Ibn Toumart', in *Mémorial Henri Basset* (Paris, 1928), II, 105–21.
28. al-Baidaq (tr. Lévi-Provençal), *op. cit.*, p. 88.
29. R. Montagne, *Les Berbères et le Makhzen dans le Sud du Maroc*, Essai sur la transformation politique des Berbères sédentaires (groupe Chleuh), Trauvaux de l'année sociologique (Paris, 1930), pp. 59–71.
30. See Ibn Abi Zarʻ (tr. Fagnan), *op. cit.*, p. 257 *et seq.*
31. al-Baidaq (tr. Lévi-Provençal), *op. cit.*, pp. 128–9.
32. Ibn Khaldun (tr. de Slane), *op. cit.*, II, 173.
33. al-Baidaq (tr. Lévi-Provençal), *op. cit.*, p. 122.
34. *Ibid.*, p. 171; and anonymous, *al-Hulal al-mawshiyya fi dhikr al-akhbar al-Marrakushiyya*, written c. 1381; for a good Arabic edition see I. S. Allouche, 'Collection des textes arabes', *I.H.E.M.*, vol. VI (Rabat, 1936)—see also bibliography, IX, Arabic Sources, *al-Hulal*, etc.
35. al-Idrisi (tr. Dozy and de Goeje), *op. cit.*, p. 105.
36. al-Ghubrīnī, *Unwān al-dirāya* (Alger, 1911), 104 biographies of personages in Bougie during the 7th century A.H./13th century A.D.; see G. Yver, 'Bougie', *Encyclopedia of Islam*, I.
37. E. Lévi-Provençal, ed., *Trente-sept lettres officielles almohades* (Paris, 1941); also E. Lévi-Provençal, 'Un recueil de lettres officielles almohades', *Hespéris*, XXVIII (1941), pp. 1–70; letters 13 and 14, pp. 35–8.
38. *al-Hulal al-mawshiyya, op. cit.*
39. E. Lévi-Provençal (1941), *op. cit.*, pp. 32–3
40. Ibn al-Athir (tr. Fagnan), *op. cit.*, pp. 584–5.
41. E. Lévi-Provençal (1941), *op. cit.*, pp. 31–2.
42. Ibn Abi Zarʻ (tr. Beaumier), *op. cit.*, p. 286.
43. *Ibid.*, p. 281.
44. Ibn Khaldun (tr. de Slane), *op. cit.*, II, 196–8.
45. Ibn al-Athir (tr. Fagnan), *op. cit.*, pp. 595–6.

The Berber Empires: the Almoravids and the Almohads

46. E. Lévi-Provençal (1941), *op. cit.*, pp. 50–1.
47. *Ibid.*, pp. 50–1.
48. Mohammed er-Rachid Mouline, *L'époque d'el Mançour l'Almohade, ou la vie politique intellectuelle et religieuse au Maghreb de l'année 580 à l'année 595* (Rabat, 1945).
49. al-Marrakushi (tr. Fagnan), *op. cit.*, pp. 241–2.
50. *Ibid.*, p. 242.
51. Ibn Abi Zar' (tr. Beaumier), *op. cit.*; for the account of the reign of al-Nasir, see p. 326 *et seq.*
52. Ibn Khaldun (tr. de Slane), *op. cit.*; for the account of the opening years of the Hafsid dynasty, see II, 226, *et seq.*
53. Ibn Abi Zar' (tr. Beaumier), *op. cit.*; see pp. 268–9.
54. *fundicum marcilliense.*
55. E. A. Sayous, *Le Commerce des Européens à Tunis depuis le XIIe siècle jusqu'à la fin du XVIe siècle* (Paris, 1929); the texts are found in the appendices, pp. 139–75.
56. *Ibid.*, p. 145.
57. *Ibid.*, p. 147; the selections are from six letters from Tunis merchants to Pisian traders who had left Tunis.
58. *Ibid.*, chapter I ('XIIe et XIIIe siècles; activité des Pisans, des Genois, et des Marseillais'), pp. 39–68.
59. H. Terrasse and H. Hainaut, *Les Arts décoratifs au Maroc* (Paris, 1925), pp. 85–6.
60. *Ibid.*, p. 86.
61. H. Terrasse (1949), *op. cit.*, I, 255–60.
62. *Ibid.*, I, 364.

CHAPTER 4

The Return to Berber Kingdoms

✽

The Almohad empire had scarcely begun to show the first signs of serious weakness when Barbary was beginning to split into three parts, as it had been split under Roman rule, in the eighth and ninth centuries, and then once more in the eleventh when the Sanhaja of Achir had broken away from the Zirids of Ifriqiya.

The governor of Ifriqiya proclaimed his independence in 1236 after breaking with Marrakesh seven years earlier; this was the foundation of the Hafsid dynasty. In 1236 the Beni ʿAbd al-Wad tribe, commanded by Yaghmorasan ibn Ziyan, assumed independent power at Tlemcen and in the surrounding region, the protection of which the Almohads had for long entrusted to them. Finally in 1248 another Berber tribe, the Beni Merin, gained possession of Fez and there established an authority which rapidly grew in vigour. It may be added that Muslim Spain too had seceded from the Almohad empire; what was left of it fell to the Nasrids, princes of Granada.

Thus, twenty years before the Almohad dynasty had finally succumbed, the empire founded by ʿAbd al-Mumin was breaking up into three sections each having at its head a Berber tribe or family. The fortunes of these groupings were varied, but included some moments of glory and times of comparative prosperity. They cannot, however, be regarded as anything but successor states. Nothing in them recalls the vitality or the vigorous personalities of the Mahdi's men; all alike ranged themselves under the aegis of the Almohads and their sole object was to restore to their own benefit the empire of their predecessors. Some of their rulers were to appear likely to succeed in doing so, but never for more than a period of a few months.

Considering it in perspective, the history of the Maghrib down to the extinction of the Hafsid, ʿAbd al-Wadid and Merinid

The Return to Berber Kingdoms

dynasties—that is, until the middle of the sixteenth century—is that of a vain attempt to revive the past, of a long stagnation and a slow decadence.

By an exceptionally fortunate chance, this process of decline was observed and described by an historian of genius, Ibn Khaldun (1332–1406). Without the help of his writings it would have been impossible for G. Marçais to reconstruct the stages of the Hilalian invasion, or for Gautier to pierce the dark ages of the Maghrib with shafts of light. In the course of his political career Ibn Khaldun was of service or disservice, at the prompting of his interests rather than of his scruples, to the Hafsids, the Merinids, the Nasrids and the 'Abd al-Wadids, and then lived among the Arabs to whom he had gone to raise troops. Everywhere this gallant man occupied high office and was thus able to follow events and pass judgment on men. He might have drawn on his experience and knowledge to produce crude annals, like those of the *Qirtas*, but he was endowed with such exceptional critical spirit and scientific curiosity that Gautier does not hesitate to set him on the same level as Hannibal and Saint Augustine.[1]

Under his father and the most renowned masters, Ibn Khaldun studied grammar, philosophy, law and poetry at Tunis. He then joined the school of the Moroccan scholars who had come with the Merinids, for training in philosophical and theological exercises. But he was an innovator, and drew his principles and his method from his own resources. Before writing his great universal history *The Book of Examples* (*Kitāb al-'Ibar*) he published his *Prolegomena* (*Muqaddima*) which consists of reflections on the most diverse subjects, from which, however, a veritable philosophy of history can be derived.[2]

Unlike the Muslim chroniclers, Ibn Khaldun was concerned with verifying the value of sources, in accordance with rational, not religious, criteria. He was not content to enumerate facts; he tried to understand them and, if possible, to explain them. On the probative value of documents or the importance of labour as an element of wealth he offers reflections rendered familiar to us by historians or economists of the nineteenth century, but which are surprising when they come from the pen of a man of the fourteenth. It is not his contemporary Froissart we should think of, but Machiavelli or Vico. Struck by the coexistence of deserts and fertile regions, the latter inhabited by settled folk, the former ranged over by nomads, he concluded that nomadic life was the forerunner and begetter of settled existence. Nomads pure and simple, entirely devoted to family and tribal interests are able, thanks to their military qualities, to effect conquests which enrich them but corrupt, and then they are swept away by another rough and valiant people. It is among nomads above all that we find persisting that solidarity and devotion to the collective interest (*'asabiyya*) which constitute a strength that states cannot do without. Their morals are superior to those of corrupt and degenerate townsmen. History shows that kingdoms are born, grow and die, passing through five stages of development, in the space of three generations, that is, 120 years. Gautier has laid stress on Ibn Khaldun's contempt for the land, the peasant and the ordinary citizen, and on the biological and genealogical ideas of this historian of genius, to whom the geographical substratum of history was always unfamiliar.[5]

This pessimistic philosophy of the relations between nomads and settled people was inspired less by Arabia than by the Maghrib. Accordingly the part of his universal history which de Slane extracted and translated under his own title of *Histoire des Berbèrs* remains the essential source, particularly for the fourteenth century, in which the kingdoms were organised that succeeded to the power of the Almohads. The remarkable intelligence displayed by Ibn Khaldun, and the robust originality of his views, are accompanied by a first-hand documentation, since the historian was also the respected adviser to the rulers about whom he wrote.

1. The Hafsid Kingdom of Tunis

ABU ZAKARIYA (1229–1249)

Of the three dynasties that shared out and quarrelled over Barbary, the Hafsid was the first to set itself up as heir of the powers and traditions of the failing Almohad caliphate. The new kingdom enjoyed genuine prestige, especially during the thirteenth century, but could not prevent the decline of Ifriqiya, where the rivalries and revolts of the Arab tribes sustained unrest and aggravated ruin. Its history has been studied in a quite remarkable and

The Return to Berber Kingdoms

exhaustive fashion by Brunschvig in his two-volume work entitled *La Berbérie orientale sous les Hafçides, des origines à la fin du XVe siècle*.[4]

It will be remembered that after defeating the rebel Yahya ibn Ghaniya in southern Tunisia, the Almohad caliph al-Nasir had in 1207 entrusted the protection of Ifriqiya to a son of Shaikh Abu-Hafs, 'Umar al-Hintati. This governor ruled there under the Almohads until his death in 1221, when his place was taken by various governors of the Muminid family. In 1226 the caliph al-ʿAdil once more appointed a Hafsid as ruler of Ifriqiya. This governor, on his refusal to acknowledge the new caliph al-Mamun, was dismissed in favour of his brother Abu-Zakariya Yahya, then governor of Gabès.

As the son of the first Hafsid governor of Ifriqiya and grandson of the famous shaikh Abu-Hafs, this young man of about twenty-six enjoyed the lustre of his family and the renown acquired by his father in protecting Ifriqiya against the encroachments of Ibn Ghaniya. To these advantages inherited from his forebearers he added a good education, great self-discipline and calculated boldness.

A few months after his appointment to Tunis he found himself under the orders of one caliph, al-Mamun, who was openly discarding the Almohad doctrine, and confronted with an anti-caliph, Yahya ibn Nasir, who was not able to establish his authority. After the adherence of a few weeks to the cause of the second of these, Abu Zakariya decided to have the Friday prayer pronounced 'in the name of the Mahdi and the orthodox caliphs' and himself to assume the title of Amir.[5] It was a discreet declaration of an independence which he rendered complete a few years later, in 1236 or 1237, by having the prayer pronounced in his own name. Meanwhile he had considerably augmented his territory. In 1230, as seems probable, Constantine and Bougie fell into his power, after which he finally expelled Yahya ibn Ghaniya from his domain. In 1235 he annexed Algiers and by good will or force secured the submission of the leading tribes of the Chélif valley. Thus the former Zirid kingdom was restored in the form in which it had existed at the end of the tenth century. The Christian powers were in no doubt about him. Treaties of good will and trade were concluded with the new sovereign by Venice in 1231, Pisa in

1234 and Genoa in 1236, while Frederick II of Sicily dispatched a consul in 1239 and the king of Aragon entered into diplomatic relations. At the same time, amid all the Almohad anarchy, Abu Zakariya appeared as the veritable upholder of Muslim strength in the eyes of the Muslims of the west threatened by the Spanish *reconquista*, and as the sole authentic repository of Almohad tradition. From 1238 for several years the Friday prayer was pronounced in Abu Zakariya's name at Valencia, Seville, Jerez, Tarifa and Granada, and likewise at Tangier, Ceuta and el-Ksar el-Kébir. About 1245 the Merinids in their turn acknowledged the Hafsid's authority. He had, in 1242, brought to reason the amir Yaghmorasan of Tlemcen, who was stubbornly supporting the cause of the Almohad caliph al-Rashid. Finally Abu Zakariya, by skilful manœuvring with the Arab tribes, succeeded in limiting their influence and making useful auxiliaries of some of them.

When he died of an illness in 1249, he had accomplished a considerable achievement in constituting a solid block of territory surrounded by vassal or friendly states and in having accustomed the peoples of Ifriqiya to the new dynasty reigning over it.

AL-MUSTANSIR

The situation he left to his son Abu ʿAbd Allah (1249-1277) was not, however, free from danger. Even within his own family the young prince found rivals ready to place themselves at the head of the Arab tribes. He had to put down four rebellions, pursue the nomadic Dawawida, the most tenacious, far into the desert, throw the remnants of the tribe back towards the west and slaughter their chiefs.

This did not prevent him from assuming in 1253 the caliphian title of *Amir al-Muminin* and the honorific surname of al-Mustansir bi'llah by which he is ordinarily known. He conducted a policy of prestige, planning the kasbah at Tunis with ostentatious splendour, creating 'magnificent gardens with stretches of water in the Tunis region' and surrounding himself with poets and men of letters.[6] The kingdoms of Tlemcen and Fez acknowledged his suzerainty. He received embassies not only from the Italian cities and practically all the states of the western Mediterranean, but also from countries as far distant as Norway (1262), and Kanem and Bornu (1257), the rulers of which sent him rich presents. In 1259

The Return to Berber Kingdoms

the sharif of Mecca even recognised him as caliph, to be followed in this by the Mamlukes of Egypt in 1260. It is true that this recognition was short-lived and that in 1261 the new sultan of Egypt, Baybars, revived the Abbasid dynasty. The Hafsid state was thus very powerful when the fleet of St. Louis appeared before Carthage in 1270.

Until the accession of Charles of Anjou to the throne of Sicily in 1266, the Hafsids had, with fair regularity, paid a small tribute first to the Normans and then to the Hohenstaufen, in order to be spared from Sicilian piracy and to be able to sell their grain freely in the island's ports. Al-Mustansir refused to recognise the rights of Charles, harboured his opponents and ceased payment. Some have sought to see in his attitude the determining cause of the eighth crusade, in which, it is said, St. Louis was involved by his brother's intrigues.

That economic questions played a considerable role in the relations between states in the thirteenth century is undoubtedly a fact. Ibn Khaldun was probably not mistaken in laying stress on the claims of Provençal traders anxious to recover outstanding debts put in jeopardy by the execution of a former minister at Tunis. In the origins of the expeditions of Justinian, St. Louis and Charles X the crusading spirit found it possible, among the ruler's entourage, to reconcile itself with a sense for business. But it is difficult to see where the interest of Charles of Anjou lay in letting himself be diverted from his plans against Constantinople when his way had been left open by a vacancy in the Holy See. It is known, however, that it was on his brother's orders that he had to abandon his enterprise and to join the army of crusaders that had embarked at Aigues-Mortes, which he and his troops did at Tunis on 4 July 1270. The crusade represented not a triumph for his diplomacy, but the failure of his policy.

The determination of St. Louis is more intelligible, inspired as it was by the friar Raymond Martin, professor of Hebrew and Arabic at the Dominican house at Tunis, and a friend of the caliph. The king of France was informed, or thought he understood, that al-Mustansir had decided to become a convert. The noble simplicity of St. Louis has been attributed, groundlessly, to Muslim duplicity. The king's mind was excited at the prospect of transforming Ifriqiya into a powerful centre of Christianity, or at the very least, a base for action against the sultan of Egypt, Baybars, whose activities were proving dangerous.

However, the formidable preparations planned for the delivery of the holy places were, not without hesitation, diverted against Barbary. The fleet moored at Cagliari and six days later, on 18 July, made a landing near Carthage. The caliph had fortified Tunis and sounded the recall of the allied tribes. The resistance took on the character of a holy war preached by 'the devout, the lawyers and the marabouts'.[7] The army was comprised of the Almohads and the *jund* of regulars and volunteers. St. Louis never suspected how near he came to succeeding. Al-Mustansir was thinking of moving his capital to Kairouan when fever and dysentery ravaged the French camp and killed the king on 25 August 1270.

Charles of Anjou, who landed a few hours after his brother's death, became the leader of the crusade and thereafter considered nothing but his own interests. He quickly concluded a treaty with the caliph much to the advantage of the kingdom of Sicily. Al-Mustansir accepted it because the exodus of Arabs towards their pastures in the south was threatening to render resistance by the Muslim army impossible. Accordingly he agreed on 5 November to pay a tribute of twice the amount that had been payable to the Hohenstaufen, together with arrears and an idemnity of war, to return Sicilian deserters, and to grant commercial guarantees to the subjects of the kings of France, of Sicily and of Navarre. All he got in compensation was the razing of the ruins of Carthage in which the Christians had sheltered.

This outcome, admittedly inglorious, was on balance favourable to Ifriqiya. It appears that, apart from a few who were irreconcilably opposed to the settlement, the people realised as much, for al-Mustansir had no trouble in collecting the sums he had undertaken to pay. He was then able without difficulty to resume the commercial relations into which he had earlier entered with Aragon (in 1271), Pisa, Venice (1271) and Genoa (1272) and to keep on good terms with his neighbour of Sicily, Charles of Anjou. The only noteworthy event in the last years of his reign was the recovery of Algiers, which had declared itself independent. It was a peaceful and powerful al-Mustansir who died of an illness on 17 May 1277.

The Return to Berber Kingdoms

RUPTURE OF HAFSID UNITY

The empire left by al-Mustansir appeared solid enough, but it quickly disintegrated in the hands of his successors. His son al-Wathiq, who took his place without opposition, let himself be dominated by a favourite of Andalusian origin who roused the whole Almohad clan against the government. A brother of al-Mustansir, Abu Ishaq, who had already rebelled in 1253, set up as his nephew's rival. Besides the malcontents of Ifriqiya who gathered round him, he had the advantage of military support from the new king of Aragon, Peter III (1276-1285). The latter, with Mediterranean ambitions at heart, had designs on Angevin Sicily and thought himself more likely to accomplish them if a ruler devoted to his cause were reigning in Ifriqiya. Having become master of Bougie in April 1279, Abu Ishaq entered Tunis during August of that year and there assumed power.[8]

The new ruler, who had remained content with the title of Amir, was no more successful than his unhappy predecessor. He very quickly disappointed his Christian protector who, in support of a rebel, made a landing at Collo in June 1282 and maintained himself there for two months without success. He then embarked for Sicily, where the Sicilian Vespers (30 March 1282) had seriously damaged Angevin rule. Relieved of this threat, Abu Ishaq strengthened his position by marrying one of his daughters to the heir apparent of the kingdom of Tlemcen. But his internal policy, 'composed of weakness and fits of brutality', had already caused discontent among the greater part of the population, particularly the Arabs of the south. It was among them that an audacious adventurer, Ibn Abi 'Umara, found a hearing. He passed himself off as a son of al-Wathiq and aided by Bedouin support made himself master of all southern Tunisia by the autumn of 1282. In January 1283 he was at Tunis and in June he defeated the troops of the Hafsids, who had taken refuge in Bougie and were trying to recover their capital.

His success was to be only short-lived. In his turn he stirred up the Arabs against him, who had no difficulty in finding a pretender in Abu Hafs 'Umar, a brother of al-Mustansir. They marched on Tunis, took it in July 1284 and had the new caliph proclaimed under the name of al-Mustansir bi'llah.

Abu Hafs (1284-1295) owed his success to the Beni Sulaim, and he rewarded their services generously. Whereas Abu Zakariya and al-Mustansir had always refused to concede towns to them and had been content to make them a money payment, Abu Hafs in 1284 granted them, as a free gift carrying not only the revenue from land but also the enjoyment of taxes (charter of *iqtā'*), three or four districts in the Sfax and Djérid country.

The concessions the Hafsids had to grant hastened the decline of the kingdom. In 1289 the traveller al-'Abdari noted that with the exception of Tunis, which continued to be a busy centre of trade and studies, the other towns were reeling under the blows of Christians and nomads.[9] Djerba had given way to the attacks of the Sicilian and Aragonese fleet of Roger of Loria in 1284; the Kerkenna Islands had suffered the same fate in 1287, Constantine was exhausted by factional strife, and Béja was in ruins and so sorely threatened by the Arabs that burials were carried out under armed guard.

The anarchy maintained by the rivalries of the Arab tribes led to the appearance of pretenders who were always certain of finding a party of nomads to support their claims. The unity of the Hafsid kingdom gave way during one of the crises. In 1284 Abu Zakariya II set up a rival kingdom to that of Tunis at Bougie, covering the greater part of the province of Constantine. For twenty-three years the two princes, supported by Arab tribes, kept up the conflict. It required the authority of the Almohad shaikhs to bring the caliph of Tunis, Abu 'Asida (1295-1309), and the sultan of Bougie, Abu al-Baqa, to agree that the survivor of the two should reunite the two kingdoms under his authority.

It was Abu al-Baqa who benefited from the restoration of Hafsid unity, but only briefly; his reign lasted only from 1309 to 1311. An aged and skilful pretender, Ibn al-Lihyani (1311-1318), soon succeeded in supplanting the caliph by handing over all power to the nomads, while a great-grandson of Abu Zakariya, Abu Yahya Abu Bakr (1318-1346), took possession of Bougie. Hafsid unity was once more re-established by Abu Bakr, and with difficulty maintained between 1315 and 1318. The Arabs did not limit themselves to setting up pretenders against him, but rather they brought about intervention by the 'Abd al-Wadids of Tlemcen. They were far from indifferent to the discords in the central Maghrib and they coveted Bougie. The caliph saved himself from the combined efforts of the Beni Sulaim, the Dawawida and the

The Return to Berber Kingdoms

'Abd al-Wadids by provoking a counter-intervention of the Merinids against Tlemcen. In the course of the struggle he had been driven out of his capital four times. With the protection of the Merinids, and the support of the leading chief of the Beni Sulaim, Shaikh Hamza, he was able to reconquer his kingdom province by province. At the same time he punished rebellious Berbers, he brought the governors and independent shaikhs back into obedience to the caliph, and he levied the tithe on the nomads. In 1335 (?) a fortunate surprise attack even brought him the recapture of Djerba from the Christians.

CONQUEST OF IFRIQIYA BY THE MERINIDS

The death of Abu Bakr in 1346 led to a new crisis. The brother of the legitimate heir was responsible for his death, as also for the death of three of Shaikh Hamza's sons. The nomads, determined in their resistance from that time, resigned themselves to swearing loyalty to the Merinid sultan Abu al-Hasan who, against the advice of his counsellors and instigated by the chancellor of Tunis, Ibn Tafragin, let himself be led into the conquest of the eastern Maghrib. After taking Constantine and Bougie without difficulty, he entered Tunis in great pomp on 15 September 1347. The fleeing caliph had been overtaken near Gabès and beheaded. From that time Abu al-Hasan held power over the whole of the Maghrib, as the Muninids, whom he claimed to succeed, had done.

But he could not calculate without taking the nomads into account, as valuable to a pretender as they were dangerous to a ruler. To ward off the danger he tried to turn the feudal leaders into officials. The tribal chiefs combined against the threat and finally defeated him near Kairouan on 10 April 1348. Notwithstanding the discord sown among his opponents by their victory, Abu al-Hasan was unable to re-establish his authority. Constantine and Bougie yielded themselves to a Hafsid, and his empire collapsed piece by piece. Finally, in December 1349–January 1350, he fled to Algiers and made his way back to Morocco. One of his sons was unable to maintain himself at Tunis despite the protection of the Arab tribe into which he had married.

The chronic rivalries of Ifriqiya soon made it possible for the Merinids to invade the Hafsid kingdom again. In 1353 Sultan Abu 'Inan completed his occupation of 'Abd al-Wadid territory by annexing Bougie, where he won over the nomads by increased grants. Then, in spite of a serious setback, he gained possession in 1357 of Constantine, Bône and Tunis. He, like Abu al-Hasan, found himself faced with the problem of how the central power was to exert its authority over the Arabs. His attempts at repression resulted in the same failure, he lost his allies and had to make a hasty return to Morocco. A further last campaign in 1358 amounted to no more than a route march between Bône and the Aurès.

RESTORATION OF HAFSID POWER

Three princes established themselves at Tunis, Bougie and Constantine after the departure of the Merinids. Of these, Hafsid Abu al-'Abbas, installed at Constantine through the sultan's friendship, succeeded in acquiring Bougie, Dellys and Bône with the support of the Dawawida, and then, on 9 November 1370, Tunis, where he reigned until 1394.

The man who once more reunited the entire eastern kingdom under his own authority deserved his success. He was a leader with a strong will but a sense of justice which the historians have applauded. He was unable to acquiesce in being reduced by the nomads to ownership of Tunis and its immediate neighbourhood. He rescinded grants of caliphian lands, contained tribal encroachments, put down revolts and subdued the shaikhs of the Djérid, Gafsa and Gabès. But he was not blind to the disadvantages of authoritarian action, and knew equally well how to employ diplomacy and distribute favour or pardon at the right moment. By this skilful policy he was able to keep himself in power. The divided Arabs were unable to inflict on the Hafsid caliph the fate suffered by the Merinid sultans Abu al-Hasan and Abu 'Inan.

It was during his reign that privateering against Christian vessels was organised, with Bougie as its focal point. The Christian powers took counter-action, primarily through a Franco-Genoese expedition against Mahdiya which failed to secure the desired result.

THE FIFTEENTH CENTURY HAFSIDS: ABU FARIS AND ABU 'AMR 'UTHMAN

While the other two Maghribi states—Tlemcen and Fez—continued their unbroken decline throughout the fifteenth century,

The Return to Berber Kingdoms

the Hafsid kingdom in the same period underwent a recovery of glory and power, due to two sovereigns who shared the common attributes of valour and longevity—Abu Faris (1394–1434) and Abu 'Amr 'Uthman (1435–1488).

The former, a son of Abu al-Abbas, acceded to power without difficulty on his father's death. He was a little over thirty years old and had shown his mettle as a military leader at the time of the Christian attack on Mahdiya. He also enjoyed a great reputation for piety and had been able to secure the support of his brothers. Accordingly he found it no great task to triumph over the few rebels who made known their opinions against him, and he was well able to handle the principal clans of the kingdom—Almohads, Andalusians and Arabs—with tact. Strong in the solidity with which he had been able to endow his government, he found it possible to subjugate one by one the semi-independent principalities his father had been obliged to tolerate in the south of the country—Tripoli in 1398, Tozeur and Gafsa in 1400 and Biskra in 1402. He even succeeded in securing Algiers, in 1410 or 1411.

Such a re-establishment of Hafsid power brought Abu Faris great prestige, a prestige which was augmented by the care the ruler took to make clear his interest in religious matters. This he did by surrounding himself with scholars and sharifs, by celebrating the Muslim festivals with splendour, by facilitating worship and by conforming as well as he could to Koranic law. The fame of Abu Faris spread far beyond the borders of his kingdom, as witness the embassies, gifts and marks of honour he received from Granada, Fez, Egypt and even the holy cities. The Christian states for their part hastened to negotiate with so powerful a ruler, and master of such a prosperous kingdom, but the encroachments of the corsairs sometimes thwarted these good relations. Thus it was that, following the sack of Torreblanca by the Barbaresques in 1397, the combined fleets of Valencia and Majorca attacked Dellys in 1398 and then Bône in 1399. In 1424 the fleet of Alphonso V of Aragon ravaged the Kerkenna Islands and in 1432 it attacked Djerba, though without much success.

The best possible proof of Hafsid recovery is to be found in the interest taken by Abu Faris in the affairs of the west, after more than a century during which the Hafsids had been content to suffer the attacks of Fez or Tlemcen or to call on one or the other for help. Twice, in 1424 and 1431, he organised expeditions against Tlemcen, where several ʿAbd al-Wadids were struggling for power, and on each occasion he installed a ruler devoted to his cause. He even marched against Fez in 1424, but as the young Merinid sultan and his Wattasid guardian had sent him a token of homage, he halted on his journey and intervened no more in Morocco except to lend the help of his fleet against the squadrons of Portugal. Likewise he took a fairly close interest in the dynastic quarrels which from 1427 to 1430 rent the kingdom of Granada. At his death, then, the Hafsid state had recovered, or very nearly so, the splendour which it had enjoyed in the reign of al-Mustansir.

He was replaced by his grandson al-Muntasir, but this young man, undermined by disease, died at the end of fourteen months, on 16 September 1435. After him power passed to his brother Abu ʿAmr ʿUthman, who was only sixteen and a half years of age, but had already given proof of his courage.

The beginning of his reign saw much unrest, for one of his uncles, Abu al-Hasan, caused him much trouble in the Constantine country and around Bougie. After eleven years of effort ʿUthman inflicted a decisive reverse on him at Bougie, but he did not effectively dispose of him until 1452. It should, however, be noted how limited this disturbance was in scope. It did not prevent the caliph from directing important expeditions against Nefta, in 1441, and Touggourt, in 1449, and security prevailed throughout Hafsid territory as a whole, as is illustrated by an official Florentine document dated 1446 cited by Brunschvig.[10] Later, in 1463, ʿUthman had to put down a rising of certain Arab tribes who had rebelled over money matters, but this was not a particularly serious episode and Hafsid power was in no danger from it. On the Ifriqiya of this period we have primary source material published by Brunschvig in the account of the Flamand Adorne,[11] who spent from 27 May to 25 June 1470 at Tunis and Sousse. ʿUthman is here represented as both powerful and good, esteemed and respected by his subjects and completely in control of his kingdom.

Relations with neighbouring states confirm this impression. Several Christian powers concluded or renewed trade treaties with him. Among these were Provençe and the France of Louis XI which until then had been in the background. 'It is probable',

The Return to Berber Kingdoms

observes Brunschvig, 'that, forced out of many points in the eastern Mediterranean by the prodigious advance of the Turks, the trade of the Italian maritime republics had for the most part fallen back on North Africa. . . .'[12] In the Maghrib, under 'Uthman as under Abu Faris, the Hafsid state played the role of a leading power. In 1462 and 1466 the caliph directed two expeditions against Tlemcen in order to restore Hafsid influence, which had been put in jeopardy by palace revolutions. We know that in 1472 Muhammad al-Shaikh, ruler of Fez and founder of the Wattasid dynasty, acknowledged himself as a vassal of the caliph 'Uthman. Relations with Egypt and Granada continued courteous, and it is almost certain that an ambassador was sent to the court of the Grand Turk in 1454.

THE END OF THE HAFSIDS

'Uthman had designated one of his grandsons, Abu Zakariya Yahya, as his successor who had scarcely been enthroned when he had to struggle with several competitors from among his uncles and brothers. He did it with great cruelty and, as brutal to his supporters as to his opponents, was soon deserted by his followers and died in combat in 1489. His vanquisher, a cousin-german, was no more successful and in 1490 was dethroned by a son of his unfortunate rival Abu Yahya Zakariya. This young man of eighteen seemed likely to impose his will, but he died of plague in the spring of 1494. Power then fell to one of his cousins-german, Abu 'Abd Allah Muhammad, 'a weak man and fond of his pleasures',[13] poorly equipped to check the abrupt decline of the Hafsid state or to stand up to the difficult situation which the clash between Turks and Spaniards was to bring about in Ifriqiya.

THE HAFSID STATE

Whatever its vicissitudes, the Hafsid dynasty succeeded in maintaining itself in the eastern half of the Maghrib for three centuries and a half and could not fail to have exerted a profound influence on the country. We can accordingly understand Brunschvig's reasons for devoting more than half of his masterly work to the study of the country and its institutions.

The first question that presents itself concerns the demography of Ifriqiya. From the eleventh to the thirteenth century Ifriqiya, more than any other part of the Maghrib, received a considerable influx of Bedouin Arabs. How did these newcomers, whose numbers are unknown, establish themselves in a country already inhabited by a Berber population which was most certainly numerous? In general, though it cannot be laid down as an absolute rule, they settled in the flat country more suitable to their pastoral ways, while the Berbers retreated towards the hills or the mountain regions. Moreover, by the Hafsid period it is very difficult to distinguish Berber from Arab regions, for linguistic frontiers no longer coincide with ethnic frontiers; Arabic had made great progress even in Berber areas. Only groups protected by their relative isolation, like the Kabyles, the people of the Aurès and Djerba, and the inhabitants of the mountain masses of southern Tunisia and Tripolitania, remained entirely Berber-speaking. It should be added that in some places religion contributed to the permanence of the Berber idiom. The Djebel Nefousa, Djerba and a part of the Djefara remained Kharijite as well as Berber-speaking. These two peculiarities, when reinforcing each other, withstood the penetration of outside influences better than did either one of them separately. The rest of what is now Tunisia was completely Arabised in the Hafsid period.

Furthermore, the distribution of urban centres was modified, without doubt as a result of Bedouin invasions. Almost all the towns that can be called such were established on the coast, in which the Bedouins were not interested and where economic relations with Christian states afforded the new townsmen some scope for activity. Apart from the maritime ports, there were to be found only oases—ports of the Sahara—and finally Kairouan and Constantine. These were the only two inland towns which were able to maintain some sort of existence, though with diminished standing. This they did by virtue of sheer size, the strategic situation of the one and the religious character of the other. Archaeology provides proof of this, at least in respect of Kairouan. In conclusion, the balance of the country had profoundly changed since the Zirid period, and it would appear that the Hafsids by their flexible policy contributed to the stabilization of the new human equilibrium in Ifriqiya.

Alongside the Muslims lived Christians and Jews. The latter had been ill-treated by the Almohads, but had survived. They were

The Return to Berber Kingdoms

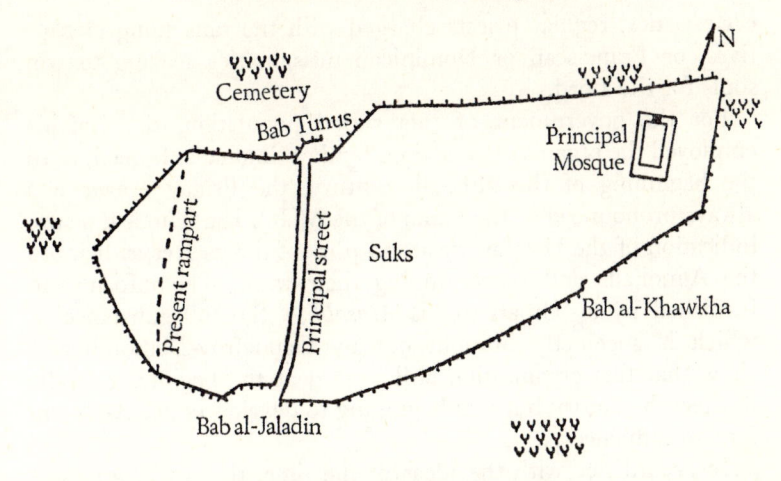

5 Kairouan during the Hafsid period

joined by Jews from Spain after the persecutions these had suffered in 1391 followed by the decree of expulsion passed against them after the fall of Granada. The Jews of Ifriqiya had not played a political role like their co-religionists in Morocco under the Merinids, but they had contributed handsomely to the country's economic activity and had benefited from the watchful protection of the Hafsid rulers. Whether they lived in a separate quarter, as was the case in Morocco from the fifteenth century onwards, extant documents do not enable us to state with certainty.

The Christians were all of European origin. The last traces of native Christianity had disappeared in the thirteenth century under the influence of the Almohad movement. Some of them were traders; most of them lived in the coastal ports, grouped by 'nations' in a *funduk* where they resided and traded under the authority of a consul accredited to the Hafsid ruler. Their situation, though subject to the chances and changes of politics, was on the whole satisfactory. Also, there was a Christian military force at the Hafsid court—some hundreds of men, nearly all Catalans at various periods, who acted as bodyguard to the prince, lived in a quarter apart, and generally remained attached to Christianity. Besides them were to be found renegades, most of them former slaves, slaves of both sexes taken by the corsairs, and finally ecclesiastics, regular priests charged with the ransoming of captives, or Franciscan or Dominican missionaries seeking to win souls for the Lord.

For the government of this varied population, the Hafsids employed the organisation devised by the Almohads. Indeed, until the beginning of the fifteenth century, the Friday prayer was always pronounced in the name of the Mahdi Ibn Tumart, a sure indication of the Hafsids' desire to present themselves as heirs to the Almohads and as continuing their work. The information furnished by al-'Umari in his *Masalik*,[14] the full substance of which is succinctly brought out by Gaudefroy-Demombynes, show that this organisation still existed at the beginning of the fourteenth century but was beginning to develop under Arab and foreign influences.

In accordance with the ideas of the time, the sovereign combined all power in his own person and was the object of marks of respect embodied in a fairly detailed code of etiquette. However, this absolutism did not mean that, on the model of the Abbasid caliphs, the Hafsid monarch lived jealously separated from his subjects. He frequently appeared before them, as the sultan of Morocco does in our day, and they gained his audience without great difficulty.

However, he did govern with the help of the ten Almohad shaikhs. The 'Shaikh of the Almohads', the veritable leader of the aristocracy, held the highest offices. Almohad society remained hierarchic, as in the time of Ibn Tumart; at the head were the great shaikhs and the assembly of the Ten, and grouped beneath were, the petty shaikhs of the Fifty, and the ordinary shaikhs. These shaikhs continued to be organised in categories under the supervision of a senior (*mazwar*) who was in the beginning a censor of morals but later became the prince's chamberlain and carried out the punishments he had ordered.

Their influence diminished markedly in the first half of the fifteenth century. The chief among them no doubt formed part of the council (*shūrā*) whose advice the ruler could ask for and on which the high officials managing the administration probably sat. Under Abu Zakariya there were three ministers (*wazīr*, plural *wuzarāʾ*). At the beginning of the sixteenth century Leo Africanus enumerates ten 'principal officers at the court of the king of Tunis'.[15] The three original viziers comprised the minister for the *jund*—the

The Return to Berber Kingdoms

only one to be a shaikh—who was head of the army and of ordnance and supply; the minister of finance, who was accountant-general as well as having charge of the tax department and who took action against defrauders; and the secretary of state in charge of political correspondence and the police. Ibn Khaldun stresses the importance of the *hājib*, who began as major-domo of the palace, later became the intermediary between the sultan and his officials and finally veritable head of the government.[16] The *Masalik* also mentions agents in charge of the commissariat and of the presentation of petitions, the chief of police, the censor of morals at Tunis (*muhāsaba*) and the provincial governors. They too, like the *muhtasib*, were responsible for the battle against evil and the encouragement of the good.[17]

The Hafsid sovereigns marked their power by formality of etiquette in public audience and above all in their processions. Surrounded by shaikhs and men-at-arms, and later by foreign guards, they paraded on horseback in great pomp, to the beating of kettledrums and tambours, the rustling of multicoloured standards of embroidered silk overshadowed by their own white standards, and popular demonstrations. Adorne has left us a vivid description of one such procession.[18]

The Almohad people constituted the *jund*. This included not only Berber elements, organised in annual contingents. There were also Turks, Andalusians, Arabs, even renegade Christians, and negro soldiers. These last, with the Christian mercenaries, formed the caliph's loyal guard. The members of the *jund* enjoyed various privileges. The shaikhs, according to their standing, received endowments of land carrying either the enjoyment of the revenue or even the raising of taxes. Four times a year every Almohad was paid a salary in money, quite apart from presents dependent on the sultan's personal decision. It has been seen that military necessities obliged the Hafsids to allow the Arabs charters of *iqtāʿ*. The army was not lacking in bravery and it can be compared favourably with European armies of the day, though it was without heavy armament. The case was not the same by sea. By the end of the Middle Ages the navy showed a fairly clear inferiority in comparison to the European fleets of the Mediterranean. Not only were the Hafsid vessels of war outclassed by the Genoese and others, but also, transports being insufficient in numbers, the foreign trade of Barbary was carried for the most part in Christian ships. The corsairs alone, owing to their mobility and their spirit of attack by surprise, maintained an important position in the western Mediterranean.

Provincial administration assumed three distinct forms, depending on whether it was concerned with the tribes of the 'cities of the south' or towns and districts coming under the direct authority of the ruler. The tribes, a large part of them Arab, were subject to shaikhs appointed from among them according to no precise rule. When these tribes were on good terms with the central authority, the shaikhs played a double role as agents of the government to their fellow tribesmen and as representatives of their fellow tribesmen to the government. In the towns of the south weak rulers were obliged to tolerate the influence of oligarchies or of great local families. Strong sultans had much difficulty in reducing to obedience these elements of autonomy, which strongly resembled the fragmentation that had occurred between 1050 and 1060 at the beginning of the Hilalian invasion. Finally, in the districts where caliphian authority could be exercised directly, the sovereign was represented by a governor. This was nearly always one of his close relatives, often one of his sons, assisted by an experienced official and enjoying, like the caliph, very extensive powers.

TUNIS AND MEDITERRANEAN TRADE

With the Hafsids Tunis assumed the character and appearance of an unchallenged capital. It comprised the former centre of the Medina, flanked on the north and south by the two former suburbs of Bab Souïqa and Bab Jazira, which were enclosed with ramparts at the beginning of the fourteenth century. To the west lay the Kasbah, of Almohad construction but remodelled and completed by the Hafsids; and to the east lay Christian *funduks* and the arsenal on the shore of the lake. The appointments of the town, as they exist today, are chiefly the work of the Hafsids. By the time of Abu Zakariya Tunis boasted two madarsas or colleges, which are still in existence. A third, not now standing, was built at the end of the thirteenth century in the suk quarter. The *Masalik* draws attention to the importance of its baths and suks.[19] It was in the thirteenth or fourteenth century that the suk for perfumes and cloth was built. Its three alleys were covered in brick cradle-

The Return to Berber Kingdoms

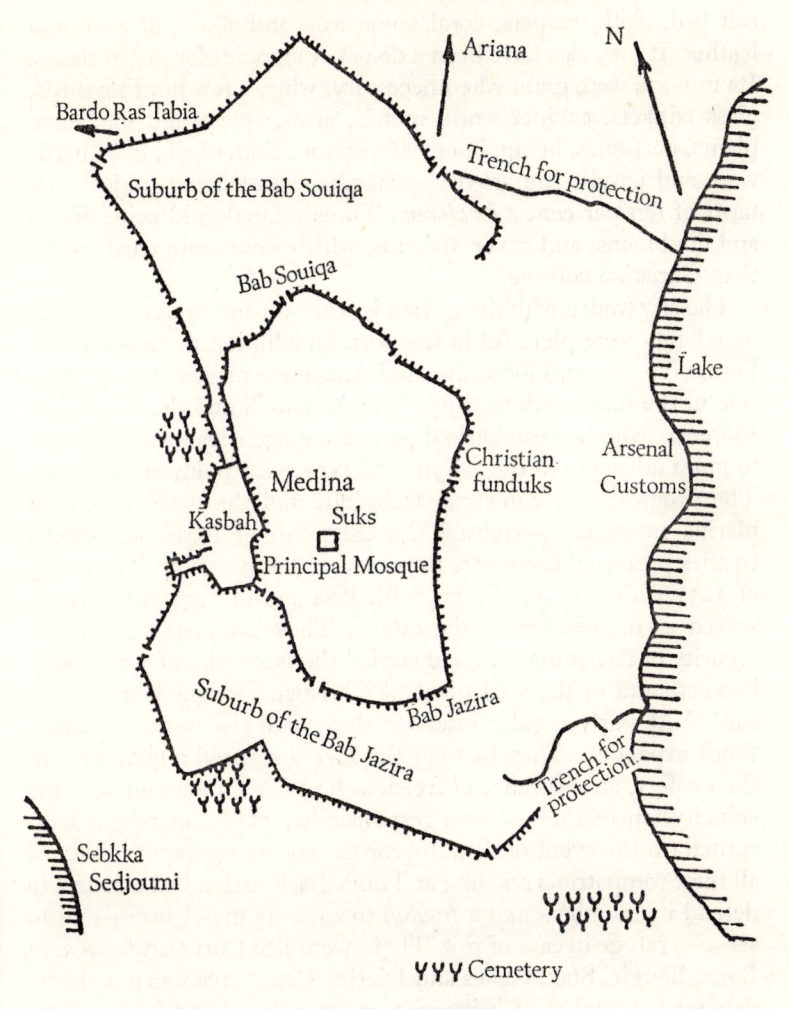

6 Tunis under the Hafsids

vaulting and on to it opened shops likewise roofed with cradles at right angles to the first set.

The building of new suks was rendered the more necessary by the increasing pace of Tunisian commercial activity. Tunis was an exporter of grain, when the harvest was good, dates, olive oil, wax, salt fish, cloth, carpets, coral, some arms and above all wool and leather. It may also have been a dispatching point for negro slaves. Its imports were grain when necessary, wine, a few hunting birds, glass trinkets, cabinet work, metals, arms, spices and medicinal plants, perfumes, hemp, linen, silk, cotton, cloth of all kinds, hardware and jewels. Imported merchandise was usually subject to a tariff of ten per cent *ad valorem*. Tunis minted gold coin, dinars and doubloons, and silver dirhems, which were more trustworthy than Christian coinage.

The city traded with the Levant by caravan and by sea. Christian merchants were plentiful in the port. In addition to Genoese and Pisans, Venetians, Florentines and Aragonese played an important role in the fourteenth century. The Acciaiuoli and the Peruzzi of Florence, who had established permanent agencies there and used to grant advances to the caliph, had very great political influence. The progress of commercial technique and the development of marine insurance permitted the extension of business. Special treaties protected foreigners in person and in property. The treaty of 1231 with Venice, of 1234 with Pisa and of 1236 with Genoa served as models for all the others. They 'stipulated reciprocal security of navigation . . . and settled the principles of conducting business and of the settlement of Christian foreigners on Islamic soil'.[20] At fairly regular intervals they were renewed and sometimes expanded. Thus in 1353 the Pisans secured a guarantee of their safety, an assurance of freedom for their transactions and the substitution of the personal responsibility of the merchant concerned (in the event of dispute) for the collective responsibility of all their compatriots residing at Tunis. Each nation had a consul to defend its members and a *funduk* to store its merchandise and to serve as refuge in case of riot. There were also Christian *funduks* at Bône, Bougie, Sfax, Gabès and Djerba. Commerce was not always dependable, and the Christians were as guilty of bad faith as were the Muslims. It was conducted chiefly on credit, either in bond—with the moral guarantee of the authorities and generally at auction with a dragoman as intermediary—or out of bond, at the merchant's own risk.

The growth of piracy, which the caliph was incapable of controlling, necessitated sailing in convoy and led to frequent conflicts. Several factors increased the tension of relations, Djerba was

The Return to Berber Kingdoms

occupied by Roger of Loria and organised by a Catalan adventurer Ramon Muntaner between 1311 and 1314. The place was recaptured by the Muslims in 1335, and then unsuccessfully attacked by the Genoese and Sicilians. Rivalry between Christian mariners and the corsairs of Mahdiya resulted in 1390 in the dispatch of a Venetian and Genoese fleet, reinforced by French galleys, against the port of Ifriqiya with the object of gaining possession of this 'city of Auffrique of manly might'.[21] The attack failed, but Mahdiya may have had to agree to pay tribute.

The development of Muslim piracy in the sixteenth century probably contributed to the Spanish attacks against Djerba and Tunis.

HAFSID CULTURE

Active as it was in the political and economic fields, the Hafsid state was also able to maintain its place in intellectual matters. It is possible to speak of a Hafsid culture. In religion this is marked by the renaissance, after its eclipse during Almohad domination, of Malikism, under the influence of the juridical schools of Tunis, Bougie and Kairouan and particularly of the celebrated doctor, Ibn 'Arafa (1316–1401). About the same time Maghribi mysticism sprang into full life following the teaching of the great mystic of Bougie, Abu Madyan (Sidi Bu Madian, who died near Tlemcen in 1197 or 1198). The movement had been inaugurated in the thirteenth century by such pioneers as Abu Sa'id al-Baji (Sidi Bu Said), Abu al-Hasan al-Shadhili (Sidi Belhassen) and 'Aisha al-Manubiya (Lalla Manoubia). It underwent a great expansion in the second half of the thirteenth century, its most celebrated representative being one of the patron saints of Tunis, Sidi Bin 'Arus, who was venerated in his own lifetime and whose body was escorted to the grave by the entire city in 1463. Secular knowledge underwent the same decline in Ifriqiya as in the Muslim world as a whole. Not a single mathematician, physician or doctor of medicine of any note is to be found throughout the Hafsid period. On the other hand, the literary genre of edifying biography was much practised and, apart from the inspired Ibn Khaldun, certain historical works of some merit are worthy of mention. Examples are the *Rihla*, an account of travel, by Tijani[22] (fourteenth century) and the *Farisiya* by Ibn Qunfud,[23] the *Adilla* by al-Hintati[24] and the *Tarikh al-dawlatain* attributed to Zarkashi[25]—all works of the fifteenth century. If to these we add accomplished prose, as an embellishment of official correspondence, and poetry only too often occasional in character, we shall have an approximate idea of the intellectual life in the Hafsid kingdom. It was uninspired, vacillating between slightly decadent Andalusian influences and oriental influences lacking in brilliance. It was a semi-conscious period of waiting, having at any rate the merit of keeping alive a long and brilliant cultural tradition.

The Hafsid sultans were also builders. In the towns they found numerous examples of Aghlabid and Sanhajan architecture. But strong as were the former traditions and oriental influences that architecture recalled, they yielded even more to the teachings of the Andalusian artists who were plentiful at the court of Tunis. 'The present sultan (Abu Zakariya)', wrote Ibn Saiyd to an émigré notable from Spain, 'is constructing public buildings, building palaces, planting gardens and vineyards, after the manner of the Andalusians. All his architects are natives of this country, likewise his masons, his carpenters, his brickmakers, his painters and his gardeners. The plans of the edifices have been drawn by Andalusians or copied directly from actual buildings of their country.' The prestige of Merinid culture, displayed by the scholars surrounding Abu al-Hasan, equally made its mark on the art of Ifriqiya.

At Tunis Abu Zakariya, following former Ifriqiyan models, hastened to raise the Mosque of the Kasbah. Its square minaret, of stone construction, though heavier in form, recalls that of the kasbah at Marrakesh. Al-Mustansir probably built a mosque at Monastir. The caliph Abu Hafs carried out important works at the Great Mosque of Kairouan in 1294. Nothing is left of the parks of al-Mustansir, which aroused Ibn Khaldun's enthusiasm,[26] but two angled doors have been preserved, one of them dating from his reign, with bays of oriental inspiration. A garden made for Abu Hafs enclosed a large lake on which his wives indulged in the pleasures of boating. In order to supply it, he restored the ancient aqueduct erected in Hadrian's time and arranged offtakes from it. At Tunis the Hafsids also constructed reservoirs and drinking fountains, the troughs of which still exist. The architects of Ifriqiya retained their taste for polychrome materials. Finally, the immediate surroundings of Tunis, which give the town its special character and appearance, are a Hafsid creation. There is the palace of Ras Tabia, built in 1225 at the north-west corner of the town and taken up again by al-Mustansir; also there is a park, laid out by him, near the present village of Ariana. The palace of the Bardo, built by Abu Faris, probably dates from the very early years of the fifteenth century. Finally, about 1500 Abu 'Abd Allah Muhammad had a country house built at La Marsa.

Thus the Hafsids were not great builders, in the sense of having left public buildings worthy of admiration like their Almohad forerunners, nor could we speak specifically of a Hafsid style of architecture. But they fixed for centuries the appearance of a city like Tunis and were able to maintain those urban centres like Kairouan which had succeeded in holding on after the Bedouin invasions.

We may look on the Hafsids as the preservers of a civilisation to which they themselves made little original contribution. However, if we remember that they continually had to hold turbulent tribes in check, and to protect themselves against ever more enterprising Christians—and all this without an expectation of outside aid, we shall allow that their achievement, for all its lack of brilliance, at least commands our respect.

11. The 'Abd Al-Wadid Kingdom of Tlemcen

THE RESURGENCE OF THE ZENATA. THE 'ABD AL-WADIDS

Eastern Barbary, where urban and administrative traditions retained their life and vigour, was able to preserve a sultanate despite Arab encroachments, but the central Maghrib reverted to grazing country, where towns were razed and cultivation destroyed. The collapse of the rudimentary authority of the Sanhaja gave the Zenata the opportunity, which they took, to gradually restore their strength. Then the Bedouins, delayed by the looting of Ifriqiya, began there too to throw their weight into dynastic quarrels and to impress their mark on the nomadic Berber tribes.

Zenata resurgence resulted in the creation in the central and western Maghrib, on either side of Taza gap, of two dynasties which though related were rivals, as formerly the Maghrawa and Beni Ifren dynasties had been. These were the ʿAbd al-Wadids of Tlemcen and the Merinids of Fez.

The founder of the ʿAbd al-Wadid or Ziyanid dynasty, Yaghmorasan ibn Ziyan, conferred great prestige on a nomadic family whose previous history, whatever Arab chroniclers have said, could not have been more humble. About the mid-eleventh century the Hilalian thrust had pushed the ʿAbd al-Wadids back as far as the confines of the far Maghrib, and for more than a century they had been content to revolve in the orbit of powerful Zenata families. ʿAbd al-Mumin rewarded them for siding with him by settling them in the western part of Orania, and there they played the role of vassals, nearly always loyal, of the Almohads.

The Muminid decline caused no break in their fortune. Indeed they had as chief a man of decision, capable of seizing the opportune moment to establish an independent dynasty which lasted for more than three centuries, from 1235 to 1554.

TLEMCEN

Tlemcen became the capital of the new Maghribi kingdom, though the city had a past stretching back into antiquity. On the neighbouring plateau, where Agadir stands today, the Romans had built the camp, later the town, of Pomaria. It may have been conquered by a lieutenant of ʿUqba ibn Nafiʿ. Certainly it became the centre of the small Kharijite community of the imam Abu Qurra, and was then taken by Idris I in 790 and remained the vassal of Fez. At the time of the collapse of the Idrisids, Agadir passed under the control of Maghrawa amirs, the Beni Khazer, followed by the Beni Yaʿla, vassals of the ʿUmaiyads of Cordova. In the eleventh century al-Bakri commented on its prosperity.[27]

It was the Almoravid prince Yusuf ibn Tashfin who at the beginning of the twelfth century built Tagrart, predecessor of the present Tlemcen, on the plateau where he had camped west of Agadir. The new city grew quickly at the expense of the old, and finally absorbed it. The Almohads fortified the two, and under them one was inhabited by officials, the other by the common folk. But it was Yaghmorasan who transformed it, in Ibn Khaldun's words, into 'the capital of the central Maghrib and the guardian metropolis of the Zenata tribes'.[28]

The Return to Berber Kingdoms

Gautier has shown how geography appears to have determined the foundation of a western capital of Algeria in the Tafna area.[29] Where the great Touat–Roussillon fault crosses the Tell, the line that runs from Tlemcen to the mouth of the Tafna, and on which rose Siga, the capital of Syphax, is not without its similarities to the line Achir–Médéa–Miliana–Algiers. However, the situation of the 'Abd al-Wadid city made it pleasant to live in and encouraged its commercial activity. Built as it was half-way up a hillside, at a height of some 2,700 feet, amid orchards from which it had got its Latin name, it offered so many charms that an Arab writer likened it to 'a young bride on her nuptial couch'. It commanded the crossing of several main roads, particularly those leading from the ports of Honeïn, 24 miles east of Nemours, and Oran to the Tafilalet.

Even in times of crisis it continued to be frequented by merchants who stocked up with products of the Sudan—ivory, gold and slaves brought by caravans along tracks furnished at intervals with wells. In exchange Tlemcen dispatched its wool, arms and books, but it was chiefly a transit point for African and European merchandise, the sale of which took place in the old quarter of the Qaïçariya. At the beginning of the sixteenth century Leo Africanus laid stress on the reputation for honesty of the merchants of Tlemcen.[30]

However, the political position of the town was precarious. It was caught as in a vice between the Hafsid and Merinid kingdoms, and furthermore open to attack by its neighbours of Fez, who looked on it as one of their dependencies, as well as by Hilalian nomads ever ready to act as forerunners of invasion. Accordingly the existence of Tlemcen, even in Yaghmorasan's reign, was precarious and never enabled it to command a powerful empire.

YAGHMORASAN IBN ZIYAN

The dynasty made a promising start with the long reign of Yaghmorasan (1235–1283). In order to resist its enemies Tlemcen needed an event as exceptional as this fifty-year period free from dynastic crisis. These enemies included Hafsids, who did, however, impose a brief suzerainty following a victorious campaign in 1242; Almohads, who were repulsed in 1248; Zenata, who, jealous of the good fortune of the 'Abd al-Wadids, allied themselves with their enemies; and finally Arab tribes, principally the Ma'qil Dawi 'Ubaid Allah, whose camps lay to the west of Ziyanid territory. Against these last, it is said, Yaghmorasan had to conduct seventy-two expeditions.

While settling the 'Abd al-Wadids, Yaghmorasan did not abandon the friendship or support of the nomads. Against the Arab-Zenata *suf* of Dawi 'Ubaid Allah and the Merinids he set up another *suf* which was joined by the Suwaid Arabs of the Beni Zoghba tribe. The Suwaid formed his makhzan and he granted them, over and above occasional bounties, fiefs on which the majority of them settled. In order to more effectively defend himself against the Dawi 'Ubaid Allah, who were on the flanks of his territory, he even sent for other more distant Zoghba Arabs, the Beni 'Amir and the Homaiyan. Due to his Zoghba militia, Yaghmorasan was able to subjugate the Dawi 'Ubaid Allah and even to venture on raids against the Merinids. But they only too easily became a burden, and that is probably why Yaghmorasan allowed the Zoghba, even the Suwaid, to move away from Tlemcen. The sedentary prince felt strong enough to break the nomadic makhzan on which he had had to rely in times of danger.

Although of the same distant origin, the 'Abd al-Wadids and Merinids were not on good terms. This mutual animosity may have been connected with quarrels over pasture lands or over *sufs*. It was certainly exacerbated by the rise of the Almohads. However, whereas the 'Abd al-Wadids came to terms with the conqueror about 1145 and profited by it, the Merinids refused to submit to the victorious mountaineers and withdrew to the borders of the desert, where they led a precarious existence. When the Almohad empire was tottering, old quarrels were complicated by political rivalries. The caliph al-Sa'id first tried, in 1245, to annihilate the Merinids with the support of the 'Abd al-Wadids, then, having failed in this attempt, in 1248 he accepted Merinid aid against Tlemcen. Thereafter, and until Yaghmorasan's death, there was a state of constant conflict between the two neighbours. Encouraged by the Almohads, who found in him an unexpected ally, Yaghmorasan tried time and again to foster the Merinids' increasing power; he fully realised what the danger to his people would be, situated between Hafsids and Merinids, but he was without success. Accordingly, his death-bed counsel to his sons

The Return to Berber Kingdoms

was to give up Morocco and to concentrate their efforts on Hafsid border territory. It was a favourable juncture, as the death of al-Mustansir had gravely weakened the eastern kingdom. For a full hundred years the Ziyanids struggled desperately but without success to subdue the Zenata of the Chélif valley and to gain possession of Bougie. The Hafsids warded off the danger by stirring up diversions amongst the Merinids.

THE MERINID INVASIONS

The reign of the Ziyanid Abu Sa'id 'Uthman (1283-1304) was spent in battle. In 1287 he suffered a reverse under the walls of Bougie after ravaging its environs, and he was four times attacked by the Merinid sultan Abu Ya'qub. Three times assaults on Tlemcen were frustrated by its ramparts. The sultan of Fez then tried, in 1299, to starve the city out. He enclosed it by a surrounding wall pierced with gates for attack. 'A spirit, an invisible being', says Ibn Khaldun, 'would have found it hard to penetrate into the city.'[31] The siege lasted eight years. Opposite the capital Abu Ya'qub built a palace, a mosque, living quarters for his staff, public baths, hostelries and markets, all of which he surrounded with walls. Thus the Merinid attempt created a rival city to the Ziyanid capital, the camp of victory (*al-Mahalla al-Mansura*) or New Tlemcen. Its markets abounded in produce, its caravanserais gave shelter to 'merchants from every land'.

In Tlemcen, meanwhile, the starving inhabitants were eating dogs and snakes. Resistance was not brought to an end by the king's sudden death in 1304. His son Abu Ziyan, we are told, was preparing for a final sortie when, in 1307 Abu Ya'qub was assassinated by one of his eunuchs. Peace was signed immediately and the Merinid troops hurriedly returned to Fez. The people of Tlemcen did not long spare the rival city, the buildings and walls of which were demolished once conflict with the Merinids was resumed. The Arabs had taken advantage of the Ziyanid weakness: if they did not join forces with Abu Ya'qub, who received their overtures unfavourably, at least they extended their field of action, chiefly in the Sersou. Freed for the moment of danger from the Merinids, Abu Ziyan (1304-1308) began to restore order in his kingdom. He carried out forays against the Berber tribes of the east who had supported the Merinids and drove the Arabs out of the Sersou. But without nomadic support any effectual action remained impossible. Realising this, the sultan employed the Beni Ya'qub Beni 'Amir tribe to reconstitute the makhzan which Yaghmorasan's imprudence had abolished.

When Abu Ziyan died, the ruins that had accumulated as a result of Abu Ya'qub's attack were far from having been rebuilt. His brother, Abu Hammu Musa I (1308–1318), took on the task himself to repair ramparts, dig ditches, accumulate reserves in his silos and replenish the treasury. The aim of all these measures was to render the city safe against another siege. He even succeeded in keeping the Merinids on the far side of the Oujda, resumed the policy of expansion in the Chélif valley and pushed as far as Constantine and Bougie. His death came by assassination which was instigated by his son, in 1318.

Abu Tashfin (1318–1337) was then only twenty-five. According to the chroniclers, whom there is no need to suspect of bias, he was a man chiefly concerned with pleasure, a lover of ostentation, cultivated and not especially devout. At the request of Arab tribes in revolt against the Hafsid caliph Abu Bakr, he besieged Bougie and Constantine. He then founded a strong point, Tamzizdikt, in the valley of the Soummam one day's march from Bougie, which was designed to cut the communications of Bougie. He was in hopes of annexing the western part of the Hafsid kingdom when Abu Bakr succeeded in persuading the Merinids to intervene. A simultaneous attack on both flanks threw Abu Tashfin back on the defensive. His position was the more serious for the abandonment of the 'Abd al-Wadid cause by the Suwaid and the Beni Ya'qub Beni 'Amir. Tlemcen was once more besieged for nearly two years, and this time was carried by assault by the sultan of Fez, Abu al-Hasan. The king, three of his sons and his commander-in-chief died, sword in hand, in 1337.

MERINID OCCUPATION AND SUZERAINTY

The victory of the sultan of Fez led to the annexation of the kingdom of Tlemcen. The Merinids rebuilt and embellished Mançoura, and constructed the best of the public buildings of Sidi Bou Médine, which became their favourite place of pilgrimage. It was probably at this time that the Great Mosque was completed and the Palace of Victory built. For nearly a quarter of a century, from

The Return to Berber Kingdoms

1337 to 1359, they governed the country directly. Even after they had lost it, they kept the ʿAbd al-Wadid princes in check, and stirred up rivals against them at the least hint of independence.

The rout of the sultan of Fez, Abu al-Hasan, on the plain of Kairouan led to the dismemberment of his empire. The Arab tribes of the central Maghrib deserted the losing side and rallied to two Ziyanid princes, Abu Thabat and Abu Saʿid. The two sultans entered Tlemcen unopposed, but their success was short-lived. In 1352 a strong Merinid army repulsed the Arab-Zenata forces of Abu Thabat in the Chélif valley. Abu Saʿid, who had been taken prisoner in a skirmish, and Abu Thabat, whom the governor of Bougie had handed over, were put to death. The Suwaid, who had supported the Merinid cause, were given the Sersou; the ʿAmir Beni Hammad of Shaikh Shigar, who had fought alongside Abu Thabat, had to take refuge in the desert. For six years the Tell folk, sedentary and nomad alike, fell once more under the authority of the sultans of Fez.

It was to Arab intervention that the Ziyanid dynasty owed its restoration. The Dawawida, in revolt against the Merinid sultan Abu ʿInan and supported by Shigar's fellow-tribesmen, chose Abu Hammu Musa II, nephew to the two last sultans and at the time a refugee at Tunis, and installed him at Tlemcen.

ABU HAMMU MUSA II (1359–1389)

This man of letters, more interested in diplomacy than in battle, spent his reign in putting down rebellion, in conflict with pretenders upheld by Arabs and Merinids, and in defending himself against the intrigues and conspiracies of his own son.

Merinid rule had borne down so heavily on certain Hilalian tribes that Abu Hammu had no difficulty in reconstituting an Arab party. He relied principally on Shigar's ʿAmir Beni Hammad, who had been constant in their loyalty to the ʿAbd al-Wadids, but also on very nearly all the Maʿqilian tribes, who had been rallied to his cause by the skill of his vizier Ibn Musillim. But, weakened by defections and by the death of Shigar, he twice had to evacuate his capital.

The future of the monarchy was decided in the central Maghrib. An attempt by the Ziyanid sultan on Bougie resulted in 1366 in a disastrous defeat, which had considerable repercussions. It afforded the Arabs unopposed access to the rich plain lands from which they had been excluded. Thus the Husain settled in the Titteri, and thereafter levied taxes there for their own benefit.

The defeated sultan tried to strike back with the support of the Dawawida, but he came up against a coalition of Arabs and Merinids instigated by the Suwaid, and in 1370 he had to abandon his capital and take refuge in the Zab. He was pursued into the desert, but owed his safety to the death in 1372 of the sultan of Fez, which enabled him to return to Tlemcen. A truce skilfully negotiated by Wanzammar, the adviser and friend of the Merinid dynasty, brought him the assistance of the Suwaid and a recovery of his authority. For ten years the 'Abd al-Wadid kingdom enjoyed a prosperity it never knew again, but all danger was not removed and Abu Hammu had even considered moving his capital to Algiers in 1378. His clumsy intervention against the kingdom of Fez provoked a rupture with Wanzammar and the Merinids, and reopened the period of invasions. There then rose up against the prince of Tlemcen an implacable enemy in the person of his own son Abu Tashfin, who eventually drove him out with the support of the Suwaid and the Merinids. The sultan was overtaken in the mountains and he perished sword in hand in 1389.

After him the kingdom of Tlemcen, as vassal either of Fez or Tunis, continued a long and inglorious existence. The Ziyanid dynasty, after having to suffer interference by Merinids and Hafsids, followed by Spanish suzerainty, succumbed after a slow death-struggle to the blows of the Turks in 1554.

ARABISATION OF THE ZENATA

Aided by the endemic unrest in the central Maghrib, the Hilalian tribes expanded through the Tell and made themselves independent. It was on their support that pretenders relied, rewarding their aid with new fiefs and the right to collect taxes. The situation depicted by Ibn Khaldun merely grew worse as time went on. 'The Arabs', he wrote in 1380, 'are masters of the plains and of the greater part of the cities. The authority of the Beni 'Abd al-Wad no longer extends to the provinces removed from the centre of the empire and scarcely runs beyond the maritime territory they possessed at the beginning. Their authority has given way before the power of the Arabs. They have themselves contributed to the strengthening of this nomadic race, by lavishing treasure on them,

The Return to Berber Kingdoms

by ceding huge areas to them and by handing over to them the revenues of a great number of towns.'[32]

But the country over which the Arabs spread like the shadow cast by mountains at the close of day, to employ an expression of Ibn Khaldun, was not an abandoned country. Notwithstanding wars and destruction, the Zenata tribes continued to be strong enough to be a constant aggravation to the Ziyanid sultans and to slow down the Bedouin advance. Nevertheless these Zenata suddenly disappeared from history. Were they driven out by the Arabs? But how could these latter have managed it, numbering as they did perhaps 200,000 odd, and swamped by millions of Berbers? And how could it have come about that the Arab tribes of today should all be descendants of the Hilalian invaders? Could it not rather be that in the course of the fifteenth century there came about a fusion of nomadic Zenata with nomadic Arabs, the process encouraged by the similarity of their manner and customs? On that basis the Arabs of the Maghrib would for the most part be none other than Arabised Zenata. This transformation would have caused the ancient rivalry between settled and nomadic Berbers, whom their common language could nevertheless bring together, to be replaced by the much more tenacious hatred between two peoples irreconcilably opposed—Arabs, or Arabised Zenata thinking themselves to be Arabs, and Berbers who resisted Arabisation. A new cause of disturbance was added to the calamities already hanging over Barbary. Such at any rate is Gautier's hypothesis, one of the most fruitful put forward to date with a view to dispersing the obscurity of the mediaeval Maghrib.[33]

'ABD AL-WADID CULTURE AND ART

Several 'Abd al-Wadid princes enjoyed surrounding themselves with artists and scholars, and Tlemcen had the reputation of an intellectual city. 'The sciences and the arts', declared Ibn Khaldun, who had long lived there, 'were successfully cultivated. It was the birthplace of scholars and eminent men whose reputation spread to other countries.'[34] Its poets took pleasure in offering classical, skilled and mannered praises to the rulers. Its society was, as G. Marçais writes, 'polished, devout and cultivated'.[35]

As a centre of Muslim studies, where the five madarsas enjoyed great fame, Tlemcen was thoroughly imbued with that oriental mysticism which was to triumph in reaction against foreign invasion. Among those venerated there were Sidi Wahhab, the companion of the Prophet who had come in 'Uqba's wake and was believed to have been buried in the city. There was also Daudi the great tenth-century saint (died 1101) and above all Sidi Bu Madian, the celebrated mystic of the end of the twelfth century— the 'master of the country' whose tomb, drawing pilgrims from the entire Maghrib, led to the growth of the village of el-'Eubad el-Fouqi.

A few 'Abd al-Wadid foundations still exist. Yaghmorasan had the two minarets of the mosques at Agadir and Tlemcen reconstructed. The Agadir minaret, dominating the Idrisid mosque, is a square brick tower over 130 feet high, classical and elegant in form. It rests on a base, the stones of which were taken from Roman buildings, and it is decorated on its four faces with miniature columns and panels ornamented with fleurons in glazed terracotta. The minaret of the Great Mosque, nearly 112 feet high, is similar in style. The charming brick qubba of the wood of Sidi Ya'qub, octagonal in plan and carried on open multi-lobed arcades, may date from the reign of Yaghmorasan, but is more probably of an earlier period.

The founder of the monarchy could not be content with the Château-Vieux, the Almoravid palace of Tagrart next to the Great Mosque, and laid the foundations of a palace-citadel, the Méchouar, of which hardly anything remains. The Méchouar became the official residence of the Ziyanid princes. There they had their living quarters, their mosque and military stores. There lived the members of the court and foreign amirs, and there were held the great receptions. To celebrate the Prophet's birthday, Abu Hammu II sat upon the throne in the main hall of the Méchouar, surrounded by grandees and in the presence of the people. The tall candelabra, the garments of silk, the reading of poems, and the banquet followed by morning prayer lent a ceremonious air to the entire festival.

Only three 'Abd al-Wadid mosques remain. The oratory of Sidi Belhassen, built by Abu Said 'Uthman at the end of the thirteenth century, is small but delightful. Horseshoe arcades springing from eight onyx columns, of which only two have been destroyed,

The Return to Berber Kingdoms

divide it into three naves each with three bays. The niche with cut-off corners forming the mihrab is covered by a vault in stalactites resting on colonnettes. The interior walls are adorned with magnificent panels in sculptured, and formerly painted, plaster. Their arabesques are evidence of incomparable skill and elegance. The cedarwood ceiling carried polychrome decorations, but of this it has been possible to save only a few fragments. The Ouled el-Imam Mosque, smaller still, with its two bays and three naves, has lost almost all its stucco ornamentation.

Nothing survives of the many public buildings erected by Abu Tashfin. The ruins of his madarsa were razed to the ground at the turn of the nineteenth century. Of the building activity of Abu Hammu II, the mosque and tomb of Sidi Brahim, intended to house the bodies of the sultan's father and uncles, stand as evidence of the swift decadence of the art of Tlemcen.

If Tlemcen represents a centre of Muslim architecture which is unique in Algeria, that is because the Merinids, in their devotion to the local saints, built at Mançoura and Sidi Bou Médine monuments, some of which are among the most beautiful in the Maghrib.

CONCLUSION

Whereas the history of the Hafsid kingdom is one of sometimes brilliant survival, that of the kingdom of Tlemcen is certainly one of almost total failure. Yet it had originated in favourable circumstances. The 'Abd al-Wadids had had no such struggle to establish themselves in their capital as had the Merinids. They had, moreover, benefited for more than fifty years from the drive of a great leader, Yaghmorasan. Finally for a lengthy period they had as neighbours Hafsids who were far away and Merinids who were occupied in conquering a kingdom. In spite of all these advantages, Tlemcen did not become the capital of a great state. The Arabs, more firmly established in the central Maghrib than in Morocco, were partly responsible for this failure. So also were the Merinids, who were able first to resist Yaghmorasan's encroachments and later to keep the 'Abd al-Wadid dynasty inactive for many years. But it certainly seems that account should here be taken of the influences of geography. It has been observed that Orania and eastern Morocco are the areas of North Africa where the high plains suitable for pastoral life come closest to the coast. There the Tell and the cultivated areas constitute an extremely narrow strip, highly vulnerable to the encroachments of invaders. The 'Abd al-Wadid kingdom, therefore, could not, like its eastern and western neighbours, constitute a state with a firm peasant base. This, it seems, is one of the reasons for its instability and lack of success. With its population dispersed in scattered groups and often at odds over pasture lands, and an economy insufficiently diversified, it was unable to achieve a point of balance.

III. The Merinids of Fez

ORIGIN OF THE MERINIDS

The tribe or confederation of the Beni Marin were, like that of the Beni 'Abd al-Wad, Zenata. They were leading a nomadic life in the Zab, the present Biskra region, when at the end of the eleventh century they were gradually pushed westward by the Hilalian tribes. In the middle of the twelfth century, when 'Abd al-Mumin conquered his empire, they were roaming the high plains of Orania and took part in the Zenata coalition formed against the Almohads. In defeat, unlike their racial brethren the Beni 'Abd al-Wad, they declined to submit and took refuge on the borders of the Sahara far from the governors and fiscal agents of the Almohads, and led a life which if precarious was free. They emerged from their retreat only in 1195 when they took part in the holy war which ended with the resounding victory of Alarcos. Their then leader, Mahyu, seriously wounded in combat, died soon afterwards. Power fell to his son 'Abd al-Haqq, who was not only father of the founders of Merinid power, but also a personage of exemplary piety endowed with a supernatural power (*baraka*) which is mentioned in several documents. At that time (in the early thirteenth century) the Beni Marin were living in what is now eastern Morocco between Figuig and the Oued Za and Oued Moulouya. In summer they ascended as far as Outat el-Hajj and even Guercif to pasture their flocks and procure the few provisions they needed for the winter. There they made contact with the Zenata tribes living in the regions of the Rif and lower Moulouya. There

The Return to Berber Kingdoms

was no basis then for seeing in these shepherd nomads the future masters of Morocco.

The death of the caliph al-Nasir afforded them an opportunity for a raid. The new caliph al-Mustansir was a young man given to pleasure, and Almohad power had been seriously shaken by the defeat of Las Navas de Tolosa. The Beni Marin felt that here was an occasion not to be ignored and in 1215 or 1216 they hurled themselves on the cultivated areas of the Tell, which previously they had never dared attack. However, it would appear that 'Abd al-Haqq and his men harboured no political design.

Against these pillagers the Almohads dispatched an army of 10,000 men. Operations first took place in the coastal region (scene of the indecisive battle of the Oued Nakour south of the Bay of Alhucemas) and later in the neighbourhood of Taza, where the Merinids utterly routed the Almohad forces in 1216. In the following year the Almohads changed their tactics and sent into battle against the Merinids, who had not returned to the desert, a dissident Merinid splinter-group and the Arab Riyah tribe. No doubt they thought these nomad contingents more suited than regular troops for repelling other nomads. The main encounter took place on 26 September 1217 in the neighbourhood of the Oued Sebou and the town of Fez. 'Abd al-Haqq lost his life but his fellow tribesmen were victorious under the command of his son, 'Uthman, and they imposed a tribute on the Riyah. According to Ibn Khaldun this victory marked the beginning of serious disorders.[36] The countryside was surrendered to anarchy while Almohad garrisons and governors entrenched themselves in the towns. Gradually, however, so far as the vague documents available allow us to be specific, the Merinids secured payment of a contribution from all the tribes of northern Morocco and got even the towns to pay tribute in return for guaranteeing the freedom of their communications. A successful raid had turned into political adventure. However, the Merinid chiefs still had no idea whatever of conquering Morocco. They took not the least advantage of the unrest in the Almohad empire from 1224 onward to make any attempt whatever at its expense. On the contrary, it was the Almohad caliph al-Sa'id who took the offensive in 1224 and inflicted a severe defeat on the Merinids near Fez. The Merinid chief Muhammad ibn 'Abd al-Haqq, who had succeeded his brother 'Uthman in 1239, met his death in the battle. The fragments of his troops first found refuge among the Ghiyata, Berber mountaineers of the Taza region, and then withdrew as far as the edge of the Sahara. It might have been supposed that the extraordinary adventure of 'Adb al-Haqq and his successors was at an end.

ABU YAHYA

But this was to discount the new Merinid leader, Abu Yahya Abu Bakr (1244-1258), also a son of 'Abd al-Haqq. He was thirty-seven when he assumed power and he had inherited the combined qualities of a leader of men and an astute politician. Once he had regrouped his men near the desert, he divided Morocco into fiefs which he distributed in perpetuity to the main groups within the Beni Marin tribe. It was a bold stroke and a blank cheque, but it revived energies and gave them a specific object. Abu Yahya and his men at once took the road to the north and installed themselves in the region of Meknès, a city of only secondary importance but very well situated. It was then, at the end of 1244, that the caliph al-Sa'id succeeded in mobilising Yaghmorasan and the Beni 'Abd al-Wad. Although at first surrounded in the Ouergha region, Abu Yahya succeeded in breaking up the coalition which al-Sa'id had mounted against him. While the caliph was suppressing a revolt in the Azemmour area, he managed in 1245 to gain possession of the town of Meknès, the first to fall into Merinid hands; there he had the Friday prayer recited in the name of the Hafsid Abu Zakariya. The bandit leader was turning himself into the political opponent of the Almohad dynasty. Al-Sa'id for his part, far from acknowledging defeat, was assembling a formidable army for the reconquest of his ancestral empire. Abu Yahya, we are told, made his way in disguise to the Almohad camp pitched near the Oued Beth. He realised that the struggle would be unequal and as soon as he returned to Meknès he called in his scattered garrisons and withdrew towards eastern Morocco. There, secure against any military surprise, he opened negotiations with the caliph, volunteering to settle the fate of Yaghmorasan unaided. Al-Sa'id barely accepted the token support of 500 Merinid warriors, who were hostages rather than combatants. It is known that al-Sa'id met his death in an ambush near Tlemcen and his army fled back

The Return to Berber Kingdoms

in disorder to the west. Abu Yahya awaited it at the Guercif ford on the Moulouya and annihilated it. The contingents of Turkish and Christian mercenaries who had been serving under the Almohads went over to the Merinids. With these reinforcements and in a better position for action than Yahgmorasan, Abu Yahya secured the domination of Morocco, made his entry into Fez on 20 August 1248 and rapidly took possession of Taza, Meknès, Salé, Rabat and the flat country as far as the Oum er-Rbia. The end of the the year 1248 can thus be taken as the date of the creation of the Merinid kingdom, the principal architect of which was incontestably Abu Yahya.

Although established, he was not, however, at the end of his difficulties. In order to ensure the safety of his capital, he wished to secure the submission of the Middle Atlas and he dispatched a military expedition there. At once certain notables of Fez fomented a conspiracy with the leader of the Christian militia and a few Almohads whose lives Abu Yahya had spared. The conspiracy succeeded and Fez returned to Almohad hands in January–February 1250. As soon as he was informed, Abu Yahya marched on Fez. He had not reached it before he had to face an attack by Yaghmorasan. He defeated his ancient rival on the banks of the Oued Isly and was eventually able, though not without difficulty, to reconquer his capital. The repression was harsh and the people of Fez were mastered for a long period afterwards.

Abu Yahya still had to repel various attempts on the part of the Almohad caliph al-Murtada. He even had to abandon Salé temporarily in 1252 or 1253 (A.H. 650), but recovered himself in the following year by inflicting a disgraceful defeat on the Almohad army in the Fez area. He took advantage of this success to conquer the Tadla and then Sijilmasa, capital of the Tafilalet, and the palm-groves in the bend of the Oued Draᶜ (Agzd, Zagora, Tagounit, etc.) thus preventing Yaghmorasan from supplanting him in these pre-Saharan regions. Thus, when Abu Yahya died of an illness in July 1258, the Merinids were masters of all eastern and northern Morocco, of the western plains as far as the Oum er-Rbia, of the Tadla and the Middle Atlas and finally of the pre-Saharan oases. There were left to the Almohads only the High Atlas, the Sous, the Marrakesh region and the coastal districts situated south of the Oum er-Rbia. This outline of territories affords a measure of the efforts put forth and the success gained by the Merinids under the command of Abu Yahya.

ABU YUSUF

For the first but not, it would appear, the last time a quarrel over the succession followed on Abu Yahya's death. One of his sons seized power at Fez, but the young man's uncle, Abu Yusuf Ya'qub (1258–1286), governor of Taza, immediately set himself up as a pretender in October 1258, and succeeded with some difficulty in imposing his authority and having it acknowledged throughout Merinid-occupied territory. The man who assumed command of the tribe was the fourth son of 'Abd al-Haqq. He was forty-six or forty-eight when he acceded to power, and the chroniclers represent him not only as a warrior, engaged all his life in battle in the Maghrib and in Spain, but also as a 'devout king' who spent his nights in prayer, read the lives of the saints, fasted regularly and protected the marabouts.

The opening of his long reign was marked by fresh dynastic quarrels. Early in 1260 one of his nephews gained possession of Salé, where the Almohads had succeeded in re-establishing themselves. Christians from Spain, Castilians most probably, took advantage of this dissension and occupied Salé by surprise in September 1260; Abu Yusuf was able to drive them out only after a siege of fourteen days. So far the Merinids had had no time to take part in the holy war in Spain. Abu Yusuf had shown signs of intending to do so about 1245 when his brother had recently taken Meknès, but the latter in his political wisdom had restrained his younger brother's noble designs. The attack on Salé, much more of a raid than a genuine attempt at establishing a foothold in Africa, certainly revived the desire which the new ruler had already shown to fight the Christians. But he first had to complete the conquest of Morocco, and so he contented himself in 1262 with sending to Spain a Merinid clan which had revolted in the Chechaouen area, simultaneously satisfying his pious intentions and the safety of his own authority.

He was thus able in all security to attack what was left of the Almohad kingdom. A first attempt on Marrakesh failed in 1262 after a desperate conflict at the very walls of the city. Abu Yusuf then changed his tactics. He entertained advances from the

The Return to Berber Kingdoms

Almohad Abu Dabbus, and furnished him with troops and money against a half-share in such booty and territory as he should acquire. Abu Dabbus conquered Marrakesh in the autumn of 1266 but immediately broke the undertakings he had given to the Merinids. As the latter had already laid siege to Marrakesh, Yaghmorasan, thwarted by Abu Dabbus, penetrated into Merinid territory. Abu Yusuf turned back against this new adversary and inflicted a serious defeat on him near the Moulouya at the beginning of 1268. Freed from this anxiety, he marched yet again on Marrakesh, defeated the troops of Abu Dabbus and entered the town on 8 September 1259. The enterprise begun by Abu Yahya had been brought to a successful conclusion by his successor. The Merinids had secured the heritage of the Almohads in Morocco. Abu Yusuf at once assumed the title of *Amir al-Muslimin* (Prince of the Muslims) which had already been used by the Almoravid rulers. It will be remembered that the caliphian title of *Amir al-Muminin* had for the past ten years been the prerogative of the Hafsid ruler al-Mustansir. Abu Yusuf had no wish to enter into dispute with him over it and even accepted the continued recitation of the Friday prayer in the name of the caliph of Tunis.

While two of his sons were conducting an expedition in the Sous and the Anti-Atlas with the intention of securing recognition there of Merinid authority, Abu Yusuf remained at Marrakesh, where delegations from all southern Morocco came in great numbers to publicly acknowledge the authority of the successor to the Almohads and to give him homage and gifts. Only the Arab Ma'qil tribes settled in the Oued Dra' area refused to submit. Abu Yusuf went in person to punish them in the spring of 1271. Thereafter all the Maghrib al-Aqsa was subject to the Merinids. There were two exceptions: the African shore of the Straits of Gibraltar, which made its submission in 1273; and Sijilmasa, which under the influence of the Ma'qil Arabs had passed under Yaghmorasan's control in 1265, and was brought back under Merinid authority in 1274 after a siege. In the course of this seige Abu Yusuf is said to have used pieces of artillery for the first time.

THE FIRST SPANISH EXPEDITION AND FOUNDATION OF FEZ JDID

The Muslims of Spain had sent Abu Yusuf a request for immediate help in 1272, when he was marching against Yaghmorasan to punish him for having supported Abu Dabbus. At once, our sources tell us, the Merinid ruler had made overtures for peace, but his rival had countered with a categorical refusal. Abu Yusuf had thus resigned himself to continuing his campaign and to putting off intervention in Spain until later. He defeated the ʿAbd al-Wadids once again near the Oued Isly on 16 February 1272, besieged Tlemcen without result and built an advanced fortress at Taount, next to the present Nemours. Yaghmorasan had been made to see reason for a time. Nevertheless, before committing himself in Spain, Abu Yusuf secured possession of Tangier and Ceuta in 1273, and then reconquered Sijilmasa in 1274. Just after the capture of this town he received a second embassy from Granada, its mission again being to ask for his help. This time there was nothing further to prevent him from assuming his part in the holy war and taking up a tradition of the Almohads whose successor he was claiming himself to be. The moment for intervention was favourable. The *reconquista*, almost brought to an end by Ferdinand III, had not been pursued with the same energy by his son. King Alphonso X the Learned (1252–1284) was endowed with qualities of the highest order, but in the fields of literature and science rather than of politics. If he regretted not having been present at the Creation so as better to order the world, he displayed too much versatility for the right ordering of his own states. In compliance with his father's wish he had fitted out fleets and armies to expel the Nasrids and to carry the war into Morocco with the pope's support, but he changed his mind before putting his project into effect. His fiscal measures aroused lively discontent among the people, and his foreign policy harmed his prestige.

The Muslims were incapable of taking advantage of the situation. In the narrow territory squeezed between the Sierra Nevada and the Sierra de Ronda the amirs spent their time fighting among themselves. The Nasrids of Granada remained on the alert. The amir Ibn al-Ahmar had had to submit to the suzerainty of the king of Castile. He realised, however, that eventually he would have to choose between submission to the Christians and calling on the help of the Maghribis. The capture of Cadiz by the Castilians and the Murcian campaign of James of Aragon showed the Christian danger to be the greater threat, but the hostility of Ibn

The Return to Berber Kingdoms

al-Ahmar towards Abu Yusuf had thrown him back on King Alphonso. His son and successor, Muhammad al-Faqih, on the instigation of Castilian refugees, had changed his attitude and had taken advantage of King Alphonso's absence to solicit Merinid intervention.

Owing to the ships of Ceuta, the Merinid advance guard crossed the Straits without difficulty in April 1275, gained some successes in the Jerez region and took possession of Algeciras, which was ceded to the Africans by the ruler of Granada. Meanwhile Abu Yusuf was negotiating with Yaghmorasan with whom he secured a satisfactory peace treaty. He was thus able in his turn to cross to Spain with the bulk of his forces on 16 August 1275. He took the field at once, raided the regions of the lower Guadalquivir and Cordova, and then on 8 September 1275 encountered a strong Castilian relieving army, commanded by the famous Castilian captain Don Nuño Gonzales de Lara. The Merinid victory was complete and was celebrated as the revenge for Las Navas de Tolosa.

While Abu Yusuf was waging war in Spain the Merinid governor of Marrakesh was marching on Tinmel, where the last of the Almohads had taken refuge. He had no difficulty in dislodging them and eliminating the last descendants of 'Abd al-Mumin. The year 1275 thus brought the Merinids a series of brilliant victories. Abu Yusuf decided to celebrate the flowering of his dynasty by founding a new capital. In this he was following the example of Sidi 'Uqba with Kairouan, Mulay Idris with Fez, 'Ubaid Allah with Mahdiya, al-Mansur with Mançouriya, Hammad with Qal'a of the Beni Hammad, Yusuf ibn Tashfin with Marrakesh and Ya'qub al-Mansur with Rabat. As the site for his new city he chose the gently sloping plateau which overlooked the town of Fez from the west and through which ran the Oued Fez before descending the slopes of the old town. The site was favourable for the development of a great city and had the further advantage of easy surveillance of the critical town of Fez, the rebellion of which in 1250 had left bitter memories in the minds of the Merinid rulers. The laying out of the city was begun in accordance with great artistic plans on 21 March 1276, and the works were pushed forward actively. With great speed ramparts, a Great Mosque, a palace, a market, a bath, and dwellings for the notables and the dynasty were erected in

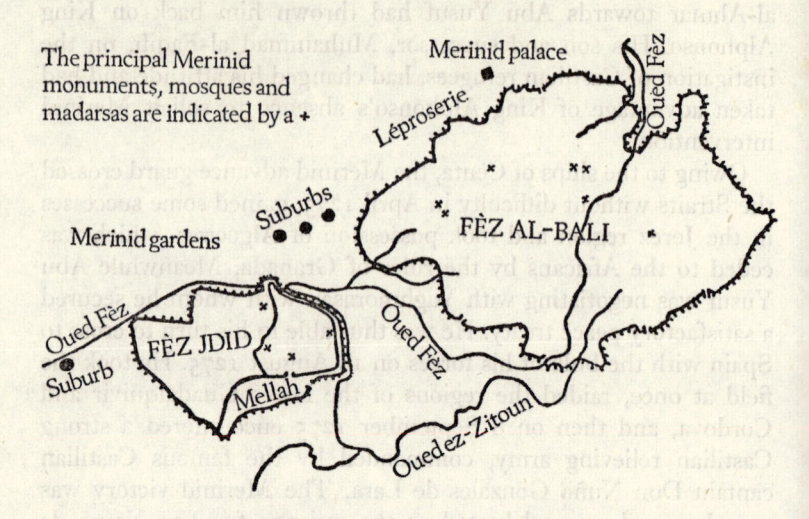

7 The city of Fez during the Merinid period

accordance with the plan laid down. The mosque was opened for worship in January 1279. The town was at first called the White City (*al-Madina al-Baida*) but was later commonly designated by the name of *Fās al-Jdid* (New Fez) in contrast to *Fās al-Bālī* (Old Fez). We may wonder at first sight whether this was a case of a genuine fresh creation. The new city, beside the old, inevitably benefited from the reputation and trade of the latter and from all the conveniences and advantages built up by the Almoravids and even more, it appears, by the Almohads. In fact it was indeed a new and original centre that Abu Yusuf built, so far at any rate as concerns its population. It was a Merinid city, a military and administrative city which, even in modern times and notwithstanding the changes it has undergone, remains very different from Old Fez.

At the same time Abu Yusuf had a kasbah with castle and mosque built at Meknès; and at Old Fez a madrasa was situated to the south of the mosque of the men of Kairouan and intended to afford lodging to students from the country. The victorious ruler thus assumed the figure of a great builder in accordance with the best Maghribi traditions.

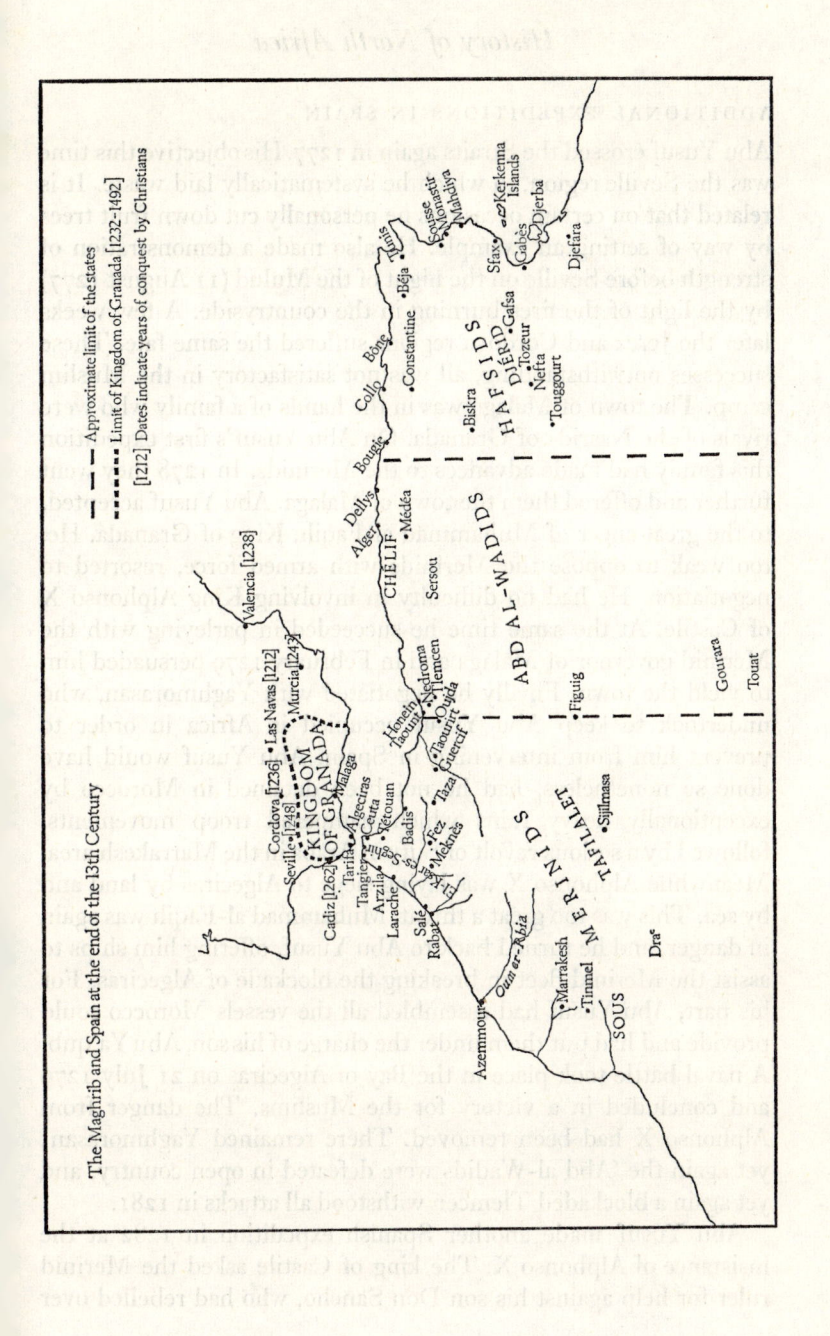

The Maghrib and Spain at the end of the 13th Century

- - - - Approximate limit of the states
―――― Limit of Kingdom of Granada [1232-1492]
[1212] Dates indicate years of conquest by Christians

Valencia [1238]
Cordova [1236]
Las Navas [1212]
Seville [1248]
Murcia [1243]
KINGDOM
OF GRANADA
Málaga
Cadiz [1262]
Tarifa
Algeciras
Tangier
Ceuta
Arzila
Tetouan
Larache
Badis
Salé
Rabat
S. S.
El-Ksar
Fez
Meknès

Azemmour
Oum er-Rbia
Marrakesh
Tinmel
SOUS
Drâ

MERINIDS
TAFILALET
Sijilmassa

Tlemcen
Hoseïn
Taount
Taza
Oudjda
Taourirt
ABD AL-WADIDS
Figuig
Gourara
Touat

Algiers
Dellys
Médéa
CHÉLIF
Sersou

Bougie
Collo
Bône
Constantine
Béja
Tunis
Sousse
Monastir
Mahdiya
Kerkenna
Islands
Sfax
Gabès
Djerba
Djefara
Gafsa
Tozeur
Nefta
Touggourt
Biskra
DJÉRID
HAFSIDS

ADDITIONAL EXPEDITIONS IN SPAIN

Abu Yusuf crossed the Straits again in 1277. His objective this time was the Seville region, to which he systematically laid waste. It is related that on certain occasions he personally cut down fruit trees by way of setting an example. He also made a demonstration of strength before Seville on the night of the Mulud (11 August 1277) by the light of the fires burning in the countryside. A few weeks later the Jerez and Cordova regions suffered the same fate. These successes notwithstanding, all was not satisfactory in the Muslim camp. The town of Malaga was in the hands of a family who were rivals of the Nasrids of Granada. On Abu Yusuf's first expedition this family had made advances to the Merinids. In 1278 they went further and offered them the town of Malaga. Abu Yusuf accepted, to the great anger of Muhammad al-Faqih, King of Granada. He, too weak to oppose the Merinids with armed force, resorted to negotiation. He had no difficulty in involving King Alphonso X of Castile. At the same time he succeeded in parleying with the Merinid governor of Malaga and in February 1279 persuaded him to yield the town. Finally he negotiated with Yaghmorasan, who undertook to keep Abu Yusuf occupied in Africa in order to prevent him from intervening in Spain. Abu Yusuf would have done so nonetheless, had he not been detained in Morocco by exceptionally heavy rains which hampered troop movements, followed by a serious revolt of Sufyan Arabs in the Marrakesh area. Meanwhile Alphonso X was laying siege to Algeciras by land and by sea. This was too great a threat. Muhammad al-Faqih was again in danger, and he turned back to Abu Yusuf, offering him ships to assist the Merinid fleet in breaking the blockade of Algeciras. For his part, Abu Yusuf had assembled all the vessels Morocco could provide and had put them under the charge of his son, Abu Ya'qub. A naval battle took place in the Bay of Algeciras on 21 July 1279 and concluded in a victory for the Muslims. The danger from Alphonso X had been removed. There remained Yaghmorasan; yet again the 'Abd al-Wadids were defeated in open country, and yet again a blockaded Tlemcen withstood all attacks in 1281.

Abu Yusuf made another Spanish expedition in 1282 at the insistance of Alphonso X. The king of Castile asked the Merinid ruler for help against his son Don Sancho, who had rebelled over

The Return to Berber Kingdoms

the question of succession. Abu Yusuf did not hesitate and crossed the Straits. His action seems to have yielded nothing but some booty and the crown of Castile which had been given him as a pledge.

Yaghmorasan died in the spring of 1283, advising his successor not to pursue the barren conflict he had himself waged against the Merinids. In the spring of 1284 Alphonso X died also and the throne of Castile passed to his rebel son Don Sancho. With no anxiety from the quarter of Tlemcen to deter him, Abu Yusuf decided to profit from the change of ruler and to intervene in Spain. He was unable to do so until 1285, having been obliged to mount a punitive expedition in the Sous and the lower Draʿ against the Maʿqil Arabs, who, as was their wont, were pillaging in those parts.

It was not until 7 April 1285 that Abu Yusuf crossed the Straits for the fourth time. There was little in the way of important operations except by sea, where the Castilian fleet tried in vain to regain control of the Straits. For the sake of peace and quiet Don Sancho sought to negotiate, and Abu Yusuf gladly seized the opportunity to bring the fruitless expedition to an end. He secured an improvement in the condition of Muslim merchants on Christian soil, and an undertaking by Don Sancho to refrain from interfering in the internal affairs of Muslim territories in the Peninsula. Also Don Sancho undertook to return to Muslim hands the Arabic manuscripts—thirteen mule-loads of them—that had come into Christian possession as a result of the *reconquista*. In return Abu Yusuf agreed to pay reparations for the damage done by his army in Christian territory. This compromise peace (21 October 1285) was celebrated as a victory in the Merinid camp and was the occasion for poetic contests, echoes of which are preserved in the *Qirtas*.[37] Shortly afterwards Abu Yusuf fell sick and died on 20 March 1286. His body was later transferred to the necropolis at Chella which he had had built.

If Abu Yahya can be regarded as the founder of the dynasty, Abu Yusuf was the founder of its glory. His reign saw the completion of Moroccan unity under the dynasty, the erection of new buildings and the resumption of traditional Moroccan involvement in Spain. After the death of the Hafsid al-Mustansir and the ensuing dynastic disturbances, and after the disappearance of

Yaghmorasan and the change of policy on the part of the kingdom of Tlemcen, Abu Yusuf was rightly regarded as the most powerful ruler in the Maghrib. But it was a brittle power. Several Merinid princes could hardly endure the authority of the ruling family. The Arabs, whether those settled in Morocco by Almohad caliphs or Ma'qil newly arrived from the south, were always ready to join a conflict against the government. The descendants of the Almohads, Sanhaja of the High Atlas, found it difficult to tolerate the rule of their conquerors. We may wonder with Terrasse whether the Merinid troops were adequate for all the tasks assigned to them by their rulers.[38] The military worth of these horsemen is undeniable, but it is significant to note that Abu Yusuf probably never succeeded in fighting simultaneously on two fronts. Finally, Merinid policy as outlined by Abu Yusuf was definitely backward-looking. His aim was to restore the Almohad empire he had himself destroyed, though he lacked the advantages both of the Almohads' military forces and of their religious prestige.

ABU YA'QUB YUSUF

His son Abu Ya'qub Yusuf (1286–1307) had long been appointed his successor and had no difficulty in securing recognition as ruler in governmental circles. But he had at once to deal with several serious revolts which demonstrated the internal weakness of the Merinid state. One of his kinsmen rebelled in the Oued Dra' area. Abu Ya'qub put a small force under the charge of one of his brothers and he, instead of punishing the rebel, made an alliance with him. The insurgents, attempting to take refuge at Tlemcen, were caught and executed at Taza in September 1286. At the same moment a tribal rebellion broke out in the mountainous area south of Fez; it was quickly suppressed. Immediately afterwards another of Abu Ya'qub's kinsmen roused a Ma'qil tribe in the Dra'; he was killed in July 1287 and the Ma'qil were punished in the following October. A year later, in November 1288, it was one of the sultan's sons who took up arms against his father at Marrakesh. This time again the revolt was promptly extinguished, but the rebel prince Abu 'Amir and his principal accomplice succeeded in escaping and taking refuge at Tlemcen. There followed nearly four years of tranquillity, and then the revolt of the Beni Wattas broke out. The Beni Wattas was a Merinid tribe settled in the Rif which,

The Return to Berber Kingdoms

in the fifteenth century, was to provide Morocco with a dynasty. It took Abu Ya'qub nearly six months to gain control over this movement, which he did in the spring of 1293. Finally from 1295 to 1298 the rebel son Abu 'Amir, who had been received back into favour, once more revolted in the Ghomara region and long held the field while his father was waging war against Tlemcen.

Spanish affairs played a secondary role in the concerns of Abu Ya'qub. It would appear probable that this prince, with an independent mind, and unencumbered by tradition, had recognised the fact that war on two fronts was likely to prove fatal to the Merinid state and that his sole object should be an honourable liquidation of his Spanish commitment. Immediately following his father's death he returned to Muhammad al-Faqih the majority of the strongpoints which Muhammad had given to the Merinids, and renewed the peace treaty concluded with Don Sancho in 1285. He made some further concessions to the Nasrid on the occasion of his own marriage to a Merinid princess of Granada.

Nevertheless, Don Sancho forced him out of his attitude of reserve in 1291, when in circumstances now obscure he ceased to observe the conditions of the treaty of 1285. Abu Ya'qub proclaimed holy war and, with some difficulty, crossed the Straits which were well guarded by the Castilian fleet. He conducted a short inglorious campaign, following which Muhammad al-Faqih once more made alliance with the Castilians against the Merinids, with the men of Don Sancho and the money of Muhammad al-Faqih. The Merinid strongpoint of Tarifa was besieged and it capitulated at the end of four months in September 1291. Don Sancho kept it, notwithstanding the terms of his agreement with the Nasrids. Resuming the vacillating policy habitual with him, Muhammad al-Faqih deserted his ambitious Christian ally and sought a Merinid alliance once more. He had to pay the price; Abu Ya'qub was weary of his partner's indecision and had little desire to become involved in Spain. In addition to territorial concessions, the Nasrids presented him with one of the four copies of the Koran edited on lines indicated by the caliph 'Uthman, which had been preserved by the 'Umaiyads of Cordova and later acquired by the Nasrids. In 1293 Abu Ya'qub laid siege to Tarifa but his troops failed in their undertaking. He did not persist, as the conflict with Tlemcen was occupying all his resources.

The Ziyanid 'Uthman had begun by following his late father's advice and directing his efforts against Hafsid territory. But in 1289 he followed his own inclinations to the point of affording hospitality to the fugitive prince Abu 'Amir and his adviser. Abu Ya'qub became reconciled with the former but demanded the extradition of the latter. 'Uthman refused and war ensued. Tlemcen was blockaded by the Merinid army from May to October 1290, though without result. Abu Ya'qub did not renew his attempts on Tlemcen in the following years, engrossed as he was by affairs in Spain and then by the rebellion of the Beni Wattas. But he remembered very clearly that the 'Abd al-Wadid ruler had had a hand in the anti-Merinid negotiations of 1292 between Don Sancho and Muhammad al-Faqih. It was only in 1295 that he was able to devote himself to a ruthless war which was to last twelve years. He proceeded methodically, occupying successively Taourirt on the Oued Za (1295), Oujda (1296), Taount and Nedroma (1298). Several times he pushed small forces forward against Tlemcen but he did not commit himself deeply until he felt sure of victory. On 6 May 1299 he stationed himself before the enemy capital determined not to leave until it had fallen. The town's defenders were no less resolute; they were prepared to fight to the end. These determined wills were opposed for eight full years, as has been mentioned above. Meanwhile Abu Ya'qub by force or negotiation was subduing all the central Maghrib as far as Algiers. His power was considerable. In his palace at Mançoura he received embassies from Ifriqiya, Egypt and Mecca. He had brought the Zenata of the Maghrib under his authority and his kingdom had been quiet since Abu 'Amir's death. Finally, despite its extraordinary and brave resistance Tlemcen, was becoming exhausted and was ready to yield. Abu Ya'qub felt victory to be so close that he paid little heed to the dissidence of Ceuta. In point of fact a Merinid from Spain, with the discreet support of the ruler of Granada, had landed at Ceuta in 1306 and had there proclaimed himself sovereign. Gradually his influence gained a hold in the mountainous region of northern Morocco. But Abu Ya'qub took no notice; the surrender of Tlemcen was no more than a matter of days when on 13 May 1307 the sultan was assassinated by one of his eunuchs because of some obscure harem intrigue.

The Return to Berber Kingdoms

THE FIRST MERINID ECLIPSE

The heir-designate was a twenty-three-year-old grandson of Abu Ya'qub, Abu Thabit. He found himself faced with three, soon to be four, competitors. Three of them were swiftly eliminated after Abu Thabit had negotiated with the people of Tlemcen and brought his troops back to Morocco. The fourth was 'Uthman ibn Idris, the Merinid who had had himself proclaimed Sultan at Ceuta in 1306 and who now held Arzila, Larache and all the Ghomara country. Abu Thabit marched against him, founded the town of Tétouan in order to have a base for operations against Ceuta and was engaged in negotiations for the surrender of that town when he died of an illness on 28 July 1308. His nineteen-year-old brother, Abu al-Rabi', succeeded him without great difficulty and managed to recover possession of Ceuta on 20 July 1309. The Nasrids, hard pressed by the Castilians, who had just secured Gibraltar, were seeking to regain the friendship of the Merinids and accordingly made a settlement easy. However, en route to put down a revolt at Taza Abu al-Rabi' fell sick and died on 23 November 1310.

Although he had one rival, Abu Sa'id 'Uthman (1310–1331) was readily acknowledged as ruler. This prince, some thirty-five years old, was the son of Abu Yusuf's epoch. Pacific and pious, he did not throw himself into great enterprises but showed himself, like his father, a lover of fine buildings. To him are due three madarsas at Fez—that of Fez Jdid (1320), that of the Basin (*madrasa al-Sahrij*, 1321) and that of the Spice-perfumers (*madrasa al-'Attarin*, 1323).

His reign was not, however, as untroubled as he might have wished. His younger son, Abu 'Ali, who was very much his favourite and whom he had designated as his heir, rebelled in 1315 and deposed his father.

The latter had accepted the *fait accompli* and resigned himself to the role of governor of Taza, but when Abu 'Ali fell sick, Abu Sa'id took courage, besieged the rebel in Fez Jdid and secured his capitulation. He deprived him of the succession to the throne in favour of his eldest son Abu al-Hasan, but appointed him governor of Sijilmasa, where Abu 'Ali organised a veritable state with its budget, and its standing army and auxiliaries recruited from the

Maʿqil Arabs. He subjected the oases of the Touat and the Gourara to his authority, as well as the valley of the Sous. In 1320 he again took up arms against his father, gained control of the Draʿ oases and then, in 1322, of Marrakesh. The Merinid state was in danger of being split into a northern and a southern kingdom. Abu Saʿid saw the danger, marched against his son and defeated his troops on the Oum er-Rbia but pardoned Abu ʿAli once more and left him in control of Sijilmasa.

At the outset of his reign he had considered the idea of intervening in Spain. The idea was short-lived, although the occasion was propitious. Ferdinand IV of Castile died in 1312 leaving an heir in the cradle. An Abu Yusuf would certainly have taken advantage of this situation. In 1316 the governor of Ceuta, Yahya ibn ʿAfzi, declared himself independent and remained so *de facto* for some ten years. Finally in 1319 Granada, under threat from the Castilians, appealed yet once more to the Merinids. Abu Saʿid, whose aspirations were towards peace, laid down unacceptable conditions and there the matter rested. As regards Tlemcen, there is nothing to record but a scarcely successful expedition in 1314.

At the end of his reign, however, Merinid policy took a new turn. The Hafsid ruler Abu Bakr, hard pressed by Abu Tashfin of Tlemcen, begged for Merinid help in 1329. Abu Saʿid mounted a feeble diversion but sought to profit from the advances made to him. Already in 1321 he had requested the hand of a Hafsid princess for his son and heir-designate Abu al-Hasan, but his request had been answered evasively. He renewed it in 1331, this time with success. In August the princess Fatima landed on the Moroccan coast, and her future father-in-law set out to welcome her. He was delayed by illness near Taza and died on 25 August.

ABU AL-HASAN

The reign of Abu al-Hasan (1331–1351) marked the zenith of Merinid power. The restoration of the Maghribi empire from the Atlantic to Gabès, the prestige of the pious sultan and his court and the great number of his buildings made him the most powerful ruler of the fourteenth century.

He was thirty-four or forty-five; sources give a range of eleven years for his date of birth. He was of imposing presence and dark-skinned, being the son of an Abyssinian woman, hence his nick-

The Return to Berber Kingdoms

name of 'Black Sultan'. He was prodigiously active. 'For him fatigues were pleasures,' says Ibn Khaldun.[39] Ibn Marzuq has described for us the programme followed by the sultan at Fez.[40] A great part of his day he devoted to recitations from the Koran, the second half of which he knew by heart, to prayer, pious readings in the company of experts in law, and to visiting the tombs of saints. His religious life was conducted under the watchful but pitiless eyes of the pietists of his court. He performed his duties as sultan conscientiously, and with his secretary, his personal adviser and his viziers looked into the cases and complaints submitted to him. 'The shaikhs of Merinid and Arab tribes were then presented, as were new arrivals at court and tribal notables.'[41] No doubt the sultan had to reckon with the chiefs of the indigenous tribes and handled them tactfully. Accordingly he invited them 'to make known to him their requests on certain days, each in his turn according to rank and a fixed order of precedence'.[42] It is a pity that Ibn Marzuq, so closely involved in the sultan's daily life, should have maintained silence on the subject of these conferences. Abu al-Hasan would probably have escaped from some of this rigid etiquette when in camp. It is, however, certain that he had to submit to it so long as he maintained his authority. But the splendour it reveals was fleeting, for his policy of conquest failed both in Spain and in Ifriqiya, and in the end he had to renounce the idea of recovering Morocco from his rebellious son.

Abu Yusuf and Abu Ya'qub had by their exertions been assured of an undisputed control over Morocco. Nevertheless the presence of Abu 'Ali at Sijilmasa was likely to jeopardise the new sultan's ventures against the Ziyanids or the Christians of the Peninsula. Accordingly Abu al-Hasan deemed it more prudent to avoid provoking a rupture by leaving to his brother the appanage of the Tafilalet. But he had to abandon an expedition conducted against Tlemcen in concert with the Hafsids in order to besiege Sijilmasa for a year. The fall of the town and the death of Abu 'Ali so weakened the kingdom of the Tafilalet that it took thirty years to recover. Abu al-Hasan also overthrew the independent principality of the Sous with the help of the Arabs, whom he rewarded by a grant of *iqtā'*, and he enforced regular payment of taxes on the nomads of the Dra'. Thus his power over the far Maghrib seemed firmly enough based to allow for active interventions abroad.

The situation in Spain following the death of Alphonso X continued to be one of confusion. Intrigues and personal ambitions, changes of alliance and the abatement of religious fervour prevented a decisive offensive on either side. Nevertheless the king of Castile had been able to take Gibraltar by surprise, and though he had to raise the siege of Algeciras, he had secured the cession of two Nasrid towns by way of compensation. The minority of Alphonso XI (1312–1350) very nearly compromised Christian progress, but the king resumed the *reconquista* in 1327 as soon as he had rid himself of his guardians. The amir of Granada escaped only by having recourse once more to the Merinids, though he expelled them once he was clear of danger. When yet again he begged for their aid he had Abu al-Hasan to deal with, who was little disposed to let himself be involved. The sultan of Fez immediately recaptured Algeciras, in 1333, and after waiting under arms for six years undertook, in concert with the Nasrids, to reconquer Spain from the Christians. Castilians and Aragonese were drawn together by the common danger, but they were unable to prevent the Merinid fleet, reinforced by Hafsid vessels, from securing temporary mastery of the Straits after a brilliant naval victory on 5 April 1340. Then, jointly with the forces of Granada, Abu al-Hasan laid siege to Tarifa. Owing to the solidity of its walls and the help of Genoese galleys, the town was able to await relief by the Christians, who had raised an army probably of 35,000 men. The clash took place north of Tarifa, on the banks of the Rio Salado, on 30 October 1340. A sortie by the besieged settled the issue, the victory being the most important gained by the Christians since Las Navas de Tolosa. The Merinids had difficulty in returning to Morocco. Four years later, on 26 March 1344, Algeciras fell to the young king of Castile after a siege of more than twenty months in which the best of English, French and Italian chivalry took part.

Abu al-Hasan, declared Ibn Khaldun, 'remained profoundly convinced that the cause of Allah would triumph in the end and that the Almighty would fulfil his promise by according the Muslims a return of good fortune'.[43] But no doubt Allah, like Hercules in the fable, helps those who help themselves, and the sultan contented himself with passive hopefulness. The Muslim crusade was completely over. While Abu al-Hasan was isolating himself in Tunis after the Kairouan disaster, Alphonso XI was

The Return to Berber Kingdoms

besieging Gibraltar (August 1349) and he [Alphonso XI] would have entered it had not an epidemic cut him down in the fullness of his youth in March 1350. He had finally eliminated the Merinids from the Spanish chess-board, and he left to his successors the easier task of fighting the single kingdom of Granada.

Abu al-Hasan had had better fortune against Tlemcen. On the request of his father-in-law, the Hafsid Abu Bakr, he had required Abu Tashfin to desist from his encroachments on Hafsid territory. Abu Tashfin assumed an arrogant attitude and a rupture took place between them in 1334. Under the command of the sultan the Merinid troops marched at the beginning of 1335. They invested Tlemcen immediately and then swept on to conquer the central Maghrib while Mançoura was being built again—it is from this reconstruction that the present imposing ruins date—and Tlemcen was being strongly besieged. The defence was desperate. Abu Tashfin resisted to the very end, going so far as to defend his palace, sword in hand, when the final assault took place on 1 May 1337. He was wounded and soon afterwards killed. For the first time the Merinids were successful in gaining possession of the town that had caused them so much trouble. Abu al-Hasan announced his victory to the principal Muslim rulers of his day and received felicitations from Egypt, the Sudan and naturally Granada and Tunis.

However, the ambitions of Abu al-Hasan were not satisfied. Haunted like his predecessors by the memory of the Almohad empire, he aspired to rule over the entire Maghrib. Already the Hafsid state was assuming the guise of vassal to that of Fez. In 1341 or 1342 Abu al-Hasan obtained from his father-in-law the surrender of the Merinid deserters expelled from Spain. In 1346 he demanded the hand of a second daughter of Abu Bakr, the first daughter having died in the unfortunate Tarifa affair in 1340. On each occasion his claims were supported by the Hafsid chamberlain Ibn Tafragin, leader of the pro-Merinid party at the court of Tunis. He took no action, however, so long as Abu Bakr's reign continued, but at the death of Abu Bakr the ensuing rivalries furnished him with the pretext he was probably awaiting. He set off at the head of his troops in the spring of 1347, entered Tunis on 18 September of the same year and established himself there with all the display of a conquering power.

We have seen above how Abu al-Hasan had displeased the Arabs by encroaching on their privileges, was defeated by them near Kairouan on 10 April 1348 and was surrounded in the town of Sidi 'Uqba. He succeeded nevertheless in extricating himself with the complicity of certain Arab clans, returned to Tunis and restored the situation. But the Merinid kingdom had not withstood the crisis. Abu 'Inan, the sultan's son, who was acting as regent in his father's absence, had himself proclaimed ruler and abandoned Tlemcen. The Beni 'Abd al-Wad returned there and restored Ziyanid sovereignty. Several Hafsid princes threw off the Merinid yoke at Bougie, Constantine and Bône. Abu al-Hasan fought on at Tunis for a year in the hope of getting the situation once more under control. Finally, at the end of December 1349, he decided to return to Morocco as he was achieving nothing at Tunis.

He went by sea, the land route being entirely closed. A storm scattered his fleet and cast him on a small island close to Bougie, where he barely escaped capture by the Kabyles. He finally reached Algiers in a sorry state, and there the Suwaid Arabs rallied round him. Strengthened by this support he marched against Tlemcen but was defeated in the Chélif plain. With the energy of despair he descended on the Tafilalet with his supporters and installed himself at Sijilmasa. The approach of the troops of Abu 'Inan and the defection of the Suwaid compelled him to abandon that position. He then threw himself on Marrakesh, where collusion enabled him to establish himself and to rebuild the semblance of a state. But Abu 'Inan took up arms once more. In May 1350 there was an encounter on the banks of the Oum-er-Rbia where Abu al-Hasan was defeated and narrowly escaped death. He then took refuge in the High Atlas, where the former Almohad tribe of the Hintata made him welcome. Abu 'Inan pursued him there, set up a rigorous blockade throughout the winter and forced his father to negotiate. Abu al-Hasan was weary, desperate and stripped of all resources. He consented to abdicate in favour of the usurper in return for money and clothes, whereupon he fell sick and had himself bled. The incision became infected and Abu al-Hasan died in a miserable condition on the mountain of the Hintata on 24 May 1351. Abu 'Inan is said to have shed tears over the corpse of his father, and to have had him interred in the royal necropolis at Chella, where his tomb is still to be seen.

The Return to Berber Kingdoms

This great and ill-starred sultan had not been merely a conqueror whose ambitions were frustrated. Like his father and his forerunners he left a very considerable architectural achievement. At Fez there were the al-Shrabliyin and Abu al-Hasan Mosques; at Tlemcen the Mançoura Mosque, most imposing of all Merinid constructions, and that of Sidi Bou Médine. Of madarsas there were el-Oued and Misbahiya at Fez, those of Taza, Salé, Marrakesh, Meknès (finished by Abu 'Inan) and Sidi Bou Médine. Finally he had the hospital (*maristan*) at Fez restored.

ABU 'INAN

His son and successor Abu 'Inan Faris (1348–1358) was born in January 1329. He was thus a young man when he assumed power, with all the fire, ambition and intransigence of his years. Tall, well-built, of great courage and not wanting in culture, he had some of the qualities of a great ruler, but showed himself strong-headed and unable to accept advice. His ambition was great; he dared to assume the caliphian title of *Amir al-Muminin*.

It seems likely that he at first thought his father had died of the plague at Tunis when he had himself proclaimed sultan. However, one of his nephews had assumed power at Fez Jdid before he himself had taken any step. In brief, his decision is to some extent explicable, but when he learned that his father was still alive his attitude was unchanged. He easily drove his competitor out of Fez Jdid and rallied Morocco under his authority, but at the same time Tlemcen and the central Maghrib were liberating themselves from Merinid control.

During the early years of his reign the sole concern of Abu 'Inan was the elimination of Abu al-Hasan. It was not until 1352 that he did his best to repeat what his father had previously done. As might be expected, he first attacked Tlemcen. On 14 June 1352, a battle in the plain of the Angad, where his personal valour assured a victory, placed the town in his hands. From that time, following his own momentum, he gained possession in one campaign of all the central Maghrib as far as Bougie. This was in the autumn of 1352, and it was then that the difficulties began. Bougie rebelled in 1353 and had to be reconquered. Two pretenders to the throne appeared in 1354, one was pushed on by the Hafsids in the Constantine region, and the other was landed on the coast of the Sous by ships from Castile. Both were taught their lesson. In 1355 the governor of Gibraltar declared his independence, and a Merinid fleet had to lay siege to the town to secure his submission.

Having finally restored tranquillity in his states, Abu 'Inan was able to put into execution his grand project, which had also been that of his father and that of the Almohads—the subjection of the entire Maghrib to Merinid authority. The enterprise opened well; Constantine was taken early in the summer of 1357 and Tunis in September. We know that the Arabs of Ifriqiya at once rebelled, as they had done against Abu al-Hasan and for the same reasons. Abu 'Inan exhausted himself in pursuing them as far as the Biskra region. There, as his troops were beginning to disband out of weariness, he was obliged to retreat, and he returned to Fez in November 1357. He did not regard this reverse as final. The following year he sent an expedition under one of his viziers to subdue the Aurès, and this having been done, he fell gravely ill. His viziers split into two camps, each supporting a son of the dying sultan. The most enterprising of the viziers, al-Fududi, secured the victory of his candidate, a child of five, and strangled Abu 'Inan, whose death, on 5 December 1358, had become somewhat protracted.

The reign of Abu 'Inan may appear to be an exact, if briefer, repetition of that of Abu al-Hasan. It was so in the way it developed, but not in its consequences. Abu 'Inan had not been vanquished by the Arabs of Ifriqiya, but by the refusal of his own troops to march any further. The Merinids had demanded of their subjects too great an effort and its limit was thereafter reached. On the other hand, the disintegration of the Merinid state was much more serious than it had been ten years before. It was now the viziers who began to make and unmake the rulers. The crisis, begun with Abu 'Inan's death, was to continue until the extinction of the Merinid dynasty. It had lasted so long, and its consequences had been so grave, as to put it beyond the power of the Wattasids to restore the situation when they assumed authority.

MERINID DECADENCE

Scarcely had Abu 'Inan died when anarchy spread like a disease through the Merinid kingdom. Viziers, Merinid pretenders, Arabs

The Return to Berber Kingdoms

and Christian militia vied in the dispute for power. There were reigns lasting a few days or months, conspiracies, and assassinations. The state, but lately still brilliant and giving every impression of power, now resembled nothing more than a machine totally out of control.

The vizier al-Fududi controlled matters in the beginning, though he had to be wary of competition from the amir of the Hintata, 'Amir al-Hintati, who ruled over the Marrakesh region. In May 1359, less than eighteen months after Abu 'Inan's death, another vizier, Ibn Masai, set himself up a pretender and endeavoured to gain power under his aegis. At this moment yet another pretender, Abu Salim, son of Abu al-Hasan, appeared on the scene with the support of the king of Castile, Peter the Cruel. The two viziers, watching carefully the devolution of power, deserted their respective sultans and each made overtures to Abu Salim, who was proclaimed sultan in July 1359. Al-Fududi was sent to Marrakesh in disgrace, there rebelled and in the spring of 1360 was caught and executed. Ibn Masai and Abu Salim thought they had the situation well in hand when on 19 September 1361 a new vizier, 'Umar ibn 'Abd Allah, upset the equilibrium and in agreement with the leader of the Christian militia, a Spaniard, proclaimed a new sultan—an idiot son of Abu al-Hasan, named Tashfin. A few months later, however, at the end of 1361, the all-powerful vizier, deeming his ruler inadequate, summoned a grandson of Abu al-Hasan, Abu Ziyan, from the court of Castile where he had taken refuge. Meanwhile the Merinid kingdom was breaking up. The 'Abd al-Wadids took advantage of every opportunity to install themselves in Tlemcen, only to be expelled every time. Southern Morocco was subject *de facto* to 'Amir al-Hintati. Finally a Merinid prince had established himself at Sijilmasa with the assistance of the Ma'qil Arabs, and was taking on there the appearance of a sovereign. At the end of some years Abu Ziyan, anxious to shake off his vizier's control, planned to have him put to death. Warned through harem channels—he had his spies there—'Umar ibn 'Abd Allah had his master strangled in the autumn of 1366, and put in his place a son of Abu al-Hasan, 'Abd al-'Aziz, who had until that time been secluded in the palace of Fez.

The prisoner become sultan was a sickly young man, but he concealed great energy in his weak body and was supported by his mother, a woman of capacity and decision. Perceiving that once more his sovereign was not what he was looking for, the vizier 'Umar contemplated causing his disappearance. His plan was discovered and in July 1367 'Abd al-'Aziz had him cut to pieces before his eyes; he then set his government in order. This did not suit al-Hintati, master of the south, and he embarked on open rebellion. 'Abd al-'Aziz marched against him, tracked him down in the mountains in midwinter and finally captured him in the spring of 1370. He then turned back against Tlemcen, where the 'Abd al-Wadid prince Abu Hammu had re-established himself. The town fell without resistance on 7 August 1370. 'Abd al-'Aziz then pursued his campaign in the central Maghrib, of which he made himself master, victorious over Arab resistance. In 1372 the Merinid kingdom had been all but restored to its state in the greatest days of Abu Ya'qub. But not for long: for all his energy, the sultan's health was failing. He died on 23 October 1372, leaving power to a quite young child, al-Sa'id.

Rule by vizier began once more. First Abu Bakr ibn Ghazi ruled in the name of the infant al-Sa'id. He was not long able to withstand the attacks of a competitor Muhammad ibn 'Uthman, who with the support of the king of Granada linked his cause with that of the pretender Abu al-'Abbas who was successful in 1374. At the end of ten years Abu al-'Abbas ceased to please his Nasrid patron, and he was forced into exile and his vizier was put to death. Then the vizier Ibn Masai reappeared with the sultans Musa (1384–1386), a son of Abu 'Inan, and an incapable invalid, followed by al-Wathiq (1386–1387), a great-grandson of Abu al-Hasan. As Ibn Masai was endeavouring to shake off the heavy yoke laid on the north of Morocco by Muhammad V, ruler of Granada, Muhammad sent Abu al-'Abbas back again to Morocco. He succeeded in gaining power and had Ibn Masai put to death under painful torture. The Ma'qil, who had made this restoration possible, took an increasing interest in the affairs of the state. Some became masters of the Tafilalet kingdom; others secured free access to the coastal plains. Under Abu al-'Abbas Morocco was again relatively tranquil for six years. The sultan was even able to send his son to conquer Tlemcen, Algers, Miliana and Dellys, but the unrest following his death at Taza in November 1393 was such as to permit Christians to carry the war into Morocco.

The Return to Berber Kingdoms

THE GOVERNMENT OF THE SULTANS

The Merinid dynasty displayed more pragmatism than originality. Whatever their ambition, its rulers contented themselves with the title of champions of Islam (*Amir al-Muslimīn*—Commander of the Muslims). Until the reign of Abu 'Inan they did not venture to assume that of Caliph, which the Almohads had borne unquestioned. Failing this, they managed to take care of their reputation among foreigners and influential Moroccan townsmen by the ostentatious display of their courts and retinues, the magnificence of their building works, the majestic quality of their monumental epigraphy and the adulatory publicity conferred by their poets and chroniclers. Thus they succeeded in making such an impression, not only on their contemporaries but on posterity, that even today the popular mind still regards them as the last representatives of Muslim grandeur. 'After the Beni Merin and the Beni Wattas,' the saying goes in Morocco, 'there is nothing.'

In general, the Merinids drew their viziers, chamberlains, secretaries and qadis from the same families. Thus it was that most of the viziers came not from the sovereign's direct kin—their ambition would have been too dangerous—but from collateral or confederate groups. These high dignitaries, simultaneously military leaders and administrators, probably did not exercise clearly defined functions, being more skilled with the sword than with the pen. Made responsible for the highest and most dangerous duties, they did not always display unfailing honesty and loyalty.

The sultans appointed their chamberlains at their own desire. These confidential agents, whether slaves, freedmen, Jews or eunuchs, controlled access to their master, arranged public audiences, supervised the execution of punishments and guarded the prisoners in their gaols. They may even have acted as censors of morals.

The administration of the kingdom was entrusted by the sultans to secretaries. These functionaries generally belonged to the circle of Andalusian men of letters, though sometimes to Maghribi families whose members had in former times served the Almohads. More frequently they came from other Muslim courts where they had acquired an expertise. When Ibn Khaldun joined the Merinids he had already had his training on the staff of the Hafsid chancellery. According to the *Musnad* there were two kinds of court secretaries.[44] Some were responsible for incoming and outgoing correspondence, others for war, survey-work and financial services—chiefly the allocation and levying of taxes.

Qadis were generally recruited locally, which indicates that there must have existed a Maghribi élite experienced in legal practice.

The Merinid *jund* comprised Zenata and Arab tribes. The soldiers were renowned for their bravery, but also for their pride. The 'volunteers of the faith' represented the core of the army. It was they who challenged Christian champions before battle. Zenata and Arabs were the chief source of cavalry, Andalusians provided crossbowmen and Asiatic mercenaries were the archers. To these should be added a Christian military force quartered in a district of Fez Jdid called *Rabad al-Nusarā* (suburb of the Christians). The sultan was always accompanied by his personal guard, the 'men of the ring' whose tents encircled his. When the army was in the field the commander-in-chief was entrusted by the sultan with a small flag in white linen, a miniature of the royal standard, in token of authority. This flag was borne at the head of the troops and planted on conquered citadels.

The army preferred raiding expeditions to set battles. When battle was to be entered, each corps occupied a prearranged position. After the challenges and single combats, the archers and crossbowmen loosed a flight of shafts on the enemy and the cavalry then charged. When fighting against unbelievers the victors seldom showed mercy, shared out the booty equitably and destroyed what they could not carry off.

The Merinid dynasty could not have survived without relying on Arab families. Its makhzan was at first recruited among the Khlot, previously reduced to a minor role but irreconcilably hostile to the Almohads, who had deported them to Morocco and treated them harshly. A marriage set the seal on the union in 1260. The favourable attitude of the Khlot lasted more than a century, though they never had the benefit of the advantages conferred by the Hafsids and the 'Abd al-Wadids on the nomads who served them. Their fall, due perhaps to their loyalty to the sultan of Marrakesh, came with the conflict in which he was opposed to the sultan of Fez, 'Abd al-'Aziz. For thirty years or so from 1310 the

The Return to Berber Kingdoms

Suwaid became the Merinids' most solid support against their rivals of the central Maghrib. The benefits they received were the greater in proportion as their distant situation rendered them less of a danger.

MERINID ART

Merinid architecture was the visible expression of the political, military and religious activity of the rulers of Morocco. As heads of state they embellished their capital of New Fez. As conquerors they built the walls of Mançoura. As pious Muslims they erected colleges or madarsas, increased the number of establishments around the tomb of Sidi Bu Madian at El-Eubbad, and placed their necropolis of Chella under the protecting shadow of the *ribat* built by the Almohads at Salé.

For a hundred years Muminid decadence and the founding of the Merinid dynasty discouraged building activity. It was not until the end of the thirteenth century that Abu Ya'qub constructed the mosques at Taza and Oujda, both still strongly marked by Almohad influences. Abu al-Hasan, whose *Musnad* catalogues the many Moroccan mosques, was unable to complete the one begun at Mançoura by Abu Ya'qub, who took as his model the Mosque of Hassan at Rabat; all he could achieve was the square courtyard, the extension of which was probably due to Merinid initiative. The imposing minaret, over 130 feet high and with a lantern above, was, unlike other edifices, remarkable for its solidity and the quality of its construction. It was also Abu al-Hasan who in 1339 built the Mosque of El-Eubbad near the tomb of Sidi Bu Madian. Access to this is by way of a monumental porch decorated with porcelain mosaics. In the prayer-hall, with its five naves, three bays and a transept, the walls and coffered ceilings are decorated with a coat of sculptured plaster; the mihrab, a niche with cut-off corners, has its arch supported by two onyx columns with elegant capitals, and is preceded by a bay crowned with a rich stalactited dome. The courtyard is surrounded by a portico with prismatic pillars, and the minaret is copiously decorated with networks of brick and ceramic.

Fourteen years later Abu 'Inan dedicated a mosque to another ascetic, Sidi al-Halwi, formerly qadi of Seville, who became a seller of sweetmeats (*halwā*) at Tlemcen. This was similar to that of Sidi Bou Médine but smaller. The prayer-hall contains eight onyx columns and the four faces of the minaret carry motifs in enamelled terracotta.

In the absence of Moroccan mosques, we may note the monuments erected in the Chella necropolis at the gates of Rabat. Here the sultans and their kin, from Abu Yusuf in 1286 to Abu al-Hasan in 1339, were laid to rest in ground sanctified by the nearby presence of the ribat. It was Abu al-Hasan, the last Merinid champion of Islam, who gave it an air of splendour by enclosing it with a wall, beautifying the sanctuary and erecting a second mosque. The pentagonal wall, some 985 by 262 feet, was constructed in coarse cement rough-coated in white, and flanked with twenty towers. Its main gate, flanked by two semi-octagonal bastions with merlons at the corners, sacrificed the requirements of defence to a wealth of ornamentation in sculptured stone, polychrome marble and faience. The sanctuary comprised Abu Yusuf's oratory, now in ruins, the mihrab of which is surrounded by a semicircular corridor, a minaret 47 feet high surmounted by a lantern and adorned with large panels of multicoloured porcelain, and the oratory of Abu Hasan. In the nearby garden the sultan had raised his sumptuous funeral chapel; this was in ashlar bonded in a remarkable fashion, the courses being joined with layers of lead, and its interior walls were of luxuriously decorated stone set off with marble.

The victory of the Merinids over the Almohads, which was also the victory of Sunni orthodoxy over Shi'a heresy, led them to build numerous madarsas for instruction in Maliki jurisprudence; the students were lodged in these establishments at the sultan's expense. Ibn Marzuq applauded the zeal of Abu al-Hasan in defending Sunni doctrine. The al-Saffarin madarsa, which we owe to Abu Yusuf, is the only one dating from the thirteenth century. Its courtyard contains a square basin in the middle and has the students' cells ranged along its sides. The small prayer-hall, square in shape, has a mihrab said to be the best positioned in Fez. The other madarsas were built in the first half of the fourteenth century. The one at Fez Jdid goes back to Abu Sa'id 'Uthman. The al-Sahrij madarsa, which has no minaret, owes its popular name to the huge rectangular basin in its courtyard. It is simple but harmonious in form. The little al-Sba'iyin madarsa, which serves as an annexe to it, was set apart for teaching the *riwāya*, that is, the seven ways of reading the Koran. The

The Return to Berber Kingdoms

al-'Attarin—or perfumers' quarter—madarsa is the most elegant. It is perhaps the most nearly perfect Merinid monument in its fitting distribution of the decorative masses of its courtyard and the ornamentation of its prayer-hall. The Misbahiya, erected by Abu al-Hasan and taking its name from the first professor who taught there, contained 117 rooms. It still has a fine screen in carved wood, a vestibule ceiling of remarkable workmanship and an entry to the prayer-hall of rare elegance. The madarsa at Salé, of the same period, is approached by a carved doorway with steps, framed in sculpture. The madarsa at El-Eubbad, built in 1347, testified to Abu al-Hasan's pious veneration for Sidi Bu Madian. The Bou 'Inaniya, which we owe to Abu 'Inan, the last and most monumental of the madarsas at Fez, was built during the years 1350–1357. Its main door, with two leaves of wood overlaid with worked bronze, leads on to a vestibule rising in steps edged with onyx and faience and flanked by benches in polychrome faience. Its vast courtyard is paved with flags of onyx and white or rose-coloured marble and lined with mosaics. The windows of the rooms open through the plaster decoration. 'Higher up, the pillars take the thrust of great imitation arches in wood which support the large upper frieze covered with Koranic inscriptions and protected by a screen of a richness never surpassed.'[45] The prayer-hall has two transverse naves with geometric ribs of intricate perfection, and is lit by two stained glass windows. At its side stood a clock built in 1357, comprising thirteen bronze bells which probably served as chimes, and latrines covered by a magnificent timber framed roof.

The Merinids also founded numerous military establishments. Abu Yusuf provided the *ribat* of Bou Regreg with an arsenal, and built ramparts and gates at Fez Jdid. Abu al-Hasan, as has been mentioned, erected the surrounding wall at Chella, though it was not as important defensively as the one at Mançoura.

The merits of the Hispano-Maghribi art of the Merinids do not derive from the architects' technique. The building material is of poor quality disguised under the wealth of decoration. Broad clean lines give way to immense detail. Nevertheless the general effect is still uncluttered, the proportions balanced and the decoration perfectly adapted to the spaces it fills. Above all, the polychrome effects show an unfailing delicacy and certainty of touch.

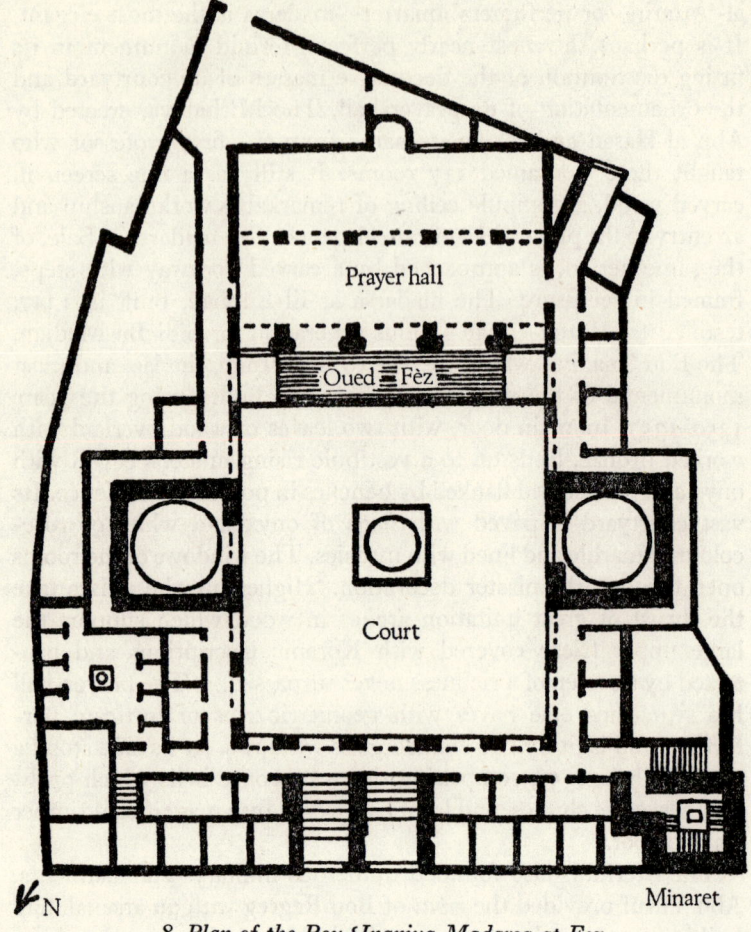

8 Plan of the Bou ʿInaniya Madarsa at Fez

Merinid art, having attained maturity, carried within itself the seeds of the decadence that was to come of the abuse of [architectural] formulae and the employment of a profusion of detail. But the influence it exercised and its prestige were unparalleled not only throughout all Barbary but in the East as well. By the end of the fourteenth century, however, it had exhausted its strength. The disturbances of the following century meant that great works were no longer possible.

The Return to Berber Kingdoms

CONCLUSION

Officially the Merinid dynasty continued until 1465. In fact we can regard it as coming to an end in 1420. It was then that the sultan Abu Sa'id 'Uthman III was assassinated by his chamberlain, and power, devolving *de jure* on to 'Abd al-Haqq, the late ruler's one-year-old child, was exercised *de facto* by a member of the Beni Wattas family. Accordingly, in evaluating Merinid achievement, 1420 would appear to be an appropriate date at which to begin.

After overthrowing the Almohads by force, the Merinids had but one objective—to restore what they had destroyed and to reconstitute an Almohad empire under Merinid colours. But neither their means nor their circumstances were the same. They did not possess the same forces as their predecessors. Being nomadic horsemen, they never had infantry of their own. Their foot-soldiers were Andalusians, Castilians, even orientals, whereas the basic element of the Almohad army had been the Moroccan mountaineer, the ancestor of the *goumier* of today. Their military instrument, therefore, remained incomplete for all its brilliance. It was also very small. Terrasse observes that the few figures available, and indeed the Merinids' military policy itself, appear to indicate clearly that their numbers were relatively weak.[46] Accordingly we see them constantly calling on the Berber tribes of Morocco, who were not always anxious to take up arms on their behalf, and on Arab tribes, or at any rate some of them—the equivalent of what were later to be called the makhzan tribes. Thus Merinid strength was not based nearly as much on troops furnished by the victorious clan as that of the Almohads had been. The Merinid armies contained a high proportion of unzealous or indifferent troops, even contingents secretly hostile. It was a force that did not measure up to the tasks demanded of it by the more enterprising rulers.

And at the same time, their opponents were more formidable than those of the Almohads; in Spain the kingdom of Castile had grown noticeably stronger. Its army and fleet shared in the progress made in the art of war throughout western Europe. In the Maghrib the Almohads had found themselves confronted by anarchic tribes or kingdoms undermined by the Arab invasion. The Merinids had to reckon with two states which had been formed before their own and which, under the impetus of rulers of the stature of Yaghmorasan, Abu Zakariya or al-Mustansir, had attained a certain cohesion. Finally the Arabs had spread throughout the Maghrib and with them had come the destructive conflict between settled agricultural life and nomadic pastoral life. In addition, the Merinid dynasty never knew the cohesion of the Muminid dynasty. No sooner was the first true Merinid ruler, Abu Yahya, dead, than power became an object of competition. Rarely indeed were successions accomplished without hindrance.

It would have been surprising if in these conditions the Merinids had been able to realise their dream. Indeed, the dream would have had to be a different one. Instead of obstinately endeavouring to revive an Almohad empire covering the whole of the Maghrib and Muslim Spain, they would have had to try to constitute a Zenata state confined to Morocco and the central Maghrib, bounded to the east by Kabylia and the Aurès. In brief, they would have had to set a limit to their ambitions. Whether in Spain or in the Maghrib their failure was complete. Their Andalusian adventure was over in 1340 even before Abu al-Hasan entertained the illusion, and a fleeting one at that, of having formed a Maghribi empire. The failure was the more serious in so far as they had squandered their strength to the point of exhaustion, and an irreversible decline set in soon after Abu 'Inan's final effort.

In political terms then, the Merinid dynasty ended in total failure. The same need not be said, however, of religion and culture. The Merinids were neither religious reformers nor descendants of the Prophet crowned with special graces. Nevertheless their influence on the religious life of Morocco is indisputable. Smoothly and without conflict they gradually brought about the disappearance of the Almohad doctrine in favour of the Malikism of former times. They encouraged the development of religious learning by founding madarsas almost everywhere. If they are not to be regarded as having founded the 'school of Fez' they contributed largely to its growth and glory. It can be said that everything in Morocco that goes to make up Islam carries the stamp of the Merinids, from the madarsas and the list of works of instruction to the practices observed in celebrating the great religious feasts, notably that of the Mulud or Birth of the Prophet. The tendency to rigorism and austerity resulting from Almohad

The Return to Berber Kingdoms

doctrine persisted, but a great part of the religious institutions is of Merinid origin. From the same period, though it received no impetus from the rulers, dates the popularity of the Moroccan mystical movement, to which we shall return later.

Anyone who has visited Fez or Tlemcen can be in no doubt about the existence of a Merinid culture, certainly more original than that of the Hafsids. But buildings are not all it has left behind. When one reads the pages devoted by Leo Africanus to Fez, it is realised that the Merinids gave to Morocco, at least to its northern part, a manner of life that is not yet entirely lost.[47] Terrasse has rightly laid emphasis on the overwhelming share in this culture of Andalusian influence.[48] It was already at work in Almohad times, though less insistent, less predominant. Under the thrust of the *reconquista* Spanish Islam withdrew slowly to nearby Morocco, and the Zenata, little encumbered with culture or traditions, let themselves be influenced by this influx of so much wealth. Thus the public buildings, a few of which have been summarily analysed above, and a certain literary flowering dominated by the Andalusian poet and historian Ibn al-Khatib. Thus too, the development of the towns in the north of Morocco; Fez Jdid and Tétouan are Merinid creations. The same could almost be said of Meknès, which, before Abu Yusuf, was hardly more than a kasbah rising near a few ancient Berber villages, and of Oujda, to which Abu Ya'qub gave the importance of a frontier town. The old town of Fez, Taza, Salé, and Ceuta all were improved at the pleasure of these builder princes, from Abu Yusuf to Abu 'Inan. It is only proper to observe that their culture remained urban in character and scarcely touched the countryside or even the centres of secondary importance. It was only where they did not closely imitate the Almohads that the Merinids created a lasting achievement.

IV. The Beni Wattas Dynasty and the Reawakening of Islam

THE CHRISTIAN OFFENSIVE IN MOROCCO

Despite the battles on Spanish soil and reciprocal acts of piracy, relations between the Muslims of Morocco and the Christians had never been interrupted. During the fifteenth century ships from Venice, Genoa, Pisa, Marseilles, Catalonia and Aragon regularly used the ports of Arzila, Tangier, Badis (which faced the islet known as Peñon de Velez), Ceuta, Arcudia or Alcudia (Alhucemas?) and Melilla. Only rarely did they touch at Salé, Azemmour, Safi and Mogador, where Muslim coastal traffic alone was active. It was exceptional for merchants to venture into the towns of the interior, though Marrakesh had a Frankish quarter (*Kassaria*). Exchanges took place at the ports, where there were Arab customs and Christian *funduks*. Every second year the Venetian fleet put into Badis, the port of Fez. Morocco's chief imports were hunting birds, metals, hardware, haberdashery, textiles, woollens, spices and wine. Its exports were slaves, leather, hides, carpets, wool, coral, grain and sugar. This busy trade did not cease during the fifteenth century in spite of the Christian offensive. Trade relations were even established between the Moroccans and the strongpoints (*fronteiras*) and these facilitated Portuguese penetration in the direction of Marrakesh.

At the beginning of the sixteenth century the most important centre was the Wattasid capital, Fez. This was linked by four roads with the ports of Chasasa or Ghassaça (Selouan, perhaps, since Melilla had been taken by the Spaniards in 1497), Badis, Ceuta and Tangier. The somewhat unsafe road from the threshold of Taza made possible relations with Tlemcen. One road led to Sijilmasa, from which the date caravans came, and three to the Haouz. Merchandise was liable to duties levied by the towns, as well as to tolls imposed by local chiefs.

The hostility of the Merinids towards the Castilians had led to the establishment of particularly cordial relations with the Aragonese, who in 1274 helped them to suppress a revolt in Ceuta, and expelled the king of Granada from that port in 1309. After thirty years of tension caused by the interventions of the sultans in Spain the rapprochement of 1345 was a matter of course, and resulted twelve years later in a political and commercial treaty aimed against Castile. Abu 'Inan and his successors followed a policy favourable to Aragon, which was in any case too fully occupied elsewhere to modify its Moroccan policy.

The Portuguese and the Castilians, however, were looking for an opportunity to intervene in Morocco. It was in the conflict against

The Return to Berber Kingdoms

Maghribi invaders that Portugal had forged its independence as a nation, and the Avis dynasty, founded in 1385 due to the support of the merchant bourgeoisie, aspired to try its new strength against the infidel. By the victory of the Rio Salado the Castilians had put an end to effectual Merinid intervention on Spanish soil. Thereafter the struggle between Castile and Granada assumed the character of a quarrel between suzerain and vassal rather than between Christian and Muslim. The real enemies of the Christians were still the Maghribis. Accordingly the Castilians were only awaiting a favourable opportunity to realise the dream of Ferdinand III by making a landing in Africa and thus to put an end to the twin dangers of a still possible invasion and increasingly active piracy. The situation in Morocco at the end of the fourteenth century facilitated such action.

After the death of Abu al-'Abbas, quarrels over the succession enabled the amir of Granada, aided by the king of Castile, to keep Morocco in a state of anarchy favourable to his ambitions by raising up or supporting pretenders. The Merinid sultan replied by allowing Maghribi corsairs to attack Andalusian and Christian vessels. Privateering proved so effective and so lucrative that it developed into an autonomous undertaking over which the government lost all control and which provoked reprisals on the part of the Castilians.

While the Merinid army was besieging Tlemcen in 1399, Henry III of Castile, obsessed with the idea of a crusade, took possession of Tétouan, destroyed it, massacred half the inhabitants and reduced the other half to slavery. This savage attack not only stimulated the pirates' zeal, but it also stirred up a wave of nationalist and religious emotion which was to result in the defeat of the Christians.

The Portuguese too profited from anarchy in Morocco. The revolution which had conferred power on 'the defender of the kingdom', Don John, grand master of the order of Avis, marked the triumph of the bourgeoisie of Lisbon and Porto over the landed aristocracy, supported by the common people living on the coast. These last had, on legitimist grounds, rallied to the cause of the king of Castile in 1385. The victory of Portuguese over Castilians demonstrated the superiority of the revolutionary tactics of the bourgeois infantry over the traditional manœuvres of the aristocratic cavalry. It also brought about a shift of policy by giving precedence to the economic interests of the victors. The bourgeoisie, in prevailing on the king to attempt a landing at Ceuta, had the support of the infantes Henry and Ferdinand who were anxious to forestall a Castilian intervention in Morocco. They also had three aims of their own—to put an end to the piracy which was halting grain convoys, to satisfy the crusading spirit now spreading throughout the Peninsula with the increasing progress of the *reconquista*, and to divert popular agitation. The Portuguese fleet easily secured possession of Ceuta on 21 August 1415 and left there a garrison of 2,500 men. The new *fronteira* had only one serious attack to undergo from Moroccans and Granadans, in 1419, and that failed because of internal Merinid dissention.

ADVENT OF THE BENI WATTAS

A year later the Merinid sultan Abu Sa'id 'Uthman was killed in a palace revolution, and his death led to a recrudescence of civil war. The Hilalian tribes took advantage of it to gain territory and to pillage the settled chiefs, and the Arab chiefs to sell themselves and their troops to the highest bidding pretenders. The Portuguese fortified themselves in Ceuta, the 'Abd al-Wadids threw off the suzerainty of Fez, and the religious party increased its influence. Thus in the closing years of the dynasty, the opposing forces reflected the rivalries which for a century were to make up the history of Morocco.

Aided by the crisis, the Beni Wattas branch of the Merinids imposed its authority. After a long period of nomadic wanderings on the edge of the High Plateaux and the Sahara, the Beni Wattas had eventually settled in eastern Morocco. The victory of their cousins, the Merinids, over the Almohads brought them a powerful fief in the Rif, and during the later reigns of the dynasty a constantly growing influence at court. In the massacre of Abu Sa'id's family, a one-year-old child was spared, 'Abd al-Haqq, against whom Granada and Tlemcen set up pretenders. Abu Zakariya Yahya al-Wattasi, at that time governor of Salé, took on the orphan's case and, not without a struggle, saw to its success. Abu Zakariya's action meant more than the restoration of Merinid authority; it marked the seizure of governmental power by the Wattasids. Their leader, while holding the office of regent, in reality held the power.

The Return to Berber Kingdoms

'Abd al-Haqq, when he came to manhood, preferred devoting himself to debauchery to shaking off his guardian's control. Nor did he take any action against that of the nephew of Abu Zakariya, 'Ali ibn Yusuf. Furthermore, for thirty years, from 1428 to 1458, the mayors of the palace showed themselves able to perform their task. They faced the Christian peril with energy as they did the revival of nationalist and religious fanaticism that was its consequence.

Within the shelter of their *fronteira* of Ceuta the only encounters the Portuguese experienced were single combats in which their lords engaged with the 'warriors of the faith' (*mujāhidūn*) who came to challenge them. During the lifetime of Don John I they showed no desire to extend their conquests. But when the infante Don Edward had become king the court was torn between the Moroccan ambitions of Don Henry and Don Fernando and the policy of national production sustained by the king's advice and by Don Pedro, both of whom refused to 'trade a good cloak for a bad bonnet'. The colonial party, fortified by pontifical approval, overcame the king's resistance, and mounted an expedition against Tangier. An army insufficient in numbers for lack of volunteers was surrounded under the city walls by the considerable forces which had reached Abu Zakariya from all parts of Morocco, and capitulated on 16 October 1437. The defeated had to agree to cede Ceuta and to hand over the infante Don Fernando as hostage pending the completion of their undertaking. But Don Edward felt obliged to sacrifice his brother rather than the commercial centre. After six years of difficult captivity, which he endured with admirable courage, the infante died at Fez on 5 June 1433. The Church, whose influence and prestige had prevented the expedition from being abandoned, enrolled him in her martyrology and in 1470 beatified him.

THE REAWAKENING OF ISLAM

Abu Zakariya's forceful activity answered the wishes of the religious party, for whom his regency represented the 'golden age'. After the Spaniards had destroyed Tétouan, Berber nationalism, under the impetus of the shaikhs of the zawiyas, had found expression in an upwelling of Muslim fervour. In the ransoming of captives the shaikhs stepped into the place of the sultans, who were prevented from intervening personally by reasons of policy. By virtue of their activity and their ardour they became the representatives of popular aspirations for holy war, thus running counter to the opportunist decisions of the makhzan, which refused to categorise as operational territory regions occupied by the infidel in which the practice of Islam was even partially maintained.

Sufism (from *suf*, a garment of coarse wool) had spread in Morocco under the Almoravids and the Almohads. This movement, embodying the doctrine of those Muslims who renounce the world, had originated in the East by way of a reaction, influenced by Christian monasticism and Neoplatonism, against the worldliness of Islam. Thereafter, there had arisen numerous local saints indwelt by the holy emanation of *baraka*; these were the marabouts (*murābit*, in colloquial usage *mrābit*). Some lived in isolation, but around others there grew up in remote spots schools (*zawāyā*) of ever increasing influence in which not only sufism was taught, but also alchemy and magic. Accordingly the rulers of Morocco banned the activity of sufism outside the limits of the zawiyas. During the struggle between Almohads and Merinids the brotherhoods exerted their influence against the Muminid dynasty. The Merinids, though they had benefited from their support, were quick to oppose their decentralising tendencies by upholding the official corps of '*ulamā*', who taught orthodox doctrine, against the shaikhs and their mysticism. The increase in the number of madarsas was partly due to the struggle against the growing popularity of sufism.

When the authority of the rulers of Fez grew weak and the makhzan showed itself incapable of effectively combating the unbelievers, the zawiyas extended their field of action. They now emerged as powerfully constituted institutions, at the same time monasteries, schools and hostelries, under the direction of the shaikhs. From them there spread throughout the country the disciples (*muqaddams*) carrying watchwords to the ardent mass of the brethren (*ikwān*). On their faithful they imposed a ritual which, though strict, was devoid of any dogmatism, together with ascetic mortifications which induced that divine ecstasy in which the sufi is absorbed in the unique reality of the Divine Being.

Two of them were ardent centres of Muslim faith. One derived from 'Abd al-Qadir al-Jilani, the Great Pole, who died at Baghdad

The Return to Berber Kingdoms

in 1066; this was directed by the Qadiri sharifs of Fez. The other went back, through Muhammad al-Jazuli who died in the middle of the fifteenth century, to ʿAbd al-Salam ibn Mshish, the great saint of the Jebala. But under the Wattasids these brotherhoods, whose political role tends to be exaggerated, were almost exclusively organs of religious propaganda. Their influence over the masses, aimed at rousing them against the sultans, was neither systematic nor effective until after the triumph of the Saadians, and then it took place apart from them.

The Wattasids tried to divert the nationalist and religious movement to their own benefit. They took command of the struggle against the Portuguese and endeavoured to turn their capital into a zawiya the prestige of which would overwhelm all the others. The year in which Abu Zakariya captured the army of the infantes under the walls of Tangier was marked by the discovery at Fez of the tomb of Mulay Idris. The body of the city's founder, which had been thought to have been interred at Oulili near that of his father, was recognised intact by the regent, the head of the Idrisid family and the *fuqahāʾ*. It was decided to leave it at the same spot where it had been found and to cover it with a monument. This renewal, after a long eclipse, of the Idrisid cult was not fortuitous. It was, so to speak, the consecration of the rebirth of Sharifism. On all sides there sprang up marabout-sharifs (or, following the dialectal plural form commonly used in the Maghrib, *shurfa*)—true or supposed descendants of the Prophet Muhammad, whose *baraka* they had inherited. Their spiritual authority was the more efficacious for the demands made on them by the Muslims for miraculous intervention against the unbelievers. Abu Zakariya's aim was no doubt to divert to the benefit of the Wattasids this reawakening of Sharifian devotion. But the chief gain from the finding of the body fell to the prestige of the Idrisid family, whose chief had been on a footing of equality with the regent in the discovery and its verification.

THE END OF THE MERINIDS

The authority of the makhzan was jeopardised by the progress of the Christian invasion and the downfall of the Wattasid mayors of the palace. In response to an appeal from the pope, who had proclaimed a crusade against the Turks immediately after the fall of Constantinople in 1453, the king of Portugal, Alphonso V, had fitted out a fleet and an army. But for him, as for the other Christian princes, a distant expedition had no attraction, and he preferred to divert his forces against a little port between Ceuta and Tangier, el-Ksar es-Seghir, of which he wished to make a military base. The place capitulated without resistance on 18 October 1458. Three attempts by the king on Tangier failed, the last one, on 12 January 1464, disastrously. Fresh revolutions in the palace at Fez enabled him finally to achieve his end.

In 1458 the sultan 'Abd al-Haqq had agreed without resistance to accept the guardianship of a third Wattasid, Yahya son of Abu Zakariya, who was far from possessing the merit of his predecessors. This was quickly realised at court, where the ruler finally took action and at the end of two months had the vizier and his family assassinated. Two of Yahya's brothers succeeded in escaping the massacre, and one of them, Muhammad al-Shaikh, secured himself behind the walls of Arzila and gathered the malcontents around him. 'Abd al-Haqq failed to properly carry out the duties of his office, and anarchy reappeared again. Apart from the kingdom of Marrakesh, which had been practically independent for twenty years and may already have been in the hands of the Hintata amirs, the tribes were in revolt. A sharif of the Sous, the imam al-Jazuli, one of the the most striking figures of Moroccan mysticism, was scouring the regions north of the Atlas, assembling, it is said, nearly 13,000 faithful followers and covering the country with zawiyas. 'Abd al-Haqq became an object of suspicion not only to the *ikwān* of Fez after the murder of al-Jazuli, in which he was suspected of having had a hand, but also to the entire population of the city, which disapproved that he had a Jew as minister. In May 1465, in the course of a revolt, the mob had him ritually murdered like an animal, and with him the Merinid dynasty came to an end.

This murder revealed the prestige of the Idrisid family. The leader of the sharifs, who had presided over the discovery of the body of Idris, like his ancestor the founder of Fez, proclaimed himself Imam. But he was unable to withstand the attacks of Muhammad al-Shaikh, who after six years of conflict entered the capital as conqueror and assumed power. From being mayors of the palace the Wattasids had become titular sovereigns.

The Return to Berber Kingdoms

THE TRIUMPH OF THE SHARIFS

The founder of the dynasty was faced with a task of great difficulty. Aided by the disturbances, the Portuguese, with 477 ships and 30,000 men, succeeded in carrying Arzila. Muhammad al-Shaikh had to resign himself to a twenty years' truce, involving not the fortified places, but the flat country. The king took advantage of the restrictive clause to have Tangier occupied without resistance on 29 August 1471. It was then that he assumed the title of *Rei de Portugal e dos Algarves daquem e dalem mar em Africa* (King of the Algarves on this side of the sea and beyond the sea in Africa).

Despite his energy, the Wattasid sultan was able to make himself master only of the Fez region; the mountain Berbers and the marabouts of the South eluded his authority. He ran into the irreconcilable hostility of the religious element, which supported pretenders against him. Notwithstanding the zeal of the zawiyas against the infidel, there was no halt to the progress of the Portuguese. A treaty with the Castilians signed in 1479 acknowledged their exclusive rights over the coast of Africa facing the Canaries, including the kingdom of Fez, and reserved to them the monopoly of trade. Despite a serious setback in 1489, in an attempt on an island in the river Loukkos, where they desired to found the fortress of Graciosa, they had succeeded in firmly establishing their four *fronteiras* of Ceuta, el-Ksar es-Seghir, Tangier and Arzila.

The Spaniards, notwithstanding their earlier undertakings, hoped to occupy certain points in Moroccan territory after the capture of Granada in 1492 had crowned the work of the *reconquista*. The Catholic kings conducted a study of the Maghribi coastline by travellers in their employ. They persuaded the Portuguese, to whom the whole kingdom of Fez was reserved by the treaties, to sacrifice it in 1494. Three years later the Duke of Medina Sidonia occupied it without striking a blow, with the fleet intended for the second voyage of Christopher Columbus (1497). From there the Spaniards followed with anxious interest the progress of the struggle between Wattasids and sharifs.

Under the successors to Muhammad al-Shaikh—Muhammad al-Burtugali (1455–1524) and Abu al-ʿAbbas Ahmad (1524–1549)—the situation grew steadily worse. Don Manuel, master of Vasco da Gama and Albuquerque, though primarily interested in outlets in

History of North Africa

Asia, nevertheless intervened in Morocco against the kingdom of Marrakesh. After establishing agencies (*feitorias*) there, he occupied Safi in 1508, followed by Azemmour in 1513. At his death in 1520 the Portuguese held the Atlantic coast of Morocco as far as the Straits of Gibraltar. It was economically important to them because from it they could purchase from the interior the wheat needed by the mother country and the horses and woollen blankets (*hambel*) which they exchanged in black Africa for gold and slaves. Moreover they were not content with their coastal fortresses; in certain cities of the interior, notably Fez, they maintained agents (*feitor*) who were both consuls and commercial agents. The correspondence of one of these agents at Fez has been partly preserved, and from it he appears much concerned with the purchase of grain.[49]

Thus, so far as the Portuguese were concerned, Morocco was not to be regarded as an end in itself, but rather as a part of the immense economic empire that Portugal was occupied with establishing on the shores of the Atlantic and the Indian Ocean.

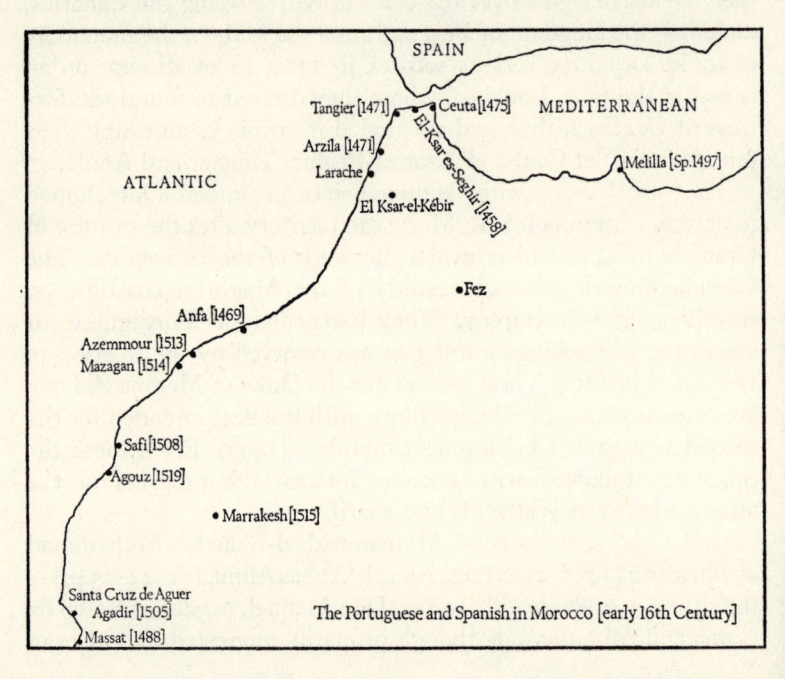

The Portuguese and Spanish in Morocco [early 16th Century]

The Return to Berber Kingdoms

This explains why the Portuguese never really sought to conquer Morocco, but tried rather to arrive at a formula fairly close to that which underlay the modern protectorates. Their soldiers remained in their strongpoints, protected by ramparts and moats, but always on the alert. High or projecting towers enabled a watch to be kept on the countryside, and mortars gave warning to gardeners, fishermen and hunters when there was danger of a Moorish attack. Mortar fire also, given a favouring wind, warned the occupation force at Tangier to come to the aid of that at Arzila, or a boat carried the news from one port to the other. Information about enemy intentions was received by interrogating prisoners. The captain of the strongpoint directed raids, collected a fifth share of booty for himself and divided the remainder among his soldiers. Expeditions launched from Arzila, Tangier and Ceuta seldom penetrated further into the countryside than 20 miles or so. The captains of the strongpoints in the south had a wide field of action. They had brought into submission the greater part of the Haouz, mainly in the province of the Dokkala, and relied on the tribute-paying peoples, 'the Moors of peace', for supplies of grain, and for aid in preparing for the investment of Marrakesh. One of these Moors, Ibn Tafuft, was the best auxiliary of the captain of Safi. In 1515 a Portuguese and Moorish corps advanced as far as the gates of Marrakesh, some 95 miles from Safi. Between conflicts there were truces, but these were soon broken by one side or the other.

The Wattasids were diverted from the struggle against the Christians by an exceptionally dangerous development—the emergence of the rival dynasty of southern sharifs. Just at the time the governors of Safi were making a great effort to gain possession of Marrakesh there arose in the Sous the Beni S'ad or Saadians. At the beginning of the sixteenth century the leader of their zawiya had taken command of the holy war against the Portuguese, who in 1505 had established themselves in Santa-Cruz of Cap d'Aguer (Agadir), and had had himself proclaimed chief in the Sous in 1511. His sons converted Taroudant into a fortified base against the unbelievers. Allies at first of the sultan of the south, they removed him in 1525 by assassination, and made Marrakesh their capital. From that time ruthless conflict occurred between Wattasids and Saadians, the latter constantly gaining at the expense of the former. The Wattasid Ahmad was unable to purchase peace even at the price of recognising the Saadians' possession of the territory of Marrakesh. He marched against them in 1537, was beaten, and then had to accept a new partition of territory under pressure from the religious elements. Successes against the unbelievers, such as the capture of Agadir in 1541, followed by Portuguese evacuation of Safi and Azemmour, consolidated Saadian prestige. In 1549, despite resistance by Bu Hassun, a brother of al-Burtugali, the sharif Muhammad al-Mahdi succeeded in taking Fez and driving out the Wattasid dynasty. Bu Hassun sought in vain for help from Europe. Charles V sent him away, and an attempt by the Portuguese met with failure. The Turks alone—recent arrivals in Africa and masters of Tlemcen, where they were apprehensive of attacks by the Saadians—gave him energetic support, and installed him as Sultan at Fez in 1553. But the restoration of the Wattasids was short-lived. The death of Bu Hassun, treacherously killed in a combat with Muhammad al-Mahdi on 13 September 1554, marked their final ruin and the seizure by the Saadians of all Morocco.

CONCLUSION

In itself the Wattasid dynasty is of no particular importance; it merely followed Merinid policy, and made no change in it. Although the Wattasids, especially in the early years, endeavoured to maintain the struggle against the Portuguese invaders, they were often driven to negotiate with them. The fact remains that they had taken over a country in an advanced stage of disintegration, reduced in area to the northern part of Morocco from the Oum er-Rbia to Tangier, and too much accustomed to anarchy to bow readily to the authority of a master with nothing fresh to contribute.

But in the second half of the fifteenth century and the first half of the sixteenth century the dynasty was not alone in the field. Other forces were appearing in Morocco beside it, and were soon to be against it. If the government admitted its incapacity for effective resistance against Portuguese enterprise, the Moroccan masses refused to accept such domination by unbelievers. Moved by a complex of feelings made up of wounded religious pride and xenophobia, they tried to put obstacles in the way of the newcomer wherever he appeared—first in the north around Ceuta and

The Return to Berber Kingdoms

Tangier, and later in the Sous plain and as far as the Dra' oases when the Portuguese founded Santa-Cruz-Agadir.

The instinctive reaction of the Moroccan people, as may be expected, assumed a religious guise. Brotherhoods, marabouts and shurfa gathered round them adepts anxious at once to gain instruction in their religion and to defend it. For the better part of a century these scattered forces worked by uncoordinated and fragmentary thrusts. Finally the Saadian shurfa succeeded in grouping Morocco around them. It is this politico-religious ferment, with all its consequences which are reflected down to our own day, that constitutes the salient fact of the Wattasid period and endows it with great importance.

Notes

1. E. F. Gautier, *op. cit.*, p. 53.
2. For an English translation of the *Muqaddima*, see F. Rosenthal, *The Muqaddimah: an introduction to history*, 3 vols. (New York, 1958). Probably the most widely accepted translation, though somewhat fulsome in interpretation, is *Les Prolegomenes*, 3 vols. (ed. M. de Slane, Paris, 1934-8).
3. E. F. Gautier, *op. cit.*, pp. 58-74.
4. R. Brunschvig, *La Berbèrie orientale sous les Hafçides, des origines à la fin du XVe siècle*, 2 vols. (Paris, 1940, 1949).
5. *Ibid.*, I, 21.
6. *Ibid.*, I, 42.
7. See *Ibid.*, I, 60 for an account of resistance in Ifriqiya.
8. See *Ibid.*, I, 78 for a portrait of Abu Ishaq.
9. al-'Abdari, *Rihala*, a traveller's account of Hafsid Ifriqiya in 1289; see A. Cherbonneau, 'Notice et extraits du voyage d'El-Adbery', *Journal Asiatique*, 5th series, IV (1854), pp. 150-66.
10. R. Brunschvig (1940), *op. cit.*, I, 255-6.
    XVe siècle. *'Abdal-basit b. Khalil et Adorne* (Paris, 1936), pp. 139–
11. R. Brunschvig, *Deux Récits de Voyage inédits en Afrique du Nord au* 225.
12. See R. Brunschvig (1940), *op. cit.*, I, 251-7 for an account of Abu 'Amr 'Uthman's commercial policy and its relation to the Italian states.
13. *Ibid.*, I, 280.
14. al-'Umari, *Masalik al-Absar fi Mamalik al-Amsar*; see M. Gaudefroy-Demombynes, ed. and trans., *L'Afrique moins l'Egypte* (Paris, 1927), I.

15. Leo Africanus (Hassan b. Muhammad al-Wazzan); see a new edition from the Italian, *Description de l'Afrique*, 2 vols. (tr. A. Epaulard, Paris, 1956), annotated by Th. Monod, H. Laote, R. Mauny, *et al.*; see II, 386–7.
16. Ibn Khaldun (tr. de Slane), *op. cit.*, see II, 404–5.
17. al-'Umari (tr. Gaudefroy-Demombynes), *op. cit.*, p. 118.
18. R. Brunschvig (1936), *op. cit.*, pp. 213–15.
19. al-'Umari (tr. Gaudefroy-Demombynes), *op. cit.*, pp. 111–12.
20. R. Brunschvig (1940), *op. cit.*, I, 27.
21. J. Froissart, *Chroniques* (ed. Kervyn de Lettenhove, Brussels, 1867–77), XIV.
22. al-Tijani, *Rihla*, trans. in part by A. Rousseau, 'Voyage', *Journal Asiatique*, I (1852–3).
23. Ibn Qunfud, *al-Farisiyya fi mabadi al-daula al-Hafsiyya*, trans. in part by A. Cherbonneau, 'Histoire de la dynastie des Beni-Hafs', *Journal Asiatique* (1848–52).
24. Ibn al-Shamma' (al-Hintati), *al-Adilla al-bayyina al-nuraniyya fi mafakhir al-daula al-Hafsiyya* (ed. Kaak, Tunis, 1936).
25. Attrib. to Zarkashi, *Tar'ikh al-dawlatain al-Mawakhidiyya wa al-Hafsidiyya*; see for an Arabic edition under the same title (ed., E. Fagnan, Tunis, A.H. 1286/A.D. 1869) and also E. Fagnan, tr., *Chronique des Almohades et des Hafçides attribuée à Zekechi* (Constantine, 1894).
26. Ibn Khaldun (tr. de Slane), *op. cit.*, II, 339–40.
27. al-Bakri (tr. de Slane), *op. cit.*, pp. 155–9.
28. Ibn Khaldun (tr. de Slane), *op. cit.*, III, 339.
29. E. F. Gautier, *op. cit.*, pp. 342–3.
30. Leo Africanus (tr. Epaulard), *op. cit.*, p. 226.
31. Ibn Khaldun (tr. de Slane), *op. cit.*, IV, 143.
32. *Ibid.*, III, 472–3.
33. E. F. Gautier, *op. cit.*, pp. 401–11.
34. Ibn Khaldun (tr. de Slane), *op. cit.*, III, 340.
35. G. Marçais (1927), *op. cit.*, II, see pp. 470–2.
36. Ibn Khaldun (tr. de Slane), *op. cit.*, IV, 31.
37. Ibn Abi Zar' (tr. Beaumier), *op. cit.*, see p. 516 *et seq.*
38. H. Terrasse (1950), *op. cit.*, II, 95–9.
39. Ibn Khaldun (tr. de Slane), *op. cit.*, IV, 212.
40. Ibn Marzuq (d. 1379), *Musnad*; see M. R. Blachère, 'Quelques détails sur la vie privée du sultan mérinide Abu 'l-Hasan', *Mémorial Henri Basset* (Paris, 1928), I, 86–9.
41. *Ibid.*, p. 87.
42. *Ibid.*, p. 87.
43. Ibn Khaldun (tr. de Slane), *op. cit.*, IV, 236.
44. Ibn Marzuq (tr. Lévi-Provençal), 'Un nouveau texte d'histoire mérinide: Le Musnad d'Ibn Marzuk', *Hespéris*, V (1925), pp. 56–61.
45. P. Ricard, *Pour comprendre l'art musulman dans l'Afrique du Nord et en Espagne* (Paris, 1921), p. 210.

The Return to Berber Kingdoms

46. H. Terrasse (1950), *op. cit.*, II, 71–4.
47. Leo Africanus (tr. Epaulard), *op. cit.*, pp. 157–319.
48. H. Terrasse (1950), *op. cit.*, II, 76–9.
49. H. de Castries, *et al.*, *Sources inédites de l'Histoire du Maroc: Portugal* (Paris, 1934–53), III. Bastião de Vargas, agent of Jean III of Portugal; documents LVI, p. 200; LXV, p. 227; LXXXIII, p. 295; and CXXXVII, p. 529: see also the account of this figure by R. Ricard, *op. cit.*, pp. 176–92.

CHAPTER 5

The Sharifian Empire: 1553-1830

1. The Saadian Dynasty

THE HISTORY OF THE SHARIFIAN DYNASTIES

For the study of the Saadian and Alawite dynasties Moroccan archives are almost entirely lacking and recourse is necessary to Christian documents and to histories in Arabic. However, the exploration of European libraries and archives undertaken by Lieutenant-Colonel de Castries has made it possible to establish an immense corpus, the *Sources inédites de l'Histoire du Maroc*.[1] A score of large volumes packed with documents place basic texts at the historian's disposal—secret treaties, correspondence of ambassadors or merchants, memoirs, charter parties, business partnerships, and travellers' narratives already published but now rare or unobtainable. De Castries supplemented them with critical introductions and valuable notes. This important work, which was continued by de Cenival and since his death has been entrusted to Ricard, gives us fresh knowledge of Sharifian Morocco.

European sources are the more useful in proportion as indigenous history has to be approached with caution. Until the fifteenth century Morocco had produced only meticulous grammarians or zealous theologians. Its concentration on resistance to foreign attack involved the creation of a national history. In an authoritative work[2] Lévi-Provençal has shown what value should properly be put on it: method—none, save a stringing together of facts lacking either a scale of values or governing ideas; content—panegyric or malicious comment, the one as suspect as the other; authors—impenitent plagiarists of the highest order. The historians, far more interested in individuals than in events, are primarily

The Sharifian Empire: 1553-1830

official biographers, with an eye for nothing but the ruler, his court and his capital. Of what constitutes the essence of Moroccan history since the sixteenth century—particularly the struggle of the central power against the religious leaders—nothing emerges from their work.

However, the Saadian dynasty had two important historians. One, whose work is not extant, was al-Fishtali (1549-1621), secretary of state responsible for correspondence, poet-laureate and historiographer to al-Mansur. The other was al-Ifrani, who died about the middle of the eighteenth century and who, out of spite against the sultan Mulay Isma'il, celebrated the praises of the fallen dynasty in his *History of the Saadian Dynasty in Morocco (Nuzhat al-Hādī)*,[3] which is still today the best indigenous source. Among all the Alawite historians al-Zayani (1734-1833?), a pure-blooded Berber,[4] is outstanding. He was a remarkable statesman and in the course of a life full of honours, as well as periods during which he fell from grace, and numerous missions and embassies, he managed to write a number of works. Among them there is a general history from the creation of the world and a history of the Alawite dynasty, which was plagiarized by his successors. We are indebted to him also for a very interesting chapter on the Saadian dynasty, a fragment of which has been published by Lévi-Provençal in Arabic in his *Extraits des historiens arabes du Maroc*.[5] In the nineteenth century an official of the makhzan, al-Nasiri, compiled a general history (*Kitāb al-Istiqṣā*)[6] which is of no great originality but is useful for his own period. Finally, al-Kattani, with the aid of earlier publications, established a catalogue of the saints of Fez (*Salwat al-anfās*).[7]

In addition to works of history proper, Moroccan literature of the sixteenth century produced a wealth of biographies of illustrious men, religious personages of every rank and travellers' tales mingled with local biographies. Any of these may enable a few facts—*rari nantes*—to be gathered from the vast amount of hagiographic matter.

ORIGINS OF THE SAADIANS

It may be useful to deal further with the beginnings of the Saadian dynasty, which in the previous chapter were touched on only in outline and in relation to the decline of the Wattasids.

That they were of Arab origin seems certain, though their Sharifian ancestry has been questioned, at least in their decadent period. The rumour was then current that they did not descend from the Prophet but only from his nurse, by birth a member of the Beni Sa'd tribe. Hence the name of Saadians given them early in the seventeenth century which carried a slightly pejorative implication, since it stressed that they were not of the *shurfa*. However, of greater importance is that they were regarded as descendants of the Prophet at the time of their rise to power. They had come from Arabia in about the twelfth century, apparently shortly before their cousins the Alawite *shurfa*, and after unknown vicissitudes they had finally settled in the oases of the Middle Dra' in the neighbourhood of the present locality of Zagora. There for some centuries they led the life of petty men of letters whose origin brought them a certain esteem. At a point in time difficult to fix, but probably in the second half of the fifteenth century, they moved to the Sous valley and there settled at Tidsi, south-west of and not far from Taroudant; there they founded a zawiya.

It was a period when anarchy was gaining ground despite the efforts of the Wattasids to assert their authority. Southern Morocco was almost completely out of their control. The Hintata amirs, reigning at Marrakesh, were not capable of exacting obedience beyond the Atlas. The plain of the Sous, the Anti-Atlas and the Dra' oases were thus *de facto* independent. But the people were concerned about Portuguese inroads, and their piety moved them to take up arms against the infidel. Half-consciously they were seeking to gather under religious leaders who would lead them in holy war; the Saadians were those leaders. Under the sponsorship of a local marabout, 'Abd Allah ibn Mubarak, a native of the Bani and disciple of the mystic al-Jazuli, the first among them, Muhammad ibn 'Abd al-Rahman, was appointed commander-in-chief in 1511 to lead the struggle against the Portuguese fortress of Founti (Agadir) which had been established in 1505. He secured no result there, but he did extend his influence over the northern slope of the Atlas. He died at Afoughal near Chichaoua, where he was buried beside the mystic al-Jazuli. His power passed to his two sons, Ahmad al-A'raj (Ahmad the Lame) and Muhammad al-Asghar (Muhammad the Younger Son) surnamed Amghar (commander-in-chief).

The Sharifian Empire: 1553-1830

THE CONQUEST OF SOUTHERN MOROCCO

Ahmad al-A'raj was his father's heir-designate. He assumed power, but he drew his brother Muhammad into association with himself. Their influence was counteracted by that of Yahya or Tafuft, the supporter of the Portuguese who was assassinated in 1518, and the two brothers gradually extended their influence as far as Marrakesh. It was not until 1525 that they established themselves there, and in doing so they were careful to acknowledge the overlordship of the Wattasids of Fez.

Despite this moderate and cautious attitude, conflict between the kingdoms of Fez and Marrakesh was inevitable. It was Ahmad al-Wattasi who opened hostilities in 1528. He almost took Marrakesh but was prevented from maintaining his attack by a revolt in his rear, and after an indecisive battle in the Tadla he resigned himself to negotiations. There was no more than a truce. Ahmad al-A'raj, fortified by his ties with the marabouts, had attracted the active sympathy of several heads of the brotherhoods and zawiyas. In this way he surrounded the Wattasid ruler with an ever-tightening net. However, he did not precipitate matters, perhaps out of natural caution and also no doubt in order to avoid appearing as the unjust aggressor. In 1537 he deemed that the right moment had arrived and marched on Fez, but a number of marabouts intervened and he negotiated once again.

The primary *raison d'être* of the Saadians being holy war, they attacked the Portuguese fortress of Agadir and took it in 1541, causing the Portuguese to abandon Safi and Azemmour as well. They were unable at once to exploit this success, which brought them so much prestige in the eyes of the Moroccans, for discord had arisen among them. Immediately after the capture of Agadir there was a clash between supporters of al-A'raj and supporters of Muhammad, who had changed his Berber surname of *Amghar* into its Arab equivalent of *Shaikh*. The former were defeated, al-A'raj retired to the Tafilalet and Muhammad al-Shaikh retained sole power.

SETTLEMENT AT FEZ

As soon as he was able, the Saadian took the offensive. In 1545 he took the sultan of Fez, Ahmad, prisoner on the banks of the Oued el-Abid. Meanwhile Bou Hassan was taking charge of affairs at Fez and trying to engage the local marabouts on his side; his most important step, however, was to pay homage to [the Ottoman] Sulaiman the Magnificent. He promptly sent an ambassador to Marrakesh to demand that the Friday prayer be said in the name of the caliph of Constantinople. Muhammad al-Shaikh refused, and the Turks and Saadians were to live on poor terms for a long period thereafter. The Saadian offensive was resumed in 1548. Fez was besieged and within its walls two classes of marabouts contended for influence—the Shadhiliya on behalf of the Saadians, and the Qadiriya on behalf of the Wattasids and their Turkish protectors. The students of Fez, gathered around the celebrated and pious doctor ʽAbd al-Wahid al-Wansharisi, remained loyal to established authority. Muhammad al-Shaikh had al-Wansharisi assassinated and succeeded in gaining possession of Fez in 1549. Immediately afterwards he launched a premature and unsuccessful offensive against Tlemcen, which was not yet in Turkish hands, followed by one against the Turkish garrison of Mostaganem. It was demanding too much of his resources, particularly that Morocco had not yet been entirely won over by the dynasty. Bou Hassan succeeded in winning over the pasha of Algiers, Salah Rais, and the Spaniards of Oran. At the head of a small army of Maghribis and Turks he succeeded in recapturing Fez in the early days of 1554 after defeating Muhammad al-Shaikh near Taza and then again at the gates of Fez. But the Turks acted as if they were in a conquered land and Bou Hassan was obliged to dismiss them. He then found himself without resources in the face of the Saadians, whom his successes had by no means overwhelmed. Although Ahmad al-Aʽraj had allowed himself to be won for the Wattasid cause and had again taken up arms against his brother, Muhammad al-Shaikh took the offensive and in September 1554 once more established himself in Fez, but on this occasion for the final time. Morocco was his, though under threat from the Turks of Algiers and burdened with Spanish and Portuguese claims in spite of the Portuguese withdrawal of 1541.

The Sharif, who had borne the title of Caliph since the capture of Fez, did not settle in that city. He was not at ease there, for he could not forget its enthusiastic welcome for Bou Hassan in 1554. It was, moreover, too refined for him, being still a Saharan of

The Sharifian Empire: 1553–1830

unpolished manners (al-Ifrani gives us a picture of the new masters of Fez taking lessons in deportment from the previous ruler's domestic servants). Perhaps, too, he judged it too greatly exposed to Turkish attacks. But of greater importance this man of the south preferred Marrakesh and its palm-trees. After three centuries of eclipse, Marrakesh became the capital of the new dynasty.

This did not prevent Muhammad al-Shaikh from thoughts of overcoming the Turks, against whom he appears to have cherished a personal hatred. In order to gain this end he did not hesitate to negotiate with the infidel, represented by the Spaniards of Oran. Warned of the danger threatening them, the Turks forestalled him by besieging Oran and thus prevented any large-scale operations. In addition, the pasha of Algiers sent a number of Turks to the Saadian's court; they, posing as deserters, won his confidence and in 1557 succeeded in assassinating him in the course of an expedition in the Atlas. One or two of them even managed to get back to Algiers after a remarkable odyssey, and they carried Muhammad al-Shaikh's head as far as Constantinople.

The man who had driven out the Wattasids and stood up to the Turks was of the stuff rulers are made of. Astute and authoritarian, he regarded himself as master of Morocco and would allow no opposition there. He had had to solve the difficult problem of establishing a regular budget in order to maintain his court and his armies, as neither commercial exchanges with the English nor industrial monopolies had been able to furnish him with sufficient revenues. Accordingly he had to extend to the mountaineers the land tax (*kharāj*) already paid by the plainsmen. This fiscal policy set the marabouts against him and caused revolts, which he repressed vigorously, searching the zawiyas, expelling the marabouts and killing the intractable. Thus this leader, born of the maraboutic movement and raised to power to conduct holy war, had not hesitated, once he had come up against the obstacle constituted by the Turks, to curb the marabouts and even to make common cause with the Spaniards against the Turks.

THE SAADIAN KINGDOM UNTIL THE BATTLE OF THE THREE KINGS (1557–1578)

His son, Mulay 'Abd Allah al-Ghalib bi-llah (1557–1574), was acknowledged as ruler readily since three of his brothers had taken refuge with the Turks upon the death of their father. Two of them, 'Abd al-Malik and Ahmad, even made their way as far as Constantinople where they entered the service of Sulaiman and his successors.

The new ruler showed himself loyal to his father's policy. He continued to seek Spanish support against the Turks and even ceded the port of Badis (Velez) to the Spaniards in 1564. Nevertheless, the disaster which overtook the Count of Alcaudete at Mostaganem in 1558, followed ten years later by the revolt of the Moriscos in Spain, prevented any large-scale operations. In the economic field, Mulay 'Abd Allah allowed English trade to develop on the coasts of Morocco, but in 1562 he tried, without success, to drive the Portuguese out of Mazagan.

As his father, he was in conflict with the marabouts and religious groups, who could not readily accept either his authority or his flexibility towards the Christians. But, though he was able to subdue the Qadiriya and the Sheraga, who were of Algerian origin, he had to come to terms with a certain number of maraboutic families of central and northern Morocco. Finally, taking advantage of the relative degree of tranquillity which now prevailed, he undertook the beautifying of his capital, which Muhammad al-Shaikh had not had time to touch. He died of an illness in 1574.

In that same year his two brothers in exile at Constantinople took part in the capture of La Goulette and were the first to announce the good news to Sultan Murad III. With the support of the captain-pasha 'Eulj 'Ali they obtained money and men for the conquest of Morocco, while their nephew Muhammad al-Mutawakkil peacefully succeeded to his father's position.

The expedition took place at the beginning of 1576. Deserted by part of his troops, al-Mutawakkil retired to the south of Morocco, held the field there and even succeeded in gaining possession of Marrakesh, but then resigned himself to crossing over to Spain.

'Abd al-Malik . . .

had the unusual quality, for a Moroccan sultan, of having seen long service abroad. Above all he had profited from his travels outside Morocco. He spoke Spanish and Italian and was

The Sharifian Empire: 1553–1830

personally fond of Spain. Nevertheless it was his sojourn in the Ottoman empire that had made the deepest mark on him. He had adopted the manners and dress of the Turks and he liked speaking Turkish.[8]

He had scarcely acceded to power when he gave proof of his very real capacities as an organiser and diplomat, creating an army and negotiating with Spain, France and England. He thus secured from Philip II the expulsion of al-Mutawakkil.

THE BATTLE OF THE THREE KINGS (4 AUGUST 1578)

At this point the fluctuations of Portuguese policy were turning the attention of the Lisbon government once more to Morocco. John III, whose efforts had been directed to the exploitation of Brazil, had abandoned Ceuta, Tangier and El-Ksar. His grandson, Sebastian (1557–1578), brought up in a deeply religious court steeped in mysticism, was led by the influence of his Jesuit preceptors to think he was to be the paladin of the Catholic faith against Protestants and Muslims. Probably, too, reaction against the African policy of John III, brought about by ruinous experiences in the Indies and Brazil, offered favourable ground for al-Mutawakkil's overtures.

Sebastian's object was to conquer Morocco, notwithstanding the opposition of his captains, the advice of his uncle Philip II of Spain and, whatever may have been said on the point, the unfavourable opinion of the great poet Camoëns, who knew about war in Africa from having taken part in it as a private soldier and having returned from it blind in one eye. He had under his command an army of fewer than 20,000 men, entirely untrained for an African war, made up of heterogeneous contingents (mainly Portuguese, with Spaniards, Germans and Italians, and also a small contingent of Moroccans under al-Mutawakkil's orders). The army was weak in cavalry, and burdened at the same time with thirty-six pieces of artillery and an imposing train of wagons highly unsuitable for the Maghribi tracks. The landing took place unopposed at Tangier and chiefly at Arzila, and the army trailed slowly along towards El-Ksar el-Kebir (Alcazar-quivir), allowing 'Abd al-Malik and his brother time to assemble a numerous army—some 50,000 men—the main strength of which lay in its cavalry and which was animated by the spirit of holy war.

Don Sebastian, who stubbornly refused all advice save his own, allowed himself to be drawn into a cul-de-sac between the Loukkos and one of its tributaries without allowing for the fact that the water level varied greatly according to the state of the tide. He was the first to attack and thereby gained an initial success, which he was unable to exploit for lack of cavalry. The Moroccan army, with the advantages of numbers and position, then took the initiative. It routed the Christian army, which tried to cross the Oued el-Makhazin in order to flee to Larache. But the river was filled by the rising tide and the greater part of the Christians were drowned or taken prisoner. Don Sebastian and al-Mutawakkil were drowned. 'Abd al-Malik, who had been gravely ill at the outset of the action but through a burst of energy had launched his troops into battle, died at the end of the morning before the outcome of the day had been decided. His death was carefully concealed until the end of the combat. The battle owes its name to the deaths of these three rulers, but Arab historians know it only as the battle of the Oued el-Makhazin.

AHMAD AL-MANSUR (1578–1603)

By this defeat Portugal, deprived of its king, was laid open to the covetous designs of Spain. In Morocco it aroused enthusiasm proportionate to the fears the crusade had inspired. Without doubt, 'Abd al-Malik died of natural causes, but the succession went by unanimous agreement to his brother Ahmad. He was proclaimed sultan on the field of battle with the surname of *al-Mansur* (the Victorious) and benefited not only from the prestige of a victory exceeding all expectations, but also from enormous booty, which enabled him to assure the goodwill of the army, together with hundreds of captives, whose ransoms brought in a flow of Portuguese gold. The Christian princes held great respect for a monarch who could strike such blows. Thereafter they regarded the Sharifian empire as a power to be reckoned with, sent their ships to its ports and their ambassadors to Marrakesh, and tried to obtain loans from a ruler so rich that he was called 'the Golden [one]' (*al-Dhahabi*).

By comparison with the eleven other Saadian sultans, who floundered amid incessant revolts and eight of whom were

The Sharifian Empire: 1553-1830

assassinated, al-Mansur stood out as a great ruler. Although immediately after his accession he had to put down mutinies in his army, frustrate the conspiracies of the zawiyas and restrain the turbulence of the Berber tribes, the Sharif was not a hardened soldier. He was rather a statesman of outstanding culture, whom the affairs of empire never diverted from his studies. His master, al-Manjur, declared that he himself gained instruction from contact with his royal pupil, 'the scholar of caliphs and the caliph of scholars'.

Rarely had Morocco known such quiet and prosperity as during his reign. The Sharif took an interest in trade, which was active at the time, exploited industrial monopolies, let out the sugar mills to Jews or Christians, controlled contraband of war and enriched himself with the profits from privateering. He increased the rate of taxation, and his *harkas* applied themselves with energy to its collection. The revolts he had to put down never endangered his rule. The most formidable—that of the Branès in 1595-1596, led by the pretender al-Nasir—failed for lack of support from Spain.

In the beginning, the Sharif ruled personally, and he did so with clarity and decision. As assistants he had secretaries, among whom figure his historian al-Fishtali and a Jew. Indeed, the influence of renegades and Jews aroused discontent on the part of the marabouts, and increased the prestige of the brotherhoods and hostility towards foreigners. However, there was no overt enmity between makhzan and marabouts, and the latter were able to prepare themselves for better times. The notables were kept in hand at the beginning of the reign but eventually freed themselves from all control. Not only did they grow rich by trade or the sale of captives; they were also able to devote themselves to exploiting their co-religionists.

Al-Mansur had a political philosophy on which he drew for the government of the tribes. 'The people of the Maghrib', he announced, according to al-Ifrani, 'are madmen whose madness can be treated only by keeping them in chains and iron collars.'[9] By way of applying his principles, he organised the government of Morocco—the makhzan—in accordance with rules which, notwithstanding later modifications, endured until the institution of the French protectorate.

The Sharifian empire consisted of a federation of tribes

administered, or rather exploited, by a central organisation, the makhzan. This had its military—or *guish*—tribes, dispensed from taxation and provided with land, its ministers, officers, governors and palace corporations. Thereafter there were two Moroccos. There was official Morocco (*bled al-makhzan*) comprising the lands of the Muslim community; these were subject to land tax, occupied by Arab tribes and administered directly by the makhzan. There was also independent Morocco (*bled al-siba*) which was not only removed from the sultan's effective authority but was always ready to encroach on the *bled al-makhzan*. In al-Mansur's time, however, the rivalry between the two parts of Morocco was nearly always no more than latent, and by no means as open as in later periods. This was the result of the ruler's prudence and prestige and of the strength of his army.

Like his brother al-Ghahib, the sultan improved Marrakesh, which recovered the splendour of the Almohad period. For his building works he called on workmen from every land, even from Europe, and bought Italian marble for its weight in sugar. Immediately after the victory of the Oued el-Makhazin he began the construction of the Badi', which continued for fifteen years. This palace, which Mulay Isma'il had entirely destroyed, stood within the perimeter of the Saadian kasbah. By way of embellishment several water-basins were dug and paved with ceramic inlay, dominated by fountains and framed with flower beds and rich pavilions. Recent works make it possible to form a fairly accurate idea of the general plan and proportions of the palace. Certainly it was exceedingly handsome. It was probably al-Mansur who chose the sacred soil where his ancestors rested, near the tomb of the marabout al-Jazuli, as the site for erecting the qubba on the east side of the Saadian cemetery, and there laid the remains of his mother.

The sultan had a brilliant court, at which he received visitors with ostentatious pomp. There influential renegades rubbed shoulders with Jewish financiers, Christian merchants, foreign ambassadors and the sultan's confidential agents, who were at once political missionaries, men of business and, if occasion demanded, procurers. Religious festivals were celebrated with splendour; their arrangement was very similar to what can still be seen in Morocco. In 1579 the Spaniard Juan de Medina went to the

The Sharifian Empire: 1553–1830

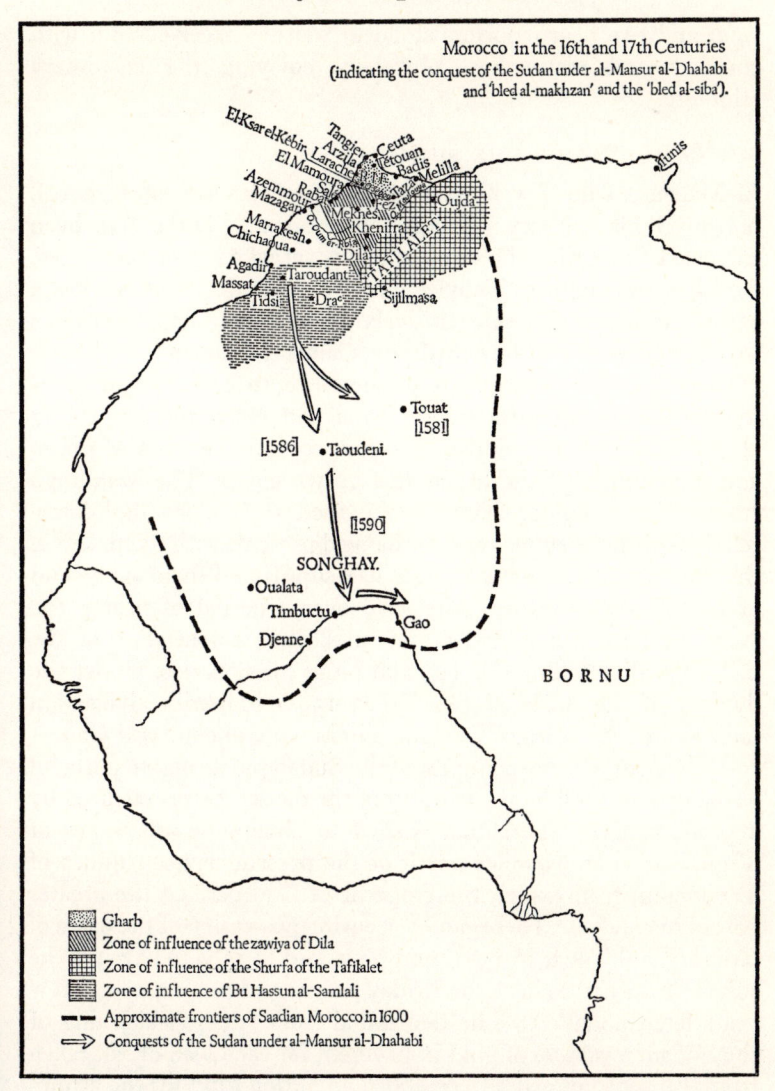

Morocco in the 16th and 17th Centuries
(indicating the conquest of the Sudan under al-Mansur al-Dhahabi and 'bled al-makhzan' and the 'bled al-siba').

Gharb
Zone of influence of the zawiya of Dila
Zone of influence of the Shurfa of the Tafilalet
Zone of influence of Bu Hassun al-Samlali
Approximate frontiers of Saadian Morocco in 1600
Conquests of the Sudan under al-Mansur al-Dhahabi

palace in great pomp. He was saluted by the hundred halberdiers, the makhzanis in their state caps adorned with plumes and the renegades clad in Turkish fashion. The sultan, seated on silken cushions in a room hung with brocades and carpets, where eight *qaids* and two negro porters stood in waiting, received him with courtesy and distinction, obviously enjoying the customary etiquette.

THE CONQUEST OF THE SUDAN

Al-Mansur, who for his receptions copied Oriental protocol, borrowed his military organisation from the Turks. He even entrusted them with the training of his varied army of renegades, Andalusians, negroes, Kabyles and Ottoman deserters. It was a corps consisting almost exclusively of renegades and Christians that he charged with the expedition against the Sudan.

Ever since the Almoravids in the eleventh century had overthrown the pagan princes of Ghana and converted the ruling classes of the western Sudan to Islam, contacts between Morocco and the country of the blacks had grown closer. The Mandingo rulers of the Upper Niger maintained permanent diplomatic relations with the sultans and exchanged presents with them. When the Songhay of the eastern Niger had supplanted them at the end of the fifteenth century, Morocco, over a period of nearly 100 years, undertook a religious and intellectual colonisation of the Sudan by dispatching scholars and pious missionaries. Under the dynasty of the Askia of Gao (1493–1591) Maghribi civilisation took root in the cities of Oualata, Timbuctoo, Djenne and Gao.

Al-Mansur's brutal conquest of the Sudan put an end to peaceful exchanges and ruined the country of the blacks. It was inspired by a profit motive. The sultan wished to obtain the salt mines of Teghazza, some 95 miles north of the present-day salt mines of Taoudenni, from which the emperor of Gao derived the greater part of his revenue. He began by securing possession of the oases of Gourara and Touat in 1581, and he is said in 1583 to have got the sultan of Bornou to have the Friday prayer said in his name. A few years later, about 1586, he demanded from Ishaq Askia, king of the Sudan, a *mithqal* of gold in payment for each load of salt taken from Teghazza in order to establish a fighting fund for the armies of Islam. It was simply a pretext, since at the time Morocco was at peace with all its neighbours. Al-Mansur was indeed in need of money, but he may have desired to establish a western caliphate which, under the authority of a descendant of the Prophet, might later rival the Ottoman caliphate. The king of the Sudan refused.

The Sharifian Empire: 1553-1830

Al-Mansur, determined to break his resistance, assembled his council and set the facts before them. Contrary to his expectations, he encountered very lively opposition, for his entourage deemed the expedition both unjust and dangerous. But in the end he silenced the objectors and the matter was settled in accordance with his intentions.

Did a first expedition then take place? An odd and obscure text in the *Chronique anonyme de la dynastie sa'dienne*[10] permits this assumption. According to this document al-Mansur, following a mutiny, dispatched a contingent of the rebellious troops in the direction of the Sudan and authorised the guide to abandon them in mid-desert. One man is said to have escaped by a miracle. Could this not be the official or semi-official version of a disaster, itself the outcome of an ill-prepared expedition?

However, in 1590 the Spanish renegade Judar was given command of a force of some 3,000 men, renegades for the most part, who were to attack the Sudan by way of the desert. He set out about the end of October and reached the Niger at the end of 135 days' march having left at least half his total strength en route. On 12 March 1591 musket fire, and the panic of the cattle which the Songhay army had formed into a rampart, quickly got the better of 20,000 negroes armed with throwing-spears, sabres and cudgels. Disappointed by the uncomfortable appointments of Gao, Judar installed himself at Timbuctoo, which from that time on continued to be the pashas' capital. He would gladly have agreed to return to Marrakesh with the 100,000 gold pieces and the 1,000 slaves the Askia proposed to present to the sultan, but al-Mansur regarded these offers as an insult and replaced the pasha by another renegade, Mahmud Zergun, who was wise enough to make Judar his lieutenant and chief adviser.

Zergun tried to re-establish the Songhay state, but he himself took part in the pillaging and massacre which were the only methods of government the renegades were acquainted with. His successors drained the country by their exactions, and destroyed a large part of the intellectual and religious aristocracy, whose influence they feared. From 1612 onward Morocco abandoned the Sudan to the will and pleasure of the occupation force. The soldiers turned into brigands and the elected pasha into a bandit chief. Between 1612 and 1660 twenty-one pashas succeeded one

History of North Africa

another; between 1660 and 1750, 128 followed. Some ruled only for a few hours before being killed by their rivals. The Spaniards lived with the Sudanese women and were gradually assimilated to the native population. Their descendants, the 'hurlers' (of musket balls), the *Armas*, did, however, constitute an aristocracy which affected a superiority over the pure-blooded negroes. Even today they stand out by virtue of their intelligence, their authoritarian and combative temper, their wealth and the cleanliness of their houses. They comprise nobles, descendants of the Roumis of Marrakesh, a middle class descended from that of Fez, a plebs and a lower class of degenerates. The only trade they follow is that of shoemaker. Their absorption into the negro population became more marked from one year to another.

According to contemporary accounts the profits al-Mansur derived from the Sudan were considerable. Al-Ifrani declares that he received so much gold dust 'that thereafter he paid his officials only in pure metal and dinars of full weight.'[11] The sultan is said to have had 1,400 hammers at work every day minting his coins. The Englishman Lawrence Madock, agent of a commercial company at Marrakesh, witnessed the arrival of thirty mule-loads of gold.[12] Moroccan ducats were at a premium with the English merchants, who tried to smuggle them out because of their high degree of fineness. However, it is possible that al-Mansur may have found it to his interest to deceive both Moroccans and foreigners over the extent of his resources. The invaders were never able to exploit directly the gold mines of the Sudan, which were too far from Gao. The gold received by the sultan came in the first instance from confiscations executed on the notables of Timbuctoo and later from exchanges negotiated by the 'king's agents' charged with exploiting the Taodeni salt mines. It is probable that the proverbial riches of the Sudan were never worth as much as the Portuguese ransoms which had gained for al-Mansur the surname of 'the Golden [one]'. A more certain result of the conquest of Songhay and of Timbuctoo was the ruin of Sudanese commerce, the intellectual decline of Timbuctoo and the retreat of Islam on the middle Niger—a process which came to an end only at the end of the eighteenth century under the influence of the Toucouleurs.

Besides loads of gold the sultan received convoys of slaves, male and female. It is probable that he enlisted negroes in his army and

The Sharifian Empire: 1553–1830

that his regimental rolls suggested to Mulay Isma'il the idea of creating a black guard.

AL-MANSUR'S FOREIGN POLICY

The conquest of the Sudan also gained for Morocco the reputation of an exceedingly rich country and for its sovereign great prestige. His power caused anxiety to the sultans of Constantinople, who desired to impose their religious supremacy on the sharif, and to the beylerbeys installed at Algiers, whose dream it was to hand the Atlantic ports over to their corsairs. Against his enemies in the east al-Mansur appealed to Europe for help. Nevertheless in 1581 he only just staved off an attack by the beylerbey 'Eulj 'Ali by heaping the Porte with gifts. 'Eulj 'Ali's death in 1587, and the disappearance of the beylerbeys in 1588, delivered him from a permanent danger. He might indeed have taken the offensive in his turn had not his attention been preoccupied by rivalries among his sons.

His advances to the Christian states were not repulsed. Indeed, the English and Spaniards contended for alliance with him. Latecomers as they were to Morocco, where they had first landed in 1551, the English had taken advantage of the Portuguese defeat to develop the exchange of their woollens for Maghribi gold, sugar, leather and saltpetre, and to organise contraband. But an attempt in 1585 to combine interests and efforts in a single organisation, the Barbary Company, was defeated in part by rivalries between independent traders and agents of the City merchants and, in part, by the self-interested influence of important personages in London. Thereafter English trade made no further progress. Nevertheless, business relations continued to draw Queen Elizabeth's attention to the political, as well as the economic, importance of Morocco. Against Philip II, who had become master of Portugal, she tried to form an alliance to be joined by the sultans of Constantinople and Marrakesh. But al-Mansur regarded the Turks as his most formidable enemies. Despite Morocco's traditional hatred for Spain, which found expression in popular enthusiasm at the news of the destruction of the Armada, al-Mansur was well aware that at his court Philip was maintaining al-Mutawakkil's brother, always ready to put himself at the head of a seditious movement. The king of Spain, fearing that Moroccan pirates might seize his Indian convoys and eventually capture the unfortunate and permanently blockaded *presidios*, or fortified posts, tried to buy the sultan's neutrality by ceding Arzila to him in 1589.

With great skill al-Mansur played off the Spaniards against the English, relying on the fear roused by the prospect of action on his part. He held out offers of help, but gave nothing away. Philip's plan for occupying the island of Arguin and the Saharan coast, with the object of acquiring for himself the gold of the Sudan, finally tilted the balance in England's favour. The sultan even reached the point of envisaging the conquest of Spain and its partitioning between himself and the English, though Elizabeth would have preferred the effort to be exerted in the Indies. In 1603 the aged Queen's death, and that of the sultan from plague, put an end to these projects of high policy.

With France, rent by the wars of religion, al-Mansur did no more than maintain commercial relations and receive French consuls. At the same time the Low Countries were only beginning to take an interest in trade with Morocco.

THE SAADIAN DECLINE

No sooner was the old ruler dead than three of his sons contended for power—Mulay Zidan, proclaimed at Fez; Abu Faris, acknowledged at Marrakesh; and Muhammad al-Shaikh al-Mamun, whom his father, shortly before his death, had had imprisoned. The last-named was a violent character who obeyed nothing but his own instincts. He had been recognised as heir as early as 1581, but he had finally worn out his father's patience by his scandals and rebellions, and he had been taken, sword in hand, in 1602 and imprisoned at Meknès. For seven years the three, in alliances of two against one, and constantly changing partners, vied for power and searched out one another, invoking the aid at one time of the Spaniards, and at another of the Turks. In 1610 Abu Faris was assassinated by his nephew 'Abd Allah, son of al-Mamun, who resembled his father only too closely. Al-Mamun succeeded in gaining possession of Fez due to the aid of the Spaniards, who were given Larache as the price of their services. With difficulty, Mulay Zidan kept Marrakesh and its surrounding region; as in the fifteenth century, Morocco was divided into two kingdoms—that of Fez and that of Marrakesh.

The Sharifian Empire: 1553-1830

This division was not a sign of peace. The fratricidal conflicts between al-Mansur's sons had awakened tendencies to violence which his own authority had imperfectly laid to rest. On all sides there sprang up religious leaders who tried to destroy each other and spread mourning and ruin around them. The Arab tribes played their part in the disorders. The mountain Berber tribes, suffering the repercussions of all this unrest, took a hand in the game in turn. It was the darkest period of anarchy that Morocco has experienced. Cities as firmly based, and usually as peaceable, as Fez became the prey of factions. For several days the call to prayer from the lofty minaret of the Great Mosque was no more heard, and whole quarters of the town fell into ruin and reverted to gardens.

In the midst of all this, the sultans of Fez and Marrakesh carried little weight. Mulay Zidan (1603–1628), the better of the two, had considerable difficulty in maintaining his power; three times he was driven out and then restored. He never succeeded in reconquering the kingdom of Fez, which remained independent. As ruler of Marrakesh he did, however, find time to build on to the Saadian burial-place that western qubba which arouses the enthusiasm of tourists by its sumptuous adornment of arabesques, the stalactites of its vault and the chased work of its tombs. None the less it is a work of decadence. Between the strong serenity of the Almohad mosques and the ordered and harmonious beauty of the Merinid madarsas, and the intemperate riches of the Saadian mausoleum, there lies, according to G. Marçais, the distance that separates the church at Brou from the north door of Chartres.

By 1626 Fez had ceased to obey any but bandit chieftains, except for the times when it might be subject to one of the clans seeking to assume supreme power. At Marrakesh the Saadians held on rather longer; the last of them, al-'Abbas, was assassinated in 1659.

THE ASPIRANTS TO POWER

While the dynasty was dying, Spain, with her overmastering anxiety to curb the encroachments of the corsairs, was occupying the Moroccan ports. We noted above how Larache had been ceded to her in 1610. She also built a fortress at the mouth of the Sebou in 1614 in order to keep a closer watch on the towns of Bou Regreg, Rabat and Salé, where piracy was increasing.

This fortress, which the Spaniards called San Miguel de Ultramar and the Moroccans al-Ma'mura, how bears the name of Mehdia. Like the Portuguese encroachments of the preceding century, this Christian seizure of a few plots of Muslim territory roused the people's anger and provided a pious pretext for the ambitions of certain religious leaders.

The Christian danger was most apparent in the north of Morocco. It was there too that reactions in religious guise were strongest, further encouraged by the weakness and inadequacy of the Saadian rulers. However, the south also had its maraboutic movements, though on a smaller scale.

The first such movement was the work of a petty scholar of the Tafilalet, Abu Mahalli. Having had his training in the Safi school, he had settled in the Saoura valley about 1593, had there acquired a great reputation for piety and had passed himself off as the Mahdi. The cession of Larache to the Spaniards impelled him to action. He marched on Sijilmasa, took possession of it, defeated a relieving army sent against him by Mulay Zidan, crossed the Atlas and took Marrakesh in a surprise attack. Mulay Zidan, unable to recover his capital unaided, launched against him another marabout who came from the Atlas, Yahya ibn 'Abd Allah al-Hahi. He attacked Marrakesh, Abu Mahalli was killed at the outset of the action and his head was hung on the ramparts of the town where, it is said, it remained for twelve years.[13] Emboldened by his success, Yahya ibn 'Abd Allah behaved as a ruler and held the countryside until 1627. Then a third personage—until then a simple supernumerary—Abu al-Hasan al-Samlali, commonly called Abu Hassun, a native of Massat, set up an independent principality in the Sous and the Anti-Atlas which disappeared only with the Alawite conquest. Finally, we should mention by way of introduction —we shall return to them later—the Alawite *shurfa* of the Tafilalet.

In the north three powers engaged in conflict with the Saadian princes of Fez—the Moriscan republic of Rabat and Salé, the marabout al-'Ayashi and the marabouts of Dila.

THE BOU REGREG REPUBLIC

Following their revolt in 1568 the Moriscos had been expelled

The Sharifian Empire: 1553–1830

from the province of Granada but not from Spain. Philip II and his advisers were not without hope of assimilating them. After a trial period lasting forty years, Philip III deemed them to be unassimilable and during the period 1609–1614 passed a series of decrees of expulsion against them. All who would not consent to abjure were thus forced to leave. They spread along the entire North African coast from Tunis to Rabat, but particularly in northern Tunisia and northern Morocco. In this latter region they formed two main groups, one at Tétouan and the other on either side of the estuary of the Bou Regreg. In 1609 the ancient fortress dominating the river from the west, 'Abd al-Mumin's Ribat al-Fath, received the Hornacheros (so called from Hornacha, a small town in Estremadura). In 1610 émigrés from lower Andalusia came to people the little town only subsisting at the foot of the fortress and to enlarge it considerably. In the beginning they lived on good terms with Mulay Zidan, whose authority extended as far as Rabat. The sultan thought of finding soldiers among them and of profiting from the revenues they were beginning to acquire from privateering. Indeed, the Hornacheros, who had considerable capital at their command, had immediately on their arrival armed several vessels for privateering, manning them with renegades and adventurers from every quarter. The Moriscos soon felt that they were being exploited and from 1627 made themselves virtually independent, encouraged by the marabout al-'Ayashi. They formed an oligarchic republic, at times linked with Salé and at times limited to the two urban centres of Rabat, sometimes united and sometimes a prey to internecine conflict. Eventually their independence proved displeasing to al-'Ayashi, who made things difficult for them from 1637 until his death in 1641. The Bou Regreg estuary then passed to the rule of the marabouts of Dila.

The Bou Regreg émigrés laid no claims to dominate Morocco and were moved by highly contradictory views. They detested the Christian Spain which had expelled them, but they also felt ill at ease in a political and economic system that was foreign to them and to which they found it exceedingly difficult to acclimatise themselves. In effect they displayed considerable indifference to the political manœuvres around them. This was by no means the case with the marabouts who were in a state of unrest in the same region.

THE MARABOUTS OF THE NORTH

The first in chronological order was Muhammad ibn Ahmad al-Zayani, known as al-ʿAyashi. A scholar and disciple of a mystic of Salé, he made himself a champion of holy war under Mulay Zidan and attacked Mazagan. By way of reward for his zeal the sultan appointed him *qaid* of Azemmour, but he soon displeased his master and had to flee. He then reached the plain of the Gharb, encouraged the independence of the Bou Regreg towns, waged holy war against al-Maʿmura and Larache and thus gained the approval and support of a large part of the marabouts in the region and indeed in Morocco generally. In 1637 he quarrelled with the Moriscos, whom he accused of maintaining suspicious relations with the English and the Spaniards. Indeed, he eventually gained possession of Rabat and Salé in 1641, which caused his downfall. The Moriscos took refuge with the marabouts of Dila and encouraged them to resort to arms. Al-ʿAyashi was defeated and killed in 1641.

The marabouts of Dila, Sanhaja Berbers, had founded a zawiya near the present town of Khenifra at the end of the sixteenth century. Hospitable, upright and chosen as arbitrators by the pastoral tribes of the Middle Atlas and the Moulouya, they had gradually extended their influence over these warlike peoples and soon had an excellent army at their disposal. They used it for the defeat in 1640 of the Saadian Muhammad al-Shaikh al-Asghar who desired to abate their rising power, and then of the marabout al-ʿAyashi in 1641. They were then masters of the entire northern region of Morocco but they became involved in rivalry with the Alawite *shurfa* of the Tafilalet who also harboured vague ideas of expansion. In the end it was between these marabout-led Berber mountaineers and the oasis folk under the aegis of the *shurfa* that the question of the successor to the Saadian dynasty was to be settled.

EUROPE AND MOROCCO

These disturbances did much less harm than might be thought to the long-standing relations between Morocco and certain European powers. Indeed, what the Christians lost through xenophobia and fanaticism they regained through rivalries and competition. A

The Sharifian Empire: 1553-1830

marabout elevated to power by the idea of holy war, like al-'Ayashi, would be quite happy to negotiate with the English or the Dutch from time to time, to get supplies of arms from them in order to crush his Moroccan opponents more easily. Thus the complexion of relations between the unsettled Morocco of those days and Europe varied greatly with circumstances and, of course, the interested parties.

Spain had been the Saadians' ally when the Turks constituted a threat. The Algiers of triennial pashas, preoccupied as it was with privateering and its internal dissensions, had ceased to represent a danger for the Moroccans. Consequently the Spanish counterweight was no further use to them. Moreover, Spain was expelling the Moriscos, persecuting Islam and acquiring Larache and al-Ma'mura. Nonetheless it was still to Spain that al-Mamun turned in 1610 when he was trying to gain possession of the kingdom of Fez, and it was in Spain that Mulay Zidan considered taking refuge when he had been forced to yield Marrakesh to Abu Mahalli. In point of fact Spain, now absorbed in European politics, had little or no thought of conquest in Morocco or even of establishing zones of political or economic influence. Her main object was to protect her Atlantic vessels against the encroachments of Moroccan corsairs.

France, though a Catholic power, was in a different position from Spain *vis-à-vis* Morocco. Indeed her role was still a minor one and her concern was less with trade than with ransoming captives, more or less successfully. She was still represented by Marseillais consuls, and by physicians whom the Saadian princes often consulted. But also, France was represented by adventurers like Antoine de Saint-Mandrier, outlawed in France but the agent of France in Morocco and a builder of ports, or Philip Castelane who recompensed himself for some shipping for Mulay Zidan by carrying off the sharif's library and baggage. Unfortunately, his ship was seized in a Spanish port and neither he nor France was in a position to restore the impounded property. This annoying incident damaged relations between France and southern Morocco for several years. Isaac de Razilly, however, managed to sign a peace treaty with the Sharif in 1631 and with the Moriscos in 1635.

Unlike Spain and France, England carried on a fairly brisk trade with Morocco. Officially this was conducted through the

Barbary Company, but it may well have principally been carried out by unscrupulous traders, the 'interlopers', who supplied material of war to any who could pay the price, to rebels like al-Samlali no less than to the legitimate sovereign. In any case the English worried far less about legitimacy than about trading results, and they might be seen in negotiation with the Bou Regreg republic at the same time as they were sending embassies to Marrakesh. They were very well informed about events in Morocco; the accounts of their travellers and agents rank among the best documents available to us for this period. Like the Spaniards they found the prevailing piracy a difficult trial and they followed a policy of blockade alternating with negotiations.

The most active trade, however, was not the work of the English, but of the United Provinces. The activity and business sense of the Dutch merchants was certainly a factor, but so too was the hatred of Spain which the Netherlanders shared with the main body of the Moroccans. Accordingly, the government of the United Provinces did not hesitate to officially supply Morocco with ships, rigging, cannon and powder, in the hope that all these things would be used against Spain. The Jewish Pallache family acted as an intermediary in all these transactions. No more than the English were the Dutch difficult to please in their choice of partner; they were on as good terms with Mulay Zidan as with the Moriscos or the marabouts of Dila. They too had sometimes to suffer from commerce-raiding; they blockaded the south of the Bou Regreg in 1651 and made van Tromp and de Ruyter responsible for organising squadrons in 1654.

II. The Alawite Dynasty

THE FILALIAN 'SHURFA'

The Alawite *shurfa*—descendants of al-Hasan, son of 'Ali and Fatima and originally from the little Arab town of Yanbo' on the Red Sea coast—arrived in the Tafilalet some years after the Saadians had settled in the Dra'. The circumstances of their arrival remain surrounded with legend and we may wonder, with Terrasse, whether they did not follow in the wake of some group of

The Sharifian Empire: 1553-1830

Ma'qil Arabs.[14] The fact remains that they established themselves in the Tafilalet oasis about the beginning of the thirteenth century and there lived for several centuries in obscurity, as personages worthy of veneration but having no political role.

At the time of the Saadian anarchy and shortly after the death of Mulay Zidan, the Tafilalet fell under the covetous eyes of two marabouts who had grown powerful, al-Samlali and Muhammad al-Hajj, who was head of the zawiya at Dila. It was at this point that in 1631 the Filalians, in an attempt to safeguard their independence, placed the leader of the Alawite *shurfa*, Muhammad al-Sharif, at their head. He succeeded more or less in warding off the danger from the two powerful rivals. He did not, however, prevent Muhammad al-Hajj from establishing himself at the gateways to the mountains—at Goulmina on the Oued Gheris and at Ksar es-Souk on the Oued Ziz—or from maintaining a garrison in the very heart of the Tafilalet. Possibly from discouragement he relinquished power in 1636, and the people of the oasis entrusted it to one of his sons, Mulay Muhammad.

He was a man of action. He began by driving the Dilaite garrison out of the Tafilalet in 1638, after which he looked for space in which to expand. Bounded in by the Dilaites to the north, by al-Samlali to the west and by the desert to the south, he made an attempt in a north-easterly direction. He rallied the warlike tribes of the High Guir to his cause, got possession of Oujda, carried out raids in the Tlemcen region and even pushed as far as Laghouat. The Turks then negotiated and secured from Mulay Muhammad an undertaking to stay on the far side of the Tafna. Thereafter he commanded a wide zone of influence and was regarded as a power to be respected. In 1649 the people of Fez appealed to him for help against the Dilaites, whose rule was proving unbearable. He complied but was unable to maintain himself in the city when the marabouts of Dila resumed the offensive, and he withdrew to the Tafilalet, accepting the defeat.

MULAY AL-RASHID

When the last Saadian died, the kingdom of Marrakesh, in the hands of the *qaid* of the Chebanat, lay confined between the High Atlas and the Oum er-Rbia. In the Sous and the Anti-Atlas Bu Hassun al-Samlali held undisputed control, and the marabouts of

Dila were still masters of the kingdom of Fez, though the Tangier zone, the Garb, the Rif and even Fez Jdid were beginning to slip out of their authority. On the Moroccan chessboard the Filalians appeared to constitute no more than a negligible piece, the more so that the king of the Tafilalet, far from being able to count on his brother Mulay al-Rashid, had every ground for fearing him as a rival.

In 1659 Mulay al-Rashid had left the Tafilalet in haste and sought asylum with the Filalians' traditional rivals; but neither the Dilaites nor the mercenary leaders who held Fez were anxious to keep within their walls a guest whose presence could only be dangerous. He had to leave and seek his fortune in the restless zone of eastern Morocco, first in the country of the Kebdana (between Melilla and the mouth of the Moulouya) and later among the Beni Snassen. There the support of the shaikh al-Lawati, and of the brotherhood in which he was probably an outstanding figure, was favourable for his first steps. It was then that he took that forceful action which legend has appropriated, preserving a distorted memory of it in the annual festival of the sultan of the *tulba* at Fez. He assassinated a wealthy Jew living in a village of Dar Ibn Mechʻal (in the Beni Snassen mountain country) who had probably played a considerable role in that part of the world. By pillaging the Jew's wealth he was enabled to form a party of supporters and to become a threat to his neighbours. Legend credits him with other assassinations and confiscations of treasure, but these are probably no more than repetitions of his first adventure. One certain fact is that in 1664 Mulay al-Rashid defeated his brother (who died in battle) on the plain of the Angad, the inhabitants of which had rallied to his cause. Thereafter the adventurer assumed the character of a pretender. Fez felt itself threatened, but Mulay al-Rashid preferred first to assure himself of a reliable base and a potential place of refuge in the Tafilalet.

From there he directed his first campaign against the master of the Rif, the shaikh Aʻras, who had refused to recognise him and whose hostility seemed likely to endanger his plans for attacking Fez. This shaikh, after failing in a campaign against rival tribes, had turned his activities in the direction of trade and had made a concession of a site to some English merchants in the bay of Albouzème (El-Mezemma = Alhucemas). The French at once put themselves in a position to share in the Rif trade. They had taken a

The Sharifian Empire: 1553–1830

favourable view of the marriage of Charles II to Catherine of Portugal, by which the port of Tangier, coveted by Spain and scorned by Mazarin eighteen years earlier, had come into the hands of England in 1661. But they soon found cause for fear in English aims on the strategic points on the Rif littoral. The cruises undertaken by Beaufort and Nuchèze, with the intention of reconnoitring the islands of Albouzème, the Zaffarines and the mouth of the Moulouya, may in Colbert's mind have been a prelude to a permanent settlement on the coast of Morocco, like that established later on the Algerian coast at Djidjelli.

It was the merchants who took up the minister's abortive projects. In 1665 financiers created the Albouzème Company under the impetus of two Marseillais businessmen, Michel and Roland Fréjus, and then secured from the king a grant for the privilege of trading and the right to negotiate with the local powers. But when Roland Fréjus landed at Albouzème, in March 1666, the power of Shaikh A'ras had just been broken in a decisive attack by Mulay al-Rashid. The sharif, who could get supplies of arms and merchandise only through the western ports, received Roland Fréjus at Taza with favour. The chief result of the enthusiastic account of his mission given by the boastful Marseillais was to reveal al-Rashid's strength, which French diplomacy then promptly tried to bring into line against the English in Tangier. However, commercial hopes were disappointed. Blunders by Roland Fréjus, acting in the name of a Levant Company which had been created in 1670 and which was strongly suspected of espionage, antagonised the sharif. He constructed a fort on his own account at Albouzème, which the Spaniards took possession of shortly afterwards and made into their *presidio* of Alhucemas.

Mulay al-Rashid had avoided French advances because in the meantime he had become master of the ports of western Morocco and had been led to take up the struggle against foreign encroachment. Shortly after the defeat of Shaikh A'ras he entered Fez, where he was proclaimed Sultan on 6 June 1666. The triumph of the founder of the Filalian dynasty was due not to the support of the brotherhoods, but to the superiority of his troops. Indeed, against the influence of the marabouts he could set that of the Idrisid chiefs who rallied to his cause and provided him with the personnel for his makhzan.

The sultan was still only in possession of the Angad country, the Taza region, the Tafilalet, the Rif and Fez. In a series of arduous expeditions he was able to expel a daring corsair, Ghailan, from the Gharb and the Tangier region where he had been receiving help from both the Turks and the English. Ghalian withdrew to Algiers in 1669. The previous year the sultan had defeated the army of the marabouts of Dila and destroyed their zawiya, and in 1669 he acquired Marrakesh, where he slaughtered a great number of Chebanat. Lastly, in 1670, he took the fortress of Iligh and put an end to the power of the marabouts of the Sous for more than a century.

At Salé the sultan found a highly organised system of piracy, which he aimed not to suppress but to utilise for his own account. The cruises of Jean d'Estrées and Château-Renaud, the blockade of Salé and the capture of a few corsairs did not divert him from his plans, any more than negotiations induced him to surrender the Christian slaves.

Despite the brevity of a reign fully occupied with battle, he succeeded in erecting a few public buildings. Moreover for strategic reasons he built an earthen bridge across the Sebou some two and a half miles from Fez, with eight unequal arches and over 490 feet in length. He strengthened the walls of Fez al-Bali, and constructed the kasbah of the Khemis (now of the Cherarda) with a view to sheltering the Cheraga of eastern Morocco, whom he made into *guish* tribes. It was also at Fez, which seems to have been his favourite seat, that, by way of replacement for an earlier madarsa allegedly polluted by student debauches, he erected the al-Sharatin madarsa, the architecture and decoration of which, despite their charm, are a long way from Merinid purity.

He seldom resided at Marrakesh, although he was there in 1672 to put down a revolt by a nephew when his horse bolted in the gardens of the Agdal, and ran him against a branch of an orange-tree, which smashed his skull. He was only forty-two years old.

MULAY ISMA'IL

Few sultans acquired so great a renown as did Mulay al-Rashid's brother Mulay Isma'il, who succeeded him at the age of twenty-six. This powerful sovereign, who succeeded in keeping Morocco under control throughout a long reign (1672–1727), did not,

The Sharifian Empire: 1553–1830

however, owe his prestige to the lofty conception he formed of his kingly calling. It was rather the buildings of the 'Moroccan Versailles', the harem escapades, the innumerable progeny of this untiring sire, and above all his plans for marriage with a daughter of France, that spread his glory abroad. All this built up a stock of legend, the picturesque character of which still appears to exert its influence on historians.

His physiognomy can easily be sketched, not only by reading his biographers, but also from the testimony of Europeans like the Sieur Mouëtte,[15] who was a captive for eleven years from 1670 to 1681, or from those who went either to ransom captives like Père Busnot[16] in 1703, or on diplomatic missions like the Frenchman Pidou de Saint-Olon[17] in 1693. At thirty-five he was seen by Mouëtte as 'fairly tall and of very slender figure', though stout-looking on account of his clothes. He had a somewhat long light brown face and 'fairly well made' features, a long beard 'slightly forked', and eyes with a 'fairly gentle' look.[18] Twenty-three years later Père Busnot also noted the thinness of face, the forked beard now turned white, the blackish complexion marked by a white spot near the nose, the burning eyes and the powerful voice. In his youth Mulay Isma'il would gallop on horseback carrying one of his sons in one hand and brandishing a lance in the other. When almost in his sixties he used to mount his horse in one bound.

All his contemporaries report his violence, his cruelty and his cupidity. A setback, a mere crossing of his will even, would make him change colour and give him the look of a savage. The effects of his rage were known to be terrible, and accordingly those who served him made their approach 'a step at a time'. He was seen by Pidou de Saint-Olon dripping with the blood of a victim he had butchered with a knife. The ambassador Saint-Amand declared that his presence alone prevented the sharif from striking off the head of the slave who had made him miss a leap, and according to Père Busnot he turned executions of this kind into an amusement. He had a passionate love of money, spoiled the Jews, pressured his subjects to the point of ruin and did not shrink from crime if he could thereby confiscate a fortune. He was moreover no spendthrift, 'concerning himself personally with horseshoes and horseshoe nails, with spices, drugs, butter, honey and other trifles that are in his stores'. All of which caused the Sieur Mouëtte, subject of a king who stinted nothing, to say that such an occupation 'is more suited to a grocer than to a great prince like him'.[19]

This powerful man had an iron constitution. Of him can be asserted what the Old Woman said to Candide concerning all Moroccans; it was not blood that ran in his veins, but vitriol, and he was an impassioned lover of women. He used them up at an incredible rate. The seraglio of Dar al-Makhzan housed 500 of every colour and every race, steeped in oil and idleness while waiting to satisfy the master's passions. Once they were past thirty they were relegated to the old seraglio at Fez or to the Tafilalet. The sultana Zidana was a blackish mastodon who wielded great influence. Much appreciated too was a young renegade Englishwoman. It was not in the sharif's nature to be unable to add a Frenchwoman to his collection. Mulay Isma'il was proud of his progeny and showed off with pleasure the year's brood swarming in the palace courtyards. He was credited with 700 sons and an uncounted number of daughters. Part of the output was reared at Sijilmasa.

So vigorous a temperament was at its happiest in war, in which he displayed remarkable courage, while being by no means unskilled in his use of the sword. Quick intelligence, prompt and pointed repartee, piety ardent to the point of proselytism, indomitable energy, contempt for luxury and the pleasures of the table, high concern for national independence and the economic development of his country—such were the essential features of a royal figure of a stamp quite different from his contemporaries Charles II of Spain or James II of England.

THE SUBJECTION OF MOROCCO

The Sharif naturally had to conquer his kingdom at the point of the sword. It took him five years. Besides the family rivalries stirred up against him by his brother Mulay al-Harran in the Tafilalet, and by his nephew Ahmad ibn Mahriz at Marrakesh and in the Sous, there were incursions by the bold pirate Ghailan and Turkish intrigues in support of his opponents.

At the time he was proclaimed Sultan he was master of Fez, of which he was the governor, of the Gharb, the Rif and the Taza region. He had to take Marrakesh, which he did on 4 June 1672, put down a sedition in Fez, defeat Ghailan (who died in a mysterious

The Sharifian Empire: 1553-1830

fashion) near El-Ksar and then undertake a fresh campaign against the territories in the south and in the Atlas, where there had been risings instigated by Ibn Mahriz. After a two-year siege he took Marrakesh and sacked it in June 1677. The city did not again escape from the sultan's grasp, but it thenceforward lost its rank as a capital, and the materials of its public buildings were used for constructing the palaces at Meknès.

Tranquillity was not entirely restored. For a further twelve years Ibn Mahriz and al-Harran kept the Sous in a state of unrest. Their deaths and the fall of Taroudant in March 1687, when he massacred all its inhabitants, secured the sharif's power. He had also to subdue the Berber revolts stirred up in the Tadla and the western provinces by a Turkish-supported descendant of the marabouts of Dila. He made his way into the Tafilalet, transported the Arab Chebanat tribes from the Oujda neighbourhood and formed them into regiments. He made raids on the Beni Snassen, who had little liking for such a neighbour, and finally crushed the tribes of the upper Moulouya under the weight of three expeditionary columns.

Almost a quarter of a century of military action had been necessary to bring Morocco into subjection, but it did not stir again.

THE BLACK ARMY OF THE 'ABID AND THE MUJAHIDUN

In order to keep the country under control and to wage war against the Christians and Turks, the sharif organised an army whose loyalty withstood every test, enlisting soldiers levied among the negroes of the Sudan.

Al-Mansur had already enrolled black slaves in his regular army, which consisted chiefly of liberated Christian captives and Andalusian renegades. Al-Rashid engaged in hostilities with the Bambara king of Ségou, who had given a welcome to one of his rivals from the Sous, 'Ali ibn Haidar (Bu Hassun?), and had no hope of getting recruits from Timbuctoo. Ibn Haidar, on the other hand, managed to gather several thousand negroes in the Sudan with the intention of invading the States of the sultan, but he disbanded them in the Sous on learning of the death of al-Rashid. It was from their ranks that Mulay Isma'il drew in order to form the nucleus of his negro guard. He may thereafter have sought out descendants of al-Mansur's negro soldiers, whose existence he had discovered from their regimental roll.

He did not send the recruits into battle immediately, but he dispatched them to Mechraʿ er-Remel (near the Sebou between Meknès and Salé) which acted as a 'remount' depot. Their essential task was to beget children, and the offspring were born as children of the regiment. When they were about ten and attaining puberty, they were taken to the sultan. This presentation was repeated regularly from 1688–1689. First they were taught a trade and during the two years following they were trained as muleteers and then as masons. The fourth year saw the beginning of their military apprenticeship by means of exercises in horsemanship, completed in the final year with archery and musketry. At the same time the young women were trained in domestic arts, and the best-looking in music. At fifteen the children of the regiment were assigned to a corps and married off. Their sons were, in their turn, destined for the army and their daughters to marriage with negro soldiers or to service in the princes' household staff.

While waiting for Mechraʿ er-Remel to furnish its annual contingents, Mulay Ismaʿil supplied his army by means of a regular draft from Timbuctoo and raids carried out on the slaves and serfs of the Saharan tribes.

By virtue of their origin, the negro soldiers were given the name of 'slaves' (*ʿabid*), or colloquially of 'negroes'. It was because they took their oath on the collection of *hadiths* of al-Bukari that they are said to have been nicknamed *ʿabid al-Bukari* or *bwakhar*, if indeed this explanation, provided by Houdas,[20] does not arise from an error in transcription.

The regular army consisted exclusively of Saharan negroes and the output of Mechraʿ er-Remel, and was thus without root in the country and entirely devoted to the master. It was comprised of as many as 150,000 men, of whom 70,000 were at the Mechraʿ depot, 25,000 constituted the sharif's private guard at Meknès, and the rest were in the kasbahs. It took part in all the great expeditions to the entire satisfaction of the sultan, who in 1697–1698 granted the right of becoming landowners to the slaves (*ʿabid*) and serfs (*harātīn*).

It did not take this professional army long to realise that it constituted the sole organised force in Morocco. The black

The Sharifian Empire: 1553-1830

praetorians put the empire up for auction and sought to direct its policy, but diminution in their strength reduced them by the end of the eighteenth century to constituting no more than the sultan's bodyguard. In addition to the black army, Mulay Isma'il brought the buccaneers of the Atlantic coast under military organisation by brigading them with the *'abīd*. These buccaneers, under pretext of fighting the Christians, used to pillage the neighbourhood of the ports and, when directed by bold leaders like al-'Ayashi or Ghailan, could on occasion form bands capable of holding their own against the sultans. In giving regular status to the 'volunteers of the faith' (*mujāhidūn*) the sharif appeared to be meeting the aspirations of the more intransigent Muslims. In fact he was relying on these fiery troops for the liberation of the Moroccan ports from Christian occupation and Turkish influence.

The army of Mulay Isma'il also included renegades, though it is impossible to establish in exactly what proportion. About them we have little information apart from that given by one of them, the Englishman Thomas Pellow.[21] They formed separate army corps and were seldom in garrison at Meknès. No case is known of their attaining high office in the makhzan, as had happened in Saadian times.

A great part of this important standing army was garrisoned outside the towns, in isolated kasbahs. Indeed, in order to keep down a still very turbulent country, Mulay Isma'il had recourse to the system of fortified support points held by permanent garrisons. He made use of the kasbahs already in existence and, according to al-Zayani, had seventy-six others built.[22] According to Terrasse these kasbahs fell into three different categories—those which kept watch on the dissident zones (the Middle Atlas in particular) and contained them, those planted along the main communication routes (the roads from Taza to Oujda, from Fez to the Tafilalet, from Fez to Marrakesh, etc.), and finally those which served as barracks for the *'abīd* in the neighbourhood of certain large towns.[23]

HOLY WAR AND THE STRUGGLE AGAINST THE TURKS

Mulay Isma'il resumed with vigour the policy of *reconquista* which had been in abeyance since the death of al-'Ayashi in 1641. He took el-Ma'moura from the Spaniards in 1681 and found 100 cannon in it. He also very nearly made his way into Tangier. After some years of tentative efforts the English had endeavoured to expand beyond the town's ramparts, within which they were suffocated. But London shrank from a policy of strength, the cost of which was high and the profit uncertain. The exploits of the 'Tangier Regiment' tore gaps in its ranks which were filled with recruits of the poorest quality. The governors made money out of their office; the officers turned merchant or falsified the muster-rolls; the common soldiers, starving and unpaid, deserted or mutinied. The main effect of the charter of 1668, which gave Tangier the same status as an English borough, was to enable the town councillors to secure commercial privileges. The port, which naval officers protected with a strong breakwater, could have furnished the English fleet with a reliable base. Trade, stimulated by French refugees expelled from Cadiz and by Dutch captures, ought quickly to have achieved prosperity. But liquid money was short and the creation of a great Morocco company failed in face of the opposition of Tangier businessmen and corrupt governors, who were equally apprehensive of competition from other Maghribi ports. The siege of Mulay Isma'il in 1679 struck a severe blow to trade, and in April 1681 obliged the English to cease erecting fortifications outside the ramparts. In London the House of Commons, fearing that the garrison of Tangier, that nursery of 'Papist soldiers', might furnish Charles II with forces for an attempt at a *coup d'état* against Parliament, refused to grant a request by the Crown for supply 'before we are effectually secured from the imminent and apparent dangers arising from the power of popish persons and counsels'.[24] The king, having dissolved Parliament, was reduced to living on subsidies from Louis XIV and had no desire to squander his resources on Tangier. He gave orders for the town to be evacuated after the destruction of everything in it, including even the large breakwater. This decision, which surrendered the town not to European rivals but to the sharif, was received by English public opinion with satisfaction. Mulay Isma'il's troops might well have believed that the siege of 1679 and their repeated assaults were the real cause of the English exodus. The sharif settled peoples from the Rif in the ruined town. The 'volunteers of the faith' took Larache in 1689 and Arzila in 1691. The Atlantic coastline, on which the Portuguese

The Sharifian Empire: 1553-1830

enclave of Mazagan alone held out, was almost freed from defilement by the presence of Christians.

On the Mediterranean coast there still remained the *presidios* of Melilla, Ceuta, the Peñon of Alhucemas and the Peñon of Velez. Reduced, like the garrison of Tangier, to relying on themselves alone, the Spanish garrisons, badly paid, badly supplied and exploited by their governors, were unable to break the close blockade imposed by the Sharifian forces. But they did not yield to their numerous attacks. It was in vain that Mulay Isma'il established a *ribat* opposite Ceuta, complete with mosque and general's palace, by way of marking his firm determination to master the place. His attention was diverted elsewhere by serious anxieties, and the anarchy that followed his death was the saving of the town.

Even more than war against the Christians, the struggle against the Turks governed his policy. Due to the 'volunteers of the faith', not a single Turkish bandit chief was now able to penetrate Morocco by way of the ports of the Gharb, but in the east the sharif had to be content with less success, for the black army was no match for the Algerian forces. The sultan was well aware that the Turks were encouraging revolts in the Maghrib. In 1679, in order to intimidate them, he pushed as far as the Djebel Amour, but Turkish artillery put the Arab auxiliaries to flight and Mulay Isma'il, like his brother al-Rashid, had to recognise the Tafna as the boundary between the two territories.

After the final submission of the Sous, he made a fresh attempt in 1692 in conjunction with the bey of Tunis, but the two allies were unable to coordinate their movements and were defeated one after the other. His son Zidan, who commanded the province of Taza, had succeeded in taking Tlemcen after a series of incursions, but he did not follow up his success. The sharif denounced his attitude and took command of an army which advanced as far as the Chérif valley, where it was crushed on 28 April 1701. Mulay Isma'il was wounded and nearly fell into the hands of the Turks, who carried the heads of 3,000 soldiers off to Tangier. Nevertheless, he did not abandon his plans. Secured against the danger of invasion by the fortresses which closed his eastern frontier, he did not give up hope of carrying war into the heart of the Regency by penetrating from the south. Already, between 1710 and 1713, one of his sons had managed to occupy the Ain Mahdi region (west of

Laghouat) and a nephew had established a garrison at Bou Semghoun (between Ain Séfra and Géryville). Military riots at Algiers and tribal revolts facilitated an invasion, but the sharif's attention was concentrated on Morocco because of dissensions among his sons and he was unable to take advantage of the opportunity presented to him.

TRADE AND EXTERNAL RELATIONS

Anxious as he was to defend Morocco against encroachments by Christians and Turks, Mulay Isma'il was no less concerned for its economic development. 'He desires', wrote a French resident, contrasting him with his predecessor, 'the aggrandisement of his subjects and of their fortunes by commerce: this he prefers to piracy, to the practice of which they were much more attached in the past than they now are.' Indeed the corsairs of Salé and Tétouan, few in number and badly armed, now hardly troubled any but the smallest vessels. 'The private citizens of Salé, who used always to maintain ten or a dozen ships, had them no longer,' declared the consul J.-B. Estelle in 1699, 'because when they came home with prizes, the king of Morocco always found some pretext for making himself master of them.'[25]

In the Moroccan economy trade held a much more important place than at Algiers or even Tunis. The sharif took an interest in it, largely because he collected ten per cent of the import and export duties levied on all merchandise and as much as twenty-five per cent on the trade in wax.

Information collected by Pidou de Saint-Olon in the course of his mission gives some details of business conditions about 1693. At that time Jews and Christians exercised a *de facto* monopoly. Salé and Tétouan were 'the places most frequented, whence merchandise is exported most easily'. Trade at Safi and Agadir was less important and was fed from the Tafilalet and the Sous. 'The town of Fez is, as it were, the general storehouse of all Barbary.' It was a centre of redistribution kept active by the presence of 5,000 Jews. In the maritime towns, skins for red moroccan leather, the finest in Barbary, were manufactured.

'The Spanish trade consists in cochineal and vermilion; the English in woollens and in cowries from Guinea, these being shells used in that country as coins. Holland brings in woollens, textiles,

The Sharifian Empire: 1553-1830

spices of all kinds, iron wire, brass, steel, benzoin, storax, cinnabar, small mirrors, muslins for turbans and from time to time arms and other munitions of war. Italy supplies alum, stick sulphur and quantities of terracotta curios made at Venice. From the Levant comes silk, cotton, yellow arsenic, quicksilver, red arsenic and opium. The English and Dutch warehoused their merchandise at Cadiz, where Portuguese vessels came to take them on board.'[26]

The *Dictionnaire Universel du commerce* by Savary de Bruslons enables us to fill out these data for the first quarter of the eighteenth century. Moors and Jews collected supplies of European merchandise from the Christian stores on the coast and distributed them among their branches at Fez, Meknès, Marrakesh, Taroudant and Iligh. Meknès was still the principal market for grain, leather and wax. Any surplus, over that which the five towns consumed, was sent to the Tafilalet, 'where in exchange for it the Arabs give tibir or gold dust, indigo, ostrich feathers, dates, or sometimes a few elephants' teeth otherwise known as morfil or raw ivory'. Caravan traffic with the Sudan continued to be active.

Christian consuls and merchants were often adventurers exploiting their co-religionists no less than the Moroccans. Mouëtte, having seen them at close quarters, accuses them of buying from the corsairs such prizes as Morocco did not use and selling them back to Europe at four times the price. A more serious charge was that they took a cut out of the ransom money they received and left captives in their fetters while leading their families to believe that they were negotiating with the sultan.[27]

At the end of the eighteenth century French commerce in Morocco occupied first place and was encouraged by the sharif. The pride and brutality of Louis XIV compromised a situation which, with a little skill and tact, might have become exceptionally favourable. Immediately after acceding to power, Mulay Isma'il had given the king's representative an undertaking to require the corsairs to respect French vessels, to grant 'the faculty of exporting from his country local merchandise of every kind, which his late brother had forbidden, notably copper and brass',[28] and to encourage the ransoming of slaves. During the last twenty years of the seventeenth century the very Christian king and the Sharif exchanged embassies, but Louis's prestige diplomacy brought these to nothing.

In 1682 Muhammad Tamin brought back from the French court a draft peace treaty guaranteeing for six years to the French, among others, freedom of navigation and trade. The sharif was preparing to sign it when the embassy of the Chevalier de Saint-Amand was sent to him accompanied by so small a retinue as to take on the character of an insult. Saint-Amand was charged with the duty of asking for modifications which altered the treaty's original purpose. Regarding the redemption of Moroccan slaves, Mulay Isma'il proposed to give one Christian captive and 300 livres for each one of them. Colbert, primarily concerned with maintaining the numbers of oarsmen for his galleys, invited his envoy to employ 'all his skill with a view to avoiding an answer on this subject'.[29] The sultan ratified the peace treaty on 14 December 1682, but in doing so rejected the additions suggested by Saint-Amand. The question of the slaves had naturally not been settled.

A second embassy under Muhammad Tamim was detained at Toulon for trifling reasons of procedure and Versailles then tried unsuccessfully to intimidate Morocco with displays of naval strength. The very Christian king and the Sharif grew obdurate in their pride, the latter being agreeable to negotiate only with ambassadors and not with merchants, and the former desiring to secure recognition of his superiority over the barbarian prince. Louis XIV did, however, consent to send an ordinary gentleman of his household to Meknès early in 1693. This was Pidou de Saint-Olon, whose negotiations were without result. French influence and commerce alike were damaged by this setback.

The victories gained by Louis XIV over the Coalition were propitious for a resumption of talks. Admiral Bin Aisha, who had sided with France after being England's agent, came to the court in 1698 where he became a personality of the day. A great lady showed herself more complaisant towards him than did the king towards the sharif. The Moroccan, refusing the concessions offered him in the matter of exchanging slaves, went home empty-handed. Mulay Isma'il was displeased and made his feelings very clear. He reproached the king for having gone back on undertakings entered into in his name by Vice-Admiral d'Estrées. 'Bin Aisha', wrote the sultan to the king, 'ought to have returned ... for we need nothing from your country. ... Peace or war with you matters to us not in the least.'[30] He did not, however, break off relations. Rather, with a

The Sharifian Empire: 1553-1830

view to establishing an alliance between Louis XIV and himself, which he considered desirable, he proposed marriage with a royal bastard, the beautiful Princesse de Conti, of whom Bin Aisha had spoken to him in terms of high praise and to whom he was prepared to guarantee the practice of her religion. The court ridiculed a proposal whose ironical aspect Mulay Isma'il was incapable of grasping and as an answer he received an insolent invitation to convert to Christianity.

At the beginning of the eighteenth century the decline and defeats of the French navy turned to the advantage of the English, who had just set foot on Gibraltar. The king's Spanish policy alienated the sharif, who dreamed of recovering Ceuta. However, the Mercedarians and the Trinitarian Fathers attempted to continue negotiations at Meknès for the redemption of slaves, though no agreement was reached and they entered into dispute with the French consul at Salé. The sole outcome was the exchange of twenty captives in 1712. After the Fathers had left the situation grew steadily worse. Commerce passed into the hands of Huguenot refugees from Languedoc, who were accused of favouring the English and the Dutch to the detriment of the 'French nation'. One of them ended as a renegade and governor of Salé. Deprived of authority by the Calvinists' influence over the mind of the sharif, the two consuls ceased to represent anyone but themselves and had to leave Salé in 1710 and Tétouan in 1712. For more than forty years France had no further representative and this enabled the English to take first place in the Moroccan trade.

Louis XIV, writes Hardy, had distinguished himself 'by his clumsiness, his failure to understand men and matters in Morocco and his lack of consideration and elementary precautions',[31] all of which were in contrast with the 'honesty' of the sharif. The ruin of French trade [in Morocco] was the price paid for the glory of the king.

MEKNÈS

Like Louis XIV, whom he is said to have imitated (though he had begun his works at Meknès long before becoming acquainted with the splendours of Versailles), Mulay Isma'il had a passion for building. Rulers give proof of their power to their subjects and to posterity in the form of bricks and mortar. The sharif, loathing Fez and Marrakesh because of their revolts, desired to raise a city worthy of himself. He chose the admirable site of Meknès, the elongated spur of which, with a watercourse to maintain its greenery and coolness, rises amid fertile plateaux and commands the outlets from the Middle Atlas and the Zerhoun. He did not create the city from nothing, but 'Meknès of the olive-trees' (*Miknasa al-zitun*), which derived its name from the great Zenata tribe of the Miknasa, had an undistinguished past. It may have been fortified by the Almoravids, was certainly maltreated by the first Almohads and had grown rich through trading in the thirteenth century. The Merinids built a kasbah there, and also, in 1276, a mosque, a zawiya, caravanserais, a drainage system and bridges. Later, in the mid-fourteenth century, they added to these the attractive Bou 'Inaniya Madarsa, with its gateway with folding doors covered in bronze, engraved and fretted, and its ribbed dome dominating the entrance. At the beginning of the sixteenth century Leo Africanus was boasting of its orchards and fields, its abundant water supply, the strength of its position and the importance of its markets.[32] But it was Mulay Isma'il who carried out the greatest part of the work.

On the works the sharif employed, not 25,000 Christians, but 2,000 at most, some 30,000 men convicted under ordinary law, prisoners taken from rebel camps and workers regularly furnished by the tribes for forced labour. He probably also made use of the young negroes during the third year of their apprenticeship.

The captives were harshly treated. Hauled out of their underground dungeons at daybreak, they were formed into teams, each under a negro slave-driver who did not spare the lash. Some demolished the old walls with 'picks of exceptional weight'. Others gathered together and rammed vigorously between two planks 'gravelly earth mixed with lime, which bind together by dint of stirring and pouring water over them.' This 'mastic' they put up as masonry. Carrying these materials was an exhausting task, the ladders cut their feet and the tackle-ropes their hands. Sometimes captives in charge of lime-kilns were burnt alive.

The sharif was a ruthless taskmaster. Mouëtte tells how he shot down a Breton 'who was drawing his breath for a moment' and twice drove a lance into another slave for the same reason. He was no more sparing of his own staff. 'In the year 1696, while visiting

The Sharifian Empire: 1553–1830

his works, he took it into his head that they were not going forward fast enough. He at once sent for the Alcaz el-Malec... and though he was at the time one of the first men in his court and in his confidence, and superintendent of his buildings, he first let loose his wrath on him and then had him given 500 strokes with a leather strap, after having himself thrashed him soundly.' Another time, finding the bricks too thin, he broke them over the foreman's head. Moreover, he did not hesitate to set an example by taking a pick in his own hands.[33]

The construction of Meknès was the task of a multitude in slavery to a master's despotic will. The result was not so much a work of art as a massive monument.

He made no noticeable change in the general plan of the old town of Meknès. He did, however, build several mosques, such as that of Bab Berdaïn at the extreme north of the town. He razed the southern quarter, which was an obstacle to the constructions he planned (the name Place el-Hedim—place of debris—preserves the memory of this demolition), and he had built a Jewish quarter (*mellah*) which formed a suburb to the west of the Muslim city.

The imperial quarter—a town in itself, surrounded on its completion with a wall some 16 miles in circumference—rose to the south of the old town. Mulay Isma'il's first step was to have a compact palace (*Dar Kabira*) built on the site of the Merinid Kasbah and the quarter he had had levelled. Three walls enclosed it to the north-east. The first and lowest of these was lined with square towers. The second, of intermediate height, had a sentry walk. The third, protecting the seraglio, was the highest. It was not so much a palace as a town; of it there remains only a mass of confused but sometimes striking ruins. The other sides were enclosed by a single wall. The principal building, according to al-Zayani, comprised twenty pavilions, whose 'fair towers square in form and covered with green tiles' dominated the countryside.[34] Not far away there rose four great pavilions facing one another. There were two imposing mosques, that of the Flowers and that of Lalla 'Awda.

Next Mulay Isma'il had designed, to the south-west of this complex, several gardens enclosed by walls and flanked by buildings. Later, to the south of these gardens, another series of palaces was built; some of these, restored in the nineteenth century, form the present Dar el-Makhzen. Finally, to the west of Dar Kebira rose a garden city (*Madina al-Riad*) reserved for the high officials of the makhzan. Of this there remains only the admirable Bab el-Khemis, 'the horseshoe opening of which is surrounded by black scutcheons and a frame of green mosaic and surmounted by a frieze of inscriptions in black cursive characters; all these decorations stand out on a brick background. Two bastions, one in ruins, stand on either side of the gate.'[35]

These four great complexes were supplemented by numerous annexes, kasbahs housing the detachments of black troops, 'wide meadows used for military parades and pasturing the sultan's flocks ... a huge basin recalling the water mirrors of Marrakesh', and finally innumerable stores and stables. There still stand the pillars and arcades of an imposing edifice which has been taken for the great stables but which must actually have been used as a grain store. The real 'Roües or stables' were, in Père Busnot's eyes, the most beautiful thing in the palace, with their two ranges of arcades three-quarters of a league in length, and the canal which supplied them.[36] The horses, tethered by all four feet to two rings by horsehair ropes, were looked after by Muslim ostlers and Christian stable-boys. Besides his stables the sultan had a menagerie, in which he staged combats of lions and wolves (?) against dogs.

The sharif was not above honouring visitors of note with a personally conducted tour of the property. The Englishman John Windus, who has left us an account of Commodore Stewart's mission in 1720,[37] admired the profusion of mosaics, the prospect of the buildings—'beautiful, magnificent and simple'—the arms depots, and the qubbas. He was also impressed by the residence of the two royal favourites or Dome of His Majesty (*Qubba al-Hadra*), the terrace overlooking the gardens for a length of half a mile, the workshops for saddlery or arms, and above all a building raised on Roman pillars which came from the ruins of Volubilis(?). In the course of the tour the visitors were served with a light meal of fruits and sweetmeats.

The sharif's last construction which was finished by his son, was Bab Mansur el-ʿEulj, the gate of Mansur the Christian convert. It is the most imposing gateway of Meknès. The gigantic bay, a slightly broken horseshoe, is flanked by two bastions raised on

The Sharifian Empire: 1553-1830

arcades. On either side rises a tall column with prismatic piers. 'The dominant motif is a curvilinear interlaced design standing out in relief on the flat background of green gilt glazed mosaic. A broad and beautiful inscription in black cursive characters, topped by a row of merlons, runs the length of the upper frieze. The proportions are heavy and the surfaces flat, but the general effect is full of majesty.'[38]

THE GOVERNMENT OF THE SHARIFS

The strong will displayed by Mulay Isma'il in liberating his territory and building Meknès was also manifest in his governmental methods. He took all decisions himself, tolerated no opposition and paid regard to no rule but his own good pleasure. During his reign Morocco and *bled al-makhzan* almost came to coincide, for even the tribes of the High Atlas acknowledged occasionally that they had found their master.

'Your king Louis', was his retort to an observation by an ambassador from Louis XIV, 'commands men while I command brutes.' Accordingly he maintained order by force. Confiscation of arms and horses, territories reduced by his harkas to a wilderness, mass executions—such were his favourite methods of making his authority felt. He was, however, always ready to negotiate with the opponent he had just raided and, if need be, to take him into his service—as he did with the Dilaites. He was ruthless in putting down revolts but was also able to anticipate them by keeping a watchful eye on disturbed areas by means of kasbahs, occupied by garrisons housing from 400 to 3,000 men and supplied by the tribes.

These kasbahs constituted independent establishments standing in open country, provided with a magazine and a mosque, and sometimes encircled by two walls, the inner one enclosing the buildings, the outer and larger one serving as potential cover for the population of the surrounding countryside. The post commander was answerable for the tranquillity of the zone under his surveillance. In this way the country enjoyed exceptional security. 'A Jew or a woman', declared al-Zayani, 'could go from Oujda to the Oued Noun without a soul daring to ask whence they came or whither they were going.'[39]

To the hostile influence of the marabouts supported by the

Turks, Mulay Isma'il set in opposition the sharifs, from among whom he chose his counsellors. The one marabout who benefited from the master's favour—the marabout of Ouezzan, whom he appointed governor of that town—was also a sharif.

MULAY ISMA'IL'S SUCCESSORS

Mulay Isma'il's makhzan was a formidable force based on the will of one man. His reign had not ended before revolts began to presage its ruin. Too tight a discipline was stifling the empire, and no sooner was the sharif dead, in 1727, than its iron framework, so painfully assembled, fell apart. The marabouts and the Turks took a hair of the dog that had bitten them, the tribes collected arms and horses with the intention of revolting, and the captives threw down the bricks they were carrying to the last buildings of Meknès.

Of greater importance, though, the *'abid* set themselves up as masters. One of the Sharif's sons, Mulay Ahmad al-Dahbi, was nominated by them for his liberality, and allowed them to massacre the governors in office. They soon replaced him by his brother 'Abd al-Malik, whom in turn they deposed as soon as they thought him too ambitious and also because he was seeking to ally himself against them with the Oudaya Arabs and the Berbers of the Middle Atlas. Al-Dahbi was recalled to power, but died of an illness a few months later, in 1729.

The *'abid* then sent to Sijilmasa for another son of Mulay Isma'il, Mulay 'Abd Allah, in order to install him in power. He quickly quarrelled with the people of Fez, then the Oudaya and finally the *'abid* themselves. With their support he could have given rein to his cruelty against Fez and the Oudaya; with the *'abid* against him he had to relinquish power in 1735 and take refuge in the region of the Oued Noun.

His brother, Mulay 'Ali al-'Araj, took his place. He was a weak and gentle man, incapable of keeping a disintegrating country in a state of order. This was Mulay 'Abd Allah's chance to return and regain the favour of the troops, which he did in 1736, but this second reign was short-lived. Fresh cruelties roused his entourage against him, and once more he had to flee and take refuge among the Berbers. From that vantage point he mounted numerous attacks against his brother and successor, Sidi Muhammad ibn 'Arbiya, who had virtually no control over the Oudiya or over the

The Sharifian Empire: 1553–1830

'abīd to whom he was indebted for his throne. Anarchy increased and a famine began. The *'abīd* revolted yet again in 1738 and tried a new sultan, another son of Mulay Isma'il named Mulay al-Mustadi. The experiment did not succeed and tired of war, they recalled Mulay 'Abd Allah in 1740. At first he was more tractable but his former character soon returned. Mulay 'Abd Allah was deposed for the third time in 1745, and took refuge once more among the Berbers, while the pasha of Tangier, Ahmad al-Rifi, had Mulay Zin al-'Abidin acknowledged as ruler at Meknès. He proved incapable of securing possession of Fez, which was unwilling to recognise him. At once the *'abīd* abandoned him and Mulay 'Abd Allah, lying in wait as before, became sultan again for the fourth time in 1745. The former sultan, al-Mustadi, then reappeared, supported by Ahmad al-Rifi. With some difficulty Mulay 'Abd Allah managed to eliminate each of them in turn, after which he gained possession of Marrakesh in 1750, and there installed his son Muhammad as governor. Under this wise and temperate governor southern Morocco experienced a period of comparative peace, while the north continued to be the scene of conflicts between *'abīd*, Oudaya and Berbers, in the midst of whom Mulay 'Abd Allah conducted his manœuvres and was sustained by his double-dealing. In 1752 the *'abīd* were about to proclaim the son as sultan in his father's place, but Sidi Muhammad magnanimously refused and Mulay 'Abd Allah was able to exercise but a shadow of power until his death in 1757.

Notwithstanding the chronic state of anarchy, the Christians continued to trade and to negotiate for the ransom of captives. The Dutch, even more than the English, gradually eliminated the French from the market. The English had a near-monopoly of commercial exchanges at Tétouan, and shared with the Dutch the business in woollens, textiles and spices handled at Salé or Safi, and also the loading of wax, goatskins and copper at Agadir. Moroccan wool was routed by the English chiefly to Marseilles by way of Livorno. French trade steadily declined. Until the mid-eighteenth century, however, if we are to believe contemporary memoirs, it was still more important than that of the three other commercial ports of Barbary. Only lack of interest on the part of the government of Louis XV prevented France from securing, like England, a trade treaty which J.-E. Rey, a Marseillais merchant at

Salé, offered to negotiate. Ransoming of captives was easier to effect. In need of money, Mulay ʿAbd Allah agreed to the sale of numerous Spanish, Dutch, English and French slaves.

SIDI MUHAMMAD IBN ʿABD ALLAH (1757–1790)

The new sovereign had already given proof of his capacity when he had been viceroy to his father at Marrakesh. He was a pious man, who yearned for the peace and justice Morocco had such need of after thirty years of disorder. He took in hand the immense task of restoring a certain balance to his distracted country. There was no lack of difficulties. The return from taxes was low, even in the *bled al-makhzan*, the army emerged from its perpetual revolts and their subsequent repression in a state of total disorganisation, and the Berber tribes of the Middle Atlas were slowly creeping down towards the plain and threatening to sever the country into two sections level with Rabat.

Patiently Sidi Muhammad set to work. He created new taxes on markets and business transactions, the legitimate nature of which was established by the learned doctors of Fez, and at the same time he had a sound coinage minted. The army was regrouped; to the corps of *ʿabīd*, dangerously reduced by the disturbances that had gone before, he added *haratin* drawn from the oases and the Arab tribes of the plain. He was even occasionally able to employ Berber contingents. At the same time he had the principal coastal towns fortified, equipping them with artillery platforms and cannon. Finally he did his best—not, it seems, with much success—to establish a naval fleet. However, these forces were still only modest and were inadequate. Accordingly Sidi Muhammad had recourse to diplomacy, at times making use of his still quite considerable prestige as a sharif, and at other times playing on the internal divisions of the Berber tribes. To this end he took into his service Berbers who had rallied to the dynasty, like the writer al-Zayani, and they, remarkably knowledgeable about the scene in which they were to act, secured far from negligible results.

Nevertheless the unsubjected zone remained very extensive and the sultan spent a great part of his reign in putting down revolts and stemming encroachments by the Sanhaja of the Middle Atlas, who were coming down northwards and north-westwards with the steady but sure force of a slow-moving landslide. He managed to

The Sharifian Empire: 1553–1830

keep subject to him the northern plains (eastern Morocco and the Fez, Meknès and Gharb regions) and also the southern plains (Oum er-Rbia and Tensift basins) but had to abandon the direct route linking Fez with Marrakesh by way of the Tadla. Thereafter, and until 1912, the sharifian *mahalla* had to go by way of Rabat and Casablanca in order to reach Marrakesh from Fez or Meknès. Also, the route from Fez to the Tafilalet was not always practical.[40]

As a man of piety, Sidi Muhammad learned through pilgrims about the Wahhabi movement then developing in Arabia with the support of the Bedouin al-Saʻud family. Its rigours were to his liking and he was accustomed to say, 'In ritual I am a Maliki, in dogma a Wahhabi'. His religious zeal even led him to destroy books, too conciliatory in his view, setting out the Ashʻarite doctrine and of certain zawiyas, such as the one at Boujad.

He was also a sultan interested in building. To him is due the town of Mogador, the plan of which was drawn by a French architect, Cournut from Avignon. At Marrakesh, where he preferred to reside, he had built the palace called Dar Baïda (now the Maisonnave hospital) and he went on to several restorations. Another Dar Baïda (now a training school for Moroccan officers) was erected at Meknès south of Mulay Ismaʻil's ruined palaces. Finally, he had the Bab Guisa Madarsa built at Fez.

He also tried to complete the work of *reconquista*, and forced the Portuguese to evacuate their last refuge at Mazagan in 1769, but he failed at Melilla notwithstanding an enormous effort. Taking Mulay Ismaʻil as a model he sought a rapprochement simultaneously with Turkey and France and negotiated with both without breaking off relations with either Algiers or Tunis. He may have hoped that a conflict between the Porte and the Algerians would enable him to intervene in the Regency.

In relations with France the Marseillais J.-E. Rey held first place. This sagacious and unscrupulous business man had first sold his influence to Denmark, which in 1751 secured through him a monopoly of trade at Safi and Agadir. He had then got the Sharif to issue in his favour a diploma entrusting him with negotiations with the European Powers. Rey thought he might profit out of this commission in negotiations with the French government, but he was badly received at the court and he returned to Morocco only to bring himself to ruin.

His initiative, though far from disinterested, was not in vain. Choiseul had his scheme for negotiations taken up by another Marseillais trader, Salva, and the result was the treaty of 1767 signed by the Comte de Breugnon. Security of trade was guaranteed anew and in the matter of customs France was assured of most favoured nation treatment. Consuls were restored, not only with their rights of precedence but also with power to employ Moroccans who would be exempt from personal charges and local jurisdiction (*censaux*). Almost the only effect of this treaty, highly advantageous as it was to the interests of business, was to restore the prestige of France. Although, Frenchmen flocked to the court of Sidi Muhammad, this intelligent prince, friend of scholars and not at all afraid of European innovations, had too much regard for his own interests to allow foreign traders to enrich themselves in any manner they wished. At the expense of Salé he bestowed favour in turn on Safi and then Agadir, and finally he founded Mogador, which he made into the chief market of Morocco and which also kept a watch for smuggling on the southern coast. The foundation of Mogador marked the beginning of an economic policy directed towards attracting foreigners in the ports and activating commercial exchanges, which alone were capable of supplying the exhausted treasury with fresh revenues. But the Christian merchants, on whom the *amin* of the customs kept a stringent check, deserted Mogador and the hoped-for taxes failed to fill the coffers. Nevertheless the new port, as a terminus for caravans and a home of a vigorous Jewish colony having relations with the communities of the Sous and the Anti-Atlas, monopolised trade with the far south. The Sous, deprived of its former maritime outlets, grew poor and ceased to be a centre of rebellion and a threat to the authority of the makhzan.

France alone retained—until 1795—her consul at Salé, or rather at Rabat, whereas the other states established theirs at Tangier. She failed to realise in Morocco the expansion envisaged by the chamber of commerce of Marseilles following the treaty of 1767, and had to be content with mediocre results.

MULAY AL-YAZID (1790–1792)

Sidi Muhammad was succeeded by his son Mulay al-Yazid, who had been a topic of conversation long before acceding to power.

The Sharifian Empire: 1553–1830

As the sultan's especially beloved son, an excellent horseman, generous, fiery, and a combatant in holy war, the prince was very popular and full of promise, but he was incapable of self-control. Having been appointed *qaid* of the Berber Garwan tribe (south of Meknès) in 1769, he had let his popularity go to his head and had allowed himself to be proclaimed sultan. Sidi Muhammad was warned of the affair, and al-Yazid took refuge in an inviolable place of sanctuary and secured his pardon. Twice again, in 1771 and 1775, he set out on the same course, in almost the same circumstances. His father then kept him out of the public eye and in 1784, having decided to conduct an expedition to the Tafilalet, sent him on pilgrimage in order to rid himself of him. As he returned earlier than expected, Sidi Muhammad sent him on pilgrimage once more. This time al-Yazid chose Cairo for an attempt to pillage an embassy which the sultan was sending to the holy cities. Sidi Muhammad, who was well informed, diverted the embassy, but al-Yazid, under pretext of making a third pilgrimage, set off again for Arabia, where he succeeded in intercepting the gifts intended for the *shurfa* of the Yemen. He then returned to Cairo with an armed band, reached Algiers by way of Tripolitania and sought his father's pardon, abandoning himself in the meantime to numerous acts of eccentricity. All he received was money, and he then made a fourth pilgrimage, on his return from which he made himself *persona non grata* wherever he went. He then tried to return to Morocco and finally was stranded at the zawiya of Sidi 'Abd al-Slam ibn Mshish, an inviolable sanctuary; there he awaited his chance. It came a few months later when his father died.

Surprising though it may seem, his accession to power gave rise to no difficulty. But he soon rendered himself unpopular by his exactions and his sanguinary whims, from which Jews and Christians were the first to suffer but from which Muslims were not spared. He even came into conflict with the Spaniards by the arbitrary arrest of the Spanish consuls at Mogador and Larache, as well as of two religious men of Tangier. He then laid siege to Ceuta but had to abandon it, for revolt was threatening in the south. One of his brothers, Mulay Hisham, had been proclaimed sultan at Marrakesh; another, Mulay 'Abd al-Rahman, had taken possession of the Tafilalet. Mulay al-Yazid marched against the former and recaptured Marrakesh, but was killed in combat in 1792 when Mulay Hisham returned to the offensive.

MULAY SLIMAN (1792–1822)

Mulay al-Yazid's brief reign had rekindled discord in Morocco. Mulay Sliman, Sidi Muhammad's favourite son after al-Yazid, was proclaimed Sultan at Fez. But he soon found three competitors ranged against him—Mulay Muslama in the mountainous area of northern Morocco, Mulay Hisham supported by the tribes in the neighbourhood of Safi and Mazagan, and somewhat later, Mulay al-Husain, who took Marrakesh and attacked Mulay Hisham.

Mulay Sliman proceeded methodically. He first attacked Mulay Muslama, the nearest to him, without concerning himself about

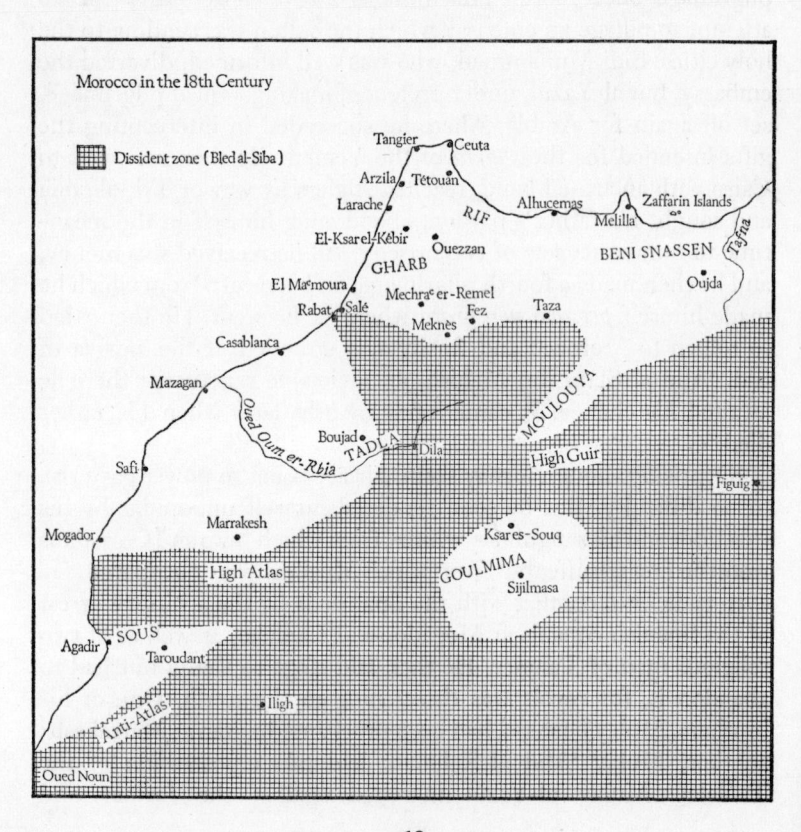

The Sharifian Empire: 1553–1830

the others. Not without difficulty he brought the north of the country under control and pacified it. Only then did he turn to the south, which was weary of the fratricidal conflict of the two pretenders, and eventually he occupied Marrakesh in 1796. He thus had in his power the *bled al-makhzan* which his father had reconstituted. He even managed to enlarge it somewhat by bringing back under control the Draʿ, Figuig and part of the Tadla. By means of constant police patrols he maintained order and levied taxes with fair regularity.

From 1811 the complexion of affairs changed. The Middle Atlas became inflamed; the greater part of the Berber tribes gathered round one of their own men, Abu Bakr Amhaush, and under his command they held in check the troops dispatched by the sultan to put down the revolt. For several years Mulay Sliman fought desperately and without result to restore order. He then suffered a very serious defeat in the Tadla in 1818, narrowly escaping owing to a Berber woman who retained some respect for the sultan's person. During the closing years of his reign the collapse intensified. It was a Morocco once more heading for anarchy that he left in the hands of his nephew and successor Mulay ʿAbd al-Rahman.

During the relatively quiet part of his reign Mulay Sliman, whose vigorous piety was similar to that of his father, had had several mosques built, among them that of the Rsif Quarter at Fez. He had also seen to the restoration of fine ancient buildings, among others the Chrabliyin Mosque and the Bou ʿInaniya Madarsa at Fez, both of the Merinid epoch. Also, he maintained correct relations both with the Turks of Algiers and with the powers of Europe; he even undertook in 1817 to suppress piracy in the territories dependent to him.

CONCLUSION

At this point our study of Sharifian Morocco concludes. With the reign of Mulay ʿAbd al-Rahman (1822–1859) it was to find itself faced with new problems.

The history of the Sharifian dynasties is one of increasingly marked withdrawal. In the sixteenth century Morocco was nearly involved in other adventures because of the Portuguese and Spaniards, who attempted to encroach there, and because, too, of the Turks, who also tried to move into Morocco. It was strong enough to repel these encroachments, hold the Turks at bay, break the last Portuguese offensive at the Battle of the Three Kings and gradually reduce the European enclaves with the exception of Ceuta and Melilla, still held by the Spaniards. Not content with holding out against political seizure, it strictly limited its commercial exchanges with the outside world. It can be said that at the death of Mulay Sliman Morocco was virtually taking no part in the economic life of a world in which commercial exchanges were developing with increasing speed.

This great desire for isolation might have been matched by the establishment of a good internal equilibrium. The Saadians, until the early seventeenth century, could hold themselves out as unifiers. On the eve of the Battle of the Three Kings, al-Mansur had the support of nearly the whole country. Throughout his reign he was able to keep the country in a fairly satisfactory state of order, but the events which followed showed that the latent centrifugal forces had been merely held in check and by no means mastered. As soon as he was dead, soldiers, Berber tribes, religious personages and town bourgeois came into collision once more. We may well speculate whether the periods of relative calm in the reigns of Mulay Isma'il and Sidi Muhammad were not rather periods of lassitude. Thereafter and until 1912 the country was divided into two sections, the *bled al-makhzan*, more or less obedient to the ruler if he was a man of energy, and the *bled al-siba*, itself rent by tribal rivalries but always obstinately resistant to the sultan's authority. He was able to rule over the zone remaining subject to him only by constantly moving from point to point, surrounded by an army and levying taxes by force of cannon and musket. No sultan had the power, perhaps not even the idea, of combining the various forces hitherto in discord or of restoring the country. Thus it was that, in a world in full and swift evolution and increasing daily in strength through improvements in means of transport and growth of the volume of trade, Morocco remained an amalgam of tribes, very unstably bound together by the link of religion—the only link they had in common—and attached to a centuries-old if not thousand-years-old economic system. In brief it was a corner of the earth becoming increasingly more of an anachronism as the years passed. All this was happening in a geographic position of the utmost importance, at the meeting-

The Sharifian Empire: 1553–1830

point of Africa and Europe, lying along essential maritime routes —down the west coast of Africa and through the Mediterranean— with its northern extremity touching the Straits of Gibraltar, one of the chief transit points of the globe, and in addition endowed with considerable natural wealth.

Inevitably the Sharifian empire—weak, out-of-date and placed in a tempting geographic position—attracted many covetous eyes. The French presence in Algeria added one further factor to a problem for which sooner or later a solution had to be found.

Notes

1. H. de Castries, Philippe de Cossé Brissac, Pierre de Cenival, *et al.*, volumes published from 1905, arranged in chronological order and by countries involved—France (series 2), Portugal and England.
2. E. Lévi-Provençal, *Les historiens des Chorfa, essai sur la littérature historique et biographique au Maroc du XVIe au XXe siècle* (Paris, 1923).
3. al-Ifrani, *Nozhet el-Hadi. Histoire de la dynastie saadienne au Maroc (1511–1670)*, 2 vols. (ed. and tr. O. Houdas, Paris, 1888–9).
4. al-Zayani (Abu al-Kasim b. Ahmad), *al-Tarjama al-mu'arib 'an dwal al-mashriq wa al-maghrib*; an extract of which has been edited and translated by O. Houdas, *Le Maroc de 1631 a 1812* (Paris, 1886).
5. E. Lévi-Provençal, *Extraits des historiens arabes du Maroc, Textes, d'explication à l'usage des Etudiants* (Paris, 1948).
6. al-Nasiri al-Slawi (Ahmad b. Khalid), *Kitab al-Istiqsa*, 4 vols. (Cairo, A.H. 1312/A.D. 1894); see E. Fumey, tr., 'Chronique de la dynastie alaouie au Maroc', *Archives Marocaines*, IX–X (1906–7).
7. Muhammad b. Ja'far al-Kattani, *Salwat al-anfas*, 3 vols. (Fes, A.H. 1316/A.D. 1898).
8. H. Terrasse, *op. cit.*, II, 184–5.
9. al-Ifrani (tr. Houdas), *op. cit.*, p. 259.
10. G. S. Colin, ed., *Chronique anonyme de la dynastie sa'dienne* (Rabat, 1934); tr. by E. Fagnan, though using a defective text, in *Extraits inédits relatifs au Maghreb* (Alger, 1924), pp. 360–457.
11. al-Ifrani (tr. Houdas), *op. cit.*, p. 167.
12. Lawrence Madock; see H. de Castries, *et al.*, *op. cit.*, 1st series, *Dynastie Sa'dienne, Angleterre* (Paris, 1935), II, 83–8.
13. al-Ifrani (tr. Houdas), *op. cit.*, p. 340.
14. H. Terrasse, *op. cit.*, II, p. 240.
15. Sieur Mouëtte, *Histoire des conquêtes de Mouley Archy connu sous le nom de roy de Tafilet, et de Mouley Ismaël* . . . (Paris, 1683) and in H. de Castries, *et al.*, *op. cit.*, 2nd series, *France*, II, 1–201; also see Sieur Mouëtte, *Relation de la captivité du sieur Mouëtte dans les*

royaumes de Fez et du Maroc, ou il a demeuré pendant onze ans (Paris, 1707), re-edited in part by Mme de Serres (Tours, 1928). For another edition see *The Travels of the Sieur Mouëtte in the Kingdoms of Fez and Morocco during his eleven years' captivity in those parts* (London, 1710).

16. Père Busnot, *Histoire de règne de Mouley-Ismaël* . . . (Rouen, 1714), 2nd edition, 1731, and *Récits d'aventures (au Maroc) au temps de Louis XIV* (Paris, 1928).
17. Pidou de Saint-Olon, *Etat présent de l'empire de Maroc* (Paris, 1694); 2nd edition, *Relation de l'Empire de Maroc* . . . (Paris, 1695).
18. S. Mouëtte (1707), *op. cit.*, p. 150.
19. *Ibid.*, pp. 150–1.
20. al-Zayani (tr. Houdas), *op. cit.*, pp. 59–60 (note).
21. Thomas Pellow, *The adventures of Thomas Pellow of Penryn, mariner*, The Adventure Series (London, 1890); see H. Terrasse, 'Les Aventures d'un renégat anglais au Maroc sous Moulay Ismail', *Bulletin de l'Enseignement public au Maroc* (1926).
22. al-Zayani (tr. Houdas), *op. cit.*, p. 31.
23. H. Terrasse, *op. cit.*, II, 258–9.
24. *Journals of the House of Commons* (27 November 1680), IX, 665–6.
25. J.-B. Estelle, 'Mémoire de J.-B. Estelle, October, 1698', in H. de Castries, *et al.*, *op. cit.*, *France*, 2nd series, *Dynastie Filalienne*, IV, 707.
26. Pidou de Saint-Olon, for his mission of 1693 see H. de Castries, *et al.*, *op. cit.*, *France*, 2nd series, *Dynastie Filalienne*, III, 552, 554, 564, 566, 570 and IV, 1, 8, 29, 33, 45, 131, 159, 212, 215.
27. S. Mouëtte (1707), *op. cit.*, pp. 308–9.
28. G. Hardy, 'La légende et l'histoire. Les relations de la France et du Maroc sous Louis XIV', *Revue de l'histoire des colonies françaises* (1927), p. 494.
29. *Ibid.*, p. 497.
30. *Ibid.*, p. 503.
31. *Ibid.*, p. 507.
32. Leo Africanus (tr. Epaulard), *op. cit.*, I, 177.
33. S. Mouëtte (1707), *op. cit.*, see chapter V, 'Des persecutions et des travaux . . . à Miguenes . . .', p. 61 *et seq.*
34. al-Zayani (tr. Houdas), *op. cit.*, p. 28.
35. See G. Marçais (1927), *op. cit.*, II, 713–15.
36. Père Busnot, *op. cit.*
37. John Windus, *A Journey to Mequinez, the Residence of the present Emperor of Fez and Morocco, on the occasion of Commodore Stewart's embassy thither for the Redemption of the British Captives in the Year 1721* (London, 1725).
38. P. Ricard, *op. cit.*, pp. 230–1.
39. al-Zayani (tr. Houdas), *op. cit.*, p. 52.
40. *Ibid.*, p. 127–57.

CHAPTER 6

Turkish Rule in Algeria and Tunisia: 1516-1830

❈

1. The Spanish Crusade, the Barbarossas and the Foundation of the Algiers Regency

THE CENTRAL MAGHRIB AT THE END OF THE FIFTEENTH CENTURY

The disintegration of the Maghrib at the end of the fifteenth century encouraged foreign invasions. Like the Portuguese in their *fronteiras* on the Atlantic, the Spaniards established themselves in the *presidios* on the coastline of Algeria and Tunisia, but their attempts were frustrated by the rival encroachments of the Turks.

As a result of increasing anarchy the eastern and central Maghrib became a political mosaic, the extraordinary diversity of which we can glimpse though we cannot achieve accuracy of detail.

In Ifriqiya the successors of the great Abu Faris found consolation for their lack of power in the patronage of men of letters and the practice of the arts. To them is probably due the enlargement of the Great Mosque at Tunis (Jamiʿ al-Zaituna), its entrance and its high-pitched exterior gallery. But the country was given over to the Arab tribes, who broke in repeated waves on the ramparts of Tunis. Though the island of Djerba escaped the control of the nomads, it was only by paying tribute to them that the towns of the Djérid and the ports were able to maintain their independence. Shut up in his capital under the protection of his Christian guard, the Hafsid sultan had to abandon venturing even as far as Djebel Ressas (17 miles to the south-east beyond the plain of the Mornag).

Later the ʿAbd al-Wadids allowed authority over the central Maghrib to slip out of their hands and had difficulty in maintaining themselves in western Algeria. Their kingdom, rent by palace rivalries or given over to the appetites of pretenders and high officials, lay at the mercy of foreign offensives.

Between the Hafsid and 'Abd al-Wadid kingdoms, the territories were parcelled out, determined by the chance of local events, into an infinite number of principalities, autonomous tribes or federations, maraboutic lands and free ports, with undefined frontiers. This process of disintegration may have been encouraged by the influence of the brotherhoods to the west: it undoubtedly was by Arab penetration in the east. The Figuig oases entered into association and formed an independent state. The tribes of the Ouarsenis organised themselves as they wished. Kabylia was subject to the kings of Kouko (a village of the Aït Yahya 5 miles east of Michelet). The Hafsid shaikh of Constantine, protected from interference by the sultan, ruled the region between Bône and Collo. The Zab and the Hodna became the fief of the Dawawida Arabs, and at Touggourt a new dynasty was founded which extended its authority over the oases of the Oued Rhir.

From Djerba to Morocco each of the ports constituted a sort of republic organised for piracy. Tunis, Bizerta, Bougie, Algiers, Oran, Honeïn—each, at its own expense fitted out galleys which scoured the Mediterranean. The corsairs of the fourteenth and fifteenth centuries were not pure robbers, as the Turks were to become, but soldiers in the holy war against the Christians. Their object was not so much the traffic in captives as the imprisonment of unbelievers. Bougie set the price of their redemption so high that it was almost impossible to pay it.

Piracy, even from motives of piety, was no less harmful to the security and trade of Christians, particularly at the end of the fifteenth century, when the Moors driven out of Spain expanded it formidably. At the same time Christian piracy, just as fierce and as keen to recruit oarsmen at the adversary's expense, was on the decline. Even more than the crusading spirit, the need to destroy the corsair's refuges helped to bring about Spanish intervention in the Maghrib.

THE BEGINNINGS OF THE AFRICAN CRUSADE

Braudel's studies[1] have clearly brought out the true [economic] character of the African 'crusade', and the religious motives under-

Turkish Rule in Algeria and Tunisia: 1516-1830

lying it have doubtlessly been exaggerated in their importance. It would obviously be impossible to dispute the religious zeal of Ferdinand the Catholic, or the dominant role of the clergy in organising the first expeditions. But material interests soon came to predominate. The king of Spain subordinated the triumph of the faith to considerations of internal and particularly external policy having nothing in common with it, while Christian soldiers behaved like mercenaries less concerned for the salvation of their souls than for coarse pleasures, loot and slaughter.

The disintegration of the Maghrib encouraged Spanish ambitions. 'The entire country', a particularly well-informed secretary of the Catholic kings wrote in 1594, 'is in such a state of mind that it seems God wills to give it to Their Majesties.' The central Maghrib was the more tempting a prey since the agreements with Portugal forbade Spain to set foot in Morocco elsewhere than at Melilla. Moreover, the occupation of that place in 1497 marked the limit of Spanish activity after the completion of the *reconquista* in 1492. This inaction would probably have continued longer if, as Braudel has shown, the insurrection of Moorish mountaineers in the kingdom of Granada in 1501 had not brought the Muslim peril back into the foreground.[2] Fanatics sought to see the hand of the Maghrib in a situation which, for the most part, represented the rebound of a people driven to extremes by the savage intransigence of Cardinal Ximenes de Cisneros. This powerful man, in a ferment of spiritual passion and temporal ambition, knew how to profit from Catholic enthusiasm. In spite of some resistance he secured agreement to war being carried on to African soil, where the Morisco refugees were kindling hatred against Spain and where it was feared there might be a coalition between the rulers of the Maghrib and the soldan of Egypt. The outset was a triumph. After corsairs from Mers el-Kébir had attacked Alicante, Elche and Malaga in the spring of 1505, the Spaniards went into action. In one and a half months, between 9 September and 23 October 1505, a Spanish armada secured the surrender of Mers el-Kébir, the best anchorage on the Algerian coast. In 1508 Pedro Navarro, who had learnt the corsair's trade by attacking Christian and Barbary vessels impartially, took the Peñon de Velez in the Spanish zone of influence in Morocco. He followed this in 1509 with the capture of Oran, which may have been handed over to him by a traitor, where the Cardinal presided over the massacre of 4,000 of the enemy, the taking of 8,000 prisoners and the consecration to Catholic use of two mosques. Finally, in January 1510, he captured Bougie, which did make a show of resistance; to add to his Maghribi successes he captured Tripoli by assault in July 1510.

A reverse at Djerba in 1511 did not compromise the prestige of the Spanish victories. The ports which were still untouched feared a fate like that of Mers el-Kébir, Oran and Bougie. One after another, Ténès (even before the capture of Oran), Dellys, Cherchel and Mostaganem asked in May 1511 to pay tribute. Algiers ceded to Pedro Navarro one of the small islands barring the entry to its port, and on this he erected the fort of the Peñon whose cannon commanded the town from a distance of little more than 300 yards. Within a few years Spain had made herself mistress of the principal points on the coast at bases on which she could have support for the conquest of the central Maghrib, but such an enterprise was never attempted. It is not even certain that Ximenes, himself, had formulated a plan for it.

THE PRESIDIOS AND LIMITED OCCUPATION

If, notwithstanding her superiority in armaments, Spain abandoned the idea of further conquest, the reason was that the African question was ceasing to be among the foremost of her preoccupations. Ferdinand the Catholic and above all King of Aragon was principally interested in the Pyrenees and Italy. His forceful intervention over a brief period—1509-1510—is to be explained by a lull in Italian affairs. At all times he had to be aware of the precarious state of a treasury which ruled out any but immediately profitable adventures. By the beginning of the sixteenth century African policy was no longer self-contained and is to be understood only if, as Braudel did, we view it in the context of Spanish policy generally.

From the reign of Ferdinand the Catholic the Spaniards were content with the system of limited occupation. They transformed the conquered ports into strongpoints with formidable walls and occupied by garrisons (*presidios*), abandoning even the suburbs to the natives. In Africa they continued the methods of the Granada war, limiting themselves to the tenure of strategic points from which at favourable moments they carried out raids (*jornadas*) in the surrounding countryside.

Throughout the whole course of the Spanish occupation the *presidios* lived in a state of siege. The soldiers led a particularly hard life, being badly fed and irregularly paid. Oran was specially favoured in being supplied by Moorish allies (*los Moros de paz*) and on information furnished by them they raided flocks on seasonal pasture in the neighbourhood. Nonetheless, the place was often in danger of famine. In other places, where reliance had to be placed chiefly on supply by sea, siege fever sometimes had a terrible effect. An official inquiry conducted at Bône in 1540 disclosed that the soldiers 'wished, out of despair, to become Moors'.[3]

'ARUJ THE CORSAIR AT ALGIERS

Unexpected intervention by the Turks not only made the situation of the *presidios* worse but also created a check on Spanish policy in Africa.

It was an initiative originating in Algiers that changed the course of African history. Nothing then seemed to presage a brilliant fortune for the little port used by Berber and Morisco corsairs. Its past was undistinguished. On the ruins of the little Roman port of Icosium, occupied by the Berber Beni Mezranna tribe, the Zirid prince Bologguin, in the second half of the tenth century, had founded the town whose four rocky islets gave it its name of el-Jazair. After being the prey of every conqueror of the central Maghrib, it was occupied in the fourteenth century by the Arab Tha'liba tribe, whose chiefs manœuvred skilfully between 'Abd al-Wadids, Hafsids and Merinids. In the fifteenth century it very nearly became the capital of the Ziyanid kingdom but shook itself free and 'formed a kind of small municipal republic administered by a bourgeois oligarchy and under the protection, by no means disinterested, of the Tha'liba'.[4]

From the tenth to the twelfth century Arab travellers noted the activity of its commerce. No doubt it declined with the disturbances of the following centuries. Nevertheless, in the fourteenth and fifteenth centuries the port was frequented by vessels from Europe and was actively devoted to piracy. The influx of Moriscos expelled from Spain after the fall of Granada in 1492 augmented the population—which in the mid-fifteenth century cannot have exceeded 20,000 inhabitants—by several thousand refugees, whose obstinate resentment found expression in a recrudescence of commerce-raiding. It was in order to ward off these attacks, from which the Spaniards were the chief sufferers, that Pedro Navarro installed the cannon of the Peñon as a permanent threat to the town. But the inhabitants disliked this 'thorn planted in their side' so much that they were driven to beg the aid of the Turkish corsair 'Aruj, who had been established as master of Djidjelli since 1514.

The Barbarossa brothers, whom it is customary to designate collectively by the nickname given to Khair al-Din alone, appear as heroes fashioned by history for the benefit of authors of romanticized biographies. They were four sons of a potter of Mételin (the Lesbos of antiquity)—'Aruj, Khair al-Din, Elias and Ishaq—and from their youth they displayed a remarkable aptitude for piracy. In the course of a surprise attack Elias fell and 'Aruj had to take an oar in the galleys of the Knights of the Order of St. John. We do not know how he was freed nor what his reasons were for leaving the Archipelago with his brothers, and shifting his theatre of action to the western Mediterranean. However, from 1504 to 1510 he acquired a great reputation among the Muslims by attacking Christian vessels, chiefly Spanish, and transporting thousands of Moriscos to Barbary. Thereafter adventurers in quest of booty flocked in their hundreds to place themselves under his command. The Hafsid sultan, with an interest in the profits to be gained, skilfully granted him licence to provision in his ports and the governorship of Gelves Island (Djerba) which became the base of the ten or twelve ships forming his squadron.

An Islam in danger soon sought the aid of these rough champions. In 1512 'Aruj tried to take Bougie at the request of its Hafsid governor, who had been expelled, but he was unable to lead the assault as a cannon ball had torn off his arm. Two years later he failed again. It was then, in 1514, that he fell back on Djidjelli. The favourable situation of this place made it possible to follow the vicissitudes of the conflict between the Kabyle 'sultans' of the Beni 'Abbès and of Kouko. By stepping in at the right moment, and bringing about the victory of the Beni 'Abbès, he acquired reinforcements and valuable intelligence.

The news that Ferdinand the Catholic was dead was then causing

Turkish Rule in Algeria and Tunisia: 1516–1830

a stir in the Spanish-occupied ports of the Maghrib. The Algerians regarded the king's death as dispensing them from their oath of personal obedience to him. But being too weak to liberate themselves they brought pressure to bear on their shaikh, Salim al-Tumi, to appeal to 'Aruj. The corsair at once realised how profitable the venture could be, and, having first occupied Cherchel, held by another Turkish soldier of fortune, made a triumphant entry in Algiers in 1516.

The Algerians were counting on being promptly freed from the Peñon, but the Turkish cannon caused little harm to the fortress, and the population began to complain. A conspiracy to expel the corsairs was quickly planned among Tha'liba, Spaniards and Algerians, but 'Aruj cut it short by having Shaikh Salim, whose restoration it aimed at, strangled and himself proclaimed Sultan by his soldiers. A few rebels were executed or imprisoned, a few promises were made to the notables, and order was restored. If not a liberator, Algiers had at least found itself a master.

For the previous five years the Spaniards had turned away from events in the Maghrib in order to concentrate their efforts in Italy against Louis XII, and accordingly Pedro Navarro had been unable to follow up his exploits. For half a century they had to undertake African expeditions with the object of diminishing the Turkish peril threatening the coastline of the peninsula and their Mediterranean trade, but they experienced little but disappointment. A first attempt on Algiers led by Diego de Vera ended in disaster on 30 September 1516. 'Aruj used the ambiguous attitude of the sultan of Ténès as a pretext for taking possession of Miliana, Médéa and finally Ténès itself. The inhabitants of Tlemcen then asked for his help against their king, who had accepted Spanish suzerainty in 1511. 'Aruj easily expelled him and then installed himself as master in the Méchouar in the place of the pretender he had promised to restore. It is said that seventy Ziyanids were drowned on his orders. The new ruler erected fortresses, made the Beni Snassen submit and entered into negotiations with the Wattasid sultan of Fez, but his triumph was fleeting. In January 1518 a Spanish army, augmented by native elements, cut his communications with Algiers and captured his brother Ishaq, who was murdered by the Arabs in defiance of promises to the contrary. An expeditionary corps set out from Oran and besieged

History of North Africa

him for six months, first in the town and then in the Méchouar. With no more than a handful of Turks left to fight for him, 'Aruj, quite undaunted, managed to get away by night, but the enemy met him near the Rio Salado, and he was murdered with his escort after a fierce resistance.

Although cut off at the age of 44 in the middle of a remarkable career as a soldier of fortune, 'Aruj had nonetheless—as was justly observed by the Benedictine Haëdo, a captive at Algiers from 1577 to 1581—'launched the powerful greatness of Algiers and of Barbary'.[5] With his habitual certainty of vision, he had grasped at once the advantage which an active minority could gain out of the rivalries between the Maghribi principalities, with the intention of building up at their expense a powerful Muslim state safe from Christian attacks. Moreover, he had conquered the Mitidja, the Chélif valley, the Titteri, the Dahra, Ouarsenis and Tlemcen, and had permanently impaired the power of the Ziyanids. His achievement would nevertheless have been doomed to ruin had it not been taken up and in large part brought to a successful conclusion by his brother Khair al-Din.

KHAIR AL-DIN, FOUNDER OF THE ALGIERS REGENCY

The man to whom 'Aruj had entrusted Algiers, and whom the Turks appointed to succeed him, had two outstanding qualities—an indomitable will and a very clear political sense. This man, whom contemporaries nicknamed Redbeard (*Barbarossa, Aenobarbus*), was the real founder of the Algiers Regency, before going on to organize the Ottoman fleet and to become its high admiral.

The disaster suffered by his brother left him in a difficult situation. Inhabitants of Ténès, Cherchel and Algiers, Kabyles of Kouko, supporters of the deposed king of Tlemcen—all tried to escape from the authority of the corsairs. It was then that Khair al-Din, by an inspired decision, linked his destiny with that of the Ottoman Empire. Alone he would have been crushed by the numerical superiority of his opponents, but with the Porte to uphold him, his prestige would be enhanced and he could call on military and financial support which would make large projects possible for him. Accordingly he hastened to swear homage to Sultan Salim, who gave him the title of Pasha and appointed him Amir of Amirs (*Beylerbey*). Of still greater value, Constantinople sent him 2,000 men equipped with artillery, followed by 4,000 volunteers having the privileges of janissaries.

These reinforcements reached him in time to ward off serious dangers—a conspiracy between the Algerians and tribesmen, which he crushed ruthlessly, and in 1519 a fresh Spanish assault led by Hugo de Moncada, which was a lamentable failure. However, he was betrayed in mid-combat by the Kouko contingents which led to his defeat by a Hafsid army in Kabylia, and even forced him to abandon Algiers and withdraw to Djidjelli. There he resumed his adventurous career as a corsair from 1520 to 1525.

However, he had not given up his ambitions. As soon as he had acquired enough wealth to bring his troops up to strength and replenish his treasury, he took Collo, in 1521, Bône, in 1522, and Constantine. Then, with the aid of the sultan of the Beni 'Abbès, he drove the Kouko Kabyles out of Algiers, where they had made themselves unpopular, and in 1525 occupied the Mitidja. The repression of various revolts in Kabylia and the Hodna and at Cherchel, Ténès and Constantine made it clear to the local people that the new master knew no pity.

There remained the fortress of the Peñon, the threat of which still hung over Algiers. Khair al-Din decided on a vigorous attack. After three weeks of bombardment the governor, Martin de Bargas, with only 25 men left out of 150 and with no hope of reinforcements, surrendered the place and was beaten to death. Khair al-Din at once had the outer perimeter of the fortress razed to the ground.

At this time Algiers provided only a mediocre anchorage, sown with reefs and swept by the winds, and the corsairs were forced to haul their vessels up on to the Bab el-Oued beach a mile west of the town. With debris from the Peñon and from the ruins of Rusguniae (Matifou) and Christian captive labour, Khair al-Din constructed a breakwater. It was 220 yards long, over 80 feet wide and some 13 feet high, and it joined the town to its collection of islets by means of a causeway. Thus the port of Algiers was created. Although it was later protected on the south-east by a new breakwater (the Great Mole) it always afforded poor shelter, lying open to the swell when the wind was easterly or north-westerly. But its situation between the Sicilian Channel and the entry to the western Mediterranean made it possible 'to keep watch over and intercept the most direct routes from Gibraltar to the eastern Mediterranean and from southern Spain to southern Italy or Sicily'.[6] Accordingly the Turks made this military port, the excellent position of which outweighed the poorness of its anchorage, the fortified base and refuge of their fleet. Spanish occupation of Bougie and Oran, and suppression of the corsairs there, enabled the Algiers of Khair al-Din to monopolise piracy in the central Maghrib.

THE CONQUEST OF TUNIS

Once master of Algiers, Khair al-Din aimed at securing unhampered control of the eastern coastline. He took advantage of dissensions at the Hafsid court, and discontent among the people against their sultan Mulay Hassan, to attempt a surprise attack on Tunis with the help of the Porte. The Turks were warmly welcomed at Bizerta and then at La Goulette, where they appeared as champions of a pretender. It cost them only a brief battle to enter the capital, on 18 August 1534. After the town had been looted, Barbarossa proclaimed the deposition of the Hafsids and a general amnesty. He stationed a garrison at Kairouan, had no trouble in winning over the coastal towns, and he even secured the assistance of powerful tribes in the southern Constantine region.

The Turks' organisation of piracy at Tunis was, however, a direct threat to the Pope and the Italian princes. It coincided with a renewal of the crusading spirit in Europe and a threat from Persia which diverted the attention of Constantinople towards the east. The king of France, François I, deprived of allies, promised to remain neutral if his enemy Charles V were to attack Barbary. The emperor hesitated over whether to direct his efforts at Algiers or Tunis. Perhaps appeals from the dethroned Sultan Mulay Hassan, and particularly the desire to isolate Algiers from Constantinople, caused him to decide on the Hafsid capital. A fleet of 400 sail, carrying 30,000 men, put in at Carthage unhindered. The Spaniards took La Goulette on 14 July 1535, and six days later Tunis, where the Christian slaves, whom Barbarossa had been unwilling to massacre, had broken their fetters and taken possession of the kasbah.

This victory uplifted the heart of Christendom, but it resolved nothing. Charles V was unwilling to attempt the conquest of

Algeria and Tunisia under the Turks

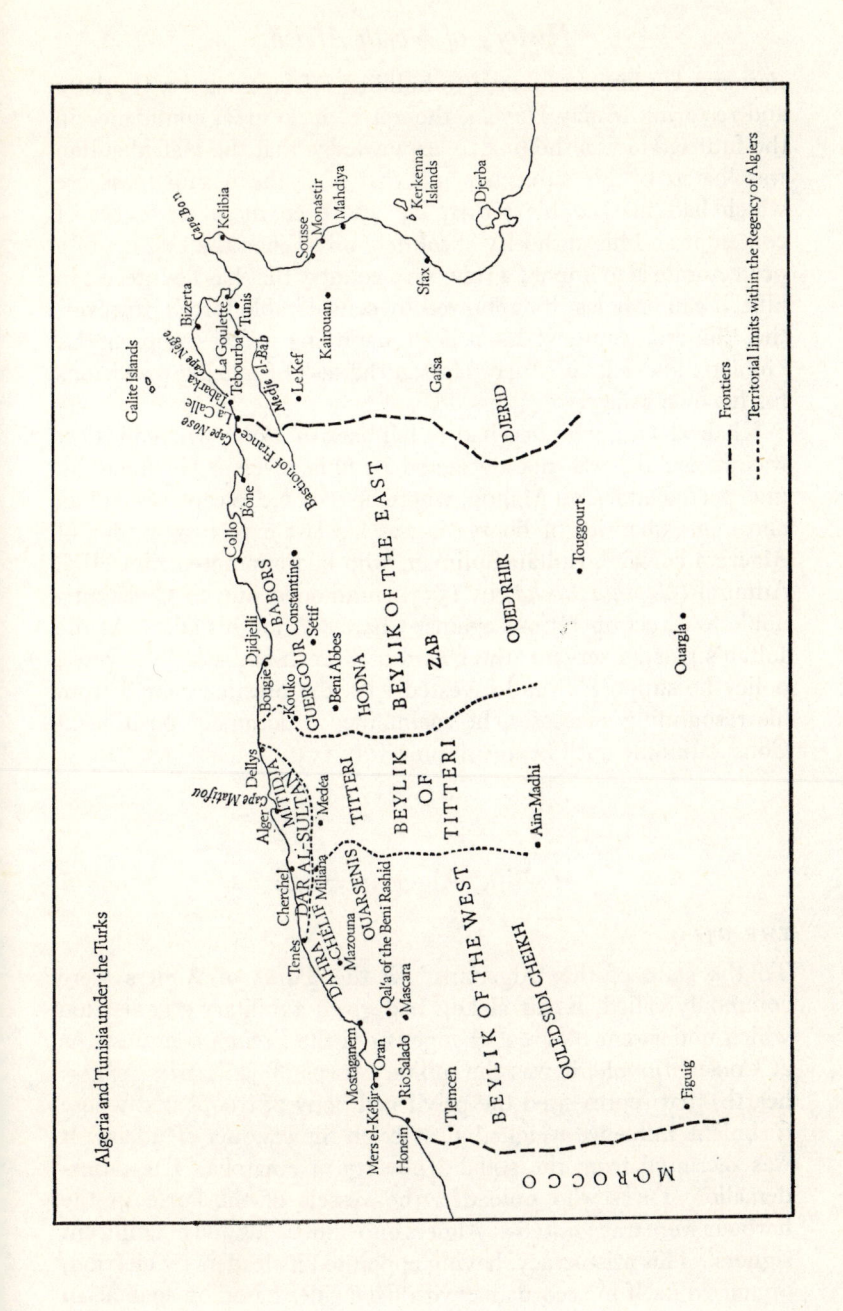

– – – Frontiers
······ Territorial limits within the Regency of Algiers

Barbary. He limited himself to building a fortress at La Goulette and restoring Mulay Hassan, though with no great confidence in the future. He was the first to acknowledge that the Hafsid sultan was 'hated by his subjects', and that after the fearful massacre which had marked his return 'he was even more an object of contempt and his authority absolutely nil'. When the first act of a protectorate is to impose a ruler on a country that has no interest in him, it can only last if supported by considerable force. However, the Emperor confined himself to stationing a few troops at La Goulette and left to Mulay Hassan the task of making provisions for his own safety.

Khair al-Din, who had had to fall back on Bône, where his fleet was at anchor, was not detracted by this reverse. He made an unexpected attack on Mahon, where he took 6,000 captives and an enormous quantity of booty; it was his last exploit as leader of Algerian corsairs. Sultan Suliman, who had appointed him High Admiral (*Captain Pasha*) in 1533, summoned him to Constantinople to direct operations against Charles V and his allies. As the sultan's trusted servant, the friend of French ambassadors whose policy he supported, and invested with the prestige gained from his resounding successes, he maintained a dominant position at Constantinople until his death on 4 July 1546.

11. The Algerian State

THE OJAQ

To the state of the 'Algerians,' as the Turks of Algiers were commonly called, Khair al-Din had given a military organisation which underwent no great changes until the French conquest. As at Constantinople, it was the military corps of janissaries (*ojaq* = hearth) that represented the privileged body of troops and whose turbulent influence weighed heavily on the conduct of affairs. It was recruited from the squalid poverty of Anatolia. The tatterdemalion Turks who unloaded the vessels of the Porte in the harbour were transmuted at Algiers into 'illustrious and magnificent signors'. This aristocracy, having appointed its leaders by election, organised itself in accordance with fixed rules based on egalitarian principles. Thereafter the private janissaries (*yoldash*) secured their promotions by seniority up to the rank of captain-general of the force (*agha*); this they held for two months, and then relinquished to become honorary agha (*mansulagha*). The force was comprised of several companies (*orta*) of varying strength, housed in very well maintained barracks and grouped in barrack-rooms (*oda*) of twelve to twenty men each. The company kept jealous watch over the great bronze cooking pot round which they gathered to eat or talk. In the event of revolt, the janissaries turned the cooking pot upside down and gave their war-cry (*istemeyiz*).

Their uniform comprised the two-cornered cap (*tortora*) in coloured woollen cloth, folded back and falling over the nape of the neck—its creation was associated with the gesture of a Turkish dervish—and topped by a wooden sheath, a gilded horn or a plume of feathers. With this they wore an open jacket with sleeves, and linen breeches held up by a strip of woollen cloth rolled round the waist. During the period of the beylerbeys the ojaq used crossbows and bolts concurrently with firearms, straight one-handed and two-handed swords, curved sabres and daggers.

The janissaries were specially favourably treated. They drew bread, meat and oil, a share in the takings of piracy and a money wage. Also, they enjoyed exemptions from taxation. The government, after carefully establishing the cost price, subjected foodstuffs to a double rate of taxation, one very low for the benefit of the members of the force, and a second, higher one, which allowed a profit to the merchant, payable by other purchasers. The customs of the ojaq governed everything, including punishments. Janissaries were exempt from normal jurisdiction and were responsible to their officers alone. These could inflict imprisonment, bastinado or death. Executions were carried out in secret.

The army consisted solely of infantry; cavalry (*spahis*) were recruited from former aghas or the local people. It was brave and was animated by a strong *esprit de corps*, but brutal and undisciplined. Its council (*divan*), which was responsible for defending its corporate interests, soon ceased to distinguish between these and those of the state. No longer content to nominate certain of its members to the pasha's divan, in which matters of government were debated and justice was administered, it endeavoured on several occasions to seize power. Its attacks were directed not only against the beylerbeys but against their supporters, the rival caste of raïs.

THE TAÏFA OF THE RAÏS

The Barbarossas had formed crews trained to the corsair's occupation which made of Algiers the most formidable pirate port. In the war against the infidel they were charged by Constantinople with holding the western Mediterranean sector. In particular they struck at the hereditary enemy of Maghribi Islam, Spain. To avoid giving themselves away by showing sail, their galliots were propelled by oars alone, the gang of galley-slaves being driven on by the lash of the *comite*. In this way the renegades and Moors who made up the crew could land unexpectedly on the eastern coasts of Spain, sacking villages and carrying off the inhabitants into captivity. Neither the building of watch-towers (*atalayas*) nor the formation of syndicates of defence managed to defeat the corsairs' cunning. The emperor, overwhelmed with complaints and petitions, provided more by way of encouragement than of effectual help. Accordingly the shore-dwellers began to desert the inhospitable *tierras maritimas*.

The pirates, treated the coasts of Sardinia, Sicily and Naples with no more respect; they threatened communications by sea between the imperial domains of Spain and Italy, boarding vessels, capturing their crews and carrying off their cargoes. French and Algerians in concert endeavoured to secure command of the western Mediterranean to the detriment of Spanish imperialism. But for the unexpected aid afforded to Charles V when the Genoese squadron of Andrea Doria joined him, the alliance of the very Christian king and the Muslim corsairs might perhaps have attained its end. At least this piratical activity damaged the development of the eastern ports of Spain and enriched Algiers at the expense of their trade. Thus holy war tended to evolve into a war of plunder.

The Christians were unable to organise against it. 'Navigating', says Haëdo, 'during winter and spring they (the corsairs) scour the sea from sunrise to sunset, making a mock of our galleys whose crews meanwhile divert themselves with feasting in port. In the knowledge that when their galliots, so well tallowed and so light, meet with Christian galleys, so heavy and so laden, the latter

Turkish Rule in Algeria and Tunisia: 1516–1830

cannot think of giving chase or of preventing them from looting and robbing to their hearts' content, their custom is to mock them by turning about and showing them their sterns.'[7] The superiority of the Algerians was due not only to the carefully thought out adaptation of galleys and brigantines to piratical warfare, but also to the training and the merciless discipline of the oarsmen. 'They have such care for the order, cleanliness and fitting out of their vessels,' the aged Benedictine also acknowledges, 'that they think of nothing else, making a point above all of good trim, in order to be able to run and tack well. ... Finally, for the same reason, no one, be he the pasha's own son himself, is allowed to change position or to budge from the spot where he is.'[8]

The corporation of corsair captains (*taïfa* of the *raïs*), companions of the Barbarossas, the Dragut and the Sinān, included only a minority of Turks or local people. For the most part its members were renegades from the poverty-stricken provinces of the Mediterranean who followed piracy as their brothers of Calabria, Sicily or Corsica did banditry. Taken captive by Algerian galliots, they had been quick to see that, in return for apostasizing, the society of the corsairs offered solid advantages over that of the land of their birth, and they became what Haëdo calls 'Turks by profession'. To the taïfa they contributed accurate intelligence concerning 'Christian lands and shores' which they knew well;[9] for themselves they were concerned less with holy war than with lucrative prizes. Nevertheless, in the time of the beylerbeys their leaders' authority secured respect for the orders of the Sultan, and they distinguished themselves in combats between the Ottoman fleet and the infidel. In 1558 the raïs had at their disposal 35 galleys, 25 brigantines or frigates and numerous lighter commerce-destroying craft.[10]

At Algiers the corsairs were held in high esteem. 'On their return', wrote Haëdo, 'all Algiers is pleased, for the merchants buy the slaves and merchandise they bring back and the tradesmen sell to those newly come ashore all the clothing and victuals they have in stock; there is nothing but eating, drinking and rejoicing.'[11]

The janissaries were jealous of the corsairs, who in return were contemptuous of the 'Anatolian oxen' and supported the beylerbeys in resisting their demands. But the raïs had to come to terms with the ojaq and in 1568 to admit its members to their crews.

This new recruiting, notwithstanding the efforts of the raïs to keep it within bounds, contributed to the decline of privateering.

ALGIERS UNDER THE CORSAIRS

As a city of pirates, Algiers had to be armed for attack and fortified against reprisals by enemy fleets. It was at the same time an arsenal and a port of refuge. From the time of the first beylerbeys it took on the aspect of a fortress bristling with defences against attacks by sea. These fortifications were augmented considerably after the expedition of Charles V in 1541, and before the attack by Don John of Austria on Tunis in 1573. The seaport of the island was protected by a parapet, and two towers were built on the site of the former Peñon and at the pierhead of the Great Breakwater. A little above the former Berber Kasbah, 'Aruj built a new kasbah which was finished only in 1590. The wall surrounding the town was reconstructed by Khair al-Din and his successors. We know from Haëdo, who likens it to a crossbow with the sea-front forming the string, that its walls—some 36 to 42 feet high and some one and a half miles in length—were constructed of unbaked brick bonded with good mortar and resting on a substructure of concrete. Even the sea-front, thicker and higher though it was, was not solid enough to withstand every conceivable assault. The wall had accordingly been protected by a moat some 20 to 26 feet deep and 37 to 48 feet across, and had been reinforced by square towers and slightly projecting bastions. Two more important works protected Khair al-Din's breakwater and the Fishery Arsenal. The parapet was crenellated and pierced with embrasures for muskets and cannon.

Access to the town was by five main gates. The New Gate was to the south-west and at the foot of the kasbah, and Bab Azoun was to the south, the most important since people came in by it from the countryside and it was linked by a long mercantile street with the Bab al-Oued to the north. The 'Island' or 'Holy War' gate (*Bāb al-Jazīra* or *Bāb al-Jihād*), through which the raïs passed, opened on to the mole, and finally the 'Fish', 'Fishery' or 'Customs' Gate, opened on to the road leading up from the harbour.

Outside the wall several forts supplemented the seafront fortifications. The 'Eulj 'Ali *burj*, built in 1568–1569 and known as the 'fort of the twenty-four hours', guarded the Bab al-Oued beach. On the landward side the approaches to the town were

Turkish Rule in Algeria and Tunisia: 1516–1830

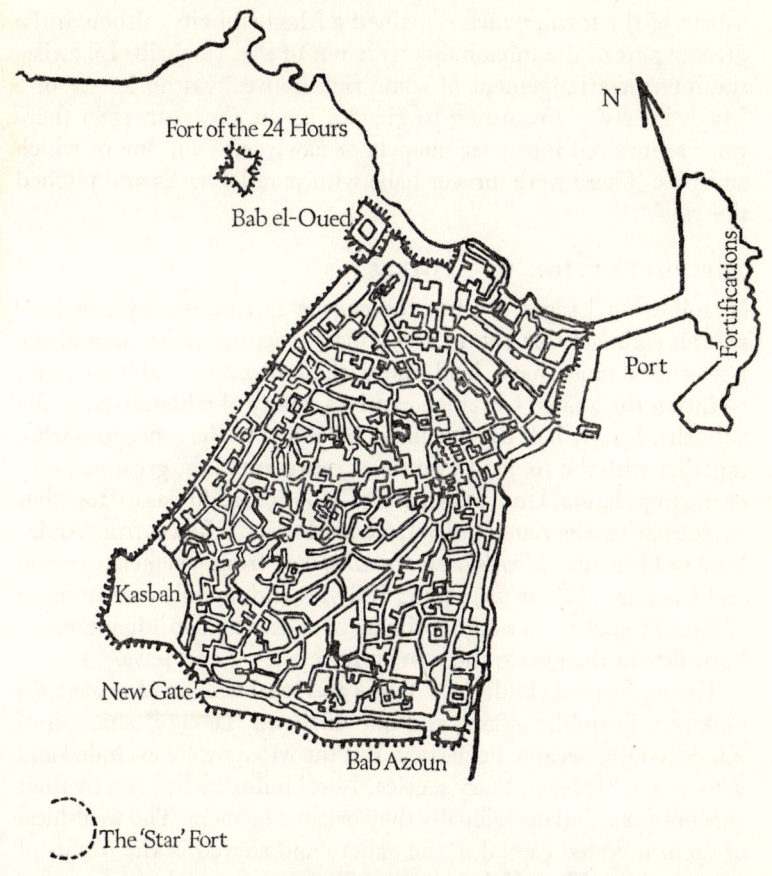

9 Algiers under the Turks

defended by the fort known as the 'Star', built above the kasbah in 1568, and the Emperor Fort (Sultan Kalassi) built facing south between 1545 and 1580 on the site of the camp of Charles V.

In the confined space enclosed within the walls white houses were grouped closely together with terraces rising in tiers, their overhangs supported on beams jutting so far out over the narrow streets as sometimes to join those across the way, thus forming a ceiling of corduroy or of groined vaulting. It was not until the end of the fifteenth century that the raïs built their costly dwellings in the lower town. These new constructions modified the outward aspect of the town, which remained a Maghribi city, although the greater part of the inhabitants were not of the Maghrib. Likewise, the interior arrangement of some rich houses was no longer of a Maghribi style. According to Haëdo, about the year 1580 there were a hundred mosques, chapels or zawiyas,[12] not one of which survives. There were 'prayer halls with parallel naves and pitched tile roofs'.[13]

THE POPULATION OF ALGIERS

If, following Lespès, we use the census carried out by Haëdo,[14] we can estimate that the 12,200 houses existing in the time of the beylerbeys must have held more than 60,000 inhabitants, not counting the 25,000 Christian captives, many of whom lived in the suburbs. Nearly half the dwellings belonged to the renegades who, together with the 10,000 Levantines, represented the great majority of the population. Under the name of Moors, Haëdo classed together 12,500 native Algerians (*Baldis*); 6,000 Morisco refugees from Andalusia or Granada (*Moudejares, Andalous*) or from Valencia, Aragon and Catalonia (*Tagarins*); 3,500 Kabyles and an unknown number of Arabs (3,000?)—a rough estimate of at least 25,000 inhabitants.[15] Crowded in the ghetto there must have been 5,000 Jews.

The half-breed children of Turks and local women (*Kouloughlis*) took part in public affairs, and one of these, Hassan Pasha, son of Khair al-Din, became beylerbey. But the Moors were excluded and were not liable for military service. Local industry was run by their corporations, and occasionally they became farmers. The wealthiest of them invested capital in the galleys and shared in the profits of privateering. The Kabyles, unskilled or day labourers, were firmly controlled. The Mzabites had the monopoly of the public baths, butchers' shops and the town mills. They also engaged in the caravan traffic and the sale of black slaves. The Biskris were water-carriers, scavengers, policemen and, particularly, porters. They lived in straw *gourbis* in the Bab Azoun suburb or slept in the open. The mixed quarter of the ghetto comprised a small number of Jews of African origin much like the native poor, together with numerous émigrés. Some of these, the *Chekliines* had come from the Balearics at the end of the twelfth century; others, the *Kiboussiines*, from Spain came a century later, and particularly after 1492. The Kiboussiines of 1391, under the powerful control

Turkish Rule in Algeria and Tunisia: 1516–1830

of their rabbis, represented an intellectual and commercial aristocracy. They were 'the true founders of Algerian Judaism'. Khair al-Din authorised the permanent settlement of the Jews in the Regency, though he placed a limit on the number of their places of business. However, they quickly gained an influential position in business, notably in the clearance of booty goods not locally consumed, and they were the target of insults from the other inhabitants, were required to wear special dress and were subject to a poll tax.

Europeans were represented by a few merchants and a large number of captives. Algiers attached no great importance to trade, however, Mediterranean businessmen, chiefly Marseillais, had begun setting up establishments there before 1550. The king of France, who was intent on keeping a check on his subjects, availed himself of his good standing with the beylerbeys to install a consul at Algiers from 1564. But it called for all the Porte's authority to master the resistance of the Algerians, which was not finally overcome until 1580. Five years later the English had their representative, though without the prerogatives of a consul. Algiers also contained a large population of captives; there were some 25,000 of them in Haëdo's time, when the raïs used to flood the Badestan market with them in their hundreds.[16]

The diversity of language was almost as great as the diversity of race. Turkish was the official language, as also that of the military and naval aristocracy, since all the renegades learned it eventually. Arabic dialect kept an important place; not only was it spoken by the old townsmen, the *Baldis*, and the émigrés from Spain, but it was also the only tongue understood by the tribes in the surrounding country. Haëdo does not mention Berber, but since he notes the presence of numerous Kabyles settled in Algiers with their families,[17] there is good ground for asserting that the Kabyle and Mzabite dialects were spoken at least in certain quarters of the town and inside houses. Finally the slaves, some European merchants and newly-arrived renegades used as a *lingua franca* a language designed for practical communication and made up of Arabic, Spanish, Turkish, Italian and Provençal words. A few Portuguese words were added after the Battle of the Three Kings, for there was then a sudden influx into Algiers of Portuguese sold into slavery by al-Mansur.

Living in Algiers seems to have been fairly easy in the time of the beylerbeys, since provisions were abundant and cheap. Occasionally, however, famine and plague created havoc. Haëdo declares that in one month (17 January–17 February 1580), 5,656 Moors or Arabs died of hunger in the streets of the town and that a severe epidemic wiped out one-third of the population in two years (1572–1574).[18] A strong and steady flow of immigrants was needed to fill gaps like these.

THE GOVERNMENT OF THE BEYLERBEYS

The beylerbeys, appointed by the sultan, governed the Regency either by direct rule or through their lieutenants (*khalīfas*) as intermediaries. They were not bound by the advice of the divan, and they wielded their suzerainty over the pashas of Tunis and Tripoli, acting as veritable 'kings of Algiers', which is what Haëdo calls them.[19] Their loyalty to the Porte was not questioned and they carried out, though sometimes under protest, the orders of the Grand Turk. It was pressure from Constantinople that in about 1560 brought them, despite the hostility of the Algerians, to grant the monopoly of coral fishing between Cap Roux and Bougie to Thomas Leche, a Corsican who had settled at Marseilles; this was the origin of the 'Africa Concessions'. They also granted him the right to found an unfortified establishment at the Bastion of France, 6½ miles west of La Calle.

At Algiers the beylerbeys lived in the 'Little Garden' (*Jenina*) which was situated in the middle of a vast complex of buildings (*Dār al-Sultān*). 'It included two courtyards; the second, smaller than the first, was adorned with a square basin and a large fountain. A large wooden staircase filled one corner which opened on to a long gallery paved with faience and flanked with marble columns. A jet of water rose from the centre of the paved floor above an octagonal basin. At the far end the pasha was enthroned on a low seat.'[20]

The pashas were not content to enrich their capital city by privateering, but they also exploited Algeria as a whole as their conquest proceeded. Their progress was facilitated not only by the prevailing anarchy, but also because they shared a common religion with local people; probably, too, the influence of the brotherhoods played its part. Of greater importance, they did not confine

Turkish Rule in Algeria and Tunisia: 1516–1830

themselves to occupying the coastline, but stationed permanent garrisons (*munas*) in towns occupying strategic positions. Their whole organisation was aimed at extracting revenue from the natives, from whom—with the support of the makhzan tribes created in 1563—they collected taxes by dispatching expeditionary columns (*mahallas*) which pillaged the countryside. Any gold not paid over to the sultan in order to ensure his favour went to swell the pasha's treasury.

The beylerbeys soon came to realise that their authority stood in greatest danger not from their subjects, but from the janissaries. Accordingly they endeavoured to form an equally valiant but more reliable army from Kabyle, principally Zwawa, contingents. They may even have aspired to establishing a maritime empire, a project which would have necessitated the assistance of all the Regency's forces. They were prevented from putting their plans into effect by the mistrust of the Porte, which feared that the army might constitute a potential independent and rival state. Nevertheless the influence of the Turks, whom contact with Europeans had accustomed to political ideas quite unknown to the Maghribi dynasties, had important consequences for the shaping of the states of Barbary. By substituting the concept of the defined frontier for that of border regions, which had been found sufficient until they arrived, they were chiefly responsible for the distinction which came into force in the sixteenth century between Algeria and Tunisia (the very names date only from the July Monarchy) and Morocco. The beylerbeys were in simultaneous conflict with the Moroccan sharifs, whose power caused them anxiety, and with the Spaniards, who kept their hold on the *presidios* and endeavoured to gain support for their influence from the vassal states of Tlemcen and Tunis both of which were hostile to the Turks.

III. The Beylerbeys and the end of the Ziyanid and Hafsid Kingdoms

THE CONFLICT OF THE BEYLERBEYS WITH THE SPANIARDS AND SHARIFS (1536–1568)

On leaving for Constantinople, Khair al-Din entrusted power to his khalifa Hassan Agha (1536–1543), whose governorship was marked by the attempt of Charles V to take Algiers in 1541. The emperor, freshly assured of the French king's neutrality, intended to strike a decisive blow at the strongholds of the raïs. In order to avoid attack by the Ottoman fleet, he deferred until the autumn, 23 October, the arrival of his armada of 516 sail, carrying 12,330 sailors and 24,000 soldiers. The landing took place at the mouth of the Harrach, and the army succeeded in gaining the heights dominating the town, but, battered by storms and torrential rains, it became disorganised and was routed by the enemy. After a retreat lasting three days which was covered by the Knights of Malta, the fugitives managed to rejoin the fleet at Cap Matifou, a storm having meanwhile destroyed 140 ships. On the advice of his admiral, Charles V abandoned the idea of attempting a fresh attack and on 3 November embarked the broken remnants of his troops. The Algerians gained enormous booty and a reputation for invincibility, though it was to the weather that the victory was in fact due.

One effect of the Turks' success was to win over to their side the king of Tlemcen, Mulay Muhammad, who denounced Spanish sovereignty and surrendered the Méchouar to the Turks. This was an excellent occasion for Christian intervention. At once the Count of Alcaudète, governor of Oran, sponsored the candidature of a young brother of the king, 'Abd Allah, and, at the head of an expeditionary column, installed him in Tlemcen on 6 February 1543. But a month had not passed before he abandoned the town and with difficulty made his way back to his base, while the people of Tlemcen recalled their former ruler. The tactic of raids into the interior which were not followed by permanent settlement was proving a serious failure.

After some months spent somewhat in disgrace, due perhaps to his lack of firmness during the siege of Algiers, Hassan Agha was replaced by Khair al-Din's son, Hassan Pasha (1544–1552), whose efforts were directed primarily to the western part of the Regency. In 1547, in order to bring aid to the strongpoint of Mostaganem, besieged by the Count of Alcaudète, the janissaries had to abandon Tlemcen, the king of which became once more a client of Spain. It was then, in 1551, that the new sharif, Muhammad al-Mahdi, conqueror of the Wattasids, took advantage of Turkish inactivity to occupy the Ziyanid capital, some of whose inhabitants

Turkish Rule in Algeria and Tunisia: 1516-1830

assisted him with intelligence information. But his son, emboldened by this first success, took possession of Mostaganem and ascended the valley of the Chélif. The Spaniards, paralysed by their difficulties in Europe, made no move. Hassan Pasha on the other hand, having become beylerbey on the death of his father in 1546, reacted vigorously. A Turkish army, commanded by the renegade Hassan Corso and supported by tribes from the west in revolt against Moroccan rule, recaptured Mostaganem, crushed the Sharifian army and pursued it as far as the Moulouya, before re-entering Tlemcen. Hassan Corso took care not to restore a vassal Ziyanid king; instead he installed a permanent Turkish governor and garrison. This permanent occupation of the great city of the west marked the end of Spanish encroachments on the Oran hinterland. Those inhabitants of Tlemcen who refused to accept an amnesty had their possessions confiscated. The proceeds enabled the victorious general to offer a magnificent installation present to the new beylerbey, Salah Raïs, who, due to the support of the French ambassador at Constantinople, replaced Hassan Pasha.

Salah Raïs had distinguished himself at the side of the Barbarossas and had commanded the Ottoman fleet. He was a rough, bold leader, whose time was spent in warfare. He compelled the *qaids* of Touggourt and Ouargla to pay tribute. In Kabylia he was unable to subdue the Beni 'Abbès, who had rebelled after helping him to conquer the south, but during the Moroccan campaign he persuaded their opponents from Kouko to join him, and these formed his cavalry. The candidature of the Wattasid Bu Hassun afforded him the pretext he sought for intervention against the Sharif, whom he routed at Taza in December 1553. His attempt to hold Fez in the sultan's name was unsuccessful, since the inhabitants forced him to proclaim Bu Hassun as ruler. He was, however, able to capture two places on behalf of the Turks. The first was the fortress of Peñon de Velez, in 1554, from which over the years 1558–1652 the daring Yahya Raïs spread destruction along the coasts of the peninsula, taking more than 4,000 captives. The second, in 1555, was the strongpoint of Bougie, to which the viceroy of Naples failed to send assistance. Philip II of Spain, threatened with bankruptcy and unable to mount an expedition, appeased the wrath of his subjects by treating the unfortunate governor of Bougie as a scapegoat and having him executed. It was no fault of his that in 1556 Oran failed to surrender in its turn. The death of Salah Raïs, and the recall of the Algerian galleys for the defence of the Bosphorus, followed by the retreat of Hassan Corso, may well have been what saved this important western *presidio*, to which no reinforcements whatever had been sent.

The sudden disappearance of Salah Raïs set the army and the taïfa against each other. The beylerbey Tekelerli, nominated by the Porte, found himself forbidden by the janissaries to enter Algiers; they demanded the appointment of Hassan Corso. Conspiracy by the raïs, however, enabled Tekelerli to enter the town and to capture Hassan Corso, who took three days to die hanging from the impaling hooks of the Bab Azoun gate. The pasha himself was assassinated shortly afterwards by the ojaq.

The disorders in the Regency led the sultan in June 1557 to decide on a fresh appeal to the prestige of Hassan ibn Khair al-Din. The situation had deteriorated in the west, where the Sharifian army was in possession of Tlemcen and was besieging the small Turkish garrison in the Méchouar. Muhammad al-Mahdi's assassination by Turkish deserters, followed by disturbances over the succession, made it possible for the beylerbey to invade Morocco, but the threat of a Spanish attack from the rear forced him to withdraw to the sea without having entered Fez. It may have been this hurried retreat that encouraged the Count of Alcaudète. The fall of the vassal kingdom of Tlemcen had ruined his hopes of keeping the Turks out of the Oran plateaux. He now hoped the capture of Mostaganem would do away with their fleet's principal port of call. He had failed twice already, in 1541 and 1547, and his third expedition also ended in disaster. In August 1558 his inexperienced troops were surprised and surrounded; the governor died, and 10,000 of his soldiers were killed or led into captivity. Spanish prestige did not recover from this blow, and thereafter the Spaniards remained blockaded in the strongpoints of Oran and Mers el-Kébir.

In June 1561 Hassan Pasha was preparing for hostilities against the Sharif when the ojaq, infuriated at the levies he was raising in Kabylia, sent him back to Constantinople in chains, on a charge of aspiring to independence. The governorship was held for a short while by a pasha who had the most deeply compromised of the

Turkish Rule in Algeria and Tunisia: 1516–1830

mutineers executed. The Porte then restored Hassan Pasha to his post as beylerbey in 1562. He at once took up his plans and laid siege to Oran and Mers el-Kébir, but Spanish resistance allowed time for Doria's fleet to bring help, and the Turks had to return to Algiers having suffered heavy losses. The campaign lasted from 3 April to 7 June 1563. Hassan was organising his revenge when the sultan recalled him from Algiers, first to take part in the siege of Malta in 1565, and then, early in 1567, to take command of the Ottoman fleet with the title of *Captain Pasha*. He left the Regency to Muhammad ibn Salah Raïs, who occupied himself with repairing the ruin which plague, famine and brigandage had brought on Algiers. It was he who, in order to pacify the rivalry between the militia and raïs, authorised the janissaries to join the crews of the galleys. He had just re-established Turkish authority at Constantine when in March 1568 he was appointed to another pashalik and replaced as beylerbey by 'Eulj 'Ali.

'EULJ 'ALI AND THE END OF THE HAFSID KINGDOM

The last beylerbey, 'Eulj 'Ali (1568–1587), was possibly, with Khair al-Din, the greatest figure of Turkish rule. He had been taken captive in youth on the Calabrian coast and rejected as a galley-slave because of a disease of the scalp. He accepted conversion to Islam only, it is said, in order to avenge himself on a Turk who had struck him. He quickly became a galley officer (*comite*), went privateering on his own account and gained distinction, particularly at Malta under the command of Hassan ibn Khair al-Din and Dragut. The Christians attributed his melancholia less to his disease than to his having abjured his faith. The ambassador of France, who saw much of him at Constantinople, declared that he was in secret a practising Christian, and the janissaries of Algiers doubted the firmness of his Muslim convictions. Nevertheless, advances made to 'Eulj 'Ali by Philip II at the Pope's instigation were badly received.

The new beylerbey knew his Regency well, having been governor of Tlemcen and having conducted the struggle against the Spaniards. His first concern was to lend support to the Morisco revolts against Catholic persecution in Granada, but he found it difficult to supply men and munitions to the rebels, and they were crushed. He was more fortunate in his efforts at ridding Tunis of the Spanish protectorate and at doing away with the Hafsid dynasty.

After the departure of Charles V, the kingdom of Tunis had relapsed into anarchy. The Hafsid king, Mulay Hassan, reduced to fighting his own people who did not support him, and his son who was trying to supplant him, was able to keep his throne only with Spanish support. Intervention by Doria was necessary in 1540 in order to secure Kélibia, Sousse, Sfax and Monastir for him. But southern Tunisia was lost to Mulay Hassan and in the course of a campaign in 1542 against Kairouan, which had become the capital of the religious principality of the Chabbiyah Arabs, he was deserted by his troops. He then resigned himself to going to Europe to beg for reinforcements. Despite these, he was defeated, captured and blinded by his son Mulay Hamida (Ahmad Sultan). After reconquering Tunis from a Hafsid pretender who was supported by the Christians, Hamida manœuvred between the Spaniards and Turks. In the archives of Simancas, Braudel has noted several treaties with the governor of La Goulette signed by Hamida.[21] Also, Monchicourt has drawn attention to the offer the Porte made him in 1552 to take La Goulette and Mahdiya on his behalf and to 'furnish him', as Sinan Pasha wrote to him, 'the troops necessary for the recovery of such of his lands as are in a state of rebellion'.[22]

It was then that the raïs Dragut, whose cunning recalls for Monchicourt the 'subtle and crafty Ulysses'[23] (have we not seen Victor Bérard making his commentary on the *Odyssey* with the help of corsairs' narratives?), re-enacted Barbarossa's adventures on the coasts of eastern Barbary. But having made Mahdiya the headquarters from which he ravaged the Italian coastline, he was unable to prevent the Spaniards from taking it from him in September 1550, and he failed in his attempt on Gafsa. It was only by means of a daring strategy that in April 1551 he escaped from Doria's galleys, which were blockading him in the Djerba channel. Once he had 'failed to realise his dream of creating for himself a principality in the Little Syrtis . . . the only course left open to the corsair chief was to renounce an independence that was proving too perilous, and to place himself under the aegis of the Sublime Porte'.[24] For nearly five years after that, from June 1551 to April 1556, the sultan directed his field of action away from the shores of Africa. Having been kept out of the post of Captain Pasha by the

Turkish Rule in Algeria and Tunisia: 1516-1830

animosity of the grand vizier Rustum, he did, however, succeed in securing the governorship of Tripoli from Sultan Suliman. Thus restored to his African career until his death in Malta in 1565, he fought the independent shaikhs of Djerba and the Tripolitanian hinterland. He entered Gafsa in triumph on 20 December 1556, drove the Chabbiya out of central Tunisia and occupied Kairouan. In less than two years, Dragut, the man of the Syrtis, had 'become a Mediterranean power'.[25]

Spain, at the critical point of her struggle with France, did not take steps to halt Dragut's progress any more than did the Algerians, but in 1559 the treaty of Cateau-Cambrésis, which marked a turning point in European history, set her free from her immediate anxieties. Her African policy then underwent a change. The Turkish danger brought Tunisia into the foreground, and Tunisia, as Braudel has observed, constituted—with Malta, Sicily and Naples—the Spanish frontier separating the western Mediterranean dominated by the Catholic king from the eastern in the power of the Sultan. The combats over points in Barbary, before Mers el-Kébir in 1563, or Peñon de Velez in 1564, were no more than incidental in character. Philip II was still very interested in La Goulette. But having gone bankrupt as recently as 1557, Spain could not afford ambitious plans.

It was perhaps to please the Pope, who was subsidising him, that in 1559 the Catholic king allowed the knights of Malta and the viceroy of Naples to organise the Djerba expedition against Dragut. Like the armada of Charles V, the fleet of the Duke of Medina Cœli waited until autumn to set sail, when the Turkish galleys were detained at Gallipoli. The admiral occupied the island with ease, but delayed far too long in organising it as a base of operations against Tripoli. As he left his moorings on 15 March 1560, he was attacked by the squadron of Piali Pasha and Dragut; 30 of his ships were sunk and 5,000 of his men imprisoned. The small Christian garrison of Djerba was annihilated after a savage defence, the bones being piled in a pyramid—the 'tower of skulls' (*burj al-rus*), which remained until 1846.

The Catholic king and the Sultan pursued their rivalry on the frontier between the two Mediterranean basins. The Turkish siege of Malta in 1565 may well have been a reply to that of Djerba; certainly the African raïs Dragut and 'Eulj 'Ali played a very large part in it. Finally the beylerbey of Algiers renewed the tradition of Khair al-Din by making war on Tunis in 1569. On his march eastwards he was easily able to repulse the weak Hafsid contingents and to expel Hamida from Tunis, who took refuge with the Spaniards. Having installed the *qaid* Ramdan as governor of Tunis, he returned to Algiers, where he occupied himself in reorganising the Barbary fleet. He was fitting out an expedition against La Goulette when he had to answer a summons from the sultan.

The Ottoman Empire was at that time faced with grave dangers. The upsurge of Catholic fanaticism caused by the new war in Granada in 1569–1570, together with the activity of Pius V, facilitated agreement between Spain, the Papacy and Venice on a league against the Turks. The Catholic king did not succeed in directing the attack towards Africa and exhausted his forces in adventures in the east. The battle of Lepanto, 9 October 1571, however, at which 'Eulj 'Ali performed prodigies of valour and gained the title of Captain Pasha, marked the victory of the coalition. As soon as the defection of Venice had brought about the dissolution of the league in 1573, Spain once more took up her plans against Tunis. In the same year Philip's brother, Don John of Austria, surprised the town and almost without a blow gained possession of it. He suggested that it be governed in the name of the Catholic king with the co-operation of the natives, who would retain their own laws. He may have dreamed of putting his own principles into practice, or rather to obtain a title for himself, but he had to be content with leaving a garrison in the town and he returned to Italy after installing a new Hafsid prince.

The Ottoman Empire could not remain inactive under the two blows of Lepanto and Tunis. In the following year, 1574, the combined forces of the Regency, Tripoli and the east, under Sinan Pasha and 'Eulj 'Ali, took La Goulette and Tunis one after another. This double victory delivered Tunisia, which became a pashalik, into the hands of the Turks, and signalled the end of Spanish influence. Ruined by another bankruptcy in 1575, paralysed by rebellion in the Low Countries and unrest in Italy, and disturbed by English and French intrigues, Philip II gave up the idea of revenge in Africa and in 1581 resigned himself to a truce with the sultan. Spain retained the unfortunate *presidios* of Melilla, Mers el-Kébir and Oran, to which the Portuguese inheritance was to

Turkish Rule in Algeria and Tunisia: 1516–1830

make a meagre addition. But as a result of the fighting, the Maghrib, though it had remained essentially itself, had taken on its modern appearance, with the three political blocs of Morocco, Algeria and Tunisia.

THE END OF THE BEYLERBEYS

After taking command of the Ottoman fleet on the day following Lepanto, 'Eulj 'Ali had entrusted the government of the Regency to khalifas. These were: 'Arab Ahmad, who assisted at the capture of La Goulette and Tunis; the *qaid* Ramdan (1574–1577), who in March 1576 succeeded in installing the pretender 'Abd al-Malik at Fez and in bringing back 500,000 ounces of gold and ten cannons by way of payment; and the pasha Hassan Veneziano (1577–1580). The last-named was a ship's writer of a Venetian merchant vessel captured by Dragut. After being sold to 'Eulj 'Ali, he had turned renegade and had made himself notorious—if we are to believe the portrait drawn by Cervantes, who was his slave—by his imperious pride and cruelty, as well as by his energy and gallantry. He governed by terror and brought both janissaries and raïs under control. But famine and plague, in addition to his exactions, eventually provoked the local people to revolt, and the aged eunuch Ja'far (1580–1582) was charged with restoring tranquillity. During Ja'far's stay at Algiers 'Eulj 'Ali went there to prepare for the conquest of Morocco from al-Mansur, but he was recalled, as was his khalifa, before he had been able to put his plan into execution, and he reappointed Ramdan as pasha of Algiers.

Ramdan was called on by the Porte to make restitution of two galleys to France in spite of the opposition of the Algerians. The taïfa took advantage of their discontent to bestow power on its leader Mami Arnaute. The triumph of the raïs was confirmed by the sudden arrival of Hassan Veneziano, who established himself as master in the Jenina from 1582 to 1588. From that time everything was subordinated to the development of privateering, which raged unchecked on the coasts of Spain and Italy and as far as the Canaries.

When 'Eulj 'Ali died at an advanced age in 1587, the sultan judged the moment opportune to bring the African conquests within the normal framework of Ottoman organisation, and he transformed Tripolitania, Tunisia and Algeria into three regencies administered by pashas subject to periodic replacement. These measures involved the abolition of the beylerbey of Algiers, and accordingly the Porte recalled Hassan Veneziano, appointed him Captain Pasha and replaced him by a pasha on a three-year posting. The Barbary provinces ceased to be a bastion of the Turkish Empire against the Spanish Empire: they became ordinary provinces, only more remote.

IV. The Golden Age of Algerian and Tunisian Piracy

THE ALGERIAN REVOLUTIONS OF THE SEVENTEENTH CENTURY

In the course of the seventeenth century the regencies of Algiers and Tunis broke loose from the authority of the Porte. Those powerful organisations, the ojaq and the taïfa, refused to take orders from transitory officials having no support in the province they were supposed to govern in the sultan's name. The point was reached at which the pashas ceased to exercise any check on janissaries and raïs except to make their own fortune when time permitted. Left to their own impulses, the factions, prompted by interest or hatred, quarrelled bitterly over public affairs. Out of the conflicts which kept the two Regencies in turmoil there emerged two new authorities. At Algiers there was that of the aghas of the army, in 1659, followed by that of the deys in 1671; at Tunis that of the deys, in 1590, followed by that of the beys in 1705. The autonomy of the African pashaliks left them free to develop piracy regardless of the politically motivated caution imposed by the Porte on the beylerbeys. Two consequences followed; the corsairs' activities provoked reprisals by European states, and rivalries between the two Regencies found expression in armed conflict.

Nothing could be more tedious than the domestic history of the Regencies in the seventeenth century. At Algiers there were continual plots, riots, and massacres, and the pasha had to be content with acting as a figurehead. Received with great pomp on arrival from Constantinople, lodged in a palace and heaped with honours, he was obliged, in order to keep his place and his head, to ratify the decisions of the janissaries' divan. This body held four meetings a week, one of them at the palace to deal with foreign

Turkish Rule in Algeria and Tunisia: 1516–1830

affairs, and in the last resort it made decisions by acclamation on questions of peace and war. The pasha had to preface official documents with the formula 'We, Pasha and Divan of the Invincible Army of Algiers.' Kheder Pasha alone tried, in 1596, to shake off the control of the janissaries with the aid of the Kouloughlis, who had been excluded from public affairs, and of the Kabyles, who were always ready for rebellion.

The time came when the army, strong in its 22,000 yoldashs, was no longer content to allow the pashas even the slightest power. It charged them with theft of pay and taxes. One of them, Ibrahim, decided at one time in 1659 to levy a tithe on the subsidies sent by the Porte to the raïs for the co-operation of the Algerian fleet. This claim provoked a riot. The divan thereupon resolved to abolish the pashas' last remaining prerogatives—issue of pay, appointment of *qaids* and jurisdiction over the Baldis—and to leave them with nothing but an honorific title. Executive power would be wielded by the agha with the assistance of the divan. This revolution, the motive of which was defence of the rights and privileges of the raïs, ultimately turned to the benefit of the army. The fortnightly change of aghas resulted either in the weakening of authority if they submitted to it, or in riots if they tried to keep themselves in power. Indeed the new regime established assassination as the regular procedure for succession. The four aghas who received the caftan of honour between 1659 and 1671 were murdered by the ojaq.

The raïs turned the situation to their advantage twelve years later. Blaming the agha 'Ali for his weakness in face of French demands, they incited a revolt of yoldashs and Algerians against him. His execution, followed by the torturing of his wife, was no encouragement to candidates for the post. The taïfa thereupon took advantage of the janissaries' default to follow the example of Tunis and to entrust power to a dey elected at first by itself, in 1671, and later by the officers of the army, in 1689. In 1711 the tenth dey, 'Ali Shaush, declined to receive the envoy of the Porte, and persuaded the Sultan to grant him the title of Pasha.

THE REVOLUTIONS IN TUNISIA

In Tunisia, Sinan Pasha's victory resulted in the establishment of a system similar to that practised in Algiers. The Tunis Regency had a pasha, an army recruited at first from the Turks (later from the Muslim Levantines and the Kouloughlis, and commanded by an agha almost independent of the pasha), a taïfa of the raïs, and makhzan tribes who were responsible for collecting taxes. Tunis went through the same disturbances as its neighbour. At the end of the sixteenth century the ojaq consisted of forty sections of one hundred men, at the head of which was a subordinate officer designated by the familiar title of 'maternal uncle' (*dey*). The ojaq suffered just as much as did the common people from arrogance and abuse of power on the part of its lieutenants (*odabashi*) and captains (*bolukbashi*) who constituted the divan and who had substituted their authority for that of the pasha. Things deteriorated to such a point that in 1590 the ojaq broke the officers' authority by a military revolution which was democratic in spirit. After slaughtering the bolukbashi, the forty deys elected one of their number to exercise command of the army jointly with the pasha. This dey steadily encroached on the pasha's prerogatives and became the real head of government. The third dey, 'Uthman, asserted his authority by two measures. Firstly he reduced the divan to the role of a ratifying chamber, and the pasha to the empty honour of receiving the caftan. Secondly, he leaned for support on two agents devoted to his service—the head of the navy (*qaptān*) and the commander of troops in charge of collecting taxes and of administering the tribes (*bey*).

The history of Tunis in the seventeenth century is that of the growth of the power of the beys at the expense of that of the deys. 'Uthman Dey (1590–1610) subdued the rebel tribes of Tunisia, and his son-in-law Yusuf (1610–1637), a protector of privateering and a great builder, fought against Arab insurrections and Algerian invasion. They were by no means weak leaders, but in comparison to their authority, which was supported by a smaller army than that of Algiers, the power of the beys increased. It was they who held the levers of power, placed in their hands through their governing the tribes and handling the state's revenues. The second bey, Murad (1612–1631), secured along with the title of Pasha the right to transmit his office to his son Hamuda. From that point the Muradids continuously and increasingly asserted their hereditary authority. Hamuda Bey (1631–1659) augmented his prestige by putting an end to defections by Arab tribes and attaching Djerba to the pashalik of Tunis. Under the two following deys he took the direction of affairs into his own hands, making good the damage caused by the attack of the Knights of Malta on the fleet of La Goulette and organising a struggle against scarcity. After him Murad Bey (1659–1675) dropped all pretence of tact or circumspection. He threw a dey into prison in 1671 and, having repressed an army revolt, installed himself in the palace of the Bardo as a ruler whose buildings witnessed to his munificence. But his death was followed by twenty years of civil war. Sword in hand, his two sons and his brother disputed the title of Bey among themselves and proclaimed and massacred deys. The resulting disorder led to victorious attacks by the Algerians and an attempt by the Porte at interference in Tunisian affairs. Eventually, the power of the Muradids collapsed in a military conspiracy. In 1702 the agha of the spahis, Ibrahim, had all of Hamuda's descendants assassinated and became bey. Not long afterwards, in 1704, he had the army confer the title of Dey on him, and the Porte that of pasha. Thus all power was for the first time concentrated in the same hands. This evolution towards monarchy was not affected by Ibrahim's defeat and capture in 1705 in an encounter with troops from Algiers and Tripoli. The agha of the spahis, Husain ibn ʿAli, rallied the runaways, shut himself up in Tunis, where the populace proclaimed him bey, and drove back the Algerians. No longer satisfied with a plurality of titles, he abolished that of dey in 1705. Thus the continued encroachments of the beys resulted in 1710 in the foundation of an hereditary dynasty.

Unsettled though Tunisia was during the seventeenth century, it suffered nothing comparable to the anarchy of its neighbour. It had a past and traditions, which did not vanish with the Hafsid dynasty. The townsfolk, anxious from Carthaginian times for a government that would maintain order, obliged Turkish authority to adapt itself to the mould that Ifriqiya had imposed on its masters for centuries past. They provided the makhzan with the personnel which it could not do without and which ensured administrative continuity. The Husainid attempt in the eighteenth century to transform a corsair state into an organised state was simply a continuation of the policy of Hafsids, Almohads and Sanhaja.

TWO CORSAIR STATES

The seventeenth century was the golden age of the Barbary

corsairs. The independence of the Regencies *vis-à-vis* the Porte, the weakness of the European fleets and the rivalries of the Christian nations made possible the most daring exploits.

Algiers above all flourished on the takings of piracy. In the mid-seventeenth century its population exceeded 100,000 inhabitants, which does not include some 25,000 to 35,000 captives. The fleet had been augmented with great galleys and 'round ships', or vessels of high freeboard, which enabled the corsairs to scour the western Mediterranean and in 1616 to make themselves felt as far as Iceland. In the course of two particularly favourable years—1615 and 1616—the value of booty exceeded two and three million livres. The entire population grew rich on trade in merchandise and the slave traffic. It was at this time that in the town and the surrounding fields there were built increasing numbers of those dwellings with a cool waiting hall (*saqīfa*) at the entrance. After this had been crossed, there was a central courtyard (*wast al-dār*), each side of which was taken up with a long narrow room opening on to a gallery and broken up by alcoves, sometimes topped with domes, such as still exist in the palace of the archbishop.

On land the raïs led the life of parvenus suddenly grown rich and greedy for vast debauches and ostentatious luxury. They were surrounded by porcelains from Delft, marble carvings from Italy, silks and velvets from Lyon or Genoa, mirrors from Venice, glass from Bohemia and clocks from England, all constituting an eclectic decor. But these Turks by birth or adoption were also fond of brasswork, arms, oriental-inspired carpets from Sétif, the Guergour (in Lesser Kabylia) or Kalʿa of the Beni Rached (between Mascara and Relizane). Particularly, they were attracted to embroidery in silk on coarse muslin or linen, of which the craftswomen (*muʿallima*) imparted the secret to the daughters of wealthy families.

Owing to the profits from piracy, Algiers increased the number of its mosques, marabouts and pious foundations. Here too the influence of Asia Minor made itself felt in large domes octagonal in plan covering prayer-halls and surrounded on the four sides by galleries supporting miniature domes or groined vaulting. Of this kind was the mosque built shortly after 1622 by the renegade Picenino, known as ʿAli Bitshnin; its character has been modified by its conversion into Notre-Dame-des-Victoires. Nearly half a

Turkish Rule in Algeria and Tunisia: 1516–1830

century later, in 1660, the ojaq, desiring a great temple of the Hanifi rite, built the most important religious building of Turkish Algiers, the Fishery Mosque (*al-Jāmiʿ al-Jdīd*). Its lofty ovoid dome on pendentives, supported by four great cradles, draws its inspiration from Constantinople. At the end of the century, in 1696, the tomb of the patron saint of Algiers, Sidi ʿAbd al-Rahman al-Thaʿlibi (d. 1648), was given shelter in a charming sanctuary, next to which is a cemetery planted with cypress trees.

Tunis too was a cosmopolitan city. Even more than Algiers it accepted Moriscos expelled from Spain in 1609. More than 80,000 of them, it is said, sought refuge within its walls, which had always been ready to receive Andalusians. This emigration, which greatly harmed the prosperity and culture of Spain, was favourably received by the Turks. "Uthman Dey', declares Ibn Abi Dinar, 'made room for them in the town, and distributed the neediest of them among the people of Tunis.'[26] The commercial, industrial and intellectual aristocracy occupied special quarters of the town. The market gardeners and makers of tarbooshes, silks and glazed porcelain followed their trades in the nearby environs. Finally the numerous peasants, who had created the wealth of the Andalusian *huertas*, for the most part developed the riverside lands of the Medjerda. Like the province of ancient civilisation that it was, Ifriqiya absorbed not only immigrants, but even those from the Orient attracted by the Turkish regime; these people quickly adopted Tunisian manners and customs. In return they contributed an improved technique of commerce-raiding, the profits from which made possible the embellishment of the town. It was this period that saw the building of a madarsa of the Hanifi rite, and of a number of mosques—that of Yusuf in an archaic local style except for the minaret, which shows oriental influence; that of the bey Hamuda the Muradid, otherwise called after Sidi bin ʿArus, built in 1654; and that of Sidi Mahraz, Turkish in inspiration and the most original, with its two superimposed oratories, built about 1675. It was also the period of the remodelling of the pleasant Sidi Sahib or 'barber's' zawiya at Kairouan, and the organising of several suks. The Berka, known as the slave market was created, a small open space with three covered ways; the aqueduct at Carthage was repaired; and fountains (*asbila*), drinking troughs, and public latrines with wash-basins for ritual ablutions (*midās*) were constructed.

Important though piracy was to the economy of Tunis, it never acquired such exclusive importance as at Algiers. Indeed the requirements of trade and of international relations ultimately obliged the government to limit its scope.

SLAVERY IN BARBARY

To the people of Barbary captives were a source of greater profit than looted merchandise. The Christian was no longer merely an infidel snatched from his own country. He had become an article of trade, to be disposed of with all speed for the best possible price. Molière's Turk, who agreed to hand over his prisoner forthwith in return for ransom, was no figment of the ingenious Scapin. There was the instance of Dragut, off Castellamare, hoisting the 'redemption pennant', according to Brantôme, as soon as the foray was over.

In order to build up stocks, the corsairs carried out coastal raids but they particularly were interested in the capture of Christian vessels. They used to parade seamen and passengers naked on deck, stopped at no indecency to uncover jewellery and examined clothes and hands in order to get an idea of social position. On the return to Algiers or Tunis the human livestock was thrown on to the market. Purchasers would look over the captives like beasts on market-day, inspect their teeth, eyes and hands, prod their flesh and make them 'walk, jump and caper to the tune of blows with a stick'. Value varied according to the use or profit the buyer expected to get. Particularly sought after were girls and boys, whom only one fate awaited; persons supposedly of quality, who might be good for ransom; and workers with special qualifications in seamanship, port work or gunnery. The master had the full and unfettered disposal of his slave, who became a speculative investment with the object of redemption.

The galley-slaves, badly fed and flogged on occasions of boarding or flight, were the most pitiable, but they were less unfortunate than the men from Barbary aboard the galleys of the king of France, for they were not branded with a red-hot iron and they were left free to practise their religion. Ashore the raïs used them as stevedores or hired them out as day-labourers. Domestic slaves, of

Turkish Rule in Algeria and Tunisia: 1516–1830

whom there were far fewer, sometimes became their masters' confidential agents. Some women were 'employed about the household or in the service of the family'. Other slaves were sent to the shipyards or set to the heavy tasks of field labour. The privileged ones, those able to pay their masters a monthly indemnity, could move freely about the town. The most enterprising became keepers of taverns, in which Christian and Muslim alike gave themselves up to drunkenness and debauchery. Because of payment, often made by the captives themselves, priests were able to exercise their ministry.

At night most of the captives were shut up in the bagnios, a sort of state prison. There were six of these at Algiers; that known as 'the king's' could hold 2,000 captives. At Tunis there were nine at the time when Père Dan visited them.[27] Masters used to send their slaves there on payment of a fee. Surveillance was provided by the warden-bashi, a dishonest character who assisted in the disposal of what goods the slaves could steal. The bagnio provided beds slung one above another, but no bedclothes. Priests used to rent small rooms from the warden-bashi and had the unimpeded use of an oratory in which according to Haëdo 'mass was celebrated throughout the year', sometimes 'with harmony'.[28]

The captives' condition was not so black as the Redemptorists painted it, but then they had to use strong measures for moving souls if they were to secure donations, and these grew steadily less. The good Fathers were unable to observe with resignation so many apostasies freely undertaken and explained them as due to force. Apart from the women, who urged their lovers to accept conversion with a view to marriage, and the raïs, who had their ship's boys 'clipped' in order to assure that no one should snatch their minions, most owners regarded an apostasy as bad business. The renegade 'Ali Bitshnin used to boast of 'having made a Christian return to Christianity by beating him'.

The captive was a piece of merchandise which it was to no one's interest to damage. If there did exist 'harsh, inconsiderate and cruel' masters, d'Arvieux had the honesty to acknowledge that 'in Europe we see masters who are no more reasonable and who would perhaps behave more barbarously, if they owned slaves, than those of Tunis'.[29] As for the twenty-three tortures which Père Dan described and had illustrated, these were quite exceptional.[30] Authors who fairly enough stigmatise the cruelty of Barbary forget that the king of France was no more sparing of the Protestants in his galleys, and that at the same period the public of Paris attended quarterings or breakings on the wheel as an entertainment.

At all times the Church had made the redemption of captives a sacred duty. Orders like that of the Trinitarians, founded by St. John of Matha in 1198, and that of Our Lady of Ransom, created by St. Peter Nolasco in 1218, devoted themselves to this work. Each nation had its redemptors. Governments of Protestant states organised collections, and even pious laymen engaged in wresting their countrymen from the fetters of captivity. But funds were beginning to run out and the zeal of the religious men to dwindle. The inquiry with a view to reforming the Trinitarians carried out in 1638 on account of the opposition of their general disclosed that their Paris house, with an annual income reaching 10,000 livres, was assessed at only 18 livres for ransom money.

The originality of St. Vincent de Paul lay in his suggesting to the Lazarists something other than a possible conversion of unbelievers, or redemption on a scale that only the state was in a position to realise. It is no great matter that, as has been irrefutably proved by Grandchamp, his captivity at Tunis, which he obstinately refused to speak of later in life, was pure invention and a piece of youthful falsehood. It was he who conceived the idea of sending his brethren 'to assist the poor enslaved Christians in Barbary, spiritually and corporally, in sickness and in health ... by means of visits, alms and instruction and by the administration of the holy sacraments'. To his dying day he was the moving spirit of this work of moral support and of struggle against apostasy. As a man full of compassion, but as an inflexible apostle, as a diplomat under the necessity of managing the rival orders and of seeking solid support in Paris, and as a humble and powerful man at the same time, Monsieur Vincent succeeded in imbuing French policy with a religious ideal.

BARBARY TRADE AND THE CONCESSIONS

Algiers never played a commercial role comparable to that of the ports of call of the Levant. The state of war, piracy, the weakness of internal trade and the competition of Oran, Bône and the

Turkish Rule in Algeria and Tunisia: 1516–1830

Bastion of France all hampered the growth of commercial exchanges. Nevertheless, and notwithstanding the dangers they ran in the event of civil commotion, there were at all times European merchants living there on a permanent footing. They trafficked, often with the connivance of the consuls, in goods of booty which the Jews sold them or dispatched to Livorno and as far as the Antilles. Their principal exports were leather, wax and wool. The English and the Dutch even managed to exchange arms for foodstuffs. The export trade—including raisins, figs, dates, textiles and tobacco—accounted for only a very small tonnage, and the government was not anxious to let it increase. The Regency sold export licences, multiplied exit duties and made its toleration dependent on the distribution of baksheesh to all the intermediaries. The Jews adapted so well to these oriental conditions of doing business that in the end they became the managers, money-changers and brokers of the beylik and masters of the country's economic life. Only the Marseillais residents, who were not scrupulously honest, were able, despite periodic massacres, to maintain their own position among them. At the end of the seventeenth century they were in opposition to the Protestant 'religionaires' of Languedoc, who after 1685 had sought asylum at Algiers, at Tunis and in Morocco.

The Christians at Tunis suffered fewer disappointments. Despite repercussions from conflicts with European nations, they generally lived at peace in their *funduks*. The English merchants moreover, even at the time when the Tunisians put their consul in prison as a reprisal for Blake's expedition of 1654, continued to trade freely.

The *funduk* of the French, built in 1659, was the largest and handsomest, for the French consul protected the merchants of all nations except the English and the Dutch. The English consul used every means to challenge his pre-eminence. Grain could not be loaded at Tunis, but there was an export trade at the end of the seventeenth century in raw hides, in competition with leather from the Levant, and also in wool, wax, sponges, dates and ostrich feathers, these last being rated less highly than those from Senegal. Imports included other wools more suitable for the manufacture of tarbooshes, which was very active at Tunis, and wine, linen and arms. Competition by Jews and the Cap Nègre Company kept down the profits of the residents, who preferred to charter their vessels to Jews and Tunisians. A small part of the trade was with Sousse. Trade with France, though three or four times greater than that done by Algiers between 1670 and 1690, was of only slight importance.

It was neither at Algiers nor at Tunis, but at the Bastion of France, at Cap Nègre and at Tabarka, that the French and the Genoese displayed the greatest activity. The Algerians had viewed with hostility the establishment of the Lenche Company at the Bastion of France, which acted in very high-handed fashion and, in breach of agreements, undertook the exportation of grain. Eventually, therefore, they seized the place in 1568. It must have been a paying proposition, for there was a bitter argument over its recapture which, when effected, yielded 'enormous riches' to Lenche's nephew. However, it resulted in 1604 in the demolition once more of the Bastion, 'by reason of the breaches of faith practised by the said French against the Moors and for having failed to pay the said tribute three years running'.

The conflict between France and Algiers prevented any agreement until the arrival of Sanson Napollon, Corsican by birth and Marseillais by adoption. He, after two years of negotiation and a considerable distribution of baksheesh, succeeded in signing the famous convention concerning the Bastion on 29 September 1628. The French secured the monopoly of trade and of coral fishing within the area of the Concessions, and the right to 'restore and, make, as they were formerly', the places that had been destroyed, 'in order to safeguard themselves against the Moors and vessels and brigantines of Majorca and Minorca'.[31] All this was in return for a rent or *lazma* of 16,000 livres, which went chiefly to pay the janissaries. This document did not permit any transformation of the Bastion, merely the putting into good order of the places in which, according to the convention of 1560, the building of 'any fortification whatsoever' was forbidden. Sanson turned it into a veritable fortress, however, and made it a centre of espionage in order to 'learn what comes to pass in Barbary', and also into a supply base for the soldiers whom he invited the king to set ashore there. 'It is necessary', he wrote without concealment, 'to keep the said places under colour of trade and coral fishing in order that the design of making the said conquests be not known.'[32] Finally he

Turkish Rule in Algeria and Tunisia: 1516–1830

enriched himself not only by the coral fishing and legitimate trade but also by the export of wheat, which he had undertaken not to engage in. In matters of cunning the ingenious Sanson could teach the people of Barbary a lesson.

This astute adventurer also had designs of taking the island of Tabarka from the Genoese. They had received it from Khair al-Din as ransom for Dragut in 1540, and had made a concession of it to the Lomellini for coral fishing and trade with Barbary. On his third attempt, in May 1633, the people of Tabarka caught him by surprise, chased him out to sea, brought him down with a musket shot and, having thrown his body into the sea, nailed his head over the gateway of their fortress.

Sanson's death was a serious blow to the Concessions. Several reasons caused the divan to decide that the Establishments should be finally destroyed and 'that the first to speak of them should loose his life'.[33] There were quarrels between the French residents of Algiers and the new captain, Sanson Lepage; the divan feared that the Bastion was acting as a supply base for the French fleet; and, of greater importance, two vessels had been seized with a cargo of contraband grain. 'Ali Bitshnin carried out the sentence rigorously on 13 December 1637. As an unexpected consequence of the destruction of the Bastion, the chief of the Hanencha, who had been making large profits out of personal trade with the Company, was impelled to bring his tribe out in revolt and to make his submission conditional on the re-establishment of the Bastion. A new convention dated 7 July 1640 distinguished between the ports of Bône and Collo, where nothing but stores might exist, and the Bastion, La Calle and Cap Rosa, where 'building would be permitted' for protection against enemy and Moorish galleys. This treaty, though, as Masson acknowledges, 'giving evidence of a great desire for conciliation' on the part of the Algerians,[34] did not put an end to the vicissitudes of the Concessions. Ruthless greed backed by unscrupulous noblemen, rivalry between Lyonnais and Marseillais and attacks by French squadrons caused every effort to fail. After 1689 peace with Algiers enabled the king to exclude the Companies from diplomatic business and to restrict them to their proper commercial function. By a final contract signed by one Company and the Algerians on 1 January 1694, the position of the Establishments was definitely settled, largely by reference to the customs of Sanson Napollon. From then until 1754 negotiations were limited to confirming the convention fourteen times without modification.

The company for exploiting the Tunisian coral fishery, founded about the same time as the Bastion on the poor site of Cap Nègre opposite Tabarka, had to contend with the Genoese and the jealousy of the residents of the port of call of Tunis. After many vicissitudes its factory was restored by some Marseillais in 1631, but shortly afterwards, in 1637, it fell into the hands of the Tunisians. Trade was soon resumed, but no convention was signed until thirty years later, in 1666. By it the French were granted no territorial concession and their establishments were forbidden any 'fortress-like appearance'. The *lazmas* were five times higher than those of the Bastion, but they constituted the Company's sole expense; moreover the Company enjoyed the formal right of trading in wheat and barley. Taking advantage of the anarchy that ensued on the death of Murad, the English made an unsuccessful attempt to evict the French. From 1691 the Company made large profits out of supplying grain to the king's army and in 1700 it attempted to ensure these profits by securing a concession in perpetuity. The double failure early in the eighteenth century of the Bastion and of Cap Nègre led to the creation of a new organisation which combined the two concessions under one development company, but left each with its own independent management. Thereafter the La Calle and Cap Nègre Companies ceased to exist; in their place was one Africa Company.

THE WARS OF THE REGENCIES

To attribute the determining factors of the policy of the Christian states towards Barbary to outbursts of indignation at acts of piracy would be to take a very superficial view. Popular opinion may have been aroused by the suffering inflicted on the captives, but governments were swayed by motives in which commercial interests and European rivalries took first place.

The policy of the Regencies was governed primarily by economic considerations. If booty diminished, the resources of the country were no longer sufficient to supply the budget and disturbances followed. Peace with the Christians involved making up a deficiency from the vessels of the protected nation and of those who fraudu-

Turkish Rule in Algeria and Tunisia: 1516–1830

lently flew its flag. A state of war, with all its risks but also with its profits, was still a worth-while proposition. At the very least, and when driven by necessity, Algiers would negotiate with only one power and increase the fury of its attacks on the rest. The peace treaty entered into with de Ruyter in 1663 was marked by a recrudescence of privateering attacks against French vessels. The treaty with Louis XIV in 1670 involved a rupture with the English and the Dutch; and the treaty with the English in 1681 was followed by a declaration of war against France. Moreover, this realistic policy accepted the coexistence of piracy and trade. Thus it was that in 1681 the Algerians advised the Marseillais that 'this rupture notwithstanding, those desirous of entering this country would always be welcome'.

Spain was too weak in the seventeenth century to react against Barbary piracy, but England with Blake, Marlborough and Allen, and Holland with de Ruyter, organised marine expeditions well prepared and ably led. The English bombarded Algiers three times, in 1622, 1655 and 1672. Nevertheless, despite their technical superiority, the results were unimpressive. Not only were they content in most cases to ransom slaves, but the Dutch in 1680, and the English in 1682, had to agree to supply rigging, spars and arms in return for the right to export grain.

French attacks, slowly prepared and reported to the divan by the Jews of Marseilles, encountered a resistance that nullified their effect. Even when the invention of heavy half-galleys made it possible to brave the fire of Algerian mortars, most of the incendiary bombs exploded before reaching the target and the result was never worth the effort expended. In 1661 and 1665 squadrons cannonaded the breakwater in vain. Duquesne twice bombarded the town. On the first occasion (20 August–20 September 1682) he succeeded in destroying only fifty houses and killing 500 inhabitants. The second attempt (June–July 1683) involved serious material damage but also a massacre of French residents, among others the aged Père Jean Le Vacher, who was blown from the mouth of a cannon. Five years later, in June–July 1688, d'Estrées fired 10,000 bombs which severely damaged forts and houses, but he had to withdraw without further success.

The attempt to occupy Djidjelli had even more unfortunate results. After a difficult landing on 23 July 1664, the soldiers, ill-fed, ill-supplied and fever-ridden, were unable to withstand the onslaughts of Turks and Kabyles. The troops had to be re-embarked, leaving 1,400 corpses and a hundred or so cannon in enemy hands. On the voyage home one ship with 1,200 soldiers on board sank within sight of Provençe.

THE KING'S CHOICE

The French attitude to Barbary becomes intelligible only if, as was done by Capot-Rey, it is seen in the context of French policy as a whole.[35] Throughout almost the whole of the seventeenth century there was no cessation of hostilities. In 1603 the French consul suffered maltreatment and the Bastion was sacked. After a brief truce from 1605 to 1609, a rupture lasting twenty years was provoked by the flight to France of the corsair Simon Dansa with two cannon belonging to the pasha, followed by the massacre of an Algerian embassy at Marseilles. After the death of Sanson Napollon the state of war continued for a further nine years, from 1636 to 1643. But at no time did France react energetically, as she did after 1661. Meanwhile other factors had made their influence felt.

Owing to St. Vincent de Paul, the Lazarists acquired the standing of a temporal power. As Apostolic Vicars and organisers of the Church of Africa, they secured, with Jean Le Vacher, a veritable episcopal authority involving control over the Italian Capuchins and the Spanish Trinitarians. Redemptorists and confidential agents of the slaves' relatives as they were, their co-operation was essential to negotiations, which always involved the ransoming of captives. Finally, as consuls they were the indispensable intermediaries between the king and the Barbary powers. This triple role often enabled them to substitute their views for those of the king and even to enforce them. But they themselves were not so much prime movers as instruments.

Not the least curious or best known feature of the Barbary policy of France in the time of Mazarin is that it was one of the forms assumed by the Devout Cabal. Behind St. Vincent de Paul, often involved against his will, stood the Company, which quietly stepped into the government's place in African affairs and directed them into paths designed to prepare for the triumph of God. While Monsieur Vincent had no desire to have the consulates, it was the Duchesse d'Aiguillon who persuaded him of their use-

Turkish Rule in Algeria and Tunisia: 1516–1830

fulness and purchased in turn that of Algiers in 1646, and that of Tunis in 1648. It was she again who, by-passing ministers, suggested in 1659 that the funds derived from collections for the captives should be used to subsidise a private expedition under the Chevalier Paul, the only squadron commander to keep alive a holy hatred for the infidel. Finally it was the company's ardent proselytizing that gave Catholic opinion, stimulated by a renewal of fervent faith, the strength to express itself and to impose its will on the government. It was against the Turk, at Candia or on Hungarian soil, that the very Christian king ought to have concentrated his efforts, if he had responded to the Pope's appeal. But, despite clashes, the alliance between Turkey and France was maintained. The great skill of Louis XIV lay in conducting his crusade at small expense by adopting a stand of national interest. The Barbary expeditions, inspired by purely commercial motives, enabled him to act agreeably to the wishes of Christendom by setting himself up as champion of the faith against the Muslims.

At the time of Monsieur Vincent's death French policy, under de Lionne and Colbert, was disengaging itself from Catholic influence. In 1672, writing to the Marquis de Feuquières, who had sent him that very odd dissertation by Leibniz on the conquest of Egypt (*Consilium Egyptiacum*), Pomponne gave the blunt reply: 'I say nothing of the plans for a holy war, but you know these wars have been out of fashion since the time of St. Louis.'[36] Leibniz stressed the need for the colonial diplomats of the future in setting their course to 'conceal the profane and the useful under the guise of the sacred and the honourable'.[37] Colbert applied to the Barbary states the principles intended by Leibniz for Egypt. The crusade for the faith and the poor captives was a purely mercantile enterprise, in which a show of force was immediately followed by commercial overtures.

Colbert subordinated everything to trade and it was in order to please the merchants that with a stroke of the pen he deprived the Lazarists of the consulates. It is true that the multiplicity of their functions had led the good Fathers to carry out some irregular transfers of funds from the captives' account to that of the residents, and to impose new duties on French vessels. Possibly, however, their condemnation was too thorough-going. Is not the true cause of the hostility to which they fell victims to be found in their loyalty to the Papal bull *In coenam Domini*, which forbade the sale of ships' supplies to the infidel, and in their opposition to the smuggling of arms by which the French residents grew rich? However that may be, a Jean le Vacher, who came to Barbary at the age of 28, admired by the dey and listened to with respect by the divan, was so zealous for his work as to exclaim, 'If on one side I saw the road to heaven open, with permission to take it, and on the other the road to Algiers, I would sooner take the latter'.[38] He died a martyr to his love of peace. Such a man represented a human value quite different from the grotesque and cowardly Dumoulin at Tunis, or the vain and pretentious Chevalier d'Avrieux at Algiers, each of whom considered avenging his failures by agitating for war.

Colbert allowed himself to be involved in expeditions against the Barbary powers by the residents who were constant advocates of strong action, and recommended him to 'ride roughshod over them'. He did not do this only when he wished to, but only as the European situation gave him some respite. As long as the Emperor was immovable, relations with the Turks deteriorated and relations with Barbary ended in marine expeditions. War with Holland in 1672 brought about reconciliation between French and unbelievers. Between the peace of Nijmegen in 1678 and the war of the Augsburg League the king resumed the policy of intimidation characterised by Duquesne's expedition to the Archipelago in 1681–1684, and the bombardments of Algiers and Tripoli. Then came the difficult period that began in 1688, and France declared herself in favour of friendly relations with the Muslims.

Colbert could have secured something better than peace—a formal alliance. He declined it not out of scruple, but because he was afraid of jeopardising his supply of galley-slaves. So too, and for the same reason, he refused a possible entente with Mulay Ismaʻil. But over and above this, he rejected it out of concern for the greatness of his king, who was in his element when at war. The insolent replies to Mulay Ismaʻil, Duquesne's summary demands and the bombardments of Salé, Algiers and Tripoli were all the outcome of the same design. This was to make plain to the barbarians the disdain of Louis XIV, and to the European powers the

Turkish Rule in Algeria and Tunisia: 1516–1830

strength of expeditions more brilliant than anything the English or Dutch could achieve. Although he had been unable to humiliate the Barbary powers as he would have liked, the king finally consented to a rapprochement, while still fully maintaining his pretensions. The hundred-years' treaty signed by Guillaume Marcel, Commissioner of the Navy, in 1689, showed that the king was renouncing holy war in favour of political and commercial advantages. Between the crusade of St. Vincent de Paul and the mercantile realism of Colbert the very Christian king had finally pronounced judgment.

At the end of the sixteenth century the Regency of Algiers had attained the frontiers which it kept until 1830. During the seventeenth century it continued to be in conflict with the Sharifs and the Muradids. The death of 'Eulj 'Ali saw the end of Turkish ambitions, but not of Turkish intrigues, in Morocco. Thereafter Algiers operated through intermediaries, chiefly religious ones, or by affording comfort to rebels. Thus it was that the raïs Ghailan secured support from Turkish notables. The conflict took on a serious character with the offensives of Mulay Isma'il, which the deys Cha'ban and Hajj Mustapha twice repulsed, in 1691 and 1701.

The Tunisians were involved by the Sharif in the conflicts with Algiers, but in 1691 the dey Cha'ban crushed their invasion of the province of Constantine and installed one of his clients at Tunis. Three years later he intervened again on his behalf, defeated his adversaries at Le Kef and returned to Algiers loaded with booty. In 1700 the bey Murad in concert with Mulay Isma'il attempted revenge, but was crushed between Sétif and Constantine. The independence of Tunisia appeared to be in danger and the dey Hajj Mustapha formed a plan for conquering it. At the outset he eliminated Ibrahim, but he was routed by Husain ibn 'Ali and was obliged to withdraw to Algiers, where he was overthrown by an uprising in 1705 and beheaded. In perspective the wars that set Morocco and the two Regencies against each other during the seventeenth century were purely incidental in character. They brought about no significant change worth mentioning in the Maghrib but contributed to the instability of authority at Algiers and Tunis by the palace revolutions that followed after them.

v. The Algeria of the Deys and Husainid Tunisia

DECLINE OF ALGIERS

In the eighteenth century Algiers lost its former prosperity. The treaties with the [European] powers, the enemy expeditions and the growing scarcity of good corsair crews impaired the effectiveness of privateering attacks. In nine years out of a quarter of a century, between 1765 and 1792, the value of booty was less than 100,000 francs. The fleet, which in 1724 comprised twenty-four vessels, declined in the course of sixty years to eight barques and two galliots in 1788. The raïs Hamidu, who held the sea until 1815, restored the fleet again to thirty ships, owing to the European wars that followed the French Revolution. Constant epidemics of plague, and famines caused by periodic droughts, hastened the decline. In a single year, 1787, Algiers lost nearly 17,000 inhabitants, and during the summer of 1817 there were 500 deaths a day. If we add the disorders due to political anarchy, we can understand the reduction of the population by the beginning of the nineteenth century to some 30,000 inhabitants. The ojaq comprised no more than 6,000 members. The number of captives, reduced to 800 in 1788 and increased to 1,642 in 1816 following the revival of piracy, was only 122 when the French took the town.

Trade suffered from the impoverishment of the town. Though Europeans enjoyed greater security, they found fewer opportunities of growing rich than in the heroic age [of privateering]. The dey, by monopolizing business, prevented its growth. In the mid-eighteenth century there remained only two or three French establishments, and these consolidated into a single Marseillais house, known as the 'Maison Française', with a monopoly of exports. It had difficulty in withstanding competition from the celebrated Africa Company.

Reduced to the three establishments of La Calle, Bône and Collo, the Africa Concessions, which since 1714 had been free to export wheat, had steadily improved their position. In the year 1741 the minister Maurepas had succeeded in getting the Marseilles chamber of commerce to take an interest in the development of the

Turkish Rule in Algeria and Tunisia: 1516–1830

Concessions and in placing the Company, thereafter the Royal Company, under close government control. About 1776 it was so prosperous that it had a medal struck representing Africa holding a cornucopia from which emerged ears of corn. The inscription—*Aucta Libycis opibus Massilia*—celebrated the enrichment of Marseilles by African trade.

The exports of other nations made no progress. In 1775 Raynal noted that Swedes, Danes, Dutch and Venetians had given up the struggle.[39] There remained the English, whose one house, much inferior to that of Marseilles, was in a perennially unstable condition. Algiers did, however, contribute to the provisioning of Gibraltar.

If Marseilles held first place for exports, Livorno did so for imports into Algiers, owing to the Jews. For the Regency as a whole the English were easily in the lead, accounting in 1822 for almost half the value of merchandise. In total the Algiers trade came to about 5,000,000 francs in 1830—a rather undistinguished figure.

Internal trade was still very steady in the first half of the eighteenth century. Algiers had active local industries which distributed their products in the provinces and were still in operation in 1830. Commerce and industry diminished as the population declined in numbers and wealth.

THE DEYS OF ALGIERS, DESPOTS WITHOUT LIBERTY

Deprived of the profits from piracy, Algiers turned to exploitation of the country. The creation of the deys had subjected the Regency to an elective but absolute monarchy. Since 1689 the officers of the army had taken the place of the raïs in designating the dey. As long as the taïfa had command over the selection it had nominated raïs, but when it came to the fifth dey the final decision, as chance would have it, fell to the army. Nevertheless most of those elected were khujat al-kheyl, aghas or khaznaji. ʽAli Malmuli (1754–1766) had once been a donkey-driver but had become an agha. The election was often no more than a formality. Of the thirty deys who succeeded one another between 1671 and 1818, fourteen were imposed [in office] by mob violence after their predecessors had been assassinated.

The dey was an autocrat, for it was only in theory that his

authority was limited by his council (*divan*) and he had free choice of its five ministers, or 'powers'. These were the officer in charge of the state treasury (*khaznaji*), the commander-in-chief of the army (*agha* of the *mahalla*), the minister of marine (*wekīl al-kharj*), his major-domo, the trustee of vacant successions (*beytulmālji*) and the receiver of tribute, known as the 'secretary of the horse' (*khujat al-kheyl*). These were assisted by the dey's personal treasurer (*khaznadār*), secretaries (*khujas*) and bailiffs (*shawshs*). The dey avoided bringing them together and, so far as possible, receiving them, preferring to communicate with them through the medium of the palace interpreter.

The dey's principal duty was to deliver justice. The Turks and the original inhabitants of the country were not answerable to the same tribunals or subject to the same police. The Turks, who were Hanifis, appeared before the *qadi* of their rite, while the Moors, who had remained Malikis, had recourse to theirs. In criminal matters the Turks were judged by the agha, the Moors by his deputy, the *kahya*. Finally, there were police officers called *shawshs* for the Turks, and other ones for the Moors. Sentences of bastinado or fine were carried out on the spot. Decapitations took place in front of the council chamber, strangulations and impalings on the curved hooks at the Bab Azoun gate. The stakes reserved for the burning of apostates and Jews were set up on the breakwater or at the Bab el-Oued gate. The dey remitted civil cases to the *qadis* or in certain instances to Maliki or Hanifi muftis. The afternoon was devoted to state business. It was then that the dey used to receive high officials, to direct diplomatic negotiations and, should occasion arise, give a final decision on questions of peace or war.

Out of respect for the pretence of equality, the deys had no civil list beyond the high pay of a janissary. But investiture fees of officials, especially beys, presents from consuls or rulers, shares in booty and profits from business ventures for which the deys provided funds combined to provide them with plentiful returns. In case of assassination their fortune, often a considerable amount, reverted to the public treasury.

Part of their wealth was devoted to pious foundations. Muhammad ibn ʿUthman (1766–1791), who was the most remarkable dey of the eighteenth century, erected the Jamiʿ al-Sayyida mosque, the

Turkish Rule in Algeria and Tunisia: 1516–1830

oratory of the heads of the Regency, next to whose palace it stood. In 1830 it was hastily, and needlessly demolished. The Fishery Mosque very nearly suffered the same fate.

The Ketchawa Mosque was built by Muhammad ibn 'Uthman's successor, Baba Hassan in 1794. The transformations it underwent in order to make it into the cathedral changed it beyond recognition, but picturesque views preserve the memory of its octagonal dome on shell pendentives covering a square space measuring 38 feet, of its lateral galleries and of its broken arches springing from columns with bulbous capitals. From the same period dates the burial mosque, in the Hamma cemetery, of Sidi Muhammad ibn 'Abd al-Rahman, commonly called Bu Qubrin—the man with two tombs—because a Kabyle village also lays claim to his sepulchre. The last dey, Hussain, had the two mosques in the kasbah built and the Jāmi' Safir mosque rebuilt. This mosque has only three galleries, as the rear part, which follows the line of the Mecca-oriented qibla, is without one.

All these Algerian mosques, 'the essential feature of which is their central hall under an eight-sided dome and the galleries that surround it'[40], were probably inspired by Anatolian models.

His power did not preserve the dey from danger. This tyrant was in fact a prisoner, with death a constant threat. As soon as he was elected he became the property of the state, which separated him from his household, allowing him one afternoon and one night a week for family life in his private house. Several deys were men of valour; nearly all of them displayed ferocity. The fact was that, like the priest of Némi, they thought they saw rivals constantly around them and were only too ready to assassinate them in order to take their places. This obsession drove even the best-natured of them to the most excessive cruelties.

To get away from the army and its sudden fits of violence, often fraught with tragedy, 'Ali Khoja in 1816 left the Jenina for the fortress of the kasbah. There he had his apartments, his harem and his audience-hall under one of the ground-floor galleries. It was from a wooden gallery set back on the second floor that the belvedere projected in which tradition sets the scene of the fly-whisk incident.[41]

A Spanish historian, Juan Cano, gave an accurate description of the dey as 'a man of wealth, but far from a master of his treasures;

a father without children, a husband without a wife, a despot without liberty, king of slaves and slave of his subjects.'

THE GOVERNMENT OF THE REGENCY

The government of the Turks was an industry from which they made every effort to derive the maximum profit.

The province of Algiers was the dey's own domain (*dār al-sultān*) and came directly under him. He administered it through the agha of the spahis, who acted as bey, and four Turkish *qaids*. He allowed the town of Algiers a special organisation superintended by the khaznaji. Each ethnic group, except that of the Kabyles, and each trade guild was answerable to a headman (*amin*) with police powers and legal jurisdiction but under the control of a mayor (*shaikh al-balad*). Special officials looked after fountains, markets, streets, baths and brothels. The town was extremely well policed.

The remainder of the Regency consisted of three provinces (*beyliks*)—the western beylik, the capital of which was in turn Mazouna, (south-east of Renault), Mascara, from 1710 and Oran, from 1792; the central or Titteri beylik, with Médéa as its seat of government; and the eastern or Constantine beylik. Each beylik had a bey at its head, who was appointed by the dey, who generally chose the most generous candidate. Within his province the bey functioned as an independent ruler. Such were Muhammad al-Kabir at Oran, and Hajj Ahmad at Constantine. The latter had a palace built by craftsmen of repute which displayed more wealth than elegance and was embellished with courtyards and two gardens. The deys mistrusted their governors. Twice a year the beys paid to the khalifa, who brought them in the taxes, a caftan of honour for their master. Every three years the beys were required to come to Algiers in person bringing with them the proceeds of customs dues. It was a hazardous ordeal, which always cost them part of their wealth, often their posts and sometimes their lives. Nonetheless, even at Algiers the dey had to reckon with them, as witnesses the account published by Emerit of the liberation of Thédenat.[42] The bey of Titteri province was particularly dangerous because of his proximity to the capital. Accordingly he was deprived of the administration of Médéa and his task was rendered more complex by interventions on the part of the head of that town, who was appointed by the agha.

Turkish Rule in Algeria and Tunisia: 1516–1830

Each beylik was subdivided into numerous districts (*outān*) which usually included several tribes and were administered by commissioners (*qaids*) armed with civil, military and judicial powers. The qaids had under their orders the tribal chiefs (*shaikhs*) who were assisted in their administration by the headman of dowars. Their main task was to supervise the division of land and to see that it was brought under cultivation. This was necessary in order to settle the assessment of taxes, the collection of which, with the aid of the shaikhs, was one of their functions. They were appointed by the beys on the nomination of the agha or other high officials, whose men they were, and they received a seal and a red burnous. They were always chosen from among the Turks, whereas the shaikhs usually belonged to the most important tribe in the outan. It sometimes happened that the outan comprised a single large tribe, in which case its shaikh then became qaid. Moreover, the powerful groups of mediæval times had been broken up and their elements incorporated into other structures. The fusion of Arab and Berber was finally complete. Secondary groups, settled on poor land outside the Turkish sphere of influence, like the Ouled Naïl and the Sahari, had withstood these changes more effectively and had indeed grown considerably in size. Finally other confederations with a religious basis had emerged; one such was the Ouled Sidi Shaikh in Orania.

For the policing of his province, and in order to ensure that taxes were collected, the bey had recourse to makhzan tribes, themselves exempt from non-canonical taxes, who 'devoured' the subject tribes (*rayah*). Their complicity guaranteed their loyalty. In addition, the Turks stationed military colonies (*zmāla*, plural *zmūl*) at strategic points. These, in return for fiscal immunities, maintained law and order in the region.

Provided their subjects paid their taxes and did not hinder the passage of troops, the deys were not interested in interfering with their customs.

REVOLTS AND WARS

The deys' effective authority, according to Rinn, extended to no more than a sixth of present-day Algeria.[43] The republics of Kabylia, the nomadic tribes of the plateaux and the south and the warrior or marabout principalities, like those of Touggourt and

Aïn Mahdi, lived in complete independence. Other groups, like that of the Ouled Sidi Shaikh, were attached to the deys by the slenderest thread of vassaldom. The government might have been apprehensive of tribal coalitions within the subject zone. In order to forestall them, it encouraged the rivalries between sharifs and brotherhoods while acknowledging their influence with respect.

However great the government's skill, it never succeeded in keeping the country under control. The Kabyles were constantly rising despite the posts established by the Turks in the valley of the Sebaou and their interference with the support of the local sharifs, in *suf* rivalries. The forceful dey Muhammad ibn 'Uthman (1766–1791) took several years to subdue them. Still more serious were the insurrections instigated early in the nineteenth century by the Derqawa brotherhood, not without some inspiration from the sultan of Fez, Mulay Sliman. It was a marabout, Bin Sharif, who caused Orania to rise, while a Derqawi chief from Morocco, Bin al-Harsh, who had some link with the English, summoned the Kabyles of the Babors to revolt. In the west the Turks had to abandon Mascara and were besieged in the Méchouar of Tlemcen, while the bey of Constantine let himself be taken prisoner and put to death. Soon the whole country from the Chélif to the Moroccan frontier was in a state of insurrection. The Turks gradually regained control but were unable to prevent the spread of centres of sedition. Between 1810 and 1815 the Kabyles of the Babors, the Flissa, the Titteri—and also the Tunisians—defeated them on all sides. To the influence of the Derqawa was added that of the Tijani marabouts of Aïn Mahdi, particularly when they could rely on the protection of the new Moroccan Sharif, Mulay 'Abd al-Rahman. When the conflict between France and the Regency broke out, the dey had still not succeeded in restoring his authority.

Occupied with the Moroccan intrigues in the west, the deys tried in the east to make use of Husainid rivalries to subdue Tunisia by armed force. After taking and looting Tunis in 1756, they obliged the beys to pay them an annual tribute. Conflicts provoked by the beys' efforts at recovering their independence went on for 65 years and were brought to an end only by the mediation of the Porte.

The European powers took advantage of the decline of Algiers to impose respect for their flags, but did so more by means of

Turkish Rule in Algeria and Tunisia: 1516-1830

money and presents in kind than of expeditions. Seven states—the United States, Holland, Portugal, the Kingdom of Naples, Sweden, Norway and Denmark—even consented to the payment of an annual tribute. Spain alone attempted attacks on Algiers in the eighteenth century. These were the final efforts of her Algerian policy. Already, in the course of the disturbances of the War of the Spanish Succession, she had allowed Oran and Mers el-Kébir to be taken in 1708, and had had to wait nearly a quarter of a century, until 1732, to recover them. The major *presidio* of Oran, which finally boasted 10,000 inhabitants, had become a garrison town in which every effort was made to imitate the etiquette of Madrid, a fact which led to its being styled, with a touch of pomposity, the Little Court (*Corte Chica*). The troops continued their forays in a radius of about 75 miles and made the subject tribes (*los Moros de paz*) pay a tax in grain (*romia*). But notwithstanding the romia and purchases from the local people, supplies were still mainly dependent on dispatches from Spanish ports, and economic crises, though less disastrous than in the time of the Count of Alcaudète, were no less serious. It was perhaps in order to deal with these difficulties that on 8 July 1775 O'Reilly landed an expeditionary force of 25,000 men near the Harrach, but it had to depart the next day, having lost a tenth of its strength. It was certainly these difficulties that prompted the two ineffective bombardments by Don Angelo Barcelo in August 1783 and July 1784 which were followed by the signing of a treaty, the terms of which were expensive for Spain. These disappointments reinforced the pessimism in certain Spanish circles hostile to involvement in Africa. The earthquake of October 1790, which destroyed Oran, furnished the providential event that without doubt enabled them to apply pressure to the royal will. However, the Spaniards ceded the place by treaty to the dey of Algiers on 12 September 1791, and they evacuated it the following year.

After 1792 relations between the Regency and Europe became more strained. It is true that the Africa Agency was able on behalf of the state to continue the operations of the former Company, which had been abolished by the Committee of Public Safety on 19 Pluviôse, Year II (8 February 1794). However it is also true that the Republic was very willing to accept the consignments of grain and the interest-free loans agreed to by the dey. But

History of North Africa

Napoleon's dream was a return to the policy of Louis XIV. Though he was unable to put his plan into execution, he did at least get Engineer Officer Boutin, in July 1808, to collect material and carry out studies in North Africa. These studies resulted in an outstanding report which proved invaluable to the expeditionary force of 1830.

Following the fall of the Empire, France refused to be associated with the plans outlined by the London Conferences in 1816 for suppressing the corsairs. At that time she preferred the continuation of piracy to reinforcing England's command of the seas. The only result of the Congress of Aix-la-Chapelle was the dispatch of a French and an English admiral whom the dey received with great reserve. The Powers were reduced to individual and separate action. It was thus that in 1815 the United States, through the use of cannon, obtained a more favourable treaty. The most forceful action was that undertaken by the English squadron under Lord Exmouth and the Dutch Admiral van Cappellen. On 27 August 1816 this made its way into the harbour under cover of a flag of truce, overwhelmed fleet and town with 34,000 projectiles but then encountered a lively resistance which cost it 883 men. Nine years later, in 1825, Admiral Neal made an attempt which produced no result, and the defences of Algiers were not seriously breached. The Regency might have long continued to exist but for underhanded transactions of which the dey was the victim, and the activities of the consul Deval, which led to the famous scene of the fly-whisk on 30 April 1827.[44] Out of this the necessities of French internal politics fabricated the occasion for the dispatch three years later of the expedition which ended with the capture of Algiers on 5 July 1830.

HUSAINID TUNISIA

The seventeenth century had brought about far-reaching changes in Tunisia. The beys of the Muradid family had established a nearly hereditary authority. Great Arab and Berber families had consolidated themselves in the centre and south of the country, and the Regency had maintained its independence against attacks by Algiers. With the eighteenth century the Husainids officially instituted an hereditary monarchy, but they had to struggle against Algerian domination and particularly against the gradual

Turkish Rule in Algeria and Tunisia: 1516–1830

ascendancy of the European powers while at the same time establishing regular relations with them.

The founder of the dynasty, Husain, a man of prudence, energy and intelligence, was not content with being proclaimed bey by the aghas in 1705. In 1710, by means of a special assembly, he assured that his position would pass regularly to his descendants. Under his rule Tunis enjoyed real prosperity. In 1724 Peysonnel noted the important place assumed by raw materials involved in the manufacture of tarbooshes, by the export of wheat, leather, wax, sponges and dates and by caravan consignments from Morocco and the Fezzan.[45] Moreover, foreign residents were numerous. The main hindrance to trade lay in 'the avarice of the bey, who has a monopoly of it and sells everything at excessive prices'. On the other hand the foreigners were unanimous in commending the honesty of the local merchants. The bey concluded treaties with France (in 1710 and 1728), England (1716), Spain (1720), Holland (1728) and Austria (1725). He thus bound himself by international understandings without being subjected to any interference by the Porte. But his influence over the corsairs was still limited, a fact which twice led to the dispatch of French squadrons to La Goulette, in 1728 and 1731.

At first the condition of the country was very good. 'The roads', wrote Muhammad Saghir, 'became safe and the country prosperous ... villas and gardens were once more occupied and palaces beyond reckoning were built in the countryside, a thing not seen in previous ages'. Husain rebuilt the walls of Kairouan and gave the town its present appearance, built several madarsas and had numerous public works constructed.

But revolts by his nephew, 'Ali Pasha, who had been excluded from power by the sons born to the bey by a Genoese captive, led to serious disorders in 1729. With the support of the Algerians 'Ali's son blockaded the ruler in Kairouan for five years, finally took him prisoner on 18 May 1740 and cut off his head.

The new bey (1740–1756) was sensitive about his independence. He made this clear to the consuls, to whom he intimated that he intended to be master in his own house. Not without reason he suspected the French of encouraging revolts, and he displayed personal animosity towards their consul, who had behaved in a very dishonourable fashion in an affair involving a woman. Finally he broke relations with France in 1741. The attitude of the Africa Company only served to increase his annoyance. Indeed he intercepted a letter from the manager at Cap Nègre, Fougasse, which disclosed a plan for the conquest of Tabarka, which the Lomellini wished to abandon. 'Not only would occupation of the island lead to a considerable expansion of French trade, but also this important post would put France in a position to dictate to the bey of Tunis and all the Barbary powers.'[46] The plan of Fougasse was modelled after that of Sanson Napollon and displayed the same imperialist designs. The bey forestalled the attack by taking possession of the place himself and then of Cap Nègre. A French lieutenant-commander then planned an attempt at a sudden attack on the island but allowed himself to be caught by surprise. To pacify the bey's resentment, Fougasse was officially removed from his post, but the *de facto* administration of La Calle was left in his hands—clear proof that the French government had been by no means displeased at his attempt at conquest. The Tunisian civil war and the liberality of a French negotiator, backed by the presence of frigates, induced 'Ali Pasha on 9 November 1742 to sign a peace treaty which restored the Concessions but required the consul of France to submit to the ceremony of kissing hands.

The bey made provision to meet the country's needs particularly by the construction of schools. His madarsas were modelled on the Egyptian madarsa in their association of school premises, founder's tomb and public fountain. The most interesting, so far as its plan is concerned, is the Bashiga at Tunis. He also embellished the former Hafsid palace at Bardo with new rooms, some of them decorated in European style, ranged round two porticoed courtyards.

The last years of 'Ali Pasha's reign were troubled by his son's rebellion. In 1756 the Algerians took advantage of the situation and invaded Tunisia. They entered the capital with ease, took the bey prisoner, beheaded him, and proclaimed in his stead one of Husain's sons, Muhammad, who had to agree to pay tribute.

Muhammad's reign lasted only three years, but in that time he managed to restore peace in the Regency. There was general praise for his uprightness, the goodness of his character and the successes which his tactful manner met with among Tunisians and foreigners alike. His brother 'Ali Bey (1759–1782) was a prince of

Turkish Rule in Algeria and Tunisia: 1516–1830

outstanding intelligence. Despite the efforts of the English, uplifted by their success in the Seven Years War, he displayed not the slightest animosity towards the French, granting them in 1768 a monopoly of coral fishing off his coast and the right to open a factory at Bizerta. A brief rupture occurred when the French annexed Corsica, which imperilled certain Tunisian interests, but it was the last break. The bey granted the Company the island of Galita (north-east of Tabarka) to make up for the loss of Cap Nègre, from which the local people had expelled the residents at musket-point. He also made a grant of Bizerta, for which the Company was asking, in 1770, followed in 1781 by permission to set up four factories on either side of Cap Bon. France owed her privileged position chiefly to the bey's son-in-law and chief minister, Mustafa Khoja, under whose administration Tunisia enjoyed a renewal of prosperity.

'Ali's son, Hamuda Bey (1782–1814), a young prince of twenty-three, of independent mind and fiery spirit, offered greater resistance to European ascendancy. He broke relations with Venice, which bombarded Sousse in 1784 and almost entirely destroyed La Goulette in 1785, without making him surrender. In 1790 he agreed to negotiate with Spain, but in circumstances in which that country was at a disadvantage. He broke the ties that bound him as a vassal to Algiers, which twice attacked unsuccessfully, in 1807 and 1813, and sent an army to restore the pasha of Tripoli. In the interim he took advantage in 1811 of a revolt by the janissaries to dissolve them, in which step he had popular support. With France he had only three short conflicts. It was the peak of French commerce, which surpassed that of all the foreign nations, including the Jews, due to the Provençal *caravaneurs*, whose coastal trade grew steadily. This favoured position, however, was compromised by the wars of the Revolution and Empire.

In the course of his long reign Hamuda built a considerable palace (*Dār al-Bey*) not far from the kasbah. Its reception chamber was T-shaped and wide, and included a large alcove; it may have been decorated by Moroccan artists. He also built the palace of the Manuba, from which a summer-house was removed to the park of the Belvedere. It is to his powerful minister Yusuf Sahib al-Taba' that we owe the Mosque of the Place Halfaouine, with its arcades separating the nine cradle-vaulted naves and other features displaying even more than those of other contemporary public buildings the European influence.

After the reign of three months of his brother 'Uthman, Muhammad bey's son, Mahmud Bey (1814–1824), found himself forced by the European powers in 1819 to abolish slavery regardless of the economic upheaval necessarily involved in taking this step so abruptly. He had realised the need to renew relations with the ojaq in order to resist pressure by the European powers, but when the two Regencies, though with difficulty, finally concluded a peace treaty in 1821, it was two years too late. The accession to power of Husain Bey (1824–1825) brought no modification of his father's policy. A new phase of Anglo-French rivalry resulted in the coral fishery at Tabarka and along the coast being conceded to England as the highest bidder. The destruction by French ships of the Tunisian fleet at Navarin in 1827 stirred up a feeling of hostility in Tunisia. The bey did not, however, take advantage of the rupture between France and Algiers to show that hostility. Like the Moroccan Sharif, with whom he communicated through the medium of mendicant marabouts, he rejoiced at the thought of the misfortunes to which the neighbouring Regency might be subject. Accordingly he made a show of the strictest neutrality and even had information regarding the situation inside Algeria conveyed to Paris. No one could then have guessed that the outcome of the expedition of 1830 would be the permanent occupation of Algiers, followed by that of Algeria, still less that it would lead to the conquest of Tunisia and Morocco.

CONCLUSION

The fortunes of the two Regencies set up by the Turks in North Africa, and kept separate and apart almost from the outset, were very different. In the Tunis Regency, a land of ancient civilisation, the Turks were gradually assimilated. It can be said that by the beginning of the nineteenth century the process was complete and the Husainid dynasty had become a Tunisian dynasty. Apart from a few terms in their administrative vocabulary and one or two Turkish customs, the beys and their officers could be regarded as belonging to the country.

At Algiers the case was different where the conquerors lived, up until 1830, somewhat apart from the country. One reason was

Turkish Rule in Algeria and Tunisia: 1516–1830

undoubtedly that the Turks took more interest in the sea than in the country itself. But it must also be said that Algeria was too deficient in culture to 'lead her fierce captor captive', and that the Berbers, still profoundly themselves, and who peopled the very regions where the Turks had settled, had far fewer affinities with the Easterners than had the Arabised peoples of Tunisia.

In short, although the two regions were at the outset subjected to the same authority, they had quickly drawn apart. The one remained conquered territory, bearing no grudge against its conqueror, but equally having no real contact with him; the other gradually absorbed the newcomers and tended to transform them into Tunisians, almost indistinguishable from the rest of the population.

Notes

1. F. Braudel, *La Méditerranée et le monde méditerranée à l'époque de Philippe II*, 2 vols. (Paris, 1949; 2nd ed. Paris, 1966); footnotes here are taken from the first edition.
2. *Ibid.*, p. 577 *et seq.*
3. *Ibid.*, for background to the Spanish empire in North Africa in this period, see pp. 516–24.
4. See G. Yver, 'Alger', *Encyclopedia of Islam*, I.
5. D. Haëdo, *Topographia e historia general de Argel* (Valladolid, 1612); see Monnereau and A. Berbrugger, tr., *Revue Africaine*, XIV (1870) and XV (1871); see XIV, 414 *et seq.*
6. R. Lespès, *Alger* (Paris, 1930), p. 35.
7. D. Haëdo (tr. Monnereau and Berbrugger), *op. cit.*, XV, 45.
8. *Ibid.*, p. 47.
9. *Ibid.*, XIV, 496, 518.
10. See *Ibid.*, XV, 50 *et seq.*
11. *Ibid.*, p. 49.
12. *Ibid.*, p. 382.
13. G. Marçais (1927), *op. cit.*, II, 777.
14. D. Haëdo (tr. Monnereau and Berbrugger), *op. cit.*, XIV, 490–5
15. R. Lespès, *op. cit.*, pp. 126–38.
16. D. Haëdo (tr. Monnereau and Berbrugger), *op. cit.*, XIV, 490.
17. *Ibid.*, p. 492–3.
18. *Ibid.*, for references to the famine see XIV, 514; XV, 225, 309.
19. *Ibid.*, XV, 465–6.
20. G. Marçais (1927), *op. cit.*, II, 799–800.

21. F. Braudel, *op. cit.*, pp. 969–70.
22. Charles Monchicourt, *L'Expédition Espagnole de 1560 contre l'île de Djerba* (Paris, 1913), see pp. 7–72.
23. *Ibid.*, 2nd part, Ch. I–V.
24. *Ibid.*
25. F. Braudel, *op. cit.*, see p. 727 *et seq.* for a further account of the career of Dragut.
26. Ibn Abi Dinar, *Kitab al-mu' nis fi akhbar Ifriqiyya wa Tunis* (Tunis, A.H. 1286/A.D. 1861); imperfectly translated by Pellissier de Reynaud, 'Histoire de l'Afrique', *Exploration scientifique de l'Algérie*, VII (1845); for portions relating to Tunis see J. Mugnin, tr., 'Description de Tunis', *Revue I.B.L.A.*, XIV (1951), pp. 150–82.
27. Père Dan, *Histoire de la Barbarie et de ses corsaires* (Paris, 1637; 2nd ed., 1649).
28. D. Haëdo (tr., Monnereau and Berbrugger), *op. cit.*, XV, 394.
29. d'Arvieux, *Mémoires du chevalier d'Arvieux . . .*, 6 vols. (Paris, 1735); see V, 57–280.
30. Père Dan, *op. cit.*, see pp. 31, 335, 402
31. Paul Masson, *Histoire des établissements et du commerce français dans l'Afrique barbaresque (1560–1793)*, (Paris, 1903), p. 30.
32. *Ibid.*, p. 53.
33. *Ibid.*, p. 102.
34. *Ibid.*, p. 107.
35. R. Capot-Rey, *La politique français et le Maghreb Méditerranéen (1643–1685)*, (Algiers, 1935) and in *Revue Africaine* (1934–5), LXXV–LXXVII.
36. *Ibid.*, LXXV, 439.
37. *Ibid.*, p. 439.
38. *Ibid.*, LXXVII, 106.
39. l'Abbé Raynal, *Histoire de commerce des Européens dans l'Afrique septentrionale* (Paris, 1775).
40. G. Marçais (1927), *op. cit.*, II, 786.
41. This is an affair arising out of a visit made by the French Consul to the Dey on 30 April 1827 on the occasion of the close of Ramadan. Evidently an argument ensued, due in part to the Dey's long fast, and the Dey struck the Consul with his fly-whisk and threatened him with imprisonment.
42. M. Emerit, 'Les aventures de Thédenat, esclave et ministre d'un bey d'Afrique XVIIIeme siècle', *Revue Africaine* (1948), pp. 143–84; a fragment of his *Mémoires*. The author was steward (*khaznadar*) to the Bey of Mascara from 1779 to 1782.
43. L. Rinn, 'La royaume d'Alger sous le dernier dey', *Revue Africaine*, 1897, pp. 121–52, 331–50; 1898, pp. 5–21, 131–9, 289–309; 1899, pp. 104–41, 297–320, and published (Algiers, 1900); *R.A.* 1897, p. 124 *et seq.*

Turkish Rule in Algeria and Tunisia: 1516–1830

44. See above, note 41.
45. Peysonnel, *Relation d'un voyage en Barbarie fait par ordre du roi en 1724 et 1725* (1714 and Paris, 1838); quoted in P. Masson, *op. cit.*, pp. 327–8.
46. P. Masson, *op. cit.*, pp. 393–4.

CHAPTER 7

General Survey

❈

When the French troops landed at Sidi Ferruch in 1830 nearly twelve centuries had passed since Islam had first come to North Africa. Although in the early stages of their conquest the Muslims encountered fierce resistance on the part of the Berbers, African Christianity does not seem to have offered vigorous opposition to Islam. It was in Judaism—assuming the Kahina was Jewish—that the plane of doctrine ran counter to the new religion and resisted it victoriously, inasmuch as autochthonous Jewish communities have survived to our own day. At the same time, the autochthonous Christian bodies of Africa finally disappeared at the end of the twelfth century. Nonetheless, in the course of three or four hundred years Islam became the religion of the great majority of the Maghribis and marked them with a stamp that may well prove indelible. It gave a style of living to every city in the land as well as to regions of easy access. In the mountainous regions, better defended by nature, it impressed its influence on beliefs but had virtually no effect on manners and customs, which remained faithful to the past.

However, through contact with the Berber peoples Islam developed subtle local variations. It is possible to speak of Maghribi Islam just as it is possible to speak of Breton or Spanish Catholicism. There was an almost complete absence of doctrinal disputes. The Shi'a beliefs of the first Idrisids, and later of the Fatimids, left no trace; Almohad doctrine, for all its early vigour, vanished without trace, no one quite knows how. Kharijism alone has lived on into our own times in two Berber communities, one in the Mzab and one in the island of Djerba—two landmarks, so to speak, that make no great difference to the human landscape. Moreover, these two heterodox communities, living as it were on the

General Survey

fringe of the Maghrib in remote and inhospitable country, have never entered into overt conflict with the orthodox population surrounding them. More important still, almost the entire Maghrib follows the rules of a single juridical school—the Maliki. Only the descendants of Turkish settlers in Algeria and Tunisia adhere to the Hanifi school, and they form quite small groups in the few principal towns of the two countries.

While remaining apart from the great theological disputes, the Muslim religion has undergone certain slight changes in the Maghrib. It has acquired an undeniable touch of the anthropomorphic. The cult of the saints developed considerably, as witness not only daily visits to venerated tombs but also annual feasts (*mausim*) commemorating the saints' deaths, as well as the hagiographic compilations that have flourished throughout North Africa from the fifteenth century. In many cases the saints are associated with trees, springs and high places, leaving no room for doubt that the veneration of the Muslim saint has been superimposed on very ancient cults to which the Berbers have remained faithfully attached. Nevertheless the animism of ancient times has found highly opportune sustenance in the belief in genies (*jnun*) permitted by Muslim orthodoxy.

Over and above these more or less disguised survivals of ancient cults, Maghribi Islam is characterised, especially from the fifteenth century onwards, by a great development of popular mysticism. It was in the countryside, not in the towns—in the souls of folk whose faith was as simple as it was ardent, and not in the subtle brains of jurists and theologians—that this religion of the heart came into being. It spread gradually under the guise of religious brotherhoods in which the adepts of one particular mystic system—of one 'way', or 'path', as the Arabic term is—are gathered together. There are modest ones accounting for no more than a score or two of adepts in some tiny country district; others extend over a great part of North Africa, sometimes over the entire country. Some are very popular and display more than a tendency towards charlatanism, like the well known Aïssaoua brotherhood; others are centres of mystic knowledge and attract the rarest and finest spirits. In our present state of knowledge it is not possible to define exactly the role of the brotherhoods in the history of the Maghrib, but it was certainly an important one, as witness, as late as the end of the eighteenth century, the rebellion of the Derqawa of Orania against the Turks.

It is impossible to leave unmentioned the prestige of individuals renowned as custodians of *baraka*, that divine charisma which extends to things temporal as well as to things spiritual. Those we commonly call marabouts—but who even more commonly go under the appellation of *walī* (friend or saint [of God])—are custodians of *baraka*. To one of their following of kinsmen and disciples they transmit the *baraka*, and it is he who continues the teaching and miracle-working after they are gone. Their field of influence is usually very limited but they are able to extend it somewhat further in the event of disturbances and anarchy. The marabouts of Dila very nearly arrogated power to themselves throughout the whole of Morocco in the mid-eighteenth century. Their rivals in *baraka* are the *shurfa* or descendants of the Prophet. Ever since the time of Idris I and 'Ubaid Allah the *shurfa* have enjoyed a great prestige in Maghribi lands at all levels of the social scale. Eventually they took on the administration of Morocco, in which country it would now be difficult to imagine the ruler being anything but a Sharif. In Algeria and Tunisia their influence was less important, but never negligible.

Finally, Maghribi Islam gives an appearance of great stability. Ever since the Almohad movement, since, that is, the mid-thirteenth century, doctrine and practice have remained recognisably the same. There is only one innovation to be noted—the commemoration of the Prophet's birth, made official by the Merinid Abu Ya'qub and very readily adopted by the entire Maghribi population. Indeed, it has been placed almost on the same level as the two canonical ceremonies of the breaking of the fast (*al-'Īd al-Saghīr*) and the sacrifice of the sheep (*al-Ī'd al-Kabīr*). But a doctrinal movement as important as Wahhabism in the eighteenth century found no echo in the Maghrib, despite the efforts put forth in its behalf by the sultan of Morocco, Sidi Muhammad ibn 'Abd Allah.

Islam, then, was victorious in North Africa. It formed scholars and drew to it almost all the inhabitants, to such a degree that the most ignorant of them and those least acquainted with orthodox practices were ready to lay down their lives in defence of their rudimentary beliefs. It stamped with an oriental mode of living a

General Survey

country which throughout the Roman period had lived in a western fashion and to all appearances was more comfortable doing so. But at the same time that Islam was taking root in the Maghrib it was drawing in on itself there, losing touch with the schools and communities of the East, allowing itself to be permeated with the ancient beliefs and former customs of the Berbers and growing sterile under the influence of Maliki casuistry. In short, this was an Islam that remained basically sound and vigorous, but had become narrow and somewhat warped by the use the Maghribis had made of it over the centuries.

The triumph of Islam did not involve the triumph of the Arabs. Their domination of North Africa as a whole did not last fifty years. By the eighth century it had finally come to an end in the entire western part of the Maghrib. The same was to be true of Ifriqiya a century and a half later.

But, paradoxically enough, though the ascendancy of the Muslim East over the Maghrib was short-lived, it was nevertheless to that same East that for centuries the Berbers looked for their leaders or their inspiration. Without so much as mentioning the extraordinary destiny of the ʿUmaiyads in Muslim Spain, we have only to recall that Ibn Rustum, Idris ibn Abd ʿAllah, ʿUbaid Allah and his forerunner Abu ʿAbd Allah were all émigrés from the East. Each of them—due to their eastern origin and, in the case of Idris and ʿUbaid Allah, to their standing as descendants of the Prophet—succeeded in taking command of a Berber tribe or confederation and was thus enabled to found a state. Ibn Rustum found support in the Zenata, Idris in the Awraba and ʿUbaid Allah in the Kotama. Later, when the Berbers would no longer give obedience to foreigners and had taken to finding their leaders from among their own numbers, it was still to the East that they looked for the ideals that stirred their energy to action. The desire for a renewal of Islam that inspired the first Almoravids sprang from a voyage to the East, and in the same way Ibn Tumart formed his doctrine during his sojourn in the East. It was only from the time of ʿAbd al-Mumin that the Berbers cut themselves off from all external influence. And it was not long afterwards that the great Berber empires vanished and the country reverted to the gradual process of disintegration.

Here, it seems, we find ourselves confronted with one of the best established constants in the history of the Berbers—their savage opposition to higher command even when it springs from their own soil, and their determination to exercise direct control over such of their numbers as attain power. At the same time we must recognise their clannish spirit, which prevents a victorious tribe from making terms with the conquered or from taking them into partnership, in short from moving forward from the ethnic group to the state proper. Not one of the Berber leaders succeeded in passing beyond the clan stage; Ibn Tumart made an attempt in that direction at Tinmel, working with tribes closely akin to each other in blood, speech and way of life. But the Almohads, as soon as they had left their mountains, opposed any collaboration with those whom they were bringing into subjection, and soon the family of the great 'Abd al-Mumin had formed a new and highly exclusive sept within the circle of the victorious clan. The Hafsids alone, too few in number to impose their exclusive sway on the rest of the population, succeeded in founding a homogeneous state because the Arab tribes made it impossible for them to accomplish this task. Yet the circumstances in which they found themselves were the most advantageous for success, since Ifriqiya is geographically the least compartmented of the Maghrib countries. It has, moreover, from earliest times been a region wide open to outside influences, peopled with folk drawn from the most diverse quarters, and rich in towns and civilisation. But the presence of the Bedouin Arabs largely nullified these conditions favouring the development of a political state.

From the time of Ibn Khaldun, no historian has failed to stress the importance of the Arab factor in North Africa. The slow but steady infiltration of the Beni Hilal and of those who followed in their wake is said to have upset the political balance of the Maghrib. Also, and of greater importance, it upset the economic balance. By virtue of its climate and relief, North Africa has a double role— agricultural and pastoral. It is difficult enough to harmonise these two ways of life, so different are their requirements. It seems that the Romans pushed the pastoralists as far south as they could. (It is, incidentally, interesting to note that the frontier of the territory under their rule, so far as we are in a position to trace it with any precision, followed fairly closely what we might regard as the natural line of demarcation between herdsman and farmer.) Their territory extended very far to the south in Tunisia and the Constantine region, drew distinctly closer to the sea with each mile westward, and finally constituted no more than a quite narrow strip in the neighbourhood of Tlemcen, at which point desert and steppe come nearest to the sea.

This balance, which was imposed by the power of Rome but which also corresponded with the country's needs, was scarcely disturbed when Roman rule came to an end. The early Muslim conquerors did nothing whatever to upset it; they were not pastoralists from Arabia but townsmen or sedentary folk from the Near East. Nor was it seriously modified by the political struggles that followed the Muslim conquest. Despite the efforts of the pastoral Zenata to compete for supremacy with the settled Kotama, the Maghrib, as described by Ibn Hawqal in the mid-tenth century, was still an agricultural country, wooded and prosperous. The Zenata may have managed to infiltrate the far Maghrib, but they had been unable to make any serious incursion in the territories of the agriculturist Ghomara, Berghwata and Masmouda.

The arrival of the Bedouin Arabs threw everything into a melting pot. Doubt has been expressed whether their numbers were at all large and the doubt is probably well-grounded. But in the desert a few thousand additional men and animals are enough to render living space inadequate. As quickly as the Arabs came on the scene, the tribes of Berber herdsmen who had continued their traditional activity were, so to speak, pushed both westwards and northwards, towards the land of the cultivators. The movement was slow but deliberate; gradually the farmers found themselves driven back by the goats and sheep, which reduced the area of sown land and were a menace to trees. It must be assumed that this imperceptible but far-reaching revolution in the country's internal equilibrium was a contributory factor to the political decline of the Maghrib between the thirteenth and the fifteenth centuries.

In the fifteenth century the play of opposing forces was complicated by a new factor, the appearance of the Christians in Africa. Until that time the Moroccans had taken part with varying success in the defence of Islam in Spain, but the defeats suffered by Abu al-Hasan in 1340 and 1343 had brought their interventions to an end. In 1415 the Portuguese crossed the Straits of Gibraltar and for the first time since the Arab conquest installed themselves on

Muslim soil. For a long time this initial success was not followed up, but it immediately involved certain important consequences. The presence of non-Muslims in Morocco, limited though their domain was to a tiny peninsula at the furthest point of the country, provoked a movement of religious fervour deeper probably than that of the Almohads. It was all the deeper for arising, not from the intellect of a doctrinaire man like Ibn Tumart, but rather from the heart and mind of the people at large. At the outset it was in the neighbourhood of Ceuta, in the Habt and the Jbel, that there began to spring up that great number of holy men, and of holy women too, who summoned the Muslims to the defence of their threatened faith. Thence the movement spread in proportion as at the end of the century the Portuguese began to extend their conquests along the Moroccan coast, and it reached as far as the distant regions of the Draʿ and the Sous, where the Saadian *shurfa* appeared. Religious fervour quickly took on a tinge of xenophobia, so much so that the Saadians did not hesitate to take the Spaniards as allies against the Turks who had settled at Algiers. They were Muslims certainly, but also foreigners threatening to make their way into Morocco, whereas the Spaniards were no longer a danger.

From that point Morocco ceased to share in the life of North Africa, withdrawing more and more upon itself, tolerating only such contacts as were barely necessary to maintain a far from flourishing trade, and no more in touch with the Muslim east than with the Christian west. Jealously closed against any outside influence, the country became engrossed in the almost unending struggle waged by the Berber tribes to break loose from the authority of government. These exhausting convulsions resulted in an extraordinary stagnation of social life just when neighbouring Europe was evolving at ever increasing speed. Morocco shut its doors against Europe at the very point when Europe was hurriedly burgeoning forth and tending to draw the rest of the world after it in the eddies of its passage.

In the other parts of the Maghrib, Spanish intervention involved different consequences. The Moors of Bougie made alliance with Turkish corsairs in an attempt to reconquer their city. These Turks seized the opportunity to settle at Algiers. Threatened in their turn, they appealed to the Sultan at Constantinople, who sent

General Survey

them troops and extended his suzerainty over the territories they occupied. For a half century Algiers became the forward bastion of the Ottoman Empire in the western Mediterranean, one of the points of friction in the wide-ranging conflict in which Charles V was opposed to Sulaiman the Magnificent. By the end of the century the Turks were established for a long time to come in the two Regencies of Algiers and Tunis. But whereas the Turks of Algiers lived on the fringe of the country, content to scour it once a year in order to raise taxes whenever they could, the Turks of Tunis, confronted with a more stable and more firmly based civilisation, gradually became absorbed into the Tunisian population and founded what can be described as a national dynasty, that of the Husainid beys. Different though development of the two Regencies was, the Turks nevertheless failed to impart any fresh impetus to the age-old Maghrib. In the one as in the other, Berber inertia won the day, so that at the beginning of the nineteenth century the entire Maghrib was living, withdrawn into its shell, in accordance with standards that had held for thousands of years, and without having been able to evolve in the direction of statehood in its modern form.

In conclusion, one cannot deny that Muslim civilisation, after a long and difficult period of adaptation, leavened the Berber dough and led to the flowering of a brilliant civilisation whose highest point is found in the Almohad epoch. It was then that the Berbers, left to themselves, fell back progressively into the pursuit of those internecine dissensions which they seemed to enjoy, and of an anachronistic way of life in close proximity to a world in a ferment of change. Such proximity could not fail to produce its effects.

Glossary

'abīd 'slaves, serfs, bondsmen'.
amīr 'commander, prince'.
amīr al-muminīn 'Commander of the Faithful', a title which appears frequently in the western part of the Muslim world, employed by dynasties which considered themselves entitled to claim the Caliphate.
amīr al-muslimīn 'Commander of the Muslims', a title which was initially accepted by the Almoravids who were content to recognise the political and spiritual supremacy of the Abbasids.
ansar 'helpers', a title given to the Prophet's followers in Medina and those who assisted him after his flight from Mecca. This title was subsequently adopted by a number of political and religious leaders in the Islamic world to designate their close associates and loyal followers.
Azrakism a Kharijite sect named after Nafi' b. al-Azrak which maintained an extreme intolerance for infidels; with the death of their leaders in 696 the Azrakites' movement disappeared.
baraka 'blessing', a quality of Divine Grace dispensed by God and by those selected by Him; of particular application in the *sufi* vocabulary and of widespread use and interpretation in North African Islam.
bey a Turkish administrative term indicating the governor of a province; the title of rulers in Tunisia from about 1705.
bled a Maghribi corruption of *balad*, country, commonly used to describe the parts of Sharifian Morocco which were under the control of the government (*bled al-makhzan*), or independent from direct governmental supervision (*bled al-siba*).
brotherhood see *tariqa*.
charter of *iqtā'* 'fief, feudal estate', land granted by feudal tenure.
dā'ī 'He who summons (men to Good or to the Faith)', a title which assumed special significance in those Shiite sects which engaged in secret propaganda.
dar al-harb 'land of war', that area of the world which is not under Muslim rule and therefore is the legitimate object of *jihad* by the Muslim peoples.

dar al-Islam 'land of Islam', a geographical area ruled by a sovereign according to Islamic law and inhabited by People of the Book (*ahl al-Kitab*) with or without non-Muslims who have submitted to Muslim control and who are not idolaters.

dervish derived from the Persian, 'medicant', generally applied throughout the Islamic world to a member of a *sufi tariqa*.

dey Turkish administrative term; the governor of Algers before 1830; a ruler or pasha of Tunis or Tripoli.

divan Turkish administrative term for the council of state.

faqih (pl. *fuqaha*') originally meaning an intelligent person but the evolved usage came to mean 'canon lawyer', one who interprets *fiqh*.

fatwa a legal opinion issued by a *mufti*, *qadi* or *faqih* of high qualification.

fiqh the name given to the Islamic science of jurisprudence.

funduk 'hotel, inn, hostel', also applied more generally to foreign commercial houses in North Africa.

guish see *jaish*.

hadith 'tradition', employed both in general terms and specifically with reference to the actions and sayings of the Prophet which supplement in varying degrees (according to the legal school of the *shari'a*) the *sunna* and *Qur'an* as sources of Prophetic guidance.

hajj 'pilgrimage', commonly applied specifically to the pilgrimage to Mecca, 'Arafat and Mina; the fifth 'pillar' of the five 'pillars' of Islam, incumbent upon every good Muslim.

Hanbali see *shari'a*.

Hanafi see *shari'a*.

haratine 'slave', a term commonly applied to negro slaves of the Sahara.

hijra 'flight', applied to the act of escaping from the control of non-believers on the pattern of the Prophet's flight from Mecca to Medina in 622 (from which date the Muslim calendar begins).

Ibadi a name applied to followers of one of the principal Kharijite branches, so named after its presumed founder, 'Abd Allah b. Ibad al-Murri al-Tamim.

ijma' 'general assent' of the Community of Islam.

imam the leader in group prayer in Islam; in Sunni usage, Caliphs and eminent scholars; in Shiite usage, a descendant of 'Ali b. Abi Talib.

iqtā' see: charter of *iqtā'*.

Islam 'submission', applied to the way of life derived from the teachings, beliefs and rituals which are based on the *Qur'an*.

jaish 'army', in Maghribi usage pronounced '*guish*'.

jihad 'holy war', encouraged in Islam to be waged by believers against non-believers.

jund 'army'.

Glossary

kalam   literally 'speech', used in reference to the scholastic theology founded by al-Ash'ari (873–935).

kasbah   'a capital city, citadel, metropolis'.

kharaj   initially, the tribute submitted by infidels living in Muslim territory, but by the end of the 1st century A.H. it had come to be a land tax.

Kharijite   literally, 'those who go out', the earliest of the Islamic religious sects which was led by 'Ali and ramifications of which caused a series of insurrections in the early years of Islam.

Koran   see *Qur'an*.

lazma   'official concession, licence, franchise'.

madrasa   an institution where the Islamic sciences are studied, generally used in reference to higher education.

al-Maghrib al-Aqsa   the far Maghrib; the third of the three regions of the Maghrib recognised by the Arab geographers. These were Ifriqiyya, the Middle Maghrib and al-Maghrib al-Aqsa; roughly modern-day Morocco.

mahdi   'the guided one', a term which came to mean the Divinely guided one who was to herald the Restoration in the preparation for the End of Time.

makhzan   'government' (in Morocco), or, more specifically, the financial organisation of the government.

Maliki   one of the four principal schools of the *shari'a*, named after Malik b. Anas, which spread throughout the Western Islamic world in the 9th century and now dominates the Maghrib and Africa.

marabout   a title of particular North and West African usage applied to a Muslim saint or a venerated man and his descendants; from the Arabic *murabit* through the Portuguese *marabuto*.

minaret   the tower of a mosque from which the *mu'zzin* calls the faithful to prayer; an architectural development in mosque construction of the early 8th century.

minbar   the 'pulpit' or stand in the mosque from which the *khutba* (sermon) is generally delivered.

mihrab   the niche or recess in the eastern end of a mosque used to indicate the direction of prayer (qibla).

mufti   a jurisconsultant who expounds the *shari'a* and is entitled to issue *fatwas*; in some Muslim governmental structures an officer of the state or assessor to a court.

Mu'tazilites   the theological school to which is attributed the creation of the speculative dogmatics of Islam.

muzarabs   name given in the Middle Ages to Christian Andalusians who had become a part of the hispano-arab civilisation and who spoke Arabic.

pasha   Turkish administrative term indicating officers of high rank.

pashalik   Turkish administrative term indicating the area under the control of a pasha.

qadi   a judge, generally in matters of civil law with particular reference to religious injunctions.

qaid (qāʾid)   a high-ranking officer; in the Maghrib the term is applied to certain officers wielding military and civil power, or to describe a member of court, government or public office.

qibla   the direction in which prayer is said; the direction of the Kaaba in Mecca; indicated in the interior of a mosque by a recess (mihrab).

Qurʾan   the sacred book of Muslims containing the collected revelations made to the Prophet Muhammad.

raïs (raïs)   'chief, head'.

ribat   a fortified Muslim monastery, frequently associated with the *jihad*, the defences and the expansion of the lands of Islam.

Rum   Arabic form of the Latin *Roma* or *Romanus* used in reference generally to the Christians.

Shafi   see *shariʿa*.

shaikh   generally an elderly and highly venerated man; frequently also used in the sense of a supreme chief, and in these terms employed in the *sufi* hierarchy as spiritual leader.

shariʿa   the law of Islam consisting of Prophetic revelation, Tradition and sayings, which is divided into four 'orthodox' schools—Maliki, Hanbali, Hanafi and Shafi.

sharif (pl. shurfa)   a term which has come to be applied to putative descendants of the Prophet.

Shiʿa   the name given to a varied and large number of sects considered apart from 'orthodox Islam', all of which recognise 'Ali as the legitimate caliph after the Prophet's death.

sufi   title given to the mystic in Islam, more popularly known as *dervish*.

sufrite   a moderate branch of the Kharijites named after 'Abdallah b. al-Saffar who broke with the Azrakites over their sanguinary policies.

suk   'market'.

sunna   'custom, wont, use'; generally used in reference to the actions of the Prophet—his deeds, utterances and un-spoken approval—which not always formally constitute a part of *hadith*.

sunni   'orthodox'; those Muslims who follow the *sunna* of the Prophet and refrain from deviating from dogma and practice.

sura   the separate revelations made to the Prophet and the name given to chapters in the *Qurʾan*.

tafsir   'explanation, commentary'; applied generally to commentaries on scientific and philosophical works and specifically applied to *Qurʾanic* interpretations; as such this Islamic science forms an important branch of *hadith* and is concerned with the external, philological exegesis.

taïfa (taʾifa)   'party, group'.

Glossary

tariqa 'way, path'; applied to the body of followers of a *sufi shaikh*, generally characterised by the name of that *shaikh*.

ta'wil technical term for the material interpretation of the *Qur'an*, relating to its content.

tawhid 'unity'; a theological notion affirming the unity of God, of particular significance to Almohad theology (*al-muwahhidun*).

radition see *sunna*.

'ulama' those who possess knowledge; specifically the custodians of canon law and theology.

vizir (wazir) 'minister'.

zakat 'alms tax'; one of the five 'pillars' of Islam.

zawiya in North African usage, a building or group of buildings used for religious study, resembling a monastery though not necessarily synonymous with a *ribat*; frequently associated with the centres of *sufi shaikhs*.

Introduction to the Bibliography

The bibliography which follows includes all the items originally in the second French edition of *Histoire de l'Afrique du Nord*, vol. II, but the format has been reorganised. References have been divided into three sections: reference and research guides, general works arranged by subject headings, and a chronological listing of specific references and monographs. The last of these is essentially Charles-André Julien's 'Bibliography by Chapters' with slight variations. Within the section dealing with general works arranged by subjects, an effort has been made to integrate all items mentioned in the final section which are not monographs of specific chronological relevance. The major changes beyond format are the addition of a section dealing with catalogues and guides to North African Arabic and Turkish manuscripts, enlarged sections on Arabic sources appearing in translation and on Islam, and the addition of more English language material. An attempt has also been made to bring the references up to date by the inclusion of books and articles which have appeared over the past eighteen years. These additions have come largely from notices of new historical work appearing during that period in *Hespéris* and *Hespéris-Tamuda*, *R.A.*, *I.B.L.A.*, and J. P. Pearson's *Index Islamicus* (Cambridge, 1958) and *Supplement* (Cambridge, 1962). All additions to the original bibliography have been indicated by an asterisk in the left margin.

EDITOR

Periodical and organisational abbreviations employed in the bibliography

Acad. Roy. Belgique Bull. Cl. Lettres	Académie royale de Belgique. Bulletin de la classe des lettres
Af. fr.	Afrique française
Af. fr. R.C.	Afrique française. Renseignements coloniaux
A.M.	Archives marocaines
Am. Hist. Rev.	American Historical Review
Ann. de Geogr.	Annales de Géographie
Annales I.E.O.	Annales de l'Institut d'Etudes Orientales
Arch. I.E.A.	Archivos del Instituto de Estudios Africanos
B.C.E.H.S.A.O.F.	Bulletin de la comité des études historiques et scientifiques d'Afrique occidentale française
B.E.P.M.	Bulletin de l'enseignement publique au Maroc
B.I.H.E.M.	Bulletin de l'Institut des Hautes études marocaines
B.S.G.A.	Bulletin de la Société de géographie d'Alger et de l'Afrique du Nord
B.S.G.O.	Bulletin de la Société de géographie et d'archéologie de la province d'Oran
B.S.O.A.S.	Bulletin of the School of Oriental and African Studies
Bull. arch. alger.	Bulletin d'archéologie algérienne
Bull. Econ. Tun.	Bulletin économique et social de la Tunisie
Bull. I.F.A.N.	Bulletin de l'Institut Française d'Afrique Noire (since 1965, Bulletin de l'Institut Fondamental d'Afrique Noire)
C.H.J.	Cambridge Historical Journal
Coll. Labor.	Colección Labor
Enc. Mens. O.M.	Encyclopédie mensuelle d'outre-mer
Engl. Hist. Rev.	English Historical Review
I.B.L.A.	Institut des belles lettres arabes
I.E.O.	Institut d'Etudes Orientales
I.H.E.M.	Institut des Hautes Etudes marocaines
Inst. Est. Isl. Madrid	Instituto Egipcio de Estudios Islámicos, Madrid
J.A.	Journal asiatique
J.A.H.	Journal of African History
J.S.A.	Journal de la Société des africanistes
M.E.A.H.	Miscelanea de estudios árabes y hebraicos
Orient.	Orientalia

History of North Africa

P.F.L.A.	Publications de la Faculté des Lettres d'Alger
R.A.	Revue africaine
R.E.I.	Revue des Etudes Islamiques
Rev. geog. Maroc.	Revue de Géographie Marocaine
R.H.	Revue historique
R.H.C.	Revue de l'histoire des colonies françaises
R.H.R.	Revue de l'histoire des religions
Rev. Inst. Eg. Madrid	Revista del Instituto Egipcio de Estudios Islámicos, Madrid
Rev. Méd.	Revue méditerranéenne
R.M.M.	Revue du Monde Musulman
R.S.A.C.	Recueil des notices et mémoires de la Société Archéologique du département de Constantine
R.T.	Revue Tunisienne
Stud. Islamica	Studia Islamica
T.I.R.S.	Travaux de l'Institut des Recherches saharienne

Index to Bibliography

PART I, RESEARCH GUIDES

I Bibliographies   *page*
  A General bibliographies relating to North Africa   359
  B Morocco   360
  C Algeria   361
  D Tunisia   362
  E Other bibliographies of relevance: Tripolitania, Sahara and West Africa, and Portugal   362

II References
  A Atlases   363
  B Encyclopedias   363
  C Dictionaries   363
  D Biographies   364
  E Museum Guides   364
  F Arabic literature   364
  G Genealogy/chronology   364

III Journals
  A General   364
  B Morocco   366
  C Algeria   367
  D Tunisia   367
  E Spain   368
  F Collective Works, *Festschriften*, Congresses   368

IV Catalogues and guides to Archives and Libraries
  A Arabic and Turkish manuscripts: Algeria   369
  B Arabic manuscripts: Morocco   370
  C Arabic manuscripts: Tunisia   370
  D Catalogues of other Archives and Libraries containing Arabic manuscript material of relevance to North African history   370
  E Published primary source material in European languages   370

PART II, TOPICAL INDEX

V Art and Archaeology
  A General   371
  B Morocco   371
  C Algeria   372
  D Tunisia   372

  E Numismatics   372
  F Epigraphy   373
 VI Islam
  A General Studies on Islamic history and civilisation   373
  B Koran   374
  C Islamic theology, law and institutions   374
  D Islam in the Maghrib   375
 VII Sociology, Anthropology, Ethnography
  A General   376
  B Morocco   376
  C Algeria   378
  D Tunisia and Libya   378
  E Islamic and Arabic music   378
 VIII Economics: commerce   379
 IX Arabic sources including those available in translation
  A Sources   381
  B Alphabetical listing of translators of Arabic and Turkish sources, indicating authors under whom the translations are listed in IX, A   389
 X History: general works pertaining to geographical areas
  A Universal histories dealing with the Maghrib   391
  B Spain and Portugal   392
  C West Africa and the Sahara   393
  D North Africa: general works   394
   1. Morocco   395
   2. Algeria   395
   3. Tunisia   396
  E North East Africa   397

PART III, CHRONOLOGICAL/HISTORICAL INDEX
 XI The Arab Conquest
  A Arab authors   397
  B Specific references and monographs   397
 XII Ibadites
  A Arab authors   398
  B Specific references and monographs   399
 XIII Idrisids, Aghlabids and Fatimids
  A Arab authors   399
  B Idrisids (specific references and monographs)   400
  C Aghlabids (specific references and monographs)   400
  D Fatimids (specific references and monographs)   400
  E Zirids (specified references and monographs)   401
  F Sanhaja and Hilalian invasions   401
 XIV Almoravids and Almohads
  A Arab authors   402
  B General works   402

Bibliography

c	Almoravids (specific references and monographs)	403
d	Almohads (specific references and monographs)	404
	1. Almohad power	404
	2. Almohad doctrine, organisation and philosophy	404
	3. Almohad art and architecture	405

XV Hafsids, Abd al-Wadids, Merinids and Beni Wattas

a	Arab authors	406
b	Portuguese sources	406
c	General works	406
d	Hafsids (specific references and monographs)	407
e	Abd al-Wadids (specific references and monographs)	407
f	Merinids (specific references and monographs)	408
g	Beni Wattas (specific references and monographs)	408

XVI The Sharifian Empire

a	Arab authors	409
b	European travellers	409
c	General works	411
d	Saadians (specific references and monographs)	411
	1. The Portuguese in Morocco	412
	2. al-Mansur al-Dhahabi	413
	3. The decline of the Saadians	414
e	Alawites (specific references and monographs)	414
	1. Mulay Rashid	414
	2. Mulay Isma'il	414
	3. The successors to Mulay Isma'il	415

XVII Turkish domination of Algeria and Tunisia (1516–1830)

a	Arab sources	416
b	European travellers	416
c	General works	417
d	The Spanish occupation in North Africa	418
e	The Regency of Algiers	419
f	Tunisia	420

Bibliography

❋

Part I. Research Guides

I. BIBLIOGRAPHIES

A. General Bibliographies relating to North Africa

* 'Bibliographie africaniste', *Journal de la Société des Africanistes* (Paris); an annual note in the *Journal* with references to North Africa.

Bibliography of Barbary States, Supplementary Papers of the Royal Geographical Society (London, 1889–92). In four parts: I, R. L. Playfair, 'Tripoli and the Cyrenaica', n.d.; II, H. S. Ashbee, 'A Bibliography of Tunisia', 1889, published first in A. Graham and H. S. Ashbee, *Travels in Tunisia*; III, R. L. Playfair, 'A Bibliography of Algeria', n.d. [1889] (covering the period 1541–1887 only), and 'Supplement to the Bibliography of Algeria', 1898 (covering the period to 1895); IV, R. L. Playfair and R. Brown, 'A Bibliography of Morocco', 1892 (from the origins to 1891).

* 'Bibliography of Current Publications', in *Africa*, published quarterly by the International Africa Institute, London, from 1928, contains sections on North Africa with especial reference to anthropology, sociology, 2nd linguistics; see also *African Abstracts* from 1950, also published quarterly and a continuation of the former 'Bibliography of Current Publications'.

Braudel, F., 'Les Espagnols en Afrique du Nord de 1492 à 1577', *R.A.*, 1928, pp. 184–233 and 351–428.

* Conover, H. F., *North and Northeast Africa. A selected, annotated list of writings 1951–1957* (Washington, D.C., 1957), Library of Congress publication (of very limited value for the historical period with which we are concerned here).

Courtois, C., 'Bibliographie de l'Histoire de l'Afrique du Nord des origines à la fin du Moyen âge', *Revue Historique*, cxcviii, 1947, pp. 228–49; and in *R.A.*, no. 412–13, 1947, pp. 278–300 (works from 1939–46, an annotated bibliography).

Creswell, K. A. C., 'A Bibliography of Muslim Architecture in North Africa (excluding Egypt)', supplement to *Hespéris*, 1954, XLI.

de Card, Rouard, *Bibliographie des ouvrages relatifs à la Berbérie au XVIIe et au XVIIIe siècle* (Paris, 1911); *Supplément* (Paris, 1917).

Despois, J., *L'Afrique du Nord* (Paris, 1949), pp. 571–87.

History of North Africa

Guernier, E. (ed.), *Encyclopédie de l'Empire français* (Paris, 1946); volumes deal with Algeria and the Sahara, Morocco and Tunisia and each is accompanied by a bibliography.

Julien, Ch.-A., *Histoire de l'Afrique du Nord* (Paris, 1931).

* Le Tourneau, R., 'Le Moyen Age et les temps modernes', *R.A.*, 100, 1956, pp. 121–44 (a continuation of the essay of W. Marçais in *Histoire et Historiens de l'Algérie* (Paris, 1931)).

* Loewenthal, R., 'Russian materials on Islam and Islamic institutions. A selective bibliography', *Der Islam*, 33, 1958, pp. 280–309; 34, 1959, pp. 174–87 and 35, 1960, pp. 128–52.

Marçais, G., *La Berbérie musulmane et l'Orient au Moyen Age* (Paris, 1946); for the 7th–13th centuries, bibliographical notices appear at the beginning of each chapter.

——, *Les Arabes en Berbérie* (Paris, 1913), pp. 741–9; for the 11th–14th centuries.

——, *Manuel d'art musulman*, 2 vols. (Paris, 1926–7), I, pp. 431–41 and II, pp. 917–29; the Arab conquest to the 19th century, divided into nine periods.

* Massignon, G., 'Bibliographie des Recueils de Contes traditionnels du Maghreb (Maroc, Algérie, Tunisie)', *Sonderdruck*, 4, 1961, pp. 111–29.

Masson, P., *Histoire des établissements et du commerce français dans l'Afrique barbaresque* (Paris, 1903); for the Spanish and Turkish occupation of Barbary, see pp. xv–xxii.

* Mylius, Norbert, *Afrika Bibliographie 1943–51* (Vienna, 1952); for anthropology and related subjects.

* Pearson, J. D., *Index Islamicus, 1906–55* (Cambridge, 1958); a collection of articles appearing in periodicals on Islamic subjects, well indexed by subject and regions of the Muslim world; 26,000 entries; and *Index Islamicus Supplement 1956–60* (Cambridge, 1962), 7,296 entries; and *Supplement 1961-65* (Cambridge, 1967), 8,135 entries.

Sauvaget, J., *L'Introduction à l'histoire de l'Orient musulman* (Paris, 1946); useful for general bibliography on the history of Islam.

* 'Travaux publiés par des historiens de l'Afrique du Nord de 1950 à 1955', *Doc. Alg. série cult.*, no. 76, 30 June 1955.

* Vajda, G., 'Notes de bibliographie maghrébine' (2nd series), *Hespéris*, 41, 1954, pp. 365–77.

B. Morocco

Archives et Bibliothèques de France, la Bibliographie de la 1re partie, Dynastie saadienne (Paris, 1926), pp. 1–10.

Bauer y Landauer, *Apuntes para una bibliografía de Marruecos* (Madrid, n.d. [1922]); includes 1,693 items of G. Robles and Cambronero up to 1912, though with many errors in the 1,331 references of Bauer covering the period 1892–1914.

de Castries, H., de Cenival, P., and Ricard, R., *Les sources inédites de*

Bibliography

l'histoire du Maroc (Paris, 1905—in progress, 23 volumes as of 1961), 2 series; see bibliography and general index to the 1st series (Paris, 1926) and appendices to subsequent volumes.

de Cenival, P. 'Note sur la bibliographie générale du Maroc', *B.I.H.E.M.*, 1920, pp. 10–16.

*de Cenival, P., Funck-Brentano, Ch., and Bousser, M., *Bibliographie marocaine* (1923–33), (Paris, 1934); a series of articles bring this bibliography up to date: for the years 1934–5 see Ch. Funck-Brentano and M. Bousser in *Hespéris*, 1939, xxvi, pp. 321–89; for the years 1936–9 see Ch. Funck-Brentano and O. Lille in *Hespéris*, 1943, xxx, pp. 3–122; for the years 1940–3 see J. Riche and O. Lille in *Hespéris*, 1947, xxxiv, pp. 103–234; for the years 1944–7 see J. Riche and O. Lille in *Hespéris*, 1951, xxxviii; for the years 1948–51 see J. Riche and O. Lille in *Hespéris*, 1955, xlii, pp. 291–708; for the years 1952–3 see J. Riche and O. Lille in *Hespéris-Tamuda*, III, 1962.

Initiation au Maroc (Paris, 1946, 3rd ed.), published by I.H.E.M.; a brief bibliography.

Lévi-Provençal, E., *Les Historiens des Chorfa* (Paris, 1922); an excellent study in bibliography and historiography of Morocco from the 16th century to the 20th century.

Meakin, Budgett, *The Moorish Empire* (London, 1899), pp. 499–518.

Playfair, R. L. and Brown R., *Bibliography of Barbary States*, IV (see above Bibliographies I.A.).

Ricard, R. in *Hespéris*, 1927, vii, pp. 33–51; 1929, ix, pp. 295–301; 1933, xvii, pp. 149–52; 1936, xxiii, pp. 55–66; 1946, xxxiii, pp. 165–73; a study of Portuguese publications.

Terrasse, H., *Histoire du Maroc des origines à l'établissement du Protectorat français* (Casablanca, 1949–50) 2 vols.; bibliographical notes are found at the beginning of each chapter.

C. Algeria

Alazard, J. and Albertini, E., *et al.*, *Histoire et historiens de l'Algérie (1830–1930)*, Collection du Centenaire de l'Algérie; IV, Archéologie et Histoire (Paris, 1931), published by *Revue Historique*. A series of essays by specialists which give a selected and critical survey of the most important works for the study of Algerian history and discuss problems of Algerian historiography including: E.-F. Gautier, 'Le cadre géographique de l'histoire'; Ely Leblanc, 'Le problème des Berbères, étude d'ethnographie physique'; W. Marçais, 'Un siècle de recherches sur le passé de l'Algérie musulmane'; A. Bel, 'Caractère et développement de l'Islam en Berbérie et plus spécialement en Algérie'; G. Marçais, 'L'art musulman en Algérie'; F. Braudel, 'Les Espagnols en Algérie'; M. Morand, 'Les problèmes indigènes et le droit musulman en Algérie'; and G. Esquer, 'Les sources de l'histoire de l'Algérie'.

* Bencheneb, S., 'Quelques historiens arabes modernes de l'Algérie', *R.A.*, 100, 1956, pp. 475–500.
Bernard, A., *L'Algérie* (Paris, 1929); select bibliography at the beginning of each chapter.
Berque, A., 'Essai d'une bibliographie des confréries musulmanes algériennes', *B.S.G.O.*, 1919, pp. 135–74 and 193–244.
Cazenave, J., 'Les sources de l'histoire d'Oran', *B.S.G.O.*, 1933, pp. 303–79.
Esquer, G., *La prise d'Alger* (Paris, 1929, 2nd ed.), pp. 553–63.
Franc, J., *Les sources d'archives* (Paris, 1926); printed sources, pp. 9–34.
Janier, E., 'Bibliographie des publications qui ont été faites sur Tlemcen et sa région', *R.A.*, xciii, 1949, pp. 314–34
Lespès, J., *Alger* (Paris, 1930), pp. 13–25.
———, *Oran* (Paris, 1938), p. 41.
Tailliart, Charles, *L'Algérie dans la littérature française. Essai de bibliographie méthodique et raisonnée jusqu'à l'année 1924* (Paris, 1925); annotation of 3,177 items.

D. Tunisia

Despois, J., *La Tunisie* (Paris, 1930), pp. 204–5.
Initiation à la Tunisie (Paris, 1950); bibliographies are found at the beginning and conclusion of each chapter.
Rousset de Pina, J., 'Informations bibliographiques', *Bulletin économique et social de la Tunisie*, published each trimester since 1949.

E. Other Bibliographies of relevance: Tripolitania, Sahara and West Africa, Portugal

Tripolitania

Despois, J., *Le Djebel Nefousa* (*Tripolitaine*), *Etude géographique* (Paris 1935), pp. 328 and 333–8; a limited but critical bibliography.
* Evans-Pritchard, E. E., 'A select Bibliography of Writings on Cyrenaica', *African Studies*, September 1945 and September 1946.
Guida d'Italia del Touring Club Italiano, xvii, *Possedimenti e Colonie* (Milan, 1929), pp. 813–15.
Playfair, R. L., *Bibliography of Barbary States*, I (see above Bibliographies I.A.).

Sahara and West Africa

* 'Bibliographie', *T.I.R.S.*, vol. 5, 1948 (covers the years 1947–8) and vol. 12, 1954, pp. 151–82.
* Brasseur, Paule, *Bibliographie Générale du Mali* (Dakar, 1964), I.F.A.N., Catalogues and Documents, no. xvi.
* Blaudin de Thé, *Essai de bibliographie du Sahara français et des régions avoisinantes* (Paris, 1960).

Bibliography

* Funck-Brentano, Ch., 'Bibliographie du Sahara occidentale', *Hespéris*, 1930, xi, pp. 203-96.
* Grandidier, G. and Joucla, E., *Bibliographie Générale des Colonies Français. Bibliographie de l'Afrique Occidentale Français* (Paris, 1937).
* Mauny, R., *Tableau géographique de l'Ouest africain au Moyen Age* (Dakar, 1961), I.F.A.N. Mémoire No. 61, pp. 547-75; the work and the references cover the period up to the mid-16th century.
* Toupet, Ch., 'Orientation bibliographique sur la Mauritanie', *Bull. I.F.A.N.*, 1959, xxi B, pp. 201-39 and 1962, xxiv B, pp. 594-613.

Portugal

Ricard, R., 'Publications portugaises sur l'histoire du Maroc', *Hespéris*, 1927, pp. 33-51.

II. REFERENCES

A. Atlases

Atlas historique, géographique, économique; l'Algérie (Paris, 1934).
Atlas historique, géographique, économique; le Maroc (Paris, 1935).
Atlas historique, géographique, économique; la Tunisie (Paris, 1936).
* Fage, J. D., *Atlas of African History* (London, 1958).
Gsell, S., *L'Atlas archéologique* (Paris, 1902-11).
* Hazard, H., *Atlas of Islamic History* (Princeton, 1951).
* Roolvink, R., *Historical Atlas of the Muslim Peoples* (Amsterdam, 1957).

B. Encyclopedias

Encyclopedia of Islam ed. M. Th. Houtsma, T. W. Arnold, R. Basset, A. J. Wensinck, E. Lévi-Provençal, H. A. R. Gibb, et al., French and English editions (Leyden, 1913-34) 4 vols. and *Supplement* Leyden, 1934-38).
* *Encyclopedia of Islam, New Edition*, H. A. R. Gibb, J. H. Kramers, E. Lévi-Provençal, J. Schacht, S. M. Stern, et al. (Leyden, London, 1960—in process). The New Edition had been completed through the Letter 'H' in 1968.
* Gibb, H. A. R. and Kramers, J. H., *Shorter Encyclopedia of Islam* (Leyden, 1964).

C. Dictionaries

* Hughes, T. P., *A Dictionary of Islam* (London, 1885).

D. Biographies

de Castries, H., et al., *Sources inédites de l'histoire du Maroc* (see above;

Bibliography, Morocco); biographies of the Saadian princes are placed at the introduction to the bibliography and general index (Paris, 1926).

Encyclopedia of Islam (see above, Bibliography, General).

Lévi-Provençal, E., *Historiens des Chorfa* (Paris, 1922) for biographies of the Moroccan authors appearing in his volume.

(For biographies of Arab authors, see below, section IX, Arabic sources available in translation.)

E. Museum Guides

Marçais, G., *Le Musée Stéphane Gsell, Musée des Antiquités et d'art musulman d'Alger* (Algiers, 1950).

Musées et Collections archéologiques de l'Algérie et de la Tunisie (Paris, 1890–1924), in 26 parts.

Note sur l'ethnographie, la préhistoire, l'archéologie, l'art musulman, les beaux arts en Algérie (Algiers, 1948); describes briefly the museums of ethnography (pp. 23–4) and of Islamic art (pp. 77–86) in Algeria.

F. Arabic literature

Abd el-Jalil, J. M., *Brève histoire de la Littérature Arabe* (Paris, 1943).

Brockelmann, K., *Geschichte der Arabischen Litteratur* (Weimar, 1898–1902) 2 vols.; and 3 supplements (Leyden, 1937–42).

Carra, de Vaux, *Les Penseurs de l'Islam* (Paris, 1921–5), 5 vols.

Huart, Cl., *Littérature arabe* (Paris, 1903).

Nicholson, R. A., *A Literary History of the Arabs* (Cambridge, 1930, 2nd ed.).

G. Genealogy/Chronology

Caetani, L., *Chronografia islamica* (Rome, 1912–23).

*Cattenoz, H. G., *Tables de concordance des ères chrétienne et hégirienne* (Rabat 1952).

*Freeman-Grenville, G. S. P., *The Muslim and Christian calendars being tables for the conversion of Muslim and Christian dates from the Hijra to the year A.D. 2000* (London, 1963).

Lane-Pool, S., *The Mohammedan dynasties* (London, 1893 and Paris, 1925).

Zambaur, E. von, *Manuel de généalogie et de Chronologie pour l'histoire de l'Islam* (Hanover, 1927).

III. JOURNALS

A. General

Pots, A., 'Etude critique des revues et périodiques de langue française

Bibliography

traitant des questions Nord-Africaines et islamiques', *R.A.* (1948), pp. 191–200.

Africa (London), (vol. I, 1928); a quarterly publication of the International African Institute; a 'Bibliography of Current Publications' appears in appendix to each issue, concentrating on anthropology, sociology, linguistics, etc.

African Abstracts (London), (vol. I, 1950; vol. XIX, 1968); a quarterly review of articles appearing in current periodicals, published by the International African Institute. The French counterpart is *Analyses Africanistes* (Paris) published by the Centre d'Analyse et de Recherches Documentaires pour l'Afrique Noire, in conjunction with the International African Institute with the assistance of UNESCO. Sections on North Africa appear in each issue.

Arabica (Paris), (vol. I, 1954).

l'Afrique française, Bulletin du Comité de l'Afrique française et du Comité du Maroc (Paris), (1909–60) and the monthly supplement, *Les Renseignements coloniaux* (Paris), (1909–60); the journal was a continuation of *Bulletin du Comité de l'Afrique française* (1891–1908).

Bulletin du Comité de l'Afrique française (Paris), (1891–1908); succeeded by *l'Afrique française*.

Bulletin du Comité des études historique et scientifique de l'Afrique Occidentale française (Paris), (vol. I, 1918; vol. 21, 1938, discontinued) and continued as *Bull. I.F.A.N.*

Bulletin de l'Institut Français d'Afrique Noire (Dakar), (continuation of *B.C.E.H.S.A.O.F.*; vol. I,1 939; title changed in 1960 to *Bulletin de l'Institut Fondamental d'Afrique Noire*: series B (sciences humaines)).

Bulletin of the School of Oriental and African Studies (London), (vol. I, 1917; vol. 31, 1968); occasional articles of principally historical content relating to North Africa.

Carnet de la Sabretache (Paris), (vol. I, 1893); memoires of officers of the African army; index for the years 1893–1902 in the volume of 1906.

Der Islam (Berlin), (vol. I, 1910; vol. 45, 1969).

Encyclopédie Mensuelle d'Outre Mer (Paris), (1952, discontinued 1957).

Journal Asiatique, (Paris), (vol. I, 1836; series 10, vol. 248, 1968).

Journal de la Société des Africanists (Paris), (vol. I, 1931; vol. 37, 1967); published annually.

Journal of African History (London, New York), (vol. I, 1960; vol. IX, 1968).

Muslim World (Hartford, Conn., U.S.A.), (vol. I, 1911; vol. LIX, 1969); contains occasional articles on principally theological matters relating to North African Islam.

Revue historique (Paris), (vol. I, 1876; vol. 248, 1968).

Revue de l'histoire des colonies françaises (Paris), (vol. I, 1913; discontinued 1958; continued in 1959 as *Revue française d'Histoire d'Outre-mer*).

Revue française d'histoire d'outre-mer (Paris), (vol. I, 1959 continuation of *R.H.C.*; vol. 53, 1966).
Revue de l'histoire des religions (Paris), (vol. I, 1880; vol. CLXXV, 1969); contains occasional articles on principally theological matters relating to North African Islam.
Revue de la Méditerranée (Paris/Algiers), (vol. I, 1944; bi-monthly (irregular); title for 1944–5 only was *Revue d'Alger*.
Revue d'Alger: see *Revue de la Méditerranée*.
Revue du Monde Musulman (Paris), (1906–26; continued as *R.E.I.*); see 'Index general', 3rd and 4th trimesters, 1926; contains numerous studies concerning North Africa.
Revue des études islamiques (Paris), (a continuation of *R.M.M.*; three issues per year since 1927, but interrupted between 1940–6).
Studia Islamica (Paris), (vol. I, 1953).

B. Morocco

Archives Berbères (Paris), (1915–21 only); succeeded by *Hespéris*.
Bulletin de l'Institut des Hautes Etudes Marocaines (Paris), (1920, single issue published); continued by *Hespéris*.
Bulletin d'Archéologie Marocaine (Rabat), (vol. I, 1956).
Bulletin économique et Social du Maroc (Rabat), (vol. I, 1933; suspended 1939–45; vol. 28, 1966); published by Société d'études économique sociales et statistiques.
Bulletin de l'Enseignement public au Maroc (Rabat), edited by la Direction de l'Instruction Publique; useful for popular accounts by specialists on a variety of subjects.
Bulletin de la Société de géographie du Maroc (Rabat), (vol. I, 1916–26; succeeded by *Revue de Géographie Marocaine*).
Hespéris, Archives berbères et Bulletin de l'Institut des Hautes Etudes marocaines (Rabat), (1921–59); published by the Institut des Hautes Etudes Marocaines; indices for 1915–35 in vol. for 1936; a continuation of *Archives Berbères* and succeeded by *Hespéris-Tamuda*; with *R. A.*, one of the most highly respected journals dealing with North Africa; principally Moroccan and Moorish Spain—history, archaeology, sociology and ethnology.
Hespéris-Tamuda (Rabat), (vol. I, 1960; vol. IX, 1968); a continuation of *Hespéris* and the Spanish language *Tamuda* (which began a new series) with articles in Spanish, French and occasionally English.
Notes marocaines (Rabat), (1951–61); published by the Société de Géographie du Maroc.; succeeded by *Revue de Géographie du Maroc*.
Revue de Géographie Marocaine (Rabat), (vol. I, 1926; new series began in 1962); contains useful bibliography; successor to *Bulletin de la Société de géographie du Maroc*.
Tamuda, Revista de Investigaeiones marroquies (Tétouan), (1953–9); succeeded by *Hespéris-Tamuda*.

Bibliography

C. Algeria

Annales de l'Institut d'Etudes Orientales (Algiers), (vol. I, 1934); includes a number of serious studies relevant to North Africa.
L'Armée d'Afrique, (1904-29; published monthly); subvention from the Ministère de la Guerre.
Bulletin d'archéologie algérienne (vol. II, 1966-7); a new publication containing valuable articles concerned with archaeological, architectural and numismatic subjects.
Bulletin de la Société de géographie et d'archéologie de la province d'Oran, published each trimester since 1878; principally concerned with archaeology, pre-history and geography, but increasingly open to historical subjects; indices are found for 1878-98 (1898), 1898-1907 (1910), and 1908-27 (1930).
Bulletin de la Société de géographie d'Alger et de l'Afrique du Nord (Algiers), founded in 1880 and published each trimester until 1940; indices appear in the 3rd trimester of 1906 (July 1896-December 1905) and 1922 (1906-22); contains both serious academic studies and popularised material on diverse subjects.
Bulletin des Etudes Arabes (Algiers), (vol. I, 1941); bi-monthly; ed. by H. Pérès; contains some useful studies and much useful bibliographic material.
Revue Africaine (Algiers), published since 1856 by the Société historique algérienne; indices appear in 1885 (1856-81) and 1924 (1882-1921); the oldest and most important of the North African publications dealing with North African and Algerian history and archaeology, Arab-Berber studies and geography.
Travaux de l'Institut de Recherches sahariennes (Algiers), (vol. I, 1942; vol. 27, 1968).

D. Tunisia

Fontaine, Jean, 'Revues tunisiennes paraissant fin 1965', *I.B.L.A.*, 29, 1966, pp. 73-80.
Van Leeuwen, 'Index des Publications périodiques parues en Tunisie (1874-1954)', *I.B.L.A.*, 69, 1955, pp. 153-67; includes a review of Arabic language journals.
Bulletin Economique et Social de la Tunisie (Tunis), monthly (1946-56).
Cahiers de Tunisie, Revue des Sciences humaines (Tunis), (vol. I, 1953; vol. 13, 1965).
Institut des Belles Lettres Arabes (Tunis), published each trimester since 1937 (now quarterly); occasional articles of historical interest and a very useful bibliography of current publications on the Islamic world, including North Africa.
Revue Tunisienne de Sciences Sociales (Tunis), vol. I, 1964.

History of North Africa

E. Spain

Al-Andalus Revista de las Escuelas de Estudios arabes de Madrid y Granada (Madrid), (vol. I, 1933); principally concerned with Islam in Spain and often contains important studies on the Almoravids and Almohades in Spain.
Revista del Instituto Egipcio de Estudios Islamicos (Madrid), (vol. I, 1953).
Tamuda (see Morocco).

F. Collective Works, Festschriften, Congresses

Actes des Congrès de la Fédération des Sociétés Savantés de l'Afrique de Nord: I, *Congrès d'Alger*, 1 vol. (Algiers, 1936); II, *Congrès de Tlemcen*, 3 vols. (Algiers, 1937); III, *Congrès de Constantine*, 2 vols. (Algiers, 1938); IV, *Congrès de Rabat*, 2 vols. (Algiers, 1939); V, *Congrès de Tunis*, 1 vol. (Algiers, 1940); all of these have been published by the Société Historique Algérienne.
Cinquantenaire de la Faculté des Lettres d'Alger (1881–1931). Articles publiés par les Professeurs de la Faculté (Algiers, 1932).
* *Etudes Maghrébines. Mélanges Charles-André Julien* (Paris, 1964).
Etudes, notes et documents sur le Sahara Occidental présentés au VIIe Congrès de l'Institut des Hautes Etudes Marocaines (Rabat, 30 mai 1930), (Rabat-Paris, 1930).
* *Etudes d'orientalisme dédiées à la mémoire de Lévi-Provençal* (Paris, 1962).
* *Homenaje a Millas-Vallacrosa*, 2 vols. (Barcelona, 1956).
* *Ignace Goldziher Memorial Volume*, pt. 1 (S. Lowinger and J. Somogyi, eds., Budapest, 1948).
Mélanges d'études luso-marocaines dédiés à la mémoire de David Lopes et Pierre de Cenival (Lisbon-Paris, 1945).
Mélanges Gaudefroy-Demombynes (Cairo, 1935–45).
Mélanges de géographie de d'orientalisme offerts à E. F. Gautier (Tours, 1937).
* *Mélanges d'histoire et d'archéologie de l'occident musulman*, vol. II, *Hommage à Georges Marçais* (Algiers, 1957).
* *Mélanges Louis Massignon* (Damascus, 1956), Institut Français de Damas.
Mélanges René Basset. Etudes nord-africaines et orientales publiées par l'Institut des Hautes Etudes Marocaines, vol. X, 2; vol. I (Paris, 1925); vol. II (Paris, 1925).
Mélanges William Marçais par l'Institut d'Etudes Islamiques de l'Université de Paris (Paris, 1950).
* *Mémorial André Basset (1895–1956)* (Paris, 1957).
Mémorial Henri Basset. Nouvelles études nord-africaines et orientales publiées par l'Institut des Hautes Etudes Marocaines, vol. XVII, 2 vols. (Paris, 1928).

Bibliography

Recueil de mémoires et de textes publiés en l'honneur du XIVe Congrès des Orientalistes; by the professors of l'Ecole Supérieure des Lettres et des Medersas (Algiers, 1905).

IV. CATALOGUES AND GUIDES TO ARCHIVES AND LIBRARIES

A. Arabic and Turkish manuscripts: Algeria

* Basset, M. R., 'Les Manuscrits arabes de la zaouyah d'El-Hamel', *Giornale della Societate Asiatica Italina*, 1897, x.
* ——, *Les Manuscrits arabes des bibliothèques des zawiyas de 'Ain Madhi et Temacin, de Ouargla et de 'Adjadja* (Algiers, 1886).
* ——, 'Les Manuscrits arabes du Bach–Agha de Djelfa', *Bulletin de correspondance africaine*, 1884, nos. 5–6.
* Cour, A., *Catalogue des Manuscrits arabes conservés dans les principales bibliothèques algériennes: Medrsa de Tlemcen* (Algiers, 1907).
* Deny, M. J., 'A propos du fonds arabo-turc des Archives du Gouvernement Générale de l'Algérie', *R.A.*, 1921, pp. 375–8.
* Fagnan, E., *Catalogue des Manuscrits arabes, turcs et persans de la Bibliothèque; Musée d'Alger*, Catalogue Général, vol. xviii (Paris, 1893).
* Mohammed Ben Cheneb, *Catalogue des Manuscrits arabes conservés dans les principales bibliothèques algériennes. Catalogue des Manuscrits arabes de la Grande Mosquée d'Alger* (Algiers, 1905).
* Schacht, J., 'Bibliothèques et manuscrits abadites', *R.A.* 100, 1956, pp. 375–98.

B. Arabic manuscripts: Morocco

* Allouche, I. S. and Regraqui, A., *Catalogue des manuscrits arabes de Rabat* (Bibliothèque générale et Archives du Maroc), (Rabat, 1958); a continuation of the Lévi-Provençal catalogue which covered acquisitions during the years 1921–53.
* Basset, M. R., 'Les manuscrits arabes de deux bibliothèques de Fas', *Bulletin de correspondance africaine*, November–December 1883, pp. 366–93.
* 'Catalogue des livres arabes de la Bibliothèque de la Mosquée d'El Qarouiyiou à Fes', *Archives Marocains*, xv, 1918.
* El-Fasi, Mohammed, 'Les bibliothèques au Maroc et quelques-uns de leurs manuscrits les plus rares', *Hespéris-Tamuda*, II, 1961, pp. 135–44.
* Lévi-Provençal, E., *Les manuscrits arabes de Rabat* (Bibliothèque Générale du Protectorat français au Maroc), (Paris, 1921).
* *Liste de Manuscrits arabes precieux exposés à la Bibliothèque de l'Université Quaraouyine à Fès à l'occasion du onzième centenaire de la fondation de cette université* (Rabat, 1380/1960).

* List de Manuscrits arabes selectionnés parmi ceux qui sont conservés à la Bibliothèque Générale et Archives du Maroc (Rabat, 1962).
* Maillard, P., 'Essai de Bibliographie Marocaine. Bibliothèque de la Grande Mosquée de Tanger', *R.M.M.*, 1917–18, xxxv, pp. 107–92.
* Salmon, G., 'Catalogue des manuscrits d'une bibliothèque privée de Tanger', *Archives Moroccains*, 1905, pp. 134–46.

C. *Arabic manuscripts: Tunisia*

* Houdas, O. and Basset, M. R., *Mission Scientifique en Tunisie* (Algiers, 1884), part ii, bibliography, pp. 45–162; also appeared in *Bulletin de correspondance africaine*, 1884, pp. 5, 97, 181.
* Roy, B., *Extrait du Catalogue des Manuscrits et des Imprimés de la Bibliothèque de la Grande Mosquée de Tunis* (Tunis, 1900).

D. *Catalogues of other archives and libraries containing Arabic manuscript material of relevance to North African history*

* Blochet, E., *Catalogue des manuscrits arabes dans la Bibliothèque Nationale, nouvelles acquisitions 1884–1924* (Paris, 1925).
* Heymowski, A. and Mokhtar ould Hamidoun, *Catalogue provisoire des manuscrits mauritaniens en langue arabe préservés en Mauritanie* (Stockholm, 1966).
* Vajda, J., *Index Général des Manuscrits Arabes Musulmans de la Bibliothèque Nationale de Paris* (Paris, 1953).
* Vajda, G., *Repertoire des catalogues et inventaires des manuscrits arabes* (Paris, 1949); a general index to the major catalogues of Arabic manuscripts to be found in European libraries.

E. *Published Primary Source Material in European Languages*

* Ayache, G., 'La question des archives historiques marocaines', *Hespéris-Tamuda*, II, 1961, pp. 311–26 (a discussion of archival collections, including the former Spanish Morocco, and bibliography for Moroccan history).

Colombe, M., 'Contribution à l'étude du recrutement de l'Odjaq d'Alger dans les dernières années de l'histoire de la Régence', *R.A.*, LXXXVII, 1943, pp. 166–83.

* de Castries, H., de Cenival, P., Ricard, R., de la Véronne, C. and de Cossé Brissac, Philippe, *Sources inédites de l'histoire du Maroc*; series 1: *Dynastie saadienne, France*, 3 vols. (1905–11), *Angleterre*, 3 vols. (1918–36), *Pays-Bas*, 6 vols. (1906–23), *Espagne*, 3 vols. (1921–61), *Portugal*, 5 vols. (1934–53); series 2: *Dynastie filalienne, France*, 6 vols. (1922–53).

de Grammont, H., *Correspondance des Consuls d'Alger (1690–1742)*, (Algiers-Paris, 1890).

Bibliography

Delvoux, A., *Archives du Consulat Général de France à Alger* (Algiers, 1865).
Esquer, G., 'Les sources de l'histoire de l'Algérie', in *Histoire et historiens de l'Algérie* (Paris, 1931); an excellent survey of archives, libraries and bibliographies relevant to Algeria.
*—— and Dermenghem, E., *Répertoire* (Archives du Gouvernment Générale de l'Algérie), (Algiers, 1953).
Monchicourt, C. and Grandchamp, P., 'Landreducci et Bosio. Costa e descorsi di Barberia. Rapport maritime, militaire et politique sur la côte d'Afrique, depuis le Nil jusqu'à Cherchell, par deux membres de l'Ordre de Malte (1re Septembre 1587)' *R.A.*, vol. 66 (1925), pp. 419–549.
* Nouschi, A., 'Archives du Gouvernement Général de l'Algérie, série HH', *Cahiers de Tunisie*, 36, 1961, pp. 1–80.
Penz, Ch., *Journal du Consulat général de France à Maroc (1767–1785)*, (Casablanca, 1943).
Plantet, E., *La correspondance des Beys de Tunis et des Consuls de France avec la Cour (1577–1830)*, 3 vols. (Paris, 1893–9).
——, *La correspondance des Deys d'Alger avec la cour de France (1579–1833)*, 2 vols (Paris, 1898).

Part II. Topical Index

V. ART AND ARCHAEOLOGY

A. General

Creswell, K. A. C., *Early Moslem Architecture*, 2 vols. (Oxford, 1932–40)
Colvin, L., *Aspects de l'Artisanat en Afrique du Nord* (Paris, 1957).
Marçais, G., *L'Architecture Musulmane d'Occident* (Paris, 1954), excellent illustrations, useful text and very complete bibliography.
——, *Art de l'Islam* (Paris, 1946), part of the collection Arts, Styles et Techniques.
——, *Manuel d'art musulman. Architecture*, 2 vols. I (9th–12th centuries), (Paris, 1926), and II (13th–19th centuries), (Paris, 1927).
Migeon, G., *Manuel d'art musulman, Arts plastiques et industriels* (2nd ed. Paris, 1927); mentions Barbary only briefly.
Ricard, P., *Pour comprendre l'art musulman dans l'Afrique du Nord et en Espagne* (Paris, 1924).
Terrasse, H., *L'art hispano-mauresque des origines au XIIIe siècle* (Paris, 1932).
* Torres Balbas, L., *Ars Hispaniae*, Vol. 4 (Arte Almohade—Arte Naziri—Arte mudéjar), (Madrid, 1949).

B. Morocco

Ricard, P., *Corpus des Tapis marocains*, 4 vols. (Paris, 1922–34).

Terrasse, H., *La mosquée des Andalous à Fès* (Paris, 1941).
——, *La Grande Mosquée de Taza* (Paris, 1944).
Terrasse, H. and Hainaut, J., *Les arts décoratifs au Maroc* (Paris, 1925).

C. Algeria

de Beylié, Général, *La Kalaa des Beni Hammad. Une capitale berbère de l'Afrique du Nord au XIe siècle* (Paris, 1900).
Marçais, G. and Dessus-Lamare, A., 'Recherches d'archéologie musulmane: Tihert-Tagdempt', *R.A.*, 1946, pp. 24–57.
Marçais, W., *Musée de Tlemcen* (Paris, 1906).
Marçais, W. and Marçais, G., *Les monuments arabes de Tlemcen* (Paris, 1903).
Pestemaldjoglou, A., 'Mers el Kébir, Historique et description de la forteresse', *R.A.*, 1942, pp. 154–85.

D. Tunisia

* Lezind, A. and Sebag, P., 'Remarques sur l'histoire de la Grande Mosquée de Kairouan', *I.B.L.A.*, 99, 1962, pp. 245–56.
Revault, J. and Poinssot, L., I, *Tapis tunisiens* (Kairouan, 1937); II, *Tapis bedouins, haute laine* (Paris, 1950); III, *Les tissus décorés de Gafsa et imitations* (Paris, 1953); vol. I was also reissued as *Tapis de Kairouan et imitations* (Paris, 1955).

E. Numismatics

Bel, A., 'Contribution à l'étude des dirhems de l'époque almohade', *Hespéris*, XVI, 1933, pp. 1–68.
* Bourouiba, R., 'Sur six dinars almohades trouvés à la Kalaa des Banu Hammad', *Bull. arch. alger.*, II, 1966–7, pp. 271–92.
Brettes, J.-D., *Contribution à l'histoire du Maroc par les recherches numismatiques* (Casablanca, 1939).
Brunschvig, R., 'Un dinar hafçide', *Bulletin de la Société historique et géographique de Sétif*, II, 1941, pp. 179–82.
Colin, G. S., 'Monnaies de la période idrisite trouvées à Volubilis', *Hespéris*, XXII, 1936, pp. 113–25.
de Candia, Farrugia, 'Monnaies aghlabites du Musée du Bardo', *R.T.*, 1935, pp. 271 *et seq.*
* de Navascues, Jorge, y de Palacio, 'Etudios de numismatica musulmana occidental', *Numario hispanico*, Madrid, 1958, pp. 49–55.
Gateau, A., 'Sur un dinar fatimide', *Hespéris*, XXXII, 1945, pp. 69–72.
Lane-Pool, S., *Catalogue of oriental Coins in the British Museum* (London, 1875–83), 8 vols.
Lavoix, H., *Catalogue des monnaies musulmanes de la Bibliothèque Nationale* (Paris, 1887–92); vol. III is devoted to North Africa and Spain.

Bibliography

* Mateu y Llopis, F., 'Hallazgos numismaticos musulmanes', IX, *Al-Andalus*, 20, 1955, pp. 454-9.
Troussel, M., 'Les monnaies d'or musulmanes du Cabinet des Médailles du musée de Constantine', *Recueil de Constantine*, 1942, pp. 124-30.
——, 'Monnaies d'argent (dirham-s) idrisites et abbassides trouvées à Ouenza', *Recueil de Constantine*, 1942, pp. 105-23.

F. Epigraphy

Basset, H. and Lévi-Provençal, E., 'Chella: une nécropole mérinide', *Hespéris*, 1922, pp. 31-45.
Basset, R., *Nédromah et les Traras* (Paris, 1901).
Bel, A., 'Les inscriptions arabes de Fès', *J.A.* (1917-19) and *Les inscriptions arabes de Fès* (Paris, 1919).
Brosselard, Ch., 'Inscriptions arabes de Tlemcen', *R.A.*, 1898 (pp. 51 *et seq.*, 241 *et seq.*, 401 *et seq.*); 1859 (pp. 1 *et seq.*, 81 *et seq.*, 161 *et seq.*, 241 *et seq.*); 1860 (pp. 14 *et seq.*, 241 *et seq.*, 401 *et seq.*); 1861 (pp. 14 *et seq.*, 161 *et seq.*).
——, 'Tombeaux des Emirs Beni Zeiyân et de Boabdil', *J.A.*, 1876.
Colin, G., *Corpus des inscriptions arabes et turques d'Algérie, I, Département d'Alger* (Paris, 1901).
Houdas, O. and Basset, R., 'Epigraphie tunisienne', *Bulletin de Correspondance africaine*, I, 1882, pp. 161 sq.
Marçais, W., *Musée de Tlemcen* (Paris, 1906).
Mercier, G., *Corpus des inscriptions arabes et turques d'Algérie, II, Département de Constantine* (Paris, 1902).
Roy, J. B. B. and Poinssot, Paule, *Inscriptions arabes de Kairouan.* (*Publiées* ... avec le concours de L. Poinssot), Paris, 1952. Published by I.H.E.T.
Terrasse, H., *La grande mosquée de Taza* (Paris, n.d.) published by I.H.E.M.
——, *La mosquée des Andalous à Fès* (Paris, n.d.), published by I.H.E.M.
Zbiss, M., *Corpus des inscriptions arabes de Tunis* (Tunis, 1955); published by the Direction des Antiquités et Arts.

VI. ISLAM

A. General Studies on Islamic history and civilisation

* Anderson, J. N. D., 'Le Droit comme force sociale dans l'histoire et la culture de l'Islam', *I.B.L.A.*, 85, 1959, pp. 29-54 and 86, 1959, pp. 157-78; also see 'Law as a social force in Islamic culture and history', *B.S.O.A.S.*, 20 (1957), pp. 13-40.
Barrau-Dihigo, L., *l'Islam en marche*.
* Brockelmann, C., *History of the Islamic Peoples* (New York, 1947).
* Brunschvig, R. and von Grunebaum, G., *Classicisme et déclin culturel dans l'histoire de l'Islam* (Paris, 1957).

* de Planhol, X., *Le Monde Islamique: Essai de géographie religieuse* (Paris, 1957); tr. *The World of Islam* (Ithica, N.Y., 1959).
Gaudefroy-Demombynes, M., *Mahomet* (Paris, 1957).
Gibb, H. A. R., *Mohammedanism, An historical survey* (Oxford, 1949).
*——, *Studies on the Civilization of Islam* (London, 1962).
* Guillaume, A., *Islam* (2nd ed., New York, 1956).
* Hitti, P., *History of the Arabs* (London, 1943; 3rd ed.).
Huart, C., *Histoire des Arabes*, 2 vols. (Paris, 1912–13).
* Lewis, B., *The Arabs in History* (London, 1950).
Muir, W., *The Caliphate, its rise, decline and fall* (ed. T. H. Weir, Edinburgh, 1915).
* Rodinson, M., *Islam et Capitalisme* (Paris, 1966).
* Rosenthal, E. I. J., *Political thought in Medieval Islam, an introductory outline* (Cambridge, 1958).
* von Grunebaum, G. E., *Islam*. Essays in the Nature and Growth of a Cultural Tradition (London, 1955).
*——, *Medieval Islam* (Chicago, 1946).
* Watt, W. M., *Muhammad at Mecca* (Oxford, 1953) and *Mohomet à la Mecque* (Paris, 1958).
*——, *Muhammad at Medina* (Oxford, 1956).
*——, *Muhammad, Prophet and Statesman* (Oxford, 1961).
* Wellhausen, J., *The Arab Kingdom and its Fall* (tr. M. G. Weir; Calcutta, 1927).

B. Koran

* Arberry, A. J., *The Quran Interpreted* (London, 1955). The most widely accepted English version of the Koran in which the translator captures some of the Arabic poetic style in his interpretation.
Rodwell, I. M., *The Koran* (London, 1876). A version in which an effort has been made to arrange the *suras* in chronological order.
Sale, G., *The Koran Translated* (London, 1734).

C. Islamic Theology, Law and Institutions

* Arberry, A. J., *Sufism, an account of the mystics of Islam* (London, 1950).
* Coulson, N. J., *A History of Islamic Law* (Edinburgh, 1964).
Depont, O. and Coppolani, X., *Les Confréries Religieuses Musulmanes* (Algiers, 1898).
Gardet, L. and Anawati, M., *Introduction à la théologie musulmane* (Paris, 1948).
Gaudefroy-Demombynes, M., *Les institutions musulmanes* (Paris, 1946; 3rd ed.); tr. J. P. Macgregor, *Muslim Institutions* (London, 1950).
Goldziher, I., *Etudes sur la Tradition Islamique* (Paris, 1952); extracts from vol. 2 of his *Muhammedanische Studien*, tr. Leon Bercher.

Bibliography

Goldziher, I., *Vorlesungen über den Islam* (Heidelberg, 1910), tr. by F. Arin, *Le dogme et la loi de l'Islam* (Paris, 1920).
Jones, E. R., (tr.), *The history of Philosophy in Islam* (London, 1903).
Juynboll, T. W., *Handleinding tot de Kennis van der Mohammedaanschewet* (Leyden, 1925; 3rd ed.).
Lammens, H., *L'Islam, croyances et institutions* (Beirut, 1926); and tr. (London, 1929).
Massé, H., *L'Islam* (Paris, 1930).
* Nicholson, R. A., *The Mystics of Islam* (London, 1914).
* Schacht, J., *The Origins of Muhammadan Jurisprudence* (Oxford, 1950).
Snouck Hurgronje, C., 'Le Droit musulman', *R.H.R.*, XXVIII, 1898, pp. 15 *et seq.*, 174 *et seq.*
Watt, W. M., *Islamic Philosophy and Theology* (Edinburgh, 1962).
——, 'Kharijite thought in the Umayyad period', *Der Islam*, 36/3, February 1961, pp. 215-31.
* Wensinck, A. J., *The Muslim Creed* (Cambridge, 1932).
Encyclopedia of Islam: see articles on Allah, Sunna and Hadith.

D. Islam in the Maghrib

* Abun-Nasr, J., *The Tijaniyya* (London, 1965).
Bel, A., 'L'Islam mystique', *R.A.*, 1927, pp. 329-72; 1928, pp. 65-111; and *L'Islam mystique* (Algiers, 1928).
——, *La Religion Musulmane en Berbérie I*, Etablissement et développement de l'Islam en Berbérie du VIIe au XXeme siècle (Paris, 1938); vol. I has an extremely useful bibliography; unfortunately volume II never appeared due to the death of the author.
Bousquet, G. H., *L'Islam maghrébin* (Algiers, 1946, 2nd ed.; 1954, 4th ed.).
Brunel, R., *Essai sur la confrérie religieuse des 'Aîssâoûa du Maroc* (Paris, 1926).
Cour, A., 'Recherches sur l'état des confréries religieuses musulmanes', *R.A.*, 1921, pp. 85-139; 291-334.
Depont, O. and Coppolani, X., *Les confréries religieuses musulmanes* (Algiers, 1897).
* Dermenghem, E., *Le culte des Saints dans l'Islam maghrébin* (Paris, 1954).
Doutté, E., *Notes sur l'Islam maghrébin: Les marabouts* (Paris, 1900).
* Drague, G., *Esquisse d'Histoire religieuse de Maroc* (Les Cahiers de l'Afrique et l'Asie, II, Paris 1951).
* Evans-Pritchard, E. E., *The Sanusi of Cyrenaica* (Oxford, 1949).
* Gellner, E., 'The Far West of Islam', *British Journal of Sociology*, IX, 1958, pp. 73-82.
Michaux-Bellaire, E., 'Conférences', *A.M.*, XXVII, 1927.
Montet, E., *Le culte des saints musulmans dans l'Afrique du Nord et plus spécialement au Maroc* (Geneva, 1909).
Rinn, L., *Marabouts et Khouan* (Algiers, 1884).

VII. SOCIOLOGY, ANTHROPOLOGY AND ETHNOGRAPHY
A. General

Basset, H., *Essai sur la littérature des Berbères* (Algiers, 1920).
* Bousquet, H., *Les Berbères* (Paris, 1957); an introduction to the subject.
* Briggs, L. C., *Tribes of the Sahara* (Cambridge, 1960).
Chapelle, Jean, *Nomades noirs du Sahara* (Paris, 1957).
* Coon, C. S., *Caravan: the story of the Middle East* (New York, 1951).
Doutté, E., *En tribu* (Paris, 1916).
——, *Magie et religion dans l'Afrique du Nord* (Algiers, 1909).
* Le Tourneau, R., *Les villes musulmanes de l'Afrique du Nord* (Algiers, 1957), published by Bibliothèque de l'Institut d'Etudes Islamiques d'Alger.
* Levy, R., *An introduction to the sociology of Islam*, 2 vols. (London, 1931-33).
*——, *Social Structure of Islam* (Cambridge, 1957).

B. Morocco

* Abdelouadeh ben Talha, *Moulay Idriss du Zerhoun, quelques aspects de la vie sociale et familiale* (Rabat, 1965), Faculté des Lettres et des Sciences Humaines de Rabat, Notes et Documents XXIII.
Basset, H., *Le culte des grottes au Maroc* (Algiers, 1920).
Bel, A., *Les industries de la céramique à Fèz* (Paris-Algiers, 1918).
Benech, J., *Essai d'explication d'un Mellah (Marrakech)* (Paris, n.d.).
* Berque, J., *Structures Sociales de Haut Atlas* (Paris, 1955).
Bourrilly, J., *Eléments d'ethnographie marocaine* (Paris, 1932).
Brunot, L., *La mer dans les traditions et industries indigènes de Rabat et Salé* (Paris, 1920).
——, 'Vocabulaire de la tannerie indigène à Rabat', *Hespéris*, III, 1923, pp. 83-124.
——, 'La cordonnerie indigène à Rabat', *Hespéris*, XXXIII, 1946, pp. 227-321.
Brunot, L. and Malka, E., *Textes judéo-arabes de Fès* (Rabat, 1939).
Brunot-David, Ch., *Les Broderies de Rabat*, 2 vols. (Rabat, 1943); Collection Hespéris, IX.
* Deverdun, G., *Marrakech des origines à 1912*, I (Rabat, 1959).
Doutté, E., *Marrakech*, I (Paris, 1905).
Goichon, A. M., 'La Broderie au fil d'or à Fès. Ses rapports avec la broderie de soie; ses accessoires de passementerie', *Hespéris*, XXVI (1939), pp. 49-97.
Goulven, J., *Les Mellahs de Rabat-Salé* (Paris, 1927).
Guyot, R., Le Tourneau, R., and Paye, L., 'La corporation des tanneurs et l'industrie de la tannerie à Fès', *Hespéris*, XXI, 1935, pp. 167-240.

Bibliography

——, 'L'industrie de la poterie à Fès', *Bulletin Economique Marocaine*, II, no. 10, pp. 268–72.

——, 'Les cordonniers de Fès', *Hespéris*, XXIII, 1936, pp. 9–54.

——, 'Les relieurs de Fès', *Bulletin Economique Marocaine*, III, no. 12, pp. 107–14.

Laoust, E., *Mots et choses berbères* (Paris, 1920).

——, *Noms et cérémonies des feux de joie chez les Berbères du Haut et de l'Anti-Atlas* (Paris, 1921).

——, *Pêcheurs berbères du Sous* (Paris, 1923).

——, *L'habitation chez les transhumants du Maroc central* (Paris, 1935), Collection Hespéris, no. VI.

Lapanne-Joinville, J., 'Les métiers à tisser de Fès. Vocabulaire des termes techniques du tissage', *Hespéris*, XXVII, 1940, pp. 21–98.

Le Tourneau, R. and Vicaire, M., 'La fabrication du fil d'or au Mellah de Fès', *Hespéris*, XXIV, 1937, pp. 67–88.

Le Tourneau, R., 'L'activité économique de Sefrou', *Hespéris*, XXV, 1938, pp. 269–86.

——, 'Fès avant le Protectorat', thesis, 1950; and *Fès avant le Protectorat* (Casablanca, 1949).

Massignon, L., 'Enquête sur les corporations musulmanes d'artisans et de commerçants au Maroc', *R.M.M.*, LVIII, 1924, and continued in *R.E.I.*, 1927, pp. 273–93.

Michaux-Bellaire, E. and Justinard, Col. (ed.), Section sociologique de la Direction des affaires indigènes, *Villes et tribus du Maroc* (11 vols.); I–II *Casablanca et les Châouïa* (Paris, 1915); III–VI *Rabat et sa région* (Paris, 1918–20); VII *Tanger et sa zone* (Paris, 1921); VIII *Les Aït Ba Amran* (Paris, 1930); IX *Districts et tribus de la haute vallée du Drâ* (Paris, 1931); X–XI *Région des Doukkala* (Paris, 1932).

* Mikesell, M. W., *Northern Morocco, a Cultural Geography* (University of California, 1961).

Montagne, R. (ed.), *Naissance du prolétariat marocain* (Paris, 1951), Cahiers de l'Afrique et l'Asie, vol. III.

* Montagne, R., *La vie sociale et vie politique des Berbères* (Paris, 1931).

Ricard, P., *Les Arts et industries indigènes du Nord de l'Afrique*, I, *Arts ruraux* (Fes, 1918).

——, *Les broderies marocaines* (Algiers, 1919).

——, *Corpus des Tapis marocains* 4 vols. (Paris, 1922–34).

——, *Dentelles algériennes et marocaines* (Paris, 1928).

* Rivers, Julian P. H. (ed.), *Mediterranean Countrymen* (Paris, 1963).

Spillmann, G., *Les Aït Atta du Sahara et la pacification du Haut-Dra* (Rabat, 1936).

Troin, J. F., 'Observations sur les souks de la région d'Azrou et de Khenifra', *Rev. Géog. Maroc*, II, 1963, pp. 102–20.

Westermark, E., *Ritual and Belief in Morocco*, 2 vols. (London, 1926).

History of North Africa

C. Algeria

Bel, A. and Ricard, P., *Le travail de la laine à Tlemcen* (Algiers, 1913).
Bousquet-Lefèvre, L., *La femme kabyle* (Paris, 1939).
Desparmet, J., 'L'ethnographie traditionnelle de la Mitidja', *B.S.G.A.*, 1918–21 and 1924; also in *R.A.* 1918, 1922–4.
Doutté, E. and Gautier, E.-F., *Enquête sur la dispersion de la langue arabe en Algérie* (Algiers, 1913).
*Gast, M., 'Evolution de la vie économique et structure sociales au Ahaggar de 1660 à 1965', *T.I.R.S.*, XXIV, 1965, pp. 129–43.
Gaudry, Mathea, *La femme chaouïa de l'Aurès* (Paris, 1929).
Goichon, A. M., *La vie féminine au Mzab* (Paris, 1927); with important preface by W. Marçais.
Golvin, L., *Les Arts populaires en Algérie*; vol. I, *Les Techniques de Tissages* vol. 3, *Les tapis de l'Algérie orientale: zone centre et sud* (Algiers, 1950).
Hanoteau, A. and Letourneaus, A., *La Kabylie et les coutumes kabyles*, 3 vols. (Paris, 1872; 1893, 3rd ed.).
Masqueray, E., 'La Formation des cités chez les populations sédentaires d'Algérie', thesis, 1886.
Maunier, R., *Mélanges de sociologie nord-africaine* (Paris, 1930).
Mercier, M., *La Civilisation Urbaine au Mzab* (Algiers, 1932).
Van Gennep, A., 'Etudes d'ethnographie algérienne', *Revue d'ethnographie et de sociologie*, 1911.

D. Tunisia (and Libya)

Bardin, P., *Les populations arabes du Contrôle civil de Gafsa et leurs genres de vie* (Tunis, 1944).
de Montéty, H., *Le mariage musulman en Tunisie* (Tunis–Paris, 1941).
Despois, J., *La Tunisie orientale, Sahel et Basse Steppe* (Paris, 1940).
* Evans-Pritchard, E. E., *The Sanusi of Cyrenaica* (Oxford, 1949).
Golvin, L., *Les tissages décorés d'El-Djem et de Djebeniana, étude de sociologie tunisienne* (Tunis, 1949).
Moreau, P., *Le pays des Negzaouas* (Tunis, 1947).
* Pellegrin, A., 'Le peuplement historique de Tunis', *Enc. Mens. O. M.*, 3, 1953, pp. 196–8.
Tlatli, S. E., *Djerba et les Djerbiens* (Tunis, 1942).

E. Islamic and Arabic Music

Chottin, A., *Tableau de la musique marocaine* (Paris, 1939).
d'Erlanger, R., *La musique arabe* (Paris, 1930), 7 vols.
* El Fasi, Mohammed, 'La musique marocaine dite "Musique andalouse"', *Hespéris-Tamuda*, III, 1962, pp. 79–106.
Farmer, H. G., *History of Arabian Music to the XIIIth century* (London, 1929).

Bibliography

Lachmann, R., *Musik des Orients* (Breslau, 1929).
Ribera, J., *La Musica de las Cantigas. Estudio sobre su originen y naturaleza* (Madrid, 1922).
Rouanet, J., 'La musique arabe', pp. 2676–812, and 'La musique arabe dans le Maghreb', pp. 2813–939 in Lavignac and La Laurencie, *Encyclopédie de la Musique* (Paris, 1922).

VIII. ECONOMICS: COMMERCE

(For indigenous industries see Sociology, Anthropology, Ethnography.)
Braudel, F., *La Méditerranée et le monde méditerranéen à l'époque de Philippe II* (Paris, 1949, and 2nd ed. 2 vols., Paris, 1966).
——, 'L'économie de la méditerranée au XVIIe siècle', *Cahiers de Tunisie*, 4, 1956, pp. 175–97.
Bousquet, G. H. and Berque, J., 'La criée publique à Fès', *Revue d'Economie Politique*, May 1940, pp. 320–45.
Brunschvig, R., *La Berbérie orientale sous les Hafçides*, vol. II (Paris, 1940; Paris, 1947).
Caillé, J., 'Le commerce anglais avec le Maroc pendant la seconde moitié de XVIe siècle', *R.A.*, 1940.
*——, *Les accords internationaux du sultan Sidi Mohammed ben Abdallah (1757–1790)* (Tanger, 1960).
Charles-Dominique, Mlle, P., 'La pénétration économique de l'Europe au Maroc durant la dynastie saadienne (1472–1660)' (unpublished).
* Colin, G. S., 'Projet de traité entre les Morisques de la Casba de Rabat et le Roi de l'Espagne en 1631', *Hespéris*, 42, 1955, pp. 17–25.
Collet, H., 'Le commerce hollandais avec le Maroc à l'époque saadienne', *B.E.P.M.*, 1942.
Heers, J., 'Le Sahara et le commerce méditerranéen à la fin du Moyen-Age', *Annales I.E.O.*, 16, 1958, pp. 247–55.
Koehler, R. P. Henry, 'Ce que l'économie privée importait d'Espagne au Maroc, au XVIIIe siècle, d'après les manuscrits inédits des procureurs de la mission franciscaine de 1766 à 1790', *Hespéris*, XXXIX, 1952, pp. 383–406.
* Lewicki, T., 'Quelques extraits inédits relatifs aux voyages des commerçants et des missionnaires nord-africains au pays du Soudan occidental au Moyan-Age', *Folia Orientalia*, II, 1960, pp. 1–27.
Mas Latrie, *Traités de paix et de commerce et documents divers concernant les relations des Chrétiens avec les Arabes de l'Afrique septentrionale au Moyen Age* (Paris, 1866; with supplement, 1872); the introduction was re-edited under the title *Relations et commerce de l'Afrique septentrionale au Maghreb avec les nations chrétiennes* (1886).
Masson, P., *Histoire des établissements et du commerce français dans l'Afrique barbaresque (1560–1793) (Algérie, Tunisie, Tripolitaine, Maroc)* (Paris, 1903).

* Mauny, R., *Tableau géographique de l'Ouest africain au Moyen Age* (Dakar, 1961) I.F.A.N. Mémoire no. 61; the work covers the period up to the mid-16th century.
* Ricard, R., 'Contribution à l'étude du commerce génois au Maroc durant la période portugaise (1415–1550)', *Annales I.E.O.*, 3, 1937, pp. 53–73; additions et corrections, 4, 1938, pp. 155–6.
*——, 'Le commerce de Berbérie et l'organisation économique de l'empire portugais aux XVe et XVIe siècles', *Annales I.E.O.*, 2, 1936, pp. 266–85.
*——, 'Les places portugaises du Maroc et le commerce d'Andalousie. Notes sur l'histoire économique de Maroc portugais', *Annales I.E.O.*, 4, 1938, pp. 129–53.
Sayous, A. E., *Le commerce des Européens à Tunis depuis le XIIe siècle jusqu'à la fin du XVIe siècle* (Paris, 1929).
*Wansbrough, J., 'A moroccan amir's commercial treaty with Venice of the year 913/1508', *B.S.O.A.S.*, 1962, XXV, pp. 449–71.

IX. ARABIC SOURCES INCLUDING THOSE AVAILABLE IN TRANSLATION

Sources are listed alphabetically by author, or, if anonymous or full name of author is not given, by translator; attributed authorships are indicated by inverted commas. For an alphabetical listing of translators, see section IX, B.

A large part of the historical texts concerning the Maghrib are available in printed Arabic editions and many are translated. Four series account for the greater part of these texts: *Archives Marocaines*, *P.F.L.A.*, *Collection des textes arabes*, published by l'Institut des Hautes Etudes Marocaines, and *Bibliothèque arabe-français*, directed by H. Pérès. Other more general and recent series include *Textes arabes relatifs à l'histoire de l'Occident musulman* and *Bibliothèque des Géographes arabes*, directed by Ferrand and which succeeded the *Bibliotheca Geographorum arabicorum* of J. de Goeje.

The list below is by no means exhaustive for either Arabic editions or translated works, but it does include a large number of historians and major geographers whose writings are relevant to North African history. The student of Arabic is referred to the sections above dealing with Arabic literature (section II, E) and Catalogues and Guides to Archives and Libraries (section IV) and to the useful introduction to Moroccan material in P. Chenel and E. Lévi-Provençal, 'Essai de Repertoire chronologique des éditions de Fès', *R.A.*, LXII, 1921, pp. 158–73, 275–90; LXIII, pp. 170–85, 333–47. For extracts from the geographers, only a few of whom appear below, a useful source is Youssouf Kamal, *Monumenta Cartographica Africae et Aegypti* (Cairo, Leyden, 1926–51), 5 vols.

Bibliography

A. Sources

(*N.B.* 'ed.', below refers to Arabic editions, unless otherwise stated, and 'tr.' refers to French, English or Spanish translations unless otherwise stated.)

'Abd al-Bāsit b. Khalīl: see R. Brunschvig (ed. and tr.), *Deux Récits de Voyage inédits en Afrique du Nord au XVe siècle. 'Abdal-bâsit b. Khalîl et Adorne* (Paris, 1936) I.E.O., vol. VII.

'Abd al-Mu'min: see E. Lévi-Provençal (ed. and tr.), *Documents inédites d'histoire almohade, fragments inédites du 'Legajo' 1999 du fonds arabe de l'Escurial* (Paris, 1928). One of three groups of works included are letters of Ibn Tumart and 'Abd al-Mumin to Almohad chiefs, containing useful information about the opening years of the Almohads, distribution of the Chleuh tribes and material of linguistic interest in Berber.

Si 'Abd al-Qādir al-Masharfī: see M. Bodin (ed. and tr.), 'Agrément du lecteur. Notice historique sur les Arabes soumis aux Espagnols pendant leur occupation d'Oran', *R.A.*, 1924, pp. 193–260.

al-'Abdarī, *Rihla*: see A. Cherbonneau (tr.), 'Notice et extraits du voyage d'El-Abdery', *J.A.*, 5th series, IV, 1854, p. 144. The account of a cultivated traveller who reported on the Maghrib at the end of the 13th century.

Abū al-'Arab, *Tabaqāt 'ulamā' Ifrīqiyya*: see Mohammed ben Cheneb (ed. and tr.), *Classes des savants de l'Ifriqiya* (Algiers, 1914–20), *P.F.L.A.*, vol. LI–LII. A valuable account of learned men and ascetics of Kairouan, which is particularly useful for the chronological account of Aghlabid Ifriqiya.

Abū al-Hassan 'Alī al-Jaznaī, *Zahrat al-Ās*: see A. Bel (ed. and tr.), *Zahrat el-As (La fleur de myrte) traitant de la fondation de la ville de Fès* (Paris, 1923), *P.F.L.A.*, vol. LIX. A work largely plagiarized from the *Rawd al-Qirtās* (see Ibn Abi Zar'); it was written about 1365.

Abū Zakariyā', *Kitāb al-sīra wa akhbār al-a'imma*: see E. Masqueray (partial tr.), *Chronique d'Abou Zakaria, Livre des Benî Mzab* (Algiers, 1878); and R. Le Tourneau (ed. and tr.), 'La Chronique d'Abu Zakariya' al-Wargalani', (ed.), *R.A.*, no. 464–5, 1960, pp. 99–176, 322–90, 402–63, and (tr.), vol. CV, 1961, pp. 117–76, 323–74. For a biography of Abu Zakariya' see *Encyclopedia of Islam*.

al-Ayashī, *Ma' al-mawa'id*, otherwise known as *Rihla* (Fes, A.H. 1306), 2 vols. An account of an educated traveller which furnishes useful information about caravans and customs in Algeria under the Turks.

al-Bakrī, *Kitāb al-Masālik*: see M. de Slane (ed. and tr.), *Description de l'Afrique septentrionale* (Algiers, 1857–8; second, corrected edition

History of North Africa

Algiers, 1911–13; third edition, Paris, 1965). For a recent translation and commentary on six chapters of the work, see V. Monteil, 'Al-Bakri (Cordoue, 1068) Routier de l'Afrique blanche et noire du Nord-Ouest', *Bull, I.F.A.N.*, XXX, series B, no. 1, 1968. *Kitāb al-Masālik* was written *c.* 1068 and is one of the most valuable of the geographers' accounts, though it is extant only in fragments. For a biography of al-Bakri see *Encyclopedia of Islam*.

Basset, R., 'Documents musulmans sur le siège d'Alger par Charles Quint (1531)', *B.S.G.O.*, 1890, pp. 172–214.

al-Baidaq: see E. Lévi-Provençal (ed. and tr.), *Documents inédits d'histoire almohade, fragments inédits du 'Legajo' 1999 du fonds arabe de l'Escurial* (Paris, 1928). One of three groups of works included is a chronicle of al-Baidaq, a companion of the Mahdi, Ibn Tumart.

al-Balādhurī, *Kitāb futūh al-buldān*: see P. Hitti (tr.), *The Origins of the Islamic State* (New York, 1916), Columbia University Studies in History, Economics and Public Law, vol. 68. Written in the late 9th century.

Colin, G. S. (ed.), *Chronique anonyme de la dynastie sa'dienne* (Rabat, 1934), Collection des textes arabes, I.H.E.M., vol. II.

Delphin, G. (tr.), 'Histoire des pachas d'Alger de 1515 à 1745', *J.A.*, 1922, I, pp. 162–233. Written about 1734 by the son of a mufti and particularly interesting for its information concerning scholars of the time.

Deny, J. (tr.), 'Documents turcs inédits relatifs à l'Algérie des années 1754 à 1829', *J.A.*, 2nd series, 3, 1914, pp. 708–9.

al-Dhakhir al-saniyya: see M. Bencheneb (ed.), *Adh-Dhakhirat as-saniyya* (Algiers, 1921), *P.F.L.A.*, vol. LVII. An anonymous chronicle of the 13th century about the Merinids, which concludes at the foundation of Fes Jdid (1276), and which is the principal source for the *Rawd al-Qirtās* (see Ibn Abi Zar').

Fagnan, E. (tr.), *Extraits inédits relatifs au Maghrib* (Algiers, 1924). Pages 1–193 consist of translations and annotations of descriptions of North Africa made by geographers of secondary importance. Included also are fragments of a chronicle by Jannabi (d. 1590); the section dealing with Saadian history was translated from a faulty text; for a good edition see G. S. Colin (ed.), *Chronique anonyme de la dynastie sa'dienne* (Rabat, 1934), Collection des textes arabes, I.H.E.M., vol. II.

Gaudefroy-Demombynes, M., 'Une lettre de Saladin au Calife almohade', *Mélanges René Basset* (Paris, 1925), II, pp. 279–304; with a lengthy commentary.

Ghazawāt 'Aruj wa khaïr al-dīn: see Sander-Rang and Denis (tr.), *Fondation de la Régence d'Alger, Histoire de la Régence d'Alger, Histoire des Barberousse. Chronique arabe du XVIIe siècle* (Paris, 1837) 2 vols.; see also A. Noureddine (tr. into Arabic from the

Bibliography

original Turkish text), *Ghazawat 'Arouj wa Khaïr ed-din* (Algiers 1934).

al-Hulal al-mawshiyya fī dhikr al-akhbār al-marrākushiyya: see I. S. Allouche (ed.), *Al-Hulal al-mawchiyya* (Rabat, 1936), Collection des textes arabes, I.H.E.M., vol. VI.; see also A. Huici Miranda (tr.), *al-Hulal al-Mawsiyya, Cronica arabe de los dinastias almoravide, almohade y Beni Merin* (Tétouan, 1952), Instituto General Franco. This anonymous chronicle of the Almoravids and Almohads, was written about 1381.

'Bey Hassan', *Tal'at al-sa'd al-su'ūd*: see M. S. Mazai (tr.), 'La brève chronique de Bey Hasan', *B.S.G.O.*, 1924, pp. 25–61. Extracts from the *Tal'at al-sa'd al-su'ūd*, attributed to a member of a family of aghas of the tribe of the Douair.

Ibn 'Abd al-Hakam, *Kitāb futūh misr wa Ifrīqiyya*: see H. Massé (ed.), *Kitâb fotouh Micr wâ Ifriqiya* (Cairo, 1914); C. C. Torrey (ed.), *The History of the conquest of Egypt, North Africa and Spain* (New Haven, 1922), Yale Oriental Research Series, III; M. de Slane (tr.), *Histoire des Berbères*, vol. I (Paris, 1925), appendix I, pp. 301–14 for the section dealing with the conquest of North Africa up to the expedition of 'Uqba b. Nafi'; A. Gateau (ed. and tr.), *Conquête de l'Afrique du Nord et de l'Espagne* (2nd ed., Paris, 1948), Bibliothèque arabe-français, vol. II, which includes a useful introduction. This account of the conquest of Egypt and North Africa was written before 871 and represents an uncritical compilation of traditions. For a biography of Ibn 'Abd al-Hakam see *Encyclopedia of Islam*.

Ibn 'Abdūn: see E. Lévi-Provençal (ed.), 'Un document sur la vie urbaine et les corps de métiers à Séville au début de XIIe siècle. La traite d'Ibn 'Abdun', *J.A.*, CCXXIV, 1934, pp. 177–299, and (tr.), in *Séville musulmane au début du XIIe siècle* (Paris, 1947), vol. II. It deals with the Almoravid occupation of Seville.

Ibn Abī Dīnār al-Karawanī, *Kitāb al-mū'nis fī akhbār Ifrīqiyya wa Tūnis* (Tunis, 1286/1861–2); see Pellissier de Reynaud (tr.), *Histoire de l'Afrique*, Exploration scientifique de l'Algérie, VII (Paris, 1845); for portions relating to Tunis see: J. G. Magnin, 'Description de Tunis', *I.B.L.A.*, 54, 1951, pp. 150–82, and 'Coutumes des fêtes à Tunis au XI/XVIIe siècle d'après Ibn Abi Dinar', *I.B.L.A.*, 60, pp. 389–421. For a biography of Ibn Abi Dinar see *Encyclopedia of Islam*.

Ibn Abī Zar', *Rawd al-Qirtās*: see C. J. Tornberg (ed. and tr. into Latin), *Annales regum Mauritaniae* (Uppsala, 1843–6); A. Beaumier, *Raud al-Kirtas, Histoire des souverains du Maghreb et annales de la ville de Fès par Abou Mohammed Salah ben Abd al-Halim Gharnati* (Paris, 1860). This author, about whom little is known, wrote an informative account which begins with the Idrisids and terminates in 1324; in part it draws on *al-Dhakhir al-saniyya* and parts may be derived from official documents consulted during the reign of the Merinids.

Ibn al-Ahmar, *Rawd al-nisrîn*: see G. Bouali and G. Marçais (ed. and tr.), *Histoire des Benî Merîn, rois de Fàs, intitulée Rawdat-en-Nisrîn (Le jardin des églantines)* (Paris, 1917), *P.F.L.A.*, vol. LV; this ed. and tr. also has an appendix by R. Dozy (tr.), 'Histoire des Benou Zaiyan de Tlemcen', of genealogical tables and chronological listings of vizirs, chamberlains and secretaries (also published in *J.A.*, 4th series, III, 1844). Ibn al-Ahmar was a Granadian, educated in Fes who then became a jurisconsult and frequented the Merinid court in the second half of the 14th century.

Ibn al-Athīr, *Kāmil fī al-ta'rīkh*: see C. J. Tornberg (ed.), *Chronicon* (Leyden, 1853–76), 14 vols., III–VIII; E. Fagnan (tr.), *Annales du Maghreb et de l'Espagne* (Algiers, 1901). This important account concludes in 1232, two years before the death of its author; for a biography of Ibn al-Athir see *Encyclopedia of Islam*.

Ibn Battūta, *Tuhfa al-nuzzār fī gharā'ib al-amsār wa 'ajā'ib al-asfār*: see C. Défrémery and B. R. Sanguietti (ed. and tr.), *Voyages* (Paris, 1853–9), 4 vols. and 1 vol. of index. (The journey from Alexandria to Tanger is in vol. I; Morocco in vol. IV); Selections also appear in H. A. R. Gibb (tr.), *Travels in Asia and Africa* (London, 1929). Ibn Battuta, who was born in Tangier, travelled from Morocco to China (1325–50) and then returned to North Africa and visited the Western Sudan, including Timbuctu, before writing his memoires in 1356.

Ibn Hammād: see M. Vonderheyden (ed. and tr.), *Histoire des rois Obaidides (Les Califes fatimides)* (Algiers, 1927), *P.F.L.A.*, 3rd series, vol. II. The author, an important Hammadid, wrote a brief history of the Fatimids about 1220 which is particularly interesting for the account of the revolt of Abu Yazid.

Ibn Hawqal, *Kitāb al-masālik wa al-mamālik*: see J. de Goeje (ed.), *Descriptio al-Maghrebi* (Leyden, 1860) for sections relevant to the Maghrib; see also M. de Slane (tr.), 'Description de l'Afrique', *J.A.*, 1842. This work was written about 977 by a merchant who travelled throughout the Islamic world and perhaps was involved in intelligence work for the Fatimids. For a biography of Ibn Hawqal see *Encyclopedia of Islam*.

Ibn 'Idhārī, *al-Bayān al-mughrib fī akhbār al-Maghrib*: see R. Dozy (ed.), *Al-bayân 'l-Mughrib* (Leyden, 1848–51), 2 vols.; E. Fagnan (tr.), *Histoire de l'Afrique et de l'Espagne* (Algiers, 1901–14), 2 vols.; see also A. Huici Miranda, 'Un fragmento inedito de Ibn 'Idāri "Sobre los Almorávides"', *Hespéris-Tamuda*, II, 1961, pp. 43–111. The *Bayan* has preserved fragments of other works, not now extant; the author is known to have lived in the 13th century. For a biography of Ibn 'Idhari see *Encyclopedia of Islam*.

Ibn Khaldūn, *Kitāb al-'Ibar*: see Noël des Vergers (ed. and tr.), *Histoire de l'Afrique sous les Aghlabides et de la Sicile* (Paris, 1841), 7 vols.

Bibliography

(reprinted, Beirut, 1950's). A very abbreviated work of less value than the editions and translations which follow: M. de Slane (ed.), *Histoire des Berbères* (Paris 1847, and tr., Algiers, 1852–6), 4 vols. (reprinted, Paris, 1925–56), 4 vols; de Slane has edited and translated those portions dealing with North Africa.

Ibn Khaldūn, *Muqaddima*: see M. de Slane (tr.), *Les Prolégomènes* (Paris, 1934–8), 3 vols., probably the most widely accepted translation, though somewhat fullsome in interpretation; see also F. Rosenthal, *The Muqaddimah: an introduction to history* (New York, 1958), 3 vols.

Ibn Khaldūn: Numerous works have been written in analysis and interpretation of Ibn Khaldun's history and more particularly, his philosophy; for some of these see:
Bouthoul, G., *Ibn Khaldoun, sa philosophie sociale* (Paris, 1930).
Maunier, R., *Mélanges de sociologie nord-africaine* (Paris, 1930), pp. 1–35.
Gautier, E. F., *L'Islamisation de l'Afrique du Nord. Les siècles obscurs du Maghreb* (Paris, 1927), pp. 53–75.
Marçais, G., 'Ibn Khaldoun et le livre des Prolegomenes', *Revue de la Méditerranée*, 1950, pp. 406–20 and pp. 524–35.
Merad, A., 'L'autobiographie d'Ibn Khaldun', *I.B.L.A.*, 73, 1956.
Fischel, W. J., 'Ibn Khaldun's use of historical sources', *Stud. Islamica*, XIV, 1961, pp. 109–19.
For a biography of Ibn Khaldun see *Encyclopedia of Islam*.

Ibn Khallikān, *Wafayāt al-A'yān wa Anbā' Abnā' al-Zamān*: see F. W. Wüstenfeld (ed.), *Wafayât al-A'yân wa Ambâ' Abnâ' al-Zamân* (Gottingen, 1835–46); see also M. de Slane *Biographical Dictionary* (Paris–London, 1843–71), 4 vols. An excellent collection of biographies written in Cairo during the 13th century.

Ibn Khurradadbih, Ibn al-Faqih al-Hamadhani, and Ibn Rustih: see Hadj-Sadok (ed. and tr.), *Description du Maghrib et de l'Europe au IXe siècle* (Paris, 1949), Bibliothèque arabe-français, vol. VI and IX. Useful, though second-hand, information contained in the extracts collected in these volumes.

Ibn Marzūq, *Musnad*: see R. Blachère (tr.), 'Quelques détails sur la vie privée du sultan mérinide Abu 'l-Hasan', *Mémorial Henri Basset* (Paris, 1928), pp. 83–9; see also E. Lévi-Provençal (tr.), 'Un nouveau text d'histoire mérinide: Le Musnad d'Ibn Marzûk', *Hespéris*, V, 1925, pp. 1–82. The author was born in Tlemcen about 1310 and knew well from first-hand experience the court of the Merinids.

Ibn al-Qattan: see E. Lévi-Provençal (tr.), 'Six fragments inédits d'une chronique anonyme du début des Almohades', *Mélanges René Basset* (Paris, 1925), vol. II, pp. 335–93. The complete version of this manuscript, only fragments of which appear in Lévi-Provençal's work mentioned here, was discovered in Fes in 1927.

Ibn Qunfūd, *al-Fārisiyya fī mabādī' al-daula al-hafsiyya*: see A. Cherbonneau (tr.), 'Farésiade, ou commencement de la dynastie des Beni Haffs', *J.A.*, 1848–52. Written by a well educated man, born in Constantine in 1340, who describes his native town; the translation by Cherbonneau is only partial and is imperfect.

Ibn Saghīr: see A. Motylinswki (ed. and tr.), 'Chronique d'Ibn Saghir sur les imams rostémides de Tahert', *Actes du XIVe Congrès des Orientalistes* (Paris, 1907), 3rd section.

Ibn Tūmart, *Muwāta'a*: see H. Massé (tr.), 'La profession de foi ('Aqîda) et les guides spirituels (morchida) du Mahdi Ibn Toumart', *Mémorial Henri Basset* (Paris, 1928), II, pp. 105–21; see also Luciani (ed.), *Le livre d'Ibn Tourmert (Mowat't'â)*, (Algiers, 1903).

Ibn Tūmart: see E. Lévi-Provençal (ed. and tr.), *Documents inédits d'histoire almohade fragments inédits du 'Legajo' 1999 du fonds arabe de l'Escurial* (Paris, 1928). One of the three groups of documents which comprise this collection are letters of Ibn Tumart and 'Abd al-Mumin to chiefs of Almohad groups.

Idris, H. R. (tr.), 'Contribution à l'histoire de l'Ifrikiya; extraits du Riyâd en-Nufûs d'Abū Bakr el-Mâlikî', *R.E.I.*, 9, 1935, pp. 105–78, 273–305; 10, 1936, pp. 45–104.

Idris, H. R. (tr.), 'Analyse et traduction de deux textes de l'époque ziride', *70ème Congrès de l'A.F.A.S.*, fasc. 3 (Tunis, 1953).

al-Idrīsī, *Kitāb nuzhat al-mushtāq fī khtirāq al-āfāq*: see R. Dozy and J. de Goeje (ed. and partial tr.), *Description de l'Afrique et de l'Espagne* (Leyden, 1866). This is one of the best accounts by the Arab geographers; it was written about 1154 and furnishes a complete description of the world known to the Arabs in the mid-12th century.

al-Ifrānī, *Nuzhatī al-Hādi*: see O. Houdas (ed. and tr.), *Nozhet al-Hâdi. Histoire de la dynastie saadienne au Maroc (1511–1670)*, (Paris, 1888–9), 2 vols.

Jannabī: see E. Fagnan (tr.), *Extraits inédits relatifs au Maghreb* (Algiers, 1924). Contains fragments of Jannabi's (d. 1590) chronique.

Col. Justinard (tr.), *La Rihla du Marabout de Tasaft* (Paris, 1940). The adventures of a marabout of the High Atlas during the period of Mulay Isma'il, written by the man's son.

al-Kattānī, *Salwat al-anfās* (Fes, 1898–9) 3 vols. An account of the saints of Fes written by a 19th-century figure who drew upon earlier works.

LaVeronne, C. (tr.), 'Deux lettres inédites d'une roi de Tlemcen (1531–1532)', *R.A.*, 99, 1955, pp. 174–80.

Leo Africanus (see al-Wazani).

Lévi-Provençal, E. (ed.), *Extraits des historiens Arabes du Maroc* (Paris, 1923).

—— (tr.), 'Six fragments inédits d'une chronique anonyme du début des Almohades', *Mélanges René Basset* (Paris, 1925), II, pp.

Bibliography

335–93. These fragments form a part of a complete manuscript found in Fes in 1927 and which is attributed to Ibn al-Qattan.

Lévi-Provençal (ed. and tr.), *Documents inédits d'histoire almohade, fragments inédits du 'Legajo' 1999 du fonds arabe de l'Escurial* (Paris, 1928), Textes arabes relatifs à l'histoire de l'Occident musulmane. This volume contains three works: letters of Ibn Tumart and 'Abd al-Mumin to chiefs of Almoravid groups, the chronicle of al-Baidaq, and a treatise about the genealogy and companions of the Mahdi. These texts contain a great deal of information about the beginnings of the Almohads and the partition of Chleuh tribes, and they contain useful Berber linguistic material.

—— (ed.), *Fragments historiques sur les Berbères au Moyen âge: extraits du kitâb Mafâkhir al-Barbar*, (Paris, 1934), Collection des textes arabes, I.H.E.M., vol. I.

—— (ed.), *Histoire de l'Espagne musulmane, extraite du kitâb A'mal al-A'lâm d'Ibn al-Khatîb* (Paris, 1934), Collection des textes arabes, I.H.E.M., vol. III.

—— (ed. and tr.), 'Les "Mémoires" de 'Abd Allah, dernier roi ziride de Grenade', *Al-Andalus*, III, IV, 1935–6. This includes, in part, important fragments of manuscripts discovered in Fes and treating the periods 1064–77 and 1080–9.

—— (ed.), *Trente-sept lettres officielles almohades* (Paris, 1941), Collection des textes arabes, I.H.E.M., vol. X; and (tr.), 'Un recueil de lettres officielles almohades', *Hespéris*, XXVIII, 1941.

al-Maqqarī, *Nafh al-tīb min ghusn al-Andalus* (Cairo, A.H. 1302–4), 4 vols.: see R. Dozy, G. Dugat, L. Krehl and W. Wright (tr.), *Analectes sur l'histoire et la littératures des Arabes d'Espagne* (Leyden, 1855–61), which is drawn from the first part of the work; see also P Pascual de Gayangos (tr.), *The History of the Muhammedan Dynasties in Spain* (London, 1840), which is drawn from the political history in the work.

al-Marrākushī, *al-Mu'jib fī talkhīs akhbār al-Maghrib*: see R. Dozy (ed.), *History of the Almohades* (Leyden, 1847–81); see also E. Fagnan (tr.), 'Histoire des Almohades', *R.A.*, 1891–2, and *Histoire des Almohades* (Algiers, 1893). The author, a Moroccan, who was in contact with the Almohad rulers and artists, wrote this work, in part his own memoirs, in the East about 1224.

al-Muqaddasī: see C. Pellat (ed. and tr.), *Description de l'Occident musulman Xe siècle* (Algiers, 1950).

al-Nāsirī al-Slawi, *Kitāb al-Istiqsā li-akhbār duwal al-Maghrib al-Aqsa* (Cairo, 1894), 4 vols.: see A. Graulle et al. (tr.), 'Kitab el-istiqça li-akhbar doual el-maghrib el-aqça (Histoire du Maroc)' *A.M.*, XXX, 1923, pp. 1–302 (a translation of vol. 1 which concerns the Berbers, Arab conquest, Kharijite revolts and the Berghwata); XXXI, 1925, pp. 1–238 (translation by A. Graulle on the Idrisids and a translation by G. S. Colin on the Almoravids); XXXII, 1927, pp. 1–283 (a translation by Ismaël Hamet on the Almohads); and XXXIII, 1934, pp. 1–621; (a translation by Ismaël Hamet on the Merinids); see also E. Fumey (tr.), 'Chronique de la dynastie alaouie au Maroc', *A.M.*, IX, 1906, pp. 1–399 and X, 1907, pp. 1–424; see also Mohammed en-Naçiri (tr.), 'Les Saadiens', *A.M.*, XXXIV (1 re partie), 1936. Al-Nasiri al-Slawi was a civil servant of the Moroccan makhzan in the 19th century and his history is useful for the 19th century, but lacks originality.

al-Nuwairī, *Nihāyat al-arab fī funūn al-adab*: see M. de Slane (tr.), *Histoire des Berbères* (Algiers, 1852; reprinted Paris, 1925), vol. I, appendix II, pp. 314–97. The author was an Egyptian writing in the 14th century.

Saghīr b. Yusuf, *Mashrūʿ al-milkī*: see V. Serres and Mohammed Lasram (tr.), 'Machra el-melkî, soixante ans d'histoire de la Tunisie', *R.T.*, 1895–1900 and in one volume (Paris, 1900). The work is devoted to the first four Husainids.

al-Shammāʿ, Ahmad (Abū al-ʿAbbās) *al-Adilla al-bayyina al-nūrāniyya ʿalā mafākhir al-dawla al-Hafsiyya*: see O. Kaak (ed.), *Al-adilla al-bayyina an-nouraniyya ʿala mafakhir ad-dawla al-Hafçiyya* (Tunis, 1936). A eulogy rather than history of the Hafsid dynasty written about 1457.

Smogorzewski, A. (tr. in Polish), *Zrodla Abadyckie* (Levon, 1926); Ibadite texts from research in the Mzab.

Tamgrūtī, *Nafaha al-miskiyya fī al-sifara al-Turkiyya*: see H. de Castries (tr.), *Nagahat el-miskiyya fi-s-sifarat et-tourkiyya. Relation d'une ambassade marocaine en Turquie (1589–1591)*, (Paris, 1929).

al-Tijānī, *Rihla*: see A. Rousseau (tr.), 'Voyage', *J.A.*, I, 1852–3, for a partial translation. An important account from a traveller who had consulted the official papers and registers of the Hafsids at Tunis at the beginning of the 14th century.

al-Tinisi: see Abbé Bargès (tr.), *Histoire des Beni Zeiyan rois de Tlemcen* (Paris, 1850). The author had lived at the court of the ʿAbd al-Waddids for whom he has written a defence; he died in 1494.

Tisserant, E. and Wiet, G. (tr.), 'Une lettre de l'Almohade Murtadâ au Pape Innocent IV', *Hespéris*, 6, 1926, 27–53. This work is particularly interesting for the chancellery forms preserved in its style.

al-ʿUmarī, *Masālik al-absār fī mamalik al-amsār*: see M. Gaudefroy-Demombynes (ed. and tr.), *L'Afrique moins l'Egypte* (Paris, 1927), vol. I, Bibliothèque des Géographers arabes. This work contains useful information about Almohad organisation, e.g., the *jund*, with copious notes.

Vajda, G. (tr.), 'Un recueil des textes historiques judéo-marocains', *Hespéris*, XXXV, 1948, pp. 311–58 and XXXVI, 1949, pp. 139–88. This article contains texts from twelve rabbis of Fes dating from the 16th to 19th centuries.

Yahyā Ibn Khaldūn, *Bughiat al-Ruwwād*: see A. Bel (ed. and tr.), *Bighiat er-Rowâd. Histoire des Beni ʿAbd el-Wâd* (Algiers, 1904–13), 2 vols.

Bibliography

This account was written in the second half of the 14th century by the secretary and confidant of Abu Hammu II, in praise of the Ziyanids.

al-Ya'qūbī, *Kitāb al-buldān*: see J. de Goeje (ed. and Latin tr.), *Specimen e literis orientalibus exhibens discriptionem al-Maghribi sumtam e libro regionum al-Jaqubii* (Leyden, 1860); see also G. Wiet (tr.), *Textes et traductions d'auteurs orientals* (Cairo, 1937), vol. I.

al-Wazānī (Leo Africanus), *Della descrittione dell' Africa et delle cose notabili che quivi sone*: see Ramusio (ed.), *Della Naviggationi et viaggi* (Venice, 1550); J. Temporal (tr.), *Historiale Description de l'Afrique* (Lyons, 1556), re-edited by C. Schefer (Paris, 1896), 3 vols. with commentaries which do not always refer back to the original text and contain some doubtful identifications: A. Epaulard (tr.) *Description de l'Afrique* (Paris, 1956), 2 vols. The author was born in Granada in about 1495 and he travelled in southern Morocco for the Beni Wattas. He was captured and made prisoner in the Mediterranean, baptised by the Pope under the name 'Johannes Leo', and he translated from the Arabic, in 1526, his description of Africa which furnished the Christian world with a large part of its information about North and West Africa. See L. Massignon, *Le Maroc dans les premières années du XVIe siècle. Tableau géographique d'après Leon l'Africain* (Algiers, 1906).

al-Zarkashī' (attributed), *Ta'rīkh al-dawlatain al-mawakhidiyya wa al-Hafsidiyya* (Tunis, A.H. 1289): see E. Fagnan (tr.), *Chronique des Almohades et des Hafçides attribuée à Zekechi* (Constantine, 1894) and *R.S.A.C.*, 1894.

al-Zayānī, *al-Tarjama al-mu'arib 'an dwal al-mashirq wa al-maghrib*: see O. Houdas (ed. and tr.), *Le Maroc de 1631 à 1812* (Paris, 1886); see also E. Lévi-Provençal (ed.), *Extraits des historiens arabes du Maroc* (Paris, 1923), contains a fragment of al-Zayani's work on the Saadian dynasty. Al-Zayani (1734–1833?), a Berber, with a remarkable experience in politics, wrote a general history of the world from the Creation, and a history of the Alawite dynasty. For both he drew heavily on the works of earlier historians.

B. *Alphabetical listing of translators of Arabic and Turkish sources, indicating authors under whom the translations are listed in IX, A*

Allouche, I. S.   *al-Hulal al-mawshiyya*
Beaumier, A.   Ibn 'Abi Zar'
Bel, A.   Abu al-Hassan
——   Yahya Ibn Khaldun
Bergès, Abbé   al-Tinisi
Blachère, R.   Ibn Marzuq
Bodin, M.   Si 'Abd al-Qadir
Bouali, G. and Marçais, G.   Ibn al-Ahmar
Brunschvig, R.   'Abd al-Basit

History of North Africa

Cherbonneau, A.   al-'Abdari
—— Ibn Qunfud
de Castries, H.   Tamgruti
Défrémery, C. and Sanguietti, B. R.   Ibn Battuta
Dozy, R.   Ibn al-Ahmar
—— Ibn 'Idhari
—— al-Marrakushi
—— al-Maqqari
Epaulard, A.   al-Wazani (Leo Africanus)
Fagnan, E.   Ibn al-Athir
—— Ibn 'Idhari
—— Jannabi
—— al-Marrakushi
—— 'al-Zarkashi'
Fumey, E.   al-Nasiri al-Slawi
Gateau, A.   Ibn 'Abd al-Hakam
Gaudefroy-Demombynes, M.   al-'Umari
Gibb, H. A. R.   Ibn Battuta
de Goeje, J.   Ibn Hawkal
—— al-Idrisi
—— al-Ya'qubi
Graulle, A.   al-Nasiri al-Slawi
Hadj-Sadok   Ibn Khurradadbih, *et al.*
Houdas, O.   al-Ifrani
—— al-Zayani
Huici Miranda, A.   *al-Hulal al-mawshiyya*
—— Ibn 'Idhari
Kaak, O.   al-Shamma'
Le Tourneau, R.   Abu Zakariya
Lévi-Provençal, E.   'Abd al-Mumin
—— al-Baidaq
—— Ibn 'Abdun
—— Ibn Marzuq
—— Ibn al-Qattan
—— Ibn Tumart
—— al-Zayani
Luciani   Ibn Tumart
Magnin, J. G.   Ibn Abi Dinar
Mohammed en-Naçiri   al-Nasiri al-Slawi
Masqueray, E.   Abu Zakariya
Massé, H.   Ibn 'Abd al-Hakam
—— Ibn Tumart
Massignon, L.   al-Wazani (Leo Africanus)
Mazari, M. S.   'Bey Hassan'
Mohammed ben Cheneb   Abu al-'Arab
—— *al-Dhakhirat al-saniyya*
Monteil, V.   al-Bakri

Bibliography

Motylinswki, A.   Ibn Saghir
Noël des Vergers   Ibn Khaldun
Pascual de Gayangos, D.   al-Maqqari
Pellat, C.   al-Muqaddasi
Pellissier de Reynaud   Ibn Abi Zarʿ
Ramusio   al-Wazani (Leo Africanus)
Rosenthal, F.   Ibn Khaldun
Rousseau, A.   al-Tijani
Sander-Rang and Denis   *Ghazawat 'Aruj*
Serres, V. and Mohammed Lusram   Saghir b. Yusuf
de Slane, M.   al-Bakri
—— Ibn ʿAbd al-Hakam
—— Ibn Hawkal
—— Ibn Khaldun
—— Ibn Khallikan
—— al-Nuwiari
Temporal, J.   al-Wazani (Leo Africanus)
Torrey, C. C.   Ibn ʿAbd al-Hakam
Tournberg, C. J.   Ibn Abi Zarʿ
—— Ibn al-Athir
Vonderheyden, M.   Ibn Hammad
Wiet, G.   al-Yaʿqubi
Wüstenfeld, F. W.   Ibn Khallikan

X. HISTORY: GENERAL WORKS PERTAINING TO GEOGRAPHICAL AREAS

A. Universal histories dealing with the Maghrib

Berr, Henri (ed.), *L'Evolution de l'Humanité* (Paris), a series of volumes.
Cambridge Medieval History, vol. II (Cambridge, 1913); see C. H. Becker, pp. 366–80 for a study of the conquest of Africa by the Arabs.
Diehl, Ch., and Marçais, G., 'Le monde oriental de 395 à 1081', in Glotz, G. (ed.) *Histoire générale*, vol. III, 'Moyen Age' (Paris, 1944, 2nd ed.).
Gaudefroy-Demombynes, M. and Platonov, 'Le monde musulman et byzantin jusqu' aux Croisades', in Cavaignac, E. (ed.), *Histoire du Monde* (Paris, 1931), vol. VII, 1.
Halphen, L. and Sagnac, P. (ed.), *Peuples et civilisations. Histoire générale* (Paris); the most useful works in the collection for the study of North Africa are:
  Halphen, L., 'Les Barbares des grandes invasions aux conquêtes turques du XIe siècle' (1940, 4th ed.), vol. V.
  —, 'L'essor de l'Europe (XIe–XIIIe siècle)' (1948, 3rd ed.), vol. VI.
  Pirenne, H., Renaudet, A., Perroy, E., Handelsman, M., and

Halphen, L., 'La fin du Moyen Age; la désagrégation du monde médiéval (1285-1453)' (1931), vol. VII, 1.

—, et al., 'La fin du Moyen Age; l'annonce des temps nouveaux (1453-1492)' (1931), vol. VII, 2.

Hauser, H., 'La prépondérance espagnole (1559-1660)' (1948, 3rd ed.), vol. IX.

de Saint-Leger, A. and Sagnac, P., 'La prépondérance français: Louis XIV (1661-1715)' (1944, 2nd ed.), vol. X.

Lavisse, E. and Rambaud, A. (ed.), *Histoire générale du IXe siècle à nos jours*, 12 vols. (Paris, 1892-9; re-edited 1927); see Vol. IV, pp. 779-85 for a chapter by Masqueray on North African revolutions down to the 16th century.

B. Spain and Portugal

Spain

Altamira, R., *Historia de España y de la civilisacion española* (Barcelona, 1900-11; 3rd ed. 1913-14).

Ballester, R., *Histoire de l'Espagne* (tr. Legrand), (Paris, 1928).

Ballesteros y Beretta, *Historia de España y de su influencia en la historia universal* (Barcelona, 1918-36), 8 vols.

Braudel, F., 'Les Espagnols et l'Afrique du Nord de 1492 à 1577', *R.A.*, 1928, pp. 184-233 and 351-428.

——, 'Les Espagnols en Algérie', in *Histoire et historiens de l'Algérie* (Paris, 1931), published in la Collection du Centenaire de l'Algérie, vol. IV.

——, *La Méditerranée et le monde méditerranéen à l'époque de Philippe II* (Paris, 1949).

de la Primaudaie, E., *Documents inédits sur l'histoire de l'occupation espagnole en Afrique* (Algiers, 1875-7).

Dozy, R., *Histoire des Musulmans d'Espagne jusqu'à la conquête de l'Andalousie par les Almohades*, 4 vols. (Leyden, 1861); new edition, 3 vols. by E. Lévi-Procençal (Leyden, 1932).

Goldziher, I. (tr. J. de Somogyi), 'The Spanish Arabs and Islam. The place of the Spanish Arabs in the evolution of Islam as compared with the eastern Arabs', *M.W.*, LIII, 1963, pp. 5-18, 91-105, 178-84, 277-86, and LIV, 1, 1964, pp. 29-38.

Gonzalez-Palencia, A., 'Historia de la España musulmana', *Coll. Labor.* VI, no. 69 (Barcelona, 1925); (2nd ed., 1929), with bibliography pp. 207-13.

——, 'Historia de la literatura arabigo-española', *Coll. Labor.*, III, no. 164-5 (Barcelona, 1928).

Lévi-Procençal, E., *L'Espagne musulmane au Xe siècle* (Paris, 1932).

——, *Histoire de l'Espagne musulmane*, I. *De la conquête à la chute du califat de Cordoue* (Cairo, 1944; 2nd ed. Leyden-Paris, 1950).

Menendez Pidal, R. (ed.), *Historia de España*, 4 vols. in progress: I,

Bibliography

'España preistorica' (Madrid, 1947); II, 'España romana' (1935); III, 'España visigoda' (1940); IV, 'España musulmana hasta la caida del califato de Cordoba' (1950, tr. by E. Garcia Gomez of E. Lévi-Provençal's *Histoire de l'Espagne musulmane*).

——, *La España del Cid* (Madrid, 1929).

Merriman, R. B., *The rise of the Spanish Empire*, 4 vols. (New York, 1918–34). I, 'The Middle Age' (1918); II, 'The Catholic Kings' (1918); III, 'The Emperor' (1925); IV, 'Philip the Prudent' (1934).

Ribera y Tarrago, *Disertaciones y opusculos . . . (1887–1927)*, 2 vols. (Madrid, 1928); with an introduction by M. Asin Palacios; vol. 1 is devoted to Arab literature and culture and vol. 2 is devoted to music and the problem of Morocco.

Sanchez Albornoz, Cl. *La España musulmana segun los autores islamitas y cristianos medievales* (Florida, Cordoba, Buenos Aires, 1946), 2 vols.

Encyclopedia of Islam: see articles on Malaga, Saragossa, Seville, Toledo, Cordoba, Grenada, and al-Andalus.

Portugal

de Almeida, Fortunato, *Historia de Portugal*, 6 vols. (Coïmbre, 1922–9). I, 'Desde os tempos preistoricos até a aclamação de D. Joao I (1385)' (1922); II, (1385 à 1580) (1924); III, 'Instituições politicas ões politicas e sociais de 1580 a 1816' (1927); VI, (1816–1910) (1929).

de Souza, Serigo, 'Historia de Portugal', *Coll. Labor.*, VI, no. 206 (Barcelona, 1929).

Legrand, Th., *Histoire de Portugal du XIe siècle à nos jours* (Paris, 1928); with incomplete bibliography, arranged by periods, pp. 165–73.

C. West Africa and the Sahara

* Baroja, Caro, *Estudios Saharianos* (Madrid, 1955), Institut de Estudios Africanos.
* Bovill, E. W., *Caravans of the Old Sahara* (London, 1933).
* ——, *Golden Trade of the Moors* (London, 1958), revised edition (London, 1967).
* Comhaire, J., 'Notes on Africans in Muslim history', *M.W.*, 46, 1956, pp. 336–344.
* Norris, H. T., 'The History of Shinqīt according to the Idaw 'Ali tradition', *Bull. I.F.A.N.*, XXIV, B, no. 3 & 4, 1962, pp. 393–413.
* Martin, A.-G.-P., *Les Oasis Sahariennes (Gourara–Touat–Tidikelt)* (Algiers, 1908).
* Mauny, R., *Tableau géographique de l'Ouest africain au Moyen Age* (I.F.A.N. Memoires no. 61, Dakar, 1961, reprinted by Swets & Zeitlinger, Amsterdam).
* Picard, C. G., 'Civilisation saharienne', *Rev. Paris*, August 1958, pp. 132–7.

History of North Africa

* Trimingham, J. S., *Islam in West Africa* (Oxford, 1959).
* ——, *History of Islam in West Africa* (Oxford, 1962).
* Vernier, S., 'Histoire d'un pays saharien: le Fezzan', *Orient.*, 14, 1960, pp. 57–72.

D. North Africa, general works

Albertini, E., Marçais, G., and Yver, G., *Afrique du Nord française dans l'histoire* (Paris, 1937).
* Barbour, N., *A survey of North West Africa* (Oxford, 1959), Royal Institute of International Affairs; Maghribi history is only briefly treated.

Carette, E., 'Recherches sur les origines et les migrations des principales tribus de l'Afrique septentrionale et particulièrement de l'Algérie' in *Exploration scientifique de l'Algérie*, III (Paris, 1853).

Cat, E., *Histoire de l'Algérie–Tunisie–Maroc* (Algiers, 1889–91).

Diehl, Ch., *L'Afrique byzantine* (Paris, 1896; New York, 1959).

Faure-Biquet, Général, *Histoire de l'Afrique septentrionale sous la domination musulmane* (Paris, 1905).
* Fisher, Sir G., *Barbary Legend (1415–1830)* (Oxford, 1957).

Gautier, E.-F., *L'Islamisation de l'Afrique du Nord. Les siècles obscurs du Maghreb* (Paris, 1927); re-edited, 1937 under the title *Le passé de l'Afrique du Nord. Les siècles obscurs* (Paris, 1952).
* Gabriele, F., 'Histoire et culture de la Sicile arabe', *Rev. Méd.*, no. 79, May–June, 1957, pp. 249–59.
* Goitein, S. D., 'The unity of the Mediterranean world in the "Middle" Middle Ages', *Stud. Islamica*, 12, 1960, pp. 29–42.

Hamet, I., *Histoire de Maghreb* (Paris, 1913).
* Hopkins, J. F. P., *Medieval Muslim Government in Barbary until the sixth century of the Hijra* (London, 1958).
* Le Tourneau, R., 'L'Occident musulman du milieu du VIIe siècle à la fin de XVe siècle', *Annales I.E.O.*, 16, 1958, pp. 147–76.

Marçais, G., *Les Arabes en Berbérie du XIe au XIVe siècle* (Paris-Constantine, 1913) and *R.S.A.C.*, 1913, pp. 1–772; especially useful for his study of Ibn Khaldun, the expansion of the Bedouins and their role in the medieval Maghrib.

——, *Berbérie musulmane et l'Orient au Moyen Age* (Paris, 1946).
* Marçais, W., 'Les siècles obscurs du Maghrib', *Revue critique d'histoire et du littérature*, 1929, pp. 255–70; a critique of E.-F. Gautier's 1927 edition of *l'Islamisation de l'Afrique du Nord*; also reprinted in W. Marçais, *Articles et Conférences*, *P.F.L.A.* (Paris, 1961), p. 77 et seq.

Mercier, E., *Histoire de l'Afrique septentrionale (Berbérie) depuis les temps les plus reculés jusqu'à la conquête français (1830)*, 3 vols. (Paris, 1888–91): I, covering the period to 1045 (1888); II, 1045–1515 (1888); III, 1515–1830 (1891).

Bibliography

Mtouggui, L., *Vue générale de l'Histoire Berbère* (Algiers–Paris, n.d.) [1949].

Pellissier, E., 'Mémoires historiques et géographiques sur l'Algérie' in *Exploration scientifique de l'Algérie*, VI (Paris, 1844); useful for Spanish expeditions and settlements in Barbary (pp. 3–120), Portuguese in Morocco (pp. 121–73) and Italian, English and French in Barbary (pp. 175–301).

* Ziadeh, N., 'From the history of Arab North Africa', *Abhath*, 9, 1956, pp. 319–25 (in Arabic).

1. Morocco

Caillé, J., *La Ville de Rabat jusqu'au Protectorat françaises. Histoire et archéologie* (Paris, 1949), 3 vols.

Célérier, J., *Maroc* (Paris, 1948).

* Charles-Roux, F. and Caillé, J., *Missions diplomatiques français à Fès* (Paris, 1955), published by I.H.E.M.; deals with the period from the 16th century to the establishment of the Protectorat.

de Castries, H. et al. (see above Bibliography I, E. Published primary source material).

Delafosse, M., 'Les relations du Maroc avec le Soudan à travers les âges', *Hespéris*, 1924, pp. 153–74.

Deverdun, G., *Marrakech, des origines à 1912* (Rabat 1959), 2 vols.

* Drague, G., *Esquisse d'histoire religieuse du Maroc*, Les Cahiers de l'Afrique et l'Asie, II (Paris, 1951).

Gaillard, H., *Une ville d'Islam, Fez* (Paris, 1905).

Initiation au Maroc (Paris, 1946, 3rd ed.), published by I.H.E.M.

Introduction à la connaissance du Maroc (Casablanca, 1942).

Le Tourneau, R., *Fès avant le Protectorat* (Casablanca, 1949).

Lévi-Provençal, E., *Les historiens des Chorfa* (Paris, 1923).

——, 'Le Maroc en face de l'étranger à l'époque moderne', *B.E.P.M.*, 1925, pp. 95–112.

* Martin, A.-G.-P., *Quatre Siècles d'histoire Marocaine* (Paris, 1923).

Montagne, R., *Les Berbères et le Makhzen dans le Sud du Maroc, Essai sur la transformation politique des Berbères sédentaires (groupe Chleuh)* (Paris, 1930).

Terrasse, H., *Histoire du Maroc des origines à l'établissement du Protectorat français* (Casablanca, 1949–50), 2 vols.; abridged edition (Casablanca, 1952; 238 pp.).

Villes et tribus du Maroc (see p. 377, Sociology, Anthropology, Ethnography).

2. Algeria

Bernard, A., *Algérie* (Paris, 1929).

Basset, R., *Histoire de l'Algérie par ses monuments* (Paris, 1900).

——, in *Mélanges africains et orientaux* (Paris, 1915), pp. 1–16 (a résumé of *Algérie musulman*).

de Grammont, H., *Histoire d'Alger sous la domination turque (1516–1830)* (Paris, 1887).

Esquer, G., 'Les sources de l'histoire de l'Algérie', *Histoire et historiens de l'Algérie (1830–1930)* (Paris, 1931).
* Feraud, Ch., *Bougie: étude historique* (Constantine, 1869), after a manuscript published by C.E.B. (Fort-National, 1953).

Garrot, H., *Histoire générale de l'Algérie* (Algiers, 1910).

Gsell, S., Marçais, G., and Yver, G., *Histoire de l'Algérie* (Paris, 1927); the best history of Algeria available.

Larnaude, M., *Algérie* (Paris, 1950).

Lespès, J., *Alger* (Paris, 1930).

——, *Oran* (Paris, 1938).

Marçais, G. et al., *Histoire de l'Algérie* (Paris, 1927), pp. 162–89.
* Marçais, G., 'Les villes de la côte algérienne et la piraterie au Moyen Age', *Annales I.E.O.*, 13, 1955, pp. 118–42.
*——, *L'Algérie médiévale* (Paris, 1957).

Marçais, W., 'Un siècle de recherches sur le passé de l'Algérie musulmane', *Histoire et historiens de l'Algérie* (Paris, 1931).

Martin, A.-G.-P., *Les Oasis Sahariennes (Gourara–Touat–Tidikelt)* (Algiers, 1908).

Encyclopedia of Islam: see articles on Algeria, Algiers, Bône, Bougie, Djijelli, Constantine, Mascara, Shershel, and Tlemcen.

3. Tunisia

Brunschvig, R., 'La Tunisie au Moyen Age', *Initiation à la Tunisie* (Paris, 1950), pp. 73–97.

Cambon, H., *Histoire de la Régence de Tunis* (Paris, 1948); of limited value.
* Chovin, G., 'Aperçu sur les relations de la France avec le Maroc des Origines à la fin du Moyen Age', *Hespéris*, 44, 1957, pp. 249–98.

Despois, J., *La Tunisie* (Paris, 1930); the first volume of the *Collection Coloniale*, published under the editorship of H. Gourdon.

——, 'Kairouan, origine et évolution d'une ancienne capitale musulmane', *Ann. de Géogr.* 1930, pp. 159–77.

——, *La Tunisie orientale, Sahel et Basse Steppe* (Paris, 1940).
* Eisenbeth, M., 'Les Juifs en Algérie et en Tunisie à l'époque turque (1516–1860)', *R.A.*, 93, 1952, pp. 114–89.
* Latham, J. D., 'Towards a study of Andalusian immigration and its place in Tunisian history', *Cahiers de Tunisie*, 5, 1957, pp. 203–55.

Marçais, G., 'L'Art musulman de Tunisie', *Initiation à la Tunisie* (Paris, 1950), pp. 116–33.

Pellegrin, A., *Histoire de la Tunisie depuis les origines jusqu'à nos jours* (Tunis, 1948, 4th ed.).

*——, 'Le peuplement historique de Tunis', *Enc. Mens. O. M.*, 3, 1953, pp. 196–8.

Pignon, J., 'La Tunisie turque et husséinite', *Initiation à la Tunisie* (Paris, 1950), pp. 98–115.

Encyclopedia of Islam: see articles on Bizerta, Djerba, Gabès, Gafsa,

Bibliography

Ifrikiya, al-Kairawan, al-Kef, Sfax, Subaitila, Tabarka, Tunis, Tunisia, and al-Mahdiya.

E. North East Africa

Amari, *Storia dei musulmani di Sicilia*, 3 vols. (Florence, 1854–68).
Hanotaux, G., *Histoire de la Nation égyptienne*, vol. IV (Paris, 1937).
Lane-Pool, Stanley, *A history of Egypt in the Middle Age* (London, 1901; 2nd ed. 1914).
Précis de l'histoire d'Egypte par divers historiens et archéologues, vol. 3 (Cairo, 1933).
Wiet, G., *L'Egypte arabe* (Paris, 1937).
——, *L'Egypte musulmane de la conquête arabe à la conquête ottomane* (Paris); see 'Les Fatimides', pp. 173–217.

Part III. Chronological/Historical Index

XI. THE ARAB CONQUEST

A. Arab Authors

See above, section IX, *Arab sources available in translation*, for the following authors: al-Ya'qubi, Ibn Hawqal, al-Bakri, al-Idrisi, Ibn Khurradadhib *et. al.*, Ibn 'Abd al-Hakam, Ibn Khaldun, Ibn al-Athir, Ibn 'Idhari, al-Nuwairi, Ibn Abi Dinar, al-Nasiri al-Slawi.

B. Specific references and monographs

Becker, C. H., in *Cambridge Medieval History* (Cambridge, 1913), II, Ch. XII, pp. 366–80, for the conquest of North Africa by the Arabs.
* Brunschvig, R., 'Un texte arabe du IXe siècle intéressant le Fezzan', *R.A.*, 89, 1945, pp. 21–5.
——, 'Ibn 'Abdalh' akam et la conquête de l'Afrique du Nord par les Arabes', *Annales I.E.O.*, VI (1942–7) pp. 108–55.
Caetani, L., 'Le condizioni generalli dell' Africa Settentrionale e il principio della conquesta arabo-musulmana', *Annali dell' Islam*, IV, 1911, pp. 521–32 (a superficial study of the works of Fournel, Mercier and Caudel).
Caudel, M., *L'Afrique du Nord, les Byzantins, les Berberes avant les invasions* (Paris, 1900), (of limited value).
——, *Les premières invasions arabes dans l'Afrique du Nord* (27–78 Hg./641–697 J.G.), (Paris, 1900), (of limited value).
Diehl, Ch., *L'Afrique byzantine* (Paris, 1896; New York, 1959), pp. 563–600.

Fournel, H., *Les Berberes. Etude sur la conquête de l'Afrique par les Arabes, d'après les textes arabes imprimés* (Paris, 1875–81), I, pp. 1–384.
* Gateau, A., 'Ibn 'Abd al-Hakam et les sources arabes relatives à la conquête de l'Afrique du Nord et de l'Espagne', *R.T.*, 1938, pp. 37–54 and 1939, pp. 203–19.
* Lévi-Provençal, E., 'Arabica occidentalia, I. i. Un nouveau récit de la conquête de l'Afrique du Nord par les Arabes (ii. Le *zagal* hispanique dans la *Mugrib* d'Ibn Sa'īd)', *Arabica*, I, 1954, pp. 17–52.
* Lewicki, T., 'A propos d'une liste de tribus berbères d'Ibn Hawqal', *Folia Orientalia*, I, 1959, pp. 203–55.

Marçais, G., *La Berbérie musulmane et l'Orient au Moyen Age* (Paris, 1946), 'L'orientalisation de la Berbérie', pp. 19–42.
* ——, 'Sîdî Uqba, Abû l-Mahâjir et Kusaila', *Cahiers de Tunisie*, I, 1953, pp. 11–17.
* Marçais, W., 'Comment l'Afrique du Nord a été arabisée', *Annales I.E.O.*, 4, 1938, pp. 1–22.
* ——, 'Comment l'Afrique du Nord a été arabisée', *Annales I.E.O.*, 14, 1956, pp. 5–17.
* Massé, H., 'La chronique d'Ibn A'tham et la Conquête de l'Ifriqiya', *Mélanges Gaudefroy-Demombynes*, (Cairo, 1935–45), pp. 85–90.
* Merad, A., ''Abd el-Mu'min à la conquête de l'Afrique du Nord 1130–1163', *Annales I.E.O.*, XV, 1958, pp. 109–63.

Mercier, E., *Histoire de l'Afrique septentrionale (Berbérie) depuis les temps les plus reculés jusqu'à la conquête français (1830)* (Paris, 1888–1891), I, pp. 179–267.
* Sebag, P., 'Les expéditions maritimes arabes du VIIIe siècle', *Cahiers de Tunisie*, 31, 1960, pp. 73–82.
* Talbi, M., 'Rapports de l'Ifriqiya et de l'Orient au VIIIe siècle', *Cahiers de Tunisie*, 7, 1959, pp. 299–305.

Terrasse, H., *Histoire du Maroc des origines à l'établissement du Protectorat français* (Casablanca, 1949–50), I, pp. 75–104.

Encyclopedia of Islam: see articles on al-Kâhina, Berghawâta, Hanzalâ b. Safwân, Hâssan b. al-Nu'mân al-Ghassâni, Kusaila, Idris I, Idris II, Idrîsides, Kulthûm, 'Abd Allâh b. S'ad, Djizya, Sidjilmâsa, 'Abd al-Rahmân b. Habib.

XII. IBADITES

A. Arab authors

See above, section IX, *Arab sources available in translation*, for the following authors: al-Nasiri al-Slawi, Abu Zakariya, and Ibn Saghir.

Bibliography

B. Specific references and monographs

Basset, R., *Etude sur la Zenatia du Mzab, de Ouargla et de l'oued Rir'* (Paris, 1892).
——, *Les sanctuaires du Djeb el-Nefousa* (Paris, 1899).
* Bekri, Ch., 'Le Kharijisme berbère. Quelques aspects du royaume rustumide', *Annales I.E.O.*, XV, 1958, pp. 55-108.
* Canard, M., 'Les traveaux de T. Lewicki concernant le Maghreb et en particulier les Ibadhites', *R.A.*, 103, 1959, pp. 356-71.
Chevrillon, A. L., *Les puritains du désert* (Paris, 1927).
Goichon, A. M., *La vie féminine au Mzab* (Paris, 1927).
* Ibn Tawit, M., 'Les Banû Rustum, reyes de Tahert (Tiaret)', *Rev. Inst. Est. Isl.* Madrid, V, 1957; Arabic section, pp. 105-28.
* Lewicki, T., 'Un document ibâdite inédit sur l'émigration des Nafûsa du žabal dans le sâhil tunisien au VIIIᵉ au IXᵉ siècle', *Folia Orientalia*, I, 1959, pp. 175-91.
*——, 'Les historiens, biographes et traditionnistes Ibadites-Wahabites de l'Afrique du Nord du VIIᵉ au XVIᵉ siècle', *Folia Orientalia*, III, 1-2, 1961, pp. 1-134.
Marçais, G., *La Berbérie musulmane et l'Orient au Moyen Age* (Paris, 1946), pp. 101-16.
——, 'La Berbérie au IXᵉ siècle d'après el-Ya'qoûbî', *R.A.*, 1941, pp. 40-61.
Marçais, G. and Dessus-Lamare, A., 'Recherches d'archéologie musulmane: Tîhert-Tagdemt', *R.A.*, 1946, pp. 24-57.
Mercier, M., *Etude sur le 'waqf' abadhite et ses applications au Mzab* (Algiers, 1927).
Motylinski, A. de C., *Les livres de la secte abadhite* (Algiers, 1885).
——, 'L'Aqida des Abadhites', *Recueil de mémoires et de textes publié en l'honneur du XIVᵉ Congrès des Orientalistes* (Algiers, 1905), pp. 505-46.
Strothmann, R., 'Berber und Ibadîten', *Der Islam*, XVII, 1928, pp. 258-79.
* Watt, W. M., 'Kharijite thought in the Umayyad period', *Der Islam*, 36/3, February 1961, pp. 215-31.
Encyclopedia of Islam: see articles on Kharâdj, Hadjdjâdj b. Yûsuf, Khâridjite, al-Sufriya, Maisara, Tâhert, Subaitila, Abâdites, Abû Hâtim, Abû 'l-Khattâb, 'Abd al-Rahmân b. Rostem, 'Abd Allâh b. al-Zubair, 'Amr, Ghomâra, Ifren, al-Kairawân, and 'Abbasides.

XIII. IDRISIDS, AGHLABIDS AND FATIMIDS

A. Arab Authors

See above, section IX, *Arab sources available in translation*, for the following authors: Ibn Abi Dinar, Ibn 'Idhari, Ibn al-Athir, al-Bakri, Ibn Hawqal, al-Idrisi, Ibn Khaldun, al-Ya'qubi, Ibn Abi Zar', Abu al-Arab, Abu al-Hasan 'Ali al-Jaznai, Ibn Hammad, Ibn Khallikan.

B. *Idrisids* (specific references and monographs)

* Eustache, D., 'El-Basra, capitale idrissite et son port', *Hespéris*, 42, 1955, pp. 217–38.
Gautier, E. F., *L'Islamisation de l'Afrique du Nord. Les siècles obscurs du Maghreb* (Paris, 1927), pp. 274–91.
Le Tourneau, R., *Fès avant le protectorat* (Casablanca, 1949), pp. 30–51.
Lévi-Provençal, E., 'La fondation de Fès', *Annales I.E.O.*, IV, pp. 23–53.
Marçais, G., *Berbérie musulmane et l'Orient au Moyen Age* (Paris, 1946), pp. 116–29.
Salmon, G., 'Les Chorfa Idrisides de Fès', *A.M.*, I, 1904, pp. 425–53.
Terrasse, H., *Histoire du Maroc des origines à l'établissement du Protectorat français* (Casablanca, 1949–50), I, pp. 107–34.
Encyclopedia of Islam articles on Idrîs I, Idrîs II, Idrîsids, Basra, Fas.

C. *Aghlabids* (specific references and monographs)

* Abdul-Wahab, H. H., 'Un tournant de l'histoire Aghlabite', *R.T.*, 1937, pp. 343–52; 1938, p. 55.
Idris, H. R., 'Contribution à l'histoire de l'Ifriqiya. Tableau de la vie intellectuelle et administrative à Kairouan sous les Aglabites et les Fatimites ... d'après le Riyād En Nufūs de Abū Bakr el Mālikî', *R.E.I.*, 9, 1935, pp. 105–78, 273–305; 10, 1936, pp. 45–104.
Marçais, G., *Manuel d'art musulman. Architecture* (Paris, 1926), pp. 7–83.
——, *Les faïences à reflets métalliques de la Grande Mosquée de Kairouan* (Paris, 1928).
——, *La Berbérie musulmane et l'Orient au Moyen Age* (Paris, 1946), pp. 55–101.
Sayous, A. E., *Le commerce des Européens à Tunis depuis le XIIe siècle jusqu'à la fin du XVI siècle* (Paris, 1929), p. 323.
Vonderheyden, M., *La Berbérie orientale sous la dynastie des Benoû'l-Arlab*, 800–909 (Paris, 1927).
Encyclopedia of Islam articles on: Aghlabides, Ibrahim b. al-Aghlab, Asad b. al-Furat, Buhlûl, Sahnûn, 'Akl, Fikh, al-Kur'an, Kalâm, Mâlik b. Anas, al-Ash'ari.

D. *Fatimids* (specific references and monographs)

* Canard, M., 'L'Autobiographie d'un chambellan du Mahdî 'Obeidallâh le Fâtimide', *Hespéris*, XXXIX, 1952, pp. 277–330.
——, 'L'impérialisme des Fatimides et leur propagande', *Annales I.E.O.*, VI, pp. 156–93.

Bibliography

Gautier, E. F., *L'Islamisation de L'Afrique du Nord. Les siècles obscurs du Maghrib* (Paris, 1927), pp. 309–30 and 354–62.
Lewis, B., *The origins of Ismaʿīlism; a study of the historical background of the Fatimid caliphate* (Cambridge, 1940).
Marçais, G., *Manuel d'art musulman. Architecture* (Paris, 1926), pp. 95 et seq.
——, *La Berbérie musulmane et l'Orient au Moyen Age* (Paris, 1946), pp. 131–90.
O'Leary, De L., *A short history of the Fatimid caliphate* (London, 1923).
Terrasse, H., *Histoire du Maroc des origines à l'établissement du Protectorat français* (Casablanca, 1949–50), I, pp. 135–208.
Encyclopedia of Islam articles on: Shîʿa, al-Mahdî, Ismâʿîlîya, Abû ʿAbd Allâh, Fatimids, al-Mahdî ʿUbaid Allâh, al-Kâʾim, al-Mansûr Ismâʿîl, al-Mahdîya, Abû Yazîd, Ketama, Djawhar.

E. Zirids

* Courtois, C., 'Remarques sur le commerce maritime en Afrique au XIe siècle', *Mélanges hist. arch. Occ. Musul.* II, *Hommage à G. Marçais*, 1957, pp. 51–9.
* Idris, H. R., 'Analyse et traduction de deux textes de l'époque ziride', *Extract du 70e Congrès de l'A.F.A.S.*, fasc. 3 (Tunis, 1953).
*——, 'Sur le retour des Zîrîdes à l'obédience fâtimide', *Annales I.E.O.*, XI, 1954, pp. 25–39.
*——, 'Une des phases de la lutte de malikisme contre le Chiʿisme sous les Zirides (XIe siècle). Al-Tunisi, juriste kairouanais et sa célèbre fatwa sur les chiʿites', *Cahiers de Tunisie*, 4, 1956, pp. 508–17.
*——, 'Contribution à l'histoire de la vie religieuse en Ifriqiya zirīde (Xème–XIème siècles), *Mélanges L. Massignon*, II, (Damascus, 1957), pp. 327–59.
*——, *La Berbérie Orientale sous les Zirides, Xe–XIIe siècle* (Paris, 1962), Pub. of I.E.O., 2 vols.
Le Tourneau, R., 'La révolte d'Abu Yazid au Xme siècle', *Cahiers de Tunisie*, I, 1953, pp. 103–25.
——, 'La revolte de Abou-Mahalli', *J. Inst. Af. du Nord*, 9, 1955, pp. 33–4.

F. Sanhaja and Hilalian invasions

de Beylié, Général, *La Kalaa des Beni Hammad. Une capitale berbère de l'Afrique du Nord au XIe siècle* (Paris, 1900).
Gautier, E. F., *L'Islamisation de l'Afrique du Nord. Les siècles obscurs du Maghreb* (Paris, 1927), pp. 331–53 and 374–94.
Marçais, G., *Les Arabes en Berbérie du XIe au XIVe siècle* (Paris–Constantine, 1913), pp. 1–149 for the Hilalian invasions.
—— *Manuel d'art musulman. Architecture* (Paris, 1926), I, Ch. 2.

―――, *La Berbérie musulmane et l'Orient au Moyen Age* (Paris, 1946), pp. 193–228 (for a *résumé* of Marçais, 1913).
* Raidris, H., 'Problématique de la période sanhâjienne en Berbérie Orientale (X–XIIᵉ siècle)', *Annales I.E.O.*, XVII, 1959, pp. 243–55.
Encyclopedia of Islam articles on: Sanhâdja, Hammadids, Ashir, Bulukkîn, Hilâl.

XIV. ALMORAVIDS AND ALMOHADS

A. Arab authors

See above, section IX, *Arab sources available in translation*, for the following authors: Ibn Abi Zarʻ, Ibn al-Athir, Ibn Abi Dinar, Ibn Khaldun, al-Nasiri al-Slawi, al-Maqqari, al-Marrakushi, al-Zarkashi, Ibn Tumart, Ibn al-Qattan, E. Lévi Provençal (1925, 1928, 1935–6, and 1941), al-ʻUmari, Tisserant and Wiet (1926), and Gaudefroy-Demombynes (1925); and for the following work: *al-Hulal al-mawshiyya*.

Bel, A., 'Documents récents sur l'histoire des Almohades', *R.A.*, 1930, pp. 113–28.

Lévi-Provençal, E., 'Notes d'histoire almohade', *Hespéris*, 1930, pp. 49–90; in which are published fragments of a chronicle probably of the 16th or 17th century.

B. General works

Altamira, R., *Historia de España y de la civilisacion española* (Barcelona, 1900–11; 3rd ed. 1913–14).

Ballesteros y Beretta, *Historia de España y de su influencia en la historia universal* (Barcelona, 1918–36), 8 vols.

Cambridge Medieval History (Cambridge, 1913), III, pp. 440–2, 'The Western Caliphate', attributed to R. Altamira.

Dozy, R., *Histoire des Musulmans d'Espagne jusqu'à la conquête de l'Andalousie par les Almohades* (Leyden, 1861), 4 vols.; new edition, by E. Lévi-Provençal (Leyden, 1932), 3 vols.

Gonzalez-Palencia, A., 'El Califato occidental', *Revue Archivos* (Madrid), 1922 (is the text of the article appearing in *Cambridge Medieval History*, III, pp. 440–2).

―――, *Historia de la España musulmana* (Barcelona, 1925; 2nd ed. 1929 in *Coll. Labor*.).

* Huici Miranda, A. (tr.), *Ibn Idari, Al-Bayan al-mugrib. Nuevos fragmentos almoravides y almohades* (Valencia, 1963).

Lévi-Provençal, E. in *Islam et Occident. Etudes d'histoire médiévale* (collection of Islam d'hier et d'aujourd'hui, VII (Paris, 1948).

Marçais, G., *Les Arabes en Berbérie du XIᵉ au XIVᵉ siècle* (Paris, Constantine, 1913).

Bibliography

——, *Manuel d'art musulman. Architecture* (Paris, 1926), I, ch. 4.
——, *La Berbérie musulmane et l'Orient au Moyen Age* (Paris, 1946), pp. 231–275.
Montagne, R. *Les Berbères et le Makhzen dans le Sud du Maroc, Essai sur la transformation politique des Berbères sédentaires (groupe Chleuh)* (Paris, 1930), pp. 59–71 and p. 322.
* Mu'nis, Hussein, 'Textes politiques de la période de transition entre les Almohades et les Almoravides 520/1126–540/1145', *Rev. Inst. Eq. Madrid*, III, 1955, Arabic section, pp. 97–140.
Terrasse, H., *L'art hispano-mauresque des origines au XIIIe siècle* (Paris, 1932), pp. 211–395.
——, *Histoire du Maroc des origines à l'établissement du Protectorat français* (Casablanca, 1949–50), I, pp. 211–367.
Encyclopedia of Islam, see article on Marrakech.

C. Almoravids (specific references and monographs)

Codera y Zaidin, *Decadencia y desaparición de los Almorávides en España* (Saragossa, 1899).
Farias, P. F. de Moraes, 'The Almoravids: some questions concerning the character of the movements during its periods of closest contact with the Western Sudan', *Bull. I.F.A.N.*, XXIXB, 1967, 794–878.
* Huici Miranda, A., 'La invasión de los almorávides y la batalla de Zalaica', *Hespéris*, 40, 1953, pp. 17–76.
*——, 'La salida de los Almorávides del desierto y el reinado de Yûsuf b. Tašfîn: aclaraciones y rectificaciones', *Hespéris*, 1959, pp. 155–83.
*——, 'El Rawd al-Qirtas y los Almorávides', *Hespéris-Tamuda*, 1960, I, pp. 513–41.
Lévi-Provençal, E., 'Réflexions sur l'empire almoravide au début du XIe siècle', in *Cinquantenaire de la Faculté des Lettres d'Alger* (Paris, 1932), pp. 307–30.
Lévi-Provençal, E., Gomez, Garcia, and Asin, J. Oliver, 'La batalla de al-Zallâqa', *Al-Andalus*, XV, 1, 1950, pp. 111–55.
* Lévi-Provençal, E., 'La fondation Marrakech (462–1070)', *Mélanges hist. arch. Occ. musul*, II, *Hommage à G. Marçais* (Algiers, 1957), pp. 117–20.
* Leinz, Cl., 'L'époque des Almoravides au 11e siècle', *Enc. Mens. O.M.*, V, 1954, pp. 41–3.
* Meunié, J. and Allain, Ch., 'La forteresse almoravide de Zagora', *Hespéris*, XLIII, 1956, pp. 305–24.
Prieto y Vives, A., *Les reyes de Taïfas, estudio historico-numismatico de los Musulmanes españoles en el siglo V de la hegira* (Madrid, 1928).
* Quiros, C., 'Dinastêas berberes I. Los almorávides', *Arch. I.E.A.*, VIII, 1955, pp. 7–26 and p. 32.
Encyclopedia of Islam: articles on Almoravids, 'Ali b. Yûsuf, Adrâr,

Litham, 'Abd Allah b. Yâsîn, Tâshfin b. 'Alî, al-Mansûr, al-Sid, al-Ghazali, Ibn Badjdja (Avenpace).

D. *Almohads* (specific references and monographs)

1. *Almohad power*

Asin Palacios, M., 'Originen de la revolución almohade', *Revue Aragon*, December 1904.
Basset, H., 'Ibn Toumert chef d'État', *Congrès international des Religions* (Paris, 1924), II, pp. 438–9.
Bel, A., *Les Benou Ghânya, derniers représentants de l'empire almoravide et leur lutte contre l'empire almohade*, *P.F.L.A.*, XXVII (Paris, 1903).
*——, 'Document récents sur l'Histoire des Almohades', *R.A.*, 71, 1930, pp. 113–28.
* Bourouiba, R., 'Sur six dinars almohades trouvés à la Kalla des Banu Hammad', *Bull. arch. alger.*, II, 1966–7, pp. 271–92.
de Cenival, P., 'L'Eglise chrétienne de Marrakech au XIIIe siècle', *Hespéris*, 1927, pp. 69–83.
* Huici Miranda, H., 'El reinado del califa almohade Al-Rashid, hijo de Al-Ma'mun', *Hespéris*, XVI, 1954, pp. 9–46.
*——, *Historia politica del Imperio Almohade*, I (Tétouan, 1956; Instituto General Franco), and II (Tétouan, 1957).
* Koehler, R. P. Henry, 'Ce que l'économie privée importait d'Espagne au Maroc au XVIIIe siècle, d'après les manuscrits inédits des procureurs de la mission franciscaine de 1766 à 1790', *Hespéris*, XXXIX, 1952, pp. 383–406.
Lévi-Provençal, E., 'Ibn Tumart et 'Abd el-Mu'min, le "fakîh du Sûs" et le "flambeau des Almohades"', *Mémorial Henri Basset* (Paris, 1928), II, pp. 21–37.
Millet, R., *Les Almohades. Histoire d'une dynastie berbère* (Paris, 1923), of limited value.
Mouline, Mohammed er-Rachid (in Arabic), *The era of al-Mansur the Almohad, or the political, intellectual and religious life of the Maghrib from the year 580 to the year 595* [A.H.] (Rabat, 1946).
* Ross, E. D., 'An embassy from King John to the Emperor of Morocco', *B.S.O.A.S.*, 3, 1923–35, pp. 555–9.
* Zniber, M., 'Coup d'oeil sur quelques chroniques almohades récemment publiées', *Hespéris-Tamuda*, VII, 1966, pp. 41–60.
Encyclopedia of Islam: articles on Almohades, 'Abd al-Mu'min, 'Abd al-Wâhid, 'Ali b. Ghâniya, Ibn Tûmart, al-Mamûn, Ibn Mardenîsh, Areshgûl.

2. *Almohad doctrine, organisation and philosophy*

Bel, A., *Religion musulmane en Berbérie* (Paris, 1938), I, pp. 233–65.
* Brunschvig, R., 'Sur la doctrine du Mahdi Ibn Tumart', *Goldziher*

Bibliography

Mem. Vol., II (Budapest, 1958), pp. 1–13; and *Arabica*, 2, 1955, pp. 137–49.

Gaudefroy-Demombynes, M., *L'Afrique moins l'Egypte* (Paris, 1927), see introduction.

Goldziher, I., 'Mohammed Ibn Toumert et la théologie de l'Islam dans le Nord de l'Afrique au XIe siècle', preface to Gaudefroy-Demombynes (tr.), *Livre d'Ibn Toumert* (Algiers, 1903).

——, 'Materialen zur Kenntniss der Almohadenbewegung in Nordafrika', *Zeitschrift der Deutsch Morgenl. Gesellschaft*, XLI, 1887, pp. 30–141 (the major work on the doctrine of the Mahdi).

Gonzalez Palencia, A., *Historia de la literatura arabigo-española* (Barcelona, 1928) and in *Coll. Labor.*, III, no. 164–5.

* Hopkins, J. F. P., 'The Almohade hierarchy', *B.S.O.A.S.*, 16, 1954, pp. 93–112.

Lévi-Provençal, E., *Documents inédits d'histoire almohade* (Paris, 1928), see introduction.

*——, 'Ibn Tumart et Abd al-Mu'min. Le "fakih de Sus" et la "flambeau des Almohades"', *Mémorial H. Basset*, II, 1928, pp. 21–37.

* Magnin, J., 'Le testament spirituel d'Abu Zakariyya', *I.B.L.A.*, 10, 1947, pp. 393–407.

Théry, G., 'Conversations à Marrakech', *L'Islam et l'Occident, Les Cahiers du Sud* (Paris, 1947), pp. 73–91.

Encyclopedia of Islam: articles on al-Kur'ân, Kâfir, Fikh, Idjmâ', Kalâm, Sifa, Sunna, Tauîl, al-Ash'arî, Ibn Rushd (Averroes), Ibn Tufail.

3. Almohad art and architecture

Basset, H. and Terrasse, H., 'Sanctuaires et forteresses almohades', *Hespéris* (a series of articles):
I, 'Tinmel', 1924, pp. 9–92;
II, 'Les deux Kotobiya', 1924, pp. 181–203;
III, 'Le minaret de la Kotobiya', 1925, pp. 311–76, and 1926, pp. 107–17;
VI, 'L'oratorire de la Kotobiya', 1926, pp. 168–207;
VI, 'La Mosquée de la Qasba', 1926, pp. 208–70;
VII, 'Le Ribat de Tit. Tasghimout', 1927, pp. 117–71;
and 'Le tradition almohade à Marrakech', 1927, pp. 287–345.

——, *Sanctuaires et forteresses Almohades*, (Paris, 1932), Coll. Hespéris, V.

Marçais, G., *Manuel d'art musulman. Architecture* (Paris, 1926).

Terrasse, H., *L'art hispano-mauresque des origines au XIIIe siècle* (Paris, 1932), pp. 211–395.

——, *La mosquée des Andalous à Fès* (Paris, 1941).

——, *La Grande Mosquée de Taza* (Paris, 1944).

Terrasse, H. and Hainaut, H., *Les arts décoratifs au Maroc* (Paris, 1925), pp. 65–73.

* Torres Balbas, L., *Ars Hispaniae*, vol. IV, 'Arte Almohade-Art mudéjar' (Madrid, 1949).

History of North Africa

XV. HAFSIDS, ʿABD AL-WADIDS, MERINIDS AND BENI WATTAS

A. Arab authors

See above, section IX, *Arab sources available in translation*, for the following authors: Ibn Abi Zarʿ, Ibn Abi Dinar, al-Jaznai, Ibn Khaldun, al-Maqqari, al-Nasiri al-Slawi, al-Zarkashi, al-ʿAbdari, Ibn al-Ahmar, Ibn Battuta, Yahya Ibn Khaldun, Ibn Qunfud, Ibn Marzuq, al-Tinisi, al-Tijani, Jannabi, ʿAbd al-Basit b. Khalil, and al-Wazani (Leo Africanus); also see the following work in the same section: *al-Dhakhirat al-saniyya*.

B. Portuguese sources

Damiao de Gois, 'Les Portugais au Maroc de 1495 à 1521', an extract of *Chronique du Roi D. Manuel de Portugal*, (R. Ricard, tr.; Rabat, 1937).

de Castries, H. et al., *Sources inédites de l'histoire du Maroc*; series 1, 'Dynastie saadienne', *Portugal*, 4 vols. (Paris, 1934–51).

de Cenival, P. (tr.), *Chronique de Santa Cruz du Cap de Gué*, (*Agadir*) (Paris, 1934).

de Souza, Luis, *Les Portugais et l'Afrique du Nord de 1521 à 1557, Extraits des 'Annales de Jean III'* (tr. R. Ricard; Lisbon–Paris, 1940).

Mascarenhas, *Historia de la ciudad de Ceuta* (ed. by A. de Dornellas; Lisbon, 1918); (important for the period 1415–1553; written in 1648 by a Portuguese in the service of Spain).

Osorio, *De rubus Emmanuelis gestis* (Paris 1791; re-edited Coïmbre, 1923), 3 vols. (contains information on Morocco at the time of D. Manuel).

Ricard, R., 'Publications portugaises sur l'histoire du Maroc', *Hespéris*, 1927, pp. 33–51 (excellent critical study).

——, 'Notes de bibliographie luso-portugaise', *Hespéris*, XVII, 1933, pp. 149–52.

Rodriguez, B., *Anais de Arzila* (ed. by D. Lopes; Lisbon, 1915–20), 2 vols. (the author lived in Arzila from 1500 to 1549; the work is the best source for the period 1508–35).

Zurara, *Cronica de tomada de Ceuta por el rei. João I* (ed. by Francisco Ma Esteves; Lisbon, 1916) (a chronicle written in 1449–50 and published first in 1640).

C. General works

Gautier, E. F., *L'Islamisation de l'Afrique du Nord. Les siècles obscurs du Maghreb* (Paris, 1927), pp. 401–41.

Bibliography

Marçais, G., *Les Arabes en Berbérie du XIe au XIVe siècle* (Paris–Constantine, 1913).

——, *Manuel d'art musulman. Architecture* (Paris, 1926), II, Ch. 5.

——, *La Berbérie musulmane et l'Orient au Moyen Age* (Paris, 1946), pp. 193–228.

D. Hafsids (specific references and monographs)

* Brunschvig, R., 'Ibn aš-Sammāʿ historien hafside', *Annales I.E.O.*, I, 1934–5, pp. 193–212.

——, *La Berbérie orientale sous les Hafsides des origines à la fin du XVe siècle* (Paris, 1940 and 1947), 2 vols. (the best study available, employing both printed Arab sources and manuscripts and numerous European archival documents).

Gaudefroy-Demombynes, M., *L'Afrique moins l'Egypte* (Paris, 1927) (see introduction for organisation of the Hafsids).

* Marçais, G., 'Les Hafsides d'après un livre récent', *R.A.*, 93, 1949, pp. 25–37.

Pellissier, E., 'Saint Louis à Tunis', in *Mémoires historiques et géographiques sur l'Algérie*, Exploration scientifique de l'Algérie, III, (Paris, 1853), pp. 190–210.

——, 'Expédition de duc de Bourbon' [against Mahdiya], *ibid.*, pp. 221–9.

* Rivals, L., 'La huitième croisade; Saint Louis à Tunis', *Enc. Mens. O.M.*, 5, 1954, pp. 41–3.

Sayous, A. E., *Le commerce des Européens à Tunis depuis le XIIe siècle jusqu'à la fin du XVIe siècle* (Paris, 1929) (contains material on Hafsid commerce).

* Solal, E., 'Au tournant de l'histoire méditerranéenne au Moyen Age: L'expédition de Pierre III d'Aragon à Collo (1282)', *R.A.*, 101, 1957, pp. 386–408.

Sternfeld, R., *Ludwigs des Heilingen Kreuzzug nach Tunis und die Politik Karls I von Sizilien* (Berlin, 1896) (this work maintains that Charles did not know of his brother's projects).

Encyclopedia of Islam articles on: Hafsides, Djerba.

E. Abd al-Wadids (specific references and monographs)

Bergès, Abbé, *Tlemcen, ancienne capitale du royaume de ce nom* (Paris, 1859).

——, 'Mémoire sur les relations commerciales de Tlemcen avec le Soudan, sous le règne des Beni Zeiyan', *Revue d'Orient*, 1853.

——, *Vie du célèbre marabout Cidi Abou-Medien* (Paris, 1884).

Bel, A., 'Sidi bou Medyan son maître Ed-Daqqâq, à Fès', *Mélanges René Basset* (Paris, 1925), I, pp. 31–68.

Brosselard, Ch., 'Les inscriptions arabes de Tlemcen', *R.A.*, 1858 pp.

151 *et seq.*, 241 *et seq.*, 401 *et seq.*; 1859, pp. 1 *et seq.*, 81 *et seq.*, 161 *et seq.*, 241 *et seq.*; 1860, pp. 14 *et seq.*, 241 *et seq.*, 401 *et seq.*; 1861, pp. 14 *et seq.*, 161 *et seq.*

——, 'Tombeaux des Emirs Beni Zeiyan et de Boadbil', *J.A.*, 1876.
Marçais, W., *Musée de Tlemcen* (Paris, 1906).
Marçais, W. and Marçais, G., *Les monuments arabes de Tlemcen* (Paris, 1903).
Marçais, G., 'Le Makhzen des Beni Abd el-Wad', *B.S.G.O.*, March–June, 1940.
——, *Tlemcen* (Paris, 1951).
Encyclopedia of Islam articles on: Tlemcen, 'Abdalwâdides, Abû Tâchfin, Abû Zaiyûn.

F. **Merinids** (specific references and monographs)

Ballesteros Beretta, A., 'La toma de Salé en tiempos de Alfonso el Sabio', *Al-Andalus*, VIII, 1943, pp. 89–128 (see review by H. Terrasse, *Hespéris*, XXXI, 1944, pp. 87–92).
Basset, H. and Lévi-Provençal, E., 'Chella, une nécropole mérinide', *Collection Hespéris*, I, 1923.
Bel, A., 'Les premiers émirs mérinides et l'Islam', *Mélanges de géographie et d'orientalisme offerts à E. F. Gautier* (Tours, 1937), pp. 34–44.
Blanchère, R., 'Quelques détails sur la vie privée du Sultan mérinide Abu'l-Hasan', *Mémorial Henri Basset* (Paris, 1928), I, pp. 83–9.
* Brunschvig, R., 'Le sac de Tripoli de Barbarie en 766/1355', *Arabicia*, 2, 1955, p. 288.
Canard, M., 'Les relations entre les Mérinides et les Mamlouks au XIVe siècle', *Annales I.E.O.*, V, pp. 41–81.
* Colin, G. S., 'La zaouya mérinite d'Anemli à Taza', *Hespéris*, XL, 1953, pp. 528–30.
* Emerit, M., 'Un document inédit sur Alger au XVIIe siècle', *Annales I.E.O.*, 17, 1959, pp. 233–42.
Gaudefroy-Demombynes, M., 'Introduction' in *L'Afrique moins l'Egypte* (Paris, 1927).
Montagne, R., *Les Berbères et le Makhzen dans le sud du Maroc* (Paris, 1930), pp. 71–81.
* Robson, J. A., 'The Catalan fleet and Moorish sea power (1337–1344)', *Engl. Hist. Rev.*, 74, 1959, pp. 386–408.
Terrasse, H., *Histoire du Maroc des origines à l'établissement du Protectorat français* (Casablanca, 1949–50), II, pp. 3–99.
Encyclopedia of Islam: articles on Abû Zaiyân Muhammad.

G. **Beni Wattas** (specific references and monographs)

Bataillon, M., 'Le rêve de la conquête de Fès et le sentiment impérial portugais au XVIe siècle', *Mélanges d'études lusumarocaines dédiés*

Bibliography

à la mémoire de David Lopes et Pierre de Cenival (Lisbon, 1945), pp. 31–9.

Cour, A., La dynastie marocaine des Beni Wattas (*1420–1554*) (Constantine, 1920).

de Castries, H., et al., Les sources inédites de l'histoire du Maroc, 1st series, Espagne, I (Paris, 1921), Plate IV, p. 162 for genealogy of the princes; and pp. 1–28, 'Melilla au XVIe siècle'.

de Dornellas, A., Elementos para a historia de Ceuta (Lisbon, 1923).

Figanier, Joaquim, Historia de Santa Cruz do Cabo de Gué *1505–1541* (Lisbon, 1945).

Goulven, J., La place de Mazagan sous la domination portugaise (*1502–1769*) (Paris, 1917).

Lopes, D., Portugal contra os Mouros (Lisbon, n.d.).

——, Historia de Arzila durante o dominio portugués (*1471–1550 e 1577–1599*) (Coïmbre, 1924).

Massignon, L., Le Maroc dans les premières années du XVIe siècle. Tableau géographique d'après Léon l'Africain (Algiers, 1906).

Pérès, D., D. João I (Lisbon, 1917), see Ch. concerning Ceuta, pp. 49–55.

Ricard, R., 'Les Portugais au Maroc', Bulletin Ass. G.-Budé, July, 1937.

Terrasse, H., Histoire du Maroc des origines à l'établissement du Protectorat français (Casablanca, 1949–50), II, pp. 103–57.

XVI. THE SHARIFIAN EMPIRE

A. Arab Authors

See above, section IX, Arab sources available in translation, for the following authors: al-Ifrani, al-Zayani, al-Nasiri al-Slawi, Fagnan (1924), Lévi-Provençal (1923), Justinard (1940), Vajda (1948–49) and Tamgrouti.

Lévi-Provençal, E., Les historiens des Chorfa (Paris, 1923).

Pianel, G., 'Une source nouvelle de l'histoire sa'dienne', Hespéris, XXXVI, 1949, pp. 243–5.

B. European travellers

Ali Bey, Travels in Morocco, Voyages d'Ali-Bey en Afrique et en Asie pendant les années *1803–1804–1805–1806–1807*, précédés d'une lettre du roi de France (Paris, 1814), 3 vols. with an atlas (written by a Spanish adventurer, Domingo Badia, who claimed conversion to Islam and later became a high functionary for Napoleon); see also P. Roussier, 'Les derniers projets et le dernier voyage de Domingo Badia (1815–1818)', R.A., 1930, pp. 36–91.

Busnot, P., Histoire du règne de Mouley-Ismaël (Rouen, 1714; 2nd ed. 1731) (useful for Meknès, where this redemptionist visited, and for a view of the conditions of slaves).

Chénier, L. de, Recherches historiques sur les Maures et l'histoire du

Maroc (Paris 1788), 3 vols. (the author was a French consul at Mogador in 1767 and was interested in Moroccan history. He drew his historical material from the *Rawd al-Qirtās*, but also reported contemporary events.)

Dan, Père, *Histoire de la Barbarie et de ses corsaires* (Paris, 1637; 2nd ed. 1649) (a redemptionist who negotiated for the period of a half-century the purchase of captives; only a small section is devoted to Morocco, but it is important as an eye-witness account).

Fréjus, R., *Relation d'un voyage fait dans la Mauritanie en Afrique . . . en l'année 1666* (Paris, 1670); see also H. de Castries *et al.*, *Les sources inédites de l'histoire du Maroc*; 2nd series, *France* (Paris, 1922–31), II, pp. 121–88.

Grey-Jackson, J., *An account of the Empire of Morocco and the districts of Sus and Tafilelt* (London, 1809; 2nd ed., Philadelphia, 1810; 3rd ed., London, 1814) (an English consul at Mogador who received a quantity of information of some value; see M. Delafosse, *Hespéris*, 1923, p. 1).

Höst, G., *Efterretninger om Marókos og Fes* (Copenhagen, 1779); and translated as *Nachrichten von Maroco und Fes* (Copenhagen, 1781) (written by a Danish consul; a very useful source for his observations, illustrations and interest, among other things, in musical instruments).

Lemprière, W., *A Tour from Gibraltar to Tangier, Sallee, Mogadore, Santa Cruz, Tarudant, and thence over Mount Atlas to Morocco* (London, 1791); tr. by Sainte-Suzanne, *Voyage dans l'Empire du Maroc et le Royaume de Fez fait pendant les années 1790 et 1791* (Paris, 1801) (the author was called to Morocco in 1779 to care for the son of the Sultan. He travelled about the country and reported in this work his observations.)

Marmol-Carvajal, *Description general de Affrica . . .*, 3 vols. (Granada and Malaga, 1573–99); tr. by Perrot d'Ablancourt, *L'Afrique de Marmol*, 3 vols. (Paris, 1867) (the author was a Spanish traveller and historian who took part in the expedition of Charles-Quint against Tunis, where he was taken prisoner in 1556. He travelled through Barbary, particularly Morocco, where he accompanied Muhammad al-Shaikh on his expeditions.)

Morsy-Patchett, M., 'La longue captivité et les aventures de Thomas Pellow', *Hespéris-Tamuda*, IV, 1963, pp. 289–312.

Mouëtte, Sieur, *Histoire des conquêtes de Mouley Archy, connu sous le nom de roy de Tafilet, et de Mouley Ismaël* (Paris, 1683); see also in H. de Castries *et al.*, *Les sources inédites de l'histoire du Maroc*; 2nd series, France (Paris, 1922–31), II, pp. 1–201 (a captive who was well-educated, a good observer and well-informed through a student who became his friend).

——, *Relation de la captivité du sieur Mouëtte dans les royaumes de Fez et de Maroc, où il a demeuré pendant onze ans* (Paris, 1863) (a less

original work than the above); incompletely re-edited by Mme. de Serres (Tours, 1928).
Pellow, Thomas, *The adventures of Thomas Pellow of Penryn, Mariner*, The Adventure Series (London, 1860); see also H. Terrasse, 'Les Aventures d'un renégat anglais au Maroc sous Moulay Ismail', *B.E.P.M.*, 1926.
Pidou de Saint-Olon, *Etat présent de l'Empire du Maroc* (Paris, 1694).
Ricard, R., *Un document portugais sur la place de Mazagan au XVIIe siècle* (Paris, 1932).
Windus, John, *A journey to Mequinez, the residence of the present emperor of Fez and Morocco, on the occasion of commodore Stewart's embassy thither for the redemption of the British captives in the year 1721* (London, 1725).

C. General Works

Berque, J., 'Petits documents d'histoire sociale marocaine: les archives d'un cadi rural', *R.A.*, 94, 1950, pp. 113–24.
* Bennett, N. R., 'Christian and negro slavery in eighteenth century North Africa', *J.A.H.*, II, 1960, pp. 65–82.
Coindreau, R., *Les corsaires de Salé* (Paris, 1948).
Cour, A., *L'établissement des dynasties des chérifs au Maroc et leur rivalité avec les Turcs de la Régence d'Alger (1509–1830)*, *P.F.L.A.* (Paris, 1904) (defines the role of the brotherhoods and the revival of Islam).
Lévi-Provençal, E., 'Le Maroc en face de l'étranger à l'époque moderne', *B.E.P.M.*, 1925, pp. 95–112.
Marçais, G., *Manuel d'art musulman. Architecture* (Paris, 1926), II, chap. 7.
Masson, P., *Histoire des établissements et du commerce français dans l'Afrique barbaresque (1560–1793)* (Paris, 1903), pp. 181–238, 338–66, and 611–76.
Montagne, R., *Les Berbères et le Makhzen dans le sud du Maroc* (Paris, 1930), pp. 87–108.
Penz, Ch., *Les captifs français au Maroc au XVIIe siècle (1577–1699)* (Rabat, 1944).
Encyclopedia of Islam: articles on Shorfa', Morocco, Makhzen.

D. Saadians (specific references and monographs)

Arribas Palau, M., 'Las comunidades israelitas bajo los primeros sa'dies', *Homenaje a Milás-Valicrosa*, I (Barcelona, 1954), pp. 45–65.
Caillé, J., 'Le commerce anglais avec le Maroc pendant la seconde moitié de XVIe siècle', *R.A.*, 1940.
*——, 'Ambassades et missions marocaines en France (à partir du XIVe siècle)', *Hespéris-Tamuda*, I, 1960, pp. 39–84.

*——, 'Ambassades et missions morocaine au Pays-Bas à l'époque des sultans', *Hespéris-Tamuda*, IV, 1963, pp. 5–68.

Charles-Dominique, Mlle P., 'La pénétration économique de l'Europe au Maroc durant la dynastie saadienne (1472–1660)' (unpublished).

* Colin, G. S., 'Project de traité entre les Morisques de la Casba de Rabat et le Roi de l'Espagne en 1631', *Hespéris*, 42, 1955, pp. 17–25.

Collet, H., 'Le commerce hollandais avec le Maroc à l'époque saadienne', *B.E.P.M.*, 1942.

de Castries, H. et al., *Sources inédites de l'histoire du Maroc*, 1st series, *France* (Paris, 1905–11); see *Bibliographie et index général* (Paris, 1926) for bibliographic references and a genealogy of the Saadians.

de Castries, H., 'Les signes de validation des Chérifs saadiens', *Hespéris*, 1921, pp. 231–52.

* Le Tourneau, R., 'La naissance du pouvoir sa'dien vue par l'historien al-Zayyanî', *Mélanges Louis Massignon*, vol. 3 (Damascus, 1951), pp. 65–80.

*——, 'Le Sultan sa'dien Mhmmed ech-Cheikh', *J. Inst. A.F.N.*, 6, 1953, pp. 273–4.

*——, 'Fès et la naissance du pouvoir sa'dien', *Al-Andalus*, 18, 1953, pp. 271–94.

* La Veronne, C. de, 'Política de España, de Marruecos y de los Turcos en los reinos de Fez y Tremecén a mediados del siglo XVI', *M.E.A.H.*, 3, 1954, pp. 87–95.

* Mauny, R., 'L'expédition marocaine d'Oudane (Mauritanie) vers 1543–1544', *Bull. I.F.A.N.*, II, 1949, pp. 129–40.

* Pianel, G., 'Une source nouvelle de l'histoire Sa'dienne', *Hespéris*, 36, 1949, pp. 243–5.

Terrasse, H., *Histoire du Maroc des origines à l'établissement du Protectorat français* (Casablanca, 1949–50), II, pp. 158–235.

Weir, T. H., *The Shaikhs of Morocco in the XVIth Century* (Edinburgh, 1904), collection of Sufi texts, principally of Ibn 'Askar, author of biographies of the shaikhs, in 1577.

Encyclopedia of Islam: see article on Sa'dians.

1. The Portuguese in Morocco

* Beazley, C. R., 'Prince Henry of Portugal and the African Crusade of the fifteenth century', *Am. Hist. Rev.*, 16, 1910–11, pp. 11–23.

de Castries, H. et al., 'Les relations de la bataille d'El-Kasr el-Kébir', in *Sources inédites de l'histoire du Maroc*, 1st series, *France* (Paris, 1905–11), I, pp. 395–405.

Dias, M., *O 'Piedoso'* [Jean III] *e O 'Desdjado'* [Sebastien] (Lisbon, 1925).

Figuereido, D., *Sebastião rei de Portugal (1554–1578)* (Lisbon, 1924; 7th ed. 1925).

Murias, M., *A politica de Africa de El Rei D. Sebastião* (Lisbon, 1926).

Ricard, P., 'Publications portugaises sur l'histoire du Maroc', *Hespéris*, 1927, pp. 33–51 for an elaboration of the renewed interest by

Bibliography

Portuguese historians in Moroccan history, marked by the fifth centenary of the taking of Ceuta.
* Ricard, R., 'Le commerce de Berbérie et l'organisation économique de l'empire portugais aux XVe et XIVe siècles', *Annales I.E.O.*, 2, 1936, pp. 266–85.
* ——, 'Le Maroc septentrional au XVe siècle d'après les chroniques portugaise', *Hespéris*, 23, 1936, pp. 89–143.
* ——, 'Contribution à l'étude du commerce génois au Maroc durant la période portugaise (1415–1550)', *Annales I.E.O.*, 3, 1937, pp. 53–73; 'Additions et corrections', 4, 1938, pp. 155–6.
* ——, 'Les places portugaises du Maroc et le commerce d'Andalousie. Notes sur l'histoire économique de Maroc portugais', *Annales I.E.O.*, 4, 1938, pp. 129–53.
* ——, 'Bastião de Vargas, agent de Jean III de Portugal au Maroc; sa correspondance et le projet d'alliance entre le Portugal et le royaume de Fès (1539–1541)', *Andalus*, 10, 1945, pp. 53–77.
* Ricard, R. and Sanceau, E., 'Un projet de remise de Tétouan aux Portugais en 1502', *Hespéris*, XLIV, 1957, pp. 21–30.

Sergio, A., *O Desejado* (Lisbon, 1924).

——, *Camoes e D. Sabastião* (Lisbon, 1925).

2. al-Mansur al-Dhahabi

Bovill, E. W., 'The Moorish invasion of the Sudan', *J.S.A.*, 1927, XXVI, pp. 245–93 and 380–7; XXVII, pp. 47–56.
* Cabanelas Rodríques, D., 'Cartas del sultán de Marruecos Ahmad al-Mansûr al Felipe II', *Al-Andalus*, 23, 1958, pp. 19–47.

Colin, G. S., 'Note sur le système cryptographique du sultan Ahmed el-Mansûr', *Hespéris*, 1927, pp. 221–8.

de Castries, H., 'Une description du Maroc sous le règne de Mouley Ahmed el-Mansoûr, 1596, d'après un manuscrit portugais de la Bibliothèque Nationale', *Sources inédites de l'histoire du Maroc*, 1st series, *France*, (Paris, 1905–11), pp. 231–41; and also (Paris, 1909).

——, 'La conquête du Soudan', *Hespéris*, 1923, pp. 433–88.

——, 'Kabara et Karabara', *Hespéris*, 1925, pp. 125–8.

Delafosse, M., 'Les relations du Maroc avec le Soudan à travers les âges', *Hespéris*, 1924, pp. 153–74; (contests the importance of the gold brought back by the conquerors).
* Hunwick, J. O., 'Ahmad Baba and the Moroccan invasion of the Sudan (1591)', *J. of the Hist. Soc. of Nigeria*, II, 3, 1962, pp. 311–28.
* Gautier, E. F., 'La conquête du Sahara', *T.I.R.S.*, XIV, 1956, pp. 13–22.
* Pianel, G., 'Les préliminaires de la conquête du Soudan par Maulāy Ahmad al-mansūr', *Hespéris*, 40, 1953, pp. 185–98.

Préfontan, Capitain, 'Les Armas', *B.C.E.H.S.A.O.F.*, 1926, pp. 153–79

Encyclopedia of Islam: see articles on al-Mansur, Sudan, Songhoy Mandingo.

3. The decline of the Saadians

Caillé, J., *La ville de Rabat jusqu'au Protectorat français. Histoire et archéologie*, 3 vols. (Paris, 1949), vol. I.
* Caillé, J., 'Le dernier exploit des corsaires du Bou-Regreg', *Hespéris*, 37, 1950, pp. 429-37.
de Castries, H., 'Les trois républiques du Bou Regreg; Salé, la Kasba, Rabat', *Sources inédites de l'histoire du Maroc*, 1st series, *Pays-Bas* (Paris, 1906-23), V, pp. I-XXVIII.
――, 'Les Moriscos de Salé et Sidi el Ayachi', *ibid.*, 1st series, *France* (Paris, 1905-11), III, pp. 187-98.
――, 'La zaouïa de Dila et la chute de la dynastie saadienne', *ibid.*, 1st series, *France* (Paris, 1905-11), III, pp. 572-83.
Henry, R., 'Où se trouvait la zaouïa de Dila?', *Hespéris*, XXXI, 1944, pp. 49-54.
* Hijji, Mohammed, *La Zaouïa de Dila. Son rôle religieu, scientifique et politique* (Rabat, 1964), in Arabic.
* Le Tourneau, R., 'La décadence sa'dienne et l'anarchie marocaine au XIIe siècle', *Annales de la Faculté des Lettres d'Aix*, XXXII, 1960, pp. 187-225.
* Ricard, R., 'Le Maroc à la fin du XVIe siècle, d'après la Journada de Africa de Jerõnimo de Mendoça', *Hespéris*, XLIV, 1957, pp. 179-204.

E. Alawites (specific references and monographs)

1. Mulay Rashid

de Cenival, P., 'La Légende du Juif Ibn Mech'al et la fête du sultan des Tolba à Fès', *Hespéris*, 1925, pp. 137-218 (very important for the accession of Mulay Rashid).
Encyclopedia of Islam: see articles on Tâfilâlt and Sidjilmâsa.

2. Mulay Isma'il

* Allouche, I. S., 'Un plan des canalisations de Fès au temps de Mawlāy Ismā'īl d'après un texte inédit avec une étude succincte sur la corporation des "kwādsīya"', *Hespéris*, 18, 1934, pp. 49-63.
* 'Aperçus bibliographie sur la vie et le règne de Moulay Ismaël', *Hespéris-Tamuda*, 1962 (special number devoted to Mulay Isma'il), pp. 87-92.
de Castries, H., *Moulay-Ismaïl et Jacques II. Une apologie de l'Islam par un sultan du Maroc* (Paris, 1903).
Defontin-Maxange, [pseud., E. R. Colin], *Le grand Ismaïl, empereur du Maroc* (Paris, 1929) (the work of a romantic in pompous style and lacking in criticism).
de la Chapelle, F., 'Le sultan Moulay Ismaïl et les Berbères Sanhaja au Maroc central', *A.M.*, XXVIII, 1931, pp. 8-64.

Bibliography

Delafosse, M., 'Les débuts des troupes noires au Maroc', *Hespéris*, 1923, pp. 1–12.
* el-Fasi, Mohammad, 'Biographie du Moulay Ismaël, suivre d'un lettre de Sidi Mhammed El Fasi adressée à son roi', *Hespéris-Tamuda*, 1962 (special number devoted to Mulay Isma'il) pp. 5–30.
*——, 'Lettres inédites de Moulay Ismaël; étude, textes et photocopies des lettres', *Hespéris-Tamuda*, 1962 (special number devoted to Mulay Isma'il), pp. 30–86.
Hardy, G., 'La légende et l'histoires. Les relations de la France et du Maroc sous Louis XIV', *R.H.C.*, 1927, pp. 489–508.
Koehler, R. P., 'Quelques points d'histoire sur les captifs chrétiens au Maroc', *Hespéris*, 1928, pp. 177–87 (a re-evaluation of the number of prisoners and cruelties of the sultan).
Malcor, H., 'Tanger sous la domination anglaise', *Afr. fr. R.C.*, 1927, 7, pp. 261–4.
Montagne, R., 'Un épisode de la "Siba" berbère au XVIIIe siècle', *Hespéris*, XXVIII, 1941, pp. 85–97.
Penz, Ch., *Les captifs français au Maroc au XVIIe siècle (1577–1699)* (Rabat, 1944).
Reyniers, Col., 'Un document sur la politique de Moulay Ismaïl dans l'Atlas', *A.M.*, XXVIII, 1931, pp. 1–7
Encyclopedia of Islam: see article on Isma'îl.

3. The successors to Mulay Isma'il

Auzoux, A., 'L'affaire de Larache (1765)', *Afr. fr.*, 1929, pp. 505–24.
* Aziman, Moh., 'Texte arabe de Traité de paix et de commerce entre le Maroc et l'Espagne en 1767', *Tamuda*, 4, 1956, pp. 87–92.
Basset, H., 'Les années d'exil de Moulay el-Yazid (1784–1789)', *B.E.P.M.*, 1923, pp. 339–49.
* Caillé, J., 'Le consulat de Chénier au Maroc (1767–1782)', *Hespéris*, 43, 1956, pp. 261–304.
*——, 'A propos d'un document inédit de Moulay Yazid', *Hespéris*, 47, 1959, pp. 239–46.
*——, 'Le consul Jean-Baptiste Estelle et le commerce de la France au Maroc à la fin du XVIIe siècle', *Rev. franç. hist. Outre-Mer*, 46, 1959, pp. 7–48.
*——, *Les accords internationaux du sultan Sidi Mohammed ben Abdallah (1757–1790)* (Tangier, 1960).
de Cenival, P., 'Lettre de Louis XVI à Sidi Mohammed ben Abdallah (19 déc. 1778)', *Mémorial Henri Basset* (Paris, 1928), I, pp. 175–86.
* Dantzig, B. M., i Zhilenko, V. I., 'Zabuitaya stranitza iz istorii russko-marokkanskikh otnosheniy v posledney chetverti XVIII veka', (A forgotten episode from the history of Russo–Moroccan relations at the end of the 18th century), *Problemui Vostokovedeniya*, 1959, I, pp. 86–93.
Terrasse, H., *Histoire du Maroc des origines à l'établissement du Protectorat français* (Casablanca, 1949–50), II, pp. 239–321.

* Slousch, N., 'Le Maroc du dix-huitième siècle. Mémoires d'un contemporain', *R.M.M.*, 9, 1909, pp. 452–66; 643–64.
Encyclopedia of Islam: see articles on Morocco, Makhzen, Sulaïmân (Mulay Sliman), 'Abd al-Rahmân.

XVII. TURKISH DOMINATION OF ALGERIA AND TUNISIA (1516–1830)

A. Arab Sources

See above, section IX, *Arab sources available in translation*, for the following authors: Basset (1890), Delphin (1922), Si 'Abd al-Qadir al-Masharfi, 'Bey Hasan', Saghir b. Yusuf, al-Ayashi; and for the following work: *Ghazawat 'Aruj*.

Esquer, G., 'Les sources de l'histoire de l'Algérie', *Histoire et historiens de l'Algérie (1830–1930)* (Paris, 1931).

Marçais, W., 'Un siècle de recherches sur le passé de l'Algérie musulmane', *Histoire et historiens de l'Algérie (1830–1930)* (Paris, 1931).

B. European travellers

* Bousquet, G. H. and Bousquet-Mirandolle, G. W. (tr.), 'Journal de Captivité à Alger de G. Metzon (1814–1816)', *Annals I.E.O.*, XII, 1954, pp. 43–83.

*——, 'Thomas Hees, Journal d'un voyage à Alger (1675–1676)', *R.A.*, 101, 1957, pp. 85–128.

Dan, Père, *Histoire de la Barbarie et de ses corsaires* (Paris, 1637; 2nd ed. 1649); the Dutch edition, *Historie van Barbaryen en des zelfs zee-roovers* (Amsterdam, 1684) includes the engravings of Ian Luyken, which are of considerable interest.

d'Arvieux, *Mémoires du chevalier d'Arvieux* ... (1735), 6 vols.; the section relevant to Algiers is vol. 5, pp. 57–280; see also, J. Bouvat, 'Le Chevalier d'Arvieux (1635–1702), d'après ses Mémoires', *R.M.M.*, 26, 1914, pp. 1–83.

d'Aranda, E., *Relation de la captivité et liberté du sieur Emmanuel d'Aranda* (Paris, 1656) (the author, an Aragonese of Bruges, was a prisoner in Algiers for one and one-half years; on his return to Bruges he wrote of his adventures (pp. 1–117), which are followed by 37 *relations particulières*, which are among the best documented sources on slavery).

Desfontaines, *Fragments d'un voyage dans les Régences de Tunis et d'Alger fait de 1783 à 1786* (Paris, 1838), 2 vols.

Emérit, M. (ed.), 'Les aventures de Thédenat, esclave et ministre d'un bey d'Afrique (XVIIIe siècle)', *R.A.*, 1948, pp. 143–84 (the author was an attendant, *khaznadar*, to the bey of Mascara from 1779 to 1782; this article is a portion of his 'Mémoires').

Esquer, G., *Reconnaissance des villes, forts et batteries d'Alger par le chef de bataillon Boutin (1808) suivie des Mémoires sur Alger par les*

Bibliography

consuls de Kercy (1791) et Dubois-Thainville (1809) (Paris, 1927), 1 vol. plus maps and plans.

Haëdo, D., *Topographia e historia general de Argel* (Valladolid, 1612), (tr. by Monnereau and Berbrugger, *R.A.*, 1870, pp. 364 *et seq.*, 414 *et seq.*, 490 *et seq.*; 1871, pp. 41 *et seq.*, 202 *et seq.*, 375 *et seq.*).

——, *Epitome de los Reyes de Argel* (tr. Grammont, *R.A.*, 1880, pp. 37 *et seq.*, 116 *et seq.*, 215 *et seq.*, 261 *et seq.*, 344 *et seq.*, 401 *et seq.*; 1881, pp. 5 *et seq.*, 97 *et seq.*).

——, *Dialogos de la captividad* (tr. Moliner-Volle, *R.A.*, 1895, pp. 54 *et seq.*, 199 *et seq.*, 321 *et seq.*; 1896, pp. 5 *et seq.*; 1897, pp. 153 *et seq.*, 249 *et seq.*); translation also published (Algiers, 1911).

Laugier de Tassy, *Histoire du Royaume d'Alger avec l'état présent de son gouvernement* (Amsterdam, 1725) (the author, a commissioner of the navy for the King of Spain, visited Algiers and gives an account of his observations).

Marmol-Carvajal, *Descripción general de Affrica...*, 3 vols. (Granada and Malaga, 1573–99) and tr. by Perrot d'Ablancourt, *L'Afrique de Marmol*, 3 vols. (Paris, 1867) (the author was a Spanish traveller and historian who took part in the expedition of Charles-Quint against Tunis, where he was taken prisoner in 1556. He travelled through Barbary, particularly Morocco, where he accompanied Muhammad al-Shaikh on his expeditions).

Monchicourt, Ch., *Documents historiques sur la Tunisie. Relations inédites de Nyssen, Filippi et Calligaris (1788, 1829, 1834)* (Paris, 1929), see vol. I: 'Voyages dans les Régences de Tunis et d'Alger publiés par Dureau de la Malle', and vol. II: Peyssonel, 'Relation d'un voyage en Barbarie fait par ordre du roi en 1724 et 1725'.

Poiret, Abbé, *Voyage en Barbarie ou Lettres écrites de l'ancienne Numidie pendant les années 1785 et 1786* (Paris, 1789), 2 vols. (the author's primary interest is in botany and zoology, but he also makes observations on the customs of the people).

Rehbinder, *Nachrichten und Bemerkungen über den Algierischen Staat* (Altona, 1798–1800, 2nd ed. 1800), 2 vols. (the author was Danish consul at Algiers).

Shaw, Thomas, *Travels and observations relating to several parts of Barbary and the Levant* (Oxford, 1738); tr. *Voyages de Monsr Shaw...* (The Hague, 1743), 2 vols.; new translation with additions by MacCarthy (Paris, 1830).

Venture de Paradis, 'Alger au XVIIIe siècle', from 'Notes sur Alger' by E. Fagnan, *R.A.*, 1895–7, the first of five volumes of manuscripts; published in one vol. (Algiers, 1898) (the author describes Algiers and its inhabitants in 1789).

C. General works

* Bennett, N. R., 'Christian and negro slavery in eighteenth century North Africa', *J.A.H.*, I, 1960, pp. 65–82.

Braudel, F., *La Méditerranée et le monde méditerranéen à l'époque de Philippe II* (Paris, 1949) (particularly useful for the 16th century).

Capot-Rey, R., *La politique française et le Maghreb Méditerranéen (1643–1685)* (Paris, 1918); more recently published in *R.A.*, 1934, 1935; and also (Algiers, 1935) (well documented).

* Carton, L., 'Un voyage en Barbarie au XVIIIe siècle', *R.T.*, 1910, pp. 468–81.

Charles-Roux, F., 'Les travaux d'Herculais ou une extraordinaire mission en Barbarie', *R.H.C.*, 1927, pp. 1–32, 201–58, 321–68, and 543–80.

* Clark, G. N., 'The Barbary Corsairs in the seventeenth century', *C.H.J.*, 8, 1945–6, pp. 22–35.

* de Montmorency, J. E. G., 'Piracy and the Barbary Corsairs', *Law Quarterly Review*, 35, 1919, pp. 133–42.

* Eisenbeth, M., 'Les Juifs en Algérie et en Tunisie à l'époque turque (1516–1830)', *R.A.*, 96, 1952, pp. 114–87 and 343–84.

* Emerit, M., 'L'essai d'une marine marchande barbaresque au XVIIe siècle', *Cahiers de Tunisie*, 3, 1955, pp. 363–70.

* Godechot, J., 'La course maltaise le long des côtes barbaresques à la fin du XVIIIe siècle', *R.A.*, 93, 1952, pp. 109–13.

Lespès, R., *Alger* (Paris, 1930); see pp. 107–91 for an account of the topography and economic activity of the Turkish city.

Masson, P., *Histoire des établissements et du commerce français dans l'Afrique barbaresque (1560–1793)* (Paris, 1903), pp. 1–180, 239–66 and 367–601.

———, 'L'Agence nationale d'Afrique (1794–1801)', *Marseille depuis 1789* (Paris, 1921), pp. 474–563 (the completion of Masson's *Histoire des établissements* ... (cited above)).

* Riggio, A., 'Esclaves et missionaires en Barbarie (1672–1682)', *R.A.*, 93, 1949, pp. 38–64.

* Sacerdoti, A., 'Venise et les Régences d'Alger, Tunis et Tripoli (1699–1763)' (tr by Mlle. M. Despois), *R.A.*, 101, 1957, pp. 273–97.

Encyclopedia of Islam: see articles on Algiers, Algeria, Dey and Kabylia.

D. The Spanish occupation in North Africa

Braudel, F., 'Les Espagnols en Algérie', *Histoire et historiens de l'Algérie (1830–1930)* (Paris, 1931).

———, *La Méditerranée et le monde méditerranéen à l'époque de Philippe II* (Paris, 1949) (for a critical appraisal of bibliography and major issues).

Cazenave, J., 'Les Présides espagnols d'Afrique, leur organisation au XVIIIe siècle', *R.A.*, 1922, pp. 225–69, 457–88.

de la Primaudaie, E., *Documents inédits sur l'histoire de l'occupation espagnole en Afrique* (Algiers, 1875–7).

Landefrucci and Bosio, *Costa e discorsi de Barberia* (1587) see ed. and tr. by Grandchamp, *R.A.*, 1925, pp. 1–166 (with preface by Ch. Monchicourt).

Monchicourt, Ch., *L'expédition espagnole de 1500 contre l'île de Djerba (Essais bibliographiques. Récit de l'expédition, Documents originaux)* (Paris, 1913).

——, 'Essai bibliographique sur les plans imprimés de Tripoli, Djerba, Tunis, Goulette et sur un plan d'Alger du XVIe siècle', *R.A.*, 1925, pp. 385 et seq.

Pestemaldjoglou, A., 'Mers el Kébir, Historique et description de la forteresse', *R.A.*, 1942, pp. 154–85.

E. The Regency of Algiers

Bonnet, Lucienne, *L'industrie à la Kalaa des Beni Rached* (Algiers, 1929).

Colombe, M., 'Contribution à l'étude du recrutement de l'Odjaq d'Alger dans les dernières années de l'Histoire de la Régence', *R.A.*, 1943, pp. 166–83.

Dehérain, H., 'La mission du commissaire général Dubois-Thainville auprès du dey d'Alger (an VIII et an X, 1800 and 1801)', *R.H.C.*, 1926, pp. 74–100.

* Deny, J., 'Les registres de solde des Janissaires conservés à la Bibliothèque Nationale d'Alger', *R.A.*, 61, 1920, pp. 19–46, 212–60.

——, 'Chansons de janissaires d'Alger', *Mémorial René Basset* (Paris, 1923), II, pp. 33–175.

* Emerit, M., 'Mémoires de Thédenat, natif d'Uzès en Langedoc, écrites à Zurich en 1785', *R.A.*, 92, 1948, pp. 157–85.

*——, 'Les quartiers commerçants d'Alger à l'époque turque', *Algérie*, 25 (January–February 1953), pp. 6–13.

——, 'Un document inédit sur Alger au XVIIIe siècle', *Annales I.E.O.*, XVII, 1959, pp. 233–42.

de Grammont, H., *Relations entre la France et la Régence d'Alger au XVIIe siècle* (Algiers, 1879–85); in 4 parts: 'La course, l'esclavage et la rédemption à Alger', *R.H.*, 1884–5, vols. XXV, XXXVI, and XXXVII; 'Correspondance des consuls d'Alger (1690–1742)', *R.A.*, 1887–9 (eleven articles); also printed (Algiers, 1890) (the articles on consular correspondance contain a notice about each consul).

——, *Histoire d'Alger sous la domination turque (1516–1830)* (Paris, 1887).

* Kuran, M., 'La lettre du dernier Dey d'Alger au grand Vizir de l'Empire Ottoman', *R.A.*, 96, 1952, pp. 188–95.

* Leclercq, J., 'Les Corsaires algériens en Islande en 1627', *Acad. Roy. Belgique, Bull. Cl. Lettres*, 1926, pp. 252–64.

Marçais, G., *Manuel d'art musulman. Architecture* (Paris, 1926), II, chap. 8.

——, *Le costume musulman à Alger* (Paris, 1930), Collection du Centenaire.

Marçais, G. et al., *Histoire de l'Algérie* (Paris, 1927), pp. 162–89.

Playfair, R. L., *The scourge of Christendom. Annals of British relations with Algiers prior to the French conquest* (London, 1884).

* Provost, R., 'Une expédition anglaise contre les pirates d'Alger (1620–1621)', *Cinquantenaire Fac. Lettres Alger* (Paris, 1932), pp. 413–35.

* *La Régence d'Alger et le monde turc*, supplement to *L'Ecole républicaine*, 4th special number (1953–4) (monthly bulletin of the Section d'Alger du Syndicat national des Instituteurs et Institutrices de l'Union français, Algiers).

Rinn, L., *Le royaume d'Alger sous le dernier dey* (Algiers, 1900) (includes a study of the distribution of tribes).

* Roy, B., 'Deux documents inédits sur l'expédition algérienne de 1628 (1037 Hig.) contre les Tunisiens', *R.T.*, 1917, pp. 183–204.

* Sacerdoti, A., 'La mission à Alger de Consul de Venise, Nicolas Rosalem 1753–1754', *R.A.*, 96, 1952, pp. 64–91.

Vayssette, 'Histoire de Constantine sous la domination turque de 1517 à 1837', *R.S.A.C.*, 1867, pp. 241–352; 1868, pp. 255–392; 1869, pp. 453–620; and in one volume (Paris, 1869) (an account based largely upon oral tradition).

Encyclopedia of Islam: see articles on: 'Arudj, Khair al-Dîn, and Dey.

F. Tunisia (specific references and monographs)

*Bacquencourt, M. de and Grandchamp, P., 'Documents divers concernant Don Philippe d'Afrique, prince tunisien, deux fois renégat (1646–1686)', *R.T.*, 1938, pp. 55–77; 289–311.

Braudel, F., *La Méditerranée et le monde méditerranéen à l'époque de Philippe II* (Paris, 1949).

* Brown, L. C. (tr.), *The surest path: the political treatise of a nineteenth-century Moslem statesman* (Harvard, 1967), Harvard Middle East Monographs.

* Conor, M., 'Les exploits d'Alonso de Contreras, aventurier espagnol en Tunisie (1601–1611)', *R.T.*, 1913, pp. 597–611.

* Emerit, M., 'L'essai d'une marine marchande barbaresque au XVIIIe siècle', *Cahiers de Tunisie*, 3, 1955, pp. 363–70.

*——, 'Trois notes d'histoire tunisienne (A propos de la Caravane de Salé. La révolte de Sidi Younès, 1752, vue par M. de Montchenu, le vrai nom du Général Yusuf)', *Cahiers de Tunisie*, 3, 1955, pp. 466–73.

* Gandolphe, M., 'Lettres sur l'histoire politique de la Tunisie de 1728 à 1740', *R.T.*, 1924, pp. 209–30, 287–303; 1926, pp. 352–67, 457–83.

* Grandchamp, P., 'Documents divers relatifs à la croisade de Saint Louis contre Tunis', *R.T.*, 1912, pp. 384–94, 447–70; 1913, 480–1.

——, 'La prétendue captivité de saint Vincent de Paul à Tunis', in *France en Tunisie* (Tunis, 1921), VI, pp. xxxii–li; 'Observations

Bibliography

nouvelles', VII, pp. xxii–xxxiii; 'Le fondouk des Français [à Tunis 1660–1661]', IV, pp. xxii–xxxii; and 'La mission de Pléville le Pelley à Tunis', VI, pp. xxii–xxxii.

Grandchamp, P., *Documents relatifs aux corsaires tunisiens* (*2 octobre 1777–4 mai 1824*) (Tunis, 1925).

*——, 'Documents turcs relatifs aux relations entre Tunis et la Toscane (1626–1703)', *R.T.*, 1940, pp. 109–14.

* Grandchamp, P. and Mokaddem, B., 'Une mission tunisienne à Paris (Février–Mai, 1853)', *R.A.*, 90, 1946, pp. 58–98.

* Mantran, R., 'L'évolution des relations entre la Tunisie et l'Empire ottoman du XVIe au XIXe siècle', *Cahiers de Tunisie*, 7, 1959, pp. 319–33.

Marçais, G., *Manuel d'art musulman. Architecture* (Paris, 1929), II, chap. 9.

* Martel, A., 'L'armée d'Ahmed Bey d'après un instructeur français', *Cahiers de Tunisie*, 4, 1956, pp. 373–407.

Monchicourt, Ch. *Episodes de la carrière tunisienne de Dragut* (Tunis, 1918) with an introduction, 'Insecurité en Méditerranée durant l'été de 1550'; also appeared in *R.T.*, 1917, pp. 317–24 and 1918, pp. 263–73.

* Pellegrin, A., 'Notes d'histoire tunisienne: Un document sur l'esclavage à Tunis', *Bull. Eco. Tun.*, 16 May 1953, pp. 98–102.

* P.G., 'Documents concernant la course dans la Régence de Tunis de 1764 à 1769 et de 1783 à 1843', *Cahiers de Tunisie*, 5, 1957, pp. 269–340.

Pignon, J., 'L'esclavage en Tunisie de 1590 à 1620', *R.T.*, 1930, pp. 18–37; 1932, 346–77.

——, 'La Tunisie turque et husseïnite', *Initiation à la Tunisie* (Paris, 1950), pp. 98–135.

——, 'Les relations franco-tunisiennes au début du 17e siècle, l'accord de 1606', *R.A.*, 100, 1956, pp. 409–21.

——, 'La milice des Janissaires de Tunis où temps des Deys (1590–1650)', *Cahiers de Tunisie*, 4, 1956, pp. 306–26.

Poinssot, L. and Lantier, R., 'Les Gouverneurs de la Goulette durant l'occupation espagnole (1535–1574)', *R.A.*, 1930, pp. 219–52 (employs records and manuscripts of the fortress).

Rousseau, A., *Annales tunisiennes ou aperçu historique sur la Régence de Tunis* (Paris–Algiers–Constantine, 1864) (to be used with great caution; covers events up to 1832).

Encyclopedia of Islam: see articles on Bizerta, Djerba, Gabès, Gafsa, Ifrikiya, al-Kairawân, al-Kef, Tabarka, al-Mahdîya, Sfax, Subaitila, Tunis, Tunisia.

Index

❋

Geographical names which appear below are followed by the abbreviations (M), (A), (T) and (L), which indicate the location of the place-names in Morocco, Algeria, Tunisia and Libya respectively.

'Abbadids, 84
al-'Abbas (Saadian sultan), 237
Abbasids, 20, 22, 24, 37–8, 41–2, 51, 56, 67–8, 89, 117, 143, 154
'Abd Allah I (Aghlabid amir), 47
'Abd Allah II (Aghlabid amir), 47, 53
'Abd Allah (Saadian sultan), 236
'Abd Allah (Ziyanid prince), 294
'Abd Allah ibn al-Bashir al-Wansharisi, 102
'Abd Allah ibn Mubarak, 222
'Abd Allah ibn Sa'd, see Ibn Sa'd
'Abd Allah ibn Yasin, 79
'Abd Allah ibn al-Zubair, 4, 11
'Abd al-'Aziz (brother of Ibn Tumart), 109
'Abd al-'Aziz (Merinid sultan), 195, 198
'Abd al-Haqq (Merinid chief), 172–4, 176
'Abd al-Haqq (Merinid sultan), 203, 208–9, 212
'Abd al-Malik (caliph), 11, 12, 13
'Abd al-Malik (Saadian sultan), 226–8, 301
'Abd al-Mumin, 96–7 (meeting with Ibn Tumart), 96–7, 99, 102–5, 106–9, 111–15, 118, 120, 122, 124–5, 130, 162, 172, 179, 239, 339, 340
'Abd al-Qadir, 28
'Abd al-Qadir al-Jilani, 210
'Abd al-Rahman III (caliph of Cordova), 58
'Abd al-Rahman ibn Habib, 22, 23
'Abd al-Rahman ibn Rustum, see Ibn Rustum
'Abd al-Salam ibn Mshish, 211, 267
'Abd al-Wadids, see Beni 'Abd al-Wad
'Abd al-Wahhab (Rustumid imam), 32
'Abd al-Wahid al-Wansharisi, 224
al-'Abdari, 146
abid, 102, 250–1, 262–4
el-Abid (Oued), (M), 223–4
abid al-Bukari, 250
el-Abiod (Oued) (A), 11
Abu al-'Abbas (brother of the shiite, Abu 'Abd Allah), 55
Abu al-'Abbas (Hafsid prince), 148–9
Abu al-'Abbas (Merinid sultan), 196
Abu al-'Abbas Ahmad (Wattasid sultan), 207, 213
Abu 'Abd Allah the shiite, 50, 52–5, 57, 61, 339
Abu 'Abd Allah Muhammad (son of 'Abd al-Mumin), 108
Abu 'Abd Allah Muhammad (Hafsid sovereign), 151, 161
Abu 'Abd Allah Muhammad ibn Tifawat, 77
Abu 'Ali (Merinid prince), 187–8, 189
Abu 'Amir (Merinid prince), 184–6

423

Abu 'Amr 'Uthman (Hafsid caliph) 148–51
Abu 'Asida (Hafsid caliph), 146
Abu Bakr (caliph), 20, 104, 166
Abu Bakr (Rustumid imam), 30, 31, 32
Abu Bakr Amhaush, 269
Abu Bakr ibn Ghazi, 196
Abu Bakr ibn 'Umar, 80–2
Abu al-Baqa (Hafsid prince), 146
Abu Dabbus, 124, 177–8
Abu Faris (Hafsid caliph), 148–51, 161, 273
Abu Faris (Saadian sultan), 236
Abu Hafs 'Umar (Hafsid prince), 145–6, 160
Abu Hafs 'Umar al-Hintati, 102, 104, 108, 109, 114, 115, 120, 141
Abu Hammu Musa I (Ziyanid sultan), 166
Abu Hammu Musa II, 167–8, 170–1, 196
Abu Hanifa, 45
Abu al-Hasan (Hafsid prince), 150
Abu al-Hasan (Merinid sultan), 147, 160, 166–7, 187–96, 199–201, 204, 341
Abu al-Hasan al-Samlali called Bu Hassun, 238, 242–3
Abu al-Hasan al-Shadhili, 159
Abu Hatim, 24, 30, 32
Abu 'Imran al-Fasi, 78
Abu 'Inan (Merinid sultan), 147–8, 167, 192–4 (struggle against his father), 196, 197, 199, 201, 204–5, 206
Abu 'Iqal (Aghlabid amir), 47
Abu Ishaq (Hafsid prince), 145
Abu al-Khattab, 23, 24
Abu Laila Ishaq, 39
Abu Mahalli, 238, 241
Abu Mansur al-Yasa', 33
Abu al-Muhajir, 2, 7, 8
Abu Muhammad (son of Abu Hafs 'Umar), 119–22
Abu Muhammad 'Abd al-Wahid (Almohad caliph), 122
Abu al-Qasim al-Qaim, 55–6, 59–60, 62, 64
Abu Qurra, 24, 162
Abu al-Rabi' (Merinid sultan), 187
Abu Sa'id (Almohad general), 121
Abu Sa'id (Ziyanid sultan), 167
Abu Sa'id al-Baji, 159
Abu Sa'id 'Uthman (Merinid sultan), 187–8, 200
Abu Sa'id 'Uthman III (Merinid sultan), 203, 208
Abu Sa'id 'Uthman (Ziyanid sultan), 165, 170, 185–6
Abu Salim (Merinid sultan), 195
Abu Tashfin (Ziyanid sultan), 166, 171, 188, 191
Abu Tashfin II (Ziyanid sultan), 168
Abu Thabat (Ziyanid sultan), 167
Abu Thabit (Merinid sultan), 187
Abu Yahya Abu Bakr (Hafsid caliph), 146–7, 188, 191
Abu Yahya Abu Bakr (Merinid sultan), 174–6, 177, 183, 204
Abu Yahya Zakariya (Hafsid prince), 151
Abu Ya'qub Yusuf (Almohad caliph), 113, 114–18, 125
Abu Ya'qub Yusuf (Merinid sultan), 165, 182–7, 189, 199, 205, 338
Abu Yazid, 59–63, 70
Abu Yusuf (Merinid sultan), 176–84, 187, 189, 200–1, 205
Abu Yusuf Ya'qub, see Ya'qub al-Mansur
Abu Zakariya', 27
Abu Zakariya (Hafsid amir), 61, 123, 140–2, 146, 154, 156, 160, 174
Abu Zakariya II (Hafsid prince), 146
Abu Zakariya Yahya (Hafsid prince), 151
Abu Zakariya Yahya al-Wattasi, 208–9, 211–12
Abu Ziyan (Merinid sultan), 195
Abu Ziyan (Ziyanid sultan), 165–6
Acciaiuoli, 158
Achir (A), 62, 64–70, 138

Index

al-'Adil (Almohad caliph), 122, 141
Adorne, 150
Adrar (Mauritania), 77
Afāriq, 43
Aflah (Rustumid imam), 32
Afoughal (M), 222
Africa (Sub-Saharan), 214, 232–4, 249–51, 270
Africa Agency, 327
Africa Company, 314, 320–1, 330
Aftasids, 84
Agadir (M), 76, 215, (taken by the Saadians), 222, 223, 254, 263, 265–6
Agadir (Tlemcen) (A), 162, 170 (mosque)
agha, 285, 302–5 (in authority), 321–2, 324
al-Aghlab ibn Salim, 41
Aghlabids, 26, 34, 37, 41–50, 52, 55–6, 59, 160
Aghmat (M), 80, 100, 103
Agzd (M), 175
ahl al-dār, 102
Ahmad (Aghlabid amir), 47
Ahmad al-A'raj, 222–4
Ahmad ibn Mahriz, 248–9
Ahmad al-Mansur al-Dhahabi, 221, 223, 226, 228–36, 270, 291, 301
Ahmad al–Rifi, 263
Aiguillon, Duchess of, 316
Aïn Beïda (A), 12
Aïn Leuh (M), 38
Aïn Madhi (A), 253, 326
'Aisha (wife of the Prophet), 11
'Aisha al-Manubiya, 159
Aïssaoua, 337
Aït Yahya, 274
Aix-la-Chapelle (Congress of), 328
Alarcos, 117–18, 119, 172
Alawites, 16, 220–2, 238, 240, 242–71
Albouzème (Company of), 244, 245
Alcala, 118
Alcantara, 117
Alcaudète (Count of), 226 (disaster of, at Mostaganem), 294, 296, 327
Alcaz el-Malec, 259
Alcudia (M), 206
Aledo, 86
Alexander II (Pope), 84
Alexander of Aphrodisias, 129
Alexandria, 56, 60, 94, 128
Algarves, 91, 213
Algeciras, 86, 179, 182, 190
Algeria, 245, 253, 271, 273–4, 275, 284–93 (Algerian state in the sixteenth century), 299, 301–3, 304–8, 320–7 (government in the eighteenth century), 327 (struggle against Tunisia in the eighteenth century), 328 (relations with Europe at the beginning of the nineteenth century), 329–33, 337–8
Algiers, 63, 66, 83, 90 (great Mosque), 92, 107, 116, 125, 144, 149, 150, 192, 196, 224, 225, 235, 241, 246, 254, 265, 267, 269, 274, 276 (the Peñon ceded to the Spanish), 277–8 (history), 279–80 (taken by 'Aruj), 280–2 (modernization of the port), 286–90 (organization of piracy), 288–93 (in the sixteenth century), 294 (expedition of Charles V), 297, 301–2 (seventeenth century), 302–3, 305–8, 309 (prisons), 310–13, 315 (bombardments by Duquesne), 316, 318, 319 (struggle against Morocco and Tunisia), 320–6 (eighteenth century), 324–5 (administration in the eighteenth century), 328 (bombardments—nineteenth century), 332, 343
Alhucemas (M), 58, 173, 206, 244–5, 253
'Ali (agha), 303
'Ali (caliph), 5, 6, 19, 38, 51, 116, 117, 242
'Ali Bey (bey of Tunis), 330–1
'Ali Bitshnin, 306, 309, 313

'Ali ibn Ghaniya, 116
'Ali ibn Haidar, 249
'Ali Khoja (dey of Algiers), 323
'Ali Malmuli (dey of Algiers), 321
'Ali Pasha (bey of Tunis), 329–31
'Ali Shaush (dey of Algiers), 303
'Ali ibn Yusuf ibn Tashfin, 87–90, 91–3, 100
'Ali ibn Yusuf al-Wattasi, 209
Alicante, 125–6, 275
el-'Aliya (M), 40
Allen, Admiral, 315
Almanzor, 83
Almeria, 84, 86, 91, 126
Almohads, ix, 12, 73, 76, 89, 91–135, 138, 144–5, 146, 153–6 (Almohad institutions under the Hafsids), 161–2, 163, 164, 173, 175, 176–80, 184, 191–2, 194, 197–200, 203–5, 209, 237, 258, 305, 336, 338, 340, 342, 343
Almoravids, 37, 76–93, 99, 100, 104–5, 111, 118, 130, 132–4, 162, 180, 209, 232, 258, 339
Alphonso the Battler, 91
Alphonso V of Aragon, 149
Alphonso VI of Castile, 84–5, 86, 91
Alphonso VII of Castile, 91
Alphonso VIII of Castile, 106, 117, 120–1
Alphonso IX of León, 116
Alphonso X the Learned, 178–9, 182–3, 190
Alphonso XI of Castile, 190–1
Alphonso V of Portugal, 212
Amergo (M), 90
amin, 266, 324
'Amir Beni Hammad, 167
'Amir al-Hintati, 195–6
amir al-muminin, 104, 177, 193
amir al-muslimin, 89 (Almoravids), 177, 197 (Merinids)
'Amr, 4
Anas ibn al-Furat, 46
Andalusia, 84, 89, 91–3, 113, 122, 123, 129–30, 132, 135

Andalusians, 44, 83, 87, 125, 132, 145, 155 (in Tunis), 160, 197–8, 203–5, 207, 232, 249, 290 (in Algiers), 307
Angad (plain of) (M), 193, 244, 246
Ansar, 5
Anti-Atlas (M), 93, 177, 222, 238, 243, 266
Aoudaghost, 80
al-Aqsa, 177
'Arab Ahmad, 301
Arabia, 222, 265, 267, 341
Arabs, 10, 11, 13 (masters of the sea), 22 (fiscal policy), 41–2 (in the Aghlabid kingdom), 49, 73 (Hilalian invasion), 103, 107 (deportation to Morocco), 108, 111, 112–13, 115, 117, 120, 122, 125, 130, 134 (problem under the Almohads), 139, 142 (in Ifriqiya under the Hafsids), 145–6 (under the 'Abd al-Wadids), 147–8, 188, 152, 154–5, 164–5, 167–9, 171, 173, 182–3, 188–9, 192 (reaction against Abu al-Hasan), 194–5 (against Abu 'Inan), 198, 206, 208, 222, 230, 237, 242, 249 (in the sixteenth century), 253, 255, 262, 264, 273–4, 277 (Algiers), 290, 292, 298, 304, 325, 328, 333, 339, 340–1 (importance of the Hilalian invasion)
Aragon, 84–5, 115, 117, 142, 144, 145, 146, 149, 158, 178, 190, 206, 276, 290
A'ras (Shaikh), 244, 245
Arguin (island of), 236
Ariana (T), 161
Aristotle, 129
Arjona, 123
Arnisol, 91
'Aruj (the Corsair), 278–80, 288
Arvieux, Chevalier d', 309, 318
Arzila (M), 187, 206, 212–13, 215, 227, 236, 252
'asabiyya, 140

Index

Asad (qadi), 50
al-Ash'ari, 45, 94, 98, 265
Asia Minor, 284, 296, 306, 323
Askia, 232–3
al-Asnam, 22
atalayas, 286
Atlantic (Ocean), 8, 18, 188
Atlas (M), 72, 76, 80, 82, 99, 103, 105, 175, 184, 192, 225, 238, 240, 243, 249, 251, 258, 261, 262, 264
Augsburg (League of), 318
Aurès (A), 7, 8, 10, 11, 12, 15, 17, 27, 42, 61, 111, 152, 194, 204
Austria, 329
Avenpace, 89
Averroes, 118, 125, 128–9
Avicenna, 129
Avis, 207
Awjala, 109
Awraba, 7, 10, 11, 14, 38–9, 339
al-'Ayashi, 238–40, 241, 251
Azagal, 86
Azemmour (M), 174, 206, 214 (taken by the Portuguese), 216 (evacuation), 223, 240
al-'Aziz (Fatimid calif), 67
al-'Aziz (Hammadid amir), 107
azrakism, 20
Azrou(M), 38

Bab Aguenaou (Marrakesh) (M), 132
Bab Azoun (Algiers), 288, 290, 296, 322
Bab Berdaïn (Meknès), 259
Bab Jazira (Tunis), 156
Bab al-Jihād (Algiers), 288
Bab el-Khemis (Meknès), 260
Bab Mansur el-'Eulj (Meknès), 260
Bab al-Oued (Algiers), 281, 288, 322
Bab er-Rouah (Rabat), 131
Bab Souïqa (Tunis), 156
Baba Hassan (dey of Algiers), 323
Babors (A), 111, 326
Badajoz, 84, 86
Badestan (Algiers), 291

Badi' (Marrakesh), 230
Badis (Zirid amir), 67, 70–1
Badis (Aurès) (A), 111
Badis (M), 206, 226
Baghai (A), 8, 47, 111
Baghdad, 41, 56, 70–1, 94, 210
al-Baidaq, 96–100, 103
Baie du Lévrier, 79
al-Bakri, 17, 33, 40, 66, 76–7, 79, 81, 162
al-Baladhuri, 2, 17
Baldis, 290–1, 303
Balearics (islands), 87, 91, 116, 290, 312
Bambara, 249
Bani (M), 222
Baqdoura (M), 22
baraka, 172, 209, 211, 338
Barbarossa (emperor), 112, 280, 298
Barbarossas (brothers), 278, 286–7, 295
Barbary, 12, 14, 18, 20, 63, 68, 109–11, 114, 116, 117, 119, 127, 130, 144, 156, 202, 254, 278, 280, 282, 293, 299, 302, 305–8, 308–14, 316
Barbary Company, 235, 242
Barcelo, Angelo, 327
Barcelona (counts of), 85, 91, 110
Bardo (Tunis), 161, 305, 330
Bargas, Martin de, 281
Barqa (L), 3, 11, 109
Bashiga (fountain in Tunis), 330
Basra (Bassora), 28
Basset, H., 132
Bastion of France (A), 292, 311–14, 316
Battle of the Nobles, 22
Battle of the Three Kings, 227–8, 270, 291
Baybars, 143, 144
Beaufort, 245
Béja (T), 62, 68, 110–11, 117, 146
Belezma (A), 42, 47, 49, 53
Beni 'Abbès, 278, 281, 295

Beni 'Abd al-Wad, 114, 123, 124, 133, 138-9, 146-7, 150, 161-72, 174, 178, 182, 186, 195-6, 198, 273-4
Beni 'Amir, 164
Beni Ghaniya, 116-17, 118, 133
Beni Isguen (A), 33
Beni Jami', 109
Beni Khazer, 162
Beni Maimoun, 128
Beni Merin, *see* Merinids
Beni Mezranna, 277
Beni S'ad, *see* Saadians
Beni Snassen, 83, 244, 249, 279
Beni Wattas, 184, 186, 197, 203, 205-17
Beni Ya'la, 162
Beni Ya'qub Beni 'Amir, 166
Beni Zoghba, 164
Benu Midrar, 33, 80
Bérard, Victor, 298
Berbers, 4, 7, 10-13, 14-18 (Butr and Branès), 19-26 (resistance), 33, 59 (revolt of Abu Yazid), 61, 72, 99, 107-11, 113, 125, 129-30 (music), 133-4 (in Ifriqiya under the Hafsids), 149, 152, 161, 169, 203, 209, 213, 221, 237, 240, 249 (eighteenth-century anarchy), 262-4, 267, 269-70 (revolt of 1811), 277, 288, 291, 325, 328, 333, 336-7, 339 (relations with the East), 340-3
Berghwata, 18, 21, 26, 33-4 (their heresy), 72, 81, 105, 113, 341
Berka (Tunis), 307
Berth (Oued) (M), 174
bey, 253, 302, 304 (Tunis), 322, 324 (Algeria), 329
beylerbeys, 235, 280, 285-6, 288, 290-301, 302
Beylie (General de), 70
beylik, 324-5
Bin Aisha, Admiral, 256
Bin al-Harsh, 326
Bin Sharif, 326
Bir el-Kahina (A), 13

Biskra (A), 117, 149, 172
Biskris, 290 (at Algiers)
Bizerta, 74, 274, 282, 331
Blake, Admiral, 311, 315
Blanchet P., 70
bled al-makhzan, 230, 261, 264, 269, 270
bled al-siba, 230, 270
Boghari (A), 62
Bohemia, 306
Bohloul, 43
Bologguin ibn Muhammad ibn Hammad, 81
Bologguin ibn Ziri, 64, 66-7, 277
bolukbashi, 304
Bône (A), 11, 42, 107, 117, 148, 149, 158, 192, 277, 281, 284, 310, 313, 320
Bornos, 14
Bornu, 142, 232
Bou Regreg (Oued) (M), 132, 201, 238-9 (republic), 240, 242
Bou Semghoun (A), 254
Bougie (A), 73-4, 96, 106-7, 109, 114, 116, 126, 127, 141, 145, 146-8, 150, 158, 159, 165, 166, 167, 192-3, 274, 276 (taken by the Spanish), 278, 282, 295-6 (taken by the Turks), 342
Boujad (M), 265
Boutin Ct., 328
Branès, 10, 14-18, 20, 229
Brantôme, 308
Braudel, 274, 275-6, 298, 299
Brazil, 227
Breugnon, Count of, 266
Brunschvig, R., 141, 150-1
Bu Hassun, 216, 224, 295
al-Bukari, 250
burnus, 15
Busnot, R. P., 247, 260
Butr, 14-18, 26
Byzacena (T), xv, 7, 11, 13
Byzantines, xv, 7, 10, 11, 12, 13, 47, 50, 63

Çabra (T), 63

Index

Cadiz, 84, 128, 178, 252, 255
Cagliari, 144
Cairo, 2, 67, 70–2, 128, 267
Calabria, 287, 297
Calvinists, 257
Camoëns, 227
Canaries (islands), 301
Cano, Juan, 323
Cap Bon, 74, 331
Cap Bougaroun (A), 111
Cap Negre, 311–12, 314, 330, 331
Cap Rosa (A), 313
Cap Roux (A), 292
Cap Timiris, 79
Capot-Rey, 316
captain-pasha, 226, 284, 297–9, 301
captives, 258 (under Mulay Isma'il), 284, 295 (Algiers), 308–10 (seventeenth century)
Capuchins, 316
Carthage (T), 8, 12, 13 (captured), 110, 143, 144, 282, 307 (aqueduct)
Casablanca (M), 265
Castelane, Philip, 241
Castile, 84, 90, 91, 115, 117–18, 122–3, 178–9, 183, 185, 187–8, 190, 194–5, 203, 206–8, 213
Castries, H. de, 220
Catalonia, 206, 290
Cateau-Cambrésis (treaty of), 299
Catherine of Portugal, 245
Cenival, P. de, 220
censaux, 266
Cervantes, 301
Ceuta (M), 58, 67, 86, 89, 123, 126, 127, 142, 178–9, 186–7, 188, 205, 206, 208 (captured by the Portuguese), 209, 213, 215–16, 227, 253, 257, 267, 270, 342
Cha'bān, dey, 319
Chabbiyah, 298–9
Chaouia, 17, 33
Charles, of Anjou, 143, 144
Charles II of England, 245, 248, 252
Charles V, 216, 282–3, 284, 286, 288–9, 294 (Algerian Expedition), 298–9, 343
Château-Renaud, 246
Chebanat, 243, 246, 249
Chebrou (A), 120
Chechaouen (M), 176
Cheklines, 290
Chélif (A), 10, 21, 22, 141, 165, 166–7, 192, 280, 295
Chella (M), 183, 192, 199, 200–1
Cheraga, 246
Cherarda, 246
Cherchel (A), xv, 110, 276, 279, 280, 281
Chevreul (A), 53
Chichaoua (M), 222
Chimeneas, 87
Choiseul, 266
Christianity, 6, 10, 18, 119, 126, 141, 143, 149, 150, 153–4 (in Ifriqiya under the Hafsids), 158, 178, 189–90, 196, 205–12, 228, 235, 238, 251, 253, 255, 263, 309, 316, 318, 337, 341
Chronique anonyme de la dynastie sa'dienne, 233
the Cid, 85, 87
Ciudad Real, 118
Colbert, 245, 256, 317, 318
Collo (A), 145, 281, 313, 320
Columbus, Christopher, 213
commerce, 106–7, 125–7 (Almohad), 141–2, 156–9 (Hafsid), 206–8 (Merinid), 229, 234–6, 241–2 (seventeenth-century Morocco), 252, 254–7, 258 (under Mulay Isma'il), 263, 266, 270 (Morocco eighteenth century), 274, 277, 279 (Algiers sixteenth century), 308, 310–14 (Barbary States), 320–1 (Algiers eighteenth century), 329–32 (Tunisia eighteenth century)
Constant II (Byzantine emperor), xvi, 6
Constantine (A), 16, 20, 60, 96, 107, 111, 116, 126, 141, 146, 147,

Constantine (A), (*cont.*)
  148, 150, 152, 166, 192–3, 194, 274, 281, 282, 297, 319, 324, 326, 341
Constantinople, 143, 211, 224, 225–6, 235, 280, 282, 284, 286, 292, 295–7, 307, 342
consuls, 214 (at Fez), 241, 255, 257, 266–7, 291 (at Algiers), 311, 316, 317 (Lazarists), 322, 330
Conti, Princess of, 257
Cordova, 23, 40, 41, 58, 61, 63, 67, 72, 80, 83–4, 89, 90, 91, 94, 106, 113, 117, 125, 126, 179, 182, 185
Corsica, 287, 312, 331
Cournut, 265
Cuenca, 76, 117, 118
Cyrenaica, 3, 4

Dahra (A), 280
daʿi, 51–3, 59
Damascus, 94
Dan, R. P., 308
Dansa, Simon, 316
Dar al-Bahr (Qalʿa of the Beni Hammad), 70
Dar Beïda (Marrakesh), 265
Dar Beïda (Meknès), 265
Dar al-Bey (Tunis), 331
Dar Kabira (Meknès), 259
Dar el-Makhzen, 260
Dar ibn Mechʿal (M), 244
Dar al-Sultān (Algiers), 292, 324
Daudi, 170
Dawawida, 142, 146, 148, 167, 168, 274
Dawi ʿUbaid Allah, 164
Delft, 306
Dellys (A), 148, 149, 196, 276
Denmark, 265, 321, 327
Derqawa, 326, 338
Dessus-Lamare, A., 28
Deval (consul), 328
dey, 302 (Algiers), 302–4 (Tunis), 321–4, 326 (eighteenth-century Algiers)
Dila (zawiyya of) (M), 238–40,
  242, 243–4, 246, 249, 261, 338
divan (of the janissaries), 285, 303, 313, 322
Djebāla, 16
Djebālīya, 16
Djebel Amour (A), 253
Djebel Jozzoul (A), 24
Djebal Lakhdar (A), 65
Djebel Maadid (A), 70
Djebel Nefousa, 4, 23, 24, 26, 30, 32, 42, 120, 152
Djebel Ressas (T), 273
Djefara (T), 152
Djenné, 232
Djerba (T), 33, 107, 110 (captured by the Normans), 146, 147, 149, 152, 158–9, 273, 276, 278, 298–9 (expedition of 1560), 304, 336
Djérid (T), 26, 42, 54, 60–1, 110, 117, 146, 148, 273
Djidjelli (A), 110, 245, 278, 281, 315
Dokkala, 105, 113, 215
Doria, Andrea, 286, 297–8
Dorsal (of Tunisia) (T), 62
Draʿ (M), 18, 80, 175, 177, 183–4, 188–9, 217, 222, 242, 269, 342
Dragut, 287, 297–9, 301, 308, 313
Dumoulin, 318
Duquesne, 315, 318
Dutch, see Netherlands

Ebro, 91
Edward, Don, 209
Egypt, 2, 3, 6, 18, 19, 23, 54, 56–7 (first expeditions of the Fatimids), 60, 64 (conquest by the Fatimids), 128, 143, 149, 151, 191, 275, 317, 330
Elche, 275
Elias (brother of Barbarossa), 278
Elizabeth (Queen of England), 235–6
Emerit, 324
England, English, 225, 226–7, 235–6 (relations with al-Mansur), 240–2, 244, 246 (and Morocco in

Index

England (*cont.*)
  the seventeenth century), 248, 252, 254–7 (and Mulay Isma'il), 263–4, 291, 300, 306, 311, 314–15, 319, 321, 326, 329, 331, 332
Enna (Castrogiovanni), 50
Estelle, J. B., 254
Estrées Jean d', 246, 256, 315
Estremadura, 117, 239
el-Eubhbad (A), 170 (mosque), 199, 201
'Eulj 'Ali, 226, 235, 288, 297–301, 319
Exmouth, Lord, 328

al-Faiyum, 56
Fakhkh, 38
Fatima (daughter of the Prophet), 38, 51, 242
Fatima (wife of Abu al-Hasan), 188
Fatimids, 28, 38, 41, 50–64, 66–7, 70, 72, 80, 112, 336
fatwa, 87, 88
Fazas (M), 38
feitorias, 214
Ferdinand I of Castile, 84
Ferdinand III of Castile, 122–3, 178, 207
Ferdinand IV of Castile, 188
Ferdinand the Catholic, 275–6, 278
Fernando (Don, infante of Portugal), 209 (captivity in Fez)
Feuquières, Marquis de, 317
Fez (M), 34, 38–41, 58, 67, 81, 82–3, 89, 90–3, 99, 105, 109, 119, 124 (captured by the Merinids), 126, 132, 138, 142, 149, 150, 151, 162, 163, 165, 168, 173, 175, 179–81, 187 (buildings of Abu Sa'id), 189, 191, 193–4, 195–6, 198 (end of the Merinids), 200, 204–5, 206, 208, 210–13, 214 (commerce with the Portuguese), 215–16, 221, 223, 224–5 (captured by the Saadians), 236–8, 241, 243–6 (captured by Mulay al-Rashid), 246 (buildings of Mulay al-Rashid), 248, 254–5 (commerce), 257, 262–5, 268–9, 279, 295–6, 326
Fez al-Bali, 246
Fez Jdid, 177, 179–80, 187, 193, 198–201, 205, 244
Fezzan (L), 4, 7, 117
Figuig (M), 172, 269, 274
Filalians, 242–6
fiqh, 88, 94
al-Fishtali, 221, 229
Flissa, 326
Florentines, 158
Fort of the Emperor (Algiers), 289
Fort of the Star (Algiers), 289
Fort of the 24 Hours (Algiers), 288
Fougasse, 330
Founti (M), 222
Fraga, 91
France, French, 60, 126, 143–4, 150, 159, 227, 236, 241, 244–5 (and seventeenth-century Morocco), 247, 248, 252, 255–7 (and Mulay Isma'il), 263–6 (and eighteenth-century Morocco), 271, 282, 284, 291, 294–5, 297, 299, 300–1, 308, 310–19 (and the Barbary States), 320–1, 327–8, 329–30 (relations with 'Ali Pasha), 331–2, 336
Francis I, 282
Frederick II of Sicily, 142
Fréjus, Michel and Roland, 245
al-Fududi, 194–5
funduk, 126, 156, 158, 206
fuqahā', 87, 88, 96, 211
furu', 88
Fustat, 56

Gabès (T), 109, 110, 117, 148, 158, 188
Gafsa (T), 115, 117, 120, 148, 149, 298–9
Galicia, 84
Galita (islands of) (T), 331
Gao, 232–4
Garwan, 267

431

Gaudefroy-Demombynes, 154
Gaul, 18
Gautier, E. F., 1, 3, 5, 8, 10, 11, 12, 13, 14, 16, 17, 20, 22, 26–7, 37, 40, 54, 139–40, 163, 169
Gennadius, 6
Genoa, 60, 107, 142, 144, 306
Genoese, 107, 126–7, 155, 158, 159, 190, 206, 286, 313–14, 329
George of Antioch, 110
Germans, 227
al-Ghahib, 230
Ghailan (raïs), 246, 248, 251, 319
Ghana (kingdom of), 80, 232
Gharb (M), 240, 244, 246, 248, 253, 265
Ghardaia (A), 33
Ghassaca (M), 206
al-Ghazali, 88, 91, 94, 98
Gheris (Oued), 243
Ghiyata, 174
Ghomara, 18, 21, 72, 115 (rebellion against the Almohads), 185, 187, 341
Gibraltar, 86, 113, 177, 187, 190, 194, 257, 271, 321
Giralda (Seville), 125, 130
Gizeh, 56
Godala, 77, 79
la Goulette (T), 226, 282, 284, 298–9, 300–1, 305, 329, 331
Goulmina (M), 243
Gourara (A), 188, 232
gourbis, 290
Graciosa (M), 213
Granada, 84, 86, 89, 113, 123, 130, 138, 142, 149, 151, 178–9, 182, 185–6, 188, 190–1, 196, 206–8, 213 (captured by the Spanish), 239, 275, 277, 290, 297, 300 (war of)
Grandchamp, H., 310
Greeks, 5, 10, 11, 13, 129
Gregory (patrician), xvi, 11
Gsell, 133
Guadalquivir, 179
Guercif (M), 99, 124, 172, 175

Guergour (A), 306
Guinea, 254
Guir (M), 243
guish or *jaish*, 230, 246

Habt (M), 342
hadith, 43, 88, 250
Hadrumetum (T), 11
Haëdo, 280, 286–7, 288, 290–2, 309
hafidh, 102, 109
Hafsids, 120–4, 127, 138–50, 151 (end of the dynasty), 152–61, 163–5, 166, 168, 171, 177, 183, 186, 188–93, 197–8, 205, 274, 278, 281, 284, 298, 300, 305, 330, 340
hajib, 155
Hajj Ahmad (bey of Constantine), 324
Hajj Mustapha (dey of Algiers), 319
al-Hajjaj, 21
hambel, 214
Hamida, 300
Hamidu (raïs of Algiers), 320
Hamma (cemetery of) (Algiers), 323
Hammad (first Hammadid prince), 67, 70–1, 179
Hammadids, 71–2, 74, 81, 96 (struggle against the Almohads), 105, 106–7, 116
Hamuda (bey of Tunis), 307
Hamuda Bey (bey of Tunis), 304–5, 331
Hamudids, 84
Hamza (A), 70
Hamza (shaikh of the Beni Sulaim), 147
Handhala ibn Safwan, 22
Hanencha, 313
Hanifism (legal school), 45–6, 307, 322, 337
Haouz (M), 206, 215
haratin, 250
Hardy, G. Y., 257
Hargha, 93, 102
Harrach (Oued) (A), 294, 327

Index

Harun al-Rashid, 39
al-Hasan, 242
Haskousa, 18
Hassan ibn al-Nu'man al-Ghassani, 12, 13, 18, 19
Hassan Agha, 293–4
Hassan Corso, 295–6
Hassan Pasha, 290, 294–7
Hassan Veneziano, 301–2
Hawara, 15
Hayy ibn Yaqzān, 128–9
Henry the Navigator, 208
Henry III of Castile, 207
Héraclius, xvi
al-Hiba, 16
Hilalians or Beni Hilal, 37, 70, 72–4, 85, 107–8, 111, 114, 116, 117, 133, 156, 162, 163, 167–8, 169, 172, 208, 340–1
Hintata, 192, 195, 212, 222
al-Hintati, 160
Hippo Regius (A), 11
Hisham ('Umaiyad caliph), 21, 22
hizb, 103
Hodna (A), 42, 62, 63, 107, 111, 274, 281
Hohenstaufen, 143, 144
Homaiyan, 164
Honeïn (A), 163, 274
Hornacheros, 239
Houdas, 250
hubus, 114
Hudids, 84–5
Huesca, 84
Huguenots, 257
al-Hulal al-Mawshiyya, 109, 119
Husain, 168
Husain (son of 'Ali), 51
Husain ibn 'Ali (bey of Tunis), 305, 319
Husain Bey (bey of Tunis), 329, 332
Husainids, 168, 305, 326, 328–33
Hussain (dey of Algiers), 323

Ibadites, 20, 23, 24, 26–7, 29–32, 42, 52, 61
Ibiza, 87

Ibn 'Abd al-Hakam, 2, 4, 8, 10, 17
Ibn Abi Dinar, 307
Ibn Abi 'Umara, 145
Ibn al-Ahmar, 123, 178–9
Ibn 'Arafa, 159
Ibn al-Ash'ath, 23–4
Ibn Askia, 233
Ibn al–Athir, 2, 57, 76, 103, 111
Ibn Bajja, 89, 129
Ibn Hammad, 60
Ibn Hawqal, 37, 341
Ibn Hazm, 94
Ibn 'Idhari, 2, 57, 59
Ibn Khaldun, 2, 10, 11, 12, 14, 15, 22, 26, 33, 37, 40, 52, 55, 62, 72, 81, 103, 114, 120, 139–40, 143, 155, 159, 160, 162, 165, 168–9, 173, 189, 190, 197, 340
Ibn al-Khatib, 205
Ibn al-Lihyani, 146
Ibn Mardanish, 113, 115, 116
Ibn Marzuq, 189, 200
Ibn Masai, 195–6
Ibn Musillim, 167
Ibn Qunfud, 159
Ibn Rushd (*see* Averroes)
Ibn Rustum, 3, 23, 24, 26, 29, 30, 33, 52, 339
Ibn Sa'd, 4, 5, 6
Ibn Saghir, 27–31
Ibn Saiyd, 160
Ibn Tafragin, 147, 191
Ibn Tafuft, 215
Ibn Tashfin, *see* Yusuf ibn Tashfin
Ibn Tufail, 125, 128–9
Ibn Tumart, 3, 93–104, 107–8, 119, 135, 154, 339, 340, 342
Ibn Yasin, 77–80
Ibn al-Zubair, 12
Ibrahim (bey of Tunis), 305, 319
Ibrahim ibn al-Aghlab, or Ibrahim I, 41, 47
Ibrahim II (Aghlabid amir), 47, 52, 53
Ibrahim Pasha (Algiers), 303
Iceland, 306
Icosium (A), 277

Idris ibn 'Abd Allah, or Idris I, 3, 38–9, 162, 338, 339
Idris II, 39–41
al-Idrisi, 76, 106
Idrisids, 34 (kingdom of Fez), 37, 58, 60, 72, 93, 162, 211–12 (restoration in the fifteenth century), 245, 336
al-Ifrani, 221, 225, 229, 234
Ifren, 15, 24, 162
Ifriqiya, 4, 6, 7, 11, 12, 14, 18, 22, 24, 26, 34, 38, 41–4 (Aghlabid kingdom), 53, 55, 59, 61, 63–6 (Fatimid caliphate), 67, 70, 72–4 (Zirid kingdom), 81–3, 89, 108, 111–13 (Almoravid occupation), 115, 117, 119–24 (at the beginning of the 13th century), 123, 126–7, 132, 133–4 (under the Hafsids), 140–1, 143–4, 145, 147–8, 150–2, 153, 159–60, 189, 194, 273, 305, 307, 339, 340
Igilliz (M), 93–4
ijma', 94
Ikjan (A), 53
Iligh (M), 246, 255
iqta', 155, 189
Iraq, 21, 29, 43
'Isa (brother of Ibn Tumart), 109
Ishaq (brother of the Barbarossas), 278, 279
Isly (Oued) (M), 175, 178
Isma'il (Shiite imam), 51–2
istemeyiz, 285
Italy, 50, 74, 110, 227, 230, 254, 276, 279, 282, 286, 298, 300–1, 306, 316

Jaen, 117, 125
Ja'far, 301
jaish (see *guish*)
Jaloula (T), 7
James of Aragon, 178
James II of England, 248
Jami' Safir (Algiers), 323
Jami' al-Sayyida (Algiers), 322
janissaries, 284–5, 293, 296–7, 301–3, 312, 322, 331
Jativa, 126
Jawhar (Fatimid general), 63–4
el-Jazair, 277
Jbel (M), 72, 342
Jebala, 211
Jedar, 10
Jenbi, 24
Jenina (Algiers), 292, 301, 323
Jerawa, 11–12, 14, 15
Jerez, 142, 182
Jews, 43, 118, 127, 152–3, 212, 229, 230, 242, 244, 247, 254–5, 259, 261, 266–7, 290–1, 311–12, 315, 321, 331, 336
jiziya, 21
jnun, 337
John of Austria (Don), 207, 288, 300
John of Matha, Saint, 310
John I (Don, King of Portugal), 209
John III of Portugal, 227
jornadas, 277
judaism, 12, 30, 291, 336
Judar, 233
Julian (patrician), 8
jund, 49–50, 52, 102 (of the Almohads), 144, 154–5 (of the Hafsids), 198 (of the Merinids)

Kabyles, 15, 63, 105, 108, 152, 192, 232, 278, 280, 281, 290–1, 293, 303, 315, 324, 326
Kabylia (A), 42, 50, 52–3, 55, 66, 74, 93, 204, 274, 281, 295–6, 306, 323, 325
Kahina, 11–12, 13, 14, 16, 17, 336
Kahya, 322
Kairouan (T), 4, 7, 11, 21, 22, 23, 24, 40, 41, 42, 43, 46, 47 (Great mosque), 52, 59, 61–2, 67, 68, 72, 74, 89, 110, 117, 152–3, 159, 160–1, 179, 190, 192 (defeat of Abu al-Hasan), 282, 298–9, 307, 329
Kal'a of the Beni Rached, 306

Index

kalam, 45, 94
Kanem, 142
Kasbah of the Oudaya (Rabat), 130
Kasbahs, 261
al-Kattani, 221
Kebdana, 244
Kef (T), 319
Kelibia (T), 298
Kenza (mother of Idris II), 39, 41
Kerbela, 51
Kerkenna (islands), 110, 146, 149
Khair al-Din (Barbarossa), 278, 280–2, 284, 288, 290–1, 293–4, 296, 297, 313
Khalid ibn Hamid, 22
kharāj, 21, 30, 114
Kharijites, 19–26 (formation of the sect), 26–34 (Kharijite kingdoms), 38, 42–3, 50, 52, 57–9, 61, 63, 152, 162, 336
khasnadar, 322
khasnaji, 321–2, 324
Khazrun ibn Falfal al-Maghrawi, 80
Kheder pasha, 303
Khemis (Cherarda), 246
Khenifra (M), 240
Khlot, 198
khuja, 322
khujat al-kheyl, 321–2
Kiboussiines, 290
Kitab al-Istiqsa, 221
Kosaila, 7, 8, 10, 11, 14, 16, 17
Kotama, 42, 50, 52–6, 61, 64, 67, 112, 339, 341
Koufa, 19, 21, 28, 29
Kouko (A), 274, 278, 280–1, 295
Kouloughis, 290, 303, 304
Koumiya, 15, 96
el-Ksar el-Kébir (M), 142, 227
El-Ksar es-Seghir (M), 212, 213, 227
Ksar as-Souk (M), 243
Kulthum (amir), 22
Kutoubiya (Marrakesh), 83, 125, 130–1, 132

La Calle (A), 292, 313–14, 320, 330
Laghouat (A), 243, 254
Lambaesis (A), 8
Languedoc, 257, 311
Larache (M), 187, 228, 236–8, 240–1, 252, 267
Laribus (T), 53
al-Lawati (Shaikh), 244
Lazarists, 310, 316, 317
Lebda (L), 109
Leibniz, 128, 317
Lemta, 18
Lemtouna, 18, 77, 79, 80
Lenche, Thomas, 292, 312
Léo VI (Byzantine emperor), 50
Leo Africanus, 154, 163, 205, 258
Leon (Kingdom of), 84, 91, 117, 123
Leontios (Byzantine emperor), 12
Lepage, Sanson, 313
Lépanto (battle of), 300
Lerida, 84, 91
Lesbos, 278
Lespès, 290
Le Vacher, R. P. Jean, 315, 316, 318
Levant, 158, 245, 254, 290, 304, 311
Lévi-Provençal, 40, 220, 221
Lionne, de, 317
litham, 77, 116
Livorno, 263, 311, 321
Lomellini, 313, 330
London, 235, 252, 328
Loria, Roger of, 146, 159
Louis II (Carolingian emperor), 50
Louis XI, 150
Louis XII, 279
Louis XIV, 252, 255–7, 261 (and Mulay Isma'il), 315, 317–18 (and Barbary), 328
Louis XV, 263
Loukkos (Oued) (M), 213
Lusitania, 84
Lyon, 306, 313

madarsa, 169, 193, 199–201, 204, 210, 237, 307, 330
Madarsa al-'Attarin (Fez), 187, 200–1
Madarsa of Bab Guisa (Fez), 265
Madarsa Bou-'Inaniya (Fez), 201–2, 269
Madarsa Bou 'Inaniya (Meknès), 258
Madarsa al-Eubbad (A), 201
Madarsa of Fez Jdid (M), 187, 200
Madarsa Misbahiya (Fez), 193, 201
Madarsa el-Oued (Fez), 193
Madarsa al-Saffarin (Fez), 200
Madarsa al-Sahrij (Fez), 187, 200
Madarsa of Salé (M), 201
Madarsa al-Sharratin (Fez), 246
Madarsaal al-Sba'iyin (Fez), 200
Madina al-Riad (Meknès), 260
Madinat Fas, 38
Madock, Lawrence, 234
Madrid, 118
Maghdis al-Abtar, 14
Maghrawa, 56, 58, 80, 82, 162
mahallas, 293
Mahdi, 51–5, 59, 61, 93 (proclamation of Ibn Tumart), 94–104, 107–8, 109, 119, 122, 124, 138, 154, 238 (Abu Mahalli)
Mahdiya (T), 56–7, 63, 62–3, (siege by Abu Yazid), 72, 74, 94, 100, 110 (taken by the Normans), 112, 117 (taken by the Almohads), 120, 148, 159, 179, 298
Mahmud bey (Tunis), 332
Mahmud Zergun, 233
Mahon, 284
Mahyu (Merinid chief), 172
Maimun, 52
Maisara, 21, 23, 33
Majorca, 13, 87, 116, 149, 312
el-Makhazin (Oued) (M), 228, 230
makhzan, 114, 198, 203, 210, 221, 229, 230, 248, 251, 304–5, 325
Malaga, 84, 86, 182, 275
Malik ibn Anas, 45
al-Maliki, 2

Malikism, 45–6, 59, 61–2, 78–9, 87–9, 93–4, 100, 119, 134, 159, 200, 204, 265, 322, 337, 339
Mallala, 96, 99
Malta, 294, 297, 299, 305
Mami Arnaute, 301
Mamlukes, 143
al-Mamun (Almohad caliph), 119, 122–3, 141, 241
al-Ma'mura (M), 238, 240–1, 251
Mançoura (Tlemcen), 166, 171, 186, 191, 193 (mosque), 199, 201
Mançouriya (T), 63, 66, 68, 70–1, 110, 179
Mandingo, 232
Manduel, 127
al-Manjur, 229
mansulagha, 285
al-Mansur (Abbasid caliph), 22
al-Mansur (Almohad caliph; *see* Ya'qub al-Mansur)
al-Mansur (Fatimid caliph), 62–4, 67
al-Mansur (Hammadid amir), 73
al-Mansur (Zirid amir), 68
al-Mansur ibn Abi 'Amir, 67, 83
Manuba (T), 331
Manuel (Don), 213
Ma'qil, 133, 164, 167, 177, 183–4, 188, 195, 242
Marçais, G., 3, 12, 28, 29, 57, 65, 70, 74, 139, 169, 237
Marçais W., 1, 2, 14–15, 17, 20, 22, 26–7
Marcel, Guillaume, 319
maristan, 193
Marlborough, 315
Marrakesh, 82–3 (foundation), 89, 90, 92–4, 100, 103 (taken by the Almohads), 105, 108, 109, 112, 118, 119, 120, 121–4, 125, 130–1, 132, 134, 175–6 (taken by the Merinids), 179, 184, 188, 192, 193, 195, 198, 206, 212, 214 (under the Wattasids), 215–16, 222–7 (taken by the Saadians), 226, 228, 230, 234, 235–8, 241–2,

Index

Marrakesh (*cont.*)
   246 (taken by Mulay al-Rashid), 248, 255, 258, 264–5, 267–9, 275
al-Marrakushi, 76, 88, 119
La Marsa (T), 161
Marseilles, 126–7, 206, 241, 245, 263, 266, 292, 311, 312–13, 314–15, 316, 320–1
Martel, Charles, 18
Martin, Raymond, 143
Masala ibn Habbus, 58
Mascara (A), 324, 326
Masmouda, 18, 72, 76, 82, 90, 101, 104, 127, 133–4, 341
Masqueray, 17, 27
Massat, 238
Masson, P., 313
Matifou (A), 281, 294
Matmata, 16
Maurepas, 320
Mauretania (A), 8, 13, 18
Mauritania, 77, 80
māusim, 337
Mazagan (M), 226, 240, 253, 265, 268
Mazarin, 245, 316
Mazouna (A), 324
Mecca, 53, 78, 94, 143
Méchouar (Tlemcen), 170, 279, 280, 294, 296, 326
Mechra' er-Remel, 250
Médéa (A), 66, 279, 324
Mèdina, 6, 44, 45, 97, 101, 156
Medina, Juan of, 230
Medina-Coeli (Duke of), 299
Medina-Sidonia (Duke of), 213
Mediterranean, 3, 57, 110, 116, 128, 155, 158–9, 271, 274, 278–9 (in the sixteenth century), 281 (position of Algiers), 286–7, 305–8 (corsairs of Algiers)
Medjerda (Oued) (T), 307
Mehdia, 238
Meknès (M), 100, 174–5, 176 (taken by the Merinids), 180, 193 (madarsa), 205, 236 (commerce), 250–1, 255–61, (under Mulay Isma'il), 262–3, 265
Melika (town of the Mzab) (A), 33
Melilla (M), 58, 206 (taken by the Spanish), 253, 265, 270, 275, 300
mellah, 259
Mellègue (Oued) (T), 61–2
Mems (T), 11
Mercedarians, 257
Merinids, 16, 92, 122, 124, 133, 138–9, 142, 147–8, 153, 160, 162, 163–8, 171–205, 206–8, 210, 211–12, 258, 269, 338
Mers el-Kébir, 275–6, 296–7, 299, 300, 327
Meskiana (A), 12
Mesopotamia, 52, 63, 70
Messina, 50, 110
Metaghra, 15
Mételin, 278
Midrarids, 54, 64
Miknasa, 18, 21, 33, 58, 84, 258
Mila (A), 53
Miliana, 66, 116, 196, 279
Mina, 31, 114
Minorca, 13, 87, 312
Mitidja (A), 280, 281
mizwar, 102
Mogador (M), 206, 265–7
Mohammed er-Rachid Mouline, 118
Monastir (T), 47, 160, 298
Moncada, Hugo de, 281
Monchicourt, 298
Montagne, R., 101
Montpellier, 127
Moors, 85, 87, 128, 130, 215 (insurrection of 1501), 255, 274–5, 277, 286, 290, 292, 312–13, 322 (Algiers), 342
Moriscos, 226, 238–9, 240, 241–2, 275, 277 (at Algiers), 278, 290, 297, 307 (at Tunis)
Morocco, 16, 20, 21, 40, 58, 72, 81, 83 (Almoravid conquest), 89, 91–3, 104–6, 114–16, 126, 150, 153, 175–6, 179, 182, 189, 192–3, 196, 199, 203–5 (Andalusian

Morocco (cont.)
  influence under the Merinids), 203–5, 205–7, 207–17 (under the Benni Wattas), 215–17, 220–32, 234–42 (under the Saadians), 243–6, 248–9, 250, 253–7, 261, 263–70 (under the Alawites), 293, 295–6, 301, 311, 319, 326, 332 (conflicts with the Turks), 338, 341–2
Mosque of Abu al-Hasan (Fez), 193; Barbier (Kairouan), 307; Chrabliyin (Fez), 269; the Flowers (Meknès), 259; Halfaouine (Tunis), 331; Hamuda bey (Tunis), 307; Ketchawa (Algiers), 323; Lalla 'Awda (Meknès), 259; Oued al-Imam (Tlemcen), 171; Fishery mosque (Algiers), 307, 323; mosque of Rsif (Fez), 269; Sidi Bin 'Arus (Tunis), 307; Sidi Mahraz, 307; Yusuf (Tunis), 307; al-Zaituna (Tunis), 273
Mostaganem (A), 224, 276, 294–6
Motylinski, 27
Moudejares, 290
Mouëtte, 247, 255, 258
Moulouya (Oued) (M), 16, 17, 83, 114, 124, 172, 175–6, 240, 245, 249, 295
Msila (A), 70
Mu'awiya (caliph), 6, 7
Mu'awiya Ibn Hudaij, 7
Muhammad (the Prophet), 2, 46, 51, 93, 101, 204, 211, 222, 338
Muhammad I (Aghlabid amir), 47
Muhammad II (Aghlabid amir), 47
Muhammad V (Sultan of Granada), 196
Muhammad ibn 'Abd al-Haqq (Merinid chief), 174
Muhammad ibn 'Abd al-Rahman (Saadian chief), 222
Muhammad Bey (Tunis), 330
Muhammad al-Burtugali, 213, 216
Muhammad al-Faqih (Nasrid sultan), 179, 182, 185–6
Muhammad al-Hajj (Dila), 243
Muhammad al-Jazuli, 211, 212, 222, 230
Muhammad al-Kabir (bey of Oran) 324
Muhammad al-Mutawaqqil (Saadian sultan), 226–8, 235
Muhammad Saghir, 329
Muhammad ibn Salah raïs, 297
Muhammad al-Shaikh (Wattasid sovereign), 151, 212–13
Muhammad al-Shaikh al-Ashgar (Saadian), 240
Muhammad al-Shaikh al-Mahdi, 216, 222–5, 294, 296
Muhammad al-Shaikh al-Mamun (Saadian sultan), 236
Muhammad al-Sharif (Alawite), 243
Muhammad Tamim (ambassador at Versailles), 256
Muhammad ibn 'Uthman, 196
Muhammad ibn 'Uthman (dey of Algiers), 322, 326
muhtasib, 102 (Almohads), 55 (at Tunis under the Hafsids)
al-Mu'izz (Fatimid caliph), 63–4, 66
al-Mu'izz (Zirid amir), 67, 71–2
mujāhidun, 249–51
al-mulathamun, 77
Mulay 'Abd Allah (Alawite sultan), 262–4
Mulay 'Abd Allah al-Ghalib billah, 225, 226
Mulay 'Abd al-Malik (Alawite sultan), 262
Mulay 'Abd al-Rahman (Alawite prince), 267, 326
Mulay 'Abd al-Rahman ibn Hisham (Alawite sultan), 269
Mulay 'Abd al-Salam ibn Mshish, 134
Mulay Ahmad al-Dahbi (Alawite sultan), 262

Index

Mulay 'Ali al-A'raj (Alawite sultan), 262
Mulay Bu 'Azza, 134
Mulay Bushaib, 134
Mulay Hamida (Hafsid prince), 298
Mulay al-Harran, 248-9
Mulay Hassan (Hafsid sultan), 282, 284, 298
Mulay Hisham, 267-8
Mulay al-Husain, 268
Mulay Idris, 211
Mulay Isma'il, 221, 230, 235, 246-8 249-54, 257-62, 265, 270, 318, 319
Mulay Muhammad (Alawite chief), 243
Mulay Muhammad (Ziyanid sultan), 294
Mulay Muslama (Alawite prince), 268
Mulay al-Mustadi (Alawite sultan), 263
Mulay al-Rashid, 243-6, 253
Mulay Sliman, 268-9, 270, 326
Mulay al-Yazid (Alawite sultan), 266-8
Mulay Zidan, 236-8, 239-43
Mulay Zidan (Alawite prince), 253
Mulay Zin al-'Abidin, 263
Mulud, 182, 204
muluk al-tawā'if, 84-9
Muminids, 108-9, 118, 133-4, 141-5, 162, 199, 204, 210
munas, 293
Munis the brave, 56
Muntaner, Ramon, 159
al-Muntasir (Hafsid caliph), 150
al-Muqtadir (Abbasid caliph), 56
murabit, 210
murābitun, 79
Murad III, 226
Murad, bey of Tunis, 304-5, 314, 319
Muradids, 305, 319, 328
Murcia, 84-5, 86, 91, 115, 123, 178
al-Murtada (Almohad caliph), *see*

'Umar al-Murtada
Musa (Merinid sultan), 196
Musa ibn Abi al-'Afiya, 58, 60
Musa ibn Nusair, 1, 17, 181-9, 23
mushrikun, 98
Mustafa Khoja (Tunisian minister), 331
al-Mustansir (Almohad caliph), 121, 172
al-Mustansir (Hafsid caliph), 142-4, 146, 160-1, 165, 177, 183
al-Mustansir bi'llah, 142-5
mutajassimun, 98
al-Mu'tamid, 85-6
Mu'tazilites, 31, 42, 44-5, 47
muwāla, 47
al-Muzaffar, 83
Muzarabs, 91
Mzab, 33, 336
Mzabites, 27, 33, 290-1

Nakkarism, 42, 52, 61
Nakour (M), 58
Nakour (Oued) (M), 173
Naples, 286, 295, 299, 327
Napoleon I, 328
Napollon, Sanson, 312-14, 330
al-Nasir (Almohad caliph), 106, 119, 121, 141, 173
al-Nasir (Hammadid amir), 73
al-Nasir (Saadian pretender), 229
al-Nasiri, 221
Nasrids, 123, 138-9, 178, 182, 185, 187, 190, 196
Navarin, 332
Navarre, 84, 117, 144
Navarro, Pedro, 275, 278-9
Navas de Tolosa, Las, 121, 173, 179
Neal, Admiral, 328
Nédroma (A), 96, 186
Nefousa, 15, 32
Nefta (T), 150
Nefzawa, 24
Nemours (A), 178
Netherlands, 236, 241-2, 252, 254, 255, 257, 263-4, 311, 315, 318, 319, 321, 327, 328, 329

439

New Gate (Algiers), 288
Nfis (Oued) (M), 101
Niger, 232-4
Nijmegen (Peace of), 318
Normans, 74, 110, 111, 112, 143
Norway, 142, 327
Noun (Oued) (M), 262
Nuchèze, 245
Numidia, xv, 14, 52, 111
Nuño Gonzales de Lara (Don), 179
al-Nuwairi, 2, 7
Nuzhat al-Hadi, 221

oda, 285
odabashi, 304
Official Almohad Letters, 115
ojaq, 284-7, 296, 302, 304, 307, 320, 332
Oran (A), 83, 126-7, 163, 224-5, 274-5 (taken by the Spanish), 276-7, 279, 282, 294-5 (abandoned by the Spanish), 295-7, 300, 310, 324-7
Orania (A), 10, 21, 162, 171, 172, 325-6, 338
O'Reilly, 327
Orontes, 51
orta, 285
Oualata, 232
Ouargla (A), 27, 28, 33, 295
Ouarsenis (A), 83, 99, 274, 280
Oudaya, 130, 132, 262-3
Ouergha (Oued) (M), 90, 104, 115, 174
Ouezzan (M), 262
Oujda (M), 83, 99, 186, 199, 205, 243, 249
Ouled Naïl, 325
Ouled Sidi Shaikh, 325
Oulili, 211
Oum er-Rbia (Oued) (M), 18, 124, 175, 188, 192, 243, 265
Ourfejjouma, 23, 24
outan, 325
Outat el-Hajj (M), 172

Palermo, 50, 112

Pallache, 242
Paul, Chevalier, 316
Pedro (Don), 209
Pellow, Thomas, 251
Peñon of Algiers, 276, 278-9
Peñon of Alhucemas, 253
Peñon de Velez, 206, 253, 275, 295, 299
Pentapolis, (L), 3
Persia, 12, 45, 52
Peruzzi, 158
Peter the Cruel, 195
Peter Nolasco, Saint, 310
Peter III (Aragon), 145
Peysonnel, 329
Philip II, 227, 235-6, 239, 295, 297, 299, 300
Philip III, 239
Piali Pasha, 299
Picenino, 306
Pidou de Saint-Olon, 247, 254, 256
Pisa, 126, 127, 141, 144, 158, 206
Pius V, 300
Poitiers, 18
Pomaria, 162
Pomponne, 317
Portugal, 121, 150, 206-7, 208 (taking of Ceuta), 209, 211-12, 213-14 (conquest of the North of Morocco), 215-17, 222-3, 224, 226-8 (expedition of 1578), 234, 235, 238, 252-3, 255, 269-70, 273, 275, 291, 300, 327, 341-2
presidios, 236, 245, 253, 273, 277, 293, 296, 300, 327
Provence, 60, 150, 331
Psichari, E., 27

Qadiri, 211
Qadiriya, 224, 226
Qaïçariya, 163
Qaisites, 21
Qal'a of the Beni Hammad, 70-2, 73, 81, 107, 116, 179
Qamouda (T), 42
qānūn, 103
Qaraqush, 115, 117, 120, 127, 128

Index

al-Qarawiyin (Fez), 90
al-Qarn (T), 22
Qasr el-Manar (Qal'a of the Beni Hammad), 70
Qasr el-Qadim (Aghlabid palace), 47
Qastiliya (T), 54
Qubba al-Hadra (Meknès), 260

*Rabad al-Nusarā*ʾ (Fez), 198
Rabat (M), 113 (foundation by 'Abd al-Mumin), 118, 125, 130 (mosque of Hasan), 131, 175, 179, 199, 201, 238–40, 264–5
raïs of the taïfas: see *muluk al-tawaʾif*
Ramdan (*qaid*), 300–1
Raqqada (T), 47, 53, 56–7, 110
Ras Tabia (T), 161
al-Rashid (Almohad caliph), 123, 142, 249
Rashid (Freeman of Idris), 38
Rawd al-Qirtas, 40, 103, 114, 119, 124, 137, 183
raʾy, 94
rayah, 325
Raynal, 321
Razilly, Isaac de, 241
Redemptorists, 309, 316
Reggio di Calabra, 63
renegades, 232–3, 249, 251 (in the army of Mulay Isma'il), 257, 286, 290–1 (corsairs at Algiers), 295, 301, 306
Reverter, 91, 105
Rey, J. E., 263, 265
Rhir (Oued) (A), 274
ribat, 44, 47, 59, 79, 199, 201, 239, 253
Ricard, R., 204
Rif, 72, 83, 90, 104, 172, 184, 208, 244–6, 248, 252
Rinn, 325
Rio de Oro, 16
Rio Salado (A), 280
Rio Salado (Spain), 190, 207

Riyah, 116, 173
Rodrigo Diaz de Vivar, see Cid
Roger II of Sicily, 110, 111, 128
Romans, xv, 43, 57, 162, 341
Rosetta, 56
Roumis, 234
Rsif (quarter of Fez), 269
Rums, 8, 13, 43
Rusquniae (A), 281
Rustum (Turkish vizier), 299
Rustumids: see Tahert
de Ruyter, 242, 315

Saadians, 211, 215–17, 220–42, 243, 251, 270, 342
Sacralias, 86
Safi (M), 206, 214 (taken by the Portuguese), 215, 216 (evacuation by the Portuguese), 223, 238, 254, 263, 265–6, 268
Sahara, 76–7 (birth of the Almoravid dynasty), 83, 92–3, 103, 152, 250, 325
Sahel (T), 74
Sahnun, 46
al-Sa'id (Almohad caliph), 124, 164, 173–4
al-Sa'id (Merinid sultan), 196
Saint-Amand (Ambassador), 247, 256
Saint Louis, 143, 144, 317
Saint Mandrier, Antoine de, 241
sakakin, 102
Saladin, 128
Salah Rais, 224 (aid to Bu Hassun), 295–7
Salamiya, 51, 53
Salé (M), 38, 100, 175 (taken by the Christians), 193 (madarsa), 199, 205, 206, 238 (corsairs), 239–40, 246, 254, 257, 263–4, 266, 318
Salih (Prophet of the Berghwata), 33
Salim, Sultan, 280
Salim al-Tumi, 279
Salobreña, 91

441

Salva, 266
Salwat al-Anfas, 221
San Migeul de Ultramar, 238
Sancho (Don), 182–3, 185–6
Sanhaja, 15, 16, 18, 58, 62, 64–74 (Zirid and Hammadid kingdoms), 76–81, 93, 115, 120, 138, 160, 161, 184, 240 (Dila), 264, 305
Santa Cruz of Cap d'Aguer, 215, 217
Santarem, 116, 117
Saoura (A), 238
saqifa, 306
Saragossa, 84–5, 86–7, 89, 91
Sardinia, 286
al-Sa'ud family, 265
Savary de Bruslons, 255
Savona, 110
Sayous, A. E., 126
Sbeitla (T), 4
Sebaou (Oued) (A), 326
Sebastian of Portugal, 227–8
Sebou (Oued) (M), 22, 173, 237, 246, 250
Sedouikech, 15
Sedrata (A), 28, 29
Ségou, 249
Selouan (M), 206
Senegal, 311
Septem (M), xv, 13, 18
Sersou (A), 165–6, 167
Sétif (A), 53, 108, 111 (battle between the Almohads and Hilaliens), 306, 319
Seville, 84–6, 91 (taken by the Christians), 93, 123, 125 (great mosque), 129, 130, 142, 182, 199
Sfax (T), 47, 48, 110, 146, 158, 298
Shadhiliya, 224
Shaikh, 108, 209, 324–5
Sharifians, 211–16, 220–71, 293, 295–6, 319
Shawshs, 322
Sheraga, 226
Shigar (Shaikh), 167
Shiites, 32, 45, 47, 49, 50–2, 53–4, 56–62, 72, 80, 99, 200, 336

Shurfa, 217, 222, 238, 240, 242–3, 267, 338, 342
Sicily, 47, 49–50, 56, 63, 74, 110, 112, 142, 143, 144, 145, 146, 159, 286–7, 299
Sidi 'Abd al-Rahman al-Tha'libi, 307
Sidi Bal 'Abbas al-Sabti, 134
Sidi Belhassen (Tlemcen), 159, 170
Sidi Bin 'Arus, 159, 307
Sidi Bou Médine (A), 166, 171, 193 (mosque), 199
Sidi Brahim (Tlemcen), 171
Sidi Bu Madian, 134, 159, 170, 199, 201
Sidi Ferruch, 336
Sidi al-Halwi (mosque), 199
Sidi Harazam, 134
Sidi Muhammad ibn 'Abd Allah (Alawite sultan), 263–6, 267–8, 270, 338
Sidi Muhammad ibn 'Abd al-Rahman, called 'Bu Qubrin', 323
Sidi Muhammad ibn 'Arbiya, 262
Sidi 'Uqba (A), 10, 11, 179, 192
Sidi Wahhab, 170
Sierra Morena, 121
Sierra Nevada, 178
Sierra de Ronda, 178
Siga (A), 163
Sijilmasa (M), 18, 31, 33–4, 54, 57–8, 64, 67, 80, 175, 177–8, 188–9, 192, 195 (Merinid kingdom), 238, 248, 262
Simancas (archives of), 298
Sinān Pasha, 287, 298, 300, 303
de Slane, M., 141
Songhay, 232–4
Soumman (Oued) (A), 166
Sous (M), 8, 18, 21, 79, 80, 93, 177, 183, 188–9, 194, 212, 215, 217, 222, 238, 243, 246, 248–9, 253, 254, 266, 342
Sousse (T), 11, 47, 48, 110, 112, 150, 298, 331
spahis, 285, 305, 324

Index

Spain, 8, 13, 18, 20–1, 58, 63, 72, 83–6 (under Yusuf ibn Tashfin), 89–90 (under 'Ali ibn Yusuf), 106, 112–13 (Almoravid interventions), 115 (under Abu Ya'qub), 116, 117–18 (Alarcos), 121 (Las Navas de Tolosa), 122–3, 125–8 (civilisation under the Almohads), 129–30 (music), 134, 138, 151, 153, 176–86 (under the Merinid Abu Yusuf), 188, 189–91 (under Abu Hasan), 203–4, 206–8, 209, 213–14 (conquest of Morocco at the end of the fifteenth century), 224–8, 228–9, 233–4, 235–6 (relations with al-Mansur), 237, 238 (occupation of the Moroccan coast in the seventeenth century), 238–9 (expulsion of the Moriscos), 240–2 (relations with Morocco in the eighteenth century), 245 (at Alhucemas), 248, 251, 253–4, 257 (relations with Mulay Isma'il), 204, 267 (conflict with Mulay al-Yazid), 269–70, 273–7 (the African crusade), 277–9 (against 'Aruj), 281–2, 286, 290–1, 293 (sixteenth-century Algeria), 294–5 (attack on Mostaganem), 295–8 (sixteenth-century Tunisia), 299–302, 307, 315–16, 327 (relations with eighteenth-century Algeria), 329, 331, 339, 342
Stewart, Commodore, 260
Sudan, 15, 77, 80, 163, 191, 232–5 (conquest by al-Mansur), 236, 255
suf, 326
Sufetula (T), 4, 5
sufism, 210
sufrism, 20, 21, 23, 24, 33
Sufyan, 182
Sulaim or Beni Sulaim, 72, 116, 117, 120, 145, 146–7
Sulaiman the Magnificent, 224, 226, 284, 299, 343

sunni, 20, 43, 62, 68, 94, 122, 200
Suwaid, 164, 166–7, 168, 192, 199
Sweden, 321, 327
Syphax, 163
Syracuse, 50
Syria, 22, 51
Syrians, 84
Syrtis, 298–9

tabaqāt, 43
Tabarka (T), 13, 312, 313, 332
Tadla (M), 175, 223, 249, 265, 269
Tafilalet, 18, 40, 80, 163, 175, 189, 192, 223, 238, 240, 242–3, 244, 246, 248–9, 254–5, 265, 267
Tafna (Oued) (A), 163, 243, 253
Tagant, 80
Tagarins, 290
Tagdemt (A), 24
Tagounit (M), 175
Tagra (A), 96
Tagrart (A), 90, 162, 170
Tagus, 84
Tahert (A), 24, 26–9, 30, 32–4 (Rustumid kingdom), 54, 56, 61, 63, 74
Tahoudha (A), 11
taïfa of the raïs, 286–8, 301–3, 321
Taïfas, reyes de, 83–5, 86–7, 125
Tamesna (M), 38, 72
Tamzizdikt (A), 166
Tangier (M), 8, 18, 21–2, 38, 40, 142, 178, 206, 209 (attack by the Portuguese), 211–12, 213, 215, 217, 227, 244–6, 252–3 (under the English), 263, 266–7
Taodeni, 232, 234
Taormina, 50
Taount (A), 178, 186
Taourirt (M), 186
Tarifa, 85, 142, 185, 190–1
Tariq, 18
Taroudant (M), 80, 215, 222, 249, 255
Tasghimout (M), 90
Tashfin (Merinid sultan), 195
Tashfin ibn 'Ali, 91, 105

tawhid, 98
tawīl, 94
Taworgha (L), 23
Taza (M), 99, 130 (mosque), 173, 174, 175, 184, 187-8, 193, 196, 199, 205, 206, 224, 245-6, 248, 253, 295
Tebessa (A), 12, 108
Teghazza, 232
Tekelerli, 296
Tell, 15, 28, 33, 66, 122, 163, 167, 168, 172-3
Ténès (A), 83, 110, 276, 279, 280, 281
Tensift (Oued) (M), 82, 90, 265
Terrasse, Henri, 38, 58, 132, 133, 134, 184, 203, 205, 242, 251
Tétouan (M), 187 (founding), 205, 207 (sacking in 1399), 209, 239, 254 (piracy), 257, 263
Thabudeos (A), 11
Tha'liba, 277, 279
Thédenat, 324
Thubunae (A), 10
Tiaret (A), 8, 24, 26 (Kharijite kingdom), 27, 66
Tidra (islands), 79
Tidsi (M), 222
Tijani, 159, 326
Timbuctoo, 232-4, 249, 250
Tingitana (*see* Mauretania)
Tinmel (M), 101-3 (Ibn Tumart), 105, 125, 130 (mosque), 179 (taken by the Merinids), 340
Titteri (A), 168, 280, 324, 326
Tlemcen (A), 7, 24, 38, 67, 83, 90 (principal mosque), 93, 96, 99, 107, 123, 126-7, 138, 142, 145, 146-7, 149-51, 162-3 (history), 165-6 (besieged by Abu Ya'qub), 166-8 (under the Merinids), 170, 178, 182-6, 187-9, 191-3, 195-6, 199, 205-6 (under the Beni 'Abd al-Wad), 207-8 (besieged by Abu Ya'qub), 216, 224, 243 (taken by Abu al-Hasan), 253 (Sidi al-Halwi), 279-80 (expedition of 'Aruj), 293-5, 296-7, 326, 341
Tobna (A), 10, 17, 24
Toledo, 84, 85-6 (captured by Alphonso VI), 117, 118
Torreblanca, 149
tortora, 285
Tortosa, 91
Touat (A), 163, 188, 232
Toucouleurs, 234
Touggourt (A), 150, 274, 295, 325
Toujibids, 84
Toulon, 256
Tozeur (T), 61, 149
Trinitarians, 257, 310, 316
Tripoli (L), 4, 23, 42, 53, 56, 60, 76, 110 (taken by the Normans), 149, 276 (captured by the Spanish), 292, 299, 300, 305, 318, 331
Tripolitania, 12, 20, 23, 24, 27, 109, 115, 117, 120, 152, 267, 299, 301
Tunis, 13, 41, 42, 48, 62, 96, 110, 112, 117, 119, 121, 123, 126-7, 140-61 (Hafsid capital), 147-8, 160, 168, 190 (captured by Abu al-Hasan), 191-2, 193, 194 (principal mosque), 253-4, 265, 273-4, 282 (captured by Charles V), 283-4, 288, 292-3, 297-8, 300-1 (in the sixteenth century), 302-8 (in the seventeenth century), 309 (prison), 311-12, 318-19, 326, 330
Tunisia, 4, 16, 20, 145, 152, 239, 273, 293, 298-9 (captured by the Turks), 301, 303-5 (in the seventeenth century), 314, 316, 326 (struggle against Algiers in the seventeenth and eighteenth centuries), 328-33 (in the eighteenth century), 338, 341
Turcomans, 117
Turia, 85
Turkey, 265
Turks, 127, 151, 155, 211, 216, 224-5 (hostilities against Mu-

Index

Turks (cont.)
 hammad al-Shaikh), 226–7, 232, 235–6 (hostilities against al-Mansur), 241, 243, 246, 248–9, 251, 253–4 (relations with Mulay Isma'il), 262, 265, 269, 270, 273–80 (in Algeria and Tunisia), 280–2 (regency in Algiers), 282–333, 337–8, 342–3
Type (edict of Constant II), 6

'Ubaid Allah, 50–2, 53–9, 179, 338, 339
Ucles, 90
'Umaiyads (Orient), 6, 7, 20, 21, 22–3
'Umaiyads (Spain), 51, 58, 60, 61, 64, 67, 72, 80, 83, 89, 162, 185, 339
'Umar (caliph), 4, 5, 20, 21
'Umar ibn 'Abd Allah, 195–6
'Umar ibn Hafs Hazarmard, 24
'Umar al-Murtada (Almohad caliph), 124, 175
al-'Umari, 154
United Provinces, 242 (*see also* Netherlands)
United States, 327, 328
al-'Uqab, *see* Navas de Tolosa
'Uqba ibn Nafi', 7–10, 17, 22, 47, 162, 170
'Uthman (caliph), 4, 5, 6, 20, 185
'Uthman (Merinid chief), 173–4
'Uthman Dey, 304, 307
'Uthman ibn Idris (Merinid), 187

Valencia, 84, 87, 91, 123, 142, 149, 290
Van Cappellen, Admiral, 328
Van Tromp, 242
Vandals, xv, 14
Venice, Venetians, 50, 126, 127, 141, 144, 158, 159, 206, 254, 300, 306, 321, 331
Vera, Diego de, 279
Versailles, 257
Vespers, Sicilian, 145

Vincent de Paul, saint, 310, 316, 317, 319
Visigoths, 8, 18
Vivar, Rodrigo Diozde: *see* Cid
Volubilis (M), 38, 260

Waddan (L), 120
Wahhabi, 265, 338
wali, 338
Walila (M), 38, 39
Wanzammar, 168
Waqadi, 1
al-Wathiq (Hafsid caliph), 145
al-Wathiq (Merinid sultan), 196
Wattasids, 151, 194, 205–17, 223–4, 225, 270, 294–5
Wellhausen, 20
Windus, John, 260

Ximénès (Cardinal), 275

Yaghmorasan ibn Ziyan, 123, 138, 142, 162–5, 166, 170–1, 174–5, 177–83, 184, 204
Yahya (Hammadid amir), 107, 116, 117, 120, 122, 123
Yahya IV (Idrisid amir), 58
Yahya ibn 'Abd Allah al-Hahi, 238
Yahya ibn Abi-Zakariya al-Wattasi, 212
Yahya ibn 'Afzi, 188
Yahya ibn Ghaniya, 141
Yahya ibn Ibrahim al-Gadali, 78
Yahya ibn al-Nasir (Almohad caliph), 122, 141
Yahya Raïs, 295
Yahya ibn 'Umar, 80
Yahya (or Tafuft), 223
Yamina (daughter of patrician Gregory), 5
Yanbo', 242
Ya'qub (Rustumid imam), 29
Ya'qub al-Mansur (Almohad caliph), 106–7, 116–18, 125, 128, 130–1, 179, 249
al-Ya'qubi, 37, 43
Yazid (governor), 21

Yazid ibn Hatim, 24, 26, 41
Yemen, 52, 267
Yemenites, 21
yoldash, 285, 303
Yunus, 33
Yusuf (Almohad admiral), 128
Yusuf (dey of Tunis), 304
Yusuf Sahib al-Taba', 331
Yusuf ibn Tashfin, 12, 81–3, 86–7, 89, 90, 92, 162, 179

Za (Oued) (M), 172, 186
Zab (A), 24, 41–2, 55, 111, 172, 274
Zaffarines (islands), 245
Zagora (M), 175, 222
Zainib (wife of Yusuf ibn Tashfin), 12, 80
Zallaqa, 86
Zarkashi, 160
Zawila (T), 112
Zawiyas, 209–10, 211–12, 213, 215, 222, 265
al-Zayani, 221, 251, 259, 261, 264
Zenata, 12, 14, 20, 21, 22, 27, 56–8, 60, 66–7, 71–2, 74, 80, 83, 93, 96, 105, 107, 109, 114, 120, 122, 123, 133, 161–2, 163–4, 165, 169, 172, 186, 198, 204–5, 258, 339, 341
Zerhoun (M), 258
Zidana (Sultana), 248
Ziri ibn Manad, 62
Zirids, 64–70, 71–2, 74, 81, 84 (Granada), 107 (end of the dynasty in Ifriqiya), 110, 112, 138, 141, 152, 277
Ziyadat Allah I (Aghlabid amir), 47, 49–50
Ziyadat Allah II (Aghlabid amir), 47
Ziyadat Allah III (Aghlabid amir), 47, 50, 53
Ziyanids, 165, 167–8, 169–70, 189, 192, 277, 279, 280, 293–6
Ziz (Oued) (M), 243
Zliten (L), 23
zmala, 325
Zmogorzewski, 27
Zuhair ibn Qais, 11
zulaij, 132
Zwawa, 293
Zwila (L), 4